Compliments of

Joe Wilson

Sixty Years of EU State Aid Law and Policy

International Competition Law Series

VOLUME 71

Editor

In its series editor, Alastair Sutton, Kluwer is fortunate to engage and benefit from the experience and expertise of one of the world's outstanding authorities on European Union and international economic law.

Introduction

In their efforts to regulate competition in an increasingly complex business environment, competition authorities face a daunting task. The European Commission and Courts, as well as national courts and legislatures, policymakers, and regulators, are constantly proposing, enacting, reviewing, and enforcing new legal measures, often addressing novel situations. Every industry and service is affected.

Contents/Subjects

With many titles currently available and new ones appearing regularly, the series' coverage includes detailed analyses of relevant legislation and case law in major global trading jurisdictions, defences used in cases involving the digital network economy, state aid cases, enforcement methodologies and a great deal more.

Objective & Readership

The purpose of Kluwer's International Competition Law Series is to follow the ever-changing contours of this dynamic area of the law, keeping the practice in sharp focus so that practising lawyers (including in-house counsel) and academics can be assured of the most up-to-date guidance and sources, in the widest possible range of applications.

The titles published in this series are listed at the end of this volume.

Sixty Years of EU State Aid Law and Policy

Analysis and Assessment

Eugene Stuart
Iana Roginska-Green

Wolters Kluwer

Published by:
Kluwer Law International B.V.
PO Box 316
2400 AH Alphen aan den Rijn
The Netherlands
E-mail: international-sales@wolterskluwer.com
Website: lrus.wolterskluwer.com

Sold and distributed in North, Central and South America by:
Wolters Kluwer Legal & Regulatory U.S.
7201 McKinney Circle
Frederick, MD 21704
United States of America
Email: customer.service@wolterskluwer.com

Sold and distributed in all other countries by:
Air Business Subscriptions
Rockwood House
Haywards Heath
West Sussex
RH16 3DH
United Kingdom
Email: international-customerservice@wolterskluwer.com

Printed on acid-free paper.

ISBN 978-90-411-8869-4

e-Book: ISBN 978-90-411-8924-0
web-PDF: ISBN 978-90-411-8965-3

Printed in the United Kingdom.

For Anna and Joe

About the Authors

Dr Eugene Stuart is an Irish a lawyer and public policy advisor, both in Ireland and internationally. He holds a PhD in Law from the University of Belgrade, a Masters' in European Law from University College Dublin, an M.A. in Public Policy and Administration from Trinity College Dublin, and he is a graduate of the Irish Institute of Public Administration. He also holds two Post-Graduate Diplomas in International Human Rights Law from Turku University, Finland.

With some twenty-five years' experience at the Irish Ministry for Economy, Dr Stuart's professional experience covers the full range of an Economic Ministry's brief, including its regulatory areas and developmental functions. In the early 1990s, Dr Stuart worked at the European Commission in several fields, including Competition Policy, and subsequently was the first Head of the State Aid Department at the Irish Ministry for Economy.

Since 1996, he has worked as an international legal and policy advisor in various capacities in over twenty different countries. In the State aid field, he has contributed to the development of State aid regulatory systems in Albania, Serbia, Montenegro, Bosnia and Herzegovina, Hungary, Estonia, Slovakia, Slovenia, Lithuania, Croatia, Bulgaria, Ukraine, Kazakhstan, Moldova and the Russian Federation. He was appointed as EU High Level Policy Advisor on Public Procurement to the Moldovan Government in 2011.

In addition, Dr Stuart has participated in a range of important international negotiations including those at European Union level and at the OECD in regard to State aid reforms and the international monitoring of public supports to industry. He has also contributed many international conferences and journals in regard to competition law and policy, State aid and subsidies controls, company law, consumer protection and industrial development.

Iana Roginska-Green is Ukrainian and graduated from the National Law Academy of Ukraine with an LLM Diploma in 2008. She started her career in the State Department of Legal Approximation in the Ministry of Justice of Ukraine as a specialist on State aid, Public Procurement, Competition, and Company Law.

In 2011, Iana Roginska-Green graduated from the Estonian School of Diplomacy in Tallinn and in 2012, from the College of Europe with a Master's in European Single Market Law. Her Master's thesis addressed the "Creation of the State aid monitoring system in Ukraine according to the acquis communautaire."

From 2012 to 2013, Ms Roginska-Green worked on legal research for the Internal Market and Consumer Protection Committee in Policy Department of Economic and Scientific Policy of the European Parliament. In 2013, she became a co-founder and Director of the Research Institute on Legal Approximation - a non-profit research organisation aimed at helping to improve policy and decision-making in Ukraine through research and analysis.

Mrs Roginska-Green is the co-author of a number of European Parliament publications on the main freedoms of the Internal Market and of the Study for the European Parliament on *Streaming and online access to content* (EP, 13 March 2014). Moreover, she is a co-author of a number of books on State aid in Ukraine, in particular, of the first *Commentary to the Law of Ukraine on State aid* (2017).

Currently Mrs Roginska-Green lives and works in Washington D.C.

Table of Contents

Preface

The EU State aid regulatory system is now sixty years old and is increasingly impacting on national development policies within the EU and more widely in over twenty-five non-EU countries. However, the origins and development of the EU State aid system since the early 1950s are somewhat murky, not generally understood and have received limited analytical attention throughout this period.

What began as a very mild and initially rarely used initiative (to complement anti-trust law and policy and avoid negative spillover effects from sovereign national industrial policies) has now come of age with extensive EU legislation in place, serious powers in the hands of the European Commission and various national policies are now being driven by a compliance imperative vis-à-vis the EU State aid rules with significant linkages to other established and evolving EU common policies and common strategies.

In *SIXTY YEARS OF EU STATE AID LAW AND POLICY – ANALYSIS AND ASSESSMENT*, we consider the evolution of the EU State aid regulatory system in this period with particular regard to the inter-connected political, legal, economic and administrative dimensions of the system, in theory and in practice. The aim, therefore, is to achieve a fuller understanding of significant developments in EU State aid law and policy up to 2017 and provide an analysis and assessment of these developments and the likely future directions of EU State aid control.

However, at this stage, the complexity of the system limits the drawing of firm conclusions as regards the logic, effectiveness, strengths or weaknesses of a system that has changed so much in response to its own needs, the evolution of the EU itself and external developments over six decades.

After sixty years, the system is undoubtedly stronger and of more importance than in the 1950s and 1960s, although certain conceptual and practical weaknesses remain. The major strengths of the system relate to its evolutionary flexibility in response to new situations and the development imperatives of the EU itself. In parallel with a much weaker WTO regulation of trade subsidies, the EU has also managed to expand the scope of application of EU State aid law and policy, in principle or in detail, to over twenty-five non-EU countries. The main weaknesses in the system relate to the uneasy interplay between political, legal and economic factors and considerations. This has hampered the full effective enforcement of the legal rules and created the rationale for reform processes that have fundamentally changed, if not reformed, the EU State aid system since the late 1990s.

Looking ahead, important future challenges arise in regard to a changing European Union and a changing world trade external environment. In addition, the changes and reforms since 2012 are still settling in and may well require further determined adaptations of the system. Even as this publication goes to print, the EU was announcing a new Industrial policy strategy: *"Investing in a smart, innovative and sustainable Industry"*[1] which, although with little direct reference to State aid regulation, is likely to become part of a new macro-context for future State aid law and policy in the coming decade.

Thus, without offering any firm prescriptions, we hope that this analysis will provide useful food for future thought as the system continues to operate, and at the same time evolve.

Eugene Stuart & Iana Roginska-Green
October 2017

1. European Commission: Communication from the Commission – "Investing in a smart, innovative and sustainable Industry - A renewed EU Industrial Policy Strategy", COM(2017) 479 final of 13 September 2017.

List of Abbreviations

BIPA	Bilateral Investment Protection Agreements
BIT	Bilateral Investment Treaties
BRRD	Bank Recovery and Resolution Directive
CAP	Common Agricultural Policy
CCCTB	Common Consolidated Corporate Tax Base
CEECs	Central and Eastern European Countries
CEFTA	Central European Free Trade Area
CETA	EU-Canada Comprehensive Economic and Trade Agreement
CFI	Court of First Instance (now the General Court of the European Union)
CJEU	Court of Justice of the European Union (formerly the European Court of Justice)
CMO	Common Organisation of (agricultural) Markets
CMLR	Common Market Law Review
COSME	Competitiveness of Enterprises and Small and Medium-Sized Enterprises (an EU support programme operating from 2014 to 2020)
DG	Directorate-General (of the European Commission)
EAFRD	European Agricultural Fund for Rural Development
EBRD	European Bank for Reconstruction and Development
EC	European Community
ECJ	European Court of Justice (now Court of Justice of the European Union)
ECOSOC	Economic and Social Council of the United Nations
ECR	European Court Reports
ECSC	European Coal and Steel Community

ECT	Energy Community Treaty
EDIS	European Deposit Insurance Scheme
EEA	European Economic Area
EEC	European Economic Community
EFTA	European Free Trade Area countries
EMFF	European Maritime and Fisheries Fund
ERDF	European Regional Development Fund
ESF	European Social Fund
ESIF	European Structural and Investment Funds
ESM	European Stability Mechanism
EU	European Union
EUROMED	Euro-Mediterranean Association Agreements
EUROSTAT	EU Statistics Office
FCRS	Fair Competition Review System of China
GATS	General Agreement on Trade in Services
GATT	General Agreement on Tariffs and Trade
GBER	General Block Exemption Regulation
GDP	Gross Domestic Product
ICT	Information and Communication Technologies
IMF	International Monetary Fund
IPCEI	Important Project of Common European Interest
IT	Information Technologies
ITO	International Trade Organisation
KETs	Key Enabling Technologies
LIPs	Large Investment Projects
MEIP	Market Economy Investor Principle
MFN	Most Favoured Nation
NACE	Nomenclature statistique des Activités économiques dans la Communauté Européenne (the statistical classification of economic activities in the EU)
NDA	National Decommissioning Authority of United Kingdom
NUTS	Nomenclature of Territorial Units for Statistics
OECD	The Organisation for Economic Co-operation and Development
OEEC	Organisation of European Economic Cooperation
OJ	Official Journal (of the European Union)
PCA	Partnership and Cooperation Agreement
PPS	Purchasing Power Standards

R&D	Research and Development
R&D&I	Research, Development and Innovation
RAGs	Regional Aid Guidelines
SAA	Stabilisation and Association Agreement
SAM	State Aid Modernisation Programme
SCMA	Subsidies and Countervailing Measures Agreement
SGEI	Services of General Economic Interest
SGI	Services of General Interest
SMEs	Small and Medium-Sized Enterprises
TEN-T	Trans-European Transport Network
TFEU	Treaty on the Functioning of the European Union
TRIMS	Trade-Related Investment Measures Agreement
TTIP	EU-USA Trans-Atlantic Trade and Investment Partnership Agreement
UK	The United Kingdom of Great Britain and Northern Ireland
US/USA	United States of America
USO	Universal Service Obligations
WTO	World Trade Organisation

List of Tables

CHAPTER 1

Introduction

1.1 STATE AID FROM THE BEGINNING

In the beginning was the word, and the word was "aid." Today the term of art has become "State aid," although, as will be seen, "aid" remains, for most purposes, the correct legal term. More generally, the European Commission uses the "notion of aid" as a catchall concept to refer to what has been regulated by the European Union (EU) since the early 1950s and to describe the conceptual changes, arising from legal and policy shifts right up to the present day, that have transformed a very simple idea into a system of regulatory oversight that concerns (and is a source of concern) for all EU Member States and many third countries.

At its simplest, State aid is essentially about the impact on competition and trade of subsidies, tax breaks and other forms of government assistance which benefit some firms and, therefore, can impact negatively on other firms (especially competing firms which do not receive the assistance).

Every country (including all Member States of the EU and the World Trade Organisation (WTO)) support economic activity (i.e., they assist industrial sectors, particular firms, regional development, innovation, investment, trade development, small business development, and key sectors such as transport, agriculture and defence industries) to a greater or lesser extent by various instruments including subsidies, tax reliefs and other less direct supports. Indeed, this type of State activity is as old as the most traditional Finance function of government (tax raising plus public spending).[1]

However, in the modern era of free trade, these types of State economic intervention are now regarded as problematic when they have a significant impact on trade and competition. With the opening up of trade and the international position of

1. *See*, for example, Adam Smith: "The Wealth of Nations" (1776) for an early classical economics critique of State aids which were referred to at the time as "bounties."

a country (including EU, EEA and WTO membership, EU integration and WTO accession processes and membership of other treaties and agreements such as the ECT, CEFTA and the EU Open Skies Agreement), a key consequence is that international rules concerning State support to economic activity (and the interests of new trading partners in the impact of State aids and subsidies on trade and competition) need to be taken fully into account.

The existence of Government supports to undertakings represents a half-way position between the economic philosophy of central planning and that of free market economics but, as with much in life, the government's role in the economy is rarely pure and never simple. Despite initial American proposals in the 1940s that barriers to free trade, and especially government subsidies, should be banned under a United Nations mandate,[2] the regulation of Government supports to undertakings under international law has developed sporadically and vacillated widely in terms of its logic, scope and effectiveness. Direct barriers to free trade have proved difficult to abolish, economic fortunes have changed over time and serious efforts to address indirect barriers to trade have proved the most difficult area to regulate in the international economic arena.

State aid is thus one subset of indirect barriers to trade from the field of international trade law i.e. subsidies under WTO rules and "State aids" under EU competition Law. Systems of regulation of subsidies and State aids range from almost zero, in countries such as the United States of America (USA), to the increasingly intrusive EU system of State aid control. The EU system continues to develop rapidly in terms of its regulatory content and impact on Government economic policy decisions by means of European Commission policy choices, new legislation and the jurisprudence of the European courts. It is also spreading rapidly in all of the new geopolitical regions of EU influence e.g. Central & Eastern Europe, many of the countries of the former Soviet Union and the Balkan States. And, somewhere between the USA and EU systems, lies the subsidies control regime of the WTO which is principally expressed in the Subsidies and Countervailing Measures Agreement, 1994.

1.2 STATE AID – GOOD OR BAD?

While dramatic differences of opinion persist among academics and practitioners about the desirability of government supports to undertakings, whether called State aid or subsidies, there is a predominant analytical view at present, largely driven by

2. While earlier examples of subsidies and their regulation under international law will be seen later, the modern story traces to the free trade agenda initially advocated by the USA as early as 1934 and the particular vision of US Secretary of State Cordell Hull. US efforts in the 1930s and 1940s culminated in the failed attempt to introduce wide ranging and substantive regulation (*inter alia* on government supports to undertakings) via the Havana Charter of 1948. The international failure concerning the Havana Charter resulted from non-ratification by the USA, for various reasons, and this eventually lead to the foundation of the GATT – the precursor of the World Trade Organisation.

economic theory, that suggests that, (in the absence of clear market failure arguments), State aids and subsidies are generally likely to be harmful (and wasteful of public funds) as they:

- hinder the smooth operations of market mechanisms of supply and demand;
- create artificial advantages which damage competition and competitiveness;
- generate a subsidies culture where businesses facing difficulties (or even starting up) expect to be supported by the State; and
- interfere with the system of comparative advantages upon which free international trade is based.

However, even this quasi-consensus recognises a wide margin for exceptions. The question of "subsidies – good or bad?" therefore remains central to any consideration of law and practice in this field. At the same time, as law is a written expression of political will, the philosophical arguments about good and bad subsidies do not affect the law, but only future directions of policy and ultimately of future law.

The emergence in practice of a subsidising role for all States suggests that there is a substantial scope for good subsidies and other State interventions that may constitute State aid. This is also suggested by the persistence of State aid in the EU after 60 years of regulation/quasi-prohibition. Moreover, the existing EU State aid rules in Articles 106 to 109 of the TFEU provide for a range of cases where government intervention in the form of State aid raises no internal market issues[3] or may be deemed not to do so in the light of other Treaty rules[4] or specific fields of EU policy priorities.[5]

Moreover, while the current regulatory emphasis of EU State aid control is very much based on classical economic theory, the justification of good aid with reference to market failures that the aid should address and the imposition of the burden of proof on to Member States proposing new aid measures, this was not always so. Accordingly, one of the analytical issues to be explored later is how the European Commission's notion of "bad" State aid has evolved.

1.3 THE EU REGULATORY APPROACH

While the origins of State aid regulation go back much further,[6] from the 1950s there was a concern in the EU that the creation of a single common market could be undermined by the unregulated subsidisation of businesses by EU Member State governments. Accordingly, the EU State aid regulatory system set out to ensure that government interventions did not distort competition and internal market trade. A further concern was that EU competition policy rules on antitrust (regulating the market behaviours of businesses)[7] would not achieve the desired results if

3. TFEU, Article 107(2).
4. *See* the phrase "Save as otherwise provided by this Treaty" in Article 107(1) of the TFEU.
5. *See* the main grounds for European Commission discretionary exemptions in Article 107(3) of the TFEU.
6. *See* Chapter 3 on this.
7. Now Articles 101 to 104 of the Treaty on the Functioning of the European Union (TFEU).

governments remained free to create distortions of competition and trade via State aids to selected business entities. Moreover, as the EU common market (or internal market) was created and further evolved, the system needed to recognise other EU policy imperatives (especially developmental ones such as Cohesion policy and environmental goals introduced by the Maastricht Treaty) which implicitly argued for increased subsidisation. These concerns continue to the present day and have become more acute with every serious economic crisis faced by the EU, with every enlargement of the EU and in the opening of trade relations and EU integration processes with non-EU countries.

In the context of the evolution of the EU over the last 60 years, EU Member States originally retained sovereignty over industrial and fiscal policies. While the EU involves a pooling of sovereignty in many areas – and resulted in definitive common policies in some (e.g., agriculture and transport) – common industrial or fiscal policies were never envisaged in the initial Treaties. This is reflected in the required and elusive unanimity regarding direct tax harmonisation[8] and in the limited prerogatives of the EU in respect of economic policies.[9] In this setting, the EU State aid rules were initially crafted in terms of competition and trade regulation, but fundamentally motivated by the desire to regulate spillover effects of national industrial policies, especially if they undermined competition or affected industrial relocations.[10] Nonetheless, by 2017 the EU effectively had created its own industrial policy, very much coordinated the industrial policies of EU Member States and was making inroads into direct tax harmonisation. The State aid prerogatives of the European Commission played a significant part in this.

Importantly, the basic notions of the purpose of the State aid rules have also evolved over the years. Thus, a further set of analytical issues must focus on the evolution of the logic for EU State aid regulation. This includes consideration of whether the competition to be regulated is competition between competing undertakings or competition between the industrial and fiscal policies of the EU Member States, of the extent to which the regulatory reach of EU State aid control now goes beyond the intended regulation of EU internal market spillover effects and applies in relation to wider world markets where EU undertakings do or might compete and the specific policy orientations of State aid control over the years.

The EU regulatory system on State aid is fundamentally a prohibition system – as Article 107 of the TFEU firmly establishes that aid within its ambit (although undefined as such) is incompatible with the internal market. Nonetheless, this prohibition is subject to de jure and discretionary exceptions that, for many years, created a permissive system in practice. Efforts to rationalise the system so that it dealt with serious cases, rather than all cases of State aid as demanded by the TFEU, proved cumbersome for many years but recently progressed via a quasi-devolution of

8. TFEU, Article 113.
9. TFEU, Article 173.
10. Intergovernmental Committee on European Integration: The Brussels Report on the General Common Market (the Spaak Report), 1956. An English summary is available at http://aei.pitt.edu/995/1/Spaak_report.pdf.

regulatory responsibilities to EU Member States. In parallel, State aid control became more focussed on the economic rationale for State aid, notification requirements were reduced, albeit with increased quantitative and qualitative content in continuing notifications, and specific concepts of "good" aid and "bad" aid emerged.

1.4 THE ANALYSIS AND ASSESSMENT OF 60 YEARS OF EU STATE AID LAW AND POLICY

The structure of this review of 60 years of EU State aid Law and policy has a focus on:

- An overview of the development of the Treaty rules on subsidies and State aid and an explanation of how the EU State aid control system currently operates in practice.
- An historical analysis of where the EU State aid system came from, its interaction with the WTO regulatory regime on subsidies and the expansion of EU State aid concepts and systems beyond the EU itself.
- The development of State aid law and policy in separate phases over the last 60 years taking into account changes in the decisional and enforcement practice of the European Commission, the political and economic context of State aid policy in the relevant era, changes of orientation by the Commission in regard to the application of the State aid rules and landmark judgments of the European Courts.
- The processes and progress of State aid system reforms since 1996.
- The degree to which the development of EU State aid law and policy has been influenced by and has contributed to the evolution and development of a wide range of other EU policies over the last 60 years.
- A consolidated assessment, of the trends in the development of the EU system, the factors underlying those trends, the inherent logic of EU State aid control, its overall effectiveness and providing some thoughts as to its future directions.

CHAPTER 2

State Aid and How the EU System Works

As a starting point in appreciating the development of the European Union (EU) State aid regulatory system in the last 60 years, it is necessary to begin with an overview of the development of the Treaty rules on subsidies and State aid and an explanation of how the EU State aid control system currently operates in practice.

2.1 STARTING WITH COAL AND STEEL

The first EU experiment with this type of regulation was contained in Article 4 of the Treaty of Paris (1951)[11] establishing the European Coal and Steel Community (ECSC). In the ECSC context, it was very clear that the creation of a conflict free common market in coal and steel would be undermined by national subsidisation policies for steel mills and coal mines – unless these were centrally regulated. Consequently, the ECSC Treaty provided that "all subsidies or aids granted by States in any form whatsoever" were incompatible with the common market for coal and steel and were to be abolished and prohibited.[12] Such aids and subsidies were absolutely banned in that there was no criterion related to effects on intra-Community trade. Article 67 of the ECSC Treaty, however, gave the Commission its only powers of intervention. The Commission was empowered to authorise aid exceptionally where a Member State had taken economic action which could create a "serious disequilibrium" for the competitive position of its coal or steel industry (e.g., a general wage increase). The Commission was also empowered to issue recommendations where the economic action of one Member State was detrimentally affecting the coal or steel industries of other Member States. In addition, Article 95(1) of the ECSC Treaty allowed for the adoption of unanimous

11. The Treaty establishing the European Coal and Steel Community (Treaty of Paris or ECSC Treaty) was signed on 18 April 1951 between France, West Germany, Italy and the three Benelux countries (Belgium, Luxembourg, and the Netherlands), establishing the European Coal and Steel Community (ECSC), which subsequently became part of the European Union. The Treaty came into force on 23 July 1952 and expired on 23 July 2002, having been in force for 50 years.
12. ECSC Treaty, Article 4(c).

Council decisions or recommendations in cases not specifically covered by the ECSC Treaty and yet requiring action to meet the objectives of Articles 2 (establishment of a common market in coal and steel products), 3 (tasks of the Institutions regarding the common market in coal and steel) and 4 (practices – including subsidies and aids – incompatible with the common market in coal and steel). Such cases arose, in particular, where coal and steel firms benefited from aids and subsidies offered generally rather than specifically or when specific action by Member States in the coal and steel sectors fell outside the specific terms of Article 67.

While it was originally envisaged that the ECSC itself would step in and replace the assistance being provided by the six founding States of the ECSC to their coal and steel sectors, this ultimately did not happen.[13]

2.2 SECTORAL WIDENING FROM THE EEC TREATY TO ARTICLES 107 AND 108 OF THE TFEU

This experiment was widened with the establishment of the European Economic Community (EEC) by the Treaty of Rome in 1957[14] and the EURATOM Treaty[15] of the same year. The State aid provisions of the original EEC Treaty have remained substantially unchanged over the years and the present Treaty provisions are to be found in Articles 107–109 of the "Treaty on the Functioning of the European Union" (TFEU) which came into force in December 2009.[16] Moreover, the same provisions took over from the ECSC Treaty from 2002 when that Treaty, with a fixed 50 year term, expired.[17]

In very broad terms, Articles 107 and 108 set up a system whereby the provision by the State of "aid" to undertakings is fundamentally prohibited if it gives a selective advantage to certain undertakings and it has an actual or potential effect on trade and competition. This prohibition is then qualified by a range of de jure and discretionary exemptions. While the right to allow an exemption rests largely with the European Commission, Member States can in some cases bypass the Commission and get a

13. On this, *see* M. Merola: "The Forces Shaping State Aid Control in the EU" in L. Rubini & J. Hawkins (eds): "*What Shapes the Law – Reflections on the History, Law, Politics and Economics of International and European Subsidy Disciplines,*" University of Birmingham, European University Institute, 2016, p. 101.
14. The Treaty establishing the European Economic Community (Treaty of Rome or EEC Treaty) was signed on 25 March 1957 by Belgium, France, Italy, Luxembourg, the Netherlands and West Germany and came into force on 1 January 1958.
15. The European Atomic Energy Community or EURATOM (sometimes more recently referred to as EAEC) was created in 1957 to create a specialist market for nuclear power in Europe, developing nuclear energy and distributing it to its Member States and to non-Member States. Since 2014, Switzerland has also participated in EURATOM programmes as an Associated State. The regulation of State aid in the context of the EURATOM Treaty is considered further in *Chapter 3*.
16. To assist the reader, these provisions are reproduced in full at *Annex 2*. The Consolidated version of the Treaty on the Functioning of the European Union was published in OJ C 115 of 9 May 2008.
17. European Commission: Communication from the Commission concerning certain aspects of the treatment of competition cases resulting from the expiry of the ECSC Treaty, OJ C 152 of 26 June 2002.

decision from the Council. Moreover, but decreasingly so, the application of the State aid rules can be blocked by certain other provisions of the Treaty.

In addition, aid measures are in principle notifiable to the European Commission which determines by decision if the measure is State aid for the purposes of Article 107 and whether or not an exemption can be granted. Where a measure is notifiable (and this has changed a lot in recent years), it cannot be implemented until the Commission takes a decision. Where the Commission has substantial doubts about a measure, it can open a full investigation into the measure and consult with interested parties such as competitors and other Member States. State aid decisions can be positive, conditional or negative. In the latter case, the State aid measure cannot be implemented.

The Treaty rules also mandate the Commission to keep existing State aid under constant review in the context of the development of the EU internal market. Existing aid refers primarily to aid which pre-dated EU membership or aid which was earlier approved by the Commission. Where the Commission finds that an existing aid is no longer compatible with the internal market (e.g., arising from technological progress, new market structures or new EU legislation), it may issue effectively binding "appropriate measures" requiring a Member State to amend or abolish a State aid scheme.

While there is a simplicity to Articles 107 and 108 of the TFEU, the meanings to be ascribed to all of its provisions from the standpoint of practice have hugely evolved via Commission decisions, new policy positions, Court judgments and (since 1999) specific secondary regulations from the Commission. Accordingly, an appreciation of how the EU State aid regulatory system works requires an examination of the interactions of these interpretative drivers.

2.3 SUBSTANCE AND EXEMPTIONS

The starting point in the EU State aid regulatory regime which emerged from the EEC Treaty and is now in Article 107(1) of the TFEU is the principle of incompatibility:

> 1. Save as otherwise provided in the Treaties, any aid granted by a Member State or through State resources in any form whatsoever which distorts or threatens to distort competition by favouring certain undertakings or the production of certain goods shall, in so far as it affects trade between Member States, be incompatible with the internal market.[18]

While this formulation neither defines aid nor directly imposes a prohibition (using much softer language than in the ECSC Treaty), it is used to determine the fundamental elements of State aid via its inherent legal tests and the incompatibility of any such aid does indeed amount to a prohibition; because relevant Member State actions under the Treaty must be compatible with EU membership and the internal market.

18. TFEU, Article 107(1).

Accordingly, Article 107 of the TFEU starts with a complex prohibition on State aid; while immediately recognising that, in some circumstances, government interventions are to be regarded as compatible with the internal market (de jure exemptions),[19] and in others, they may well be necessary for a well-functioning and equitable economy (discretionary exemptions).

Without a definition of "aid," Article 107(1) of the TFEU creates the basis on which questionable or prohibited public support measures (whether direct or indirect) are generally identified by applying to those measures the *six tests* contained in this provision viz:

- it is not covered by the opening phrase of Article 107(1) – "Save as otherwise provided in this Treaty…";
- the measure is provided by or through State resources;
- it creates a selective advantage;
- the recipient of the advantage is (generally) an "undertaking";
- it actually or potentially distorts competition; and
- it affects trade.

These elements are the cumulative test for whether or not a State measure constitutes State aid. Over the years, the scope and meaning of these elements have evolved via the jurisprudence of the European Courts and via decisional practice and soft law measures developed by the European Commission. They have become what is known as "the notion of aid" in EU State aid law and policy[20] and are considered in further detail later in this Chapter.

Even if a State measure comes within the scope of Article 107(1) of the TFEU, it can benefit, in appropriate cases, from either the de jure exemptions of Article 107(2) or the discretionary exemptions of Article 107(3).

19. Article 107(2) of the TFEU provides for three such cases: (a) aid having a social character, granted to individual consumers, provided that such aid is granted without discrimination related to the origin of the products concerned; (b) aid to make good the damage caused by natural disasters or exceptional occurrences; and (c) aid granted to the economy of certain areas of the Federal Republic of Germany affected by the division of Germany, in so far as such aid is required in order to compensate for the economic disadvantages caused by that division – unless repealed. This latter case of compatible aid is of general historical interest and has not been used since the 1990s. The TFEU also anticipates that "five years after the entry into force of the Treaty of Lisbon, the Council, acting on a proposal from the Commission, may adopt a decision repealing this point." This has not yet been initiated, perhaps underlining both its historical and political importance.

20. *See*, in particular, European Commission: "*Notice on the notion of State aid as referred to in Article 107(1) of the Treaty on the Functioning of the European Union*," OJ C 262 of 19 July 2016.

Article 107(2) provides for the following de jure exemptions:

State aid – de jure exemptions:

(a) aid having a social character, granted to individual consumers, provided that such aid is granted without discrimination related to the origin of the products concerned;
(b) aid to make good the damage caused by natural disasters or exceptional occurrences;
(c) aid granted to the economy of certain areas of the Federal Republic of Germany affected by the division of Germany, in so far as such aid is required in order to compensate for the economic disadvantages caused by that division. Five years after the entry into force of the Treaty of Lisbon, the Council, acting on a proposal from the Commission, may adopt a decision repealing this point.

Article 107(3), in turn, allows the European Commission to exempt a State aid measure where it meets one of the following criteria:

State aid – discretionary exemptions:

(a) aid to promote the economic development of areas where the standard of living is abnormally low or where there is serious underemployment, and of the regions referred to in Article 349, in view of their structural, economic and social situation;
(b) aid to promote the execution of an important project of common European interest or to remedy a serious disturbance in the economy of a Member State;
(c) aid to facilitate the development of certain economic activities or of certain economic areas, where such aid does not adversely affect trading conditions to an extent contrary to the common interest;
(d) aid to promote culture and heritage conservation where such aid does not affect trading conditions and competition in the Union to an extent that is contrary to the common interest;
(e) such other categories of aid as may be specified by decision of the Council on a proposal from the Commission.

The scope and meaning of the exemption categories has also evolved over time; primarily on the basis of Commission soft law measures with various titles including frameworks, communications, notices, etc. which serve to pre-define the Commission's assessment orientation across a wide range of horizontal and sectoral State aid measures. Both types of exemption and related soft law measures are also considered further below.

Some soft law measures have also become hard law since the emergence of Commission Regulations in the State aid field in the late 1990s. Of particular importance in that regard are the Regulation on *De Minimis* Aid[21] and the so-called General

21. European Commission: Regulation No 1407/2013/EU of 18 December 2013 on the application of Articles 107 and 108 of the Treaty on the Functioning of the European Union to *de minimis* aid,

Block Exemption Regulation (GBER);[22] both of which have significantly reduced the State aid case load of the European Commission (in particular, to allow it to concentrate on major cases likely to seriously impact on competition in the internal market).[23]

2.4 GENERAL PROCEDURAL APPROACH

Under the original EEC Treaty, an outline of the procedures to be applied by the Commission in reviewing State aid measures was established by what is now Article 108 of the TFEU.

Although the ordering of the provisions of Article 108 is somewhat out of sequence, there is a clear obligation on national governments to notify new or altered aid proposals to the European Commission and not to implement them until a positive decision has been received as regards their compatibility with the internal market. In appropriate cases, the European Commission may also force a Member State to abandon its plans to grant State aid or change the content of particular aid measures. Moreover, the notification requirement has direct effect under EU Law[24] and the adoption of legislation creating State aid without prior notification and approval, even if no State aid is actually granted, constitutes an infringement of the requirement to notify. Commission decisions may be positive, conditional or negative. In practice, and with a marked consistency over time, the vast majority of Commission State aid decisions in notified cases are positive, a small minority are conditional and very few are negative.[25]

OJ L 352 of 24 December 2013. This is the latest edition to the general regulation of *de minimis* aid. *De minimis* in the agriculture sector is covered by Commission Regulation No 1408/2013/EU of 18 December 2013 on the application of Articles 107 and 108 of the Treaty on the Functioning of the European Union to *de minimis* aid in the agriculture sector, OJ L 352 of 24 December 2013 and the fisheries sector is covered by Commission Regulation No 717/2014/EU of 27 June 2014 on the application of Articles 107 and 108 of the Treaty on the Functioning of the European Union to *de minimis* aid in the fishery and aquaculture sector, OJ L 190 of 28 June 2014. *De Minimis* in regard to compensation for services of general economic interest (SGEIs) is addressed in Commission Regulation No 360/2012/EU on the application of Articles 107 and 108 of the Treaty on the Functioning of the European Union to *de minimis* aid granted to undertakings providing services of general economic interest, OJ L 114 of 26 April 2012.

22. European Commission: Regulation No 651/2014/EU of 17 June 2014 declaring certain categories of aid compatible with the internal market in application of Articles 107 and 108 of the Treaty, OJ L 187 of 26 June 2014. *See also*: Commission Regulation No 702/2014/EU of 25 June 2014 declaring certain categories of aid in the agricultural and forestry sectors and in rural areas compatible with the internal market in application of Articles 107 and 108 of the Treaty on the Functioning of the European Union, OJ L 193 of 1 July 2014 and Commission Regulation No 1388/2014/EU of 16 December 2014 declaring certain categories of aid to undertakings active in the production, processing and marketing of fishery and aquaculture products compatible with the internal market in application of Articles 107 and 108 of the Treaty on the Functioning of the European Union, OJ L 369 of 24 December 2014.
23. European Commission: Press Release "*State aid: Commission exempts more aid measures from prior notification*," 21 May 2014.
24. Meaning that it can be relied upon before national courts and that no specific national legislation is required to transpose Article 108(3) – established in Case C-77/72: *Capolongo v. Maya*, [1973] ECR 611 and Case C-120/73: *Lorenz v. Germany*, [1973] ECR 1471.
25. For example, according to 2005 figures, of 701 cases decided that year, positive decisions were 91% of total decisions, 4% of decisions approved aid with conditions, 3% of cases after full

A somewhat different pattern emerges in regard to unnotified State aids that are subsequently detected and investigated. In those cases, around 25 % result in negative decisions with orders for recovery of illegal State aid.[26] Indeed, recovery orders have become the corrective factor in the enforcement of the State aid rules since 1982.[27]

As well as examining new aids or alterations in existing aids, the European Commission is also empowered to keep *existing aids under constant review*. An existing aid is one that existed either before the Treaty rules came into force in a Member State (typically before accession to the EU) and aids which have previously been approved or exempted. This important power allows the Commission to indicate that things have changed[28] and, on that basis, to reopen an investigation into existing aid. In proper cases, the Commission may issue "appropriate measures" requiring the abolition or alteration of existing aid measures.

While the Commission's power to issue appropriate measures seems somewhat gentle, practice has shown that appropriate measures can be a strong and persuasive instrument in challenging existing State aids. As a matter of EU Law, appropriate measures for the purposes of Article 108(1) amount to non-binding recommendations.[29] However, the procedure works in such a way that the Commission review is done with the full co-operation of the Member State concerned. If the Commission concludes that an existing aid is no longer compatible with the internal market, it issues its recommendation to the Member State for changes that may include the substantive amendment of an aid scheme, the introduction of procedural requirements (e.g., to limit or refine the scope of application of the aid scheme) or the abolition of the aid scheme. The Member State concerned is given a period of time to accept the appropriate measures proposed and the Member State then becomes bound by its acceptance. Any subsequent aid that is not in compliance with the appropriate measures is considered new aid and must be notified. If a Member State refuses to accept the appropriate measures, the Commission cannot directly enforce its view but must, in practice, open the formal investigation procedure of under Article 108(2).

As well as dealing with specific national aid schemes as part of its authority to keep existing aid under constant review, the European Commission, in the elaboration of its various guidelines and notices ("Soft law"), has developed the practice of

investigation were found not to involve State aid and 2 % were the subject of negative decisions. More recent data from the Commission no longer reports these data – possibly due to the increased attention to unnotified cases and the continuing reduction in notifications as a result of the GBER.

26. European Commission: Facts and figures on State aid in the EU Member States – 2012 Update of 21 December 2012 and the Facts and figures on State aid in the EU Member States – 2010 Update of 1 December 2010 accessible at: http://ec.europa.eu/competition/state_aid/studies_reports/archive/scoreboard_arch.html.

27. This possibility was first identified in Case C-70/72: *Commission v. Federal Republic of Germany (Kohlegesetz)*, [1973] ECR 813, but not actually used until Decision No 1982/312/EEC of 19 May 1982, OJ L 138 of 1982.

28. Based specifically on an interpretation by the European Commission of the reference to the progressive development or the functioning of the internal market in Article 108(1) of the TFEU.

29. Joined Cases T-132/96 & 143/96; *Freistaat Sachsen v. Commission*, [1999] ECR II-3663, para. 209; Case C-313/90: *CIRFS v. Commission*, [1993] ECR I-1125, Advocate General Lenz at p. 1154 and Case C-135/93: *Spain v. Commission*, [1995] ECR I-1651, Advocate General Lenz at p. 1161.

addressing these to Member States as appropriate measures under Article 108(1). This has proved of particular importance in the past in imposing new disciplines under the State aid control system in regard to regional State aid and State aid for the motor vehicle sector. Where a Member State refuses to accept guidelines as appropriate measures or does not register its acceptance in writing, the Commission normally commences a formal investigation into all relevant existing State aid schemes in that Member State in order to evaluate them in the light of the guidelines at issue. This has the effect, in practice, of forcing Member States to accept the guidelines.[30]

A negative decision concerning an existing aid probably cannot have retrospective effect for reasons of legal certainty[31] and, consequently, it is unlikely that the question of recovery could arise. Moreover, Article 108(1) of the TFEU is not directly effective[32] and, as a result, a third party may not bring an existing aid before a national court seeking a declaration that it is incompatible with the Treaty unless the Commission has adopted a negative Decision to that effect. Third parties, accordingly, have little protection against an aid scheme lawfully introduced by a Member State. The Commission may, however, be held liable in damages in certain cases.[33]

From the 1950s until 1999, the only formal procedural rules in the EU State aid system were those to be found in Article 108 of the TFEU. Article 108 also provides generally for a preliminary procedure on State aid assessment and a deeper investigation (or "contentious" procedure) where the Commission has serious doubts as to the acceptability of the aid. As a result, the European Courts developed a range of detailed procedural requirements concerning these assessments and Commission State aid decisions. Following a lengthy political process, a Procedural Regulation was adopted in 1999 which reflected Article 108, the Court's procedural jurisprudence and the requirements of the Commission. From the Member States' perspective, the most important innovation in the Procedural Regulation was the time limit of 10 years set for the application of any State aid recovery order by the Commission. Prior to that, State aid recipients risked an unlimited possibility of demands for State aid recovery in the event that the aid was held to be illegal.[34]

Article 108 also provides that a Member State may apply to the Council of Ministers of the EU for a unanimous decision that aid which that State is granting or intends to grant shall be considered to be compatible with the internal market, in derogation from the provisions of Article 107 or from the regulations provided for in Article 109, if such a decision is justified by exceptional circumstances. Where the Commission has already initiated a full investigation into the aid under Article 108(1),

30. In the context of an earlier series of State Aid Framework rules for the Motor Vehicle sector, such an investigation was opened against Sweden in October 1997. In the course of the investigation, the Framework rules were accepted by the Swedish authorities (Twenty-Eighth Report on Competition Policy – 1998), p. 227.
31. *See* opinion of Advocate General Mayras in Case C-70/72: *Commission v. Germany*, [1973] ECR 813 at 836.
32. Case C-77/72: *Capolongo v. Maya*, [1973] ECR 611.
33. Case C-40/75: *Produits Bertrand v. Commission*, [1976] ECR 1.
34. The updated version of the 1999 Procedural Regulation is Council Regulation No 1589/2015/EU of 13 July 2015 laying down detailed rules for the application of Article 108 of the Treaty on the Functioning of the European Union, OJ L 248 of 24 September 2015.

the application to the Council has the effect of suspending that procedure until the Council has made its decision. However, if the Council has not decided within three months of the application being made, the Commission is free to adopt its decision on the case.

The Article 108(2) Council referral provision allows the Council to restrict the Commission's power to refuse the authorisation of State aids if the representatives of the Member States agree on the existence of overriding political considerations.[35] These are referred to by the text as "exceptional circumstances" and the earliest record of such clearance by the Council concerned a scheme of French aid to the paper-pulp industry in 1960.[36] One commentator notes that:

> such circumstances would indeed have to be exceptional for all Member States to agree to permit one of their number to grant an aid otherwise incompatible with the common market.[37]

It may be observed, however, that the clearance of State aid here is solely a political matter and is not, of necessity, subject to any of the legal, economic or administrative constraints, procedures or assessments normally arising in the control of State aid under European Law.

There are strong indications that the earliest, and possibly primary, beneficiary of this provision over the years has been France. In the 1967, the paper-pulp concession was given to France in return for the lifting of that country's veto on the adoption of the common customs tariff[38] and extended by a further Article 108(2) Council Decision the following year.[39] In 1975 and 1976, French vineyards were recipients of aid cleared under this provision because of price disruption caused by exceptionally good harvests.[40] A similar basis was used in 1976 to approve an aid scheme for Danish chicken producers.[41] In 1970, a German scheme of aid was approved by Council Decision where the exceptional circumstances were the need to compensate farmers for the loss of income suffered because of the introduction under the Common Agricultural Policy (CAP) of a common price for cereals.[42] These examples have set the trend for the use of the referral provision and it is understood that it had become virtually the norm at a certain point for France, in particular, to raise exceptional circumstances in some

35. D. Schina: "*State Aids under the EEC,*" Oxford, 1987, p. 151.
36. Council Decision of 19 December 1960, OJ [1967] 548.
37. D. Vaughan (ed.): "*The Law of the European Communities,*" Vol. I, Butterworths, London, 1986, pp. 716–717.
38. Council Decision of 19 December 1960 on the system of aid in existence in France for certain types of paper pulp, OJ No 84 of 31 December 1960.
39. Council Decision No 68/160/EEC of 27 March 1968 extending until 30 June 1968 the authorisation granted in Article 1 of the Decision of 19 December 1960 on the system of aid in existence in France for certain types of paper pulp, OJ L 76 of 28 March 1968.
40. Council Decision of 21 April 1975 on the system of aids to be applied in France for the private storage of table wines, OJ L 103/24 of 23 April 1975 and Council Decision of 15 March 1976 on the system of aid to be applied in France for certain wine-growers, OJ L 72/15 of 18 March 1976.
41. Council Decision of 22 June 1976 on the system of aid applicable to the slaughter of hens in Denmark, OJ L 168/12 of 28 June 1976.
42. Council Decision No 70/355/EEC of 13 July 1970 concerning the implementation by the Federal Republic of Germany of compensation measures for cereal producers, OJ L 157 of 18 July 1970.

agricultural sector in order to achieve aid concessions in return for agreement to the fixing of annual prices under the CAP.[43] It is also to be noted that certain Council Decisions were actually silent on the matter of the "exceptional circumstances" leading to their adoption.[44] This was resolved by the European Courts in 1996 by requiring the Council to explain the exceptional circumstances motivating its decision.[45]

While resort to this provision has declined very much in recent years, the Council used this power in 2000 for German and Italian wine[46] and for the Italian sugar sector.[47] It was also used to approve debt relief for Italian milk producers in 2003[48] and for aid to assist Cypriot farmers in repaying debts arising from the Turkish invasion in 1974 and a seven year drought in the 1990s (long before Cyprus joined the EU in 2004).[49] Subsequently, the Council approved aid measures related to the purchase of agricultural land in Latvia, Lithuania, Poland and Hungary citing the impact of the credit crisis on agriculture as the exceptional occurrence. These latter decisions were upheld by the European Courts in 2013.[50]

In several cases, the Commission has successfully challenged Council decisions of this type before the European Court of Justice where there has been any hint that the Council may have exceeded the precise parameters of its powers under Article 108(2). The most recent case was *Commission v. Council* in 2006[51] which invalidated a decision of the Council of 16 July 2003, that cleared the extension of the Belgian coordination centre tax scheme (which had been rejected by the Commission) for those coordination centres whose authorisations expired between 2003 and 2005. In that case, the Court also made clear that the Council could not use Article 108(2) of the TFEU to circumvent a Commission decision requiring the recovery of illegal State aid.

2.5 ARTICLES 106 AND 109 OF THE TFEU

Alongside Articles 107 and 108 of the TFEU, which establish the essence of the EU State aid regulatory system, Articles 106 and 109 are important also because they:

43. Case C-122/94: *Commission v. Council*, [1996] ECR I-881.
44. For example: Council Decision of 27 February 1975 on *the system of aid for the slaughter of beef cattle in the United Kingdom*, [1975] OJ L 52/35 of 28 February 1975 and Council Decision of 24 July 1973 on *a system of aids existing in the United Kingdom for refining raw sugar*, [1973] OJ L 207/47 of 16 August 1973.
45. Case C-122/94: *Commission v. Council*, [1996] ECR I-881 at para. 12.
46. Council Decision No 808/2000/EC of 19 December 2000 on *the distillation of certain German wine products*, OJ. L 328/49 of 23 December 2000 and Council Decision No 809/2000/EC of the same date on *the distillation of certain Italian wine products*, OJ L 328/51 of 23 December 2000.
47. Council Decision No 257/2000/EC of 20 March 2000 on *aid granted in Italy by RIBS SpA on the restructuring of the Italian sugar beet sector*, OJ L 328/51 of 23 December 2000.
48. Council Decision No 530/2003/EC: *Italian aid to milk producers*, [2003] OJ L 184.
49. Council Decision No 39/2006/EC: *Cypriot farmers*, [2006] OJ L 23 of 27 January 2006.
50. Case C-111/10: *Commission v. Council* ECLI:EU:C:2013:785, para. 98; Case C-117/10: *Commission v. Council* ECLI:EU:C:2013:786, para. 114; Case C-118/10: *Commission v. Council* ECLI-:EU:C:2013:787, para. 105 and Case C-121/10: *Commission v. Council* ECLI:EU:C:2013:784, para. 99.
51. Case C-399/03: *Commission v. Council*, [2006] ECR I-5629.

- Reinforce the application of the State aid rules to public undertakings and undertakings to which Member States grant special or exclusive rights while creating a separate basis for exemption in respect of undertakings entrusted with the operation of Services of General Economic Interest (SGEI) or having the character of a revenue-producing monopoly if the application of Treaty rules could "obstruct the performance, in law or in fact, of the particular tasks assigned to them" and if the development of trade is not affected to such an extent as would be contrary to the interests of the EU (*Article 106*).
- Allow the Council, on a proposal from the Commission and after consulting the European Parliament, to make any appropriate regulations for the application of Articles 107 and 108 – including regulations determining the conditions in which the notification and standstill obligations of Article 108(3) shall apply and the categories of aid exempted from this procedure (*Article 109*).

2.5.1 State Enterprises and Enterprises with Special or Exclusive Rights – Article 106 of the TFEU

It is a fundamental principle of EU Law that the EU remains neutral on the issue of the organisation of Member States' markets as between the public and private sectors. Thus, Article 345 of the TFEU provides that:

> The Treaties shall in no way prejudice the rules in Member States governing the system of property ownership.

This means, that Member States are free to organise their public sector, they have the right to run a mixed economy and to create and maintain public undertakings, to nationalise whole sectors of the economy and to acquire and increase shareholdings in companies. At the same time, the State aid rules should apply equally where public undertakings are actually or potentially competing with private firms.

In EU Law, there is an important distinction to be drawn between *Services of General Interest (SGIs)* and *SGEIs*. The former are pure public services such as health and education services. The operations and regulation of these services *normally* do not fall within the competence of EU Law, including the State aid rules. Member States are allowed to designate activities as SGI under national law. Such services may co-exist with similar services provided by the private sector (e.g., private education, private hospitals). In 1994, the Court of Justice of the European Union (CJEU) set the following criteria for SGIs:

- they must be important for the daily lives of consumers;
- they must be open to all consumers; and
- they must be provided on uniform terms and pre-determined quantity, price and regularity.[52]

52. Case C-393/92: *Municipality of Almelo et al. v. NV Energiebedriif,* [1994] ECR I-1477.

The broader and undefined concept of "services of general economic interest" is mentioned in Articles 14 and 106(2) of the TFEU, in Article 36 of the EU Charter of Fundamental Rights of the Union[53] and referred to in the Protocol on Public Broadcasting to the TFEU.[54] In short, these provisions create a right to public services and various Treaty rules (notably the transport, competition and State aid rules) are precluded from preventing the fulfilment of SGEI by the undertakings responsible for their provision.

In effect, SGEI are economic activities that public authorities identify as being of particular importance to citizens and that would not be supplied (or would be supplied under different conditions) if there were no public intervention.

In economic terms, the concept of SGEI is closely related to that of "Universal Service Obligations" (USO) that refers to obligations imposed on one or more firms of a given industry to supply particular products or services to all citizens often, although not always, on a non-discriminatory basis. For example, a regional bus service (which was the case in the landmark SGEI/State aid *Altmark* case in 2003)[55] can be thought of as an obligation to serve a particular segment of bus users. Indeed, SGEIs typically concern citizens within a certain relevant category (such as the sick in the case of certain medical services, or those living in vulnerable areas in the case of measures of protection against natural disasters).

Article 14 of the TFEU provides the core logic for the approach to SGEIs in EU law:

> Without prejudice to Article 4 of the Treaty on European Union or to Articles 93, 106 and 107 of this Treaty, and given the place occupied by services of general economic interest in the shared values of the Union as well as their role in promoting social and territorial cohesion, the Union and the Member States, each within their respective powers and within the scope of application of the Treaties, shall take care that such services operate on the basis of principles and conditions, particularly economic and financial conditions, which enable them to fulfill their missions.

In practice, many such services cannot be viably provided on the basis of market mechanisms alone and, therefore, specific arrangements are necessary in order to ensure the financial equilibrium of the provider. For instance, the market itself may not offer universal access or full geographical coverage. Currently, it is for the EU Member States to ensure the financing of such services and to calculate the extra cost of the provision of such services. Depending on historical traditions and the specific characteristics of the services concerned, Member States apply different mechanisms in order to ensure the financial equilibrium of providers of SGEI. These financing methods include:

- direct financial support through the State budget (e.g., subsidies or other financial advantages such as tax reductions);

53. Charter of Fundamental Rights of the European Union, OJ C 364 of 18 December 2000.
54. Protocol 29 to the TFEU.
55. Case C-280/00: *Altmark Trans GmbH and Regierungspräsidium Magdeburg v. Nahverkehrsgesellschaft Altmark GmbH, and Oberbundesanwalt beim Bundesverwaltungsgericht*, [2003] ECR I-7747.

- special or exclusive rights (e.g., a legal monopoly);
- contributions by market participants (e.g., to universal service funds);
- tariff averaging (e.g., a uniform country-wide tariff in spite of considerable differences in the cost of provision of the service); and
- solidarity-based financing (e.g., social security contributions).

While different forms of financing exist, (e.g., *subsidies or other financial advantages such as tax reductions, the creation of a legal monopoly by granting special or exclusive rights, contributions by other market participants to fund the SGEI provider*), a clear trend has developed in recent decades. EU Member States have increasingly withdrawn exclusive rights for the provision of SGI and opened markets to new entrants.

Examples of industries where SGEIs have been used and/or continue to be used in many countries are: telecommunications, broadcasting, water supply, electricity, gas, railways and postal services.

The complex issue of the treatment of SGEI supports by the State under the State aid rules arises from Article 106 of the TFEU which provides that, in regard to public undertakings and undertakings to which Member States grant special or exclusive rights, Member States shall neither enact nor maintain in force any measure contrary to the rules contained in the Treaties, in particular to those rules provided for in Article 18 and Articles 101–109.[56] However, undertakings entrusted with the operation of SGEI or having the character of a revenue-producing monopoly are subject to the rules contained in the Treaties, in particular to the rules on competition, only in so far as the application of those rules does not obstruct the performance, in law or in fact, of the particular tasks assigned to them.[57] Moreover, there is a general requirement that the development of trade must not be affected to such an extent as would be contrary to the interests of the EU and the European Commission is charged with ensuring the application of Article 106 of the TFEU and addressing directives or decisions to Member States in appropriate cases.[58]

A European Court of Justice ruling in 1985[59] held that compensation for the extra obligation imposed on certain waste disposal firms to dispose of waste oil did not constitute State aid – it was compensation for SGEI. As a result, from 1985 until 1995, the European Commission took the view that compensation for the provision of SGEI was not State aid. In 1995, this position became problematic following a Commission Decision which decided that tax concessions to certain postal service providers in France (to offset the cost of public service obligations) did not constitute State aid. On this occasion, the Court took the opposite view: the measure was a State aid which could, nonetheless, be deemed compatible under Article 106(2). Thereafter, the European Commission took the view that compensation for the provision of SGEI was State aid that could, nonetheless, be exempted under either Article 106(2) or Article 107(3) of the TFEU. This view was subsequently challenged before the Court.

56. TFEU, Article 106(1).
57. TFEU, Article 106(2).
58. TFEU, Article 106(3).
59. Case C-240/83: *Procureur de la Republique v. ADBHU,* [1985] ECR I-531.

The *Ferring* case, decided in 2000, concerned a French Sales tax imposed on pharmaceutical companies selling directly to pharmacies. The tax was not imposed where distribution was made via wholesalers, resulting in the presumption of a selective advantage (and thus State aid) to the French wholesale pharmaceutical sector. However, the wholesalers were required to keep a permanent stock of certain products and to ensure speedy delivery in their geographic area. In this case, the Court held that the sales tax exemption of wholesalers might be compensation for the provision of SGEI if the cost of the exemption was equivalent to the extra costs for wholesalers in meeting their additional legal obligations.[60]

Thus, a key issue as between Articles 106 and 107 became whether there was over-compensation to the SGEI provider. In effect, the case opened up the possibility that a measure of this type might be "compensation" covered by Article 106(2) rather than "State aid" covered by Article 107 – provided that the compensation was equivalent to the extra costs arising from the public service obligation.

However, the Altmark judgment (considered below) now rules out the application of the State aid rules in respect of compensation for SGEI where four cumulative conditions are met.[61] This issue has a particular importance in regard to the transport, energy, telecommunications and postal services sectors. In addition, it has proven important in other sectors such as private health insurance, etc.

In *Altmark*, the Court developed the ideas of the Ferring judgment further and held that the State aid control regime does not apply to *compensation* given to any undertaking in consideration for public service obligations imposed on them (because there is no advantage conferred) where four conditions are met:

(1) the beneficiary has effectively been entrusted with clearly defined public service obligations;
(2) the parameters for calculating the compensation must be established in advance in an objective and transparent manner;
(3) the compensation does not exceed what is necessary to cover all or part of the costs incurred in discharging the public service obligations, taking into account the revenue such obligations may generate and the fact that the beneficiary is entitled to make a reasonable profit for discharging these obligations;
(4) either the undertaking selected to discharge the public service obligation is chosen by means of a public procurement procedure or, failing this, the level of compensation is determined on the basis of an analysis of what it would cost a typical, well-run undertaking to discharge these obligations, again taking into account the revenue such obligations may generate and the right for the beneficiary to make a reasonable profit.

60. Case C-53/00: *Ferring v. ACOS*, [2001] ECR 1-9067.
61. A detailed discussion of the Altmark ruling and its impact on EU State aid control can be found in P. Anestis & S. Drakakakis Howrey: "*State Aid Policy and Services of General Economic Interest: Shedding Some Light on a Controversial Area,*" European Antitrust Review, 2006 and in F. Louis & A. Vallery: *"State Aid and Financing of Public Services – A Comment on the Altmark Judgment of the Court of Justice"* Competition Law Insight, September 2003.

This judgment has several significant procedural and practical implications for EU State aid law enforcement. First, the judgment confirms that public service compensation falls outside the legal scope of State aid as defined under Article 107 of the TFEU. This means that, where funding qualifies as compensation, there is no prior notification or standstill requirement. Second, the judgment provides a substantive test for judging when State funding of public services goes *beyond compensation* and must be assessed under the EU State aid rules. This is particularly important insofar as it increases the risk of recovery orders against public service providers and opens up new bases for legal action for the European Commission and for competitors.

While EU Member States need not notify such compensation to the Commission, the Commission remains free to take up cases on its own initiative or on the basis of a competitor's complaint. It may order compensation payments to be recovered, when it considers that the conditions set out by the Court are not met. Also, as these are cumulative criteria, where only one condition is not met, the compensation constitutes State aid and (unless exempted e.g., on grounds of *de minimis*) is subject to the notification requirement and standstill obligation laid down in Article 108(3) of the TFEU. The aid measure can still be declared compatible under Articles 107(2) and (3) of the TFEU (or under Article 93 of the TFEU and secondary legislation where applicable to transport).

2.5.2 Rule-Making and Article 109 of the TFEU

Article 109 provides that the Council, on a proposal from the Commission and after consulting the European Parliament, may make any appropriate regulations for the application of Articles 107 and 108 and may, in particular, determine the conditions in which Article 108(3) shall apply and the categories of aid exempted from this procedure.

This was first used in 1970 in regard to transport aid[62] and not used again until 1998.[63] In 1998, Article 109 was the legal basis for the adoption of the so-called Enabling Regulation[64] which first gave the Commission the power to issue block exemption (Commission) Regulations declaring categories of horizontal State aid (regional aid, aid for Small and Medium-Sized Enterprises (SMEs), aid for research and development, aid for employment, aid for environmental protection and training aid) compatible with the internal market and exempt from notification. A range of such Commission Regulations followed between 2001 and 2006.[65] It also facilitated the first

62. Council Regulation No 1107/70/EEC on the granting of aids for transport by rail, road and inland waterway, OJ L 130 of 1970.
63. For reasons examined further in *Chapters 4 and 5*.
64. Council Regulation No 994/98/EC of 7 May 1998 on the application of Articles 92 and 93 of the Treaty on the Functioning of the European Union to certain categories of horizontal State aid, [1998] OJ L 142 as amended [2013] OJ L 204.
65. European Commission: Regulation No 68/2001/EC of 12 January 2001 on the application of Articles 87 and 88 of the Treaty to training aid, [2001] OJ L 10 of 13 January 2001 as amended in 2004; Commission Regulation No 70/2001/EC of 12 January 2001 on the application of Articles 87 and 88 of the Treaty to State aid to small and medium-sized enterprises, [2001] OJ L

De Minimis Regulation[66] at a time when the Commission's policy on *de minimis* was still in doubt before the European Courts. *De Minimis* Regulations were later adopted for SGEIs and for Agriculture.[67] This ultimately developed into the first GBER in 2008.[68] More recently, further categories (cultural and heritage conservation, natural disasters, remedying damage caused by weather in the forestry and fisheries sectors, the promotion of food sector products, certain infrastructures, marine and freshwater conservation, transport in remote regions and basic broadband infrastructure) were added by Council Regulation (EU) 733/2013 and a further enabling Regulation was adopted in 2015.[69]

2.6 A CLOSER LOOK AT THE NOTION OF AID

As already seen, Article 107(1) of the TFEU declares any aid falling within the parameters of that provision to be incompatible with the internal market – and by extension prohibited unless it can benefit from an exemption under Article 107(2) or (3). Thus, the identification of a measure falling within the scope of the EU State aid rules involves the application of six tests which are now considered further.

2.6.1 Measures Excluded by the Treaty (Test 1)

Article 107(1) is made subject to other prevailing Treaty provisions by the phrase "*save as otherwise provided by this Treaty.*" In effect, this allows for different rules to apply in various areas of the CAP, the common fisheries policy and the common transport policy. It also explains why different Directorates General in the European Commission are responsible for State aid issues in some of these sectors[70] while Directorate-General (DG) Competition is responsible for State aid regulation in regard to all other sectors. In addition, it excludes State aid for military or security purposes – but not State aid supporting the production of "dual-use" goods.

---

10 of 13 January 2001 as amended in 2004; Commission Regulation No 2204/2002/EC of 12 December 2002 on the application of Articles 87 and 88 of the Treaty to State aid for employment, OJ L 337 of 13 December 2002 and Commission Regulation No 1628/2006/EC of 24 October 2006 on the application of Articles 87 and 88 of the Treaty to national regional investment aid (Block Exemption Regulation for regional aid), OJ L 302 of 1 November 2006.

66. European Commission: Regulation No 1998/2006/EC on the application of Articles 107 and 108 of the Treaty to *de minimis* aid, [2006] OJ L 379.
67. Considered earlier in this Chapter.
68. The original Regulation was European Commission: Regulation No 800/2008/EC, OJ L 241 of 9 August 2008. Currently this is European Commission: Regulation No 651/2014/EU of 17 June 2014 declaring certain categories of aid compatible with the internal market in application of Articles 107 and 108 of the Treaty, OJ L 187 of 26 June 2014.
69. Council Regulation No 1588/2015/EU of 13 July 2015 on the application of Articles 107 and 108 of the Treaty on the Functioning of the European Union to certain categories of horizontal State aid, OJ L 248 of 24 September 2015.
70. The Commission's Directorate-General for Agriculture and Rural Development deals with aid in the agriculture sector, the Directorate-General for Maritime Affairs and Fisheries deals with aid in the fisheries sector. All other cases and sectors are regulated by the Directorate-General for Competition.

While the resultant exclusions gave considerable leeway to the Council in regard to EU common policies and were initially intended to largely exclude the agriculture, fisheries and transport sectors (which were heavily supported by many of the founding Member States), both policy and law in the last 60 years have increased the scope of application of Article 107 of the TFEU to those sectors, especially in the setting of CAP reforms and progressive phases of liberalisation in the transport sector.

2.6.1.1 Agriculture

In general terms, the EEC Treaty provided from the outset that the competition rules of the Treaty could only apply to agriculture to the extent that the Council decided to make them applicable. This is now reflected in Article 42 of the TFEU.

TFEU – Article 42

The provisions of the Chapter relating to rules on competition shall apply to production of and trade in agricultural products only to the extent determined by the European Parliament and the Council within the framework of Article 43(2) and in accordance with the procedure laid down therein, account being taken of the objectives set out in Article 39.

The Council, on a proposal from the Commission, may authorise the granting of aid:

(a) for the protection of enterprises handicapped by structural or natural conditions;
(b) within the framework of economic development programmes.

Following the changes introduced by the Lisbon Treaty (resulting in the TFEU), references to agriculture include reference to fisheries.[71]

In the period prior to the CAP (which established detailed market organisation rules by Regulation across most of the agricultural sector) the approach of the Council was one of reluctance as regards the competition rules[72] – although the scene was set as early as 1962 for the monitoring of agricultural aid by the establishment of a Community inventory of such aid.[73] With the advent of the CAP, the Regulations governing the organisation of the various markets generally provided for the

71. *See* Article 38(1) of the TFEU which provides that: "References to the common agricultural policy or to agriculture, and the use of the term 'agricultural', shall be understood as also referring to fisheries, having regard to the specific characteristics of this sector."
72. For example, Council Regulation 26 of 4 April 1962, OJ 993 of 1962, which applied Article 87(1) and 87(3) first sentence of the Treaty (now Article 107(1) and (3) of the TFEU) to production and trade of Annex II products resulting in a supervisory role for the Commission without the remaining enforcement powers of Article 88 (now Article 108 of the TFEU).
73. For a strong critique of this system in practice, however, *see* House of Lords Select Committee on the European Communities: State Aids to Agriculture, 1981–1982, Seventh Report, HMSO London.

application of what are now Articles 107–109 of the TFEU in full "save as otherwise provided in this Regulation."[74] The European Court of Justice subsequently confirmed that this had two effects. First, the State aid provisions of the Treaty are subordinate to any Regulation on the organisation of a particular market[75] as a *lex specialis* and, second, infringement of a CAP Regulation precludes an exemption of an aid under what is now Article 107(3) of the TFEU.[76] Thus, in particular, where a common organisation on an agricultural market had not been achieved (e.g., in regard to potatoes, horsemeat or honey) the State aid rules could be partially applied.

An attempt by the Commission to revise this in 1966 to introduce a framework Regulation on State aid to agriculture was recast by the Council into a (non-binding) Resolution.[77] In the 1970s, various Directives were adopted to improve the structural adaptation of the agricultural sector. These promoted farm modernisation, early retirement, training, hill farming and marketing and processing.[78] Various Community interventions to support the farming sector were introduced under these Directives and financial assistance from what was then the EAGGF provided the Community support. These arrangements directly encouraged Member States to introduce aid schemes where they had not previously done so and allowed national schemes to supplement Community interventions. In the case of national schemes for the consolidation of holdings[79] and processing and marketing,[80] it was stipulated that the State aid rules applied.

Most recently, as part of the CAP reforms, a single Regulation on the common organisation of agricultural markets (known as the Single CMO Regulation) was introduced to coordinate and consolidate the legislation governing the different CAP organised markets.[81] This provides, in particular, that the State aid rules of Articles 107–109 of the TFEU shall apply to cereals, rice, sugar, dried fodder, seeds, hops, olive oil and table olives, flax and hemp, fruits and vegetables, bananas, wine, live plants

74. For example: Article 22 of Council Regulation No 27427/75/EEC, OJ L 281/1 of 1975, on the cereals market.
75. Case C-177/78: *Pigs & Bacon Commission v. McCarren*, [1979] ECR 2161 at 2187.
76. Case C-72/79: *Commission v. Italy*, [1980] ECR 1411 at 1425. *See also* the positions taken by the Commission in Decision No 81/601, on aid to maintain farm incomes in 1980 granted by the French Government, OJ L 220/37 of 6 August 1981 and Decision No 82/401, OJ L 173/20 of 1982 concerning French income maintenance aid to farmers and aid to Sicilian wine, fruit and vegetable sectors respectively.
77. The Commission reopened the issue of regularising the treatment of State aid in the *Twentieth Report on Competition Policy*, (1990) point. 337 and the *Sixteenth Report on Competition Policy* (1986) sets out a list of Annex II products not covered by a common organisation.
78. Council Directive No 72/159/EEC; Council Directive No 72/160/EEC and Council Directive No 72/161/EEC of 17 April 1972 concerning the provision of socio-economic guidance for and the acquisition of occupational skills by persons engaged in agriculture, OJ L 96 of 23 April 1972 Spec. Ed. 324, Council Directive No 75/268/EEC of 28 April 1975 on mountain and hill farming and farming in certain less-favoured areas, OJ L 128 of 19 May 1975 and Council Regulation No 355/77/EEC on common measures to improve the conditions under which agricultural products are processed and marketed, OJ L 51 of 23 February 1977.
79. Council Directive No 72/160/EEC, *supra*, Article 14.
80. Council Regulation No 355/77/EEC, *supra*, Article 23.
81. Council Regulation No 1234/2007/EC of 22 October 2007 establishing a common organisation of agricultural markets and on specific provisions for certain agricultural products (Single CMO Regulation), OJ L 299 of 16 November 2007.

and the products of floriculture, raw tobacco, beef and veal, milk and milk products, pigmeat, sheepmeat, goatmeat, poultrymeat, eggs, ethyl alcohol of agricultural origin, apiculture products and silkworms and to several other products.[82] Specific provisions apply for milk and milk products[83] and for a range of national situations (e.g., reindeer farming in Finland, the alcohol monopoly in Germany) and for the payment of temporary aid where sugar quotas have been reduced by more than 50%.[84]

In regard to rural development, the rules governing the current European Agricultural Fund for Rural Development (EAFRD) provide that the State aid rules do not apply to Member State co-financing of EAFRD rural development schemes. Instead, these are subject to specific rules under the Rural Development Regulation.[85] For example, ceilings are set for aid to support farm modernisation – such as a ceiling of €70,000 to assist young farmers.[86]

In the fisheries sector, a similar approach to the Single CMO Regulation was earlier set out in Council Regulation No 104/2000 which provides that Articles 107–109 of the TFEU shall apply to the production and trade in fishery products[87] and in Council Regulation No 1198/2006 on the European Fisheries Fund (EFF).[88]

Thus, the apparent original exclusion of the agriculture and (subsequently) fisheries sectors from the application of the State aid rules is no longer absolute and separate and increasingly stringent State aid rules have developed in each of these sectors over the years. At present, the State aid rules in these sectors (also including forestry) are based on three different principles:

(1) They follow the general principles of EU competition policy.
(2) They have to be coherent and consistent with the EU's common agricultural and rural development policies.
(3) They take into account the EU's international commitments (including under the World Trade Organisation (WTO) Agreement on Agriculture, 1994).[89]

In regard to the fisheries and aquaculture sectors, these are covered by the general State aid rules only to the extent determined by the European Parliament and the Council in

82. *Ibid.*, Article 180. The other products are set out in Annex 1 Part XX1 of the Single CMO Regulation.
83. *Ibid.*, Article 181.
84. *Ibid.*, Article 182.
85. Regulation No 1305/2013/EU of the European Parliament and of the Council of 17 December 2013 on support for rural development by the European Agricultural Fund for Rural Development (EAFRD) and repealing Council Regulation No 1698/2005/EC, OJ L 347 of 20 December 2013.
86. *Ibid.*, Annex 1.
87. Council Regulation No 104/2000/EC of 17 December 1999 on the common organisation of the markets in fishery and aquaculture products, OJ L 17 of 21 January 2000.
88. Council Regulation No 1198/2006/EC of 27 July 2006 on the European Fisheries Fund, OJ L 223 of 15 August 2006.
89. WTO: Agreement on Agriculture, 1994 (accessible at: http://www.wto.org).

line with Article 42 of the TFEU. In practice, this means that funding for these sectors emerges from two directions:

(1) from the European Maritime and Fisheries Fund (EMFF) – in principle not State aid;[90]
(2) by means of State aid granted by EU countries to the fishing and aquaculture industry other than financing under the EMFF within the scope of Article 42 of the TFEU.

The main State aid rules in the agriculture, forestry rural development and fisheries sectors are set out in the following instruments:

- Guidelines on State aid for Agriculture, Forestry and Rural Development (2014).[91]
- Agriculture Block Exemption Regulation (2014).[92]
- The Agriculture *De Minimis* Regulation (2013).[93]

90. EMFF funding is co-financed by the EU and EU Member States in line with EMFF Regulation No 508/2014/EU of the European Parliament and of the Council of 15 May 2014 on the European Maritime and Fisheries Fund and repealing Council Regulations No 2328/2003/EC, No 861/2006/EC, No 1198/2006/EC and No 791/2007/EC and Regulation No 1255/2011/EU of the European Parliament and of the Council, OJ L 149 of 20 May 2014.
91. European Commission: European Union Guidelines for State aid in the agricultural and forestry sectors and in rural areas 2014 to 2020, OJ C 204 of 1 July 2014. These set out the criteria which will be used by the Commission when assessing the compatibility of such aid with the internal market and the conditions which will be verified in order to determine whether a measure constituting aid to make good the damage caused by natural disasters or exceptional occurrences is indeed covered by Article 107(2) of the TFEU. Moreover, the use of State aid can be justified only if it is in line with the objectives of the Common Agricultural Policy (CAP) and, in particular, the underlying objectives of the CAP reform towards 2020.
92. European Commission: Regulation No 702/2014/EU of 25 June 2014 declaring certain categories of aid in the agricultural and forestry sectors and in rural areas compatible with the internal market in application of Articles 107 and 108 of the Treaty on the Functioning of the European Union, OJ L 193 of 1 July 2014. In particular, this Regulation provides for block exemption from prior notification of: (1) aid in favour of SMEs active in primary agricultural production, the processing of agricultural products and the marketing of agricultural products; (2) aid for investments in favour of conservation of cultural and natural heritage located on agricultural holdings; (3) aid to make good the damage caused by natural disasters in the agricultural sector; (4) aid for research and development in the agricultural and forestry sectors; (5) aid in favour of forestry; and (6) aid in favour of SMEs in Rural Areas co-financed by the EAFRD or granted as additional national financing to such co-financed measures. These exemptions are subject to the conditions laid down in the Regulation.
93. European Commission: Regulation No 1408/2013/EU of 18 December 2013 on the application of Articles 107 and 108 of the Treaty on the Functioning of the European Union to *de minimis* aid in the agriculture sector, OJ L 352 of 24 December 2013. This Regulation applies to aid granted to undertakings active in the primary production of agricultural products, with some exceptions. The total amount of *de minimis* aid granted per Member State to a single undertaking shall not exceed €15,000 over any period of three fiscal years, provided that the global amount of such aid does not exceed 1% of the annual agricultural output.

- Fishery and Aquaculture Block Exemption Regulation (2014).[94]
- *De minimis* fisheries and aquaculture (2014).[95]

It is also important to note that food processing industries are not excluded by any special rules applying to these sectors as the special rules essentially relate to State aid for primary production. Furthermore, as much agricultural aid in the EU is given in response to natural disasters affecting farming, the tightening up of the de jure exemption of State aid to relieve natural disasters (*see infra*) under Article 107(2) of the TFEU is also relevant and has been reflected in the relevant sectoral rules.[96]

2.6.1.2 Transport

In regard to transport, Article 93 of the TFEU provides that:

> Aids shall be compatible with this Treaty if they meet the needs of co-ordination of transport or if they represent reimbursement for the discharge of certain obligations inherent in the concept of a public service.

The effect of this in combination with "save as otherwise provided in this Treaty" in Article 107(1) is not, however, to exempt transport aid from Articles 107 and 108. This was firmly ruled out by the Court in 1978 in *Commission v. Belgium*.[97] What Article 93 does, in fact, is provide an additional basis for compatibility or exemption for State aid. Thus, if a transport aid is compatible with Article 107(1), no further examination is required. If not, it may be held compatible under Article 107(2) or Article 93. In other cases, it may be exempted under Article 107(3). At the same time, the terminology of

94. European Commission: Regulation No 1388/2014/EU of 16 December 2014 declaring certain categories of aid to undertakings active in the production, processing and marketing of fishery and aquaculture products compatible with the internal market in application of Articles 107 and 108 of the Treaty on the Functioning of the European Union OJ L 369 of 24 December 2014. In particular, this Regulation applies to State aid measures to assist small and medium-sized enterprises (SMEs) active in the production, processing or marketing of fishery and aquaculture products and to aid granted to undertakings active in the production, processing or marketing of fishery and aquaculture products to make good damage caused by natural disasters, independently of the size of the beneficiary of the aid. The Regulation provides generally that any project with eligible costs of less than €2 million, or where the amount of aid is less than €1 million per beneficiary per year, is exempt from prior notification.
95. European Commission: Regulation No 717/2014/EU of 27 June 2014 on the application of Articles 107 and 108 of the Treaty on the Functioning of the European Union to *de minimis* aid in the fishery and aquaculture sector, OJ L 190 of 28 June 2014. This provides that State aid not exceeding €30,000 per beneficiary over any period of three years is deemed not to meet all the criteria laid down in Article 107(1) of the TFEU. In addition, each EU Member State has to respect a maximum cumulative amount while granting aid to undertakings active in the fishery and aquaculture sector and *de minimis* aid granted to all undertakings in the fishery and aquaculture sector over a three-year period cannot exceed 2.5% of the annual catching, processing and aquaculture turnover of a Member State. Moreover, *de minimis* aid may not be used for the purchase of fishing vessels, for modernisation or replacement of the main or ancillary engines of fishing vessels or to increase the fishing capacity of a vessel or equipment increasing the ability of a vessel to find fish.
96. European Commission: Guidelines for State aid in the agricultural and forestry sectors and in rural areas 2014 to 2020, *supra*, para 223.
97. Case C-156/77: *Commission v. Belgium*, [1978] ECR 1881 at p. 1894 para. 10.

Article 93 is very vague and has required detailed elaboration under a variety of Council instruments[98] which clarify when transport aid properly meets "the needs of co-ordination of transport" or involves "reimbursement for the discharge of certain obligations inherent in the concept of a public service."

Council Regulation No 1107/70/EEC,[99] in particular, provided for the clearance of State aid under Article 93 where it promoted fair competition (especially for railways), assisted adaptation or was part of a plan to reduce sectoral capacity. By way of illustration, the road haulage sector could not receive State aid (e.g., grants to buy rolling stock) unless this was part of a national plan to reduce overall capacity levels in national haulage.

In regard to *air and sea transport*, Article 100(2) of the TFEU provides that Article 93 and the other provisions of the Transport Title of the Treaty shall not apply to these sectors pending a Council decision to apply them. The *French Sailors* Case[100] held, however, that the general rules of the Treaty applied to those sectors. Accordingly, they are covered by Articles 107–109. Commission work in these sectors evolved gradually since the 1970s and was first reflected in a policy Statement on shipping aid and later Commission Guidelines on State aid to Maritime Transport (1997, updated in 2004), which defined the conditions under which such aid would be considered compatible with the internal market.[101] In particular, the 2004 Maritime Guidelines were inspired by the view that the EU should ensure freedom of access to shipping markets across the world for safe and environmentally friendly ships, preferably registered in EU Member States with EU nationals employed. A further factor was that, in parallel with an increase in the number of EU registered ships, there was a significant decline in the number of EU seafarers – partly due to higher tax and social security payments in EU countries. Accordingly, the Maritime Guidelines reflect a need to relax State aid rules to promote the competitiveness of EU ships versus those of other countries.

98. The seminal instrument here was Council Decision No 271/65/EEC, on the clarification of the application of Articles 107 to 109 in regard to taxation, social security and State intervention in relation to competition in rail, road, and inland waterway transport (1965–1966), OJ 1500 Spec. Ed. 67. Subsequently, the Council adopted three Regulations: *Council Regulation 1191/69/EEC on public service obligations in transport,* [1969] OJ L 156/1, Spec Ed. 276 (which imposed a free market criterion on the concept while allowing notably for the safeguarding of adequate transport supply); *Council Regulation 1192/69/EEC,* [1969] OJ L 156/8, Spec. Ed. 283 (which dealt with common rules for the calculation and compensation via State aid of the social costs of railways) and *Council Regulation 1107/70/EEC* OJ L 130/1 Spec. Ed. 360 (which set out detailed rules for the granting of aids for road, rail and inland waterway transport).
99. Council Regulation No 1107/70/EEC on the granting of aids for transport by rail, road and inland waterway, OJ L 130 of 1970.
100. Case C-167/83: *Commission v. France,* [1974] ECR 359 at 371.
101. The original rules emerged as *Guidelines for the examination of State Aids to Community Shipping companies* of 3 August 1989 referred to in *Nineteenth Report on Competition Policy,* (1989) point 211. These were updated by the Community guidelines on State aid to maritime transport, OJ C 205/5 of 5 July 1997 and the most recent policy guidelines are the Community guidelines on State aid to maritime transport, OJ C 13 of 17 January 2004.

Table 1 Main Provisions of 2004 Maritime State Aid Guidelines

- Endorses special tax measures for shipping (e.g., accelerated depreciation allowances, allowances for re-invested profits and tonnage based profits taxation) as acceptable State aid. - Allows such measures also for full shipping fleets. - Allows aid to ship-management companies where they manage the entire crew and the technical management of a ship or ships (*this elaborated further in separate Communication on State aid to ship management companies of 2009*).[102] - Allows State aid to reduce employment costs and taxes related to seafarers. - Allows aid to repatriate sailors. - Allows aid for ship renewal (investment aid) if in accordance with the Shipbuilding sectoral State aid rules. - Also allows investment aid to improve equipment, safety and hygiene on ships.

To regulate air transport, three Regulations on the liberalisation of air transport[103] and guidelines on rescue aid in the air transport sector and on the financing of airports and start-up aid to airlines departing from regional airports were adopted between 1994 and 2005.[104] In February 2014, new *Commission Guidelines on State Aid to Airports and airlines* replaced both the 1994 and the 2005 aviation guidelines.[105]

It is important to note that the airlines sector was previously regulated by bilateral agreements between Member States. However, the liberalisation of the sector since the 1970s meant that the State aid position became very important for actually achieving the benefits of liberalisation. Thus, as early as 1993 and 1994, the Commission examined the restructuring programmes of Aer Lingus, TAP, Air France and Olympic Airways[106] and made its authorisation of State aid subject to much stricter conditions. These cases then, in effect, set the conditions for the 1994 aviation Guidelines,

102. European Commission: Communication from the Commission providing guidance on State aid to ship-management companies, OJ C 132 of 11 June 2009.
103. Council Regulation No 2407/92/EEC of 23 July 1992 on licensing of air carriers, OJ L 240 of 24 August 1992, Council Regulation No 2408/92/EEC of 23 July 1992 on access for Community air carriers to intra-Community air routes, OJ C 178 of 30 June 1993 and Council Regulation No 2409/92/EEC of 23 July 1992 on fares and rates for air services, OJ C 293 of 29 October 1993.
104. European Commission: Community guidelines on the application of Articles 87 and 88 of the EC Treaty and Article 61 of the EEA Agreement to State aids in the aviation sector (OJ C 350 of 10 December 1994) and European Commission: Community guidelines on financing of airports and start-up aid to airlines departing from regional airports, OJ C 312 of 9 December 2005. The general background to the 1994 guidelines is set out in the Twenty-Fourth Report on Competition Policy (1994), point 375.
105. European Commission: Communication from the Commission - *Guidelines on State aid to airports and airlines*, OJ C 99 of 4 April 2014.
106. European Commission: Decision No 94/118/EC of 21 December 1993 concerning aid to be provided by the Irish Government to the Aer Lingus group, OJ L 54 of 25 February 1994, Decision No 94/698/EC of 6 July 1994 concerning increase in capital, credit guarantees and tax exemption in favour of TAP, OJ L 279/29 of 28 October 1994, Decision No 94/653/EC of 27 July 1994 concerning the notified capital increase of Air France, OJ L 254/73 of 30 September 1994 and Olympic Airways of 7 October 1994 on the aid granted by Greece to Olympic Airways, OJ L 273/22 of 25 October 1994. The Air France approval of 20 billion francs was overturned by the Court of First Instance in Cases T-371 & T-394/94: *British airways and British Midland Airways v. Commission,* [1998] ECR II-2405.

including special rules for the rescue and restructuring of airlines. Under the 2014 guidelines, however, the special airline rescue and restructuring rules were abolished and the general State aid rules on rescue and restructuring[107] now apply also to airlines. However, the 2014 guidelines do allow State aid to airlines for launching new routes in special circumstances (e.g., to improve the transport connectivity of EU regions) and for certain types of aid to airports. A summary of the present position is provided below.

Table 2 Main State Aid Rules on Airlines and Airports

- State aid for investment in airport infrastructure is allowed if there is a genuine transport need and the public support is necessary to ensure the accessibility of a region.
- The new guidelines define maximum permissible aid intensities depending on the size of an airport, in order to ensure the right mix between public and private investment.
- The possibilities to grant aid are therefore higher for smaller airports than for larger ones.
- Operating aid to regional airports (with less than 3 million passengers a year) will be allowed for a transitional period of ten years under certain conditions, in order to give airports time to adjust their business model.
- To receive operating aid, airports need to work out a business plan paving the way towards full coverage of operating costs at the end of the transitional period.
- As under the current market conditions, airports with an annual passenger traffic of below 700,000 may face increased difficulties in achieving full cost coverage during the transitional period, the guidelines include a special regime for those airports, with higher aid intensities and a reassessment of the situation after five years.
- Start-up aid to airlines to launch a new air route is permitted provided it remains limited in time. The compatibility conditions for start-up aid to airlines have been streamlined and adapted to recent market developments.

In regard to railways, this is perhaps the transport sector with the lowest scrutiny of State aids within the EU system. This arises because of the relatively limited liberalisation and the very high level of public service obligations in that sector. In line with the Court's judgment in the *Altmark Case (2003)*,[108] the State aid control regime does not apply to compensation given to any undertaking in consideration for public service obligations imposed on them (because there is no advantage conferred) where the four Altmark conditions are met and this has a particular importance in regard to the transport sector.[109]

It is also to be noted that, while the solutions adopted within the Common Transport Policy to State aid issues were quite different to those in the agricultural sector, in both areas the development of EU policies has had regard to the State aid

107. These are considered further in *Chapter 4*.
108. Case C-280/00: *Altmark Trans GmbH and Regierungspräsidium Magdeburg v. Nahverkehrsgesellschaft Altmark GmbH, and Oberbundesanwalt beim Bundesverwaltungsgericht*, [2003] ECR I-7747.
109. Although it also applies *mutatis mutandis* to other sectors including postal services, telecommunications and energy.

rules – albeit as secondary to the sectoral imperatives in the Treaty. Unlike industrial policy (where the pooling of sovereignty was not accepted by the authors of the Treaty),[110] the separate development of law and policy in agriculture and transport reflects the evolution of the original consensus to develop these sectors in a common EU context. Accordingly, the control of aid in agriculture and transport can be generally regarded as a separate instrument of those common policies which, in practice, were separately administered for that reason. In both cases, however, there has been a trend to gradually increase the application of the State aid rules in those sectors (especially but not solely in regard to problematic types of aid, problematic sub-sectors and parts of the sectors which are more peripheral to the operations of both common policies). As a result, the apparent exemption of agriculture and transport under the phrase "save as otherwise provided by this Treaty" in Article 107(1) is no longer clear-cut and demands specialised navigation through the common policy rules, court jurisprudence and the secondary rules applying Articles 107 and 108 of the TFEU.

2.6.1.3 Defence and Security

Article 346 of the TFEU provides that the provisions of the Treaty are without prejudice to the right of a Member State to take necessary measures for the "protection of the essential interests of its security which are connected with the production of or trade in arms, munitions and war material." Accordingly, ordnance factories can be subsidised without regard to Articles 107 and 108. However, the measures contemplated by Article 346 must not adversely affect the conditions of competition in the internal market regarding products which are not intended for specifically military purposes (so-called dual-use goods). Should this occur, Article 348 provides that the European Commission and the Member States concerned must examine how these measures can be adjusted to the rules laid down in the Treaty. Article 348 also provides that the Commission or any Member State may bring an action to the Court if they consider that a Member State is making improper use of the provisions of Article 346. The Court must give its ruling *in camera*.

There have been few cases related to this provision. In *Commission v. Greece (1994)* the Commission brought an action against Greece for prohibiting exports into or through its territory from the Former Yugoslav Republic of Macedonia. The *in camera* ruling of the Court rejected the Commission's application for interim measures.[111] Later, in *BFM v. Commission (1998)*, restructuring aid was granted to an Italian firm which was allegedly working in the defence sector. This aid was refused by the Commission and BFM argued that the aid in question was not covered by Article 107(1) of the Treaty. The Court of First Instance held that none of the aid at issue was specifically connected to military projects closely linked to national defence policy and that the causal link between the proposed injection of fresh capital and its specific

110. As discussed later, it nonetheless seems to have been largely created, and somewhat by default, by the extensive use of the GBER by EU Member States.
111. Case C-120/94: *Commission v. Greece*, judgment of 29 June 1994 [1996] ECR I-1513.

application to the protection of the essential interests of security connected with the production of or trade in arms, munitions and war material could not be established.[112]

Reflecting the traditional EU logic of the phrase "save as otherwise provided by this Treaty," the exclusions related to the phrase are also reflected in EU agreements with non-EU countries requiring national State aid systems in the latter.[113] Generally, non-EU countries are also not required to regulate the areas excluded from the scope of Article 107(1) of the TFEU by this phrase. However, given the complex interactions between the general State aid rules and EU common policy areas such as agriculture, fisheries and transport (which are not mirrored in the national policies of non-EU countries in regard to those sectors), third countries tend towards a blanket exclusion of these sectors. A possible exception to this is the application of the Altmark criteria as the EU encourages a harmonised approach to SGEI situations (another area generally unknown in non-EU countries) in applying State aid rules under these agreements.

2.6.2 By or Through State Resources (Test 2)

The second criterion for a State aid measure is direct or indirect involvement of State resources and the imputability of the measure[114] with reference to the phrase "by or through State resources" in Article 107(1) of the TFEU.

Following the evolution of EU practice and case law, the term "resources" is to be interpreted widely and the EU Courts have expanded this beyond obvious public expenditure support to explicitly include cases where:

- revenues that would otherwise be payable to the State are foregone;
- the State makes a firm and concrete commitment to make State resources available in the future;
- revenues do not reach the State budget, but the State imposes contributions and controls their collection and spending; or
- the measure leads to a sufficiently concrete risk of an additional burden on the State's budget for the future.

It is clear that the notion of "State" includes central government authorities, decentralised authorities (provincial, departments, municipalities and local authorities), autonomous regions (such as Sicily)[115] and States within States (e.g., the German Lander).[116] It is also clear that aid can be passed on within the various layers of a national system (e.g., central government aid decided and delivered at municipal level)

112. Joined Cases T-126-127/96: *Breda Fucine Meridionale SpA v. Commission*, [1998] ECR II-3437 at 89.
113. *See* discussion of these in *Chapter 3*.
114. In its legal meaning, *imputability* refers to legal responsibility because of a particular relationship resulting in liability, financial or otherwise.
115. The Italian Constitutional Court ruled in two cases (*State Commissioner for the Sicilian Region v. Regional Government of Sicily*, [1963] CMLR 315 and *State Commissioner for the Sicilian Region v. Regional Government of Sicily*, [1970] CMLR 35) that the Italian autonomous regions were bound by Articles 107 and 108 of the TFEU.
116. European Commission: *First Report on Competition Policy*, (1971) points 158 and 159.

or generated and granted from the resources of any type of authority covered by the broad descriptions above. Accordingly, the scope of "State" is wide-ranging and includes the Government directly as well as all other public authorities – Ministries, regional authorities, municipalities, and other public institutions. It also encapsulates public enterprises and other undertakings (even private) acting in the name of the State or authorised by public institutions.

Only advantages granted directly or indirectly through State resources can constitute State aid within the meaning of Article 107(1) of the TFEU. State resources include all resources of the public sector, including resources of intra-State entities (decentralised, federated, regional or other) and, under certain circumstances, resources of private bodies. Moreover, it is irrelevant whether an institution within the public sector is autonomous. Funds provided by the central bank of a Member State to specific credit institutions generally fall within the scope of the State aid rules. Resources of public undertakings also constitute State resources within the meaning of Article 107(1) of the TFEU because the State is capable of directing the use of these resources. Furthermore, the financial resources of private undertakings controlled by the State can also be subject to the TFEU State aid rules.

"By a Member State or through State resources" excludes aid from a private body e.g. a philanthropic foundation or a charity. However, it does not exclude assistance from a private body which is itself assisted by the State as, for example, where Italian banks were encouraged by tax advantages to form consortia for rescue operations in the private sector.[117] Moreover a formalistic approach to the status of a body giving aid does not preclude the application of Article 107 of the TFEU. In *Firma Steinike und Weinlig v. Germany (1977)*, where the body concerned was established by public law and financed its food marketing operations from State grants and producer contributions, the Court held:

> It is not necessary to make a distinction whether the aid is granted directly by the State or by public or private bodies established or appointed by it to administer the aid. In applying [Article 107], regard must primarily be had to the effects of the aid on the undertakings or producers favoured and not the status of the institutions entrusted with the distribution and administration of the aid.[118]

In *Italy v. Commission (1974)*[119] the measure at issue was a 33% reduction for the textile sector in statutory contributions to family allowances. Italy argued that the losses to the social security fund were made up by another unemployment fund financed by the private sector and, accordingly, there was a double entry that meant the reduction did not constitute aid under Article 107. The Court rejected this as the contributions were a compulsory obligation in law and the replacement funds "must be regarded as State resources within the meaning of [Article 107] even if they are administered by institutions distinct from the public authorities."[120]

117. European Commission: *Tenth Report on Competition Policy*, (1980), point 220.
118. Case C-78/76: *Firma Steinike und Weinlig v. Germany*, [1977] ECR 595 at 611.
119. Case C-173/73: *Italy v. Commission*, [1974] ECR, 709.
120. *Ibid.*, at 720.

The position may be summarised by the application of the following tests to an apparently private body:

- is it established or appointed by the State to administer aid?;[121]
- does it get its funding from compulsory contributions under public law?;[122]
- does it manage and distribute funds in accordance with legislation?;[123] and
- is it, de facto or de jure, predominantly under State influence in its decision-making[124]?

In regard to imputability, an aid measure is imputable to the State when it can be linked to the decision of a public authority and it is clear that the State ultimately has control over the decision to transfer the relevant resources. Such a link is present when the aid is granted directly by a public authority or when the public authority appoints a private or public body to administer the measure, regardless of whether that public authority has some degree of autonomy. However, it is harder to prove imputability to the State when the advantage is granted through intermediate bodies (public or private). In such cases, the fact that a measure is taken by an intermediate body is insufficient to establish the link. In the *France v. Commission (Stardust) (2002)* case, [125] the European Court of Justice concluded that State aid may be established only where State funds are used and that the use of the funds of State enterprises alone was insufficient to meet this condition. In addition, it was necessary to prove that public authorities had been involved in the adoption of the measure and/or that they were instructed by the State.

To help to clarify imputability, the European Commission has suggested a list of indicators through which imputability can be established. If the advantage is granted through a public undertaking such indicators are: that the undertaking had to take into account directives issued by governmental bodies; or the integration of the undertaking into the structures of public administration. By contrast, a measure is not imputable to the State if it is the mere result of the implementation of EU law and the State had no discretion in the matter.[126]

According to the Commission, the origin of the resources is not relevant provided that, before being directly or indirectly transferred to the beneficiaries, they enter under public control and are, therefore, available to the national authorities, even if the resources do not become the property of the public authority. This policy position has allowed the Commission in various recent legislation and soft law instruments to include most EU structural funds as State aid. This is a controversial position and emerged from political complaints by Member States not in receipt of structural funds. In essence, structural funds are EU funds which are fundamentally directed by the EU.

121. The Steinike und Weinlig principle.
122. The *Italy v. Commission case.*
123. Case C-290/83: *Commission v. France (Credit Agricole),* [1985] ECR 439 and Case C-222/82: *Apple and Pear Development Council v. Lewis,* [1983] ECR 4083.
124. Case C-67/85: *Van der Kooy v. Commission,* [1988] ECR 219 and Case C-303/88: *ENI-Lanerossi,* [1991] ECR I-1433.
125. Case C-482/99: *France v. Commission* (Stardust), [2002] ECR I-4397.
126. European Commission: *Commission Notice on the notion of State aid pursuant to Article 107(1) TFEU,* 19 May 2016, OJ 262 of 19 July 2016.

In some cases, structural funds are added to by national funds but in some cases they are not. In the case of other EU funding, the funds are entirely administered and distributed by the EU. An alternative approach would have been to only view State matching funding as State resources and, indeed, this was the previous Commission position. However, in its latest policy Statement on this, the Commission points out that:

> Resources coming from the Union (e.g. from structural funds) or international financial institutions, such as the IMF or the EBRD, should also be considered as State resources if national authorities have discretion as to the use of those resources (in particular the selection of beneficiaries). By contrast, if such resources are awarded directly by the Union or the international financial institutions, with no discretion on the part of the national authorities, they do not constitute State resources (e.g. funding awarded in direct management under the Horizon 2020 framework programme or the COSME programme)[127]

Moreover, regulation that leads to financial redistribution from one private entity to another without any further involvement of the State does not entail a transfer of State resources, if the money flows directly from one private entity to another, without passing through a public or private body designated by the State to administer the transfer. An example of this is an obligation imposed by the State on private electricity suppliers to purchase electricity produced from renewable energy sources at fixed minimum prices. This does not entail the direct or indirect transfer of State resources to undertakings which produce that type of electricity. In this case, the undertakings concerned (i.e., the private electricity suppliers) are not appointed by the State to manage an aid scheme, but are only bound by an obligation to purchase a specific type of electricity with their own financial resources.[128]

A further consideration here is that, while the concept of aid has clearly widened over the years, the European Courts have paradoxically taken a strict position of interpretation against widening the scope of "aid" to include any *measures with equivalent effect to aid.*[129] This has generally arisen where the Commission found it difficult to confirm that a particular measure was aid and, nonetheless, wanted to see it broadly regulated as if it was aid.

A final aspect here is that, because of the potential for evading the State aid rules, the Commission adopted a Directive in 1980 to make the financial relations between Member States and public bodies operating in the professional, industrial, agricultural or business sectors transparent.[130] Under the Directive, Member States are required to

127. *Ibid.*, para. 62. This citation also notes that, in the case of funding directly from the EU, principles similar to the substantive provisions of State aid law are often applicable by virtue of secondary Union legislation which frequently imposes consistency requirements.

128. *Ibid.*, paras 63 and 64.

129. This was confirmed in Case C-290/83: *Commission v. France ("Poor farmers")*, [1985] ECR 439, para. 18. The point also arose in Case C-349/98: *Preussen Elektra*, [2001] ECR I-2099, paras 63–65.

130. European Commission: Commission Directive No 80/723/EEC on the transparency of financial relations between Member States and public undertakings, OJ L 195 of 29 July 1980. This Directive is based on the view that the fair and effective application of the competition rules requires a detailed knowledge of companies' financial and organisational structures, especially

ensure the transparency of financial relations between public authorities and undertakings which have benefited from public resources and they must take the necessary measures to guarantee transparency in respect of:

- setting-off of operating losses;
- provision of capital;
- non-refundable grants or loans on privileged terms;
- financial advantages granted by forgoing profits or debt recovery;
- forgoing of a normal return on public funds used;
- compensation for financial burdens imposed by public authorities.

EU Member States are also required to make available to the Commission all data concerning financial relations between the Member States and public undertakings. Moreover, the Directive creates an obligation to keep separate accounts which reflect the financial and organisational structure of undertakings with special or exclusive rights, so that it is possible to determine the costs corresponding to the different activities and the method whereby costs and revenues are assigned or allocated to the different activities. The Directive applies, in particular, to public undertakings operating in the manufacturing sector if their annual turnover exceeds €250 million. However, it does not apply to small-scale public and private undertakings supplying services (which are unlikely to affect trade between EU countries to an appreciable extent),[131] central banks, public credit institutions, as regards deposits of public funds placed with them by public authorities on normal commercial terms and undertakings which have been entrusted with the operation of SGEI – if the compensation they receive in any form whatsoever was fixed for an appropriate period following an open, transparent and non-discriminating procedure. The Directive was amended and updated in 2005[132] to clarify the requirements for separate accounts in the light of the *Altmark Case* on SGEI and, in particular, to require separate accounting – even in cases

as regards the financial relations between public authorities and public undertakings. This Directive was needed also because of the fact that what is now Article 345 of the TFEU stipulates that the Treaty does not prejudice the rules in Member States governing the system of property ownership and that no unjustified discrimination may be made between public and private undertakings in the application of the competition rules. Accordingly, EU Law is agnostic as between public enterprises and private firms in its market economy.

131. In effect, public undertakings whose net annual turnover in the two financial years preceding that in which the public resources were made available was less than €40 million (or a balance sheet total of €800 million in the case of public credit institutions) and public and private undertakings whose net annual turnover in the two financial years preceding any year in which it enjoys special or exclusive rights granted by an EU country or in which it is entrusted with the operation of a service of general economic interest was less than €40 million (or a balance sheet total of €800 million in the case of public credit institutions).

132. European Commission: Commission Directive No 2005/81/EC of 28 November 2005 amending Directive No 80/723/EEC on the transparency of financial relations between Member States and public undertakings as well as on financial transparency within certain undertakings, OJ L 312 of 29 November 2005.

where the transfer of State resources does not constitute State aid. The consolidated version of the Directive was published in 2006.[133]

2.6.3 Providing a Selective Advantage (Test 3)

The *a priori* prohibition of State aid under Article 107(1) of the TFEU requires that aid "favours certain undertakings or the production of certain goods." Accordingly, there must be an advantage and it must be a selective, rather than a general, advantage. Moreover, the recipient of the aid must be an undertaking, rather than a private individual (*see Test 4 infra*).

Accordingly, not all measures which favour economic operators fall under the notion of aid, but only those which grant *an advantage in a selective way* (sometimes referred to as a "specific advantage") to certain undertakings or categories of undertakings or to certain economic sectors. In particular, an advantage granted to *all* undertakings in a Member State is a general measure, rather than a State aid as it does not "favour certain undertakings or the production of certain goods." This is important for several reasons. First, it effectively excludes such interventions as generalised tax reliefs, general reductions of social security payments and most forms of general initiatives to promote employment, improve the investment climate and the business environment. Indeed, it is clear that general economic policy measures (such as those providing advantageous crediting terms, reduction of interest rates, reduction of the general tax burden e.g., corporate income tax) in respect of *all* undertakings do not constitute State aid. Second, specificity under Article 107(1) demands the presence of favourable treatment within the same Member State as between firms objectively in the same position.

Despite extensive but rather erratic case law on the subject, the selectivity test can be somewhat difficult to apply, in certain situations. This is because not every measure that produces an advantage for certain undertakings over others is regarded as selective within the meaning of Article 107(1) of the TFEU. In particular, the case law of the European Courts has held that a differential measure (one that applies differently to undertakings) may escape classification as State aid based on the selectivity criterion where:

(1) The favoured undertakings are not correctly comparable to the identified group of non-favoured undertakings.
(2) The different treatment may be justified by the nature and scheme of the relevant system.

Increasingly, EU law focuses on material selectivity and regional selectivity.

133. European Commission: Commission Directive No 2006/111/EC of 16 November 2006 on the transparency of financial relations between Member States and public undertakings as well as on financial transparency within certain undertakings (Codified version), OJ L 318 of 17 November 2006.

Material selectivity can be established de jure or de facto. De jure selectivity results directly from the legal criteria for granting a measure that is formally reserved for certain undertakings only (for instance, those of a certain size, those located in a certain area, firms active in certain sectors, firms having a certain legal form, firms incorporated during a particular period, firms belonging to a group having certain characteristics or firms entrusted with certain functions within a group). De facto selectivity can be established in cases where, although the formal criteria for the application of the measure are formulated in general and objective terms, the structure of the measure is such that its effects significantly favour a particular group of undertakings. De facto selectivity may be the result of conditions or barriers imposed by Member States preventing certain undertakings from benefiting from the measure. For example, applying a tax measure (e.g., a tax credit) only to investments exceeding a certain threshold may mean that the measure is de facto reserved for undertakings with significant financial resources.

Equally, selective advantage can also stem from discretionary administrative practices. Measures which prima facie apply to all undertakings, but are (or may be) limited by the discretionary power of administration, are selective.[134]

At the same time, it is clear that it is not necessary to identify State aid beneficiaries in advance for the measure to be selective. Where a measure requires beneficiaries to meet certain requirements to benefit from the aid, this still means that it is selective.[135] Equally, where there is only one beneficiary (an individual or "ad-hoc" aid), it is not necessary to determine whether the measure is selective vis-à-vis other undertakings in a similar situation.[136]

Regional selectivity refers to measures only available to undertakings in a particular region or area of an EU Member State. Indeed, the Court judgments in the *Azores* and *Gibraltar* tax cases provide detailed guidance on regional selectivity.[137]

A further consideration in regard to selectivity, especially in taxation or social security cases, is the exclusion of selectivity where the differential nature of a measure can be justified by the "nature or scheme of the system." This arises, for example, in tax systems involving progressive rates – the fact that one taxpayer pays more or less than others is regarded as a systemic function of the progressive tax system and, thus, lower rates are not per se selective.

In addition, investments in public infrastructure that benefit society and/or all undertakings generally are general measures rather than measures conferring a selective advantage. This includes the construction of roads, railways, canals, etc. However, if a particular infrastructure project can be linked to the needs of one or more particular firms, then infrastructure investment can be considered to create a selective

134. This has been an important consideration in recent EU State aid cases involving discretionary setting of tax arrangements between EU Member States and Starbucks, FIAT and Amazon.
135. Case T-468/08: *Tisza Eromu tft v. Commission*, ECLI:EU:T:2014:235, para. 164.
136. Case T-135/12: *France v. Commission*, ECLI:EU:T:2015:116 where the General Court considered French legislation reducing pension payments due from France Telecom. Here the selectivity was clear and an examination of the market position of other telecom operators was not relevant or needed to establish selectivity.
137. These cases are examined in further detail in *Chapter 4*.

advantage.[138] Another important consequence (e.g., in relation to the establishment of industrial parks as part of national industrial policy) is that the public financing of the preparation of land for industrial use, including the installation of electricity, water sewage and other utilities, does not create a selective advantage provided that the company or companies that eventually use the site pay for the use of the infrastructure provided via direct or indirect charges.[139]

Moreover, selectivity can arise from the abnormal market behaviour of the State. For example, where the State invests on the same basis as a normal private investor, there is no State aid passed on via the investment. Where the conditions of the investment are not in accordance with normal market investment, a selective advantage is likely to arise. Similar selective advantage considerations arise when the State grants loans, makes purchases or assists a commercial restructuring on conditions that are not typical for a private creditor, purchaser or debtor respectively.

Thus, in order to establish whether or not an undertaking receives an exceptional economic benefit or selective advantage, the so-called *market economy investor principle* may be applied. This principle is applicable where public institutions provide funding to undertakings in which the major share of the capital is State-owned, in order to establish whether or not a private investor operating under market conditions would behave the same way, i.e. whether or not a private investor under identical conditions would provide funding to the undertaking. If the State behaves as any private investor or creditor, then there is no State aid and no need for a public tender.

When providing funding to an undertaking suffering from economic difficulties, the issue whether a private investor would behave the same way needs to be carefully considered. In practice, the so-called *private creditor test* is applied. This test is used to examine whether debt renegotiations by public creditors involve State aid; comparing the behaviour of a public creditor to that of hypothetical private creditors that find themselves in a similar situation. Finally, the EU Courts have developed the "private vendor test" to assess whether a sale carried out by a public body involves State aid; considering whether a private vendor, under normal market conditions, could have obtained the same or a better price. These principles or tests are variations of the same basic concept that the behaviour of public authorities or undertakings should be compared to that of similar private economic operators under normal market conditions to determine whether the economic transactions carried out by such authorities or undertakings grant a selective advantage to their counterparts.

The search for a clear dividing line between measures which are selective and general measures has proved difficult; not least as EU Member States have produced a

138. *See* Case C-80/01P: *Aéroports de Paris v. Commission*, [2002] ECR I-9297 and Case C-288/11 P: *Mitteldeutsche Flughafen AG v. Commission* ECLI:EU:C:2012:821 where the close linkages between infrastructure and airport operations was held to involve State aid and European Commission: Decision No 91/390/EEC of 26 March 1991 *on aid granted by the French Government to the undertaking Saint-Gobain (Eurofloat) at Salaise-sur-Sanne (glass sector)*, OJ L 215 of 20 June 1991, where improved local infrastructure was held not to involve State aid to a major local undertaking.

139. On this, *see* European Commission: *Seventeenth Report on Competition Policy* (1988), p. 120 and *Twenty-Fifth Report on Competition Policy* (1995), point 158 together with Commission Decision: *Daimler Benz*, No 92/465/EEC, OJ L 263 1992.

range of arguments in an attempt to avoid the classification of various measures as selective. However, it is reasonably clear at this point that general measures, which are effectively open to all undertakings operating within a Member State, on an equal basis, are not selective. For measures to be genuinely general in character, they must not be reduced in scope in their application by factors that restrict their practical effect. Neither a large number of eligible undertakings (which can even include all undertakings of a certain sector), nor the diversity and size of the sectors to which they belong, provide grounds for concluding that a State initiative constitutes a general measure of economic policy, if not all economic sectors can benefit from it. Moreover, the fact that the scope of application of a measure is determined in an objective manner is not in itself sufficient to establish the general character of the measure and does not exclude selectivity.[140]

As a final remark here, it is to be noted that the phrase "favours certain undertakings or the production of certain goods" means that both goods and *services* are covered by the selective advantage test. This is, of course, because undertakings can produce goods or supply services.[141]

2.6.4 Only if Supporting an Undertaking or an Economic Activity (Test 4)

State aid only arises where the recipient of a support measure is an "undertaking" which performs economic activity. On this, it is also clear that the application of the State aid rules does not depend on whether an entity is set up to generate profits.[142] Moreover, the status of the entity under national law is not decisive. An entity that is classified as an "association" under national law may have to be regarded as an undertaking within the meaning of Article 107(1). The same applies to an entity that is formally part of the public administration. Thus, the application of the State aid rules does not depend on the legal status of an entity or on the way it is financed. In addition, the State aid rules apply regardless of whether an entity intends to make profit and regardless of whether it offers its services free of charge to end users or customers.[143]

Nonetheless, an entity that carries out both economic and non-economic activities is to be regarded as an undertaking only with regard to its economic activities. EU case law has made clear that Article 107 of the TFEU does not apply where the State acts "by exercising public power" or where public entities act "in their capacity as

140. Case C-143/99: *Adria-Wien Pipeline GmbH and Wietersdorfer & Peggauer Zementwerke GmbH v. Finanzlandesdirektion für Kärnten*, [2001] ECR I-8365, para. 48.
141. *See* European Commission: *Commission Notice on the notion of State aid pursuant to Article 107(1) TFEU*, 19 May 2016, OJ 262 of 19 July 2016 e.g. at points 9 and 12.
142. Joined Cases 209/78 to 215/78 and 218/78: *Heintz van Landewyck SARL and others v. Commission*, [1980] ECR I-3125, para. 88; Case C-244/94: *FFSA and Others v. Ministère de l'Agriculture et de la Pêche*, [1995] ECR I-4013, para. 21 and Case C-49/07: *MOTOE v. Elliniko Dimosio*, [2008] ECR I-4863, paras 27 and 28.
143. Joined Cases C-180/98 to C-184/98: *Pavlov and Others v. Stichting Pensioenfonds Medische Specialisten*, [2000] ECR I-6451, para. 74; and Case C-222/04: *Ministero dell'Economia e delle Finanze* v. *Cassa di Risparmio di Firenze SpA and Others*, [2006] ECR I-289, para. 107.

public authorities."[144] An entity may be deemed to act by exercising public powers where the activity in question is a task that forms part of the essential functions of the State or is connected with those functions by its nature, its aim and the rules to which it is subject. Unless the Member State concerned has decided to introduce market mechanisms, activities that intrinsically form part of the prerogatives of official authority and are performed by the State do not constitute economic activities.

Examples of non-economic activities are activities related to:

- the army or the police;
- air navigation safety and control;
- maritime traffic control and safety;
- anti-pollution surveillance;
- the organisation, financing and enforcement of prison sentences; and
- the collection of data to be used for public purposes on the basis of a statutory obligation imposed on the undertakings concerned to disclose such data.

In so far as a public entity exercises an economic activity which can be separated from the exercise of public powers, that entity, in relation to that activity, acts as an undertaking. On the contrary, if that economic activity cannot be separated from the exercise of public powers, the activities exercised by that entity as a whole remain connected with the exercise of those public powers and therefore fall outside the notion of an undertaking.[145]

Another very clear consequence of the test regarding undertakings/economic activity is that State supports to private individuals (e.g., in the form of welfare payments or educational or training grants to students) do not give rise to State aid.[146]

2.6.5 Impact on Competition (Test 5)

The purpose of controlling and, if necessary prohibiting, State aid is to avoid *undue* actual or potential distortions of competition and negative effects on trade. Accordingly, public support to undertakings is only prohibited under Article 107(1) of the TFEU if it "distorts or threatens to distort competition by favouring certain undertakings or the production of certain goods" and only insofar as it "affects trade between Member States." These are two distinct and necessary elements of the notion of State aid.

Before reviewing the elements of competition distortions and trade effects, it can be noted that some degree of such impacts is generally to be presumed in any public support to undertakings. Moreover, the extensive possibilities allowed for de jure and

144. Case C-118/85: *Commission v. Italy*, [1987] ECR I-2599, paras 7 and 8 and Case C-30/87: *Bodson v. SA Pompes funèbres des régions libérées*, [1988] ECR I-2479, para. 18.
145. Case C-138/11: *Compass-Datenbank GmbH*, ECLI:EU:C:2012:449, para. 40.
146. *See* European Commission: *Commission Notice on the notion of State aid pursuant to Article 107(1) TFEU*, 19 May 2016, OJ 262 of 19 July 2016 at paras 2.3 to 2.6 for a full discussion of circumstances in which the delivery of social security, health and education may involve the activities of undertakings.

discretionary exemptions under Article 107(2) and (3) of the TFEU mean, in practice, that what is really prohibited are excessive or undue distortions of competition and effects on trade. As the regulator, the European Commission has a wide margin of appreciation in delineating the line between acceptable and unacceptable distortions of competition and effects on trade.

Several commentators point out that the two tests of distortion of competition and effect on trade are conceptually linked with the permissible exemptions in Article 107(3) as, in practice, they argue, that:

> the Commission will accept distortions of competition to speed the rate at which markets move towards long-run competitive equilibrium.[147]

In this view, such accepted distortions include schemes designed to speed-up industrial restructuring and to relieve the problems of depressed areas and underdeveloped regions. However, these are linked to the Commission's assessment of particular cases under Article 108 in the application of the permissible exemptions of Article 107(3). Acceptable distortions, therefore, are subject to the *compensatory justification principle* which holds that the grant of aid falling within Article 107(1) will be permitted only when necessary to accomplish one of the goals of Article 107(3).[148]

While there is a close linkage between the impact on competition test and the effect on trade test (Test 6 *infra*) these two criteria are often considered together.[149] Nonetheless, a measure may distort competition but not affect trade, due to its very-localised market situation. In turn, there may be a clear impact on a market in which there is intra-EU trade but the actual or potential distortion of competition may not be adequately demonstrated.

On the impact on competition test specifically, a measure granted by the State is considered to distort or threaten to distort competition when it is liable to improve the competitive position of the recipient compared to other undertakings with which it competes.[150] As noted earlier, State aid is identified, not from its purpose, but from its effects.

Moreover, there is often a presumption under Article 107(1) regarding the distortive effects of State aid on competition. This was the view of Advocate General Capotorti in the *Philip Morris* case where he argued:

> It is permissible... to start from the presumption that any public aid granted to an undertaking distorts competition - or threatens to distort it where the aid is only proposed and not yet granted - unless exceptional circumstances exist.[151]

Such exceptional circumstances might exist, for example, if the products produced by the recipient are unique in the EU internal market and there are no identifiable

147. A. Evans & S. Martin, "*Socially Acceptable Distortion of Competition: Community Policy on State Aids*" (April 1991), European Law Review, p. 110.
148. European Commission: *Tenth Report on Competition Policy,* (1980) p. 149.
149. Joined Cases T-298/97, T-312/97, etc.: *Alzetta,* [2000] ECR II-2325, para. 81.
150. Case C-730/79: *Phillip Morris Holland BV v. Commission,* [1980] ECR 2671, para. 11 and Joined Cases T-298/97 and T-312/97: *Alzetta,* [2000] ECR II-2325, para. 80.
151. Case C-730/79: *Philip Morris Holland BV v. Commission,* [1980] ECR 2671 at 2698.

substitutes produced in the EU. This view – which is very much based on classical economics – has been endorsed by the Commission.[152]

However, in the *Philip Morris* case, the Court did not hold that State aid automatically distorted competition as, in that case, there was ample evidence to support the distortive effect of the investment from the Dutch Government designed to rationalise cigarette production in Holland by producing a 30% capacity increase where 80% of Dutch output was for export. Accordingly, the Court found sufficient justification for the application of the prohibition and held:

> When State financial aid strengthens the position of an undertaking compared with other undertakings competing in intra-Community trade, the latter must be regarded as affected by the aid.[153]

The Court had previously held in 1970[154] that a qualitative rather than a quantitative analysis was required. Taken together, the apparent view of the Court was interpreted by the Commission as reinforcing the perception of the latter that they were relieved of any requirement to give a detailed assessment of distortion on competition once there was inter-State trade in the relevant product or a close substitute. This created a "due process" problem later when decisions opposing aid were challenged as being insufficiently reasoned under Article 296 of the TFEU. For this reason, the Court held in three later lead cases that Article 296 of the TFEU required the presentation of reasoning regarding the distortive effects of aid.[155] In the earliest of these, the Court held that the opposing decision had set out nothing supporting a view on distortion of competition:

> Even if in certain cases, the very circumstances in which the aid is granted are sufficient to show that the aid is capable of affecting trade between Member States and of distorting or threatening to distort competition, the Commission must at least set out those circumstances in the Statement of reasons for its decision.[156]

In the more recent case of *Germany v. Commission (1987)*, the Court held that, in the case of an aid programme, the Commission could confine itself to examining the characteristics of the programme in question in order to determine whether, by reason of the high amounts or percentages of aid, the nature of the investments for which aid is granted or other terms of the programme, it gives an appreciable advantage to recipients in relation to their competitors and is likely to benefit, in particular, undertakings engaged in trade between Member States.

Taken together, these cases spurred a major improvement in Commission practice in subsequent decisions on State aids where an economic impact assessment supported by market and trade statistics has been used to support the distortion of

152. European Commission: *Eleventh Report on Competition Policy* (1981), point 176.
153. Philip Morris, *supra*.
154. Case C-47/69: *France v. Commission*, [1970] ECR 487 at 502.
155. Cases C-296, 318/82: *Netherlands and Leeuwarder Papierwarenfabriek BV v. Commission*, [1985] ECR 809; Case C-323/82: *Intermills v. Commission*, [1984] ECR 3809 and Advocate General Sir Gordon Slynn in Case 223/85: *RSV Machinefabrieken en Scheepswerven NV v. Commission*, [1987] ECR 4617 at 4658–69.
156. Cases C-296, 318/82, *supra*, at 824.

competition test. In recent years, the European Commission specifically further developed its economic analyses in State aid cases and this further improved the application of the distortion of competition criterion under Article 107(1) of the TFEU by bringing its assessment closer to relevant market analysis under the EU antitrust competition rules.

At the same time, no *actual* effects on competition and trade need to be established.[157] This would be impossible in several cases, especially in the case of a notified new State aid. Accordingly, it is enough to demonstrate that the measure *might* distort competition and affect trade. Moreover, any requirement to show an actual distortion would favour those Member States that failed to notify a new aid measure.[158] However, the Commission is also allowed, of course, to strengthen its case by presenting evidence of actual distortions of competition or effects on trade.[159] Thus, even though the threshold of proof is quite low, any decision that fails to set out the Commission's basis for believing that the measure involves actual or potential distortions of competition and effects on trade (or that contains no examination of the effects of the aid) is likely to be annulled.[160]

Three further issues within the distortion of competition test deserve to be briefly noted. First, the use of aid to produce countervailing distortions or, in effect, economic retaliation for distortions that exist in the internal market arising from the actions of others is not an acceptable defence for a State aid measure.[161] On this the Court has held that several distortions do not cancel each other out vis-à-vis the internal market but rather accumulate the distortive damage.[162] Moreover, the fact that competitors of the beneficiary of the aid receive State aid, even illegal aid, is irrelevant in classifying the measure as aid.[163]

Second, unlike the position under the antitrust competition rules of Article 102 of the TFEU, the market to be assessed by the Commission in its reasoning need not be a "substantial part of the internal market."[164] Moreover, while the Commission was previously relieved of any obligation to precisely use the correct product market in its

157. Case C-327/97: *Italy v. Commission*, [2004] ECR I-3679, para. 44; Case C-494/06 P: *Commission v. Italy and Wam SpA*, [2009] ECR I-3639, para. 50 and Case T-211/05: *Italy v. Commission*, [2009] ECR II-2777, para. 152.
158. Case C-301/87: *France v. Commission (Boussac)*, [1990] ECR I-307, para. 33; Case C-298/00: *Italy v. Commission*, [2004] ECR I-4087, para. 49 and Joined Cases C-346 and 529/03: *Atzeni v. Regione autonoma della Sardegna*, [2006] ECR I-1875, para. 74.
159. Case C-142/87: *Belgium v. Commission (Tubemeuse)*, [1990] ECR I-959, para. 39; Cases T-447 – 449/93: *AITEC v. Commission*, [1995] ECR II-1971, para. 141 and Case C-415/96: *Spain v. Commission*, [1998] ECR I-6993, para. 41.
160. As in Cases C-15/98 and 105/99: *Italy and Sardegna Lines*, [2000] ECR I-8855, para. 66; Case T-34/02: *EURL Le Levant v. Commission*, [2006] ECR II-267 and Case T-1/08: *Buczek Automotive v. Commission*, [2011] ECR II-2107, paras 102 to 108 (upheld on appeal in Case C-405/11 P judgment of 21 March 2013).
161. Cases C-6, 11/69: *Commission v. France*, [1969] ECR 523, Case C-173/73: *Italy v. Commission*, [1974] ECR 709 and Case C-78/76: *Steinike und Weinlig v. Germany*, [1977] ECR 595.
162. Case C-78/76 at 612.
163. Case T-214/95: *Vlaamse Gewest v. Commission*, [1998] ECR II-717, para. 54.
164. This point is made in R. Whish: "Competition Law," Butterworths, London, 1994, at VIII para. 49.

assessment of distortion of competition,[165] stricter requirements emerged from the Court of First Instance in the *SIDE Case* of 2002.[166] In that case, a Commission Decision was annulled concerning aid for the export of French language books on the basis that the Commission had used the market for books in its assessment rather than the market for agency services for the export of French language books.

Third, it is necessary to consider whether the principle of appreciable effect or *de minimis* – a test which features in the application of Articles 101 and 102 of the TFEU – applies in the assessment of distortion of competition for the purpose of Article 107(1). The importance of this issue can be seen readily from the position taken by the Court of First Instance in the *Friuli Venezia Giulia Case (2001)*, concerning aid for road haulage, where the Court held that, because of the structure of the market (including a very large number of small-scale road hauliers), even relatively modest aid was liable to strengthen the market position of an aid recipient as compared to its competitors.[167]

2.6.5.1 **De Minimis** ***Aid***

Until relatively recently, the European Courts rejected any idea that State aid could be too small to actually or potentially affect competition and trade, although there were occasional references to the need for the economic advantage from the measure to be appreciable.[168] The general view of the European Courts was reflected in the *Vlaamse Gewest dictum* of 1998:

> Where a public authority favours an undertaking operating in a sector which is characterised by intense competition by granting it a benefit, there is a distortion of competition or a risk of such distortion. Where the benefit is limited, competition is distorted to a lesser extent, but it is still distorted.[169]

Notwithstanding the consistent position of the Court, the European Commission has taken the view that small amounts of aid, especially for SMEs should be exempt from notification. This resulted in the formulation of the first *de minimis* rule in 1992 in Guidelines for SME State aid[170] and its extension in 1996 in a Commission Notice on *de minimis* aid.[171] The legal status of the Commission's approach versus the position of

165. Philip Morris *supra* and Cases C-62 & 72/87: *Executif Regional Wallon v. Commission,* [1988] ECR 1573, para. 15.
166. Case T-155/98: *SIDE v. Commission,* [2002] ECR II-1179.
167. Case T-288/97: *Regione Autonoma Friuli Venezia Giulia v. Commission,* [2001] ECR II-1169 at para. 46.
168. Case C-57/86: *Greece v. Commission,* [1988] ECR 2855, paras 17 to 18; Case C-142/87: *Belgium v. Commission,* [1990] ECR I-959, para. 43; Case C-310/99: *Italy v. Commission,* [2002] ECR I-2289, para. 86; Case C-172/03: *Heiser,* [2005] ECR I-1627, para. 32.
169. Case T-214/95: *Vlaamse Gewest v. Commission,* [1998] ECR II-717, paras 46 to 50.
170. European Commission: *Community Guidelines on State aid for small and medium-sized enterprises (SMEs),* OJ C 213 of 19 August 1992.
171. European Commission: *Commission Notice on the De Minimis rule for State aid,* [1996] OJ C 68 of 6 March 1996.

the Court remained unsettled, however, until the Commission adopted a series of *de minimis* Regulations in 1998. These were subsequently absorbed into the General *De Minimis* Regulations of 2001, 2006[172] and, most recently, Commission Regulation No 1407/2013/EU of December 2013.[173] In addition, separate legislation governs *de minimis* State aid related to SGEI,[174] primary agricultural production and the fisheries sector[175] and applied for a period under the temporary rules applicable from 2008 to the banking sector.[176] In general, the *de minimis* threshold does not apply to export aid and to aid favouring domestic over imported goods, the acquisition of road freight transport vehicles and aid for undertakings in difficulty (rescue aid). The current general level of *de minimis* is €200,000 per firm over a period of three fiscal years, although this is lower in the case of the transport sector (€100,000) and the fisheries sector (€30,000) and was (until end-2011) higher under the temporary banking sector rules (€500,000).

At present, the main legal act on *de minimis* State aid is Commission Regulation No 1407/2013/EU[177] which applies to aid granted to undertakings in all sectors, with the exception of the fishery and aquaculture sector and the primary production of agricultural products. In part because of requirements of WTO Agreement on Subsidies and Countervailing Measures, the *de minimis* Regulation does not exempt export aid or aid favouring domestic over imported products. The transport sector is covered by the Regulation except in respect of the acquisition of road transport vehicles. Regulation No 1407/2013/EU is in force from 1 January 2014 until 31 December 2020.

172. European Commission: Commission Regulation No 69/2001/EC of 12 January 2001, OJ L 10/30 and Commission Regulation No 1998/2006/EC of 15 December 2006, OJ L 379 of 28 December 2006.
173. European Commission: Commission Regulation No 1407/2013/EU of 18 December 2013 on the application of Articles 107 and 108 of the Treaty on the Functioning of the European Union to *de minimis* aid, OJ L 352 of 24 December 2013.
174. European Commission: Commission Regulation 360/2012/EU on the application of Articles 107 and 108 of the Treaty on the Functioning of the European Union to *de minimis* aid granted to undertakings providing services of general economic interest, OJ L 114 of 26 April 2012.
175. European Commission: Commission Regulation No 1408/2013/EU of 18 December 2013 on the application of Articles 107 and 108 of the Treaty on the Functioning of the European Union to *de minimis* aid in the agriculture sector, OJ L 352 of 24 December 2013 and Commission Regulation No 717/2014/EU of 27 June 2014 on the application of Articles 107 and 108 of the Treaty on the Functioning of the European Union to *de minimis* aid in the fishery and aquaculture sector, OJ L 190 of 28 June 2014.
176. European Commission: *Temporary Community Framework for State aid measures to support access to finance in the current financial and economic crisis*, OJ C 16 of 22 January 2009, Article 4.2, as amended and *Communication of the Commission - Temporary Union framework for State aid measures to support access to finance in the current financial and economic crisis*, OJ C 6 of 11 January 2011, Article 2.2. In its report on the evaluation of the Temporary Frameworks, the Commission notes that the use of *de minimis* schemes was the most popular measure used by EU Member States (Commission Staff Working Paper: "*The effects of temporary State aid rules adopted in the context of the financial and economic crisis*," 5 October 2011).
177. European Commission: Regulation No 1407/2013/EU of 18 December 2013 on the application of Articles 107 and 108 of the Treaty on the Functioning of the European Union to *de minimis* aid, OJ L 352 of 24 December 2013.

In its core provision, the current Regulation defines the concept of *de minimis* as follows:

> Aid measures shall be deemed not to meet all the criteria in Article 107(1) of the Treaty, and shall therefore be exempt from the notification requirement in Article 108(3) of the Treaty, if they fulfill the conditions laid down in this Regulation.[178]

Two points are interesting here. First, the measure is "aid" and can still potentially amount to prohibited State aid if it is not applied in accordance with the Regulation. Second, whether or not it fulfils the tests of Article 107(1) of the TFEU, up to the thresholds set in the Regulation, it is to be *deemed* not to meet the criteria of Article 107(1) for potentially prohibited State aid – but again only if the conditions of the Regulation are met. This leaves open the question as to which one or more of the tests is being relieved. Traditionally, the approach has been that *de minimis* aid is too small to affect competition and/or trade in the EU internal market. Accordingly, *de minimis* aid may now be regarded as having a wider scope of exemption vis-à-vis Article 107(1).

The present Regulation No 1407/2013/EU, unlike the one it replaced, does not exclude from the scope of its application firms which are in financial difficulty (as long as *de minimis* aid is not in the form of a loan or guarantee). Such firms are excluded from all other State aid regulations and guidelines with the exception, of course, of the Rescue and Restructuring Guidelines.[179]

The general requirement laid down in the Regulation is that the total amount of *de minimis* aid granted by a Member State to a single undertaking may not exceed €200,000 over any period of three fiscal years. The total amount of *de minimis* aid granted by a Member State to a single undertaking performing road freight transport for hire or reward must not exceed €100,000 over any period of three fiscal years. This *de minimis* aid may not be used for the acquisition of road freight transport vehicles. If an undertaking performs road freight transport for hire or reward and also carries out other activities to which the ceiling of €200,000 applies, the ceiling of €200,000 applies to the undertaking, provided that the Member State concerned ensures, by appropriate means such as a separation of activities or distinction of costs, that the benefit to the road freight transport activity does not exceed €100,000 and that no *de minimis* aid is used for the acquisition of road freight transport vehicles.

The ceilings of permissible aid apply irrespective of the form of the *de minimis* aid or the objective pursued and regardless of whether the aid granted by the Member State is financed entirely or partly by resources of EU origin (e.g., EU structural or cohesion funds). When an aid amount exceeds the ceiling, the total amount is not *de minimis*. Moreover, the ceiling applies to all companies belonging to the same group.

The ceiling of €200,000 takes into account all public assistance given by a Member State as *de minimis* support over the three financial years. Such assistance may have various forms (grants, loans, tax exemptions) and may arise from several

178. European Commission: Regulation No 1407/2013/EU of 18 December 2013 on the application of Articles 107 and 108 of the Treaty on the Functioning of the European Union to *de minimis* aid, *supra*, Article 3(1).
179. European Commission: *Guidelines on State aid for rescuing and restructuring non-financial undertakings in difficulty*, OJ C 249 of 31 July 2014.

different support measures. In appropriate cases, amounts which are not in the form of a cash grant must be converted into their grant equivalent. All figures have to be gross, before the deduction of any applicable direct taxation. Aid payable in several instalments has to be discounted to its value at the moment it is granted. For this, the interest rate to be used for discounting purposes is the discount rate applicable at the time the aid is granted. The Regulation is applicable only to aid in respect of which it is possible to calculate precisely the gross grant equivalent of the aid *ex ante* without any need to undertake a risk assessment and this is generally referred to in the Regulation as "transparent aid."

De minimis aid granted in accordance with the Regulation may be cumulated with *de minimis* aid granted in accordance with other *de minimis* Regulations (covering agriculture and fisheries) up to the €200,000 ceiling. *De minimis* aid may also be cumulated with *de minimis* aid for the provision of a service of general economic interest (SGEI) up to a ceiling of €500,000. However, *de minimis* aid may not be cumulated with State aid in relation to the same eligible costs if the relevant ceilings defined in a block exemption regulation or any guidelines are exceeded. *De minimis* aid which is not granted for, or attributable to specific eligible costs, may be cumulated with other State aid.

As regards the time limits for *de minimis* aid, the period of three years has to be taken into account for the purposes of the Regulation. This period has to be assessed on a rolling basis. So for each new grant of *de minimis* aid, the total amount of *de minimis* aid granted in the fiscal year concerned and during the previous two fiscal years needs to be taken into account. The relevant period in all such cases starts when a beneficiary is legally eligible to receive aid (not when it actually gets it).

The Member State may only grant new *de minimis* aid after having checked that this aid will not raise the total amount of *de minimis* aid received during the relevant period of three years over the €200,000 threshold. In order to ensure compliance with this rule, Member States have two options when granting *de minimis* aid, either:

(1) the Member State must inform the enterprise of the *de minimis* character of the aid and obtain from the enterprise concerned full information about other *de minimis* aid received during the previous three years; or
(2) the Member State can set up a central register of *de minimis* aid containing complete information on all *de minimis* aid granted by any authority within that Member State, while ensuring at least that the register covers a period of three years.

Under the Regulation, EU Member States must keep records for a period of ten years from the date on which individual *de minimis* aid was granted and ten years from the last individual aid granted under a *de minimis* scheme. Upon request this information must be provided to the European Commission.

Over the years, the general *de minimis* level has risen from €50,000 to its current €200,000 level and the current Regulation, as seen above, now has several quite detailed constraints and conditions on the legitimate use of *de minimis* in the State aid context. This evolutionary process has underlying political and administrative elements. At the political level, the emergence of any *de minimis* threshold obviously resulted in a reduction of the power and scope of the Commission's regulatory mandate. However, for administrative reasons (essentially the convenience of the Commission) the Commission was prepared to relinquish control of smaller cases to keep its workload within a reasonable level. For EU Member States, the general view over the years was that *de minimis* gave sovereignty back to national authorities, reduced their administrative burden vis-à-vis the Commission and was, therefore, to be welcomed. At one point, France proposed increasing *de minimis* to €4 million in the run-up to the most recent revisions of the threshold. However, a countervailing influence was regularly introduced by some countries (notably Denmark which uniquely controls State aid below the EU *de minimis* level via its national competition law)[180] to push for restraint in raising the *de minimis* threshold. Moreover, the United Kingdom, in particular, continued to notify *de minimis* cases until the European Courts supported the Commission's position on the actual legality of *de minimis*.

2.6.6 Effect on Trade (Test 6)

While, as noted earlier, there are strong conceptual links between the distortion of competition test and the test of effect on trade, the latter may be independently considered. An aid that meets the criteria of *Tests 1 to 5* may not be a prohibited aid under Article 107(1) where no trade effect can be shown. However, it is only in very marginal cases that this may happen. Fundamentally, if intra-EU trade exists in a sector and if the aid is not localised or in such a small amount as to have insignificant effect on competition in the internal market, then the effect on trade test is met.[181]

> ***Example: A UK measure did not affect trade, but now it does***
>
> The Commission position on the development of an offshore supplies industry illustrates the effect on trade test and also provides an interesting example of the Commission's review of an existing State aid under Article 108(1) of the TFEU.
>
> In 1973, a UK scheme of interest reliefs in support of the exploitation of North Sea Oil was held by the Commission not to constitute aid. This scheme, which was open to suppliers and purchasers of offshore supplies, tended to primarily benefit UK suppliers/manufacturers. The 1973 decision was based on the desirability of building a new technological sector in the Community and the UK scheme was assessed as not affecting trade. In 1979, however, the Commission declared the scheme incompatible with Article 107(1) on account of the fact that it benefited UK suppliers and that there now was trade in these supplies.[182]

180. *See* the Danish Competition Act (Consolidation Act No 700 of 18 June 2013), Article 11a.
181. Case C-52/76: *Benedetti v. Munari,* [1977] ECR 163 at 190 where the essence of the test was set out by Advocate General Reischl.
182. Commission Decision No 79/496/EEC of 2 May 1979 on the UK scheme of assistance in favour of the offshore supplies industry, OJ L 127 of 24 May 1979.

It is irrelevant, moreover, that the effect is to increase or decrease EU trade. Moreover, it is an insufficient defence to show that an assisted undertaking does not export outside the donor Member State or that there is spare capacity in a sector.[183] The reasoning on this is that aid to such firms has an effect on the volume of domestic production and therefore affects imports from other Member States.

As noted above, most types of aid below a total amount of €200,000[184] are now regarded by the European Commission as not constituting a level sufficient to affect trade. Apart from this, the Commission "accepts no critical market share below which possible distorting effects on trade could be overlooked." This was made clear in a Decision opposing a German grant to a firm with only 0.03% of Community trade[185] and later affirmed by the European Courts in 1990[186] and again in 2000[187] and 2003.[188]

It is also to be noted that, unlike Articles 101 and 102 of the TFEU which address *potential* effects on trade in regard to the antitrust competition rules, the wording of Article 107(1) does not use the word "may" but addresses aid which "affects trade." This does not mean, however, that potential effects are excluded or that only actual effects need be examined. Indeed, an interpretation that did not read in *actual or potential effects on trade* would fail to take account of the fact that, in the advance notification of aid, only potential effects on trade can be assessed. This was made particularly clear in the *AITEC* cases where the Court of First Instance annulled a Commission Decision for failing to examine the effect that the aid was likely to have on future inter-State trade.[189] At the same time, the European Courts have been clear that a focus on potential effects on trade is sufficient[190] and that, where State financial aid strengthens the position of an undertaking as compared with other undertakings competing in intra-[Union] trade, the latter must be regarded as affected by the aid.[191]

Furthermore, in establishing an effect on trade, it is not necessary for the Commission to define the market or to investigate in detail the impact of the measure on the competitive position of the beneficiary and its competitors.[192] At the same time, an effect on trade between Member States cannot be merely hypothetical or simply presumed. At a minimum, the Commission is required to establish why the measure

183. Case C-102/87: *France v. Commission*, [1988] ECR 4067.
184. As of 1 January 2007.
185. Commission Decision No 88/175/EEC of 17 November 1987 on Lander aid of 2 million DM to BUG- Alutechnik GmbH, OJ L 79 of 28 March 1977.
186. Case C-5/89: *Commission v. Germany*, [1990] ECR I 3453.
187. Case T-55/99: *Confederación Espanola de Transporte de Mercancías v. Commission*, [2000] ECR II-3207, para. 89.
188. Case C-280/00: *Altmark Trans GmbH and Regierungspräsidium Magdeburg v. Nahverkehrsgesellschaft Altmark GmbH, and Oberbundesanwalt beim Bundesverwaltungsgericht*, [2003] ECR I-7747, para. 81.
189. Cases T-447 to 449/93: *AITEC v. Commission*, [1995] ECR II-1971, paras 139 to 140.
190. Case C-518/13: *Eventech v. The Parking Adjudicator*, ECLI:EU:C:2015:9, para. 65 and Joined Cases C-197/11 and C-203/11: *Libert and others*, ECLI:EU:C:2013:288, para. 76.
191. Case C-518/13: *Eventech v. The Parking Adjudicator*, ECLI:EU:C:2015:9, para. 66; Joined Cases C-197/11 and C-203/11: *Libert and others*, ECLI:EU:C:2013:288, para. 77 and Case T-288/97: *Friulia Venezia Giulia*, [2001] ECR II-1169, para. 41.
192. Case C-730/79: *Philip Morris*, ECLI:EU:C:1980:209; Case T-211/05: *Italy v. Commission*, [2009] ECR II-2777, paras 157 to 160 and Joined Cases T-298/97, T-312/97, etc.: *Alzetta*, [2000] ECR II-2325, para. 95.

distorts or threatens to distort competition and is liable to have an effect on trade between Member States, based on the foreseeable effects of the measure.[193]

Support to an individual undertaking has the potential to affect trade between Member States even where the undertaking concerned does not export its production. It is sufficient that the goods concerned are traded with other Member States. Even a public subsidy granted to an undertaking which provides only local or regional services and does not provide any services outside its State of origin may, nonetheless, have an effect on trade between Member States where undertakings from other Member States might provide such services (also through the right of establishment) and this possibility is not merely hypothetical. In principle, trade can also be affected even if the recipient exports all or most of its production outside the EU; but, in such situations, the effect is less immediate and cannot be assumed from the mere fact that the market is open to competition.[194]

Indeed, some commentators suggest a degree of ambiguity in the European Commission's approach to the effect on trade test in regard to aid related to the export of goods outside the EU. However, such cases rarely arise independently of any intra-EU trade facts. In cases where this could arise, the logical position by the Commission would be to defend the level playing field in third countries of EU exporters, unless, of course, there were other political considerations involved.[195]

In addition, the European Commission has in several cases considered that, due to their specific characteristics, certain activities had a purely local impact and consequently did not affect trade between Member States. These are the cases where:

(a) the aid does not lead to demand or investments being attracted to the region concerned and does not create obstacles to the establishment of undertakings from other Member States;
(b) the goods or services produced by the beneficiary are purely local or have a geographically limited attraction zone;
(c) there is at most a marginal effect on the markets and on consumers in neighbouring Member States.

Some examples of such cases are:

- swimming pools and other leisure facilities intended predominantly for a local catchment area;
- museums or other cultural infrastructure unlikely to attract visitors from other Member States;

193. Joined Cases T-447/93, T-448/93 and T-449/93: *AITEC and others v. Commission*, [1995] ECR II-1971, para. 141.
194. A point made in the European Commission Notice on the Notion of Aid, *supra*, para. 193 with reference to Case C-142/87: *Belgium v. Commission ("Tubemeuse")*, [1990] ECR I-959, para. 35 and Case C-494/06 P: *Commission v. Italian Republic and Wam SpA*, [2009] ECR I-3639, para. 62.
195. *See*, for example, C. Quigley & A.M.Collins: *"EC State Aid Law and Policy,"* Hart Publishing, Portland Oregon, USA, 2003, p. 63.

- hospitals and other health care facilities aimed essentially at servicing the needs of a local population;
- news media and/or cultural products which, for linguistic and geographical reasons, have a locally restricted audience;
- a conference centre, where the location and the potential effect of the aid on prices is unlikely to divert users from other centres in other Member States.

2.6.7 Cumulative Application of the Tests

To summarise the concept of State aid based on the above analysis, *all* of the six tests have to be met even if, in some cases, they cannot be proven in detail or in advance of the application of a State support measure and even though some of them are closely and sometimes inextricably linked.[196] *De minimis* State aid is still State aid, although, subject to fairly demanding conditions, it is deemed not to be and thus exempt from notification. The six tests are in the box below.

Table 3 The Six Tests for a Support Measure to Constitute State Aid for the Purposes of Regulation

TEST 1: the measure is not excluded by the phrase "Save as otherwise provided by this Treaty..." which generally relates to primary agricultural production, services of general economic interest and security and defence industries.
TEST 2: the support is provided by or through State resources (covering both public expenditure and revenue foregone to the public budget).
TEST 3: the measure creates a selective advantage.
TEST 4: the measure supports an undertaking or an economic activity.
TEST 5: there is an actual or potential impact on competition.
TEST 6: there is an actual or potential effect on trade.

A very significant element of EU practice in regard to State aid control is dedicated to establishing whether or not a proposed State measure is a State aid. While the analysis is objectively based, it is not always an easy or undisputed final determination.

The most typical cases where government measures *do not* constitute State aid, and indeed where there can be some confusion on this point, are:

- General economic measures giving rise to no specific advantage.
- State investment in general infrastructure (provided that normal public procurement practices are followed and there is nothing specific about the infrastructure project).

196. Specifically: selectivity and advantage and effect on competition and trade.

- International Donor aid (including humanitarian aid).
- Aid whose recipients are not enterprises will generally not be considered as State aid, for example aid to households, handicapped, infrastructure, educational institutes, hospitals, public housing, aid for public vocational training centres.
- Where an incidental effect of a State measure is a reduction in State tax revenues, the State measure is not State aid.
- Misapplication of tax rules.
- Aid which compensates for the performance of SGEI is not State aid if certain conditions are fulfilled.[197]
- Aid to the armaments and munitions industries linked to national defence and security policy.
- Agricultural subsidies under the EU CAP.

Given the possible range of government measures that may be potential State aids, it is always important to check if the Article 107(1) tests *all* apply in regard to any particular measure.

When it is clear that a measure is a State aid, the next question is whether any of the de jure or discretionary exemptions of Article 107(2) and (3) of the TFEU can be applied so that the State aid is not prohibited under Article 107(1) of the TFEU.

2.7 THE APPLICATION OF EXEMPTIONS – ARTICLE 107(2) AND (3) OF THE TFEU

As with the concept or notion of State aid, the de jure exemptions of Article 107(2) of the TFEU and the Commission's discretionary exemptions under Article 107(3) of the Treaty require careful navigation and, especially in regard to discretionary exemptions, have evolved significantly – and mostly on the basis of extensive Commission soft law measures.

2.7.1 De Jure Exemptions – Article 107(2) of the TFEU

Article 107(2) of the TFEU provides for specific cases where State aid is automatically considered compatible with the EU internal market. Exemption is automatic if the Commission considers that a State aid measure falls within the specified categories. The categories of measures in Article 107(2) are still State aid and control continues to apply to them insofar as the European Commission needs to ensure that measures claiming the benefit of de jure exemption are, in fact, correctly categorised within the scope of Article 107(2) of the TFEU.

197. Specifically, the *Altmark* criteria.

The three categories of de jure exemptions are:

(1) aid having a social character, granted to individual consumers, provided that such aid is granted without discrimination related to the origin of the products concerned;
(2) aid granted to make good the damage caused by natural disasters or caused by exceptional occurrences;
(3) aid granted to the economy of certain areas of the Federal Republic of Germany affected by the division of Germany, in so far as such aid is required in order to compensate for the economic disadvantages caused by that division.

2.7.1.1 Aid Having a Social Character – Article 107(2)(a) of the TFEU

In relation to the first category, the aid must be to individual consumers and not to enterprises, it must be of a "social character," it must not be linked to quantities of product and, from the wording itself, it must not discriminate on the basis of the origin of the products concerned.[198]

A number of examples of the application of Article 107(2)(a) have arisen and give some useful illustration of the provision. In the landmark case of *Benedetti v. Munari*, the below cost sale of hard wheat by a State agency to millers in order to lower bread prices generally was regarded by Advocate General Reischl as aid of a social character but it conferred an advantage on selected millers and thus failed to be "granted to individual consumers."[199] In a 1990 decision, the European Commission considered tax relief for the purchase of cars fitted with pollution reduction devices to be within the scope of this derogation but went on to challenge the scheme on the basis of origin discrimination.

In a 1967 Decision, the Commission ruled that aid failed to be of a social character when applied to a whole nation. This case involved Dutch aid for the transformation of certain cereals into products for human consumption. In more recent cases, the Commission initially rejected the application of Article 107(2)(a) in respect of an aid scheme for the free zone of Gorizia in Italy on the basis that the entire population of Gorizia could not be regarded as in need of social aid.[200] A further case involved French

198. This was first clarified in this form in a response given by the then Commissioner M. Vredeling to Written Question 112/70 [1970] OJ C 123/2. It can be noted here that there is an apparent contradiction in the notion that aid which benefits private individuals is in fact State aid in the first place (Test 4 considered earlier). This is largely explained by the fact that the type of measures relevant to Article 107(2)(a) tend to be structured in a manner where an undertaking receives the State aid in the first instance and then passes it on fully to the private individuals, thereby giving it its social character.
199. Case C-52/76: *Benedetti v. Munari*, [1977] ECR 163.
200. European Commission: *Twenty-Second Report on Competition Policy* (1992), para. 495. In this case the aid scheme was later approved following the introduction of certain limiting conditions.

"social aid" to 630,000 French small farmers where the Commission regarded the aid as equivalent to a price supplement improving the competitive position of French products.

In its *Guidelines on State Aid in the Aviation Sector*, the Commission has consistently recognised that Article 107(2)(a) can have application as regards the direct operational subsidisation of air routes if the full benefit is passed on to travelling consumers or particular categories (e.g., children, the handicapped or low-income travellers). Moreover, where such subsidies relate to linking remote areas with the mainland, the social aid could, exceptionally, cover the entire population of the region.[201]

Finally, the Commission's Decision on *Ferries Golfo de Vizcaya* (2001) has confirmed the extension of the concept of aid having a social character granted to individual consumers to include services, even though the precise wording refers only to products.[202] It is also to be noted that this derogation disregards any anticompetitive effects of "social aid" provided that the origin discrimination rule is respected.[203] This may arise, for example, in relation to substitute products. The significance of this lies in the fact that the two other categories in Article 107(2)(a), by contrast, allow aid targeted at the reinstatement of competitive positions where the stated causes of disadvantage arise.

2.7.1.2 Aid to Address Natural Disasters and Exceptional Occurrences – Article 107(2)(b) of the TFEU

Article 107(2)(b) of the TFEU creates a de jure exemption in respect of aid to compensate for the damage caused by natural disasters and exceptional occurrences. This provision is related to measures to compensate damages caused by natural disasters, such as flooding or earthquake destruction. In this case, the aid cannot be larger than the damage incurred. Any aid provided under this provision must be related solely to the economic disadvantages arising directly out of the national disaster (or other exceptional occurrences) in question and Member States must demonstrate a

201. European Commission: *Community Guidelines on the application of Articles 87 and 88 of the EC Treaty to State aids in the aviation sector*, OJ C 350 of 10 December 1994 and *Thirtieth Report on Competition Policy* (2000), para. 378. The current guidelines are in *Communication from the Commission - Guidelines on State aid to airports and airlines*, 4 April 2014, OJ C 99/2014 and Article 51 of the General Block Exemption Regulation (Commission Regulation No 651/2014/EU of 17 June 2014 declaring certain categories of aid compatible with the internal market in application of Articles 107 and 108 of the Treaty, OJ L 187 of 26 June 2014) exempts from notification social aid for transport to benefit residents of remote regions.

202. European Commission: Decision No 2001/247/EC of 29 November 2000 on the aid scheme implemented by Spain in favour of the shipping company Ferries Golfo de Vizcay, OJ L 89 of 29 March 2001.

203. D. Schina, *supra*, p. 40 points out that this is the only genuine exception to Article 107(1) for this reason.

clear and direct link between the natural disaster, the resulting damage caused by the disaster and the proposed compensation. However, the scope of this exemption does not extend to preventive measures.[204]

According to the Commission, "natural disasters" include extraordinary natural phenomena such as floods, droughts, tornadoes, forest fires, earthquakes, volcanic eruptions and diseases of plants or animals if they are of catastrophic proportions.[205] In practice, this has included reconstruction aid for flood damage in the Liguria Region of Italy and low-interest loans for the rebuilding of industrial plant following an earthquake in the Friuli-Venezia Giulia Region.[206] In another French case, involving aid to the sheepmeat and pigmeat sectors in response to an outbreak of foot and mouth disease, it appears that the outbreak in question was insufficiently catastrophic for the derogation to apply.[207] More recent examples of acceptable natural disaster aid include aid to offset the rain and flood damage in Valle D'Aosta in 2001.[208] Under the recent Agriculture Guidelines, specific conditions are set for the compensation of natural disasters and exceptional occurrences in the agriculture sector of up to 100% of the costs of remedying the damage caused but all such schemes of support must be notified in advance and pre-suppose in all cases that the Government has declared an event to be a natural disaster. The concept is further extended under the Guidelines to similarly include aid to compensate for damage caused by an adverse climatic event which can be assimilated to a natural disaster, aid for the costs of the prevention, control and eradication of animal diseases and plant pests, aid to make good the damage caused by animal diseases and plant pests, aid for fallen stock and aid to compensate for the damage caused by protected animals.[209]

"Exceptional occurrences" is potentially a very open-ended term. According to commentators, it apparently includes war, serious internal political disturbances, explosions and mine accidents.[210] Moreover, the term does not cover strikes on the basis that strikes are not exceptional phenomena. However, absent a testing of this, one could envisage extreme types of disruptive strikes akin to internal political disturbances that might, at least, be argued as falling within the scope of the derogation. Others argue that the term is, in practice, construed *eiusdem generis* and point to its extreme application in 1963 in relation to a German plan for rescue assistance to certain lead and zinc mines where the exceptional occurrence was peculiar distortions in the world market prices for base metals.[211] Further

204. This was decided in the European Commission: Decision No 72/251/CEE of 26 May 1972 on the award of aid for the setting up of a fund to cover the risks of hail damage to apple and pear crops in the Netherlands, OJ L 163/19 of 19 July 1972. Nonetheless, such measures may still be exempted under Article 107(3)(a) or (c).
205. European Commission: *Eighth Report on Competition Policy* (1978), point 164.
206. *Ibid.*
207. European Commission: Decision No 82/261/EEC of 31 March 1982 concerning aid granted by the French Government in the sheepmeat and pigmeat sectors, OJ L 113 of 27 April 1982.
208. European Commission: *Thirty-First Report on Competition Policy* (2001), para. 474.
209. European Commission: *Guidelines for State aid in the agricultural and forestry sectors and in rural areas* 2014 to 2020, OJ C 204 of 1 July 2014 at paras 327 et seq.
210. Schina, *supra*, p. 41.
211. A. Campbell: "*Common Market Law*," Longman (London), 1975, p. 698.

commentaries suggest that such matters as compensation for the damage caused by the Second World War or in response to racial or social persecution also come within the scope of this term.[212]

As with the natural disasters exception, practice on the exceptional occurrences point has focused largely on agricultural issues. Since the 2000 Agriculture Guidelines, in particular, it is clear that the concept of exceptional occurrences does not extend to purely financial losses caused by the commercial decisions of business undertakings and that risks which are otherwise insurable and normal commercial preventative measures are likewise excluded. This arose in the Commission Decision on *Gaelic Ferries* where the Commission refused to regard the need for more expensive transport services to export live cattle in response to pressure from animal rights activists as an exceptional occurrence under Article 107(2)(b).[213] It also arose in 1998 where agricultural damage caused by field mice was held not to constitute an exceptional occurrence.[214] On the other hand, the BSE ("Mad Cow Disease") crisis in agriculture was held to be an exceptional occurrence justifying huge amounts of State aid in the UK, Belgium and Italy.

Some examples illustrate further the reasons for notifying and approving State aid under the de jure exemption of Article 107(2)(b) and on the use of these exemptions:

- Natural disasters cover material damage caused by earthquakes,[215] floods[216] tornadoes[217] avalanches landslides and rockslides.[218]
- Exceptional occurrences cover wars, internal disturbances, some strikes and (with some reservations) nuclear disasters and fires.[219]
- Repeated flooding in Venice was neither a natural disaster nor an exceptional occurrence;[220]

212. For example, J. Thiesing in Wohlfarth, Everling, Glaesner and Sprung: *Die Europaische Wirtschaftsgemeinschaft, Kommentar zum Vertrag*, Verlag Franz, 1960, Artikel 92, p. 276.
213. European Commission: Decision *Gaelic Ferries*, OJ L 263 of 2000.
214. European Commission: *Twenty-Eighth Report on Competition Policy* (1998), para. 237.
215. European Commission: Decision No 459/A/2009 *Earthquake in Abruzzo*, OJ C 278 of 18 November 2009 and Decision No SA.35482 of 19 December 2012: Earthquakes of 20 to 29 May 2012, OJ C 31/2013 of 31 January 2013.
216. European Commission: Decision No 436a/2006 of 11 December 2006: Flood reconstruction loans, OJ C 23 of 1 February 2007 and Decision No 235a/2010 of 6 August 2010: Floods in Poland, OJ C 283/2010 of 20 October 2010.
217. European Commission: Decision No 294/2010 *Tornadohilfe Sachsen*, OJ C 311/2010 of 16 November 2010.
218. European Commission: Decision No 424/2009 *Aid for the damage caused by natural disasters*, OJ C 275 of 14 November 2009.
219. The effects of the Chernobyl disaster were argued by Greece in Case C-278/00 *Greece v. Commission*, [2004] ECR I-3997, paras 78–89. Also European Commission: Decision No 622/2008 *Palmitos Park Fire*, OJ C 101 of 20 April 2010. On strikes, these need to be accompanied by public disorder – European Commission: Decision of 3 April 2002 concerning the aid provided for by Article 4 of Law No 290 of 17 August 1999 (notified under document number C(2002) 1188) (*Italian agricultural credit operations*), OJ L 194 of 23 July 2002.
220. Joined Cases C-71/09 P, C-73/09 P and C-76/09 P: *Comitato "Venezia vuole vivere" and Hotel Cipriani Srl and Società Italiana per il gas SpA (Italgas) v. Commission*, [2011] ECR I-4727, para. 175.

- An exceptional occurrence is by its nature unforseeable and the exemption cannot therefore be applied to preventive measures.[221]
- Bad weather is not normally accepted as a natural disaster or exceptional occurrence.
- Normally plant and animal diseases are not covered by the exemption (e.g., an attack by field mice on Greek melon and watermelon crops was rejected as this was a recurring phenomenon in Greece)[222] but the BSE (mad cow disease) outbreak in the United Kingdom was accepted as was aid to compensate Irish pigmeat producers following the discovery of dioxin contamination.[223]
- Compensation for the short-term effects on civil aviation of the 11 September 2001 terrorist attacks in New York and the Icelandic volcanic cloud disruptions in 2011 were accepted as exemptible, but with specific limitations as to what could be compensated.[224]
- The exemptions do not cover compensation related to normal commercial conduct[225] and may not be used to compensate for the absence of commercial due diligence (this is the point especially on insurance).[226]

Under Article 50 of the current GBER, aid schemes to make good the damage caused by earthquakes, avalanches, landslides, floods, tornadoes, hurricanes, volcanic eruptions and wild fires of natural origin shall be compatible with the internal market within the meaning of Article 107(2)(b) of the Treaty and shall be exempted from notification to the Commission, provided that certain conditions are fulfilled. In particular, the natural disaster must be declared officially, there must be a direct causal link between the natural disaster and the damages to be compensated by the aid, the amount of damage must be assessed by an independent expert or by an insurance undertaking and the total aid, including any insurance payments, must not exceed 100% of the assessed damage.[227]

221. European Commission: Decision No 2000/625/EC of 13 June 2000 on the aid scheme implemented by Ireland to promote the transport of Irish livestock by sea to continental Europe (Gaelic Ferries), OJ L 263 of 18 October 2000.
222. European Commission: Decision No 2001/259/EC of 31 January 2001 on the State-aid scheme proposed by Greece for fruit and vegetable growers, OJ L 93 of 3 April 2001.
223. European Commission: Decision No NN 46/2001 of 25 July 2001 on aid to stock farmers hit by the BSE crisis, OJ C 247 of 5 September 2001 and Decision No 643/2008 of 23 December 2008: Special measures relating to meat products of animal origin from Pigs following a dioxin contamination in Ireland, OJ C 36 of 13 February 2009.
224. European Commission: *Communication on the repercussions of the terrorist attacks in the United States on the air transport industry*, COM (2001) 574 Final.
225. European Commission: Decision No 2000/625/EC of 13 June 2000 on the aid scheme implemented by Ireland to promote the transport of Irish livestock by sea to continental Europe (Gaelic Ferries), OJ L 263 of 18 October 2000.
226. European Commission: Decision No 147/2009 of 8 April 2009: Pigmeat processors, OJ C 147 of 27 June 2009, para. 40.
227. European Commission: Regulation No 651/2014/EU of 17 June 2014 declaring certain categories of aid compatible with the internal market in application of Articles 107 and 108 of the Treaty, OJ L 187 of 26 June 2014.

2.7.1.3 Aid Concerning the Former Division of Germany – Article 107(2)(c) of the TFEU

The third category of derogation in Article 107(2), while largely of historical interest, retains a certain current relevance. Its appearance in Article 107 reflects a West German concern at the time of the original EEC Treaty to reserve the right to assist areas affected by the Second World War and the borders agreed in the division of Germany. From what has been said above, it is arguable that this derogation might have been subsumed into exceptional occurrences although, for political rather than legal certainty, it put the German situation at the time largely beyond doubt. The provision does not, however, identify the "certain areas" to which it applies. In practice, its main applications have been in respect of the old Berlin corridor and West Berlin[228] and the Zonenrandgebiet border area between the former East and West Germany. Other applications have included the integration of the Saar region into West Germany and aid to assist refugees, displaced persons and war victims. This derogation is further reflected in Article 98 of the TFEU which continues a similar derogation from the Transport policy rules and had resulted in 1971 in the clearance of a German tax on the transport of goods by road.[229]

The unification of Germany on 3 October 1990 ought to have made this derogation redundant and seen its removal in the Maastricht revisions of February 1992. It is interesting that this did not happen either under the Maastricht, Amsterdam, Nice or the most recent Lisbon Treaty (TFEU) changes and the reason, quite simply, was German political opposition to any change on this point or on Article 98 of the Treaty. A Commission Communication prior to reunification notes that, from unification, the State aids rules should apply in full in the unified Germany and accepts that aid in West Berlin needed to be phased out.[230] Subsequently, investment loans for new investment in West Berlin were challenged by the Commission and held incompatible with Article 107(1)[231] and when new regional aid schemes for the new Lander were approved in 1991, West Berlin was excluded.[232] The possible application of the Article 107(2)(c) derogation in regard to Daimler- Benz[233] and Opel[234] investments in West Berlin reappeared in 1992 and 1993 respectively. In the former case, the derogation was

228. European Commission: *Ninth Report on Competition Policy*, [1979] point 143.
229. European Commission: Decision No 71/295/CEE of 23 July 1971, OJ L 179 of 9 August 1971.
230. European Commission: *Communication on the Community and German Re-unification*, COM (90) 400 final, Vol. I, 69.
231. *See* European Commission: *Notice concerning subsidised loans to promote investment in West Berlin*, [1992] OJ C 164/3.
232. European Commission: *Twenty-First Report on Competition Policy* (1991) at point 181.
233. European Commission: Decision of 14 April 1992 concerning aid granted by the Land of Berlin to Daimler-Benz AG Germany (C 3/91 ex NN 5/91), OJ L 263 of 9 September 1992.
234. European Commission: Decision of 18 December 1991 regarding the proposal by the German Government to award State aid to the Opel group in support of its investment plans in the new Lander, OJ C 43 of 16 February 1993.

held applicable as Daimler-Benz had decided to invest in West Berlin in 1988 and had acquired the site in 1989 before unification. However, the reduced price paid for the site fell to be considered under Article 107(3)(c) and was not exempted. The Opel case involved a sale of land at a reduced price and this was held by the Commission to be exemptible under Article 107(3)(c) and the question of automatic exemption under the derogation of Article 107(2)(c) was not answered.

In 2000, the European Court of Justice recognised that, while Article 107(2)(c) remained in force, it was to be interpreted narrowly and applied solely to compensation for economic disadvantage caused by the isolation resulting from the creation and maintenance of the old frontier, including the breakdown of communication links and the loss of markets.[235] In a series of cases decided between 2003 and 2004, the European Courts rejected the view that aid to support the relatively low economic development of German regions (or Lander) which had previously been part of East Germany was covered by this de jure exemption.[236]

Finally, it is to be noted that the sentence: "Five years after the entry into force of the Treaty of Lisbon, the Council, acting on a proposal from the Commission, may adopt a decision repealing this point" was added in the TFEU version of this de jure exemption. This clearly reflects a political compromise vis-à-vis the prospect of repealing this exemption from Article 107(2). To date, no such proposal from the Commission has emerged.

2.8 DISCRETIONARY EXEMPTIONS – ARTICLE 107(3) OF THE TFEU

Article 107(3) refers to cases where State aid may be considered compatible with the internal market. Thus, the exceptions in Article 107(3) to the general prohibition of Article 107(1) are not applied automatically – they are at the discretion of the European Commission. Based on notifications, the Commission is obliged to evaluate the State aid and to establish whether or not the Member State can be authorised to grant such aid. This contrasts with the de jure exemptions of Article 107(2) where exemption is automatic once the Commission is satisfied that the aid falls within any of the three categories listed.

In Article 107(3) the use of the word "may" creates the discretionary nature of the exemptions covered by this provision and confers considerable discretion upon the Commission, the exercise of which is only subject to marginal review by the European Courts. In making its assessment, the Commission takes into account various factors including the objective of the aid and its necessity and proportionality.

235. Case C-156/98: *Germany v. Commission,* [2000] ECR I-6857, para. 49.
236. Case C-334/99: *Germany v. Commission,* [2003] ECR I-1139, para. 120; Case C-301/96: *Germany v. Commission,* [2000] ECR I-9919, para. 67; Cases C-57/00P and C-61/00p: *Freistaat Sachsen v. Commission,* [2003] ECR I-9975, para. 25 and Case C-277/00: *Germany v. Commission,* [2004] ECR I-3925, para. 53.

In applying its discretion, the Commission must accept certain distortions of competition and trade inherent in most State aid measures. To that end, Commission practice has applied the so-called *compensatory justification principle* which holds that the grant of aid falling within Article 107(1) will be permitted only when necessary to accomplish one of the goals of Article 107(3).[237] As early as 1980, the Commission explained:

> if the Commission has to use its discretionary power not to raise objection to an aid proposal, it must contain a compensatory justification which takes the form of a contribution by the beneficiary of aid over and above the effects of normal play of market forces to the achievement of Community objectives as contained in the derogations of [Article 107(3) of the TFEU].[238]

The *compensatory justification principle* is thus viewed as an essential aspect of Article 107(3) exemption. In 1983, the European Commission elaborated this position by identifying key factors in its consideration of exemptions:

1) *the aid must promote or further a project that is in the EU interest as a whole;*
2) *the aid must be necessary for the achievement of this result and the objective must not be capable of achievement without the aid;*
3) *the duration, intensity and scope of the aid must be proportional to the importance of the intended result.*[239]

In its 1992 decision on *Hytasa*, the Commission specifically pointed out that the exemptions are applicable in situations where:

> Without the aid, market forces alone would be insufficient to guide recipients towards patterns of behaviour that would serve one of the objectives of the said exemption.[240]

It is not coincidental, therefore, that the actual exemptions permitted under Article 107(3) are closely inter-linked, in most cases, with various other EU policies and notably: regional policy, policy on specific sectors, culture and heritage policy and the specific case of Important Projects of Common European Interest (IPCEI).

237. European Commission: *Tenth Report on Competition Policy*, p. 149.
238. European Commission: *Tenth Report on Competition Policy*, [1980] at point 213.
239. European Commission: *Twelfth Report on Competition Policy*, [1983] point 160.
240. European Commission: Decision No 92/317/EEC, of 25 March 1992 on State aid in favour of Hilaturas y Tejidos Andaluces SA, now called Mediterráneo Técnica Textil SA and its buyer *(Hytasa)*, OJ L 171/54 of 26 June 1992 where exemption was refused and the recovery of 4,200 million pesetas ordered.

Table 4 The Categories of Discretionary Exemptions under Article 107(3) of the TFEU

(a) aid to promote the economic development of areas where the standard of living is abnormally low or where there is serious underemployment, and of the regions referred to in Article 349, in view of their structural, economic and social situation; (the so-called "A" Regions of the EU with per capita GDP at less than 75% of the EU average);
(b) aid to promote the execution of an important project of common European interest or to remedy a serious disturbance in the economy of a Member State;
(c) aid to facilitate the development of certain economic activities or of certain economic areas, where such aid does not adversely affect trading conditions to an extent contrary to the common interest; (the so-called "C" Regions of the EU);[241]
(d) aid to promote culture and heritage conservation where such aid does not affect trading conditions and competition in the Union to an extent that is contrary to the common interest;
(e) such other categories of aid as may be specified by decision of the Council on a proposal from the Commission.

2.8.1 Article 107(3)(a) of the TFEU – Seriously Underdeveloped Regions

The exemption categories under paragraphs (a) and (c) of Article 107(3) of the TFEU both refer to regional development aids. The key difference between the two provisions is that, on account of the extremity of the situation contemplated by paragraph (a), aid may be exempted under paragraph (a) of Article 107(3) *even if it "adversely affects trading conditions to an extent contrary to the common interest."* Under Article 107(3)(c), however, the EU interest regarding effect on trade is safeguarded. The result is that the sole test under paragraph (a) is whether the aid meets the objective of the exemption and it is then assumed to be in the EU interest.

Central to the application of exemption under Article 107(3)(a) is the Commission satisfaction that the area concerned suffers from an abnormally low standard of living or from serious underemployment. While this is done in an EU context, regard may also be had to the national context.[242] The current basis of assessment under this exemption category is to be found in the *Guidelines on Regional State Aid 2014 to*

241. Under the EU regional policy in coordination with the State aids rules, the EU refers to "assisted regions" as those where investment and job creation aids are seen as justified based on different degrees of national or regional handicaps and general market failures. The linkage to the grounds for State aid exemption emerges from Article 107(3)(a) referring to serious development handicaps ("A" regions) and Article 107(3)(c) which provides the basis for exemption of State aid to address development issues in areas within a Member State ("C" regions).

242. Thus, in the European Commission: *Ninth Report on Competition Policy* (point 142), the Commission scrutinises the application of an investment subsidy in the former Federal Republic of Germany where the eligible areas covered 60% of the country and 34% of the population. The analysis looked at GDP, population, regional migration, unemployment, employment and economic structures and concluded that economic development in several eligible areas was above the German and the EU GDP averages.

2020[243] and the related provisions of the GBER which exempts from notification any State aid measure which is compatible with the Guidelines. The effect of these measures, *inter alia,* is that the areas covered by Article 107(3)(a) are NUTS 2 regions[244] of the EU that have a gross domestic product per capita below or equal to 75% of the EU average based on the average of Eurostat data in the preceding three years.

Building on its earlier general approach, the Commission has elaborated its bases for assessment of the regional aid exemption in the following terms.

Table 5 Bases of Assessment under the Regional State Aid Guidelines 2014 to 2020

(a) contribution to a well-defined objective of common interest: a State aid measure must aim at an objective of common interest in accordance with Article 107(3) of the Treaty; (Section 3.2) (b) need for State intervention: a State aid measure must be targeted towards a situation where aid can bring about a material improvement that the market cannot deliver itself, for example by remedying a market failure or addressing an equity or cohesion concern; (c) appropriateness of the aid measure: the proposed aid measure must be an appropriate policy instrument to address the objective of common interest; (d) incentive effect: the aid must change the behaviour of the undertaking(s) concerned in such a way that it engages in additional activity which it would not carry out without the aid or it would carry out in a restricted or different manner or location; (e) proportionality of the aid (aid to the minimum): the aid amount must be limited to the minimum needed to induce the additional investment or activity in the area concerned; (f) avoidance of undue negative effects on competition and trade between Member States: the negative effects of aid must be sufficiently limited, so that the overall balance of the measure is positive.

2.8.2 Article 107(3)(b) of the TFEU – Projects of Common European Interest and Aid to Remedy a Serious Disturbance in the Economy

There are two types of exemption here; neither of which are defined. However, practice and recent Commission Guidelines give a substantial appreciation for the factors

243. European Commission: *Guidelines on Regional State aid for 2014-2020,* (2013/C 209/01), OJ C 209 of 23 July 2013.

244. EU NUTS regions are established by Commission Regulation No 31/2011/EU of 17 January 2011 amending annexes to Regulation No 1059/2003/EC of the European Parliament and of the Council on the establishment of a common classification of territorial units for statistics (NUTS), OJ L 13 of 18 January 2011. NUTS 2 Regions are usually regions within a Member State having a minimum population of 800,000 and a maximum population of 3 million. In the case of Estonia, Latvia, Luxembourg, Lithuania, Malta and Cyprus, the concept covers the entire country.

necessary for an aided project to be in the common European interest while some appreciation from practice is to be found regarding aid to remedy a serious disturbance in the national economy.

2.8.2.1 Projects of Common European Interest

The Commission has regarded projects as diverse as a road tunnel under the Alps, a hydro-electric dam in Luxembourg supplying adjoining Member States,[245] German aid to the Airbus project[246] and aid for the Channel Tunnel as projects in the common European interest. On the other hand, the manufacture of cigarettes was held not to be such a project.[247] During the 1970s, moreover, aid to projects that served to apply or advance EU policies in regard to the rational use of energy and the protection of the environment were exempted under this provision.[248] Equally, aid that opposed such EU policies was refused exemption.[249] In the *Glaverbel* case (1988), the Court endorsed Commission policy in this regard and held that a project is not of common European interest unless it forms part of a transnational programme supported jointly by a number of EU Member States or arises from concerted action by a number of Member States to combat a common threat such as environmental pollution.[250]

A particularly useful source of parallel assistance on interpretation on this exemption is to be found in the nature of projects financed by the EU itself via the European Investment Bank (EIB) and in the transport field. Article 309(c) of the TFEU dealing with the EIB refers to "projects of common interest to several Member States which are of such a size or nature that they cannot be financed by the various means available in the individual Member States." While this is clearly not the same as Article 107(3)(b), it certainly provides elements for projects of a common European interest when read with *Glaverbel* and Commission practice. The EIB, for example, has been a heavy financier of the Trans-European Networks in the areas of transport, telecommunications and energy infrastructures. In that regard, Article 171 of the TFEU requires the EU to identify such common interest projects and allows it to aid "feasibility studies, loan guarantees or interest-rate subsidies" and to finance transport infrastructure from the EU Cohesion fund. The EIB also developed its activities further into the area of interest rebates for job creation in SMEs via its global loan facilities to

245. These examples are cited in Campbell *supra*, p. 699.
246. Bulletin EC No 4, 1974, point 2112.
247. A point made by Vaughan, *supra*, p. 711 on the *Philip Morris* case.
248. *See*, for example, European Commission: *Seventh Report on Competition Policy*, [1977] point 250 regarding energy and the *Tenth Report on Competition Policy*, [1980] point 223 on environment.
249. On this point, exemption in respect of aid to Belgian Shell was refused as contrary to environment policy in European Commission: Decision No 85/254/EEC of 15 November 1988: relating to aid which the Belgian Government has granted to a petrochemicals company at Ottignies/Louvain-la-Neuve (SA Belgian Shell), OJ L 106 of 18 April 1989 and a preferential natural gas tariff to glasshouse growers in the Netherlands also failed to qualify as *"it ran counter to the objectives of the common energy policy which aims at energy saving and the rational use of energy"* - Decision No 82/73/EEC of 15 December 1981 *on preferential natural gas tariff to glasshouse growers in the Netherlands*, OJ L 37/29 of 10 February 1981 at p. 34.
250. Cases C-62 and 72/87: *Executif Regional Wallon v. Commission (Glaverbel)*, [1988] ECR 1573.

commercial banks under the so-called 2% Edinburgh facility in 1994 ultimately claiming credit for the creation of some 30,000 jobs in the EU in response to the Delors *White Paper on Growth, Competitiveness and Employment*[251] and, in 1995, the Bank provided a 4% subsidy on its lending rate to 11 Irish banks to promote SME development under the 1995 *Programme for Peace and Reconciliation in Ireland and Northern Ireland*.[252]

In 2014, the Commission, for the first time, issued official guidance on criteria for the assessment of State aid to promote the execution of IPCEI.[253] In this Communication, the main points concerning IPCEIs are the following:

- An IPCEI is a single project which is clearly defined in respect of its objectives as well as the terms of its implementation, including its participants and its funding.
- The project must contribute in a concrete, clear and identifiable manner to one or more EU objectives and must have a significant impact on competitiveness of the EU, sustainable growth, addressing societal challenges or value creation across the EU.
- The project must represent an important contribution to the EU's objectives, for instance by being of major importance to implementing a major EU Strategy.
- The project must normally involve more than one Member State and its benefits must not be confined to the financing Member States, but extend to a wide part of the EU. The benefits of the project must be clearly defined in a concrete and identifiable manner.
- When assessing the compatibility with the internal market of aid to promote the execution of an IPCEI on the basis of Article 107(3)(b) of the Treaty, the Commission will carry out a balancing test to assess whether the expected positive effects outweigh the possible negative effects and the Commission may presume the presence of a market failure or other important systemic failures, as well as the contribution to a common European interest, where the project fulfils the eligibility criteria for an IPCEI.
- The maximum aid level will be determined with regard to the identified funding gap in relation to the eligible costs. If justified by the funding gap analysis, the aid intensity could reach up to 100% of the eligible costs.

251. European Commission: *White Paper on Growth, Competitiveness and Employment*, Bulletin EC Supplement 6/93.
252. Irish Department of Finance: Programme for Peace and Reconciliation in Ireland and Northern Ireland, (Stationery Office, Dublin) 1995.
253. European Commission: Communication from the Commission - *Criteria for the analysis of the compatibility with the internal market of State aid to promote the execution of important projects of common European interest*, OJ C 188 of 20 June 2014.

The Commission will also take a generally positive approach towards IPCEIs where:

- the project has been designed so as to make it possible for all interested Member States to participate, having regard to the type of project, the objective pursued and its financing needs;
- the design of the project involves the Commission or any legal body to which the Commission has delegated its powers, such as the EIB;
- the selection of the project involves the Commission or any legal body to which the Commission has delegated its power, provided that this body is acting in that purpose as an implementing structure;
- the governance structure of the project involves the Commission – or any legal body to which the Commission has delegated its powers – and several Member States;
- the project involves important collaborative interactions in terms of the number of partners, the involvement of organisations of different sectors, or the involvement of undertakings of different sizes;
- the project involves co-financing by an EU Fund.

2.8.2.2 Aid to Remedy a Serious Disturbance in the Economy

One of the earliest examples of the use of this derogation was in 1971 when Italy faced such a serious disturbance in its economy involving a decline in economic activity, increasing unemployment and a slowdown in investment. Aid in the form of reduced social security charges for SMEs and all Italian textile firms was approved but the duration was limited to one year.[254] This type of economic difficulty became more widespread during the 1970s as the Oil Crisis deepened and energy prices continued to rise. It is apparent that most Member States responded to this situation either by reorienting existing general aid schemes or by introducing new schemes of limited duration to cope with the crisis. Article 107(3)(b) was only used to exempt aid, however, where the recipient firms were experiencing short-run problems discretely linked to the Oil Crisis and where a restructuring plan was being put in place.

In 1991, exemption on the basis of a serious disturbance in the economy was cited as the basis for approving aid for a Greek privatisation programme having regard to undertakings given by the Greek Government concerning the recovery of the Greek economy.[255] In its decision on aid to the Opel Group in 1993, however, the Commission rejected the submission that the aid was exemptible under this heading citing the reunification of Germany as the serious economic disturbance.[256]

254. European Commission: *Second Report on Competition Policy*, [1972] at point 120.
255. European Commission: *Twenty-First Report on Competition Policy*, [1991] at point 251 referring to Commission Decision No NN 11/91 of 31 July 1991: Greek privatization aid, OJ C 88/6.
256. European Commission: Decision of 18 December 1991 regarding the proposal by the German Government to award State aid to the Opel group in support of its investment plans in the new Lander, OJ C 43 of 16 February 1993.

From the wording of the provision itself, it is clear that the disturbance at issue must affect the entire country. Something affecting part of a country would fall for consideration of exemption under Article 107(3)(a) or (c).

Exemption on the basis of remedying a serious disturbance in the economy became very important since the international financial crisis of 2007 to 2009. At issue generally was the rescue and recapitalisation of banks across the EU. Normally State aid measures for such purposes would be considered under Article 107(3)(c) as aid to facilitate the development of certain economic activities or sectors and under the general Rescue and Restructuring Guidelines.[257] However, building on an extensive analytical preparation dating back to 1999,[258] the Commission decided to introduce temporary rules to ensure the survival of banks in response to the crisis.[259] From 2008 to end-2014, some 500 decisions were taken by the Commission authorising State aid measures to banks across the EU worth over €5,000 billion and mostly in the form of guarantees or other liquidity support. Over 95% of EU banks were eligible for the various measures permitted and only five EU Member States adopted no measures to support banks (Bulgaria, the Czech Republic, Estonia, Malta and Romania) and three Member States which did so did not apply them (Poland, Slovakia and Lithuania).[260]

By 2010, although aspects of the financial crisis persisted, revised measures were introduced and the conditions under the special rules were tightened up. By 2013, a revised Banking Communication was issued replacing the earlier version of the Banking rules and rules concerning impaired assets, recapitalisation and restructuring.[261] This continued to use Article 107(3)(b) as the basis for exemption of State aid to banks; although more detailed scrutiny was now involved.

Since 1 January 2015, the *Bank Recovery and Resolution Directive (BRRD)* applies in all EU Member States[262] and substantially shifts the burden of rescuing and

257. The current edition of these is European Commission: *Guidelines on State aid for rescuing and restructuring non-financial undertakings in difficulty*, OJ C 249 of 31 July 2014.
258. On this see the extensive discussion covered in C.D. Ehlermann & M. Everson (ed.): "*European Competition Law Annual 1999 – Selected Issues in the Field of State Aid,*" Oxford, 2001.
259. European Commission: Communication from the Commission - *The application of* State aid rules to measures taken in relation to financial institutions *in the context of the current global financial crisis*, OJ C 270 of 25 October 2008, Communication from the Commission – *Temporary framework for State aid measures to support access to finance in the current financial and economic crisis* (consolidated version), OJ C 83 of 7 July 2009 (as amended) and Communication of the Commission: *Temporary Union framework for State aid measures to support access to finance in the current financial and economic crisis*, OJ C 6 of 11 January 2011.
260. A point made in C. Quigley: "*European State Aid Law and Policy*" (Third Edition), Hart Publishing, Oxford and Portland, Oregon, 2015 at p. 468.
261. European Commission: *Communication from the Commission on the application, from 1 August 2013, of State aid rules to support measures in favour of banks in the context of the financial crisis* ("Banking Communication"), OJ C 216 of 30 July 2013.
262. Directive No 2014/59/EU of the European Parliament and of the Council of 15 May 2014 establishing a framework for the recovery and resolution of credit institutions and investment firms and amending Council Directive 82/891/EEC, and Directives 2001/24/EC, 2002/47/EC, 2004/25/EC, 2005/56/EC, 2007/36/EC, 2011/35/EU, 2012/30/EU and 2013/36/EU, and Regulations No 1093/2010/EU and No 648/2012/EU, of the European Parliament and of the Council, OJ L 173 of 12 June 2014.

restructuring banks away from tax payers (State aid) towards the bank's shareholders and creditors.[263]

2.8.3 Article 107(3)(c) of the TFEU – Assisted Regions, Economic Activities and Sectors

Article 107(3)(c) deals with sectoral and regional aid and exemption may be granted in respect of aid to facilitate the development of certain economic activities (i.e., sectors) or of certain economic areas (i.e., regions), where such aid does not adversely affect trading conditions to an extent contrary to the common interest. This paragraph is generally regarded as the most important discretionary exception to the general prohibition on State aids in Article 107(1).[264]

As with the exemption basis in paragraph (a) of Article 107(3), paragraph (c) also deals with regional aid. However, in *Germany v. Commission*,[265] the Court held that paragraph (c) of Article 107(3):

> is wider in scope inasmuch as it permits the development of certain areas without being restricted by the economic conditions laid down in Article 107(3)(a), provided such aid does not adversely affect trading conditions to an extent contrary to the common interest. That provision gives the Commission power to authorise aid intended to further the economic development of areas of a Member State which are disadvantaged in relation to the national average.[266] (Emphasis added).

This is now fully reflected in the Regional State Aid Guidelines as they apply to the exemption of State aid in regions which are not covered by Article 107(3)(a).[267]

Exemption is not permissible under Article 107(3)(c) for the purpose of creating a competitive advantage but is intended rather to offset identifiable regional or sectoral disadvantages.[268] This was clearly demonstrated in one of the Commission's earliest State aid decisions in 1964 where an interest allowance granted by the Belgian Government on a loan to Ford Tractor (Belgium) Ltd in order to aid the firm in the

263. A point made by EU Commissioner for Financial Stability, Financial Services and Capital Markets Union, Jonathan Hill in the European Commission's Press Release of 31 December 2014: "A single rulebook for the resolution of failing banks will apply in the EU as of 1 January 2015."
264. A point made by several commentators including Butterworths (*supra*, VIII para. 186) and Schina (*supra*, p. 60). It is open to contention, however, that the most important discretions on State aid arise in respect of the interface between the Community's competition rules on State aid and its regional policy which generally give rise to the clearance of very large numbers of schemes of aid under Article 107(3)(a). This alternative viewpoint as to the relative importance of the exemption clauses is given particular support in the coverage of State aid in Sir Leon Brittan: *European Competition Policy - Keeping the Playing-Field Level*, Brassey's (UK) for the Centre for European Policy Studies, 1992 where the exemption potential of Article 107(3)(c) is not mentioned.
265. Case C-248/84: *Germany v. Commission*, [1987] ECR 2671.
266. *Ibid.*, at 4042, para. 19.
267. European Commission: *Guidelines on Regional State aid for 2014-2020*, OJ C 209 of 23 July 2013.
268. A point made in Campbell *supra*, p. 699.

assembly of tractors and the manufacture of gear boxes and axles was held incompatible with Article 107. The Decision pointed out:

> On the Common Market in agricultural tractors, the production capacity is not smaller than the demand. Certain undertakings which already exist within the Community have reached a high degree of technical development. In these circumstances, the grant of aid intended to favour the creation of a new unit of production could not be justified as an increase in the or a stimulus to the competition, so as to make the sector in question healthy. The support given to the creation at Antwerp of manufacture of axles and gear boxes for tractors and assembly of these vehicles could not be based on the economic situation of the Antwerp region which is prosperous by comparison with that of numerous other regions of the Community. The aid can only contribute to aggravating the already difficult situation in the Community production of tractors.
> Thus, even if the aid contributes to facilitating the development of the production of agricultural tractors - and so of the Antwerp region - nevertheless the application of the provisions of [Article 107(3)(c)] is not only inexpedient, because the aid is not in the common interest, but is also excluded because it alters the conditions of trade by a measure which is contrary to the common interest.[269]

This position was developed further by the Commission setting the criteria for the facilitation of development in 1972 by indicating that, to avail of exemption, sectoral and regional aids must be:

(1) Selective: they must only be granted to undertakings whose development or reorganisation justifies the assumption that they will be competitive in the long run having regard to anticipated developments in the industrial sector concerned.[270]
(2) Degressive: the aid must eventually be phased out, leaving the undertakings to manage without further assistance; the aid must not, therefore, allow a situation of less than optimum allocation of resources to continue indefinitely (unless at the EU level it is decided to continue them in order to compensate for distortions of competition outside the EU).
(3) Transparent: it must be possible for the EU institutions and other interested parties to evaluate the aid.
(4) Well adapted to the intended objective: the instrument used having the least effect on intra-EU competition and the common interest.[271]

Further guidance was offered on this in 1982 focusing, in particular, on the point that aids must not lead to the transfer of industrial difficulties and unemployment from one Member State to the rest of the EU.[272]

---

269. European Commission: Decision No 64/651/EEC: *Re Subsidies to Ford Tractor (Belgium) Ltd.*, OJ 3257/64 of 18 October 1964.
270. *See*, for example, Case C-142/87: *Belgium v. Commission (Tubemeuse)*, [1990] ECR I-959 where the Commission rejected the applicability of Article 107(3)(c) to the development of a region where the aided undertaking was not in a position to ensure its own viability.
271. European Commission: *First Report on Competition Policy* (1972) at point 130.
272. European Commission: *Eleventh Report on Competition Policy* (1982) at point 180.

From the Commission's practice it can be further deduced that development within the meaning of Article 107(3)(c) is not facilitated where:

(a) the aid has no appreciable and direct impact on regional or sectoral development[273] or its effect is of limited scope and duration, as in the case of operating aid;[274]
(b) free market forces provide a better means of ensuring this development;[275]
(c) aid is notified to the Commission *ex post facto*;[276]
(d) specific aid for regional or sectoral development has already been given to the same undertaking;[277]
(e) the need for the investment was highly foreseeable and it was, therefore, in the undertakings own interests to carry out the expansion.[278]

It emerges from the *Glaverbel*[279] and *Boussac*[280] cases that State aid for replacement investment, even when it incorporates new technology, is likely to fail to fulfil the requirements for exemption here as this is normal commercial investment. Commission policy, moreover, indicates that the facilitation of development need not necessarily involve new investment or increased capacity. Closures, the adaptation of

273. European Commission: Decision No 81/797/EEC of 18 September 1981, on a proposal by the Netherlands Government to grant aid for the creation of new production capacity by an undertaking in the chemical industry (magnesium oxide), OJ L 296 of 15 October 1981.
274. *See*, for example, European Commission: Decision No 80/932/EEC of 15 September 1980 concerning the partial taking-over by the State of employers' contributions to sickness insurance schemes in Italy, OJ L 264 of 8 October 1980; Decision No 82/401/EEC of 5 May 1982, OJ L 173 of 19 June 1982; Decision No 82/651/EEC of 10 September 1982, OJ L 274 of 24 September 1982 and Decision No 82/73/EEC of 15 December 1981, on preferential natural gas tariff to glasshouse growers in the Netherlands, OJ L 37 of 10 February 1981.
275. European Commission: Decision No 81/716/EEC of 23 July 1981, on a proposal by the Netherlands Government to grant aid for increasing the production capacity by an undertaking in the chemical industry (polyethylene), OJ L 256 of 10 September 1981 and Decision No 82/295/EEC of 10 March 1982, on an aid scheme by the Belgian Government in respect of certain investments carried out by a Belgian undertaking to increase its production capacity for high-density polyethylene, OJ L 132 of 14 May 1982.
276. This of course is at the heart of the necessity test and typified in European Commission: Decision No 80/1157/EEC of 28 November 1980 on a scheme of aid by the Belgian Government in respect of certain investments carried out by the Belgian subsidiary of an international oil group at its Antwerp refinery, OJ L 343 of 18 December 1980.
277. On this, *see* European Commission: Decision No 82/829/EEC of 27 October 1982, on a proposed aid by the Belgian Government in respect of certain investments carried out by an oil company at its Antwerp refinery OJ L 350 of 10 December 1982.
278. *See* European Commission: Decisions No 82/774/EEC on a Belgian Government aid scheme concerning the setting-up of a new factory by a soft drinks manufacturer, 82/775/EEC on a Belgian Government aid scheme concerning the expansion of the production capacity of an undertaking manufacturing mineral water and soft drinks and 82/776/EEC on a Belgian Government aid scheme concerning the expansion of the production capacity of an undertaking manufacturing mineral water, hot spring water and soft drinks, OJ L 323 of 19 November 1982.
279. Cases C-62 and 72/87: *Executif Regional Wallon v. Commission (Glaverbel)*, [1988] ECR 1573.
280. Case C-301/87: *France v. Commission (Boussac)*, [1990] ECR I-307.

production and other forms of rationalisation can also facilitate development for the purpose of the exemption contemplated by Article 107(3)(c).[281]

While State aid which facilitates the development of certain economic activities or of certain economic areas is *eligible* for exemption under Article 107(3)(c), the substantive test is whether or not the aid adversely affects trading conditions to an extent contrary to the common interest. This test is strictly applied by the Commission who regard themselves as under a duty here to balance the beneficial effects of the aid against its adverse effects on trading conditions and the maintenance of undistorted competition.[282] Recalling the earlier coverage of the "effect on trade test" in relation to the prohibition of State aid in Article 107(1), it can be said that the test here amounts to a declaration that either the effect on trade is small (and thus counter-balanced by the sectoral or regional benefits), or that the nature of the aid scheme at issue can be justified by recognising a stronger economic development interest which over-rides the interest of EU competition policy per se.

In its assessment in this regard, the Commission takes account of the increased output and the percentage of the undertakings total production which will probably be exported within the EU after the aid is received.[283] Several Decisions have taken the position that, as a result of the prevailing competitive conditions, even a small amount of aid may impact on trading conditions to an extent contrary to the common interest.[284] This seems to be the view especially where there is declining demand or surplus capacity on account of the inherent transfer of the resultant economic problems to other Member States arising from any State aid response to these situations.[285] The

281. This position was upheld in Joined Cases 296 and 318/82: *Netherlands & Leeuwarder Papierwarenfabriek v. Commission*, [1985] ECR 809.
282. European Commission: *Fourteenth Report on Competition Policy* (1984), point 202.
283. European Commission: Decision No 80/1157/EEC of 28 November 1980 on a scheme of aid by the Belgian Government in respect of certain investments carried out by the Belgian subsidiary of an international oil group at its Antwerp refinery, OJ L 343 of 18 December 1980; Decision No 81/738/EEC of 31 July 1981, on a proposal by the Netherlands Government to grant aid for the creation of new production capacity by an undertaking in the petro-chemical industry (aromatic solvents), OJ L 262 of 16 September 1981; Decision No 81/626/EEC of 10 July 1981, on a scheme of aid by the Belgian Government in respect of certain investments carried out by a Belgian undertaking to modernise its butyl rubber production plant, OJ L 229 of 13 August 1981; Decision No 82/295/EEC of 10 March 1982, on an aid scheme by the Belgian Government in respect of certain investments carried out by a Belgian undertaking to increase its production capacity for high-density polyethylene, OJ L 132 of 14 May 1982 and Decision No 82/829/EEC of 27 October 1982, on a proposed aid by the Belgian Government in respect of certain investments carried out by an oil company at its Antwerp refinery, OJ L 350 of 10 December 1982.
284. European Commission: Decision No 82/401/EEC of 5 May 1982, OJ L 173 of 19 June 1982; Commission Decision No 82/651/EEC of 10 September 1982, OJ L 274 of 24 September 1982 and Commission Decision No 82/744/EEC of 11 October 1982 concerning Italian national Law No 423/81 of 1 August 1981 on measures for agriculture, OJ L 315 of 11 November 1982.
285. European Commission: Decision No 81/738/EEC of 31 July 1981 on a proposal by the Netherlands Government to grant aid for the creation of new production capacity by an undertaking in the petro-chemical industry (aromatic solvents), OJ L 262 of 16 September 1981; Decision No 82/295/EEC of 10 March 1982 on an aid scheme by the Belgian Government in respect of certain investments carried out by a Belgian undertaking to increase its production capacity for high-density polyethylene, OJ L 132 of 14 May 1982 and Decision No 82/829/EEC

logic of this type of approach by the Commission was upheld in the 1980 *Philip Morris* case.[286]

In a recent case, where the development of corporate listings was envisaged by means of an Italian aid tax relief scheme to support the cost of flotations on the stock exchange, exemption on the basis of Article 107(3)(c) was refused.[287]

The method by which aid is financed became a critical element in the application of this test following the 1970 case of *France v. Commission*.[288] This case considered the scope of Commission discretion under paragraph (c) with particular regard to the second test concerning contributions towards research and restructuring in the French textiles sector. The Court said that it was necessary for the Commission to consider all the legal and factual circumstances regarding the aid and to explore any imbalances between the charges imposed on undertakings and the benefits from the aid.[289] In this case, the Court said that the method by which the aid was financed (a parafiscal charge) could not be divorced from the provision of the aid itself and upheld the Commission's objection to the method of financing; holding that method to adversely affect trade to a degree contrary to the common interest.[290] At issue in that case was the imposition of a restructuring levy on all textiles sales in France in order to fund research and the restructuring of the French textiles sector. The Court agreed that this method of financing had an adverse effect far exceeding the aid in question.[291]

Article 107(3)(c) allows for the approval of various horizontal aid measures (or measures applying to all sectors) such as aid to SMEs, for environmental protection and for research, development and innovation. Accordingly, it is the main point of reference for secondary rules and soft law measures concerning these categories of aid. Moreover, it may also be invoked where the objective of a State aid measure relates to some other Treaty objective such as a high level of public healthcare under Article 168 of the TFEU.[292] The current EU horizontal State aid rules are listed below.

---

of 27 October 1982 on a proposed aid by the Belgian Government in respect of certain investments carried out by an oil company at its Antwerp refinery, OJ L 350 of 10 December 1982.

286. Case 730/79: *Philip Morris v. Commission*, [1980] ECR 2671 at 2692. European Commission: Decision No 81/738/EEC of 31 July 1981 on a proposal by the Netherlands Government to grant aid for the creation of new production capacity by an undertaking in the petro-chemical industry (aromatic solvents), OJ L 262 of 16 September 1981; Commission Decision No 82/295/EEC of 10 March 1982, on an aid scheme by the Belgian Government in respect of certain investments carried out by a Belgian undertaking to increase its production capacity for high-density polyethylene, OJ L 132 of 14 May 1982 and Commission Decision No 82/829/EEC of 27 October 1982 on a proposed aid by the Belgian Government in respect of certain investments carried out by an oil company at its Antwerp refinery, OJ L 350 of 10 December 1982.
287. Case T-211/05: *Italy v. Commission*, [2009] ECR II-2777 at para. 183.
288. Case C-47/69: *France v. Commission*, [1970] ECR 487.
289. *Ibid.*, at 494.
290. *Ibid.*, at 493–494.
291. *Ibid.*, at 496.
292. European Commission: *Thirtieth Report on Competition Policy* (2000), point 411 concerning the approval of a Swedish aid measure to reduce the level of toxic substances in building citing Article 168 of the TFEU.

Table 6 EU Horizontal State Aid Regulations and Soft Law Measures

General Block Exemption Regulation[293] *De Minimis* Regulation[295] SGEI *De minimis* Regulation[297] SGEI Decision[299] Regional State aid[301] Risk capital State aid[303] Research and Development and Innovation (R&D&I) aid[305]	State aid for employment of disadvantaged or disabled workers[294] Training aid[296] Environmental and Energy State aid[298] SGEI Communication and Framework[300] Guarantees[302] Export Credit Insurance[304]

293. European Commission: Regulation No 651/2014/EU of 17 June 2014 declaring certain categories of aid compatible with the internal market in application of Articles 107 and 108 of the Treaty, OJ L 187 of 26 June 2014.
294. European Commission: Communication from the Commission - *Criteria for the compatibility analysis of training state aid cases subject to individual notification*, OJ C 188 of 11 August 2009.
295. European Commission: Regulation No 1407/2013/EU of 18 December 2013 on the application of Articles 107 and 108 of the Treaty on the Functioning of the European Union to *de minimis* aid, OJ L 352 of 24 December 2013.
296. European Commission: Communication from the Commission - *Criteria for the compatibility analysis of state aid to disadvantaged and disabled workers subject to individual notification*, OJ C 188 of 11 August 2009.
297. European Commission: Regulation No 360/2012/EU on the application of Articles 107 and 108 of the Treaty on the Functioning of the European Union to *de minimis* aid granted to undertakings providing services of general economic interest, OJ L 114 of 26 April 2012.
298. European Commission: Communication from the Commission - *Guidelines on State aid for environmental protection and energy* 2014-2020, OJ C 200 of 28 June 2014 and *Guidelines on certain State aid measures in the context of the greenhouse gas emission allowance trading scheme post 2012*, OJ C 154 of 5 June 2012.
299. European Commission: Decision No 21/2012/EU of 20 December 2011 on the application of Article 106(2) of the Treaty on the Functioning of the European Union to State aid in the form of public service compensation granted to certain undertakings entrusted with the operation of services of general economic interest, OJ L 7 of 11 January 2012.
300. European Commission: *Communication on the application of the European Union State aid rules to compensation granted for the provision of services of general economic interest*, OJ C 8 of 11 January 2012 and Communication from the Commission: *European Union framework for State aid in the form of public service compensation*, [2011] OJ C 8 of 11 January 2012.
301. European Commission: *Guidelines on Regional State aid for 2014-2020*, OJ C 209 of 23 July 2013.
302. European Commission: *Notice on the application of Articles 87 and 88 of the EC Treaty (now Articles 107 and 108 of the TFEU) to State aid in the form of guarantees*, OJ C 155 of 20 June 2008 as corrected by Corrigendum in OJ C 244 of 25 September 2008.
303. European Commission: *Guidelines on risk finance aid for 2014-2020*, OJ C 19 of 22 January 2014.
304. European Commission: *Communication from the Commission to the Member States on the application of Articles 107 and 108 of the Treaty on the Functioning of the European Union to short-term export-credit insurance*, OJ C 392 of 19 December 2012, as amended.
305. European Commission: *Framework for State aid for research and development and innovation*, OJ C 198 of 27 June 2014.

Article 107(3)(c) also allows for the approval of sectoral aid and is the exemption-link in Article 107 as regards the important field of State aid for the rescue and restructuring of undertakings in difficulty. At the same time, as the purpose of Article 107(3)(c) is to facilitate the development of economic areas or activities, its purpose is not to assist individual firms. For that reason, the use of the exemption in rescue and restructuring cases has been applied with increasing strictness over the years and with particular regard to the overall position of a sector within which a rescue and restructuring measure is proposed. The current sectoral State aid rules (including the rules on rescue and restructuring) are listed below.

Table 7 EU Sectoral Regulations and Soft Law Measures

Coal sector[306]	Postal sector[307]
Rescue and Restructuring State aid[308]	Transport sector (Road and rail)[309]
The Steel sector[310]	Transport sector (Air)[311]
The Electricity sector (stranded costs)[312]	Transport sector (Maritime and Inland Waterway)[313]

306. Council Decision No 787/2010/EU of 10 December 2010 on *State aid to facilitate the closure of uncompetitive coal mines*, OJ L 336 of 21 December 2010.
307. European Commission: *Notice from the Commission on the application of the competition rules to the postal sector and on the assessment of certain State measures relating to postal services*, OJ C 39 of 6 February 1998.
308. European Commission: *Guidelines on State aid for rescuing and restructuring non-financial undertakings in difficulty*, OJ C 249 of 31 July 2014.
309. Regulation No 1370/2007/EC of the European Parliament and of the Council of 23 October 2007 on public passenger transport services by rail and by road and repealing Council Regulations Nos 1191/69/EEC and 1107/70/EEC, OJ L 315 of 3 December 2007 and European Commission: *Communication from the Commission - Community guidelines on State aid for railway undertakings*, OJ C 184 of 22 July 2008.
310. European Commission: *Communication from the Commission: Rescue and restructuring aid and closure aid for the steel sector*, OJ C 70 of 19 March 2002.
311. European Commission: *Guidelines on State aid to airports and airlines*, OJ C 99 of 4 April 2014.
312. European Commission: *Commission Communication relating to the methodology for analysing State aid linked to stranded costs*, adopted by the Commission on 26 July 2001 and issued as Commission letter SG (2001) D/290869 of 6 August 2001. This is accessible from http://ec.europa.eu/competition/state_aid/legislation/specific_rules.html but has not been published in the Official Journal.
313. European Commission: *Communication from the Commission providing guidance on State aid to ship-management companies*, OJ C 132 of 11 June 2009; *Communication from the Commission providing guidance on State aid complementary to Community funding for the launching of the motorways of the sea*, OJ C 317 of 12 December 2008 and Commission Communication C (2004) 43 - *Community guidelines on State aid to maritime transport*, OJ C 13 of 17 January 2004.

Financial sector[314] Film and Audiovisual sector[316] Broadcasting sector[317] Broadband sector[318]	Agriculture, Fisheries, Forestries and Rural sectors[315]

2.8.4 Article 107(3)(d) of the TFEU – Aid Supporting Culture and Heritage

This new exemption category was introduced by the Maastricht Treaty (Treaty on the European Union) signed in 1992. It is understood that the initiative for this text came from the Government of the Netherlands. The idea was first mooted in a paper to the Dutch Parliament on 26 October 1990 on European Political Union in a section dealing with culture where it was suggested that one possible solution to the "tension between on the one hand the working of the Treaty (particularly as regards national support measures and competition) and on the other the widely felt need to protect or promote expressions of national culture" would be "the formulation of an exception to existing Community law, which would take the form of redefining Articles [42 and 107 of the TFEU]." The text of the Article 107(3) amendment started with a blanket exemption facility for the promotion of culture and heritage conservation in early 1991. The criteria on effects on trade and competition were added in Council negotiations and the Foreign Ministers added the "common interest" wording at the end of 1991.[319]

The Maastricht Treaty on European Union first introduced an EU role in contributing to "the flowering of the cultures of the Member States"[320] and also introduced what is now Article 167 of the TFEU mandating the EU to:

> "contribute to the flowering of the cultures of the Member States, while respecting their national and regional diversity, and at the same time bringing the common cultural heritage to the fore"... and to "take cultural aspects into account in its action under other provisions of this Treaty"[321]

314. European Commission: *Communication from the Commission on the application, from 1 August 2013, of State aid rules to support measures in favour of banks in the context of the financial crisis ("Banking Communication")*, OJ C 216 of 30 July 2013.
315. Guidelines on State aid for Agriculture, Forestry and Rural Development (2014), *supra*; the Agriculture Block Exemption Regulation (2014), *supra*; the Agriculture *De Minimis* Regulation (2013) *supra*; the Fishery and Aquaculture Block Exemption Regulation, *supra* and the *De minimis* Fisheries and Aquaculture Regulation (2014), *supra*.
316. European Commission: *Communication from the Commission on State aid for films and other audiovisual works*, OJ C 332 of 15 November 2013.
317. European Commission: *Communication from the Commission on the application of State aid rules to public service broadcasting*, OJ C 257 of 27 October 2009.
318. European Commission: *EU Guidelines for the application of state aid rules in relation to the rapid deployment of broadband networks* of 15 January 2013, OJ C 25 of 26 January 2013.
319. The authors are indebted to the Irish Department of Foreign Affairs for the background material provided on this provision.
320. Maastricht Treaty, Article 3(p).
321. TFEU, Article 167(1) and Article 167(4).

Accordingly, it is clear that the provision of Article 107(3)(d) sets the framework for the State aid rules to take appropriate account of the new cultural objectives of the EU. It may also not have been coincidental that in July 1991 the Commission exempted a fund for literary productions and translations notified by the Dutch Government.[322]

On the wording of Article 107(3)(d), it is to be noted first that the two tests considered in the previous section regarding Article 107(3)(c) are essentially reproduced for cases of culture and heritage aid. A distinct reference to "competition" is added, however, suggesting a more in-depth substantive analysis for the application of the Article 107(3)(d) exemption. Moreover, the eligibility test is worded in terms of "promote" rather than "facilitate" suggesting a closer affinity to Article 107(3)(b) and perhaps a more relaxed test of eligibility for that reason.

It is clearly arguable that culture and heritage aid could have been subsumed into Article 107(3)(b) as a priority project of common European interest in the light of the objectives of the new Article 167. This view is supported further by suggestions from two sources that the insertion of paragraph (d) would not change practice and merely confirmed existing Commission policy.[323] However, a view that law and practice regarding cultural aid was far from clear in the early 1990s is evident from the *SIDES Case*[324] where a package of aid to promote the export of French language books to minority foreign markets (e.g., Africa, the French Overseas Territories and Eastern Europe) was exempted under Article 107(3)(c) in June 1993 (rather than under the new Article 107(3(d)) expressly on the grounds of the cultural objective of the aid.[325]

In its subsequent practice, the European Commission has applied this exemption primarily in cases involving the audiovisual sector – notably in regard to the approval of aid for the film industry, the production of television programmes in regional languages, the plastic arts and the export of books to countries where the language of those books is not widely spoken. In the earlier era, where cultural aids were generally assumed not to be covered by the State aid rules, the primary concern had been situations where the nature or structure of a scheme had given rise to potential infringements of other Treaty articles by virtue of in-built discriminations against the nationals of another Member State or the creation of barriers to the free movement of workers, freedom of establishment and freedom to provide services.[326] By 1999, the position regarding the new Article 107(3)(d) was described as follows:

322. This is referred to in L. Hancher, T. Ottervanger & P.J. Slot: "*EC State Aids*" (First Edition), Chancery Law Publications, 1993, p. 63 and in by Loman, Mortelmans, Post & Watson: "*Culture and Community Law*," Kluwer, 1992.

323. This was the position of Loman, Mortelmans, Post & Watson: "*Culture and Community Law*," Kluwer, 1992, p. 192. It was also the line taken by the Commission in a draft "*Guideline on State Aid for the arts and culture with particular reference to the audio-visual sector*" circulated to Member States in March 1995.

324. Case T-49/93: *Societe Internationale de Diffusion et d'Edition (SIDE) v. Commission*, [1995] ECR II-2501.

325. European Commission: Decision No 92/127/EEC of 25 June 1993, *Aid to Exporters of French Books*, OJ C 174 of 17 July 1993.

326. *See*, for example, European Commission: Decision No 89/441/EEC of 21 December 1988 - Greek Film Industry, OJ L 208 of 20 July 1989, where a scheme of aid to the Greek Film industry was declared incompatible with Article 107(1) of the Treaty unless a provision requiring the producers of assisted films to be Greek was removed.

> All Member States have adopted policies for the promotion and expression of their culture.... However, in the field of culture and arts there is frequently competition for audiences and advertising. Therefore, competition policy has a role to play. The Commission normally takes a positive attitude towards State aid for the audiovisual sector, which is identified as a fast growing industry ... [and] approval will normally be given as long as the aid is in proportion to the objectives and does not discriminate on grounds of nationality. Almost all notified aid schemes aiming at a derogation under this new article concerned the film industry. The European film industry is still not commercially viable, despite some recent major box office successes. In 1996, for instance, among the top 10 films in terms of admissions, there was only one film from Europe (Sense and Sensibility, a US/UK co-production). Therefore, many Member States run schemes to aid the production of films on their territory and/or in the national language.[327]

The EU's liberal and developmental approach to the promotion and strengthening of the European film industry is focussed on improving its competitive capabilities (particularly at the level of small and medium enterprises) taking into account, at the same time, the cultural dimension of the sector. This is done largely by allowing the Member States considerable freedom to provide a wide range of financial support mechanisms (generally in form of subsidies or repayable advances) to all aspects of the industry. It is also mirrored in a number of EU support initiatives and the background of the *European Convention on Cinematographic Co-production*[328] which aimed to promote the development of European cinematographic co-production by simplifying procedures and production on the basis of criteria established by the "Eurimages." Moreover, it is clear from the Convention that there are different rules governing State support for cinema production and that the main objectives of the Convention were to minimise these differences and to harmonise multilateral relations between States when they enter co-production agreements.

The EU's own measures to provide financial support were introduced to enable the European industry to take advantage of the Europe-wide market. EU policy also recognises that it is often difficult for producers of audiovisual works to access funds to finance and expand their activities. Indeed, while SMEs may have difficulty in accessing finance generally, the position is viewed as significantly more difficult for SMEs operating in the cultural and creative sectors.[329] Various measures have been

---

327. European Commission: "*European Economy*," 1999 p. 49.
328. Council of Europe: *European Convention on Cinematographic Co-production*, Strasbourg, 2 October 1992. A revised Council of Europe Convention on Cinematographic Co-production (ETS No 220) to take account of technology changes and to open up the Convention to non-European countries was adopted on 29 June 2016 and opened for signature on 30 January 2017.
329. Regulation No 1295/2013/EU of the European Parliament and of the Council of 11 December 2013 establishing *the Creative Europe Programme (2014 to 2020)* and repealing Decisions No 1718/2006/EC, No 1855/2006/EC and No 1041/2009/EC, OJ L 347 of 20 December 2013, pp. 221–237.

introduced over the years at EU level to facilitate the promotion of this sector. These have included the MEDIA 2007 Programme[330] and the Creative Europe Programme.[331]

In its 2001 *"Communication on the future of the Cinema and the Audiovisual Industry in Europe,"* the European Commission pointed out that:

> The audiovisual sector in Europe, which is a strategic industry because of its cultural importance and its potential for the creation of wealth and jobs, continues to suffer from numerous handicaps that hinder the circulation of films and other audiovisual works.[332]

In this important Communication, the European Commission analysed these handicaps and proposed ways of overcoming them. It also provided the cinema sector with greater legal security by explaining the criteria that the Commission would be using when examining national cinema support schemes under the Treaty's rules on State aid. This resulted also in a specific Communication on cinematographic and other audiovisual works which applied until end of 2013.[333]

The essential approach of the Communication on cinematographic and other audiovisual works was that support to the film sector, for example, cannot be restricted on the basis of nationality, that there must be an objective cultural dimension to such support based on national criteria (which the Commission must accept unless it identifies manifest errors in national criteria), that at least 20% of the film making must be free to take place in a country other than that providing the aid and that the intensity of government support (except for low budget and "difficult" films) must not exceed 50%. The latter condition was designed to stimulate normal commercial decisions without resulting in a bidding war and this was augmented by a further condition that support for supplementary film activities (e.g., post-production) was prohibited. In

---

330. The *MEDIA* Programme 2007-2013 (with a budget of €755 million) was jointly run by the European Commission Directorate-General for Education and Culture (DG EAC) and the Education, Audiovisual & Culture Executive Agency (EACEA), which is in charge of the operational management of the Programme. The MEDIA Programme aims at strengthening the competitiveness of the European audiovisual industry with a series support measures dealing with: the training of professionals; the development of production projects and companies; the distribution of cinematographic works and audiovisual programmes; the promotion of cinematographic works and audiovisual programmes; support for cinematographic festivals (including the annual Cannes Film Festival) and the development and use of new technologies in the sector.
331. *Creative Europe* is the European Commission's new framework programme for support to the culture and audiovisual sectors and the successor to the earlier Culture Programme and MEDIA programme, Creative Europe, with a budget of €1.46 billion is specifically supporting culture sector initiatives (including those promoting cross-border cooperation, platforms, networking, and literary translation) and audiovisual sector initiatives (such as those promoting the development, distribution, or access to audiovisual works). Accordingly, the Programme intends to support 250,000 artists and cultural professionals, 2,000 cinemas, 800 films, 4,500 book translations and provide a financial guarantee facility of up to €750 million for small businesses active in the sector.
332. European Commission: *Communication on the future of the Cinema and the Audiovisual Industry in Europe,* 27 September 2001.
333. European Commission: *Communication from the Commission to the Council, the European Parliament, the Economic and Social Committee and the Committee of the Regions on certain legal aspects relating to cinematographic and other audiovisual works,* OJ C 43 of 16 February 2002. This was subsequently extended on several occasions until the end of 2013.

addition, in its recent decisions, the Commission has applied these rules by analogy to the development of films, including the writing of screenplays and the promotion and distribution of films.[334]

While this has been referred to recently as "a policy in motion," it is still the general view of both governments and the film industry that, in the absence of public support to film production in most Member States, most European productions would already have disappeared. Indeed, in the four years 2002–2005, EU governments provided over €6.5 billion of State aid for film production,[335] which helped to produce over 3,600 films. France provided the highest overall amounts of State aid for films, followed by the UK, Germany, Italy and Spain and government support in these five countries accounted for 83% of the total. Moreover, there are over 600 film support schemes operating across the EU. Currently, EU Member States provide an estimated €3 billion per year in film support: €2 billion in grants and soft loans, as well as €1 billion in tax incentives. Around 80% of this is for film production and France, the UK, Germany, Italy and Spain continue to offer the majority of this financial support.[336]

Even in the context of a largely liberal State aid approach to the sector, a new debate arose in recent years about how to strike a better balance in regard to territorial conditions in the future that require film making to be carried out in the donor country.

On a different point concerning the culture and heritage exemption, State aid measures to support public broadcasting tend *not* to be regarded as related to culture and are generally not covered by the possible exemption of Article 107(3)(d). In practice, State aid cases of this type are normally examined for possible exemption as compensation for SGEI (Article 106), as aid of a social character (Article 107(2)(a))[337] or as aid covered by Article 107(3)(c).[338] Moreover, the Commission has expressly rejected the exemption of State aid to public broadcasters under Article 107(3)(d) of the TFEU to promote culture, because the notion of "culture" is to be interpreted restrictively and the Commission considers that Article 107(3)(d) should only be relevant if a measure was specifically aimed at promoting cultural objectives, as

334. A point made by J. Broche, O. Chatterjee, I Orissich & N. Tosics: "*State Aid for Films – A Policy in Motion?*," Competition Policy Newsletter, DG Competition, Spring, 2007, p. 45. Particular examples of this include: European Commission: Decision No 181/2004 - Germany, *Förderung von Film- und Fernsehproduktionen in Baden-Württemberg: Medien-und-Filmgesellschaft Baden-WürttembergmbH, 2004* and Commission Decision: No 368/2005 - Spain, *Ayudas a lapromoción de obras audiovisuales por Andalucía, 2005.*

335. Copenhagen Think Tank/European Audiovisual Observatory. http://www.dfi.dk/NR/rdonlyres/1BE19F2D-F61F-403F-934C-B0AB2447D9D8/0/CTT_Information_Notes_300606.pdf.

336. European Commission: Press Release "*State aid: Commission consults on new film support rules,*" 30 April 2013.

337. European Commission Decision: *Fund for digitalisation, Austria* (Case No 622/2003) of 16 March 2005, OJ C 228 of 17 September 2005 and European Commission: Decision No 546/2006 of 6 December 2006 *French digital television*, OJ C 23 of 1 February 2007. In that Decision, the Commission found that subsidies to enable low-income consumers to purchase equipment, enabling them to receive digital broadcasting, fell within the scope of Article 107(2)(a).

338. European Commission: Decision No C 52/2005 of 24 January 2007 - *Digital decoder subsidy*, OJ C 147 of 8 June 2007; Decision No C19/2009 of 20 April 2011 - *TV2/Denmark*, OJ L 340 of 21 December 2011 and Case T-21/06: *Germany v. Commission*, [2009] ECR II-197.

opposed to the educational and democratic needs of society.[339] Thus in its Decision on *BBC News 24*, the Commission took the view that:

> the provision of a 24-hour news channel is aimed more at fulfilling the information needs of UK citizens than at promoting culture or national heritage within the meaning of Article 107(3)(d).[340]

2.8.5 Article 107(3)(e) of the TFEU – Other Categories of Aid Authorised by the Council on a Proposal from the Commission

The final, and apparently open-ended, provision for discretionary exemption under Article 107(3)(e) applies to such other categories of aid as may be specified by a decision of the Council adopted by a qualified majority on a proposal from the Commission. Article 107(3)(e) provides for the creation of other bases for discretionary exemption to the general prohibition on aid. In effect, it is a contingency provision allowing a new exemption to be created if others cannot be applied and if there is a policy imperative to do so.

Such a policy imperative arose in the past in regard to the EU shipbuilding industry and this provision was used to adopt seven directives to address the particular State aid challenges which had arisen in the shipbuilding sector and most recently the Framework on State aid for shipbuilding which operated from 2012 until 30 June 2014.[341] With the expiry of these rules, and a considerable restoration of competitiveness in the shipbuilding sector, the Commission integrated the provisions on innovation aid laid down in the Framework into the revised version of the general EU Framework for State aid for Research and Development and Innovation[342] and the provisions on regional aid in the most recent Regional Aid Guidelines.[343]

In the context of the most recent State aid rules applicable to the coal sector, the Council adopted a Decision on aid to facilitate the closure of uncompetitive coal mines, using Article 107(3)(e) as the legal basis.[344]

Two other points are of note. First, this provision merely permits the Council, on a proposal from the Commission, to create new categories of exceptions to the basic provisions of Article 107(3). It cannot, therefore, make any adjustments to categories (a) to (d) and it cannot act without a Commission proposal. Second, this provision is

339. European Commission: *Communication from the Commission on the application of State aid rules to public service broadcasting, supra*, paras 34 and 35.
340. European Commission: Decision No 88/1998 of 14 December 1999 - *BBC News 24*, OJ C 78 of 18 March 2000, para 36.
341. European Commission: *Framework on State aid for shipbuilding*, OJ C 364 of 14 December 2011.
342. European Commission: *Framework for State aid for Research and Development and Innovation* OJ C 198 of 27 June 2014.
343. European Commission: *Guidelines on regional State aid for 2014-2020*, OJ C 209 of 23 July 2013.
344. Council Decision No 2010/787/EU on State aid to facilitate the closure of uncompetitive coal mines, OJ L 336, of 21 December 2010.

entirely separate to the Council's powers to intervene in individual State cases under Article 108(2) and does not create any separate basis of intervention in individual cases.

Finally, the Article 107(3)(e) basis for exemption may be less important following the activation of Article 109 regulations since 1998 (enabling regulations) and the subsequent addition of Article 108(4) in the Lisbon Treaty. Article 108(4) provides as follows:

> The Commission may adopt regulations relating to the categories of State aid that the Council has, pursuant to Article 109, determined may be exempted from the procedure provided for by paragraph 3 of this Article.[345]

In particular, it would seem that, while Article 107(3)(e) offers a basis for substantive exemption, it does not provide a sufficient basis for a procedural exemption e.g. block exemption from notification of certain types of State aid measures. This has become the function of Article 108(4) in combination with Article 109 since the Lisbon Treaty came into force as the TFEU.

2.9 BLOCK EXEMPTIONS

Since 2008, the EU introduced a GBER which allowed Member States to apply many categories of (horizontal) State aid without prior notification and up to the maximum levels allowed in the GBER. The most recent edition of the GBER (Commission Regulation No 651/2014/EU of 17 June 2014)[346] made several important changes which effectively further extended the scope of the GBER:

- It raised the exemption thresholds for many measures that were previously covered by the 2008 GBER, allowing Member States to grant higher aid amounts without prior notification. For some categories of aid, the scope was also increased through more flexible eligibility conditions, more favourable maximum aid intensities and higher aid amounts.
- The European Commission added several new categories, such as aid for local, broadband, research and energy infrastructures, innovation clusters, regional urban development funds, culture and heritage conservation, audiovisual works, sports and recreational infrastructures and aid to make good damage caused by certain natural disasters.
- Other aspects of the 2014 GBER involved some degree of simplification of the 2008 GBER conditions that aid measures should meet to benefit from the exemption.
- European Commission monitoring of the aid granted under the GBER was tightened up; allowing the Commission to request Member States to carry out

345. TFEU, Article 108(4).
346. European Commission: Regulation No 651/2014/EU of 17 June 2014 declaring certain categories of aid compatible with the internal market in application of Articles 107 and 108 of the Treaty, OJ L 187 of 26 June 2014.

evaluations of the effects of some large aid schemes in order to better assess their actual impact and facilitate future improvements.
- Aid measures under the GBER were to become more transparent, by requiring Member States to publish lists of the aid beneficiaries.

As a result, the position now is that some fourteen main categories of aid are allowed to be granted immediately by EU Member States without prior notification to the Commission, up to the maximum aid amounts as defined in the Regulation. The position, in summary is set out in the following Table.

Table 8 2014 GBER Limits to Block Exemptions for Horizontal State Aids

The GBER does not apply to any individual aid, whether granted ad hoc or on the basis of a scheme, the gross grant equivalent of which exceeds the following thresholds:

- Regional investment aid where the "adjusted aid amount" of aid for an investment with eligible costs is €100 million or more.
- Regional urban development aid greater than €20 million.
- SME investment aid of €7.5 million per undertaking per investment project.
- Aid for consultancy for SMEs: €2 million per undertaking, per project.
- Aid to SMEs for participation in fairs: €2 million per undertaking, per year.
- Aid to SMEs for cooperation costs incurred by participating in European Territorial Cooperation projects: €2 million per undertaking, per project.
- Risk finance aid: €15 million per eligible undertaking.
- Aid for start-ups up to the following limits: (A) SUBSIDISED LOANS with a duration of ten years and with a maximum nominal amount greater than €1 million (For loans with a duration of between five and ten years, the maximum amounts may be adjusted by multiplying the amounts above by the ratio between ten years and the actual duration of the loan. For loans with a duration of less than five years, the maximum amount shall be the same as for loans with a duration of five years; (B) GUARANTEES with premiums which do not conform with market conditions, with a duration of ten years and up to a maximum guaranteed amount of €1.5 million (€2.25 million for undertakings established in "A regions" and €3 million for undertakings established in "C regions"); similar adjustment for duration apply as in the case of subsidized loans and the guarantee provided must not exceed 80% of the underlying loan; (C) GRANTS, including equity or quasi equity investment, interests rate and guarantee premium reductions up to €400,000 (or €600,000 for undertakings established in "A regions" and €800,000 for undertakings established in "C regions"); (D) For small and innovative enterprises, the maximum amounts set out in (A) to (C) may be doubled:
- Aid for research and development: (A) Fundamental Research – €40 million per undertaking, per project; (B) Industrial Research – €20 million per undertaking, per project; (C) Experimental Development – €15 million per undertaking, per project; (D) Eureka Programme projects – €80, €40 and €30 million respectively; (E) well-structured repayable advances, €60, €30 and €22.5 million respectively; (F) Feasibility Studies – €7.5 million per study; (G) Investment Aid for Research Infrastructures – €20 million per infrastructure; (H) Innovation Clusters – €7.5 million per cluster; (I) Innovation Aid to SMEs – €5 million per undertaking, per project; (J) Process and Organisational Innovation – €7.5 million per undertaking, per project.

- Training aid: €2 million per training project.
- Aid for the recruitment of disadvantaged workers: €5 million per undertaking, per year.
- Aid for the employment of workers with disabilities in the form of wage subsidies: €10 million per undertaking, per year.
- Aid for compensating the costs of assistance provided to disadvantaged workers: €5 million per undertaking, per year.
- Investment aid for environmental protection, excluding investment aid for the remedial work on contaminated sites and aid for the distribution network part of energy-efficient district heating and cooling installation: €15 million per undertaking per investment project.
- Investment aid for energy efficiency projects: €10 million.
- Investment aid for remedying contaminated sites: €20 million per undertaking per investment project.
- Operating aid for the production of electricity from renewable sources and operating aid for the promotion of energy from renewable sources in small-scale installations: €15 million per undertaking per project (and €150 million where the aid is granted on the basis of a competitive bidding process).
- Investment aid for the district heating or cooling distribution network: €20 million per undertaking per investment project.
- Investment aid for energy infrastructure: €50 million per undertaking, per investment project.
- Aid for broadband infrastructures: €70 million total cost per project.
- Investment aid for culture and heritage conservation: €100 million per project.
- Operating aid for culture and heritage conservation: €50 million per undertaking per year.
- Aid schemes for audiovisual works: €50 million per scheme per year.
- Investment aid for sports and multifunctional infrastructures: €15 million or the total costs exceeding €50 million per project.
- Operating aid for sport infrastructure: €2 million per infrastructure per year.
- Investment aid for local infrastructures: €10 million or the total costs exceeding €20 million for the same infrastructure.

These thresholds may not be circumvented by artificially splitting up the aid schemes or aid projects.

Accordingly, only State aid measures which are not covered by *de minimis* regulations and/or by the GBER (or similar regulations in areas such as agriculture) currently need to be notified and pre-approved under Article 108(3) of the TFEU. Where a measure continues to require notification, specific horizontal or relevant sectoral rules set further State aid limits and the basis for Commission assessment. Where such rules do not exist, a notified measure will be assessed on the basis of the general provisions of the TFEU and the Commission's general principles for State aid assessment - notably regarding the necessity, proportionality and duration of the proposed aid.

The importance of these exclusions from notification and pre-approval should not be underestimated. In launching the 2014 GBER, the European Commission noted that the previous GBER covered 60% of all aid measures and almost 30% of all aid amounts in the EU. The new GBER, in turn was estimated to relieve the Commission and the Member State from the need to notify some 75% of all State aid measures (and 66% of total EU State aid by value) for pre-approval.[347] This huge change was further expanded by the following statement:

> Even more aid measures could be exempted if Member States make smart use of the possibilities offered by the Regulation, designing their aid schemes so that they meet the conditions required.[348]

Moreover, the Commission expressly stated that the new Regulation:

- encourages "good aid" which stimulates economic growth, job creation and other objectives of common interest;
- reduces the administrative burden for Member States;
- allows the faster deployment of aid for companies; and
- enables the Commission to concentrate its scrutiny on the aid measures which are most likely to distort competition in the Single Market.

2.10 WHAT HAPPENS WHEN STATE AID IS ILLEGAL?

Prior to Regulation No 659/1999/EC, liability for recovery in cases of illegal aid was open ended following the ruling in *Commission v. Federal Republic of Germany (Kohlegesetz)* of 1972. The 1999 Procedural Regulation introduced a ten-year time limit on recovery orders on the basis that, after ten years, most of the actual or potential impacts of such State aid on competition could be considered to have disappeared from the market.

In regard to recovery, the updated Procedural Regulation[349] contains a chapter on the procedure regarding unlawful aid.[350] The Commission's power to order recovery is restricted to unlawful aid[351] and cases of misused aid.[352] The Commission may typically act on its own initiative or in response to a complaint. In appropriate cases, following the initial comments of the Member State concerned, the Commission may order the suspension of the contested measure[353] and the provisional recovery of the

347. European Commission: Press Release "*State aid: Commission exempts more aid measures from prior notification,*" 21 May 2014.
348. *Ibid.*
349. Council Regulation 1589/2015/EU of 13 July 2015 laying down detailed rules for the application of Article 108 of the Treaty on the Functioning of the European Union, OJ L 248 of 24 September 2015.
350. *Ibid.*, Chapter III – Articles 12–16.
351. *Ibid.*, Article 16.
352. *Ibid.*, Article 16.
353. *Ibid.*, Article 13(1).

unlawful aid.[354] The Commission's investigation must not only establish that the measure was not notified but that it is/was also incompatible with the internal market.[355]

The definition of unlawful aid is the key concept relevant for recovery. The concept of unlawful aid is defined as "new aid" put into effect in contravention of Article 108(3).[356] First, this definition covers situations where aid is implemented without notification. In that regard, it can be noted that, in practice, EU Member States and the Commission may legitimately hold a different view of the notion of State aid in specific circumstances; especially given the constant evolution of the concept. This will usually translate into a "good faith" failure to notify.[357] Similarly, EU Member States may also be of the opinion that a certain State aid does not have to be notified because it has already been approved as a part of a general State aid scheme. Furthermore, the present complexity of secondary rules and Commission soft law measures (including the GBER) may also give rise to differences of opinion on the need to notify. Second, the term unlawful aid covers notified aid which is, notwithstanding the standstill obligation, implemented before the Commission has given its approval.

Recovery can also arise when lawfully implemented State aid is subsequently misused.[358] If the Commission considers that there has been a misuse of State aid, it is required to open a formal procedure under Article 108(2).[359] The usual rules for this procedure apply. If the Commission imposes conditions in its decision on State aid compatibility, it may derogate from the procedure only in the event of relatively minor deviations from the initial conditions, which leave it in no doubt as to whether the aid is still compatible with the internal market. When the Commission has no doubts that the conditions have not been observed, it may refer the case directly to CJEU.[360]

Here it can be noted that Article 108(2) of the TFEU specifically provides that: "If the State concerned does not comply with [a] decision within the prescribed time, the Commission or any other interested State may, in derogation from the provisions of Articles 258 and 259, refer the matter to the Court of Justice of the European Union direct."

The Commission will normally do so when it considers that the damage done by the disregard of the conditions is such that the aid has to be stopped and recovered. If the Commission is of the opinion that the failure can be remedied or is not a serious failure or only a minor failure to observe the conditions, it will reopen the formal investigation procedure. The Regulation does not provide rules as to how the

354. *Ibid.*, Article 13(2). For a provisional recovery decision, there must be no doubts about the aid character of the measure concerned; there must be an urgency to act and there must be an established serious risk of substantial and irreparable damage to a competitor.
355. *Ibid.*, Article 15.
356. *Ibid.*, Article 1(f).
357. *Ibid.*, Article 20.
358. Misused State aid is any State aid that has not been used in accordance with the Decision of the Commission declaring it compatible with the internal market.
359. Council Regulation 1589/2015/EU of 13 July 2015, *supra*, Article 20.
360. TFEU, Article 108(2).

Commission should handle conditions and obligations. Thus, there may still be a question to be addressed as to how far the Commission powers may go in imposing conditions when it approves aid.

Recovery is the consequence primarily of an aid that is unlawfully granted and incompatible with the internal market. The recovery aims at reinstating the position *ex ante* before the distortion of competition caused by the granting of the aid took place.[361] The Commission's power to recover aid where it takes a negative decision is laid down in the Regulation. It provides that the Commission shall decide that the Member State concerned shall take all necessary measures to recover the aid. Recovery shall be affected without delay and in accordance with the procedures under the national law of the Member State concerned; provided that they allow the immediate and effective execution of the Commission's decision. To this effect and in the event of a procedure before national courts, the Member States concerned shall take all necessary steps which are available in their respective legal systems.[362]

The power of the Commission to recover aid is subject to a limitation period of 10 years.[363]

The amount to be recovered, if it is not included in the Commission Decision, must be determined by the Member State concerned. The Commission is not required to fix the amount; but, at a minimum, the decision must include information which is sufficient to enable the Member State to determine the amount, without too much difficulty.[364] The Commission decision will also require interest to be paid from the date on which the unlawful aid was at disposal of the beneficiary until the moment of recovery.[365] The interest rate to be applied is normally *the reference rate* applicable to the Member State that granted the aid. Reference rates are communicated by the Commission to the Member States from time to time.[366]

It is for the Member State to decide how the unlawful and incompatible aid measure is recovered. Recovery does not necessarily have to be in the form of a cash payment. Recovery by way of a cash payment is the Commission's preferred method because it is easy to supervise. However, alternative methods are allowed provided that the Member State ensures that the measure chosen is transparent and eliminates the distortion of competition caused by unlawful aid. Measures must be unconditional (not related to uncertain future events) and immediately applicable. A Member State is free to choose the means of fulfilling the recovery order, provided that the measures chosen do not adversely affect the scope and effectiveness of EU law.[367]

361. Case C-277/00: Germany v. Commission ("SMI"), [2004] ECR I-3925, paras 74 to 76.
362. Council Regulation 1589/2015/EU of 13 July 2015, *supra*, Article 16.
363. *Ibid.*, Article 17.
364. Case C-480/98, Spain v. Commission, [2000] ECR I 8717, para. 25 and Joined Cases C-67/85, C-68/85 and C-70/85, Kwekerij van der Kooy BV and others v. Commission, [1988] ECR 219.
365. Council Regulation 1589/2015/EU, *supra*, Article 16(2).
366. The latest reference rates are available at: http://ec.europa.eu/competition/state_aid/legislation/reference_rates.html.
367. *See*: European Commission: Notice from the Commission (2007/C 272/05) - *Towards an effective implementation of Commission decisions ordering Member States to recover unlawful and incompatible State aid*, OJ C 272 of 15 November 2007.

In regard to the concept of the immediate and effective execution of the Commission's decision requiring recovery, such decisions previously required execution within two months of the decision, and this was endorsed by the European Courts.[368] Since 2007, however, the Commission has recognised that two months is too short in the majority of cases. Thus, the requirement now, and generally reflected in the relevant decisions, is for two time limits to be respected:

- the Member State must *inform* the Commission of the measures planned or taken within two months;
- the decision must be fully executed within four months.[369]

Recovery is excluded where it would be contrary to a general principle of EU law or where it would be entirely impossible.[370] However, the term "impossibility" is interpreted very narrowly by the European Courts. It is almost excluded to construe a case where total impossibility would be accepted. Practical administrative difficulties, such as the multitude of beneficiaries and authorities involved, is insufficient to show total impossibility. Recovery is also not impossible solely because the company has gone bankrupt and ceased its economic activities, since recovery can be achieved by registration as one of the liabilities of the undertaking in a bankruptcy procedure.[371] Many Commission decisions involve considerations touching on the principle of legitimate expectations. However, it is only the beneficiary, and not the Member State concerned, that may argue the existence of legitimate expectations - and only in exceptional circumstances. First, there is a general duty of diligence on aid recipients that prevents them from pleading total ignorance of the illegality of aid to prevent recovery.[372] Second, protection via the principle of legitimate expectations can only be invoked successfully if the beneficiary was misled as a result of conduct by the Commission or other EU institutions, and if the aid was granted in compliance with the procedure laid down in Article 108.[373]

Normally, a failure to comply with a recovery order is pursued by an application to the Court under Article 108(2) of the TFEU, although cases involving unnotified aid or aid implemented in breach of the standstill obligation are frequently pursued via

368. Case C-207/05: *Commission v. Italy,* [2006] ECR I-70, paras 31 to 36; Case C-378/98: *Commission v. Belgium,* [2001] ECR I-5107, para. 28 and Case C-232/05: *Commission v. France* ("Scott"), [2006] ECR I-10071.
369. Notice from the Commission (2007/C 272/05) - *Towards an effective implementation of Commission decisions ordering Member States to recover unlawful and incompatible State aid, supra,* paras 40 to 43.
370. *Ibid.*
371. This is reviewed in European Commission: Notice from the Commission (2007/C 272/05) - *Towards an effective implementation of Commission decisions ordering Member States to recover unlawful and incompatible State aid,* OJ C 272 of 15 November 2007 at points 18 to 20.
372. Case C-5/89: *Commission v. Germany,* [1990] ECR I-3453, para. 14; Case C-169/95: *Spain v. Commission,* [1997] ECR I-135, para. 5; Joined Cases C-183/02 and C- 187/02 P *Demesa v. Commission,* [2004] ECR I-10609, para. 44; Joined Cases C-346/03 and C-529/03: *Atzeni v. Regione autonoma della Sardegna,* [2006] ECR I-1875, para. 64.
373. *See*: European Commission: Notice from the Commission (2007/C 272/05) - *Towards an effective implementation of Commission decisions ordering Member States to recover unlawful and incompatible State aid,* OJ C 272 of 15 November 2007.

Article 258 of the TFEU (which deals with Treaty infringements generally). Where the Commission's position is upheld by the Court and that judgment is not complied with, the Commission can bring a further action under Article 260 of the TFEU requesting a lump sum or penalty payment which the Court may then impose on the Member State concerned. This was first used against Greece in 2007 in the context of failure to recover illegal State aid granted to Olympic Airways ordered by a decision in 2002.[374] This resulted in a €2 million lump sum penalty against Greece together with a €16,000 per day penalty dating back to the original 2003 judgment until the unlawful aid was recovered. More recently, it was also used in cases against Italy and Spain.[375] The Italian case involved aid granted unlawfully by Italy since November 1995 for employment under training and work experience contracts and the Court awarded a €30 million lump sum penalty plus a pro-rata penalty payment for every six months of delay in recovery as a proportion of €30 million. The Spanish case, concerned a December 1989 Commission Decision which declared the aid granted by the Spanish central Government, and several autonomous regional governments, to the companies in the Magefesa group, in the form of loan guarantees, a loan at other than on market conditions, non-repayable subsidies and an interest subsidy to be unlawful and incompatible with the common market. This resulted in a lump sum award of €20 million in 2012 against Spain together with a €50,000 daily penalty until the original Court judgment was complied with.

While the possibility of recovery of illegal State aid was clear from 1972, it was first used only in 1982.[376] In recent years, its importance has increased enormously. This is evidenced, in particular, by the following three cases which recently imposed record recovery amounts.

Table 9 Recent Record State Aid Recovery Orders

Case	*Estimated Recovery Amount*
Spanish football clubs[377]	Valencia €20.4 million, Real Madrid €18.4 million, Hercules €6.1 million and Elche €3.7 million and up to €5 million in tax repayments in respect of each of the clubs Real Madrid, FC Barcelona, Athletic Bilbao and Atlético Osasuna.

374. Case C-369/07: *Commission v. Greece*, [2009] ECR I-5703.
375. Case C-496/09: *Commission v. Italy*, [2011] ECR I-11483 and Case C-610/10: *Commission v. Spain*, ECLI:EU:C:2012:781.
376. European Commission: Decision No 1982/312/EEC - Aid to an industrial and commercial group manufacturing wall coverings (Belgium) of 10 March 1982, OJ L 138 of 19 May 1982.
377. European Commission: Press Release "*State aid: Commission decides Spanish professional football clubs have to pay back incompatible aid*," 4 July 2016.

Case	*Estimated Recovery Amount*
Belgian Excess Profit tax scheme [378]	(€700 million from 35 multinationals)
Irish tax rulings - Apple 2016[379]	€13 billion (plus €2.5 billion estimated interest)

The chronic problem with recovery as a matter of State aid enforcement is highlighted in the Commission's Recovery Notice of 2007,[380] which noted that there was practically not a single case where recovery was completed within the deadline set out in the recovery decision. Moreover, 2014 Commission statistics reveal an interesting experience in the overall enforcement of recovery orders.

Table 10 DG Competition Statistics on Recovery of State Aid 2004–2014

- Only 52% of State aid recovery required by Commission Decisions was actually achieved in ten years (€ 7.2 billion + interest).
- The Commission is still pursuing € 5.1 billion + interest (36%).
- 12% of all State aid to be recovered was lost as a result of the bankruptcies of the undertakings concerned.[381]

The most recent 2016 statistics indicate that, in respect of 257 recovery decisions taken and finalised since 1999, almost €9.5 billion had been recovered and some 2.4 billion was categorised as non-recoverable ("aid lost"). Founding EU Member States and Spain accounted for 76% of all recovery orders issued in this period.[382]

In the next Chapter, we look at State aid regulation in the context of international trade treaties

378. European Commission: Decision No 2016/1699/EU of 11 January 2016 on the excess profit exemption State aid scheme SA.37667 (2015/C) (ex 2015/NN) implemented by Belgium, OJ L 260 of 27 September 2016.
379. European Commission: Decision on State aid SA.38373 of 30 August 2016 on State aid implemented by Ireland to Apple, OJ L 187 of 19 July 2017.
380. European Commission: *Notice from the Commission - Towards an effective implementation of Commission decisions ordering Member States to recover unlawful and incompatible State aid*, OJ C 272 of 15 November 2007, pp. 4–17, para. 3.
381. European Commission, DG Competition: *Statistics for 2004-2014, Recovery of illegal and incompatible State aid.*
382. European Commission: http://ec.europa.eu/competition/state_aid/studies_reports/recovery.html.

CHAPTER 3
The Evolution of Treaty Rules on State Aid

While the European Union has developed a unique, complex and far-reaching system of State aid control over the last 60 years, the regulation of subsidies under international trade law has developed in parallel. However, the content of international regulation is different, it has developed more slowly and cautiously, and today it operates quite differently to the EU State aid system. Both systems, however, have the same conceptual roots in the Havana Charter and, since 1990 in particular, the EU has been expanding the scope of its system into non-EU countries, including those aspiring to EU association or eventual membership.

This Chapter traces these developments and explains and contrasts WTO subsidy regulation with EU State aid control. First, however, we consider even earlier attempts at regulation (from the fifteenth century) and trade concerns with subsidies first articulated by classical economics in the eighteenth century.

3.1 CHRISTOPHER COLUMBUS, THE POPE AND THE FIRST REGULATION OF SUBSIDIES

It appears that one of the earliest imperatives to regulate subsidies centred on the voyages of Christopher Columbus. If the voyages of Christopher Columbus are considered as regards their funding, beneficiaries and objects and effects, a particularly strong and early example of State aid can be discerned as early as the fifteenth century.[383] The Columbus voyage of 1492 was funded by Spain's Ferdinand and Isabella. The reason was that, from the early 1400s, most spices and other goods from India and China were brought overland to Europe by Arab merchants. Italian ships

383. The view here that this was perhaps the earliest example of State aid is supported by a range of literature including W.C. Atkinson: "*A History of Spain and Portugal*," Penguin, London, 1960. However, historians continue to differ as to the primary motives of the voyage with some, notably K.A. Miller: "*Why did Columbus sail?*" in Christian History, Issue 35, (Volume XI, No 3) emphasising religious proselytisation as the primary motive.

then carried the spices and goods to European ports. This spice trade with India and Asia was very profitable, and both Spain and Portugal hoped to find a sea route to India and China because they wanted to bypass the Arab and Italian traders. Thus, the key tests for the presence of State aid seem to have been fully met in the Spanish support for Columbus.[384]

The subsidised exploration efforts of Spain and Portugal in the fifteenth century culminated in international regulation by the Pope under the *Treaty of Tordesillas* in 1494[385] which was designed to keep the peace between these two countries in the context of a growing trade war. The Treaty of Tordesillas drew an imaginary North/South line 370 leagues west of the Cape Verde islands and all newly discovered lands to the east of this line would belong to Portugal and all newly discovered lands to the west of this line would go to Spain. In effect, this was the first, albeit indirect and ultimately failed, international regulation of government State aids/subsidies.

3.2 THE DEVELOPMENT OF THE ROLE OF THE STATE AND THE EMERGENCE OF THE "SUBSIDISING STATE"

By the 1700s, the first systematic body of thought devoted to the role of the State in regard to trade emerged based on the international interactions and economic effects of the then bigger world. *Mercantilist theory* advocated a particular approach by the State to economic policy which had a rapid impact. In particular, it advocated action by the State to generate a balance of trade surplus by promoting exports, to be paid for in precious metals, thereby increasing the State's revenue. It also proposed that colonial exports of manufactured goods should be limited and that imports from colonies should be restricted to raw materials. In this way, mercantilism provided a justification for highly interventionist State economic policies to tax imports, to build up domestic industries and, in a wider sense, to strengthen the national defence. While Mercantilism proved immensely popular in the eighteenth century with governments, reaction to it was the proximate cause of the American Revolution[386] and the direct cause of the emergence of an economic philosophy on the role of the State which carries an influence forward to the present day in regard to various matters including free trade and the validity of State subsidies.

Thus, in Adam Smith's *Wealth of Nations* (1776),[387] there is a vigorous attack, not only on general government intervention in the economy but also on the protectionism

384. In October 2014, the Christopher Columbus case was the basis of a Moot Court exercise on the application of the EU State aid rules held at the Anti-Monopoly Committee of Ukraine. For further information on this, *see*: http://www.eupublicprocurement.org.ua.
385. Treaty of Tordesillas, 7 June 1494 accessed at: http://avalon.law.yale.edu/15th_century/mod001.asp.
386. J. Edelman Spero: "*The Politics of International Economic Relations*," London, 1982, notes that the key mercantilist policies objected to by the American colonies not only covered the often quoted "no taxation without representation" point but also the regulation of production, of exports and imports and the control of shipping (p. 6).
387. Adam Smith: "*Inquiry into the Nature and Causes of the Wealth of Nations*," Glasgow, 1776.

inherent in mercantilism and the use of export subsidies (or "bounties" at that time).[388] In regard to protectionism, Smith argued that, while this would benefit certain domestic industries, it diminished competition and afforded those producers a monopoly in the home market which was both damaging and inefficient.[389] In regard to export subsidies, similar arguments applied:

> Bounties were given for the encouragement either of some beginning manufactures, or of such sorts of industry of other kinds as supposed to deserve particular favour....The trades, it is to be observed, which are carried on by means of bounties, are the only ones which can be carried on between two nations for any considerable time together, in such a manner as that one of them shall always and regularly lose, or sell its goods for less than it really costs to send them to market. .... The effect of bounties, like that of all the other expedients of the mercantile system, can only be to force the trade of a country into a channel much less advantageous than that in which it would naturally run of its own accord.[390]

More generally, the emergence of economic and political theory in the eighteenth and early nineteenth centuries gradually changed the basis for consideration of the nature of the State and its role generally and in regard to economic matters. It is particularly clear, moreover, that the earliest economic philosophy was driven by concerns about the purposes and effects of the then established economic role of the State, especially as regards protectionism and subsidies. Responses to crises in the first part of the twentieth century (e.g., the Great Depression) involved a renewed use of subsidies and trade protectionism as part of many national economic policy responses. Indeed, it was in this period that one can speak of the emergence of the concept of the "subsidising State."

Whether as an international political concept or from an economic theory perspective, free trade is an idealised market model in which the trade of goods and services between countries flows unhindered by government-imposed tariff and non-tariff barriers. Classical laissez-faire economists (e.g., Adam Smith) considered that no other requirements were needed, while more modern welfare economics theory takes the view that the conditions of perfect competition are also required in order for the general equilibrium theorems of free trade theory to apply.

More specifically, modern free trade theory focuses on the international trade of goods and international trade in services without tariffs (taxes on imports) or other trade barriers (e.g., quotas on imports or subsidies for domestic producers); the absence of trade-distorting policies (such as taxes, subsidies, regulations or laws) that give domestic firms, households or factors of production an advantage over foreign ones; free access to markets, free access to market information and the inability of firms to distort markets through monopoly or oligopoly power. Thus, nearly all modern

388. Later writers – notably John Stuart Mill: *Essays on Some Unsettled Questions of Political Economy* (1844) and *Principles of Political Economy* (1848) – revised some of this basic analysis in support of the "infant industries" defence of short-term protection and provided the first analysis of multilateral versus unilateral tariff reductions.
389. Adam Smith, *supra,* Book IV, Chapter 2.
390. *Ibid.*, Book IV, Chapter 5.

non-Marxist economic theories and writings support the view that free trade involves a net gain to all trading partners and that the gains from free trade outweigh the losses.

Even though free trade theory and free trade government policies became progressively influential throughout the twentieth century, all developed countries have used protectionism to develop and strengthen their economies although there has also been the tendency to reduce protectionism as national wealth increased.

3.3 MODERN REGULATION – FROM THE HAVANA CHARTER TO THE WTO

The commencement of modern international regulation of subsidies in the interests of free trade emerged after the Second World War when there was a strong recognition that trade disputes could provide the basis for further international conflict. In particular, the United Kingdom and the United States submitted proposals in the immediate post-war period to the Economic and Social Council (ECOSOC) of the United Nations regarding the establishment of an international trade body that was to be named the International Trade Organisation (ITO). The ECOSOC convened a conference, the United Nations Conference on Trade and Employment, in 1946 to consider the UK and US proposals and a Preparatory Committee drafted the ITO Charter which was approved in 1948 at the conference in Havana. The Charter of the ITO became known as the *Havana Charter*. The first round of trade negotiations, focussing on tariff reductions, took place while the Preparatory Committee was still working on drafting the Charter because the participants were anxious to begin the process of trade liberalisation as soon as possible. Their results were incorporated into the *General Agreement on Tariffs and Trade (GATT)*, which was signed in 1947. However, ratification in some national legislatures proved impossible. The most serious opposition was in the US Congress, even though the US government had been one of the driving forces. In 1950, the United States government announced that it would not seek Congressional ratification of the Havana Charter, and the ITO was effectively dead. So, the GATT became the only multilateral instrument governing international trade from 1948 until the World Trade Organisation (WTO) was established in 1994.

Despite its very provisional nature, the GATT completed eight rounds of multilateral trade negotiations over the years culminating in the Uruguay Round (the eighth round) which was concluded on 15 April 1994 with the signing of the Final Act on 15 April 1994, in Marrakesh and established the World Trade Organisation (WTO). The development of the GATT can be divided into three phases: the first, from 1947 until the Torquay round (1951)[391] was largely concerned with which commodities would be covered by the agreement and freezing existing tariff levels. A second phase, encompassing three rounds, from 1959 to 1979, focused on reducing tariffs.[392] The third phase was the Uruguay Round from 1986 to 1994 which, *inter alia*, extended the GATT

391. GATT 1947 was followed by the Annecy Round in 1949 and the Torquay Round in 1951.
392. These were the Geneva Round of 1955, the second Geneva (or "Dillon") Round from 1960 to 1962, the third Geneva Round ("Kennedy Round") from 1964 to 1967 and the Tokyo Round from 1973 to 1979.

agreement fully to new areas such as intellectual property, services, capital, and agriculture. A fourth phase is currently underway under the mandate of the WTO Doha Round.

It is clear that the continuing international focus on free (and even fair) trade and the imperative to regulate emerged as an alternative to earlier more bellicose historical options (e.g., trade wars) and with a particular foundation in economic theories, such as those of Adam Smith. In addition, while priority was given to tariff barriers to trade in international treaties, non-tariff barriers including subsidies, while discussed and drafted into international agreements, only became a big issue in the international regulatory context when most of the tariff issues had been resolved and in response to the increased use of non-tariff barriers as a domestic policy option.

At the same time, the Havana Charter of 1948, which was the unsuccessful precursor of the GATT, had contained proposals for the regulation of subsidies that would inspire the development of EU State aid regulation in the 1950s but would only re-emerge as an important topic of international law in the early 1990s as the basis for the WTO was being created. The Havana Charter provided for subsidy regulation in the following terms:

> If any Member grants or maintains any subsidy, including any form of income or price support, which operates directly or indirectly to maintain or increase exports of any product from, or to reduce, or prevent an increase in, imports of any product into, its territory, the Member shall notify the Organisation in writing of the extent and nature of the subsidization, of the estimated effect of the subsidization on the quantity of the affected product or products imported into or exported from its territory and of the circumstances making the subsidization necessary. In any case in which a Member considers that serious prejudice to its interests is caused or threatened by any such subsidization, the Member granting the subsidy shall, upon request, discuss with the other Member or Members concerned, or with the Organisation, the possibility of limiting the subsidization.[393]

The fundamental reason for the regulation of government supports to undertakings under international law is the fact that, in the period since the 1930s, developed countries, in particular, have taken a large measure of responsibility for the development of each of the factors of production in the economic system. This has necessitated a variety of policies, across a spectrum from minimalist to maximalist intervention, affecting the use and distribution of land, labour, capital and enterprise. Among the types of policies developed have been those concerning employment creation, the attraction of foreign investment, the continued development of public enterprise, the rescue of ailing firms and industries, the balanced regulation of private enterprise, the control of inflation and the control of the balance of payments and the national debt. Within capitalist economies, and more recently in transition economies, the citizens of the modern State have looked increasingly, and primarily, to national government in the last 80 years to properly analyse and purposefully resolve the economic problems of the nation. This in part has created the subsidising State and the pressure to regulate the cross-border and international trade impacts of subsidisation.

393. Havana Charter, Article 25.

At the same time, this was never going to be an easy process at the international level:

> From the first discussions to regulate trade at the international level, the Parties involved perceived the importance of including some provisions to regulate subsidies in international trade. They also understood that reaching a general consensus to deal with this issue at the international level was going to be complicated. The reasons were varied. On the one hand, it was difficult to draw the line to distinguish general governmental policies from other government policies that were costly and did nothing but distort trade at the international level. On the other hand, in the context of negotiations where the objective was to reduce barriers, the negotiating Parties did not want to give up such an important instrument of trade protection as subsidies, which were important for both domestic production as well as exports.[394]

3.4 MODERN REGULATION – THE PARALLEL DEVELOPMENT OF THE EU STATE AID SYSTEM

While there is limited historical information available on the political discussions underlying the approach taken in the Treaty of Rome in designing the original State aid regulatory system, it is clear that competition and the location of industries were at the heart of the legal drafting in the Treaty. It is also clear that the original intention was to give a key role to the European Commission, subject to Court review, in parallel with a consultative role of the Council in deciding the compatibility (rather than the prohibition approach of the ECSC Treaty) of notified State aids. Moreover, the drafters took account of the special position of agriculture, the range of social interventions of the State and presented important foresight as regards the distinction between specific State aid measures and general measures. All of this is reflected in the following extract from the 1956 Spaak Report.

State Aid Regulation under the Treaty of Rome – Drafting Considerations 1956

Section 2. Rules Concerning Financial Assistance Granted by the States

The following general principles will be incorporated in the treaty:

(1) Financial assistance, no matter in what form it is granted, is incompatible with the common market if it distorts competition and the distribution of economic activities by favoring certain enterprises or certain types of production.
(2) The following exceptions are allowed:
   (a) Subsidies to individual consumers and to disinterested institutions (schools and hospitals) used as instruments of social policy.

394. G.E. Luengo Hernandez de Madrid, "*Regulation of subsidies and State aids in WTO and EC law*," Kluwer Law International, 2006, p. 35.

(b) Subsidies for the development of certain regions.
These two categories of exceptions will be of a continuing type.
(c) During the transitional period only:

- direct re-adaptation aid for certain marginal activities.
- temporary aid to compensate for distortions.

The procedures for intervention will be as follows:
(1) A study of the various types of aid will be carried out by the European Commission which will learn of them from information submitted by the State in question or from inquiries that it will make on its own initiative or on the request of another state.
(2) After consultation with the Council and under the reserve of recourse to the Court, the European Commission will decide on the compatibility of the various forms of financial assistance with the common market or on the conditions and the time periods included in authorizations. As regards systems of governmental intervention affecting the general economy of a country, decisions of the Commission will require unanimity on the part of the Council during the first stage, with a qualified majority thereafter.[395]

As the Treaty provisions of the original EEC Treaty developed, however, it is clear that the Council's role was reduced and that of the Commission strengthened. Looking at the Treaty more generally, it is also important to note that neither harmonisation nor shared sovereignty was envisaged in two important fields of national policy – industrial policy and taxation. This, of course, was very much in contrast to the planned development of common policies in regard to agriculture, transport and later regional policy where a common approach and shared sovereignty was foreseen.

Accordingly, it is possible to conclude that the drivers of the State aid provisions were twofold:

(a) *The Competition factor* – A concern that the antitrust regulation of business behaviours under the Treaty[396] could be undermined by anticompetitive subsidisation of business firms.
(b) *The Industrial policy factor* – Reflecting a concern that industrial policy interventions, especially by richer Member States, could create negative spillover effects in the common market as a whole.

The Maastricht Treaty changes in 1992 changed the position to some degree by inserting a new Article dealing with Industrial policy for the first time. This is now Article 173 of the TFEU and provides:

- That the EU and EU Member States are to ensure, in accordance with a system of open and competitive markets, the conditions necessary for the

395. Intergovernmental Committee on European Integration: The Brussels Report on the General Common Market (the Spaak Report), 1956. An English summary is available at http://aei.pitt.edu/995/1/Spaak_report.pdf.
396. Now TFEU, Articles 101–105.

competitiveness of EU industry with particular regard to speeding up the adjustment of industry to structural changes, encouraging an environment favourable to initiative and to the development of undertakings (especially small and medium-sized undertakings), encouraging an environment favourable to cooperation between undertakings and fostering better exploitation of the industrial potential of policies of innovation, research and technological development.
- For Member States to consult each other in liaison with the Commission and, where necessary, to coordinate their action.
- That the Commission may take any useful initiative to promote such coordination – in particular initiatives aimed at the establishment of guidelines and indicators, the organisation of exchange of best practice, and the preparation of the necessary elements for periodic monitoring and evaluation.
- The EU shall contribute to the achievement of these through the policies and activities it pursues under other provisions of the Treaties and that the European Parliament and the Council may decide on specific measures – but excluding any harmonisation of the laws and regulations of the Member States.

However, Article 173 also expressly provides that it shall not provide a basis for the introduction by the EU of any measure which could lead to a distortion of competition or contains tax provisions or provisions relating to the rights and interests of employed persons.[397]

Several points can be noted here, especially in regard to the cautious wording of Article 173. First, the approach in Article 173 is that of joint action between the EU and the Member States and coordinated action is only envisaged "where necessary." Second, taxation measures, law harmonisation and measures of social policy are excluded. At the same time, the EU is empowered to pursue the stated aims of Article 173 via "the policies and activities it pursues under other provisions of the Treaties."

Even before the entry into force of Article 173, the Commission in 1990 issued a paper on *Industrial policy in an open and competitive environment - Guidelines for a Community approach.*[398] This broadly defined the Commission's concept of an EU industrial policy in terms of balancing the following key elements:

- laying down stable and long term conditions for an efficiently functioning market economy: maintenance of a competitive economic environment, as well as a high level of educational attainment and of social cohesion;
- providing the main catalysts for structural adjustment;
- developing the instruments to accelerate structural adjustment and to enhance competitiveness.

397. The full text of TFEU, Article 173 is reproduced and discussed further in Chapter 7.
398. European Commission: *Communication of the Commission to the Council and to the European Parliament – "Industrial policy in an open and competitive environment - Guidelines for a Community approach," COM (90) 556 final, 16 November 1990.*

In respect of State aid, the paper noted that:

> financial support by public authorities must be rigourously examined and controlled. As other forms of protectionism recede, the importance of state aids as an anti-competitive mechanism tends to grow. Beyond their negative effect on competition, state aids can also have serious implications for economic convergence within the Community. Large and well developed Member States will always be able to outbid less developed Member States on the periphery of the Community. The four largest Member States account for 88% of all aid granted. The objective of industrial policy should be to create the conditions which allow better control of such subsidies.[399]

In addition, the paper signalled a need for tighter control on regional aid, to reduce sectoral aid and (in the context of international trade) it pointed out that:

> Putting a stop to the international subsidy race is an important prerequisite for a further reduction in state aids in the Community. Stricter disciplines on state aids should be applied by the Community's international partners.[400]

Article 173 has also proved important as a basis for several subsequent initiatives to promote competitiveness in the EU:

- The *1993 Delors White Paper on Growth, Competitiveness and Employment*[401] which recommended increased cooperation in research and development, the adoption of a new development model taking into account the environment and qualitative needs, and action to be taken regarding the employment market.
- The *1994 Bangemann Report*[402] which recommended that actions be taken at European level and by Member States to strike down entrenched positions which put Europe at a competitive disadvantage by fostering an entrepreneurial mentality to enable the emergence of new dynamic sectors of the economy and by developing a common regulatory approach to bring forth a competitive, Europe-wide market for information services. (In addition to its specific recommendations, the Report set out an action plan of concrete initiatives based on a partnership between the private and public sectors to carry Europe forward into the information society).
- The *2000 Lisbon Strategy*[403] which sought to deal with the low productivity and stagnation of economic growth in the EU, through the formulation of various policy initiatives to be taken by all EU Member States. The broader objectives set out by the Lisbon Strategy were to be attained by 2010 and

399. *Ibid.*, p. 8.
400. *Ibid.*, p. 8.
401. European Commission. "*Growth, competitiveness, and employment - The challenges and ways forward into the 21st century,*" 5 December 1993 COM (93) 700 final.
402. "Europe and the Global Information Society – Recommendations to the European Council," Recommendations of the high-level group on the information society to the Corfu European Council, 1994 accessed at: http://aei.pitt.edu/1199/1/info_society_bangeman_report.pdf.
403. European Council: Presidency Lisbon Council Conclusions of 23 and 24 March 2000.

included the objective of transforming Europe into the world's largest knowledge-based economy by 2010.[404]

- The *Europe 2020 Strategy*, adopted in 2010, which set out a vision for Europe's market economy over the next decade with reference to three interlocking and mutually reinforcing priority areas: (a) smart growth, developing an economy based on knowledge and innovation; (b) sustainable growth, promoting a low-carbon, resource-efficient and competitive economy; and (c) inclusive growth, fostering a high-employment economy delivering social and territorial cohesion.

In broad terms – and consistent with the mandate of Article 173 to use "the policies and activities it pursues under other provisions of the Treaties" – the evolution of the EU State aid rules since 2000 has reflected the objectives of both the Lisbon Strategy and the current Europe 2020 Strategy. This is also a reflection of the original State aid ideas in the 1990 paper on *Industrial policy in an open and competitive environment* and provides the basis for a fuller discussion of how the State aid rules have been used to effectively create an EU common industrial policy.

3.5 THE CURIOUS CASE OF EURATOM

The objectives of the *EURATOM Treaty* were and are the promotion of the development and use of nuclear energy.[405] The Treaty contains no specific prohibition on aid for the sector and, by virtue of the Treaty objectives, it was unclear from the outset whether the EEC Treaty rules on State aid could or should be applied. Moreover, the objectives of the EURATOM Treaty are limited by an untested provision of Article 6(a) which provides that the Commission may:

> provide financial assistance within the framework of research contracts, **without, however, offering subsidies** [emphasis added].[406]

While the EEC Treaty provided that its provisions could not derogate from the rules establishing the EURATOM Treaty,[407] this provision was repealed by the TFEU.[408] Moreover, Article 194 of the TFEU gave the EU general competence for energy policy for the first time. This gradually opened up a policy view (also somewhat fuelled by the

404. The Lisbon Strategy was ultimately judged a failure by most commentators, *see* e.g. http://www.euractiv.com/section/eu-priorities-2020/news/eu-seeks-new-narrative-for-growth-and-jobs-strategy/.
405. EURATOM Treaty, Article 2.
406. Hancher et al. (1993), *supra*, also point out that one exemption in the nuclear sector was granted by the European Commission in respect of the British Non-Fossil Fuel levy after a preliminary assessment under Article 93(2) of the EEC Treaty and highlight the position of Advocate General Reischl in Joined Cases C-188-190/80: *France, Italy and United Kingdom v. Commission*, [1982] ECR 25-45, that Articles 92–94 of the EEC Treaty (now Articles 107–109 of the TFEU) should be applied to regulate State aids to the nuclear sector.
407. EEC Treaty, Article 305(2) – now repealed.
408. Hancher et al. (Fourth Edition), 2012, p. 730 notes that there was a certain political appetite in the preparation of the TFEU to abolish EURATOM altogether.

earlier application of the general State aid rules to the coal and steel sectors following the expiry of the ECSC Treaty) that the general TFEU State aid rules could apply to the nuclear sector, provided that such application did not directly infringe the EURATOM Treaty. This interpretation was given additional credibility based on the extensive powers of the European Commission to coordinate nuclear research by Member States,[409] to regulate various aspects of investments in the nuclear sector[410] and to prohibit unfair competitive practices setting prices otherwise than on a market basis.[411]

In general, the European Commission has moved cautiously in regard to actual or potential State aid in the nuclear sector; primarily finding that measures were either not State aid or could be held to be compatible. Thus, in 1989, the UK authorities notified several pre-privatisation support measures for its nuclear industry, including State guarantees of £2.5 billion, a consumer levy and a debt write-off for the Scottish producer of £1.4 billion. These measures were approved.[412] In 2001, the Commission ruled that the German tax treatment of reserves for the decommissioning of nuclear plants and the disposal of nuclear waste did not constitute State aid as they applied to all other sectors required to keep similar reserves.[413] In its 2002 Decision on compensation to electricity entities Electrabel and SPE in Belgium of €377 million to dismantle experimental nuclear facilities, the Commission referred, without explanation, to the fact that this would be compatible with the discretionary exemption under what is now Article 107(3)(c) of the TFEU (aid to facilitate the development of certain economic activities or of certain economic areas, where such aid does not adversely affect trading conditions to an extent contrary to the common interest).[414] In the EDF Decision of 2003 the Commission ordered the abolition of an open-ended guarantee to EDF and noted that this was without prejudice to the application of, or respect for, the provisions of the EURATOM Treaty. A more complex attempt by the Commission to navigate around the EURATOM Treaty in a State aid investigation is also to be found in the Decision on aid to British Energy.[415] In that case, some of the measures involved were EURATOM Treaty measures, although the UK argued that they all were. The investigation focussed on whether the transfer of decommissioned assets from nuclear producer British Nuclear Fuels to a National Decommissioning Authority (NDA) allowed the firm to avoid environmental liabilities related to the decommissioning; thereby involving a selective advantage and constituting State aid. In launching this enquiry in 2003, the Commission noted:

> In view of the complexity and the novelty of the case, as well as the importance of the sums involved, the Commission decided that an in-depth enquiry would be

409. EURATOM Treaty, Article 5.
410. EURATOM Treaty, Articles 34, 37 and 40–44.
411. EURATOM Treaty, Article 67.
412. European Commission: Press Release IP/90/267 of 28 March 1990.
413. European Commission: Decision No of 30 October 2001 on German Reserves for nuclear power station waste management and decommissioning (No NN 137/01), OJ C 77 of 28 March 2002.
414. European Commission: Decision on Belgian Transitional regime for the electricity market (C 31/2002 (ex N 149/2000)), OJ C 222 of 18 September 2002.
415. European Commission: Decision No 2005/407/EC of 22 September 2004 on the State aid which the United Kingdom is planning to implement for British Energy plc (British Energy), OJ L 142 of 6 June 2005.

> necessary in order to analyse the balance of the positive and negative aspects of the aid. This in-depth enquiry will allow the Commission to judge, in particular, whether the contribution of the setting up of the NDA to the achievement of the Euratom Treaty's objectives outweighs the impact of the aid on the internal market.[416]

In the event, the Decision in 2006 found that the measures did not constitute State aid to British Nuclear Fuels and were in accordance with the EURATOM Treaty. At the same time, the Decision imposed some conditions on the National Decommissioning Authority regarding possible similar relations with other decommissioning nuclear entities.[417]

Around the same time, the main general rules on State aid in the energy sector were first set out in the 2008 Environmental State aid Guidelines which specifically excluded the nuclear sub-sector.[418] The most recent revision of these Guidelines in 2013 initially proposed detailed rules for State aid in the nuclear sector[419] but these were later removed from the text.[420]

As a result, and contrary to earlier interpretations, it emerges that State aid in the nuclear sector is now viewed as covered by the TFEU regime – except in regard to the supply of minerals and materials under Article 197 of the EURATOM Treaty and State support for Nuclear research (Articles 7 et seq. and within the parameters laid down in Annex 1 to the Treaty). This has a basic logic. First, the full exclusion of State aid in the nuclear sector would undoubtedly put that energy sub-sector at a distinct advantage versus other energy sub-sectors (e.g., coal, oil, water and renewable generation). Moreover, it would be at variance with overall EU liberalisation policy in regard to the electricity sector and the creation of a single Electricity market which has been actively pursued since 2011.[421] That policy is based on free competition between all electricity undertakings, regardless of the source of electricity generation.

In 2014, planned British Government aid for the construction and operation of a nuclear facility at Hinkley Point in Somerset was assessed directly under Article 107 of the TFEU. Following some changes by the UK, the Commission approved the measures

416. European Commission: Press Release *"State aids: Commission opens formal investigation into UK Nuclear Decommissioning Authority,"* IP/04/1430 of 1 December 2004.
417. European Commission: Press Release *"State aid: Commission authorises transfer of nuclear assets from British Nuclear Fuels to Nuclear Decommissioning Authority subject to conditions,"* IP/06/428 of 4 April 2006.
418. European Commission: *Community Guidelines on State aid for environmental protection*, OJ C 82 of 1 April 2008, Article 2.1.
419. European Commission: *Draft Guidelines on State aid for environmental protection and energy 2014–2020,* accessible at: http://ec.europa.eu/competition/consultations/2013_state_aid_environment/draft_guidelines_en.pdf.
420. European Commission: *Guidelines on State aid for environmental protection and energy 2014–2020,* OJ C 200 of 28 June 2014.
421. Conclusions of the European Council of 4 February 2011, accessible at: https://www.consilium.europa.eu/uedocs/cms_data/docs/pressdata/en/trans/119253.pdf and European Commission: Progress towards completing the Internal Energy Market, 2014 accessed at: https://ec.europa.eu/energy/en/topics/markets-and-consumers/single-market-progress-report.

as constituting a genuine response to market failures.[422] This case was subsequently challenged on its reasoning by Austria.[423] Finally, it can be noted that the European Courts have not, to date, ruled on the interactions between the EURATOM Treaty and the TFEU in regard to State aid in the nuclear sector.

3.6 THE GENERAL AGREEMENT ON TARIFFS AND TRADE (GATT)

As a result of the failure to ratify the Havana Charter, its approach to subsidy regulation remains primarily of historical interest. Nonetheless, the work done at Havana continued to influence the subsequent development of international rules on non-tariff barriers to trade.

Under Article XVI of the GATT 1947 Agreement,[424] any trade-distorting subsidy requires notification of the extent and nature of the subsidy, its trade impact, and its rationale. The same Article also requires discussion with any Contracting Party experiencing "serious prejudice" about "limiting" the subsidy. The GATT 1947 Agreement also recognised the particular adverse impact of export subsidies on other Contracting Parties and required GATT States to "seek to avoid the use of subsidies on the export of primary products." Moreover, and reflecting the approach of the Havana Charter, the GATT provided that any subsidy on primary products should not result in a "more than equitable share of world export trade." The GATT 1947 provisions also sought to prohibit by 1958 all export subsidies on products, other than of primary products, which resulted in dumping.[425]

Under Article VI of the GATT, the ultimate remedy for a breach of Article XVI that could not be resolved amicably was the introduction of "countervailing measures" (in effect punitive tariffs) against another GATT member maintaining subsidies in contravention of GATT Article XVI.

The use of these provisions posed major procedural, conceptual, economic and political difficulties that the Subsidies and Countervailing Measures Agreement (SCMA) sought to remedy in 1994.

In the meantime, the Tokyo Round of the GATT in the 1970s, which continued GATT's successful efforts to progressively reduce tariffs, had tried also to address problems in non-tariff areas, including subsidies. While the Tokyo Round faced major problems in regard to non-tariff barriers in agricultural trade, a series of agreements on non-tariff barriers did emerge from the negotiations, in some cases interpreting existing GATT rules, in others breaking entirely new ground. In most cases, only a relatively small number of, mainly industrialised, GATT members ascribed to these agreements

422. European Commission: Decision No 2015/658/EU of 8 October 2014 on the aid measure SA.34947 (2013/C) (ex 2013/N) which the United Kingdom is planning to implement for support to the Hinkley Point C nuclear power station, OJ L 109 of 28 April 2015.
423. Case T-356/15: *Austria v. Commission* (judgment pending).
424. General Agreement on Tariffs and Trade, 1947 ("GATT 1947"), accessible at: http://www.worldtradelaw.net/uragreement/gatt.pdf.
425. *Dumping* essentially involves the sale of goods below production cost on export markets.

and arrangements which, as a consequence, have been referred to since as "codes." One of these was the Subsidies Code which had a distinct focus on interpreting and elaborating the GATT 1947 rules.[426]

The *Tokyo Subsidies Code* was based on the political agreement of GATT Ministers in September 1973 that the Multilateral Trade Negotiations should, *inter alia*, reduce or eliminate the trade restricting or distorting effects of non-tariff measures, and bring such measures under more effective international discipline. In the Preamble to the Code, the political balancing on the question of subsidies is clear. The Code recognised that subsidies are used by governments to promote important objectives of national policy, although subsidies may have harmful effects on trade and production. Second, the stated emphasis of the Code was "on the effects of subsidies" and their assessment taking due account of the internal economic situation of the signatories concerned as well as of the state of international economic and monetary relations. Thus, the aim was to ensure that:

- the use of subsidies did not adversely affect or prejudice the interests of any GATT signatory and that countervailing measures did not unjustifiably impede international trade;
- relief was made available to producers adversely affected by the use of subsidies within an agreed international framework of rights and obligations;
- the particular trade, development and financial needs of developing countries were taken into account;
- the provisions of Articles VI, XVI and XXIII of the GATT 1947 Agreement, in so far as they related to subsidies and countervailing measures, were to be fully applied and elaborated via rules for their application in order to provide greater uniformity and certainty in their implementation; and
- there could be speedy, effective and equitable resolution of subsidy disputes.

Because the Tokyo Subsidies Code was not accepted by the full GATT membership, it did not become a proper multilateral agreement. Most of the other Tokyo Round agreements on non-tariff issues met the same fate. Even when the Subsidies Code was used in some GATT disputes, the following fundamental problems remained in the GATT system:

- the absence of a definition of "subsidy";
- continuing uncertainty as to whether the GATT dispute settlement was an adjudicative system (the US position and that of developing countries from the 1980s) or a diplomatic negotiation (the EU position).

The EU position was supported by the emphasis in the Subsidies Code on consultation and conciliation and a view that lawsuits could create damaging legal precedents and

426. This is reflected in the title of the Agreement: Agreement on the interpretation and application of Articles VI, XVI and XXIII of the General Agreement on Tariffs and Trade (Subsidies Code) – accessible at: http://www.worldtradelaw.net/tokyoround/subsidiescode.pdf.

were unsuitable to the complexity of trade disputes.[427] On the other hand, the USA became the major GATT litigant on subsidies, whether with or without substantive merit, and this has been viewed as a political tactic in this period to resist or delay domestic political pressures to introduce protectionist countervailing measures in the US.[428] In this situation, the inception of EU litigation against US subsidies (the *DISC Case* which began in 1973 and was dealt with in a GATT Panel Report of 1976[429] and a GATT Council decision in 1981) was seen as retaliation against a whole series of US subsidy actions against the EU.[430]

Even as this type of litigation increased and diplomacy decreased in this period of the GATT, the fundamental problems remained and grew more acute and obvious. It was not then until the Tokyo Codes were later amended in the Uruguay Round that they were turned into multilateral commitments accepted by all WTO members. In the context of subsidies, the result was the Subsidies and Countervailing Measures Agreement (SCMA) of 1994.

3.7 THE SUBSIDIES AND COUNTERVAILING MEASURES AGREEMENT (SCMA)

The GATT Uruguay Round started in 1986 and concluded in 1994. This Round substantially extended the GATT into new areas and created fully binding agreements covering several aspects of government supports to undertakings. The so-called *Punta*

---

427. R. Hudec: *"Regulation of Domestic Subsidies under the MTN Subsidies Code"* in Wallace et al. (eds): *"Interface Three – Legal Treatment of Domestic Subsidies,"* Washington, International Law Institute, 1984.

428. *See*, for example, R. Hudec: *"Legal issues in US-EC Trade Policy: GATT litigation 1960-1985"* in Baldwin, Hamilton & Sapir (eds): *"Issues in US-EC Trade Relations,"* Chicago, Chicago University Press, 1988, pp. 24 et seq.

429. The Domestic International Sales Corporation, Panel Report, (1976), BISD, 23rd Supplement, 98.

430. R. Behboodi, *supra,* at p. 56 and R. Hudec, *"GATT Dispute Settlement After the Tokyo Round: An Unfinished Business"* (1980), 13 Cornell International Law Journal, Issue 2. The *DISC Case* involved an EU challenge under GATT Article XVI to US tax legislation (The 1971 US Domestic International Sales Corporation Act) that allegedly favoured US exporters in an unfair manner. The US responded with a similar challenge to French, Belgian and Dutch export-promotion tax provisions. This case, in particular marked the end of diplomacy in GATT disputes, and it took three years to form an acceptable panel covering both cases. In effect, the challenged US and EU Member State legislations were similar in effect but different in method. The US legislation allowed exporters to set up a separate domestic corporation as an intermediary in exportation and benefiting from indefinite tax deferrals while the European variant involved the establishment of subsidiary companies and tax benefits via transfer pricing. The Panel concluded that the DISC legislation in some cases had effects which were not in accordance with US obligations under Article XVI on export subsidies and had resulted in a large increase in US exports. The Panel also concluded that, again in some cases, the EU Member State tax legislation was also incompatible with Article XVI. There was strong international diplomatic reaction to the finding against the EU Member State tax laws and, in 1981, a decision of the GATT Council adopting the 1976 Panel ruling but with an understanding that the GATT-illegal ruling on the EU Member State tax laws should be considered repealed. The DISC Case was to re-emerge later before the WTO as the Foreign Sales Corporation Case – *EC v. US: Tax Treatment for Foreign Sales Corporations*, Report of the Panel, 8 October 1999, WT/DS108/R and Appellate Body Report, 24 February 2000, WT/DS108/AB/R.

del Este mandate on subsidies and countervailing measures provided the basis for the SCMA negotiations and called for a review of GATT Articles VI and XVI and the Tokyo round Code on subsidies and countervailing measures, and for negotiations "with the objective of improving GATT disciplines relating to all subsidies and countervailing measures that affect international trade." By 1988, several positions were emerging around the key subsidy issues to be addressed in the Round and with a focus on greater legal clarity and on political balance as between harmful and less harmful subsidies. India, for example, made many of the initial proposals on improving definitions and fully incorporating the Tokyo Code with much needed amendments into the SCMA. They identified particular concerns that:

> ambiguities and deficiencies in the provisions have resulted in a number of unresolved problems, which have become the starting point for non-observance of the letter and spirit of rules and use of countervailing measures for trade harassment.[431]

This focussed in particular on the undefined concept of "injury" or "material injury" in the Subsidies Code which India argued had been diluted so far in US legislation as to allow US countervailing measures based on the most inconsequential allegation of injury.

Switzerland originally proposed the introduction of three different classes of subsidies – *prohibited subsidies* permitting unilateral countervailing measures without proof of material injury, *actionable subsidies* requiring such proof, and *non-actionable subsidies* that have to be tolerated even if there are negative effects to trading partners. In suggesting new classifications, the Swiss argued that the existing GATT system, based on motivations and the objectives of the exporter, classifications on primary and non-primary exports and the test of material injury, had become difficult to manage and should be substantially overhauled. In particular, the Swiss took the position that GATT law should be based, not on motivations and objectives, but on legal effects, both procedural and substantive.

The US negotiating position was initially focused on the inclusion of developing countries into the GATT regulation of subsidies[432] and ignoring the problems of countervailing measures. The EU also wanted developing countries included in GATT subsidies disciplines more fully and the EU, Canada,[433] Brazil, Argentina and Japan all wanted better disciplines to apply to countervailing measures which they regarded as, de facto, more distortive of trade than subsidies.[434]

With the adoption of the SCMA, together with the new WTO dispute settlement procedures, international trade law now contains the substantive and procedural tools

431. Press Release of 11 February 1988: "*GATT Provisions on Subsidies need clarifications,*" Geneva accessible at http://www.sunsonline.org/trade/process/during/uruguay/other/01110088.htm.
432. Very few developing countries at that time had adopted the Tokyo Subsidies Code.
433. For a comprehensive review of Canadian problems with US countervailing measures, *see*: P. Morici, "*Resolving the North American Subsidies War*" (September 1996), Journal of Canadian-American Public Policy, Issue 27.
434. Press Release of 4 July 1988: "*U.S. call for new GATT rules on subsidies,*" Geneva accessible at: http://www.sunsonline.org/trade/process/during/uruguay/country/07040088.htm.

for addressing the problems faced by companies confronting subsidised competition anywhere in the world. Specifically, the SCMA improved the Tokyo Subsidies Code by:

- defining, for the first time in any GATT agreement, certain key terms, such as "subsidy" and "serious prejudice";
- prohibiting export subsidies and subsidies contingent on the use of domestic instead of imported goods, including de facto export subsidies that are tied to exports or export earnings in practice though not in law;
- creating a special presumption of serious prejudice for certain subsidies;
- defining and significantly strengthening the procedures for showing when serious prejudice exists in foreign markets;
- establishing a category of government assistance that will be non-actionable and non-countervailable only when strict conditions and criteria are satisfied;
- requiring all developing countries, other than the least developed, to phase out export subsidies and import substitution subsidies, and accelerating the phase-out of export subsidies in situations where a developing country has achieved global export competitiveness in a particular product sector; and
- applying the WTO dispute settlement mechanism, with a view to ending the veto powers of WTO parties and the blocking of the adoption of panel reports.

Because of its novelty and the absence of definitions in other important international rules on State aids/subsidies, the SCMA definition of subsidy is very significant.

The SCMA Definition of Subsidy[435]

1.1 For the purpose of this Agreement, a subsidy shall be deemed to exist if:

(a) (1) there is a financial contribution by a government or any public body within the territory of a Member (referred to in this Agreement as "government"), i.e. where:

(i) a government practice involves a direct transfer of funds (e.g., grants, loans, and equity infusion), potential direct transfers of funds or liabilities (e.g., loan guarantees);

(ii) government revenue that is otherwise due is foregone or not collected (e.g., fiscal incentives such as tax credits);[436]

(iii) a government provides goods or services other than general infrastructure, or purchases goods;

(iv) a government makes payments to a funding mechanism, or entrusts or directs a private body to carry out one or more of the type of functions illustrated in (i) to (iii) above which would normally be vested in the government and the practice, in no real sense, differs from practices normally followed by governments; <u>or</u>

435. Subsidies and Countervailing Measures Agreement, 1994, Article 1.

436. In accordance with the provisions of Article XVI of GATT 1994 (Note to Article XVI) and the provisions of Annexes I through III of the SCMA, the exemption of an exported product from

(a) there is any form of income or price support in the sense of Article XVI of GATT 1994; and
(b) a benefit is thereby conferred.

1.2 A subsidy as defined in paragraph 1 shall be subject to the provisions of Part II or shall be subject to the provisions of Part III or V only if such a subsidy is specific in accordance with the provisions of Article 2.

This definition is a very wide one. However, to be regulated under the SCMA a subsidy must be *specific* to an enterprise or industry or group of enterprises or industries, within the jurisdiction of the granting authority. On this, the following terms apply:

(a) Where the granting authority, or the legislation pursuant to which the granting authority operates, explicitly limits access to a subsidy to certain enterprises, such a subsidy is specific.
(b) Where the granting authority, or the legislation pursuant to which the granting authority operates, establishes objective criteria or conditions[437] governing the eligibility for, and the amount of, a subsidy, specificity does not exist, provided that eligibility is automatic and that such criteria and conditions are strictly adhered to. The criteria or conditions must be clearly provided for in law, regulation, or other official document, so as to be capable of verification.
(c) If, notwithstanding any appearance of non-specificity resulting from the application of principles (a) and (b), there are reasons to believe that the subsidy may in fact be specific, other factors may be considered. Such factors are: the use of a subsidy programme by a limited number of enterprises, its predominant use by certain enterprises, the granting of disproportionately large amounts of subsidy to a limited number of enterprises, and the manner in which discretion has been exercised by the granting authority in the decision to grant a subsidy.[438]
(d) Any determination of specificity under the provisions of this Article shall be clearly substantiated on the basis of positive evidence.
(e) A subsidy which is limited to certain enterprises located within a designated geographical region within the jurisdiction of the granting authority is regarded as specific.
(f) The setting or change of generally applicable tax rates by all levels of government entitled to do does not result in any specific subsidy under the Agreement.
(g) Subsidies prohibited by the SCMA are in all cases specific.[439]

---

duties or taxes borne by the like product when destined for domestic consumption, or the remission of such duties or taxes in amounts not in excess of those which have accrued, are not be deemed to be a subsidy.

437. Objective criteria or conditions, in the SCMA, mean criteria or conditions which are neutral, which do not favour certain enterprises over others, and which are economic in nature and horizontal in application, such as the number of employees or the size of an enterprise.
438. In this regard, in particular, information on the frequency with which applications for a subsidy are refused or approved and the reasons for such decisions are to be considered.
439. Subsidies and Countervailing Measures Agreement, 1994, Article 2.

Table 11 Main Provisions of the WTO Subsidies and Countervailing Measures Agreement (SCMA) 1994

The Agreement contains an important definition of "subsidy" and introduces the concept of a "specific subsidy" — essentially meaning a subsidy available only to an enterprise or industry or group of enterprises or industries within the jurisdiction of the authority granting the subsidy.
Only specific subsidies are subject to the disciplines set out in the Agreement.
The SCMA establishes three categories of subsidies.
First, ***"prohibited subsidies"*** are those contingent, in law or in fact, whether solely or as one of several other conditions, upon export performance; and those contingent, whether solely or as one of several other conditions, upon the use of domestic over imported goods. Prohibited subsidies are subject to WTO dispute settlement procedures and, if it is found that the subsidy is indeed prohibited, it must be immediately withdrawn. If this is not done within the specified time period, the complaining member is authorized to take countermeasures e.g. trade sanctions.
The second category is ***"actionable subsidies."*** The Agreement provides that no WTO member should cause, through the use of subsidies, adverse effects on the interests of other WTO members, i.e. injury to domestic industry of another contracting state, nullification or impairment of benefits accruing directly or indirectly to other WTO members under the GATT (in particular the benefits of bound tariff concessions), and serious prejudice to the interests of another WTO member. "Serious prejudice" is presumed to exist for certain subsidies including when the total ad valorem subsidisation of a product exceeds 5%. In such a situation, the burden of proof is on the subsidising WTO Member State to show that the subsidies in question do not cause serious prejudice to the complaining Member State. Members affected by actionable subsidies may refer the matter to the Dispute Settlement body. In the event that it is determined that such adverse effects exist, the subsidising member must withdraw the subsidy or remove the adverse effects.
The third category involves ***"non-actionable subsidies,"*** which could either be non-specific subsidies, or specific subsidies involving assistance to industrial research and pre-competitive development activity, assistance to disadvantaged regions, or certain type of assistance for adapting existing facilities to new environmental requirements imposed by law and/or regulations. Where another member believes that an otherwise non-actionable subsidy is resulting in serious adverse effects to a domestic industry, it may seek a determination and recommendation on the matter.

The SCMA addresses the use of countervailing measures on subsidised imported goods. It sets out disciplines on the initiation of countervailing cases, investigations by national authorities and rules of evidence to ensure that all interested parties can present information and argument. Certain disciplines on the calculation of the amount of a subsidy are outlined as is the basis for the determination of injury to the domestic industry. The agreement requires that all relevant economic factors be taken into account in assessing the state of the industry and that a causal link be established between the subsidised imports and the alleged injury.

Countervailing investigations shall be concluded within one year after their initiation and in no case more than 18 months. They must be terminated immediately in cases where the amount of a subsidy is *de minimis* (the subsidy is less than 1% ad valorem) or where the volume of subsidised imports, actual or potential, or the injury is negligible.

All countervailing duties have to be terminated within five years of their imposition unless the authorities determine on the basis of a review that the expiry of the duty would be likely to lead to continuation or recurrence of subsidisation and injury.

The reporting provisions of the SCMA (Article 25) require WTO Members to notify all specific subsidies by 30 June each year. The information provided must be sufficiently specific to enable other Members to evaluate the trade effects and to understand the operation of notified subsidy programmes and include details of the type of subsidy (grant, loan, tax concession, etc.), the subsidy per unit or, in cases where this is not possible, the total amount or the annual amount budgeted for the subsidy, the policy objective and/or purpose of the subsidy, the duration of the subsidy and/or any other time limits attached to it and statistical data permitting an assessment of the trade effects of the subsidy. If subsidies are granted to specific products or sectors, the notifications must be organised by product or sector. Even if a country has no specific subsidies, it is required to submit a zero notification to that effect.

3.7.1 Definitions

A few brief observations regarding the SCMA provide some further context. First, while the EU has taken a large degree of credit for the *SCMA subsidy definition*,[440] the EU State aid regulatory system, as noted earlier, offers no definition of aid or State aid in order to avoid circumvention measures by EU Member States. This has meant that several hundred cases have been heard before the European Courts to determine the evolving "notion of aid" under the EU regulatory system. In one important ECJ case, the court held that State aid was per se wider than a subsidy[441] – but that was before

440. C.D. Ehlermann: *"State aid Control – Success or Failure?,"* 18 January 1995, Fordham International Law Journal, 1995.
441. Case C-30/59: *Steenkolenmijnen v. High Authority of the European Coal and Steel Community*, [1961] ECR 1.

the very wide SCMA definition. It also appears that the SCMA had no major implications for the application of the EU State aid rules although the Agreement has been used in a number of EU/US trade cases. In the early years of the SCMA it was the case that, in some areas at least, the SCMA was more generous in what it allowed than the EU regulatory system (e.g., regional aid and R&D aid) while, on the other hand, environmental aid rules under the SCMA imposed restrictions on some aid levels for SMEs in the EU system. However, the steady revision of EU rules and guidelines in the ensuing years removed any significant policy disparities. On this point, it remains interesting to many observers that the SCMA contains detailed Treaty definitions on subsidies and types of subsidy unlike the approach of the TFEU that continues to avoid definition but approaches the concept of "aid" on a case by case teleological basis. In the 1990s, the general consensus from observers and practitioners was that the two systems were definitionally compatible for 99.9% of practical purposes.[442] However, as the EU concept of "aid" is continuously evolving, there was always the risk that the EU concept and the concept of the WTO subsidy could diverge over time; not least due to the expansion of the scope of EU State aid control (e.g., in the area of taxation or regarding matters not previously within Article 107(1) of the TFEU prohibition).[443]

At this stage, one of the main elements that differentiates the notion of State aid in Article 107(1) of the TFEU from the definition of Subsidy in Article 1 of the SCMA is whether the resources used stem from State resources or not. The concept of "subsidy" under Article 1 of the SCMA can also include measures which do not involve a cost to the government. On the other hand, current European Court interpretation of the concept of State aid deriving from Article 107(1) of the TFEU requires that government measures have to involve a charge on the public account to constitute State aid.

Second, both the TFEU and the SCMA require that a State aid and a subsidy be specific in the sense of conferring an advantage only on certain economic operators. In the TFEU, Article 107(1) refers to "favouring certain undertakings or the production of certain goods." Article 2 of the SCMA refers to subsidies which are specific to certain enterprises, i.e. to an enterprise or industry or group of enterprises or industries.

The EU selectivity and WTO specificity elements are fundamental as they serve to distinguish between government measures which will be regarded as State aid or subsidies or not. While these very similar concepts are generally interpreted similarly in both systems, this is not the case in the context of geographical or regional selectivity/specificity.

Under Article 107(1) of the TFEU, State aid granted to all undertakings located in a geographic area is to be considered selective. In contrast, under Article 2.2 in the first sentence of the SCMA, subsidies are considered to be specific if they are limited to certain enterprises located within a designated geographical region within the

442. F. Wishlade: *"Subsidies and State Aids – the definition of acceptable measures under the EU and WTO rules,"* European Policies research Centre, University of Strathclyde, September 1996.

443. Indeed, in some cases before the ECJ, the Court has rejected any direct reference to the WTO definition for State aid regulatory purposes e.g. the position taken in Case T-55/99: *Confederación Espanola de Transporte de Mercancías v. Commission,* [2000] ECR II-3207, para. 50. For a further examination of State aid versus subsidy, *see* L. Rubini: *"The Definition of Subsidy and State Aid: WTO and EC Law in Comparative Perspective,"* Oxford University Press, 2009.

jurisdiction of the granting authority. Subsidies granted by subnational entities, such as autonomous communities, regions, provinces, etc. to all enterprises located within a designated geographical region would therefore not be considered specific, and will, as a result, be regarded as general subsidies – akin to general measures in EU law. Second, the second sentence of Article 2.2 of the SCMA reads:

> It is understood that the setting or change of generally applicable tax rates by all levels of government entitled to do so shall not be deemed to be a specific subsidy for the purpose of this agreement.

As will be seen later, this is a totally different position to that taken in the *Azores (2006)* and *Gibraltar (2011)* cases under the EU system.[444]

Moreover, there is some further scope for conflict where an EU Member State adopts a measure considered to be "State aid" according to Article 107(1) of the TFEU and the Commission, in the light of its objectives, expressly authorises or does not object to its implementation. In these cases, it is possible that the objectives that the aid validly pursues may clash with the interests of other WTO Members (actionable subsidies of Article 5 of the SCMA) or be prohibited according to Article 3 of the SCMA. In these cases, both the EU and the Member States that granted the measure in question would be jointly responsible to other WTO Members.

3.7.2 Scope and Procedures

Non-actionable subsidies lapsed as a category in 1999, and this was not extended. While there have been some suggestions that there is a tacit understanding within the WTO not to pursue these types of subsidy, they are now potentially actionable under the Agreement.

It can also be noted that the SCMA *applies also to agricultural products* – unless excluded by the WTO Agreement on Agriculture. As with other forms of actionable subsidy, to be actionable, the subsidy must damage another country's industry or create serious prejudice (this includes actions resulting in a price effect of more than 5%, ongoing underwriting of losses, debt write-offs, import or export displacement or impediment, contributions to below cost selling i.e., dumping). In regard to actionable subsidies, a complaining country has to show that the subsidy has an adverse effect on its interests – otherwise the subsidy is permitted. The SCMA defines three types of damages they can cause. Thus, actionable subsidies may damage:

- a domestic industry in an importing country;
- rival exporters from another country when the two compete in third markets; or
- exporters trying to compete in the subsidising country's domestic market.

444. Case C-88/03: *Portugal v. Commission*, [2006] ECR I-7115 and Joined Cases C-106/09 P and C-107/09 P *Commission and Spain v. Government of Gibraltar and United Kingdom*, [2011] ECR I-11113, considered in Chapter 4.

The *remedy* provided by the SCMA goes through different stages:

(1) the views of an allegedly offending State are sought;
(2) the complaining State may then call for a WTO panel to investigate;
(3) WTO recommendations are issued;
(4) provision is made for a possible appeal phase; and
(5) if the recommendations of the WTO are not complied with, the complaining State may raise *countervailing measures* against the offending State.

Furthermore, the *notification and reporting system* under the SCMA has moved de facto to a system of reporting every two years. Reports are considered by the Subsidies and Countervailing Measures Committee of the WTO.

At the same time, very little consolidated information flows from the SCMA notification and reporting system. In the first major report on WTO subsidies published by the WTO, the *World Trade Report of 2006*[445] noted that the incidence and the impact of subsidies remained seriously under-researched, that many governments maintained extensive subsidy programmes at the national and subnational levels and that they invoked a multiplicity of objectives to justify the programmes. Dealing with WTO practice, the Report underlined that, because subsidies can be trade distorting, WTO Member governments must notify the organisation of any such support. However, the Report confirmed that few governments fully meet their notification obligations under the WTO, contributing to a serious lack of information and transparency on the use and effect of subsidies.

In World Trade Report 2006, the WTO also estimated global subsidies in the region of a trillion dollars per year or 4% of world GDP. It also noted that the information was not solid enough to conclude that there was any systematic downward trend in subsidies to industry and services. In some cases, however, evidence existed of a tendency to redirect subsidies towards "horizontal" objectives which would generally make subsidies less distorting. The Report concluded that the GATT/WTO rules on subsidies had evolved considerably over the years, becoming more precise and detailed. At the same time, it recognised that there remained strongly competing views as to whether the rules are tight enough to limit trade-distorting subsidies, or accommodating enough to allow governments to pursue their legitimate objectives, including development.

Finally, there is a degree to which the WTO SCMA has yet to prove itself as a powerful international agreement beyond major trade cases between the EU and the US[446] and certain other major international trading WTO

445. WTO: "*World Trade Report 2006 – Exploring the links between subsidies, trade and the WTO,*" 24 July 2006, Geneva.

446. Up to 2008, the EU had been a complainant in 72 WTO Dispute settlement cases. Of these at least 16 concerned the Subsidies and Countervailing Measures Agreement and in 7 of those cases the EU complained against measures applying in the USA. In the same period, the USA was a complainant in some 84 WTO Dispute settlement cases. Of these, at least 18 concerned the Subsidies and Countervailing Measures Agreement and in 3 of those cases the USA complained against measures applying in the EU.

Members.[447] Nonetheless, it provides useful points of reference in interpreting key concepts which often lack definition in the EU regime.[448] From the broad policy perspective of transition countries (e.g., the Western Balkans and the countries of the former Soviet Union), the view here is that full compliance with the type of EU system being generally advocated under new trade agreements will, at least from a legal perspective, ensure full compliance also with the WTO regime – while compliance with the WTO system will *not* ensure compliance with even the basic concepts of the EU system. Moreover, the current contentious debates in the Doha multilateral trade round offer only the smallest prospect of any progressive consensus on the further regulation of government supports to undertakings via the WTO system.[449]

3.8 THE TRADE-RELATED INVESTMENT MEASURES (TRIMS) AGREEMENT[450]

The WTO *TRIMS (Trade Related Investment Measures) Agreement* was the first multilateral treaty to address problems associated with foreign direct investment. Prior to its conclusion in the Uruguay Round, the GATT contained no such provisions and international law in this area was covered by an ever-expanding number of bilateral investment treaties[451] of individual countries and two binding Codes of the Organisation for Economic Cooperation and Development (OECD) which covered most developed countries.[452]

A further factor in the evolution of the TRIMS Agreement was the *FIRA Case* brought to a GATT Panel by the USA against the Canadian Foreign Investment Review Act of 1973. Under this Canadian legislation, introduced to limit the takeover of Canadian firms by US firms under the guise of foreign investment, the Canadian Government was authorised to decide on the extent to which these businesses were likely to benefit Canada based on an analysis of several factors, including local employment, use of local resources, components and services, export potential, impacts on competition and compatibility with national industrial and economic policies. The USA argued that these rules breached GATT rules (Articles III and XI) by

447. Including Canada, Australia and Brazil and more recently China.
448. But even on this, there are indications that definitions remain problematic – World Trade Report 2006, *supra*.
449. For the purposes of this overview, the continuing debates under the WTO Doha Round, which have a focus *inter alia* on new fields of and approaches to subsidy regulation, are not included. This is because of the continuing uncertainty as regards outcomes in the Doha process.
450. WTO: Trade Related Investment Measures Agreement, 1994 (accessible at: wto.org).
451. These were known as Bilateral Investment Treaties (BITs) in the US and the European version were generally called Bilateral Investment Protection Agreements (BIPAs). As of 1992, EU Member States had over 400 such BIPAs (Dillon *supra*, p. 99) although some Member States, notably Ireland, had none.
452. BITS largely focussed on the protection of foreign investments against expropriation by the State (which had been a major problem in Latin America in the 1970s and 1980s) and rules on the entry of specialised foreign employees. The OECD Codes imposed national treatment in respect of inward investments, required the removal of restrictions on the free movement of capital in OECD countries and liberalisation on the transfer of profits. While binding, the OECD Codes have no dispute resolution system, but rely on periodic peer review meetings.

forcing foreign investors to use local inputs even where these were commercially unattractive. Canada argued that a nation's investment laws were outside the scope of the GATT. The Panel Report on the FIRA Case confirmed that the GATT did not affect the sovereign right of Canada to regulate inward investment. However, the Panel did find a breach of GATT rules on national treatment in this case and the Canadian FIRA was repealed following the Panel Report.[453]

The TRIMS Agreement focuses on the main cases where certain investment measures restrict and distort trade, and some commentators regard it as a first step in this area and, in effect, multilateral legislation on the FIRA Case.

Table 12 Main Provisions of the WTO Trade-Related Investment Measures (TRIMS) Agreement 1994

The Agreement recognises that certain investment measures restrict and distort trade.
It provides that no contracting party shall apply any TRIM inconsistent with Articles III (national treatment) and XI (prohibition of quantitative restrictions) of the GATT.
An illustrative list of TRIMs agreed to be inconsistent with these articles is appended to the Agreement. The list includes measures which require particular levels of local procurement by an enterprise ("local content requirements") or which restrict the volume or value of imports such an enterprise can purchase or use to an amount related to the level of products it exports ("trade balancing requirements").
The Agreement requires mandatory notification of all non-conforming TRIMs and their elimination within two years for developed countries, within five years for developing countries and within seven years for least-developed countries.
The Agreement establishes a Committee on TRIMs which is to monitor the implementation of these commitments.
The Agreement also provides for consideration, at a later date, of whether it should be complemented with provisions on investment and competition policy more broadly.

There is an interesting and important cross-over between the TRIMS Agreement and the SCMA which makes the former Agreement relevant to the question of government supports to undertakings. In effect, subsidies and other forms of investment incentives are often provided with reference to some local economy conditions including, for example, local hiring, use of local materials and requirements to export production. Thus:

453. *Administration of the Foreign Investment Review Act (FIRA)*, 1984, BISD, 30th Supplement, 140 et seq.

> The underlying TRIMS concept is that foreign investors will only be allowed to enter or remain, depending upon how well they help to fulfill the host country's national objectives.[454]

Accordingly, the TRIMS Agreement removed a range of conditions that could be imposed by WTO countries giving subsidies to foreign investment undertakings.[455]

3.9 THE GENERAL AGREEMENT ON TRADE IN SERVICES (GATS)[456]

The *General Agreement on Trade in Services (GATS)* emerged as a multilateral trade response to the growing importance of services in world trade. Indeed, during the Uruguay Round, wealthier States were not willing to provide increased market access to other countries unless freer trade access for them to services markets was also covered by the Uruguay Round accords.[457] As a result of the GATS Agreement, the multilateral trading system commenced the process of extending its reach into the services sectors and creating a much wider basis for the WTO regime to attack national laws.[458] According to the WTO, in 2013, services constituted about 60% of global GDP. Moreover, trade in services has particularly increased in developing countries and total trade in services accounted for more than 50% of the exports of developing countries.[459]

The GATS Agreement is structured primarily as a framework agreement containing basic obligations which apply to all member countries. This is supplemented by national schedules of commitments containing specific further national commitments which are intended to be the subject of a continuing process of liberalisation and by a number of annexes addressing the special situations of individual services sectors.

In Part I, the scope of the GATS is defined in terms of services supplied from the territory of one party to the territory of another; services supplied in the territory of one party to the consumers of any other (e.g., tourism); services provided through the presence of service providing entities of one party in the territory of any other (e.g.,

454. S. Dillon: "*International Trade and Economic Law and the European Union,*" Hart Publishing, Oxford and Portland Oregon, 2002, p. 97. On this, *see also* R.E. Edwards & S. Lester: "*Towards a More Comprehensive World Trade Organization Agreement on Trade Related Investment Measures*" (1997), 33 Stanford Journal of International Law, pp. 172–174.
455. This is well illustrated by two important WTO cases: (1) the case brought by the US, EU and Japan against the Indonesian Car Production Programme in the late 1990s focussed on a package of Indonesian financial incentives, investment restrictions and selective protectionism (*US, EC and Japan v. Indonesia: Certain Measures Affecting the Automobile Industry, Panel Report of 2 July 1998, WT/DS54, 55, 59 and 64/R)* and (2) the more recent case brought by the EU and Japan against the Canadian conditions for customs duty exemptions on imported cars (*EC and Japan v. Canada: Measures Affecting the Automotive Industry, Panel Report of 11 February 2000, WT/D139, 142/R).*
456. WTO: General Agreement on Trade in Services, 1994 (accessible at: wto.org).
457. Dillon, *supra,* p. 251.
458. For example, it has already emerged that the GATS can be used to attack the conditions of the service of providing or distributing a tradeable good – *see* WTO Cases – *Ecuador, US and others v. EC: Regime for the Importation, Sale and Distribution of Bananas - Panel Report, 22 May 1997, WT/DS27/R* and *European Communities – Regime for the importation, sale and distribution of bananas,* Report of the Appellate Body of 25 September 1997, WT/D27/AB/R.
459. At http://www.wto.org/english/res_e/booksp_e/serv_profiles13_e.pdf.

banking); and services provided by nationals of one party in the territory of any other (e.g., construction projects or consultancies).

Part II sets out general obligations and disciplines. A basic most-favoured-nation (*MFN*) obligation states that each party "shall accord immediately and unconditionally to services and service providers of any other Party, treatment no less favourable than that it accords to like services and service providers of any other country." However, it is recognised that MFN treatment may not be possible for every service activity and, therefore, it is envisaged that parties may indicate specific MFN exemptions. Conditions for such exemptions are included as an annex and provide for reviews after five years and a normal limitation of 10 years on their duration.

Transparency requirements include publication of all relevant laws and regulations. Provisions to facilitate the increased participation of developing countries in world services trade envisage negotiated commitments on access to technology, improvements in access to distribution channels and information networks and the liberalisation of market access in sectors and modes of supply of export interest. The provisions covering economic integration are analogous to those in Article XXIV of GATT, requiring arrangements to have "substantial sectoral coverage" and to "provide for the absence or elimination of substantially all discrimination" between the parties.

Since domestic regulations provide the most significant influence on services trade, the GATS provides that all such measures of general application should be administered in a reasonable, objective and impartial manner. The agreement also contains obligations with respect to recognition requirements (educational background, for instance) for the purpose of securing authorisations, licences or certification in the services area and it specifically encourages recognition requirements achieved through harmonisation and internationally agreed criteria. Further provisions state that parties are required to ensure that monopolies and exclusive service providers do not abuse their positions and that restrictive business practices should be subject to consultations between parties with a view to their elimination.

This Part of the GATS also envisages negotiations with a view to the development of disciplines on trade-distorting subsidies in the services area in Article XV which provides that:

> 1. Members recognize that, in certain circumstances, subsidies may have distortive effects on trade in services. Members shall enter into negotiations with a view to developing the necessary multilateral disciplines to avoid such trade-distortive effects.[460] The negotiations shall also address the appropriateness of countervailing procedures. Such negotiations shall recognize the role of subsidies in relation to the development programmes of developing countries and take into account the needs of Members, particularly developing country Members, for flexibility in this area. For the purpose of such negotiations, Members shall exchange information concerning all subsidies related to trade in services that they provide to their domestic service suppliers.

460. A future work programme is to determine how, and in what time-frame, negotiations on such multilateral disciplines will be conducted.

2. Any Member which considers that it is adversely affected by a subsidy of another Member may request consultations with that Member on such matters. Such requests shall be accorded sympathetic consideration.

Part III of the Agreement contains provisions on market access and national treatment which are not general obligations but commitments to be made in national schedules. Thus, in the case of market access, each party "shall accord services and service providers of other Parties treatment no less favourable than that provided for under the terms, limitations and conditions agreed and specified in its schedule." The intention of the market-access provision was to progressively eliminate the following types of measures: limitations on numbers of service providers, on the total value of service transactions or on the total number of service operations or people employed. Equally, restrictions on the kind of legal entity or joint venture through which a service is provided or any foreign capital limitations relating to maximum levels of foreign participation were to be progressively eliminated.

The national-treatment provision contains the obligation to treat foreign service suppliers and domestic service suppliers in the same manner. However, it does provide the possibility of different treatment being accorded the service providers of other parties to that accorded to domestic service providers although, in such cases, the conditions of competition should not, as a result, be modified in favour of the domestic service providers.

Part IV of the Agreement established the basis for progressive liberalisation in the services area through successive rounds of negotiations and the development of national schedules. Part V of the Agreement contains institutional provisions, including consultation and dispute settlement and the establishment of a WTO Council on Services. Finally, the GATS contains specific rules in a series of annexes.[461]

461. The first of the annexes to the agreement concerns the movement of labour. It permits parties to negotiate specific commitments applying to the movement of people providing services under the agreement and requires that people covered by a specific commitment shall be allowed to provide the service in accordance with the terms of the commitment. Nevertheless, the agreement does not apply to measures affecting employment, citizenship, residence or employment on a permanent basis. The annex on financial services (largely banking and insurance) lays down the right of parties, notwithstanding other provisions, to take prudential measures, including for the protection of investors, deposit holders and policy holders, and to ensure the integrity and stability of the financial system. The annex on telecommunications relates to measures which affect access to and use of public telecommunications services and networks. In particular, it requires that such access be accorded to another party, on reasonable and non-discriminatory terms, to permit the supply of a service included in its schedule. Thus, for example, the conditions attached to the use of public networks should be no more than is necessary to safeguard the public service responsibilities of their operators, to protect the technical integrity of the network and to ensure that foreign service suppliers do not supply services unless permitted to do so through a specific commitment. The annex also encourages technical cooperation to assist developing countries in the strengthening of their own domestic telecommunications sectors. The annex on air-transport services excludes from the agreement's coverage traffic rights (covered by bilateral air-service agreements conferring landing rights) and directly related activities which might affect the negotiation of traffic rights. Nevertheless, the annex also states that the agreement does apply to aircraft repair and maintenance services, the marketing of air-transport services and computer-reservation services.

The GATS Agreement has adopted a very different approach to subsidy disciplines to that found on the goods side. First, Article XV of the GATS, which deals with subsidies, is primarily a negotiating mandate, not a set of rules. The Article calls for negotiations in recognition both that subsidies may distort trade and that they may have a role to play in development. The Article calls for recognition of the need for flexibility in this area. The negotiating mandate is also to consider the appropriateness of countervailing procedures. Members are required to exchange information on all subsidies related to trade in services that they provide to their domestic service suppliers.

Second, there is a right established under Article XV to seek consultations with another Member State if its subsidy practices are considered to be the source of adverse trade effects. In the absence of explicit subsidy disciplines, there is, however, a degree of indirect discipline as the rules on non-discrimination – the most-favoured-nation and national treatment provisions – apply. National treatment is particularly relevant, since Members can schedule national-treatment commitments with respect to particular service activities. If these commitments do not contain explicit exemptions that permit subsidies to be granted in a discriminatory manner, then the national treatment principle will require that "like" foreign and national services and service suppliers must be given the same treatment in relation to subsidies. While this discipline does not directly regulate the granting of subsidies, it was intended to impose some restraint on the willingness of governments to subsidise.

Third, the regulatory structure under the GATS Agreement is different from the GATT, since Article III:8(b) of the GATT excludes subsidies on goods from the scope of national treatment. However, as the WTO points out:

> What on the face of it might look like stronger GATS discipline than that on goods will not in fact amount to a significant difference unless Members have chosen to assume national treatment commitments in important sectors without any carve-out for subsidies.[462]

Subsequent negotiations on possible further approaches to subsidy disciplines in the services context have not gone very far, although there appears to be some appetite in the Doha Round to use the SCMA definition of subsidies, appropriately modified, as a working basis upon which to carry forward further negotiations. Moreover, there appears to be a widespread disregard of the obligation under Article XV to engage in an information exchange on subsidies.[463]

462. WTO: "*World Trade Report 2006 – exploring the links between subsidies, trade and the WTO,*" Geneva, 2006, p. 195.

463. *Ibid.*, p. 195. *See also* M. Wall and d Vis-Dunbar: "*The Standstill in Subsidies – Update,*" International Institute for Sustainable Development, November 2005 at http://www.iisd.org who point out, *inter alia*, that "*The debate in services remains at its most basic stage, as it has since 1996. It continues to founder upon the so-called "chicken and egg" problem: without a definition, members cannot provide information to the WTO about their service subsidies; yet without this information, members cannot make a definition. And without either, creating subsidy disciplines is impossible. This problem is perceived by some members as an excuse for some developed countries to avoid disciplines.... The major cause of the impasse in Rules is said to be the outstanding dispute between Boeing and Airbus.*"

In 2006, the WTO noted that subsidies in the services sectors were widespread, but particularly frequent in transport, tourism and banking.[464] With a particular emphasis on providing "universal access," most WTO countries subsidised transport. Estimates for OECD countries suggested that subsidies to the transport sector amounted to nearly one-third of total OECD subsidies and that transportation represented the second most important sector after agriculture in terms of the flow of subsidies, while in non-OECD countries the importance of transport subsidies was much lower. Moreover, EU data at the time indicated that State aid to the transport sector represented the largest share of total EU State aid (around 46%) and State aid granted to the transport sector as a whole, excluding railways, averaged €1.5 billion annually over the period 2001–2003, representing a 50% increase compared to the period 1999–2001.[465]

In regard to tourism, the WTO Report viewed this as one of the sectors most frequently targeted by services subsidies, according to the information collected by WTO Trade Policy Review Reports. Indeed, subsidy programmes targeting tourism were mentioned in 62 of the 97 of these Reports completed between January 1995 and February 2004. In that regard, many developing countries consider tourism to be a sector with significant growth potential and governments wish to stimulate the sector by using subsidies. This is notably the case in Africa, a region that is widely recognised for the quality of its resource endowment for tourism, but where the industry is far from reaching its full potential, notwithstanding promising growth figures at the beginning of the millennium.[466]

In the WTO assessment of the banking sector (but before the international financial crisis), it emerged that the approach to subsidisation differed considerably as between countries, although most supports to the financial services sector did focus on banks. In the EU, most subsidies to the financial sector at the time took the form of equity participation; while soft loans, credit guarantees and tax exemptions represented only a very small share of total subsidies to the sector. In contrast, national data on subsidies to the financial sector in Australia revealed that about 90% of total assistance to the financial sector took the form of tax concessions. In both industrialised and developing countries, however, the WTO reported that restructuring aid had frequently been given to banks during the process of privatisation and, more generally, governments had a strong tendency to intervene to rescue a bank that was in trouble, thus avoiding bank closure or the sale of assets to new investors. Indeed, in the European Union, for example, the financial sector already featured prominently among the sectors receiving rescue and restructuring State aid. Between 1995 and 2003, the number of approved rescue and restructuring State aid cases to all sectors in the European Union was 87, of which 34 were rescues and 53 involved restructuring aid.

464. *Ibid.*, pp. 178–179.
465. *Ibid.*, pp. 179–181.
466. *Ibid.*, p. 183.

Next to construction and engineering firms, the financial services sector was the second most frequent recipient of rescue and restructuring aid (10 companies). Most of the cases in the financial sector involved restructuring aid and focussed on cases involving banks in different countries and including: Banco di Sicilia and Sicilcassa, Banesto, Crédit Lyonnais, Crédit Agricole, and Westdeutsche Landesbank.[467]

And, of course, this situation changed dramatically in the 2008–2012 period where enormous amounts of "crisis aid" were permitted and facilitated across the EU in response to the "exceptional occurrence" that was the international financial crisis.

3.10 CLASHES BETWEEN THE WTO AND EU SYSTEMS – AN EXCURSUS INTO BOEING AND AIRBUS

Throughout the 1950s, 1960s and 1970s, the global aircraft manufacturing industry was dominated by the American firm Boeing. In response, European industrial-policy concerns prompted the French, German and British governments to band together and to challenge American domination and, in 1969, the Airbus Consortium was established with heavy subsidisation by these governments. The Airbus initiative was also viewed by the EU as an important project of common European interest and, accordingly, State aid to Airbus was exempted by the European Commission.[468] By the early 1980s, Airbus slowly started to gain market share in competition with Boeing and by 1997 the share of gross aircraft orders of Airbus and Boeing were 44.7% and 53.6% respectively. By the end of the 1990s, Airbus caught up and exceeded Boeing in terms of gross aircraft orders.

The allegations of unfair subsidisation and the subsequent dispute commenced between the US and the EU ultimately led to the multilateral WTO Agreement on Trade and Subsidies for Civil Aircraft of 1992. That agreement, among other things, capped the limits of direct government subsidies for the development of aircraft with a capacity of at least one-hundred seats and prohibited production subsidies. Yet both Boeing and Airbus continued to receive different types of State financial support. The dispute reached a climax when Airbus started to develop the "superjumbo" Airbus A380 that required development financing. In October 2004, the US unilaterally withdrew from the 1992 Agreement and requested consultations under the WTO Dispute Settlement Understanding.

The tit-for-tat EU-US WTO civil aviation dispute established itself in earnest in 2004 when the US urged the WTO to act against European government loans to help

467. *Ibid.*, pp. 185–187.
468. European Commission: "Answer given by Mr Monti on behalf of the Commission, to written question E-2718/00," in OJ C 113E of 18 April 2001, p. 157 confirms that Article 107(3)(b) of the TFEU was used in 1970s and 1980s to promote European industries, in particular Airbus. Mario Monti, EU Commissioner for Competition stated that the aid to Airbus was qualified for the exception under Article 107(3)(b) (case No 369/98 – repayable advance to the Airbus).

Airbus develop new jets, followed by a counter-claim from the EU over US federal and local aid for Boeing. Both sides claimed that the other had ignored all previous findings and sought WTO permission to draw up sanctions. While the total amounts of subsidies are unknown or at least not publicly available, Boeing calculated that Airbus received illegal subsidies in the amount of $18 billion. By comparison, the Appellate Body held that Boeing had received between $5 to 6 billion of WTO-inconsistent subsidies in the years 1989–2006.[469]

In 2015, the EU complained that Boeing was set to receive unfair support for its latest plane, the 777X, from Washington State thanks to an $8.7 billion package of expanded tax breaks. Here, the EU argued that the US 2013 package of preferential business tax rates, tax credits and tax exemptions represented subsidies to Boeing in return for securing the coveted 777X jetliner work. The EU submitted that the US measures were specific subsidies within the meaning of Articles 1 and 2 of the SCMA and that they constituted prohibited subsidies under Articles 3.1(b) and 3.2 of the SCMA, involving the use of domestic over imported goods. For its part, the US industry argued the measures were available to any aerospace company in the state, including even a few suppliers to Airbus, and did not fall within the scope of the SCMA. However, Washington State's 2013 tax package for aerospace companies was largely the same as an earlier 2003 package, which the WTO found in 2011 to have caused "serious prejudice" to Airbus.

In 2011, the WTO determined that France, Germany, Spain, and the UK provided Airbus with support that breached international trade rules. The EU responded that some $2.3 billion in launch-aid loans had been repaid and that other assistance had since been modified. Unconvinced, the US submitted that Europe's subsidies for the Airbus A380 remained in place and in 2012 asked a WTO compliance panel to investigate the matter. The most recent WTO decisions in both cases were issued in 2016.

3.10.1 The 2016 Boeing Decision[470]

The Issues in the Boeing Case

This case concerned $8.7 billion in tax breaks which the Washington Legislature extended to the State's aerospace industry in exchange for Boeing building a 777X wing production plant in Everett, next to Boeing's giant wide-body assembly plant. It was this specific quid-pro-quo that violated WTO rules.

Boeing argued that the cost to the company was only $50 million a year over 20 years and that no benefit arose until the first 777X is delivered in 2020.

469. K. Brown & T. Tiemann: "*EU State Aid Policy and the EC – Airbus Case,*" Maastricht University, 2012, pp. 13–14.
470. WTO, DS487: United States — Conditional Tax Incentives for Large Civil Aircraft, 28 November 2016.

Airbus claimed that this was an attempted deception by Boeing as, under Boeing's programme accounting, Boeing had already taken its $5.7 billion share of the $8.7 billion in tax breaks with the balance going to the Washington State aerospace supply chain in general (some of which ironically indirectly supported Airbus).

The 2016 WTO Panel decision held that the US aircraft manufacturer Boeing had received prohibited subsidies for its 777X wide-body passenger jet as the US measures at issue encouraged the use of domestic materials and created unfair trade distortions. The subsidy came in the form of a renewed cut in Washington State's main business tax for aerospace agreed in 2013, when Boeing was considering where to base the assembly of its latest long-haul jet. The Panel also found that the US had acted inconsistently with Article 3.2 of the SCMA. This ruling was the third in Boeing-Airbus disputes over illegal subsidies. While the WTO did not give a value for the banned subsidisation, the EU estimated it at $5.7 billion (€5.2 billion) out of an $8.7 billion package of tax measures granted to the planemaker by Boeing's home state of Washington. Boeing responded that it was confident the ruling would be overturned on appeal and insisted that its tax breaks were not nearly as high as the $22 billion Airbus had received in subsidised loans from European governments.

The Panel report of 28 November 2016 was appealed on 16 December 2016 by the US and, on 17 January 2017, the European Union notified the Dispute Settlement Board of its decision to cross-appeal.

European Union Trade Commissioner Cecilia Malmström welcomed the ruling, calling for the prohibited tax break to be scrapped immediately and added that EU expected the US to respect the rules, uphold fair competition and withdraw these subsidies without any delay.[471] Meanwhile, the Airbus Chief Executive said that he continued to think that the only way out of the ridiculous series of disputes initiated by the US was to agree on a set of globally applicable rules for the support of the civil aircraft industry, which would benefit both sides of the Atlantic.[472] American commentators have strongly criticised the ruling with some arguing that it is meaningless:

> Entire process is nonsense. The WTO is a joke. It has no enforcement powers of its own. It can't impose sanctions for non-compliance. It can authorize the governments to impose sanctions, but they don't have to. Even if they do, the sanctions don't have to be against the companies involved, and often aren't. It's highly unlikely the US or European Union will ever impose sanctions on Airbus and Boeing. They have too much to lose. The WTO should be disbanded.[473]

471. European Commission – Press Release: "*Major Win for the EU in the WTO Dispute on Boeing,*" Brussels, 28 November 2016, IP/16/3947.
472. At http://www.dw.com/en/wto-rules-against-boeing-in-us-subsidies-case/a-36559632.
473. S. Hamilton, "*The WTO Ruling against Boeing is Meaningless*" (28 November 2016), Forbes Magazine, accessed at: https://www.forbes.com/sites/scotthamilton5/2016/11/28/wto-boeing-ruling-gives-airbus-good-pr-but-its-meaningless/#25700c937d7c.

3.10.2 The 2016 Airbus Decision[474]

> ***Issues in the Airbus Case***
>
> This case argued that Airbus had been supported primarily by the European Union, France, Germany, the UK and Spain and that the subsidies amounted to more than 300 separate measures over a period of almost 40 years. The benefits allegedly comprised below market interest rates and generous repayment obligations, design and development financing loans from the European Investment Bank (EIB) for several purposes, including R&D and design; infrastructure and related grants by the EU and the Member States for the development of infrastructure and facilities for the benefit of Airbus; the write-off of launch-aid debts and the provision of equity infusions and grants.

In June 2011, the WTO had already found that the EU and four of its Member States had provided billions of dollars in subsidised financing to Airbus. As noted earlier, the EU claimed that it had subsequently stopped the measures complained of – prompting an unconvinced US to request a compliance panel to intervene.

In its 2016 decision, the WTO decided that the European Union's so-called launch aid loans provided for the development of Airbus fleets had been a "genuine and substantial" cause of significant lost sales for its US competitor Boeing and that Airbus had received additional illegal subsidies, thus harming Boeing's sales business.

US Trade Representative Michael Froman said that the Panel's finding was "a sweeping victory for the United States and its aerospace workers" and called on Germany, France, Britain and Spain to finally respect WTO rules and immediately end subsidised financing of Airbus.[475] Airbus, in turn, filed an appeal against the ruling.

Taken together, it is clear that the WTO Panels found both sides had breached the SCMA in doing what they had both been doing for decades in support of their civil aviation industries. At present, both sides are uninterested in negotiating and it appears, therefore, that the process will continue to develop through the WTO dispute resolution process.

3.11 THE EU AND WTO SYSTEMS – COMPARATIVE STRENGTHS AND WEAKNESSES

The following Table summarises the main strengths and weaknesses of the EU and WTO systems of regulation of government supports to undertakings on the basis of the earlier analysis and practice generally.

474. WTO: DS316: European Communities — Measures Affecting Trade in Large Civil Aircraft, 22 September 2016.
475. Office of the US Trade Representative – Press Release: United States Presses for Rapid Enforcement of Two World Trade Organization (WTO) Victories, October 2016.

Table 13 Comparative Overview of the Main Strengths and Weaknesses of International Regulation of Government Supports[476]

Element	*EU State Aid Regime*	*WTO Agreements (GATT, SCMA, and GATS)*
Definitions	Weak but flexible	Strong generally (especially SCMA) - but not in the GATS
Scope of application	Strong in Industry and Services sectors. Weak in regulating agricultural sector supports.	Medium in regard to industrial subsidies. Weak in regulating services sector subsidies and very weak in regard to agriculture.
Regulatory mechanisms	Strong supranational control mechanism	Weak: reliant on action initiated by a WTO member country
Remedies	Strong, including recovery of illegal support with interest	Weak: based on countervailing measures only.
Application of remedies	Strengthening but some major difficulties	Some difficulties
Transparency	Strong and growing stronger	Weak and low levels of compliance
Legal certainty	Weak due to evolutionary nature of law and policy	Strong due to limitations on coercive action.
Impact on national sovereignty	Strong and strengthening in EU Member States and EU/third country relations.	Limited
Legitimacy	Weak due to the evolutionary nature of law and policy	Strong due to the detailed treaty making mechanism involved and the WTO Dispute Settlement understanding
Economic logic	Strong in principle but weak in practice	Strongly based on free trade theory
Flexibility/Rigidity of law	Flexible	Rigid
Extent of political influence in cases	Increasingly weak as regards individual nations.	Very strong.
Simplicity of Law	Weak - rules now very complex.	Medium to Strong
Effectiveness	Medium	Weak
Prospects for systemic reform	Only incremental change likely	Weak due to collapse of Doha Round

476. E. Stuart: "*Analysis and Assessment of Key Issues in the Regulation of Government Supports to Undertakings under International Law*," Belgrade, 2008 (unpublished).

In these comparative terms, the EU State aid regime is more developed than the WTO system. This results from an earlier and fuller regulatory consensus in the EU system which was reinforced later by pro-active interpretations and strengthened enforcement. Thus, the EU system has developed organically as a result of EU case law, the process of EU integration, relatively recent political consensus and innovative approaches to rule-making and enforcement practice. In contrast, the WTO regime is more reliant on difficult reform processes to adapt to modern needs; it retains a focus on major cases and suffers, in particular, from a lack of political consensus, poor transparency and effective compliance only *in extremis*.

At the same time, as the EU is a WTO Member, it must respect its commitments with respect to the regulation of subsidies in the WTO. This means that the EU State aid rules must conform to the WTO rules on subsidies, while they may also be stronger than the WTO rules.

It is clear also that the objectives of the EU State aid control system have shown a broad (and arguably imaginative) inconsistency over the years. This has facilitated the broader evolution of law, it has contributed to the use of Article 107 of the TFEU in a pragmatic and dynamic way that has allowed substantive law on State aid to steer through important policy conflicts with other areas of EU policy based on the tendencies of prevailing policies towards the facilitation or the prohibition of certain types of support measures.

However, the EU system has become exceedingly complex, it is not always as effective as it seeks to present and important legal, economic and policy issues persist in this "prohibition" regime. These include legal certainty and definitional clarity, the uniform application of the regulatory regime and the overall effectiveness of control, enforcement practice and deterrent effect, the rights and duties of States and businesses, the extent of real transparency, questions about the economic philosophy of the system and the State aid control regime's contribution to competition, to economic development, trade and investment, the challenges it poses for transition economies, policy issues regarding sovereignty, current taxation dilemmas and the extent to which the application of substantive law is driven by the law itself or by evolving political perspectives of what the law might evolve to mean. At the same time, it must be recognised that the three phases of reform in the EU system[477] have at least attempted to address some of these weaknesses.

With its strong diplomatic basis, the WTO regime, in contrast, is somewhat less pretentious as regards its substantive regulatory content. It is also a more effective and coherent system as a result of the Uruguay Round accords; including their improved dispute settlement and their clarity of definitions. While its importance can be mostly seen from high profile international trade disputes, these have not generally produced solutions to subsidy problems (*see* Airbus and Boeing above). However, it can also be argued that the political consensus underlying the WTO accords was perhaps never intended to be more wide ranging.

477. Considered in detail in Chapter 5.

While the WTO system also gives rise to various legal and economic issues, policy issues are few as the WTO system is not under supranational control and the WTO is not engaged in a similar evolutionary process regarding the regulation of subsidies as is the case with the European Commission.

Under strong US influence, the WTO system retains a focus on trade remedies (akin to traditional anti-dumping regulation) and has failed to date to come to terms with the real concerns in international trade regarding government supports that concern smaller, less developed and developing countries, notably as regards supports in the agriculture sector in developed countries. It has also failed to develop in line with the apparent EU agenda of harmonising the rules of international trade (examined in the next Section) with the disciplines applying in the European Union, thereby providing the impetus for the EU to promote stricter disciplines in its new bilateral trade agreements with third countries.

3.12 THE EXPANSION OF THE EU SYSTEM VIA NEW TRADE AND INTEGRATION TREATIES

Given the uniqueness of the EU State aid control system, it can be somewhat surprising to note the extent to which the EU approach has, in fact, been extended beyond the borders of the European Union Member States. This trend began during the Uruguay Round negotiations which resulted in the creation of the WTO and the adoption of the SCMA. By 1991, the EU had already extended the State aid control concept in full to other European countries via the provisions of the *Agreement on the European Economic Area (EEA)*[478] and the Europe Agreements with the countries of Central and Eastern Europe were being put in place.

From an international trade perspective, the EU clearly had concerns that its State aid disciplines would not put it at a trading disadvantage with international competitors where no such rules applied. As the then Head of DG Competition of the European Commission has indicated:

> the EU has every interest in advancing the scrutiny of subsidies at the international level. This is true of both substance and procedure, i.e. monitoring. If such rules do not exist or if they are not effectively implemented, non-member countries will benefit gratuitously from the EU's internal control mechanism. Such a situation is clearly not desirable. It might in the end even jeopardize the correct functioning of the EU's own State aid control. Contrary to commonly held views about the risks of subjecting oneself to international rules, the EU has nothing to lose and can only win in exporting its own State aid discipline to other parts of the world.[479]

478. Accordingly, in Norway, Iceland and Liechtenstein, the EFTA Surveillance Authority applies similar State aid rules to those under the TFEU. Austria, Sweden and Finland were members of EFTA but not EU Member States at the time of the EEA.
479. C.D. Ehlermann: *"State aid Control – Success or Failure?," supra,* 18 January 1995.

The same commentator also pointed out that, in the WTO SCMA, the EU definition of subsidy was adopted[480] and EU State aid rules and procedures largely gained admittance with respect to subsidies, in particular those regarding regional aid.

3.12.1 From the Stockholm Convention to the EEA

The European Free Trade Association (EFTA) was at its inception, and continues to a certain extent to be, a reaction against the EU. While both the European Union and EFTA emerged from the Organisation of European Economic Cooperation (OEEC) set up after the Second World War to manage the distribution of US Marshall Aid, EFTA broke away from the EU track because the UK, Switzerland and the Nordic countries would not accept a common external tariff or harmonisation in the economic and social spheres to the extent proposed by France in the early 1950s.[481] Accordingly, the Stockholm Convention, establishing a looser free trade association (EFTA), was signed on 3 May 1960.

As in the EU regime, the original Stockholm provisions on State aid were in the competition section of the Convention in Article 13 and were further elaborated by EFTA Council interpretations in 1968 and in 1988.

Table 14 Article 13 of the Stockholm Convention 1960

Article 13 - Government Aids
"Member States shall not maintain or introduce: (a) the forms of aid to exports of goods to other Member States which are described in Annex C; or (b) any other form of aid, the main purpose or effect of which is to frustrate the benefits expected from the removal or absence of duties and quantitative restrictions on trade between Member States. If the application of any form of aid by a Member State, although not contrary to paragraph 1 of this Article, frustrates the benefits expected from the removal or absence of duties and quantitative restrictions on trade between Member States ... the Council may, by majority decision, authorise any Member State to suspend to the Member State which is applying the aid, the application of such obligations under this Convention as the Council considers appropriate. The Council may decide to amend the provisions of this Article and of Annex C."[482]

480. This is an interesting point as the EU system of State aid control provides for no definition. Nonetheless, it would appear that the EU advanced the text of what became Article 1 of the SCMA.
481. R. Middleton: "*Negotiating on Non-Tariff Distortions of Trade – the EFTA Precedent,*" London, Macmillan, 1975, p. 9.
482. At http://www.worldtradelaw.net/fta/agreements/eftascfta at p. 11.

Annex C aids included currency retention schemes or any similar practices involving a bonus on exports or re-exports, direct government subsidies to exporters, tax and social security reliefs calculated in relation to exports, below-cost export credit insurances and export credit guarantees, support for exporters obtaining credits and reduced State transportation charges for exporters.[483]

It has been observed that EFTA, from the outset, adopted a policy of applying Article 13 of the Stockholm Convention regarding State aids with a strong emphasis on laissez-faire economics and the Smith-Ricardo theories but also with a degree of political pragmatism.[484] In 1968, the EFTA Council agreed that government grants, loans, guarantees and equity would be covered by Article 13; while aids to research and development, aids to restructuring within overall economic policy (if not directed at exports or at import substitution), regional development aids, production subsidies to goods not widely traded in EFTA countries and aids to support general public services were not to be included.[485] In 1988, not least in response to the ongoing economic crises of the 1970s and 1980s, the EFTA Council also excluded subsidies for the creation of employment in sectors not suffering from overcapacity, environmental aid and aid to support small and medium-sized enterprises. At the same time, tax concessions were to be considered covered by Article 13 of the Convention.[486]

Prior to the transformation of EFTA into the EEA, there was only one major subsidies dispute in EFTA, between the UK and Norway and involving UK subsidies to the aluminium industry, which the EFTA system totally failed to resolve.[487] Moreover, there were real difficulties in the legal application of the term "frustration of benefits" and, absent a litigious culture among EFTA Member States, there were only six disputes in EFTA and a resultant lack of case law. On the other hand, EFTA completed its First State Aid Survey before the EU and in 1989 the EFTA Surveillance Authority was strengthened to allow the recovery of State aid based on a majority vote by the EFTA Council. Several commentators indicate that the weaknesses of the EFTA regime in tackling the trade distortion effects of subsidies was a major factor in seeking to resolve this issue via the EEA accord in the early 1990s.[488]

The EEA Agreement was negotiated between the European Commission, the then EU Member States, and the then seven member countries of the EFTA and was signed in May 1992. Subsequently, Switzerland decided not to participate following a referendum, and three other EFTA Members joined the EU. The EEA Agreement entered

483. The original Stockholm Convention has since been substantially amended, including the deletion of Annex C. The present version, known as the Vaduz Convention, was signed on 21 June 2001 and entered into force on 1 June 2002. State aid matters are dealt with in Article 16 – *see: http://www.efta.int/sites/default/files/documents/legal-texts/efta-convention/Vaduz%20 Convention%20Agreement.pdf.*

484. R. Behboodi: "*Industrial Subsidies and Friction in World Trade*," Routledge (London & New York), 1994, pp. 56–67.

485. *EFTA Agreement on Government Aid*, EFTA Bulletin, October 1968, at 9(7).

486. EFTA, Economic Committee, *Working Party on Government Aids, Final Report*, Geneva, 1986.

487. The British Aluminium Smelter Case, Behboodi, *supra,* at p. 65.

488. Behboodi, *supra. See also*, R. Middleton: "*Negotiating on Non-Tariff Distortions of Trade – the EFTA Precedent*," London, Macmillan, 1975, V. Price-Curzon: "*Free trade areas: The European Experience*," Toronto, Howe Institute, 1987.

into force on 1 January 1994. The EEA was maintained because of the wish of the three remaining countries – Norway, Iceland and Liechtenstein – to participate in the EU Internal Market, while not assuming the full responsibilities of EU membership. In effect, the EEA (or EEA-EFTA as it is sometimes known) includes the EU plus the three remaining EFTA Member States. The EEA Agreement is concerned principally with the "the four freedoms" of the EU Internal Market, i.e. free movement of goods (excluding agriculture and fisheries, which are included in the Agreement only to a very limited extent), persons, services and capital. Further horizontal provisions relevant to these four freedoms in the areas of social policy, consumer protection, environment, company law are also covered. As one of the primary obligations under the Agreement is to ensure equal conditions of competition, the substantive competition rules of the Agreement correspond to the TFEU in this area, covering the rules concerning cartels, abuse of dominant positions, merger control, State monopolies and State aid. The EEA Agreement is implemented through a set of special institutional arrangements, including the EEA Joint Committee, whose main function is to adopt decisions extending EU regulations and directives to the EEA-EFTA States. The EU is represented by the European Commission in the Joint Committee and decisions in the Joint Committee are taken by unanimous agreement between the EU and the EEA-EFTA States. The EFTA Surveillance Authority (ESA) was established in 1992,[489] and the ESA has been given powers corresponding to those of the European Commission. In particular, the ESA monitors the fulfilment of obligations under the EEA Agreement, ensuring the provisions of the Agreement are properly implemented in the national legal order of the EEA-EFTA States and that their authorities correctly apply these rules. In the fields of public procurement, State aid and competition, the Authority, like the European Commission in the EU, has extended competence.[490]

3.12.2 The Europe Agreements

In the 1990s, the *Europe Agreements* provided for the application of State aid rules similar to those applying in the EU system in the then candidate countries of Central and Eastern Europe (CEECs). However, and for the first time, this was to be done under the authority of national regulatory authorities and laws. This was an ambitious experiment in the view of the EU State aid controllers:

> They will have to ensure the respect of their international obligations towards the EU through strictly national control mechanisms. Whether such a mechanism can be implemented effectively remains to be seen. In the light of the EU's own internal experience, it seems almost impossible. The CEECs have, however, one powerful incentive to succeed: in implementing correctly the State aid disciplines of the

489. Agreement between the EFTA States on the establishment of a Surveillance Authority and a Court of Justice on 2 May 1992.
490. In the context of the detailed State aid rules of the EU, it is noteworthy that "*The EFTA Surveillance Authority's State aid Guidelines*" of 19 January 1994 provide a comprehensive manual of State aid rules (over 400 pages) and include 67 specific amendments as of April 2007 http://www.eftasurv.int/fieldsofwork/fieldstateaid/legaltexts.

> Europe Agreements, they can avoid protective measures which the EU might otherwise apply to their exports to the EU. The Europe Agreements place thus a high premium on self-discipline.[491]

By 1999, it was still far from clear that this had been a successful experiment:

> We are undertaking a bold experiment with regard to our relationship with the applicant countries. We have asked them to set up their own state aid monitoring authorities and to apply the state aid rules within their own legal and administrative systems. Although there are signs that this is beginning to work in some places, this is not the case overall and, frankly speaking, it is an extraordinary request... As regards aid, the initial need is for transparency and a proper knowledge of what state aid is being paid. Yet in our own Member States, it took us 35 years to reach this level of information and interest.[492]

Nonetheless, the insistence on the creation of State aid systems in the candidate countries, at the time, clearly prepared the new EU Member States for the full rigours of State aid control after membership when national controls were, in effect, transferred to the European Commission. While the specific focus in the Europe Agreements was on monitoring (as noted in the above quotation) and on more specific commitments in the coal and steel sectors (of greatest single concern to the EU), the screening processes with candidate countries and the later membership negotiations increased the pressure on the national State aid systems of those countries to start actually *controlling* State aids.

While most Central and European countries had adopted laws aimed at protecting competition in the early 1990s, the regulation of State aid had not been anticipated and, therefore, took time. Between 1997 and 2001 all CEECs adopted national State aid laws. In many cases, these laws were simply viewed as temporary acts which contained only the main elements of European State aid rules. In other cases, certain provisions of those acts went beyond what was required e.g. in providing lists of potential types of State aid or implementing State aid permission/prohibition systems (even if the country was not formally required at that point to do so). However, as already noted, the establishment of monitoring evolved into an expectation of control before the major enlargement of the EU in 2004.

Similar requirements faced Bulgaria and Romania prior to their accession to the European Union. However, in both cases, the systems had not been completed prior to accession and special clauses were included in both accession treaties requiring the further development of the systems (together with a range of also uncompleted anti-corruption measures) as a pre-condition for accessing EU structural funds.

Typical forms of problematic State aid which were very commonly used in pre-accession countries were fiscal measures (operating aid) and subsidies provided to certain industries with structural overcapacity. Indeed, because of the budgetary constraints in most of these countries, indirect State aid, in particular fiscal measures

491. C.D. Ehlermann: *"State aid Control – Success or Failure?,"* *supra*.
492. J. Faull: *"Prospects for Decentralisation of EU State Aid Control"* in Ehlermann & Everson (eds): *"European Competition Annual 1999: Selected Issues in the Field of State Aids,"* Hart Publishing, 2001, p. 472.

(such as tax waivers and deferrals) were widely used measures of industrial policy. Some countries applied such tax measures to attract foreign investors. During the negotiations with these countries, the European Commission found that a number of tax schemes did not comply with State aid rules and these incompatible fiscal measures were considered a major obstacle to accession. In the run-up to the 2004 Enlargement, in particular, important efforts were made to convert such aid measures into permissible aid. Usually candidate countries agreed to a phasing-out of these measures after a transitional period of some years post-accession or to convert the measures into compatible horizontal aid with clearly defined objectives such as regional, environmental or training aid.

In regard to the provision of subsidies to certain sensitive sectors of the economy facing problems of structural overcapacity, this problem was especially acute in the steel sector. For some new Member States, such as Poland or the Czech Republic, the steel industry was an extremely important part of their economies. In the past, the mostly State-owned steel companies had been heavily supported by a wide range of State measures, including operating aid, to compensate for the problems of overcapacity. As the steel sector was in continuing economic difficulties during the 1990s, the Protocols of the Europe Agreements concluded with Bulgaria, the Czech Republic, Hungary, Poland, Romania, Slovakia and Slovenia provided detailed rules for the implementation of restructuring plans for steel companies. According to those protocols, the aid beneficiaries had to be viable at the end of the restructuring period, the extent of aid had to be limited to the amount absolutely necessary for restoring viability and the restructuring had to be linked to capacity reductions. Poland, Bulgaria, the Czech Republic and Romania did not complete their steel sector restructuring processes within the five-year deadlines required by the Europe Agreements and each requested a further five years. Moreover, the rules on State aid for restructuring in the steel sector were incorporated in the Accession Treaties of the Czech Republic, Poland and Romania. This was necessary, as restructuring aid to the steel sector had already been prohibited in the EU since 2002, and they would not, therefore, be regarded as protected "existing aid" following membership. Moreover, on this basis, the European Commission was entitled to order the recovery of incompatible aid even in respect of aid granted before the accession of non-Member States.

While the Commission, in principle, required the candidate countries either to abolish incompatible aid measures or to align them with the EU acquis prior to accession (and based on the Europe Agreements), in some cases consultations resulted in special limited transitional regimes for certain countries when they joined the EU. These were granted to Cyprus, the Czech Republic, Hungary, Malta, Poland and Slovakia when they became EU Member States on 1 May 2004.

3.12.3 Partnership and Cooperation Agreements with the Countries of the Former Soviet Union

Analogous disciplines were later applied in the *Partnership and Co-operation Agreements* with the countries of the former Soviet Union which, in some cases, required fully operational national systems of State aid control within a short transitional period.[493] As these countries (for the most part) had and have no aspirations towards EU membership, these requirements were less successful. In fact, only Moldova introduced State aid legislation during the effective period of its PCA, while Ukraine did so just before the signature of the successor agreement – the EU-Ukraine Association Agreement.[494]

3.12.4 Stabilisation and Association Agreements in the Balkans

Consistent with the EU approach to all new economic and trade agreements examined above, the *Stabilisation and Association Agreements* (SAAs) in the Balkan countries included explicit requirements for the *control* of State aids in those countries in line with the EU system and approach.[495]

The content of the Croatian Agreement in regard to State aid exemplifies the approach in the Western Balkans. Specifically, the Croatian SAA provided that any State aid which distorts or threatens to distort competition by favouring certain undertakings or certain products would be incompatible with the proper functioning of the Agreement, in so far as it could affect trade between the European Union and Croatia. Moreover, any aid actually or potentially contravening the Agreement was to be assessed on the basis of criteria arising from the application of the competition rules applicable in the EU, in particular from Articles 106–109 of the TFEU and interpretative instruments adopted by the EU institutions. In addition, Croatia was required to establish an operationally independent authority entrusted with the powers necessary for the full application of the State aid commitments under the Agreement within one year from the date of its entry into force. According to specific SAA terms, this authority was required to have, *inter alia*, the powers to authorise State aid schemes and individual aid grants in conformity with the SAA as well as the powers to order the recovery of State aid that had been unlawfully granted.

The EU/Croatian SAA further provided that Croatia must establish a comprehensive inventory of aid schemes instituted before the establishment of the State aid control authority and subsequently align such aid schemes with the EU rules within a period of no more than four years from the entry into force of the Agreement. Croatia was also required to provide the EU with a regular annual report, or equivalent (following the methodology and the presentation of the EU Survey on State aid)[496] and

493. For example, Article 53 of the Agreement on Partnership and Cooperation establishing a partnership between the European Communities and their Member States, of the one part, and the Russian Federation, of the other part, OJ L 327 of 27 November 1997.

494. This is considered further below.

495. The earliest of these were the Stabilisation and Association Agreement between the European Communities and their Member States, of the one part, and the former Yugoslav Republic of Macedonia, of the other part of 26 March 2001, Article 69; EU/Croatia SAA, Article 70 and Interim Agreement on trade and trade-related matters between the European Community, of the one part, and the Republic of Croatia, of the other part (October 2001), Article 35; EU/Albania SAA (2006) Article 71 and EU/Montenegro SAA of March 2007.

496. This was the EU reporting system that preceded the present State Aid Scoreboard.

provide information on particular cases of State aid at the request of the EU. These transparency requirements were reciprocal.

To deal with how to approach economic development (regional aid) in the context of exemptions based on underdevelopment (Article 107(3)(a) and (c) of the TFEU), the SAA declared that Croatia would be regarded, for a period of four years from the entry into force of the Agreement, as an area identical to those areas of the EU described in Article 107(3)(a) of the TFEU. In other words, Croatia was to be regarded as an "A" region for four years. In the same context, it was provided that, within three years from the entry into force of the Agreement, Croatia should submit to the European Commission its GDP per capita figures harmonised at NUTS II level. The Croatian State aid control authority and the European Commission were then to jointly evaluate the eligibility of the regions of Croatia as well as the maximum aid intensities for each region to create a regional aid map on the basis of the relevant Community guidelines.

Agriculture and fisheries products were excluded from the scope of these commitments and separate Protocols to the Agreement dealt with specific restructuring issues in the shipbuilding and steel sectors.

As regards the enforcement of these rules, the EU/Croatia SAA provided that:

> If one of the Parties considers that a particular practice is incompatible with the terms of paragraph 1 of this Article, it may take appropriate measures after consultation within the Stabilisation and Association Council or after thirty working days following referral for such consultation...Nothing in this Article shall prejudice or affect in any way the taking, by either Party, of antidumping or countervailing measures in accordance with the relevant Articles of GATT 1994 and WTO Agreement on Subsidies and Countervailing Measures or related internal legislation.

The (earlier) EU/Macedonian SAA contained similar provisions[497] requiring compliance within a period of five years from the entry into force of the Agreement. However, it is notable that the Macedonian Agreement did not require an independent State aid controlling authority to be established nor did it provide for regional State aid mapping in Macedonia. Under the more recent SAA with Albania, Albania was also required to establish an operationally independent State Aid and a comprehensive inventory of aid schemes instituted before the establishment of the authority within four years from the date of entry into force of the SAA. It was also required to align such aid schemes with the EU State aid rules in the same period.[498] Albania was given "A" Region status for a period of 10 years and the mapping exercise was to apply after 5 years.

As regards the implementation of these provisions in the Western Balkans, the Macedonian Law on State Aid was enacted in March 2003 but, this was heavily

497. Stabilisation and Association Agreement between the European Communities and their Member States, of the one part, and the former Yugoslav Republic of Macedonia, of the other part of 26 March 2001, Article 69.

498. While there is an apparent contradiction in the application of the four-year time limits to the establishment of the authority, the pre-control inventory and, more particularly, the alignment of existing aid schemes, it was undoubtedly driven by the establishment of State aid legislation and a supervisory function (at the Ministry for Economy in Albania) since 2005.

criticised in the European Commission's *Analytical Report for the Opinion on the application from the Macedonia for EU membership* (November 2005).[499] The range of EU concerns included disquiet about the implementation of notification requirements, the extent of coverage of secondary law and the administration and capacity of the Macedonian State Aid Commission.[500] In Croatia, a (third) State Aid Act came into force in 2005. Under the new State Aid Act, legislative proposals involving State aid had to be submitted to the Croatian Competition Agency for its prior opinion, before being sent to the Government or the Parliament. This opinion was binding on the Government, but could be overturned by the Parliament. Even with this very strict regime in place, the European Commission was highly critical of the extent of the country's achievements[501] in its 2005 Progress Report on Croatia, noting that there were serious issues to be resolved vis-à-vis the SAA.[502]

By 2012, significant progress had been made in Croatia which became an EU Member State on 1 July 2013. Just before accession, the Commission was able to point out that "A proper system of ... state aid control is in place." Moreover, the recovery of

499. European Commission: Analytical Report for the Opinion on the application from the Former Yugoslav Republic of Macedonia for EU membership (COM (2005) 562 final) of 9 November 2005.

500. The same Report also notes key EU concerns regarding (1) the amount of work needed to ensure that the country's industrial policies were made compatible with the State aid rules; (2) the low level of awareness among government institutions and the general public, including the business sector, of the notification process and of the functioning of the State aid control system in general; (3) the widespread and systematic non-payment of social security contributions and taxes by many industrial companies created State aid issues and resulted in unfair competition and (4) the absence of transparency in the form of a comprehensive inventory and reporting mechanism for all State aid measures in force. On this basis, a revised Accession Partnership Decision was adopted by the EU Council on 30 January 2006 requiring Macedonia, in the short term, to establish a credible enforcement record, ensure the independence of the State Aid Commission, provide it with adequate staff and premises, establish a comprehensive inventory and reporting of all aid measures in force, further align State aid legislation with the EU State aid rules and raise awareness among government institutions and the business sector.

501. European Commission: *Croatia 2005 Progress Report,* (COM (2005) 561 final) of 9 November 2005. This Report indicated various problems regarding State aid issues in specific sectors: (a) the fiscal aid regime, especially the Profit Tax Act, Investment Promotion Act and Free Zones Act needed to be aligned with State aid rules, (b) Croatia had not yet submitted a proposal for a regional aid map, (c) viable restructuring plans in the shipbuilding sector had not been adopted in order to comply with the State aid rules, (d) Croatia had not fulfilled its obligation under the SAA to establish a restructuring programme for its steel industry by March 2004 at the latest, and (e) the need for a full review of legislation and of other sector-specific aid, including aid to the textile industry and for tourism.

502. In its *Accession Partnership Decision of 20 February 2006 with Croatia,* the EU Council set various short-term priorities in the field of State aid including requirements for Croatia to: (a) ensure further alignment of primary and secondary legislation so as to allow effective State aid control with binding decisions for both aid schemes and individual aid measures; (b) strengthen the achievement, administrative capacity and the independence of the Competition Agency (especially by ensuring respect for notification obligations and a proactive assessment of all aid measures); (c) ensure that existing aid schemes and all fiscal legislation were aligned with the EU State aid rules; (d) establish a comprehensive inventory and reporting of all aid measures in force at all administrative levels, and (e) adopt and implement viable restructuring programmes in the steel and shipbuilding sectors, in line with EU requirements.

State aid from a major steel mill remained an issue and the detailed restructuring and privatisation of the shipbuilding sector was proceeding and being continuously monitored.[503]

3.12.5 The EUROMED Agreements

EU-Southern Mediterranean trade relations at bilateral level are managed mainly through the Euro-Mediterranean Association Agreements which the EU entered into with all countries in the region except Libya and Syria[504] between 1995 and 2002. The eventual aim of this process is to establish a free trade area across the region between the EU and the "Euromed" countries.

Under these agreements, the EU has sought to apply its State aid regime in the Euromed countries, and in a manner which broadly built upon the experience of the SAAs with the Balkan countries – but with somewhat different rules. Accordingly, the Agreements with Jordan,[505] Egypt,[506] Morocco,[507] Tunisia[508] and the Palestinian Authority,[509] for example, have the following State aid provisions:

- Any public aid which distorts or threatens to distort competition by favouring certain undertakings or the production of certain goods is declared incompatible with the proper functioning of the Agreement, in so far as they may affect trade between the parties.
- Any practice contrary to the general rule on public aid is to be assessed on the basis of the criteria resulting from the application of the TFEU rules on State aid, including secondary legislation.
- The Association Council is mandated to adopt by decision the necessary rules for the implementation the public aid provisions of the Agreement. In the interim, the WTO SCMA rules apply.
- For the purposes of applying the rules on public aid, the EU partner country is to be considered an Article 107(3)(a) region.

503. European Commission: *Communication from the Commission to the European Parliament and the Council - Monitoring report on Croatia's accession preparations*, 24 April 2012.
504. In effect, Algeria, Egypt, Israel, Jordan, Lebanon, Morocco, Palestinian Authority and Tunisia – *see* http://ec.europa.eu/trade/policy/countries-and-regions/regions/euro-mediterranean-partnership/index_en.htm.
505. Euro-Mediterranean Agreement establishing an Association between the European Communities and their Member States, of the one part, and the Hashemite Kingdom of Jordan, of the other part, OJ L 129 of 15 May 2002.
506. Euro-Mediterranean Agreement establishing an association between the European Communities and their Member States, of the one part, and the Arab Republic of Egypt, of the other part, OJ L 345 of 31 December 2003.
507. Euro-Mediterranean Agreement establishing an association between the European Communities and their Member States, of the one part, and the Kingdom of Morocco, of the other part,, OJ L 70 of 18 March 2000.
508. Euro-Mediterranean Agreement establishing an association between the European Communities and their Member States, of the one part, and the Republic of Tunisia, of the other part, OJ L 97 of 30 March 1998.
509. EU-Palestinian Authority of the West Bank and the Gaza Strip Interim Association Agreement, OJ L 187 of 16 July 1997.

- Each Party is to ensure transparency in the area of public aid, *inter alia*, by reporting annually to the other Party on the total amount and the distribution of the aid given and by providing, upon request, information on aid schemes. Upon request by one Party, the other Party is to provide information on particular individual cases of public aid.

Morocco negotiated special interim arrangements for the restructuring of its steel sector (within five years plus a possible negotiated extension)[510] and the Egyptian Agreement contains safeguard provisions where the implementing rules are either non-existent or considered inadequate by the EU.[511]

3.12.6 The Energy Community Treaty[512] and CEFTA[513]

The EU agenda on extending the requirements of the State aid regime has also been embedded in two multilateral treaties since 2005 – the Energy Community Treaty (ECT) and the agreement establishing the Central European Free Trade Area (CEFTA).

The Energy Community Treaty was signed in Athens in October 2005 and entered into force in July 2006. The Treaty created the Energy Community as an international organisation dealing with energy policy. The Treaty brings together the European Union, on the one hand, and the countries of South East Europe and the Black Sea region.[514] The key aim of the organisation is to extend the EU internal energy market to South East Europe and beyond on the basis of a legally binding framework. Moreover, the ECT seeks to:

- attract investment in power generation and networks to ensure stable and continuous energy supply that is essential for economic development and social stability;
- create an integrated energy market allowing for cross-border energy trade and integration with the EU market;
- enhance the security of supply;
- improve the environmental situation in relation with energy supply in the region; and
- enhance competition at regional level and exploit economies of scale.

Under the latter heading, the ECT provides as follows in respect of State aid to the energy sector.

510. EU-Morocco Agreement, Article 36(4).
511. EU-Egypt Agreement, Article 34(5).
512. Energy Community Treaty 2005, as amended, accessed at: https://www.energy-community.org/portal/page/portal/ENC_HOME/ENERGY_COMMUNITY/Legal/Treaty.
513. Central European Free Trade Agreement (CEFTA) 2006 (accessed at http://cefta.int/).
514. In addition to the European Union, the contracting parties to the ECT are Albania, Bosnia and Herzegovina, Kosovo, FYROM, Moldova, Montenegro, Serbia and Ukraine.

Table 15 State Aid Provisions – Energy Community Treaty 2005

Article 18
1. The following shall be incompatible with the proper functioning of the Treaty, insofar as they may affect trade of Network Energy between the Contracting Parties:
... (c) any public aid which distorts or threatens to distort competition by favouring certain undertakings or certain energy resources.
2. Any practices contrary to this Article shall be assessed on the basis of criteria arising from the application of the rules of Articles 81, 82 and 87 of the Treaty establishing the European Community (attached in Annex III).
Article 19
With regard to public undertakings and undertakings to which special or exclusive rights have been granted, each Contracting Party shall ensure that as from 6 months following the date of entry force of this Treaty, the principles of the Treaty establishing the European Community, in particular Article 86 (1) and (2) thereof (attached in Annex III), are upheld.[515]

Several points of interest arise here. First, there is no transition period to apply these rules so they apply once the ECT enters into force in a particular country. Second, there are no specific ECT provisions related to the implementation of these provisions in the national laws of the countries concerned. Third, there is compelling evidence from the ECT Secretariat that these rules are generally not working in the non-EU countries which are party to the ECT.[516]

The main purposes of the CEFTA Agreement are to:

- expand trade in goods and services and foster investment by means of fair, stable and predictable rules;
- eliminate barriers to trade between the Parties;
- provide appropriate protection of intellectual property rights in accordance with international standards;
- harmonise provisions on modern trade policy issues such as competition rules and State aid.
- provide for clear and effective procedures for dispute settlement; and
- facilitate the gradual establishment of the EU-Western Balkan countries zone of diagonal cumulation of origin, as envisaged in the European Commission's Communication of 27 January 2006.

515. The Articles referred to are now Articles 101, 102, 107 and 106 of the TFEU respectively.
516. At https://www.energy-community.org/portal/page/portal/ENC_HOME/INST_AND_MEETINGS?event_reg.category=E14861.

The Agreement fully conforms to the WTO rules and procedures and EU regulations. According to CEFTA Secretariat:

> Effectively implemented, the Agreement provides an excellent framework for the Parties to prepare for EU accession, thus continuing the tradition of the original CEFTA, whose founding members are now in the EU.[517]

The CEFTA 2006 Agreement resulted from the updating of the earlier 1997 CEFTA accord and the expansion of its membership.[518] In addition to provisions and general terms related to the trade in agricultural and industrial goods, the current CEFTA includes a series of new provisions, including provisions on the regulation of State aid.

Table 16 State Aid Provisions of the CEFTA 2006 Agreement

Article 21 – State Aid

1. Any aid granted by a Party or through State resources in any form whatsoever which distorts or threatens to distort competition by favouring certain goods shall, in so far as it may affect trade between the Party concerned and other Parties to this Agreement, be incompatible with the proper functioning of this Agreement.
2. The provisions of paragraph 1 shall not apply to products referred to in Chapter III.
3. The Parties undertake to apply their respective laws with a view to ensure the application of the principles referred to in paragraph 1.
4. Any practice contrary to this Article shall be assessed on the basis of the principles of the state aid rules applicable in the European Community, in particular from Article 87 of the Treaty establishing the European Community.
5. If a Party considers that a particular practice is incompatible with the terms of paragraph 1 and causes or threatens to cause serious prejudice to the interest of that Party or material injury to its domestic industry, it may take appropriate measures under the conditions of and in accordance with the provisions laid down in Article 24.
6. Nothing in this Article shall prejudice or affect in any way the taking by any Party of countervailing measures in accordance with the relevant Articles of GATT and the WTO Agreement on Subsidies and Countervailing Measures or related internal legislation.
7. Each Party shall ensure transparency in the area of state aid, inter alia by reporting annually to the Joint Committee on the total amount and the distribution of the aid given and by providing to the other Parties, upon request, information on aid schemes and on particular individual cases of state aid.

Thus, under the CEFTA provisions, any aid granted by a party or through State resources, in any form whatsoever, which distorts or threatens to distort competition by favouring certain goods shall be incompatible with the proper functioning of the Agreement in so far as it may affect trade between the party concerned and other parties to the Agreement.

Agricultural products are excluded from this provision, and the CEFTA parties undertake to apply their respective laws with a view to ensuring the application of

517. At http://cefta.int/.
518. The present CEFTA membership comprises Albania, Bosnia and Herzegovina, FYROM, Kosovo, Moldova, Montenegro and Serbia.

these principles. Moreover, echoing the approach in Stabilisation and Association Agreements in the Balkan region, any practice contrary to Article 21 is to be assessed on the basis of the principles of the State aid rules applicable in the EU, in particular from Article 107 of the TFEU.

The CEFTA State aid rules in Article 21 are given additional force by the Joint Declaration annexed to the Agreement requiring, *inter alia*, that the CEFTA countries each establish an operationally independent authority in charge of the application of the competition and State aid rules[519] by 2010.

3.12.7 The Evolving Model – From National Monitoring to Control

Based on these trends and developments, it is clear that a fully functioning State aid supervision system has been progressively required by the EU in its third country trade agreements – and with close supervision of implementation where those agreements are linked to the possibility of future EU membership. While the nature, intensity and phasing of State aid supervision systems in so-called third countries has varied considerably in response to national situations, engagement in certain multilateral agreements and stages in EU Integration, the structure and content of the systems now being required essentially consist of the following elements.

Table 17 State Aid Supervision System Requirements on Non-EU Countries[520]

(1) A State Aid Inventory.
(2) Legislation to create the basis for monitoring changes in the inventory and reporting it annually to the EU (and the WTO).
(3) A functioning monitoring mechanism co-ordinated at national level.
(4) Annual State aid international (possibly also national) reporting.
(5) Eventual national regulatory controls (in the legislation) to provide for:

- approval, non-approval or conditional approval of new State aids or substantial changes to existing aids;
- a process of review and alignment of existing State aid;
- a state aid mapping process to match maximum investment and job creation State aid to real and relative economic disadvantage; and
- a right of recovery of illegal State aid.

519. In the light of the different approaches in different EU agreements, it is interesting that this provision seems to require a single authority to regulate State aids and that, based on a very strict interpretation, this may have to be the same authority as the one regulating competition. In over 40 countries where EU State aid rules currently apply, few give the predominant role to a national competition authority even though this might be a highly desired result, and the obvious choice, from the standpoint of the European Commission.
520. E. Stuart & D. Vuletić: *"Introduction to the Regulation of State Aid under the Law of the European Communities – A Handbook for Bosnia and Herzegovina,"* Sarajevo, 2006, p. 103.

Clearly, this is much more than was originally required or expected under the Europe Agreements, and the SAAs provided a particular opportunity for the EU to refine and develop its requirements in respect of national State aid systems.

In its new generation of Association Agreements with Ukraine, Moldova and Georgia, the requirements have been developed in further detail and include various additional elements (notably compliance with relevant judgments from the European Courts). In the context of earlier comments here concerning the PCA requirements, it is notable that the new Association Agreements do not offer the prospect of EU membership that was a missing incentive in the PCAs and a serious driver of progress in the Europe Agreements, the SAAs and the CEFTA accord.

3.12.8 The Ukrainian, Georgian and Moldovan Association Agreement Requirements

In 2014, the EU concluded a new type of Association Agreement with Georgia, Ukraine and Moldova establishing a "Deep and Comprehensive Free Trade Area" with each of these countries. State aid disciplines were at the centre of the trade provisions of these agreements. While these generally reflect a growing sophistication in the requirements of such rules, there are differences. The Ukrainian Agreement is the most advanced and this is probably due, primarily, to its relatively greater size and significance as a trade partner with the EU.

In the 2014 EU-Georgia Agreement,[521] State aid related provisions are very limited. State monopolies are required to be subject to competition laws,[522] and each party to the Agreement is required to ensure transparency in the area of subsidies via a report every two years to the other Party (electronically or otherwise) on the legal basis, the form, the amount or the budget and, where possible, the recipient of any subsidy granted in relation to the production of goods. At the request of either side, the other party is required to promptly provide information and respond to questions pertaining to particular subsidies relating to the supply of services. Otherwise, the WTO SCMA rules apply.[523]

State aid provisions of the 2014 EU-Ukraine Association Agreement are set out in Articles 262–267 of the Agreement.[524] These are the most detailed State aid provisions to date of any EU trade agreement with a non-EU country. Under these provisions, and reflecting the thrust of Article 107(1) of the TFEU:

> any aid granted by Ukraine or the Member States of the European Union through State resources which distorts or threatens to distort competition by favouring

521. Association Agreement between the European Union and the European Atomic Energy Community and their Member States, of the one part, and Georgia, of the other part, OJ L 261 of 30 August 2014.
522. EU-Georgia Agreement, Article 205.
523. EU-Georgia Agreement, Articles 206–208.
524. Association Agreement between the European Union and its Member States, of the one part, and Ukraine, of the other part, OJ L 161 of 29 May 2014.

> certain undertakings or the production of certain goods is incompatible with the proper functioning of this Agreement insofar as it may affect trade between the Parties.[525]

Equally, and to reflect the de jure exemptions of Article 107(2) of the TFEU, the Agreement provides that the following shall be compatible with the proper functioning of the Agreement:[526]

> (a) aid having a social character, granted to individual consumers, provided that such aid is granted without discrimination related to the origin of the products concerned;
> (b) aid to make good the damage caused by natural disasters or exceptional occurrences.[527]

As a reflection of the EU approach to discretionary exemptions (Article 107(3) of the TFEU), the Agreement provides that the following *may* be considered compatible with the Agreement:

> (a) aid to promote the economic development of areas where the standard of living is abnormally low or where there is serious underemployment;
> (b) aid to promote the execution of an important project in the common European interest or to remedy a serious disturbance in the economy of one of the Member States of the European Union or Ukraine;
> (c) aid to facilitate the development of certain economic activities or of certain economic areas where such aid does not adversely affect trading conditions contrary to the interests of the Parties;
> (d) aid to promote culture and heritage conservation where such aid does not adversely affect trading conditions contrary to the interests of the Parties;
> (e) aid to achieve objectives allowed under the EU horizontal block exemption regulations and horizontal and sectoral state aid rules granted in line with the conditions set out therein;
> (f) aid for investment to comply with the mandatory standards of the EU directives listed in Annex XXIX to Chapter 6 (Environment) of Title V of this Agreement, within the implementation period provided for therein, and involving adaptation of plant and equipment to meet the new requirements, can be authorised up to the level of 40 % gross of the eligible costs.[528]

525. EU-Ukraine Association Agreement, Article 262(1).
526. The absence here of any reference to the German clause in Article 107(2) of the TFEU suggests, *inter alia*, that Ukraine could complain under the Agreement if the EU were to use of that clause in the future.
527. EU-Ukraine Association Agreement, Article 262(2).
528. EU-Ukraine Association Agreement, Article 262(3). Here it can be noted that aid to promote the execution of an important project in the common European interest appears to be a one-sided basis for exemption but that circumstances could indeed arise where Ukraine decided to exempt an aid measure on the basis of its contribution or linkage to an important project of common EU interest. Second, paragraph (f) goes beyond the provisions of Article 107(3) of the TFEU but does reflect, at least in part, the TFEU requirements to take environmental factors into account in the application of other EU policies, including that of competition.

Finally, and reflecting Article 106 of the TFEU, the Agreement requires that:

> Undertakings entrusted with the operation of services of general economic interest or having the character of a revenue-producing monopoly shall be subject to the rules contained in [Article 262], in so far as the application of such rules does not obstruct the performance, in law or in fact, of the particular tasks assigned to them. The development of trade must not be affected to such an extent as would be contrary to the interests of the Parties.[529]

The Agreement contains a range of requirements in regard to the transparency of State aid which must be implemented in full within five years of the entry into force of the Agreement and, in particular:

- Each Party to the Agreement is required to ensure transparency in the area of State aid and specifically to notify annually to the other Party the total amount, types and the sectoral distribution of State aid, including information concerning the objective, form, the amount or budget, the granting authority and, where possible, the recipient of the aid.
- Any aid below the threshold of €200,000 per undertaking over a period of three years does not need to be notified.[530]

Moreover, the Parties are required to ensure that the financial relations between public authorities and public undertakings are transparent, so that public funds made available directly or indirectly (e.g., through the intermediary of public undertakings or financial institutions) by public authorities to public undertakings are published together with information on the use to which these public funds are actually put. In addition, there are obligations for undertakings enjoying any special or exclusive rights or providing services of general economic interest to have separate accounts and to follow EU rules on cost-revenue allocation.[531]

Establishing the basis for the future discussion of problematic State aids, the Agreement provides that, if requested by a Party, the other Party shall provide further information on any State aid scheme and particular individual cases of State aid affecting trade between the Parties and that the Parties shall exchange this information taking into account the limitations imposed by the requirements of professional and business secrecy.[532]

Article 267(1) of the Agreement sets out the important requirements for the establishment and functioning of the Ukrainian national system of State aid control. In particular, Ukraine is required to:

529. EU-Ukraine Association Agreement, Article 262(4).
530. EU-Ukraine Association Agreement, Article 263(1).
531. EU-Ukraine Association Agreement, Article 263(3). This in effect requires the transposition of the Transparency Directive (Commission Directive: 2006/111/EC of 16 November 2006 transparency of financial relations between Member States and public undertakings as well as on financial transparency within certain undertakings (Codified version), OJ L 318 of 17 November 2006) into Ukrainian law.
532. EU-Ukraine Association Agreement, Article 263(2).

- Implement national State aid legislation and establish an operationally independent authority which is entrusted with the powers of this Agreement (within three years of the entry into force of the Agreement).[533]
- Ensure that any new aid granted in Ukraine must be consistent with the provisions of Articles 262 and 264 of the Agreement within one year of the date of establishment of the authority.
- Establish a comprehensive inventory of aid schemes instituted before the establishment of the authority within five years of the entry into force of the Agreement.
- Align aid schemes with the criteria referred to in Articles 262 and 264 within a period of no more than seven years from the entry into force of the Agreement.

For the purposes of applying State aid discretionary exemptions linked to Article 107(3) of the TFEU (as reflected in Article 262(2) of the Agreement), it is provided that Ukraine shall be regarded as an area identical to those areas of the European Union described in Article 107(3)(a) of the TFEU (NUTS II regions with a GDP per capita in purchasing power standards (PPS) that is equal to or less than 75% of the EU-28 average).[534] This "A region" status will apply for the first five years after the entry into force of the Agreement. Before its possible expiry (within four years after the entry into force of the Agreement), Ukraine is required to submit to the European Commission its gross domestic product per capita figures harmonised at NUTS II level. Thereafter, the Ukrainian State aid regulator and the Commission will jointly evaluate:

> the eligibility of the regions of Ukraine as well as the maximum aid intensities in relation thereto in order to draw up the regional aid map on the basis of the relevant EU guidelines.[535]

On this latter point, it can be noted here that a *preliminary State aid mapping* exercise carried out in 2014[536] revealed (on the basis of data from 2012) that Ukraine's national GDP per capita was 11.3% of the EU average and that the range of regional GDP per capita across the country vis-à-vis the EU average ranged between 5.2% (in the Chernivtsi Oblast) and 31% (in Kyiv). Accordingly, it appears that the likelihood of Ukraine (or any part of it) reaching the critical point of 45% of EU average GDP where differentiated mapping begins to be a consideration (or 75% of the EU average where "A region" status would come into question), under the current Regional Aid Guidelines within the next five years is somewhat remote.

More generally, the Agreement requires both the EU and Ukraine to interpret and apply the State aid requirements of the Agreement using the criteria arising from the

533. This authority is required, *inter alia*, to have the powers to authorise State aid schemes and individual aid grants in conformity with the criteria referred to in Articles 262 and 264 of the Agreement and the powers to order the recovery of State aid that has been unlawfully granted.
534. EU-Ukraine Association Agreement, Article 267(3)(a).
535. EU-Ukraine Association Agreement, Article 267(3)(b).
536. Dr E. Stuart, S. Cemnolonskis & I. Roginska: "*Report on State Aid Mapping for Ukraine*," November 2014, accessible at http://www.eupublicprocurement.org.ua.

application of Articles 106, 107 and 93 of the TFEU, including the relevant jurisprudence of the Court of Justice of the European Union and relevant secondary legislation, frameworks, guidelines and other administrative acts in force in the European Union.[537] This is a far-reaching requirement that goes much further than most of the earlier generation EU trade agreements and effectively means that all EU legislation, soft law measures, interpretative guidelines from the European Commission and case law[538] must be fully applied in the Ukrainian State aid system to be established under the terms of the Agreement.

The State aid provisions of the Agreement are also without prejudice to the rights of the EU and Ukraine to impose trade remedies or pursue dispute settlement in accordance with relevant WTO rules (e.g., under the WTO Subsidies and Countervailing Measures Agreement).[539] Moreover, it is clarified that agricultural production subsidies are not within the scope of the rules on State aid to be applied under the Agreement.[540]

The EU-Moldova Association Agreement[541] of 2014 contains essentially similar State aid requirements although Moldova achieved an eight year transition for the alignment of existing aid schemes, with a possible extended period in respect of Moldovan Free Economic Zones. In addition, the EU-Moldova Agreement does not contain the same degree of detailed provisions on the national system (e.g., on *de minimis*, on regional status and on the application of exemptions) as set out in the EU-Ukraine Agreement.

3.12.9 What about CETA, TTIP and BREXIT?

In the recently concluded Comprehensive Economic and Trade Agreement (CETA) between the EU and Canada,[542] the parties essentially reaffirm the application of the WTO SCMA while carving out subsidies or government support with respect to audiovisual services for the European Union and to cultural industries for Canada.[543]

In respect to the negotiations of the EU-USA Trans-Atlantic Trade and Investment Partnership (TTIP) Agreement, a similar reluctance to push State aid issues beyond the bounds of SCMA provisions is evident. However, in 2016, there were at least some indications that this remained an open issue in the dialogue moving towards this

537. EU-Ukraine Association Agreement, Article 264.
538. On the wording of Article 264 it is arguable that any new judgments of the General Court of the European Union need not be followed by Ukraine unless further reflected in a Commission instrument or confirmed (e.g. on appeal) by the superior Court of Justice of the European Union.
539. EU-Ukraine Association Agreement, Article 265.
540. EU-Ukraine Association Agreement, Article 266.
541. Association Agreement between the European Union and the European Atomic Energy Community and their Member States, of the one part, and the Republic of Moldova, of the other part, OJ L 260 of 30 August 2014, Articles 339–344.
542. European Commission: Proposal for a Council Decision on the provisional application of the Comprehensive Economic and Trade Agreement between Canada of the one part, and the European Union and its Member States, of the other part, COM/2016/0470 final of 5 July 2016.
543. *Ibid.*, Article 7.7.

Agreement[544] and the latest EU proposals include provisions safeguarding the right of the EU to operate its State aid regulatory system.[545] By 2017, however, following the inception of a new administration in the USA, the future fate of TTIP remains very much in doubt.

The result of the United Kingdom's Brexit Referendum in June 2016 and the commencement of Article 50 of the TFEU withdrawal process almost exactly on the sixtieth anniversary of the Treaty of Rome pose a range of unique legal and policy questions – both for the UK and for the EU. In regard to State aid regulation, the British issues will revolve around how much and what type of State aid/subsidy controls it will wish to apply if and when the Brexit process is concluded. From the EU side, the core issue will be what demands in regard to State aid regulation the EU will wish to impose in a post-Brexit trade agreement with the UK.

The British opening position in the Brexit negotiations is very clearly based on two points:[546]

- "taking back a control of (...) our own laws," including bringing an end to the jurisdiction of the CJEU; and
- establishing the "freest possible" free trade with the European Union – thus substituting "single market membership" with "single market access."

Moreover, the Brexit White Paper, published in February 2017, goes into considerable detail as to how the UK will seek to achieve a Strategic Partnership (and not an Association Agreement) with the EU, and within that, a "bold, ambitious and comprehensive Free Trade Agreement." However, what the UK wishes to achieve or to do in regard to EU competition policy is completely unclear. Apart from noting that "...a common competition and consumer protection framework deals with mergers, monopolies and anti-competition activity and unfair trading within the EU on a consistent basis..."[547] no further enlightenment is offered.[548]

While the UK has traditionally been a strong supporter of a robust control on State aid by the European Commission and has for many years been among the lowest State aid donors in the EU[549] (based in large measure on Thatcherite philosophy and economic policy), the development of an effective and attractive UK industrial and

544. *See* E. Stuart & I. Roginska, "*State aid regulation and Ukrainian Industrial Policy*" (March 2016), 15 European State Aid Law Quarterly, Issue 1.
545. European Commission: "Guide to the Draft text on Investment Protection and Investment Court System in the Transatlantic Trade and Investment Partnership (TTIP)," accessible at: http://trade.ec.europa.eu/doclib/press/index.cfm?id = 1365.
546. Speech of Prime Minister Teresa May of 17 January 2017, accessible at: http://www.independent.co.uk/news/uk/home-news/full-text-theresa-may-brexit-speech-global-britain-eu-european-union-latest-a7531361.html.
547. "*The United Kingdom's exit from and new partnership with the European Union,*" UK White Paper, Cm. 9417, 2 February 2017.
548. For a fuller discussion of the UK White Paper, *see* M. Emerson, "*After the UK's Brexit White Paper – What's the next move towards a CFTA?*" (February 2017), CEPS Policy Insights, Issue 2017/07.
549. European Commission: State Aid Scoreboard, 2016 available at: http://ec.europa.eu/competition/state_aid/scoreboard/index_en.html. This notes that total EU State aid was some €98 billion while UK State aid was €9 billion.

taxation policy post-Brexit may put pressure on the UK to move in the opposite direction, even under the stewardship of a conservative Government.

As State aid law is entirely based on the TFEU, the United Kingdom has no domestic implementing system, apart from a coordination and advisory service split between the State Aid Team of the Department of Business, Innovation and Skills (BIS) in London and the State Aid Unit of the Scottish Government Business Directorate in Edinburgh. Accordingly, assuming a "hard BREXIT," as soon as the United Kingdom ceases to be a party to the TFEU, State aid law will vanish in the United Kingdom – with the only remaining issues being transitional ones, such as the extent to which State aid granted before withdrawal is liable to be challenged after withdrawal.

In the context of a likely post-Brexit trade agreement with the EU, the EU has already flagged its State aid concerns in the following terms:

> Any free trade agreement should be balanced, ambitious and wide-ranging. It cannot, however, amount to participation in the Single Market or parts thereof, as this would undermine its integrity and proper functioning. It must ensure a level playing field in terms of competition and state aid, and must encompass safeguards against unfair competitive advantages through, inter alia, fiscal, social and environmental dumping.[550]

From this, it can be reasonably speculated that Association Agreement type provisions on State aid regulation will be pushed for by the EU side and that the terms of the EU-Ukraine Association Agreement (discussed earlier) provide the best indication of what is likely to be sought in a post-Brexit trade agreement with the UK This will not be easy for the UK to accept as the Association Agreement model in respect of State aid requires the application of continuously evolving EU rules (as expressed in Commission guidelines, etc.) together with the application of CJEU judgments on the concept of State aid and in individual landmark cases concerning the implementation of State aid law. These latter points are clearly at variance with the overall Brexit philosophy of taking back control of laws and excluding the jurisdiction of the CJEU. In addition, the reference to "safeguards against unfair competitive advantages through, inter alia, fiscal, social and environmental dumping" in the EU negotiating guidelines may also indicate a broader concern about the emergence of new State aid measures in future UK industrial and taxation policy.

There is no doubt, of course, that the UK can set up a State aid regulatory body and liaise with the EU on State aid issues – as indeed many non-EU countries have done.[551] But a tough EU negotiation on State aid is to be anticipated primarily to avoid any scenario in which the UK might develop aggressive economic policies to bolster its

550. European Council: Draft Negotiating Guidelines adopted by the European Council on 31 March 2017, point 19, accessible at: http://news.bbc.co.uk/2/shared/bsp/hi/pdfs/31_03_17_eu_draft_guidelines.pdf.

551. For a discussion on some key issues in doing so, *see* P. Nicolaides: "*State Aid on the Day after the Exit of the UK from the EU*," 4 February 2017, accessible at: http://www.stateaidhub.eu/blogs/stateaiduncovered/post/8330.

post-Brexit competitive position. More generally, the outcome of this negotiation is important both for the Brexit process and for the future direction of EU State aid law and policy.

3.12.10 The New Eurasian Economic Union

Inspired by a proposal by the President of Kazakhstan in 1994, the Eurasian Economic Union (EEU) was established between the Russian Federation, Belarus and Kazakhstan on 1 January 2015 following the entry into force of the Eurasian Economic Union Treaty.[552] One day later, Kyrgyzstan became a full member and Armenia acceded to the EEU in August 2015. This Treaty established a Single Market covering a total population of nearly 200 million people, enshrining principles of free movement of goods, capital, services and people, providing for common macroeconomic policies and common approaches to policies in regard to transport, industry and agriculture, energy, foreign trade, investment, customs, technical regulation, public procurement, intellectual property, anti-trust regulation and the supervision of industrial subsidies. Common institutions include institutions similar to those of the EU – the Supreme Eurasian Economic Council (Heads of State), the Eurasian Inter-governmental Council (Prime Ministers), the executive Eurasian Economic Commission and the Court of the EEU. The EEU also envisages further integration in the future and, although not included in the founding Treaty, the adoption of a common currency (the Altyn) is apparently planned for 2025.

An interesting feature of the EEU generally is the extent to which it is inspired by a blend of EU and WTO rules and methodologies. The EEU Treaty has dedicated rules on industrial subsidies (with a focus on banning specific subsidies causing material injury to another EEU member together with export subsidies) which broadly mirror the WTO subsidies rules and which came into force on 1 January 2017.[553]

Table 18 Treaty on the Eurasian Economic Union – Article 93 Industrial Subsidies

(1) In order to enable stable and efficient development of the economies of the Member States and to create a proper environment for the promotion of mutual trade and fair competition between the Member States, common rules for granting subsidies for industrial goods shall be applied on the territories of the Member States, including for the provision or receipt of services that are directly related to the manufacture, sale and consumption of industrial goods, according to Annex 28 to this Treaty.
(2) Obligations of the Member States arising from the provisions of this Article and Annex 28 to this Treaty shall not apply to legal relations between the Member States and third countries.

552. Treaty on the Eurasian Economic Union, accessible at: http://www.un.org/en/ga/sixth/70/docs/treaty_on_eeu.pdf.
553. EEU Treaty, Article 105.

(3) For the purposes of this Article, a subsidy shall refer to:

(a) financial contribution provided by a subsidising authority of a Member State (or an authorised institution of a Member State), used for generating (ensuring) benefits and carried out through: direct transfer of funds (for example, in the form of impaired and other loans), acquisition of a share in the authorised capital or an increase thereof, or an obligation to transfer such funds (e.g., loan guarantees); full or partial waiver of the collection of payments that would have been otherwise included in the income of the Member State (e.g., tax exemptions, debt relief). In this case, the exemption of exported industrial goods from duties and taxes levied on like products when intended for domestic consumption or any reduction of duties and taxes and refund of such duties and taxes in an amount not exceeding the amount actually accrued, shall not be considered as a subsidy; provision of goods or services (except for industrial goods or services intended for the maintenance and development of the common infrastructure); purchase of industrial goods;

(b) any other form of income or price support (directly or indirectly) reducing the importation of industrial goods from the territory of any Member State or increasing the exportation of industrial goods into the territory of any Member State with resulting advantages.

The types of subsidies are specified in Annex 28 to this Treaty.

(4) The subsidising authority may designate or instruct any other organisation to perform one or more of its functions related to the provision of subsidies. Actions of such an organisation shall be regarded as actions of the subsidising authority.

Acts of the head of a Member State aimed at providing subsidies shall be regarded as actions of the subsidising authority.

(5) Any investigation aimed at analysing the conformity of subsidies granted on the territory of a Member State to the provisions of this Article and Annex 28 to this Treaty shall be conducted in accordance with the procedure described in Annex 28 to this Treaty.

(6) The Commission shall ensure the control of the implementation of the provisions of this Article and Annex 28 to this Treaty and shall have the following powers:

(1) to monitor and conduct comparative legal analysis of the legislation of the Member States for compliance with the provisions of this Treaty in respect of subsidies, as well as to prepare annual reports on compliance of the Member States with the provisions of this Article and Annex 28 to this Treaty;

(2) to facilitate the organisation of consultations between the Member States on the harmonisation and unification of their legislation on the provision of subsidies;

(3) to adopt binding decisions for the Member States provided for by Annex 28 to this Treaty on the basis of voluntary coordination of planned and provided specific subsidies, including: adoption of decisions on the admissibility or inadmissibility of specific subsidies in accordance with paragraph 6 of Annex 28 to this Treaty on the basis of the criteria outlined in the international agreement within the Union stipulated in paragraph 7 of Annex 28 to this Treaty; holding a hearing on provision of specific subsidies and adoption of related binding decisions in cases determined by the international agreement within the Union stipulated in paragraph 7 of Annex 28 to this Treaty; resolution of disputes on matters relating to implementation of the provisions of this Article and Annex 28 to this Treaty and provision of explanations on their application;

> (4) to request and obtain information on subsidies granted in the procedure and on the terms determined under an international treaty within the Union stipulated in paragraph 7 of Annex 28 to this Treaty. Sub-paragraphs 3 and 4 of this paragraph shall be applied with account of the transitional provisions of paragraph 1 of Article 105 of this Treaty.
>
> (7) All disputes concerning the provisions of this Article and Annex 28 to this Treaty shall be primarily settled through negotiations and consultations. If a dispute may not be settled through negotiations and consultations within 60 calendar days from the date of a formal written request for holding thereof sent by the Member State that initiated the dispute to the respondent state, the claimant state shall be entitled to apply to the Court of the Union. If the decisions of the Court of the Union are not enforced within a determined period or if the Court of the Union decides that the measures notified by the respondent state are inconsistent with the provisions of this Article and Annex 28 to this Treaty, the claimant state shall be entitled to take proportionate response measures.
>
> (8) The period within which the Member States shall be entitled to challenge a specific subsidy provided in violation of Annex 28 to this Treaty shall amount to 5 years from the date of such specific subsidy.

However, in its detailed Annex 28, the Treaty also very much reflects the use of the market economy investor principle in identifying specific subsidies together with various pre-2012 EU rules identifying permissible subsidies in regard to regional development, R&D support and subsidies to facilitate measures of environmental protection. The Eurasian Economic Commission may approve a specific subsidy notified by an EEU member and this may not be subsequently challenged. In a provision that seems to reflect a contrary position to the EU approach (as reflected, in particular, in the Azores and Gibraltar cases),[554] the detailed rules on the specificity of subsidies include the following:

> Introduction or modification by a state authority of a Member State of tax rates in force within the entire territory of its operation shall not be regarded as a specific subsidy.[555]

Under the EEU Treaty, specific subsidies must be prohibited if they lead to a serious infringement of the interests of another EEU member e.g. by:

> 1) a displacement of like products from the market of the subsidising Member State or a restraint on the increase in the importation of like products originating from the territory of another Member State into the market of the subsidising Member State;
> 2) a significant underpricing of industrial goods manufactured, transported or exported from the territory of the subsidising Member State using a specific subsidy as compared to the price of like products originating from the territory of another Member State on the same market of any of the Member States or a significant regulation of price increases, price reductions or lost sales in the same market.[556]

554. Considered in Chapter 4.
555. EEU Treaty, Annex 28, para. 4.
556. EEU Treaty, Annex 28, para. 12.

Moreover, there is a detailed complaints and investigation procedure (which must be completed within six months) and a rigorous reporting mechanism to the Eurasian Economic Commission.[557] While the Treaty envisages harmonious resolution of subsidy disputes between EEU countries, if this is not achieved, the Court of the EEU may permit responsive measures for a period of up to five years to correct for the trade damage calculated by the Commission's investigation.

Clearly, it is too soon to consider how these rules will be applied or will further evolve. Nonetheless, it is interesting that the EEU has taken subsidy regulation on board; evidently recognising both its value in the EU and indeed the shortcomings of the WTO multilateral system in enforcing trade disciplines concerning subsidies.

3.12.11 The New State Aid Dialogue with China

In response to long-standing international concerns and more recent internal concern that the Chinese government intervenes excessively in markets and private economic activities, the China State Council established a Fair Competition Review System (FCRS) in 2016. The FCRS is intended to reduce business regulation by the administrative authorities and minimise the extent of government interference in China's economy.

In June 2016, the Opinions of the State Council on Establishing a Fair Competition Review System came into force and note that the FCRS should, *inter alia*, seek to prevent new policies and measures that exclude competition and gradually revise and ultimately abolish existing provisions that impede fair competition. The Fair Competition Review commenced in July 2016 under the aegis of four authorities – the National Development and Reform Commission, the Legislative Affairs Office of the State Council, the Ministry of Commerce and the State Administration for Industry and Commerce – which are to provide guidance on the work of the Fair Competition Review. Apart from the Legislative Affairs Office of the State Council, these authorities are also responsible for the enforcement of the Chinese Anti-Monopoly Law in conjunction with the Anti-Monopoly Committee of the State Council. In general terms, the FCRS mechanism requires every policy-making authority in China to gradually review and improve existing regulations and practices that hinder fair competition.

While this has been hailed as a major reform in China,[558] others are more cautious:

> Although the issuance of the Opinions is a welcome development, many concerns about their implementation remain. For instance, what implementing rules will the Four Authorities institute? How can relatively inexperienced and traditionally bureaucratic policy-making authorities conduct self-review and provide an objective evaluation of the self-review results? How will the Four Authorities coordinate with each other and provide effective guidance when they face such a broad a

557. EEU Treaty, Annex 28.
558. W. Jinglian, "*A Key Step to Establish the Fundamental Status of Competition Policies*" (22 June 2016), Chinese Government Network, accessible at: http://finance.sina.com.cn/roll/2016-06-22/doc-ifxtfsae6008165.shtml.

> range of policy-making authority? How can the public be involved effectively in the supervision work, including whether the exceptions to the FCRS are being abused? And what actions/punishment measures will attach to violations of the Opinions? Nonetheless, there is no doubt that the Chinese government has taken an important step forward, and questions about how far and how fast it will go will be answered in due course.[559]

China is the world's third largest economy and the EU's second trading partner. The EU is China's biggest trading partner.

In a very quick response to the creation of the FCRS, the EU (DG Competition) established a *State Aid Dialogue* with the Chinese National Development and Reform Commission in June 2017 by means of a Memorandum of Understanding.[560] Under this arrangement, which is to operate for five years, a forum of consultation and transparency between the EU and China has been set up to explore and consider matters of State aid control and the FCRS, to strengthen cooperation and coordination in this area and to increase mutual understanding and awareness of current and forthcoming trends and expected developments. The Memorandum makes clear that the Dialogue is without prejudice to the rights of the EU and China to address similar issues before the WTO and it notes, in particular, that:

> State aid control is an important factor in ensuring consumer welfare and in providing a level playing field as well as legal certainty for the business community in the market... [and that] this dialogue at technical level shall also contribute to smooth and sustainable trade relations between China and the EU.[561]

Among the matters to be explored via the Dialogue are:

- developments in State aid control and experience in the enforcement of this legislation;
- the enhancement of the operation of the State aid control authorities;
- multilateral State aid control initiatives;
- State aid control advocacy including in regard to raising the awareness of authorities, companies and the wider public of State aid control;
- a coordinated approach to technical cooperation between the EU and China in the area of State aid control.[562]

559. S. Zhang, "*China's Fair Competition Review System: China Takes Another Significant Step Eight Years After Enacting the Anti-Monopoly Law*" (1 July 2016), Anti-Trust Watch, accessible at: http://blogs.orrick.com/antitrust/2016/07/01/chinas-fair-competition-review-system-china-takes-another-significant-step-eight-years-after-enacting-the-anti-monopoly-law.
560. Memorandum of Understanding on a dialogue in the area of the State aid control regime and the Fair Competition Review System between on one side the Directorate-General for Competition of the European Commission and on the other side the National Development and Reform Commission of The People's Republic of China, 2 June 2017, accessible at: http://ec.europa.eu/competition/international/bilateral/mou_china_2017.pdf.
561. *Ibid.*, Article 1.1.
562. *Ibid.*, Article 3.1.

According to the European Commission,[563] the Dialogue will be used to share with China the European experience in enforcing State aid control, it will further the EU and Chinese mutual interest and joint work to promote fair global competition, and it is part of the Commission's broader strategy to address the distortion that national subsidies policies put on the promotion of a global level playing field where companies can compete on their merits. Operationally, the Dialogue will be supported by bilateral working groups at technical level and will formally take place at least once a year, alternating between Brussels and Beijing.

The detailed development of the EU State aid regulatory system via European Commission policy initiatives and decisional practice in parallel with the case law of the European Courts is considered in the next Chapter.

563. European Commission: Press Release "*State aid: Commission and China start dialogue on State aid control,*" 2 June 2017.

CHAPTER 4

Milestones and Landmark Cases in the Development of State Aid Law and Policy from 1957 to 2017

4.1 INTRODUCTION

In this Chapter the development of State aid law and policy is reviewed in separate phases over the last 60 years. In looking at each phase, several aspects need to be considered. These include the decisional and enforcement practice of the European Commission, the political and economic context of State aid policy in the relevant era, changes of orientation by the Commission in regard to the application of the State aid rules and landmark judgments of the European Courts. In the case of the latter, the focus is on those judgments and decisions which have contributed to the understanding and clarification or the further elaboration of EU State aid law and policy in the 60 year period from 1957 until 2017.

The development of State aid law and policy was managed by eleven Commissioners for Competition (Table 19 *infra*) although it was perhaps only the last five Commissioners who began to see the State aid area as pivotal to achieving broader aims within the EU internal market.

Table 19 EU Competition Commissioners 1957–2017

Commissioner	*Nationality*	*Period*
Hans von der Groeben	German	1958–1967
Maan Sassen	Netherlands	1967–1971
Albert Borchette	Luxembourg	1971–1976
Raymond Voeul	Luxembourg	1976–1981
Frans Andriessen	Netherlands	1981–1985

Commissioner	*Nationality*	*Period*
Peter Sutherland	Ireland	1985–1989
Leon Brittan	United Kingdom	1989–1993
Karel Van Miert	Belgium	1993–1999
Mario Monti	Italy	1999–2004
Neelie Kroes	Netherlands	2004–2010
Joaquin Almunia	Spain	2010–2014
Margrethe Vestager	Denmark	2014 to date

In overall terms, the 60 years of EU State aid policy can be divided into four phases, each of which was quite different in terms of the intensity of developments, their specific direction and the relative influence of different stakeholders, actors and factors. Thus, the four distinct phases considered here are:

(1) From the 1950s to the 1970s – *the era of slow progress and the pursuit of policy in a time of crisis.*
(2) The 1980s – *the Commission tightens the rules in a recession period.*
(3) The 1990s – *rule-making and new issues in a time of change.*
(4) From 2000 until the beginning of 2017 – *the millennium era and State aid reform.*

4.2 PHASE 1 – 1950s–1970s (SLOW PROGRESS AND THE PURSUIT OF POLICY IN A TIME OF CRISIS)

The period from the 1950s to the end of the 1970s saw the European Commission adopt a generally low profile in regard to State aid cases. This was brought about by several factors. First, until the 1970s, the Commission´s focus was on the elimination of barriers to trade and discrimination between undertakings in different Member States. In addition, the nine Member States[564] were also not willing to cooperate with the Commission and, therefore, State aid enforcement was of very limited effect. In fact, the Commission essentially started to act against the opposition of Member States in this field only as the deadline for the completion of the customs union (1968) approached.[565] At the same time, the Commission was willing throughout this early period to generally accept the granting of national aid with one limitation: discrimination against foreign producers.

Indeed, the case law of the early years shows that the Commission was primarily concerned with aids that subsidised exports to other Member States; and, if the aid measures were benefitting only, or mostly, domestic consumption, they would not be

564. On 1 January 1973 the six become nine when Denmark, Ireland and the United Kingdom formally acceded to the EU.
565. J.J. Piernas López: "*Understanding the Notion of State Aid through Policy*," European University Institute, Dubrovnik, April 2012, p. 8.

considered as aids under what is now Article 107(1) of the TFEU – because they were considered not to affect competition and/or trade at Community level.[566]

In one of its earliest significant cases, the Commission rejected the granting of an exemption for investment aid which did not facilitate the development of certain economic activities or of certain economic areas.[567] In its Ford Tractor decision in 1964, an interest allowance granted by the Belgian Government on a loan to Ford Tractor (Belgium) Ltd in order to aid the firm in the assembly of tractors and the manufacture of gear boxes and axles was held incompatible with the common market. The Decision points out:

> On the Common Market in agricultural tractors, the production capacity is not smaller than the demand. Certain undertakings which already exist within the Community have reached a high degree of technical development. In these circumstances, the grant of aid intended to favour the creation of a new unit of production could not be justified as an increase in the or a stimulus to the competition, so as to make the sector in question healthy. The support given to the creation at Antwerp of manufacture of axles and gear boxes for tractors and assembly of these vehicles could not be based on the economic situation of the Antwerp region which is prosperous by comparison with that of numerous other regions of the Community. The aid can only contribute to aggravating the already difficult situation in the Community production of tractors.
> Thus, even if the aid contributes to facilitating the development of the production of agricultural tractors - and so of the Antwerp region - nevertheless the application of the provisions of [now Article 107(3)(c)] is not only inexpedient, because the aid is not in the common interest, but is also excluded because it alters the conditions of trade by a measure which is contrary to the common interest.[568]

This position was developed further by the Commission setting the criteria for the facilitation of development in the *First Report on Competition Policy* in 1970. In that Report, the Commission said that to avail of exemption, sectoral and regional aids must be: (1) *Selective* (they must only be granted to undertakings whose development or reorganisation justifies the assumption that they will be competitive in the long run having regard to anticipated developments in the industrial sector concerned[569]); (2) *Degressive* (the aid must eventually be phased out, leaving the undertakings to manage without further assistance; the aid must not, therefore, allow a situation of less than optimum allocation of resources to continue indefinitely -unless at the

566. Case C-40/75: *Produits Bertrand v. Commission*, [1976] ECR 1; Case C-52/76: *Benedetti v. Munari*, [1977] ECR. Also: European Commission: Fifth Report on Competition Policy, 1975, points 126–129 on "*Sale of hard wheat at reduced prices to pasta manufacturers; Italy.*"
567. TFEU, Article 107(3)(c).
568. European Commission: Decision No 64/651/EEC: *Re Subsidies to Ford Tractor (Belgium) Ltd.*, OJ P 195 of 28 November 1964. The only other negative decision before 1970 was Decision No 69/266/CEE: *Recherche et rénovation des structures industrielles et commerciales dans le secteur textile*, 18 July 1969, OJ L 10 of 13 January 1972.
569. *See*, for example, Case C-142/87: *Belgium v. Commission (Tubemeuse)*, [1990] ECR I-959 where the Commission rejected the applicability of what is now Article 107(3)(c) of the TFEU to the development of a region where the aided undertaking was not in a position to ensure its own viability.

Community level it is decided to continue them in order to compensate for distortions of competition outside the Community); (3) *Transparent* (it must be possible for the Community institutions and other interested parties to evaluate the aid); and (4) *Well adapted to the intended objective* (the instrument used having the least effect on intra-Community competition and the common interest).[570,571] This general framework for the assessment of compatible State aid has stood the test of time to the present day – despite many further elaborations (and sometimes complex redefinitions) of its essential rationale.

From 1957 until the first Enlargement of the EEC in the early 1970s there were very few cases taken up in regard to the State aids of the original six Member States. Indeed, from 1957 to 1973, the Commission only took five negative decisions.[572] However, the first Enlargement, which saw the entry of the United Kingdom, Denmark and Ireland into the EEC, reopened concerns about State subsidies. The existing Member States were concerned that subsidies would be used to undermine the effects of the dismantling of tariffs (ostensibly for the purposes of industrial restructuring). For their part, the new countries (Ireland, UK and Denmark) feared that their economic development efforts would be curtailed by a strict application of the State aid rules or by new State aids emerging in the existing Member States. Indeed, it has been noted that, until 1974, the system of control envisaged by the Treaty had failed to make any major impact on the levels and practices of government supports to industry across the EU.[573]

Detailed Commission reporting on State aid matters only began in 1970. Between 1970 and 1980, the Commission took 710 State aid decisions (with a significant growth in the mid-1970s – *see* Table 20 *infra*). Of these, 73% gave rise to no concern and the balance involved an investigative procedure. However, only 21 negative decisions (3%) were taken. This pattern, especially as regards limited negative decisions was to continue for several decades.

570. European Commission: *First Report on Competition Policy* (1972) at point 130.
571. These principles resonate to the present day – *see* the examination of State aid reforms in Chapter 5.
572. *See* http://ec.europa.eu/competition/state_aid/register/state_aid_negative_decisions_1969-1994_en.pdf. The five negative decisions concerned Ford Tractor Belgium (1964), Commission Decision of 18 July 1969 on the French systems of aid for research and the reorganisation of production and distribution in the textile industry (OJ L 220 of 1 September 1969), Commission Decision No 72/34/CEE of 15 December 1971 on the abolition of Belgian aid to undertakings in difficulty (OJ L 10 of 13 January 1972) Commission Decision No 72/248/CEE of 22 June 1972 on granting aid for the growing of lucerne in Belgium (OJ L 156 of 12 July 1972)and Commission Decision No 72/262/CEE of 28 June 1972 concerning aid granted by Italy under Law No 471 of 14 July 1969 for imports of scientific instruments and advanced technological equipment (OJ L 166 of 24 July 1972).
573. K. Middlemas: "*Orchestrating Europe – The Informal Politics of European Union 1973-1995*," Fontana, London, 1995, p. 57.

Table 20 Positions Taken by the European Commission Concerning State Aids from 1970 to 1980[574]

Year	*Total*	*Of Which*		*Formal Negative Decisions Published in the OJ*
		No Objections Raised	*Procedures Undertaken*[575]	
1970	21	15	6	1
1971	18	11	7	3
1972	35	24	11	3
1973	22	15	7	4
1974	35	20	15	–
1975	45	29	16	2
1976	47	33	14	2
1977	112	99	13	1
1978	137	118	19	–
1979	133	79	54	3
1980	105	72	33	2

The 1970s brought two international oil crises which were to profoundly impact on the economies of the EU Member States. In that regard, the Commission noted that:

> Faced with a serious economic recession and resulting employment difficulties, Member States have extended the scope of their general regional aid schemes and taken temporary measures to boost the economy. While the Commission did not object to these schemes, it kept a close watch on how they were applied to ensure that they did not simply preserve obsolete industrial structures or transfer difficulties from one Member State to another.[576]

Some commentators suggest, however, that the Commission believed that the national protectionist measures adopted during the latter part of the oil crisis period would be temporary and, for that reason, refrained from actively intervening.[577] Nonetheless, whether by accident or design, the 1970s saw the first phase of accelerated application of the State aid rules by the European Commission. Moreover, in the 1970s a more rigorous enforcement of State aid policy in the EU was politically reinforced by the Commission view that State aid control could assist governments in dealing with the

574. European Commission: *Tenth Report on Competition Policy*, 1980, p. 112.
575. Here the procedure refers to Article 93(2) of the EEC Treaty *(now Article 108(2) of the TFEU)* or Article 8(3) of the Commission Decision No 2320/81/ECSC of 7 August 1981 establishing Community rules for aids to the Steel industry, OJ 1981 L 228 of 13 August 1981.
576. European Commission: *Fifth Report on Competition Policy*, 1975, point 84.
577. *"Understanding the Notion of State Aid through Policy," supra*, p. 6. and K.A. Lavdas and M.M. Mendrinou: *Politics, subsidies and competition: the new politics of state intervention in the European Union*. Cheltenham, UK, Edward Elgar, 1999, p. 31.

hyper-inflationary effects of the oil crises of that era.[578] At the same time, recourse to the exemption under Article 107(3)(b) – to remedy a serious disturbance in the economy of a Member State – was generally used in the approval of notified measures.

By 1978, the Commission emphasised that the role assigned by the Treaty to the Commission in handling State aid cases was principally one of reaction to the proposals of the Member States:

> The Commission does not consider it advisable to define systematically the types of aid to which it is favourably and unfavourably disposed in the case of each industrial sector. To elaborate such guidelines for aids would risk encouraging a more general recourse to aid by Member States even where it is not strictly necessary. It would, moreover, result in some inflexibility since such frameworks could not take into account the specific situation of the industry concerned in each Member State. However, in cases where it has become evident that an industry faces a situation of particular difficulty throughout the Community, or is likely to face such difficulty, it is appropriate to develop guidelines which indicate the Commission's policy on aids to this industry.[579]

In regard to sectors, sectoral State aid became widespread in the 1970s as national policies continued to battle the impacts of the oil crises and various initiatives of investment aid also grew in response to a new wave of US and Japanese industrial locations into Europe from the late 1970s. In particular, the shipbuilding sector was politically sensitive from the inception of the European Union for reasons linked to international economic competitiveness. From the 1950s onwards, the EU was obliged to grapple separately with declining world demand for ships, excess capacity in EU shipyards, the growing competitive advantages (often supported by aid) of Japanese and US production and the political problems posed for the original Member States which together sought to maintain some 250,000 jobs in the shipbuilding sector. Another critical factor disadvantaging the Community industry was the high levels of social security charges in the EU shipbuilding sector which these yards had no hope of reducing to the levels applying in Japan and the US.[580]

Thus, the original version of what is now Article 107(3) of the TFEU made specific provision for aid to the shipbuilding sector[581] in order to allow flexibility vis-à-vis a sector where State aid was widespread. Its presence in the Treaty facilitated the evolution of separate policy and law on the shipbuilding sector which was planned to eventually result in the virtual total ban on shipbuilding aid both in the EU and in the OECD. This was mostly done by Seven Council Directives between 1969 and 1990. The State aid regime under the Shipbuilding Directives sought to achieve a combination of reduced export aid, an emphasis in aid programmes on restructuring and especially the

578. European Commission: *Fourth Report on Competition Policy*, 1974, p. 85; *Fifth Report on Competition Policy*, 1975, points 3 and 131.

579. European Commission: *Eighth Report on Competition Policy*, 1978, p. 125.

580. European Commission: *"Reorganisation of the Community Shipbuilding Industry,"* Communication from the Commission to the Council of 9 December 1977.

581. The original text provided that *"the aids granted to shipbuilding as of 1 January 1957 shall, in so far as they serve only to compensate for the absence of customs protection, be progressively reduced under the same conditions as apply to the elimination of customs duties, subject to the provisions of this Treaty concerning common commercial policy towards third countries."*

production of high technology vessels and the maintenance of the European industry for strategic reasons as a world market player. Moreover, the complex development of EU rules on shipbuilding aids closely tracked OECD agreements on aid intensities and production capacity at the international level to the point where, by 1978, the OECD rules on export credits in the sector were confirmed as having the full binding effect of EU Law.

While aid to shipbuilding had virtually been eliminated by 1975, the 1977 shipbuilding crisis saw the process permit new maximum ceilings of 30% of contract price which was precisely the problematic starting point at the inception of the Community.[582]

Also in the 1970s, several Member States had taken action to help the motor industry, which was facing serious economic and structural difficulties. The Commission then tried to ensure in its decisions that the schemes helped to bring about improvements in the industry without affecting the terms of trade to an extent contrary to the common interest.[583] Nonetheless, State aid to the motor vehicle industry, essentially in the form of capital injections or extensive debt write-offs, accelerated from 1977 onwards and this was addressed by the first specific sectoral rules almost a decade later.[584]

Moreover, in 1977, in recognition of the low average rate of capacity utilisation for the production of synthetic fibres and yarns (about 70%), the consequent job losses and the risk that further aid would exacerbate the situation and distort competition, the Commission adopted certain measures in order to impose further control on the freedom of Member States to award aid to producers of the fibres and yarns concerned. The measures became known as "The Code on aid to the synthetic fibres industry"; and operated until 1996. Under the Code, the Commission insisted that it would be essential for it to exercise control over all aids granted to the industry and therefore informed the Member States that it expected them to notify it in advance of all proposals to grant aid and that the Commission intended to examine each such proposal with a view to ensuring that aids were used to encourage a reduction in capacity to a level where actual and prospective demand and potential supply are more nearly in balance.

The Commission's continuing tension with Member States in the context of the State aid rules also impacted on the scope of further rule-making and, in particular, the elaboration of procedures. In 1966, the Commission presented a draft Regulation to the Council on the conditions and methods of application of certain provisions of what is now Article 108 of the TFEU.[585] This text focussed on State aid control procedures and proposed an eight week preliminary procedure period, following the expiry of which approval of notified aid could be assumed. It also proposed a definitive list of

582. Council Directive No 78/338/EEC on aid to shipbuilding of 4 April 1978 (Fourth Shipbuilding Directive), OJ L 98/19 of 11 April 1978.
583. European Commission: *Fifth Report on Competition Policy*, 1975.
584. European Commission: *Framework on State Aid to the Motor Vehicle Industry*, OJ C 123 of 18 May 1989.
585. European Commission: COM (66) 95 final of 30 March 1966 communicated to the Council on 18 April 1966 and amended by COM (66) 457 of 10 November 1966 and COM (72) 1523 of 4 December 1972.

exemptions, related to what is now Article 107(2) and (3) of the TFEU, including social aid, cultural aid, certain public services (such as water, gas, electricity and telecommunications). The reduction or abolition of identified existing aids in the agricultural sector was also proposed. Within months, this proposal was amended to change the agricultural aid list. Faced with little likelihood of progress, the Commission formally withdrew the proposal by a decision of 28 February 1975.

A similar fate met a further Commission proposal put forward in the interim in 1970 and designed to introduce a quarterly system of reporting on significant cases of regional aid.[586] This proposal was withdrawn by Commission Decision on 14 December 1976 and no further attempts of this type emerged until 1990.

While the State aid rules remained a limited instrument in the hands of the Commission in this period, this was already changing by the late 1970s. It is clear that (for several reasons including their innovative character, the lack of a procedural regulation concerning their application and the reluctance of Member States' to notify State aids[587]) the first twenty years or so constituted a somewhat quiet era of State aid regulation. At the end of this period, the Commission stated in 1980 that "in some cases, indeed, the extent of the tendency towards non-notification [of aids] would appear to indicate the possible existence of a general decision not to respect the provisions in question."[588]

In any event, the Commission focused on cases strictly related to the creation of the common market, such as export aid or parafiscal levies that were clearly discriminatory against out of State traders, particularly towards the earlier-than-planned achievement of the customs union in 1968, and these were among the first cases on State aid that reached the European Court of Justice.[589] The Court supported the Commission's decisions in these cases, in which it underlined their importance for the creation of the common market, the main goal pursued by the Commission, and the latter's important role and prerogatives under the Treaty.

The Court's view of the State aid provisions of the Treaty, however, was much broader and more teleological (more related to the goal of the creation of the common market) than that of the Commission at the time. It therefore emerged, to paraphrase Judge Pescatore, that the judges of the Court had, from the very beginning, "une certain idée des aides."[590]

586. European Commission: *Proposal for a Council Regulation laying down in accordance with Article 94 EEC the methods of supervision by the Commission of the application in the central regions of the Community of the principles for the coordination of general regional aid schemes*, COM (72) 1523 Final of 4 December 1972.
587. J.J. Piernas López: "*The Concept of State Aid under EU Law: From Internal Market to Competition and Beyond*," Oxford University Press, 2015, p. 16. *See also* European Commission: *Tenth Report on Competition Policy*, 1980, point 162.
588. European Commission: *Tenth Report on Competition Policy*, 1980, point 162.
589. J.J. Piernas López, "*The Evolving Nature of the Notion of Aid under EU Law*" European State Aid Law Quarterly, 3/2016, pp. 400–415.
590. P. Pescatore, "*The Doctrine of "Direct Effect": An Infant Disease of Community Law*" (1983), European Law Review, 155, at 157 where Judge Pescatore affirms that the reasoning of the Court in the Van Gend & Loos case shows that the judges had "une certaine idée de l'Europe," cited in J.J. Piernas López, "*The Evolving Nature of the Notion of Aid under EU Law*" European State Aid Law Quarterly, 3/2016, pp. 400–415.

4.2.1 Main Trends in the Jurisprudence of This Period

4.2.1.1 1961 – Aid Is Wider than Subsidy

The first important judgment from the Court in 1961 determined, in particular, that *"aid" in the ECSC Treaty is a wider concept than "subsidy" (also in the ECSC Treaty).* This was confirmed by the European Court of Justice with reference to Article 4 of the ECSC Treaty which declared "subsidies or aid granted by States, or special charges imposed by States, in any form whatsoever" to the coal and steel sectors to be incompatible with the common market under that Treaty and, therefore, abolished and prohibited.[591] In the *Steenkolenmijnen case (1961),* 10 years after the ECSC Treaty was signed, the European Court of Justice held that:

> A subsidy is normally defined as a payment in cash or in kind made in support of an undertaking other than the payment by the purchaser or consumer of the goods or services which it produces. An aid is a very similar concept, which, however, places emphasis on its purpose and seems especially devised for a particular objective which cannot normally be achieved without outside help. The concept of aid is nevertheless wider than that of a subsidy because it embraces not only positive benefits, such as subsidies themselves, but also interventions which, in various forms, mitigate the charges which are normally included in the budget of an undertaking and which, without therefore being subsidies in the strict meaning of the word, are similar in character and have the same effect [592]

Thus, it emerged that aid includes subsidies but aid, nonetheless, has a wider scope. Accordingly, within the scope of Article 107(1) of the TFEU, State aid can take a variety of forms: subsidies; preferential rates on loans; cash injections to public enterprises; deferrals of tax, social security or other payments; sale or rental of land or property at discounted rates; preferential electricity or natural gas rates; infra-structural projects benefiting identifiable end users; and others. In effect, any intervention by an EU Member State (i.e., by a State body or through the direction of the State), where the intervention benefits a firm or a group of firms by increasing the resources they would normally obtain or by decreasing the firm's costs (including taxes) which they would otherwise incur, qualifies as a State aid irrespective of whether the benefit is conferred in money or in kind.

In the political context in 1961, this approach was coherent with the goal of removing all national support, in any form whatsoever, to the coal and steel industries by means of aid or similar measures based on a full delegation of sovereignty to the ECSC High Authority that Member States had made for the coal and steel sectors. As noted in the judgment:

> A strict wording of the Article 4 itself emphasises the exclusive character of the Community's jurisdiction within the Community...[moreover] Article 4 is designed to enable the jurisdiction of the Community to impinge on national

591. European Coal and Steel Community Treaty (1951), Article 4.
592. Case C-30/59: *Steenkolenmijnen v. High Authority of the European Coal and Steel Community,* [1961] ECR 1, para. 19.

> sovereignty in cases where, because of the power retained by the Member States, this is necessary to prevent the effectiveness of the Treaty from being considerably weakened and its purpose from being seriously compromised.[593]

The ECSC Treaty did not provide for any definition of "subsidy" and the reference to "aid" created confusion. Consequently, it was for the Court of Justice to interpret these concepts. In doing so, the Court decided to interpret these technical terms in accordance with some fundamental principles, (specifically those set out in Articles 2–5 of the ECSC Treaty); taking the view that any article of the Treaty could be interpreted in accordance with the general scheme represented by those four articles. With this crucial decision, already stated in its first judgment,[594] the Court of Justice initiated its interpretation of the Treaty provisions based on fundamental principles of the Treaty.

Moreover, some commentators have suggested that this broad definition of "aid" was also coherent with the lack of limitations or qualifications of Article 4(c) of the ECSC which promoted the recognition of its immediate application by the Court, the forerunner of the notion of direct effect.[595] In particular, it was clear that the notion of subsidy or other forms of aid addressed in the ECSC Treaty did not require any sort of distortion of competition or selectivity criteria, and did not contain any *de minimis* rule. Accordingly, the judgment in the *Steenkolenmijnen case* provides a key insight into the initial position of the Court concerning subsidies in the early days of the European integration process and in the future shaping of the State aid law and policy.

Although the judgment expressly urged the High Authority to adopt the necessary steps towards the cancellation of the forbidden subsidy,[596] the High Authority did not show any immediate intention to act in that respect. One year later, during the summer of 1962, the High Authority adopted formal measures to enforce the judgment. However, these measures were later suspended in order to treat them in the framework of a "mixed committee."[597] In that regard, it has also been suggested that the absolute prohibition of *subsidies or State assistance, or special charges imposed by the State* contained in Article 4(c) proved to be excessive and hence was totally disregarded.[598]

593. Case C-30/59: *De Gezamenlijke Steenkolenmijnen in Limburg v. High Authority of the European Coal and Steel Community*, Judgment of the Court of 23 February 1961, pp. 21 and 24.
594. *See* Case C-1/54: *France v. ECSC High Authority*, ECR 1954–1956 p. 1. *See also* Case C-8/57: *Groupement des hauts fourneaux et aciéries belges v. ECSC High Authority*, ECR 1957–1958 p. 245.
595. For example, *see*: J.J. Piernas López, "*Understanding the Notion of State Aid through Policy*" (April 2012), European University Institute, p. 4.
596. An application made by a Dutch association of undertakings, *De Gezamenlijke Steenkolenmijnen*, in view of the refusal by the High Authority to take action on the complaint that the association had made to the High Authority in 1959.
597. C.D. Ehlermann, "*State Aid Control in the European Union: Success or Failure?*" (1994), 18 Fordham International Law Journal, Issue 4, p. 1216.
598. *Ibid.*, p. 9.

4.2.1.2 1964 – The Supremacy of European Law

Shortly afterwards (in 1964), the European Court of Justice delivered its landmark judgment, applicable to the entirety of European Union law, in *Costa v. ENEL (1964)*.[599] This case established the supremacy of European Union law over the laws of its Member States. In particular, the Court held as follows:

> As opposed to other international treaties, the Treaty instituting the E.E.C. has created its own order which was integrated with the national order of the Member States the moment the Treaty came into force; as such, it is binding upon them. In fact, by creating a Community of unlimited duration, having its own institutions, its own personality and its own capacity in law, apart from having international standing and more particularly, real powers resulting from a limitation of competence or a transfer of powers from the States to the Community, the member-States, albeit within limited spheres, have restricted their sovereign rights and created a body of law applicable both to their nationals and to themselves. The reception, within the laws of each member-State, of provisions having a Community source, and more particularly of the terms and of the spirit of the Treaty, has as a corollary the impossibility, for the member-State, to give preference to a unilateral and subsequent measure against a legal order accepted by them on a basis of reciprocity. [...] It follows from all these observations that the law stemming from the treaty, an independent source of law, could not, because of its special and original nature, be overridden by domestic legal provisions, however framed, without being deprived of its character as community law and without the legal basis of the community itself being called into question.[600]

The State aid rules in the Competition Chapter of the Treaty should also be read in the context of its Preamble which recognises the importance of "the removal of existing obstacles calls for concerted action in order to guarantee steady expansion, balanced trade and fair competition." In 1966, the Court expressly stated that "the elimination of barriers" and "fair competition" were both necessary to bring about a Single Market.[601]

4.2.1.3 1969–1977 – Selectivity, the "Effects Doctrine," Advantage and State Resources

In 1969, with regard to the test of selectivity in determining whether aid is within the scope of what is now Article 107(1) of the TFEU, the Court advanced a very broad notion of selectivity in the *French exports case*[602] and held that any measure not benefitting all undertakings in a given Member State was to be deemed selective. Here the Court followed an internal market rationale by focusing, not on competition concerns, but on trade ones. The Court stated:

599. Case C-6/64: *Flaminio Costa v. E.N.E.L.*, judgment of the Court of 15 July 1964, [1964] ECR 1141.
600. *Ibid.*
601. Case C-32/65: *Italy v. Council*, [1966] ECR 389, 404, [1969] CMLR 39, 60–61.
602. Cases C-6/69 and C-11/69: *Commission v. France*, [1969] ECR from p. 546.

> A preferential rediscount rate for exports, granted by a State in favour only of national products exported and for the purpose of helping them to compete in other Member States with products originating in the latter, constitutes an aid within the meaning of [now Article 107 of the TFEU] the observance of which it is the Commission's task to ensure.[603]

Furthermore, on the purpose of the measure at stake the Court held:

> Neither the fact that the preferential rate in question is applicable to all national products exported and only to them, nor the fact that in establishing it the French government may have resolved to approximate the rate to those, applied in the other Member Countries, can remove from the measure in question the character of aid which is prohibited except in the cases and procedures provided for by the Treaty.[604]

In other words, the measure was aid because its effect and purpose was to distort trade between Member States by favouring domestic exported products over those produced in other Member States. Moreover, in this case the Court for the first time recognised the importance of the effect of a State aid measure which was later confirmed in 1974.

Thus, in the *Italian textiles case (Italy v. Commission, 1974)*,[605] the Court held that the form and purpose of a measure had no bearing on whether or not a measure was State aid and that *State aid was to be identified fundamentally based on its effects (advantage concept).* This important principle has become known as the "effects doctrine." In the case, the Italian Government had argued that a social security reduction for the textile sector should be considered a measure of social policy rather than economic policy and thus not classified as State aid. However, the Court held that:

> [Article 107(1)] of the Treaty does not distinguish between measures of State intervention by reference to their causes or their aims but defines them in relation to their effects.

The measure at issue in the case was a 33 % reduction for the textile sector in statutory contributions to family allowances. Italy argued that the losses to the social security fund were made up by another unemployment fund financed by the private sector and, accordingly, there was a double entry that meant the reduction did not constitute aid under what is now Article 107 of the TFEU. The definition of aid measures by reference to their effects also means that the aim of the State in granting the aid is, in principle, not relevant. Accordingly, it is no defence for a Member State to claim that the measure in question pursues particular types of non-economic policy objectives such as the protection of the environment[606] or social protection. On the other hand, the motivation for the State aid measure generally will become relevant regarding the Commission's assessment as to whether or not the aid can be justified by one of the exceptions in Article 107(2) or (3) of the TFEU.

603. *Ibid.*, para. 20.
604. *Ibid.*, para. 21.
605. Case C-173/73: *Italy v. Commission*, [1974] ECR 709.
606. This was rejected by the Court in Case T-109/01: *Fleuren Compost BV v. Commission*, [2004] ECR II-127, para. 54.

In the Italian textiles case, the Court also favoured State aid enforcement by stating that, to check the existence of an "advantage," a comparison of the company´s financial situation before and after the State intervention was needed – thus rejecting the argument advanced by Italy that the comparison must be carried out at a Community level. Therefore, it was underlined by the Court that:

> in the application of [now Article 107(1) of the TFEU] the point of departure must necessarily be the competitive position existing within the Common Market before the adoption of the measure in issue...The Italian textile industry is in competition with textile undertakings in the other Member States...and the modification of production costs in the Italian textile industry by the reduction of the social charges in question necessarily affects trade between the Member States.[607]

The same case also developed the basic dictum that was to confuse the distinction between State aid and general measures and, at the same time, create the basis for later inroads by the Commission into "unfair taxation" measures in the State aid context. Concerning the substance of an advantage, the Court held that:

> It must be concluded that the partial reduction of social charges pertaining to family allowances devolving upon employers in the textile sector is a measure intended partially to exempt undertakings of a particular industrial sector from the financial charges arising from the normal application of the general social security system, without there being any justification for this exemption on the basis of the nature or general scheme of this system.[608]

Subsequently, the concept of State resources in what is now Article 107(1) of the TFEU was considered in the Court's *Steinike and Weinlig (1977)* judgment.[609] In that case, the Court of Justice held that "aid" covered any aid distributed by public and private bodies, regardless of the status of the body that administered and distributed the aid. Accordingly, it was not necessary to make a distinction according to whether the aid was granted directly by the State or by public or private bodies established or appointed by it to administer the aid.[610] This judgment provided an important clarification of the wide-ranging notion of State resources that has proved of central importance ever since.

4.2.1.4 1973–1980 – Development of Procedures

From a policy and enforcement point of view, the Commission began to receive some clear support from the Court of Justice in procedural cases that started to fill the gap that Member States had created by refusing to adopt a procedural regulation under what is now Article 109 of the TFEU. In particular, the Court clarified in 1973 that Member States were obliged to refrain from implementing any aid until the Commission had had sufficient time to review its compatibility with the Common Market

607. Case C-173/73: *Italy v. Commission,* [1974] ECR 709, paras 17 and 19.
608. *Ibid.*, at para. 15.
609. Case C-78/76: *Steinike & Weinlig v. Germany,* [1977] ECR 595.
610. *Ibid.*, para. 4.

pursuant to a State aid notification.[611] The Court even held, in this period, that the Commission could ask for the repayment of illegally granted aid;[612] something that the Commission would not be able or willing to do until more than a decade later – not least because the economic situation of the companies that would have had to repay the illegal aids was often disastrous.[613]

By 1980, the Court was in a position (in the *Phillip Morris case (1980)*[614]) to decide the general basis for carrying out State aid analysis – whether to use antitrust competition standards (i.e., defining the relevant product and geographic markets) or to apply internal market standards (focussed on the effects of the measure on competition and trade). The Court explicitly ruled in favour of the internal market approach stating that:

> [the circumstances of the case...] justify the Commission's deciding that the proposed aid would be likely to affect trade between Member States and would threaten to distort competition between undertakings established in different Member States.[615]

4.3 PHASE 2 – THE 1980s (THE COMMISSION TIGHTENS THE RULES IN A RECESSION PERIOD)

The development of State aid law and policy during the 1980s saw the Commission starting to use the formal investigation procedure[616] more frequently, having also sent letters to Member States in the early 1980s reminding them of their obligation to notify new aid measures to the Commission.[617] The Commission had found that, in the period 1985–1987, some Member States had granted a relatively large number of aids without notifying them, or had notified them after the award. In the case of France, the percentage of unnotified aids in relation to aids examined by the Commission was 37%, followed by Belgium with 32%, Greece with 28%, Spain with 23% and Italy with 16%.[618] Therefore, in 1989 the Commission again expressed its concern at the growing tendency of Member States to fail to fulfil this obligation by failing to notify aids and "putting it into effect."[619] The Commission therefore explained that:

> By 'putting into effect' it means not the action of granting aid to the recipient but rather the prior action of instituting or implementing the aid at a legislative level according to the constitutional rules of the Member State concerned. Aid is

611. Case C-120/73: *Lorenz*, [1973] ECR 1471.
612. Case C-70/72: *Commission v. Germany*, [1973] ECR 813, at para. 13.
613. "*Understanding the Notion of State Aid through Policy*" *supra*, p. 6.
614. Case C-730/79: *Philip Morris Holland BV v. Commission of the European Communities*, ECR 1980 Page 02671, paras 10–12.
615. *Ibid.*, para. 19.
616. European Commission: *Tenth Report on Competition Policy*, 1980, para. 158.
617. European Commission: letters (SG(77) D/122; SG(80) D/9538; SG(81) 12740; SG(83) D/13342), OJ C 252 of 30 September 1980, p. 2 and OJ C 318 of 24 November 1983, p. 3). *See also* European Commission: *Tenth Report on Competition Policy*, point 158.
618. European Commission: *Nineteenth Report on Competition Policy*, 1990, point 132.
619. Commission letter to Member States SG(89) D/5521 of 27 April 1989.

therefore deemed to have been put into effect as soon as the legislative machinery enabling it to be granted without further formality has been set up.[620]

Even then, as some authors argue, the goal was not so much to prohibit all aids but to achieve "coordination with the aim of ensuring that [aids] would not endanger inter-State trade or export economic difficulties from one Member State to another."[621]

Of major importance in this period was the Commission's new policy ordering the recovery of illegally granted State aid. The first recovery decision was taken in 1982 in regard to loans and loan guarantees to Belgian wallpaper manufacturers.[622] This created a new situation with regard to Member States which did not take the State aid rules seriously and were prepared to flout a negative State aid decision or implement unnotified aid. As the Treaty did not envisage a mechanism such as recovery of illegal aid, this was purely a court inspired reinforcement of State aid control. Only political considerations can explain the Commission's delay in activating this possibility. Indeed from 1973 to 1981, the Commission took 25 negative decisions which should have offered some possibility to do so.[623] Later, in the 1990 Case BUG-Alutechnik, the Court would establish that there was a duty of care on aid recipients to know that the State aid they received was lawful,[624] thereby further reinforcing the recovery concept. And indeed, (from November 1993) under the Maastricht Treaty changes, financial sanctions for failing to implement a court judgment following an infringement procedure would reinforce this development further. At the same time, the Commission in the 1980s was not chasing the recovery of *all* illegal aid but (and justifying this on the basis of its limited resources) focussed its recovery policy on large cases (undefined) in order to maximise overall cost-effectiveness.[625] As then Commissioner Andriessen stated in 1983: "the Commission recently decided gradually to start demanding repayment of aid that has been granted without prior Commission approval."[626]

Another important development in this period was the adoption of the *Transparency Directive*[627] in June 1980. This imposed upon Member States the obligation to supply information to the Commission, at its request, concerning the nature and effect of their financial links with their public undertakings. The Commission was paying

620. Commission letter to Member States SG(89) D/5521 of 27 April 1989, para. 1.
621. J.J. Piernas López: "*The Concept of State Aid under EU Law: From internal market to competition and beyond*," Oxford University Press, 2015, p. 17.
622. European Commission: *Thirteenth Report on Competition Policy*, 1983, point 220 and European Commission: Decision No 82/312/EEC: *Aid to an industrial and commercial group manufacturing wall coverings – Belgium*, 10 March 1982, OJ L 138 of 19 May 1982.
623. At http://ec.europa.eu/competition/state_aid/register/state_aid_negative_decisions_1969-1994_en.pdf.
624. This was clarified by the European Court of Justice in Case C-5/89: *Germany v. Commission (BUG-Alutechnik)*, [1990] I ECR 3453 at 3457.
625. M. Merola: "*The Forces Shaping State Aid Control in the EU*," in "*What shapes the law? Reflections on the history, law, politics and economics of international and European subsidy disciplines*," European University Institute, June 2016.
626. F. Andriessen, "*The Role of Anti-Trust in the Face of Economic Recession: State Aids in the EEC*" (1983), European Competition Law Review, pp. 340–350.
627. European Commission: Directive No 80/723/EEC of 25 June 1980 on the transparency of financial relations between Member States and public undertakings, OJ L 195 of 29 July 1980 pp. 35–37.

careful attention to the danger that Member States might start providing aids indirectly and avoid State aid control in this way. For example, as noted in its 1980 Report, the Commission found in one case that an aid scheme which the Commission had insisted be terminated was being continued through the national employers organisations using funds contributed and collected "voluntarily" from firms through the national insurance system.[628]

Moreover, in 1982 a new principle of EU State aid law was established – *the Market Economy Investor Principle (MEIP)*. The earliest iterations of the MEIP emerged in a Council Directive on aid to shipbuilding[629] and a Commission Decision establishing Community rules on aids to steel industry.[630] The Commission also set out the principle in a 1984 Communication.[631] The essential idea of the MEIP is that State aid does not arise in circumstances where the investment measure is undertaken by the State on similar terms to a private or "market economy" investor. Thus, if the State contributes fresh capital to an undertaking in circumstances that would not be acceptable to a private investor operating under normal market economy conditions, State aid will arise. The MEIP proved highly controversial and it was challenged in the landmark case of *Belgium v. Commission (Meura)*[632] (considered *infra*). Nowadays, this principle has become a "yardstick for the determination of the State aid"[633] and has been further developed and refined via the market creditor principle, the market debtor principle etc.

Nonetheless, critics of this approach continue to the present day – largely focused on its theoretical incoherence and complex practical applications which have sometimes resulted in "inconsistent and unpredictable" decisions. Some even question the justification of the test and have suggested specific alterations or modifications.[634] One particular difficulty when applying the MEIP test concerns the case of capital injections into private or public firms. If the Member State invests in a manner similar to a private investor, expecting a normal return on its investment, then there is no State aid. If the Member State invests where a private investor would not have invested, then there is a State aid. Thus, when private and public investors inject capital simultaneously and in comparable amounts, it is presumed that there is no State aid. However, when only the Member State injects capital, the Commission evaluates whether a private investor would have been likely to invest given the financial and industrial circumstances of the firm. The hypothetical private investor is assumed to seek a normal rate of return given a reasonable delay. However, one of the most difficult situations is where the

628. European Commission: *Tenth Report on Competition Policy*, 1980, point 163.
629. Council Directive No 81/363/EEC on aid to shipbuilding, OJ 1981 L 137 of 25 May 1981.
630. European Commission: Decision No 2320/81/ECSC of 7 August 1981 establishing Community rules for aids to the Steel industry, Second Recital, OJ 1981 L 228.
631. Application of Articles 92 and 93 of the EEC Treaty to public authorities' holdings, Bulletin EC 9- 1984, extracts available at: http://ec.europa.eu/competition/state_aid/legislation/ec1984_en.html.
632. Case C-234/84: *Belgium v. Commission (Meura)*, [1986] ECR I-3671.
633. M. Köhler, "*New Trends Concerning the Application of the Private Investor Test*" (2011), 1 EstAL, 21.
634. Karim, Md. Rezaul: "*The EU Market Economy Investor Principle: A Good Paradigm?*," University of Birmingham – School of Law, 28 April 2014, p. 2.

beneficiary is already in an "aid environment." If an enterprise has already received aid then further provision of capital, which depends for its remuneration on that aid, cannot necessarily rely on the MEIP to lift it out of the definition in Article 107(1).[635]

An important new initiative to revitalise and better inform EU State aid policy started with the establishment in 1985 of a *Task Force on State aid*, which was mandated to review all aid granted in the Community and to help Member States identify aid that posed a risk to the achievements of the single market. During the European summit in Milan in 1985, the White Paper "*Completing the Internal Market*"[636] was presented to the European Council, which contained a detailed programme of hundreds of measures. The internal market programme, also called the 1992 initiative, became the legal basis for the *1986 Single European Act*. In accordance with the White Paper, the Commission underlined the importance of reinforcing the "Community discipline on State aids" and emphasised the link between a strong competition policy and the accomplishment of the internal market. The Community's efforts to complete a single unified internal market by 1992 added more importance to the enforcement of competition rules, particularly the rules on State aid[637] and helped the Commission shape new legislation and screening tools.[638]

In 1988, the *First Survey of State Aids in the European Community*, carried out by the Task Force established in 1985, demonstrated that, on average, aid represented 3% of GDP and 10% of government expenditures in the EU.[639] In the manufacturing sector, for example, State aid was estimated to represent over 6% of value added in 1986. In most Member States, expenditure on aids exceeded the corporate taxes paid by companies.[640] Based on these findings, the Commission decided to review existing aid schemes more systematically. Moreover, based on the Survey, the Commission concluded that, following the forthcoming completion of the Internal Market by 1992, State aid would be one of the few means available to Member States to apply protectionist policies in their intra-Community trade where competition would be far greater.[641] As a result, the Commission announced new policy orientations in 1990. These focussed on:

- The introduction of regular reviews of existing aid schemes (under which most State aids were granted in practice) and with reference to schemes where the economic conditions underlying an earlier Commission approval have since changed.

635. B. Slocock, "*The Market Economy Investor Princ*iple" (June 2002), Competition Policy Newsletter, Issue 2.
636. European Commission: Completing the Internal Market, COM (85) 310, http://europa.eu/documents/comm/white_papers/pdf/com1985_0310_f_en.pdf.
637. For example, *see* European Commission: *Fifteenth Report on Competition Policy*, 1986.
638. M. Merola: "*The Forces Shaping State Aid Control in the EU*," European University Institute publication "What shapes the law? Reflections on the history, law, politics and economics of international and European subsidy disciplines," June 2016.
639. European Commission: *First Survey on State aids in the European Community*, 1989.
640. European Commission archive, available at: http://europa.eu/rapid/press-release_IP-88-355_en.htm.
641. European Commission: *Nineteenth Report on Competition Policy*, 1990, point 119.

- A review of why investment aid had increased significantly without an increase in notifications regarding this type of measures.
- A review of export aids to promote exports to non-EU countries.
- The initiation of an examination of the criteria for a more accurate definition of cases where transfers of State resources (capital contributions, loans, guarantees, dividends, etc.) to firms, constitute aid and the establishment of a methodology to monitor such contributions.
- The preparation of proposals to strengthen the provisions concerning rescue and restructuring aid (often granted before they are notified) to ensure that the aids are notified beforehand and to tighten the rules on exemption.
- The introduction of annual State aid reporting in the interests of transparency.[642]

In regard to sectors, action was taken in the 1980s to address the situation in the motor vehicle industry. Because of its considerable importance in the fields of employment, trade and technological development, the motor vehicle industry was generally regarded as a strategic industry by most Member States. In the period 1970–1980, the Governments of several Member States injected massive amounts of aid into the modernisation and development, or indeed the survival, of their domestic car industry. This action caused a subsidy race among Member States. As a result, the Commission introduced a Community framework for State aid to the motor vehicle industry in 1989[643] with the twofold aim of increasing the transparency of aid flows and imposing stricter discipline in the granting of such aid in order to reduce distortion of competition in the Community industry to a minimum. While the industry in Europe had not experienced surplus production capacity, intra-Community trade in vehicles and engines was extensive and that alone ensured that the industry was a sensitive one.[644] In the period 1977–1987, State aid to the motor vehicle industry, essentially in the form of capital injections or extensive debt write-offs, was estimated at €26 billion. Between 1989, when the framework entered into force, and July 1996, the Commission approved €5.4 billion of aid to the industry. Accordingly, in December 1988, the Commission decided to adopt the Community framework on State aids to the motor vehicle industry which entered into force on 1 January 1989.[645] The framework required, for a two-year period, all vehicle and engine manufacturers to give prior notification of plans to award aid under approved schemes where costs exceeded €12 million. It also required Member States to draw up an annual report on all aid awarded in the sector. In one of the first significant uses of what is now Article 108(1) of the TFEU (review of existing aid and appropriate measures proposed by the Commission), the Commission proposed that the Member States approve the framework. However,

642. European Commission: *Nineteenth Report on Competition Policy*, 1990, points 119–115.
643. European Commission: *Framework on State Aid to the Motor Vehicle Industry*, OJ C 123 of 18 May 1989.
644. European Commission: *Community Framework for State aid to the Motor Vehicle Industry*, OJ C 279 of 15 September 1997 – *see* Preamble.
645. European Commission: Community framework for State aid to the motor vehicle industry, OJ C 123 of 18 May 1989.

Germany and Spain refused to accept these "appropriate measures" and, in July 1989, the Commission responded by initiating a full investigation of all State aid in the Motor sector in both countries.[646]

This development is interesting for several reasons. First, it created a new and forceful instrument to compel Member States to accept Commission policy changes regarding existing aid measures. Second, it reinforced the Commission's ability to establish quasi-binding soft law measures (such as the Framework) at a time when secondary legislation remained problematic due to Member State resistance. This has subsequently allowed the Treaty rules to be supplemented by a wide range of Commission Guidelines, notices and, more recently, Regulations setting out detailed rules for "sensitive" economic sectors, trying to balance the development needs of parts of the EU with the State aid regime (especially in the context of regional policy), setting a *de minimis* threshold below which aid is not a problem, ultimately codifying procedural rules on the notification, approval and recovery of aid[647] developed by the European Courts and providing various degrees of lenient[648] or strict interpretation[649] of the rules for aid of particular types.[650] Third, the German and Spanish objections are of interest. On the one hand Germany argued that the framework pursued undesirable industrial policy objectives and was liable to jeopardize the effectiveness of regional aid. The Commission's view was that, far from pursuing an industrial policy, the framework aimed at improving the influence of economically sound market forces. On the other hand, Spain stated that they would apply the framework provided it formed part of a Community industrial policy which extended to the whole of the sector concerned.[651]

Also, in regard to the Steel industry, the Commission adopted the Steel Aid Code[652] in early 1989 with the agreement of the Council. This updated EU rules for aid to the steel industry; allowing very limited State aid for the steel sector (essentially R&D aid, environmental protection aid and aid for the closure of steel plants, under certain conditions). At the international level, under an agreement concluded between the

646. A similar approach was taken with Sweden in 1997. In the course of that investigation, the Framework rules were accepted by the Swedish authorities – European Commission: *Twenty-Eighth Report on Competition Policy* (1998), p. 227.
647. *See* Council Regulation No 2015/1589/EU of 13 July 2015 laying down detailed rules for the application of Article 108 of the Treaty on the Functioning of the European Union, OJ L 248 of 24 September 2015.
648. For example, the measures covered by the GBER, the *De Minimis* Regulation and the various temporary regulations related to the international financial crisis and the restructuring and recapitalisation of banks.
649. For example, under European Commission: *Guidelines on State aid for rescuing and restructuring non-financial undertakings in difficulty*, OJ C 249 of 31 July 2014.
650. There are currently two remaining specific instruments on this: (1) European Commission: *Communication from the Commission to the Member States on the application of Articles 107 and 108 of the Treaty on the Functioning of the European Union to short-term export-credit insurance*, OJ C 392 of 19 December 2012 and (2) European Commission: *Notice on the application of Articles 87 and 88 of the EC Treaty [now Articles 107 and 108 of the TFEU] to State aid in the form of guarantees*, OJ C 155 of 20 June 2008.
651. European Commission: *Nineteenth Report on Competition Policy*, 1990, point 127.
652. European Commission: Decision No 322/89/ECSC of 1 February, establishing Community rules for aid to the steel industry, OJ L 38 of 10 February 1989.

European Community and the United States, a two and a half year extension to voluntary restraint arrangements (VRA) on exports of European steel to the USA was agreed and both sides reached agreement on a code of good conduct for the award of State aid to the steel industry (based on the steel aids code applied within the Community since 1 January 1986). According to the Commission, this consensus was intended to help create the right conditions for the worldwide liberalisation of the steel trade.

Table 21 gives an overview and a comparison of the Commission actions in the State aid field from 1981 until 1989. The adoption of certain frameworks, a better understanding of the Commission's policy in this area, the effort made by the Commission to improve compliance with Article 108(3) of the Treaty and the accession of Greece, Spain and Portugal in this period all contributed to the relatively large increase in the number of aid notifications.[653]

Table 21 European Commission Activity in the Control of State Aids (Excluding Aids to Agriculture, Fisheries and Transport) in the 1980s

Year	*Number of Proposals Notified*	*Action Taken by the Commission*				*Proposals Notified and Later Withdrawn by Member States*
		Raised No Objections	*Opened the Procedure*[654]	*Closed the Procedure*	*Final Decision Taken*	
1981	92	79	30	19	14	–
1982	200	104	86	30	13	–
1983	174	101	55	18	21	9
1984	162	201	58	34	21	6
1985	133	102	38	31	7	11
1986	124	98	47	26	10	5
1987	326	205	27	32	10	1
1988	375	311	31	32	13	–
1989	296	254	37	27	16	7

Source: European Commission: Nineteenth Report on Competition Policy, 1990.

653. European Commission: *Nineteenth Report on Competition Policy*, 1990, point 132.
654. Here the procedure refers to Article 93(2) of the EEC Treaty *(now Article 108(2) of the TFEU)* or Article 8(3) of Decision No 2320/81/ECSC.

In the period from 1981 to 1985, of 761 notifications, 118 (16%) related to the steel sector and of the 409 cases which resulted in full investigation procedures in this period, 67 were investigations related to the steel sector.

4.3.1 Main Trends in the Jurisprudence of This Period

Throughout the 1980s, the European Courts continued to contribute to State aid law and policy. However, a tendency emerged in the Court's case law towards less activism. During this period, the Court, while continuing to generally support Commission positions, began to require stricter minimum standards and a more solid legal basis in order to uphold measures fostering integration. In the State aid field, this trend was initiated by the *Philip Morris Case (1980)* and became clearer in other cases decided later in the 1980s.

4.3.1.1 1980 – Effect on Trade

The judgment of the Court in the case of *Philip Morris (1980)*[655] clarified the interpretation of the scope of application of the Treaty in regard to State aids and, in particular, to general aid schemes. The depth of the economic recession of the previous decade of the 1970s opened up the possibility of using State aids to assist industries with some degree of viability. This was strengthened by the Court's decision of 17 September 1980 in the *Philip Morris case*, where the Commission considered that the grant of such aids was compatible with the common interest only in so far as the aids contributed, at Community level, to reducing unemployment or stimulating investment or encouraging restructuring operations.[656] In this particular case, the Court found that since the aid under consideration concerned a company heavily engaged in inter-State trade, and the aid would contribute to its productive capacity and thus reinforce its position in international trade, the criteria of what is now Article 107(1) of the TFEU were fulfilled. Moreover, the aid diminished the cost of the concentration in question, thus giving the company a competitive advantage over others which have or had the intention of carrying out similar activities at their own expense. In the *Philip Morris case*,[657] the Court of Justice held that:

> If an aid granted by a State strengthens the position of an undertaking in comparison to other undertakings with which it competes in intra Community trade, the latter can be said to be affected by the aid.[658]

Moreover, after this case it was stated that the Commission might in future look favourably on certain measures planned specifically to combat crises in certain sectors.

655. Case C-730/79: *Philip Morris Holland B.V. v. Commission*, [1980] ECR 2671, [1981] 2 CMLR 321.
656. *Ibid.*
657. Case C-730/79: *Philip Morris Holland B.V. v. Commission*, [1980] ECR 2671, [1981] 2 CMLR 321.
658. *Ibid.*, para. 11.

In addition, the Commission indicated the possibility of sympathetic consideration being given to measures likely to promote policies of common European interest, such as the grant of aids to investments in, for instance, energy conservation or environmental protection where, under certain conditions, State aid could help in implementing positive adjustment policies.[659]

The Commission also considered that the judgment of the Court in *Philip Morris* considerably clarified the position in regard to State aids in general. In particular, this concerned the point that, although the Commission has considerable discretionary power given to it by what is now Article 107(3) of the TFEU, the basic principles of the Treaty clearly provide that State aids are in principle incompatible with the common/internal market. Thus, the idea took root that the discretionary power of the Commission should only be exercised when the aids proposed by Member States contribute to the achievement of the Community objectives and interest set out in Article 107(3) of the TFEU. However, the national interest of a Member State or the benefits, obtained by the recipient of aid in contributing to the national interest, do not by themselves justify the positive exercise of the Commission's discretionary powers.[660]

4.3.1.2 1983–1985 – State Resources and First Annulments of Commission Decisions

In the same period, three cases involved the first annulments of State aid decisions, precisely for faulty motivation or because of an incorrect legal basis. This was the situation with the *Intermills case (1984)*, and with the *Poor farmers' case (1983)*, where the Court rejected the existence of "measures having an effect equivalent to State aid" as the Commission had suggested.[661]

In 1983, the Court of Justice for the first time confirmed, in its decision in the case *Commission v. France (Poor farmers) case,*[662] that the concept of aid could fall not only on the State but also on the public or private intermediaries instituted by the State. In particular, the Court held that:

> aid need not necessarily be financed from State resources to be classified as State aid. [Article 107 of the TFEU] covers all aid granted by a Member State or through State resources and there is no necessity to draw any distinction according to whether the aid is granted directly by the State or by public or private bodies established or appointed by it to administer the aid.[663]

At the same time, in this case the Court rejected the existence of "measures having an effect equivalent to State aid" as the Commission had strongly advocated.

659. European Commission: *Tenth Report on Competition Policy*, 1980, point 161.
660. European Commission: *Tenth Report on Competition Policy*, 1980, point 260.
661. Case C-323/82: *Intermills v. Commission,* [1984] ECR I-3809 and Case C-290/83: *Commission v. France,* [1985] ECR I-439.
662. Case C-290/83: *Commission of the European Communities v. French Republic,* judgment of 30 January 1985, ECLI:EU:C:1985:37.
663. *Ibid.*, para. 14.

On 22 July 1982, the Commission had decided to authorise Belgium to grant aid in the form of a low-interest loan and two repayable advances to the *Intermills* paper firm. It had considered these aids to be compatible with the Treaty as they supported an investment programme which allowed the firm to concentrate on the production of speciality papers, without affecting trading conditions to an extent contrary to the common interest. However, the Commission had declared incompatible a third aid in the form of a capital injection to Intermills by the Wallonia Regional Executive, since the firm's severe financial difficulties would have made it difficult or impossible to raise this money on the capital markets. The Commission had considered that, regardless of the form of this measure, it constituted a rescue aid which could have a very adverse effect on competitive conditions. *Intermills* appealed against the Commission's Decision.[664]

The Court held that the Treaty applies to aid granted by a State or through State resources "in any form whatsoever." Thus, it followed that no distinction could be drawn between aid granted in the form of loans and aid granted in the form of a holding acquired in the capital of an undertaking. Aid taking either form falls within the prohibition laid down in Article 107 of the TFEU where the conditions set out in that provision are fulfilled. Moreover, the granting of aid, especially in the form of capital holdings acquired by the State or by public authorities, cannot be regarded as being automatically contrary to the provisions of the Treaty. Thus, in Intermills, the Court held that, irrespective of the form in which aid is granted, it is the Commission's task to examine whether it is contrary to Article 107(1) and, if so, to assess whether there is any possibility of its being exempt under Article 107(3) while also giving the grounds on which its decision is based.[665]

In this judgment, the Court recognised clearly that the provisions of capital to companies could be the equivalent of State aid[666] (unless, of course, provided on the terms acceptable to a normal private investor). This reflects the statement that there should be no discrimination as to the form of State aid. Aid is not only constituted by grants or advances, but also by loans on more favourable terms than are available on the market, guarantees, tax concessions, relief of social security contributions, and by the State putting up new capital for enterprises in circumstances in or on terms on which a private investor would not do so.[667] Second, it strengthened the content of Commission decisions by requiring specific reasoning rather than per se judgments. Third, the judgment gave the Commission more confidence, and from that time onwards the Commission started using Article 108(2) of the TFEU (which provides that the Commission must take a decision in relation to aid granted "after giving notice to the parties concerned to submit their comments") more frequently. The "parties concerned" are not only the undertaking(s) receiving aid but equally the persons, undertakings or associations whose interests might be affected by the grant of aid.

664. *See* European Commission: *Fourteenth Report on Competition Policy*, 1984.
665. Case C-323/82: *Intermills v. Commission*, [1984] ECR I-3809, paras 1–3.
666. European Commission: *Fourteenth Report on Competition Policy*, 1984, point 198.
667. *Ibid.*, point 201.

4.3.1.3 1986 – Court Endorsement of the Market Investor Principle

Concerning the criterion of "advantage" in determining State aid, the Court endorsed the Market Economy Investor Principle (MEIP) in 1986 in the *Belgium v. Commission (Meura)* case.[668] This arose from a Commission decision of April 1984[669] ordering Belgium to withdraw the aid it had provided to Meura, a firm manufacturing mainly brewery equipment, in the form of subscriptions of new equity by the Wallonian Regional Investment Corporation. The Commission had decided that the capital subscriptions amounted to rescue aid, which was ineligible for an exemption under what is now Article 107(3)(c) of the TFEU. The Court agreed with the arguments of the Commission in the decision and rejected the submission of the Belgian Government, holding that:

> To ascertain whether such a measure is in the nature of State aid, it is right to apply the criterion set out in the Commission's decision (and not contested by the Belgian Government), based on the company's ability to raise finance on the private capital markets. **In the case of a company almost all of whose shares are held by State bodies the major question is whether a private shareholder would in similar circumstances, in the light of the company's prospects of future profitability, have invested the capital without regard to social, regional or industrial policy considerations**"[emphasis added].[670]

The Court also accepted the Commission's evidence that the difficulties of the company were of more than a passing kind and that a restructuring would not have made it profitable again. In Meura's case, the company had been heavily lossmaking for several years and, to keep it afloat, the Belgian authorities had had to inject new funds to recapitalise it on several previous occasions also. Furthermore, the company was in an industry suffering from overcapacity.[671] In addition, in the *Meura* case, the Court departed from the traditional case law on the importance of the effects of the measure as opposed to its aims (initiated in the *Italy v. Commission case*[672]) as the aim of the measure had to be taken into account to properly distinguish between State aids and grants to public undertakings by the State in its capacity as a private operator.[673] However, in upholding the MEIP test, the Court also sent a message to the Commission that the use of the State aid rules to maintain competition in the marketplace would have to be coupled with a minimum showing of the situation in that market place – something that the Court had not required only five years before in the Philip Morris decision.[674]

668. Case C-234/84: *Belgium v. Commission (Meura)*, [1986] ECR I-3671.
669. European Commission: *Fourteenth Report on Competition Policy*, 1985, point 252.
670. Case C-234/84: *Belgium v. Commission (Meura)*, [1986] ECR I-3671, point 13 and European Commission: *Sixteenth Report on Competition Policy*, 1987.
671. European Commission: *Sixteenth Report on Competition Policy*, 1987, para. 313.
672. Case C-173/73: *Italy v. Commission*, [1974] ECR 709.
673. Opinion of AG Lenz in Case C-234/84: *Belgium v. Commission (Meura)*, [1986] ECR p. 2271.
674. J.J. Piernas López: "*Understanding the Notion of State Aid through Policy*," European University Institute, Dubrovnik, April 2012, p. 16.

Thus, by the end of the 1980s, the following elements of the State aid system had been clarified by the Court:

- If an aid granted by a State strengthens the position of an undertaking in comparison to other undertakings with which it competes in intra-Community trade, the latter can be said to be affected by the aid (*Phillip Morris case, 1980*).
- The concept of aid could fall not only on the State but also on the public or private intermediaries instituted by the State (*Poor farmers case, 1983*).
- Provision of capital to companies could be the equivalent of State aid (*Intermills case, 1984*).
- When a public authority invests in an enterprise on terms and in conditions which would be acceptable to a private investor operating under normal market economy conditions, the investment is not a State aid (*Meura case, 1986*).

4.4 PHASE 3 – THE 1990s (RULE-MAKING AND NEW ISSUES IN A TIME OF CHANGE)

The 1990s marked a dramatic phase of legal and policy development in regard to the EU State aid regulatory system. As many Member States pulled out of the recession of the 1980s, stricter State aid control was seen as a vehicle for preparing for eventual European Monetary Union. Consistent with the envisaged need to coordinate economic and fiscal policies in the context of monetary union, the drive against State aid in the form of tax measures started in the mid-1990s. In parallel, the Commission fought to decrease its workload via *de minimis* initiatives and a focus on favouring horizontal over sectoral measures. Meanwhile, the GATT Uruguay Round adopted a landmark agreement on subsidies (of key concern to the EU State aid regulators) and a new situation in Europe was emerging from the collapse of the Soviet Union with former USSR countries turning to the EU for liberalised trade relations and EU membership. Moreover, the scope of EU State aid control was further expanded by several Court decisions, the Commission got its first taste of the complexities of State aid in banking cases and State aid reform was considered for the first time.

A major milestone in the 1990s was the adoption of State aid procedural rules in the form of a Council Regulation i.e. with Member State consent. Given the continuing adversarial relations between the Commission and the Member States and the failure of earlier legislative initiatives, this outcome was by no means certain. The road to a procedural regulation began when the Council of Industry Ministers examined a proposal in 1990 to invite the Commission to propose a draft Regulation under what is now Article 109 of the TFEU to comprehensively define the scope and criteria of application of Articles 107 and 108. This was known as the "Battaglia initiative." However, Council agreement on the initiative foundered on the point of whether the Council was competent to ask the Commission to make an Article 109 proposal, rather than await a Commission initiative. This, of course, suggests in turn that there was little Commission enthusiasm and the matter concluded with Sir Leon Brittan agreeing that the Commission would henceforth present to the Council of Industry Ministers the draft annual Report on Competition Policy, that a multilateral consultative group on State aids would be established and meet twice yearly and that the Commission would publish a compendium of the rules in force regarding State aid control.[675]

Signalling growing concerns with the State aid system and a readiness to work with the Commission, the Council of Industry Ministers, in November 1995, identified transparency, legal certainty and the effectiveness of the system as key areas of common concern.[676] By 1996, the Irish Presidency tabled general proposals to reform the State aid system following the first State aid recovery order addressed to Ireland.[677] Ultimately, these proposals paved the way for a codification of State aid procedures via the Procedural Regulation of 1999[678] (including a 10-year moratorium on the recovery of illegal aid)[679] and the Enabling Regulation of 1998[680] which allowed the Commission to substantially develop mainstream regulations for the State aid system (even though soft law measures were destined to continue in several spheres).

Throughout the 1990s, efforts by the Commission to establish a *de minimis* rule in the State aid system reflected the overall experience of approving some 98% of notified measures, a growing caseload and the desire of the Commission to concentrate on major cases. Until relatively recently, however, the European Courts rejected any idea that State aid could be too small to actually or potentially affect competition and trade, although there were occasional references to the need for the economic advantage from the measure to be appreciable.[681] The general view of the European Courts was reflected in the *Vlaamse Gewest* dictum of 1998:

> Where a public authority favours an undertaking operating in a sector which is characterised by intense competition by granting it a benefit, there is a distortion of competition or a risk of such distortion. Where the benefit is limited, competition is distorted to a lesser extent, but it is still distorted.[682]

Notwithstanding the consistent position of the Court, the European Commission took the view that small amounts of aid, especially for small and medium-sized enterprises

675. European Commission: *Twentieth Report on Competition Policy* (1991), point 170.
676. Council Press Release (11172/95 – Press 307) on the conclusions of the 1880th meeting of the Industry Council of 6 and 7 November 1995, p. 30.
677. European Commission: Decision No 94/814/EEC (Irish Mushrooms), OJ L 335 of 23 December 1994.
678. Council Regulation No 659/1999/EC of 22 March 1999 laying down detailed rules for the application of Article 93 of the EC Treaty (now Article 108 of the Treaty on the Functioning of the European Union), OJ L 83 of 27 March 1999, pp. 1–9.
679. *Ibid.*, Article 15. In the latest version of the Procedural Regulation (Council Regulation No 1589/2015/EU of 13 July 2015 laying down detailed rules for the application of Article 108 of the Treaty on the Functioning of the European Union, OJ L 248 of 24 September 2015) this is retained in Article 17.
680. Council Regulation No 994/98/EC of 7 May 1998 on the application of Articles 92 and 93 (*now Articles 107 and 108 of the Treaty on the Functioning of the European Union*) to certain categories of horizontal State aid, OJ L 142 of 14 May 1998, as amended in 2013 - OJ L 204 of 31 July 2013.
681. Case C-57/86: *Greece v. Commission*, [1988] ECR 2855, paras 17–18; Case C-142/87: *Belgium v. Commission (Tubemeuse)*, [1990] ECR I-959, para. 43; Case C-310/99: *Italy v. Commission*, [2002] ECR I-2289, para. 86; Case C-172/03: *Heiser*, [2005] ECR I-1627, para. 32.
682. Case T-214/95: *Vlaamse Gewest v. Commission*, [1998] ECR II-717, paras 46–50.

(SMEs) should be exempt from notification. This resulted in the formulation of the first *de minimis* rule in 1992 in Guidelines for SME State aid[683] and its extension in 1996 in a Commission Notice on *de minimis* aid.[684] The legal status of the Commission's approach versus the Court remained unsettled, however, until the Commission adopted a series of *de minimis* Regulations in 1998. These were subsequently absorbed into the General *De Minimis* Regulations of 2001, 2006[685] and, most recently, Commission Regulation No 1407/13 of December 2013.[686] In addition, separate legislation governs *de minimis* State aid related to Services of General Economic Interest,[687] primary agricultural production and the fisheries sector[688] and under the temporary rules applicable since 2008 to the banking sector.[689] In general, the *de minimis* threshold does not apply to export aid and to aid favouring domestic over imported goods, the acquisition of road freight transport vehicles and aid for undertakings in difficulty (rescue aid). The current level of *de minimis* is €200,000 per firm over a period of three fiscal years, although this is lower in the case of the transport sector (€100,000) and the fisheries sector (€30,000) and was (until end-2011) higher under the temporary banking sector rules (€500,000).

In regard to the monitoring of State aid levels, the Sixth[690] and Seventh surveys[691] on State aid revealed the overall pattern of State aid in the EU from 1993 until 1997.

683. European Commission: *Community Guidelines on State aid for small and medium-sized enterprises (SMEs)*, OJ C 213/2.
684. European Commission: *Commission Notice on the De Minimis rule for State aid,* [1996] OJ C 68 of 6 March 1996.
685. European Commission: Commission Regulation No 69/2001 of 12 January 2001, OJ L 10 of 13 January 2001 and Commission Regulation No 1998/2006/EC of 15 December 2006, OJ L 379 of 28 December 2006.
686. European Commission: Commission Regulation No 1407/2013/EU of 18 December 2013 on the application of Articles 107 and 108 of the Treaty on the Functioning of the European Union to *de minimis* aid, OJ L 352 of 24 December 2013.
687. European Commission: Commission Regulation No 360/2012//EU on the application of Articles 107 and 108 of the Treaty on the Functioning of the European Union to *de minimis* aid granted to undertakings providing services of general economic interest, OJ L 114 of 26 April 2012.
688. European Commission: Commission Regulation No 1408/2013/EU of 18 December 2013 on the application of Articles 107 and 108 of the Treaty on the Functioning of the European Union to *de minimis* aid in the agriculture sector, OJ L 352 of 24 December 2013 and Commission Regulation No 717/2014/EU of 27 June 2014 on the application of Articles 107 and 108 of the Treaty on the Functioning of the European Union to *de minimis* aid in the fishery and aquaculture sector, OJ L 190 of 28 June 2014.
689. European Commission: *Temporary Community Framework for State aid measures to support access to finance in the current financial and economic crisis*, OJ C 16 of 22 January 2009, Article 4.2, as amended and *Communication of the Commission – Temporary Union framework for State aid measures to support access to finance in the current financial and economic crisis*, OJ C 6 of 11 January 2011, Article 2.2. In its Report on the evaluation of the Temporary Frameworks, the Commission notes that the use of *de minimis* schemes was the most popular measure used by EU Member States (Commission Staff Working Paper: *"The effects of temporary State aid rules adopted in the context of the financial and economic crisis,"* 5 October 2011).
690. European Commission: *Sixth Survey on State Aid in the European Union in the Manufacturing and Certain Other sectors*, COM (98) 417, 1998.
691. European Commission: *Seventh Survey on State Aid in the European Union in the Manufacturing and Certain Other sectors*, Brussels, 30 March 1999.

According to the Commission, overall State aid levels had reduced (by 13%) in comparison with the period 1993–1995. Aid to manufacturing represented 2.8% of value added and average aid per person employed had also reduced.[692]

Table 22 Main State Aid Statistics – 1990s

Period	*1993–1995*	*1995–1997*	*1995–1997*
Geographic area	EU-12	EU-12	EU-15
Overall aid (million EUR)	101,464	88,466	95,064
Aid to the manufacturing sector (million EUR)	41,809	36,365	37,680
Aid per person employed (EUR)	1,460	1,298	1,261

EU-12: Belgium, Denmark, Germany, Greece, Spain, France, Ireland, Italy, Luxembourg, the Netherlands, Portugal and the United Kingdom.
EU-15: EU-12 + Austria, Finland and Sweden.

Based on these trends and data, the Commission noted important differences in aid levels in certain Member States and stressed that, in absolute terms, the level of State aid remained too high. The Commission also emphasised that a tough State aid policy, together with an appropriate monitoring mechanism, must be maintained in order to reinforce the competitiveness of the EU on world markets and to achieve the benefits of the single market and of economic and monetary union.[693]

1999 saw the arrival of a new Commission and the transfer of Commissioner Mario Monti from the taxation portfolio to the competition policy arena. Within months, the new Competition Commissioner was emphasising a new direction for State aid cases building on "harmful tax competition" research since 1997, noting that "There is a general consensus on the need to combat harmful tax competition" and that the active pursuit of apparently harmful or unfair tax measures would be pursued via the State aid rules with reference to the broad guidelines set out in the Commission's Notice on the application of the State aid rules to measures relating to direct business taxation finalised in 1998.[694]

692. European Commission: *Twenty-Ninth Report on Competition Policy*, 1999.
693. *Ibid.*, p. 67.
694. European Commission: *Notice on the application of the State aid rules to measures relating to Direct Business Taxation*, OJ C 384 of 10 December 1998. This has now been repealed and replaced by European Commission: *Notice on the Notion of State aid as referred to in Article 107(1) of the Treaty on the Functioning of the European Union*, OJ C 262 of 19 July 2016.

4.4.1 SCMA and Europe Agreements

Several important legal and policy developments in the international arena took place in the early 1990s. First, the scope of EU law was extended into the former EFTA countries by the European Economic Area Agreement of 1992[695]

Second, the GATT Uruguay Round negotiations were completed in 1994; establishing the World Trade Organisation (WTO) and its landmark Subsidies and Countervailing Measures Agreement (SCMA)[696] and other agreements touching on the State aid sphere.[697] While the SCMA necessitated minor changes in EU State aid rules concerning the coal sector and aid supporting research and development, it is very clear that the European Commission saw the SCMA as an achievement in reflecting the State aid regime in an accord at the international level.[698]

In the early 1990s, a new approach to the preparation of candidate countries for EU membership was adopted as eight former Soviet Union countries clamoured for EU membership. Together with the Copenhagen criteria and the detailed screening process established by the EU, the *Europe Agreements* were trade liberalisation treaties with Estonia, Latvia, Lithuania, Hungary, Poland, Slovakia, Slovenia and the Czech Republic which provided for a range of ancillary approximation measures. In particular, the Europe Agreements provided for the application of State aid rules similar to those applying in the EU system in these countries. This was to be done under the authority of national regulatory authorities and laws. As noted earlier, this was an ambitious experiment and, by 1999, it was still far from clear that this was going to be successful.[699] While most Central and Eastern European countries had adopted laws aimed at protecting competition in the early 1990s, the regulation of State aid had not been anticipated and, therefore, took time. Moreover, while the specific focus in the Europe Agreements was on monitoring and on more specific commitments in the coal and steel sectors (of greatest single concern to the EU), the screening processes with candidate countries and the later membership negotiations increased the pressure on the national State aid systems of those countries to start actually *controlling* State aids. Between 1997 and 2001 all eight Europe Agreement countries adopted national State aid laws.

In the same period, attempts were made to apply similar disciplines on other post-Soviet countries via a separate set of trade agreements with the EU, known as the Partnership and Cooperation Agreements (PCAs).[700] These would be far less successful in the absence of either an interest in or a commitment towards EU membership.

695. Agreement between the EFTA States on the establishment of a Surveillance Authority and a Court of Justice on 2 May 1992, OJ L 344 of 31 January 1994 and EFTA States' official gazettes, at http://secretariat.efta.int/Web/legaldocuments/EsaAndEFTACourtAgreement/Documents.
696. WTO: *Subsidies and Countervailing Measures Agreement*, 1994 (accessed at: wto.org).
697. *See* Chapter 3 regarding the WTO: General Agreement on Trade in Services (GATS), 1994 and the Trade Related Investment Measures Agreement (TRIMS), 1994.
698. C.D. Ehlermann, *"State aid Control – Success or Failure?"* (18 January 1995), Fordham International Law Journal, 1995.
699. *See* earlier discussion of the Europe Agreements in Chapter 3.
700. Ten Partnership and Co-operation Agreements were concluded with the countries of the former Soviet Union and with various provisions regarding State aid disciplines and systems. Ukraine

4.4.2 Other Developments in Rule-Making

In line with the fundamental approach of the EU legal order, EU Law is based primarily on Treaty provisions, various international agreements and five types of instrument under Article 288 of the TFEU – Regulations, Directives, Decisions, Opinions and Recommendations. Under the Treaty, Regulations, Directives and Decisions are legally binding while opinions and recommendations (as suggested by the words themselves) have a generally exhortative effect. However, the legal order of the EU also recognises the importance of decided case law in the evolution of EU Law (including the recognition by the European Courts of a range of general principles of law underpinning the EU system[701]) and the European Court of Justice (since 1971) also regards the Article 288 package of instruments as not necessarily exhaustive.[702]

In the early 1990s, the Commission was firmly of the view that any cooperation with EU Member States in the development of secondary legislation in regard to State aid control would undermine the Commission's powers and prerogatives in this field which were seen as "constitutionally" derived from the Treaty provisions.[703] Faced with a range of legislative problems in regard to progressing EU Regulations and Directives (including Member State vetoes and the requirements of unanimous agreement of Member States in certain areas), the European Courts recognised various "soft law" measures as legitimate means of pursuing EU objectives and these have proved of considerable importance in the State aid field. As the European Commission has significant discretion in deciding whether measures constitute State aid and whether, and on what basis, they can be exempted from Article 107(1) of the TFEU, the Commission has issued many "soft law" measures designed to clarify its approach in the interests of legal certainty. The various titles of these measures, including Frameworks, Notices, Communications, Guidelines and even letters to the Member States, are indicative of the caution with which the Commission moved into soft law measures in regard to State aid.[704] However, in the CIRFS Case (1993) (and in later cases), the European Court of Justice endorsed this approach in the following terms:

> The rules applicable to State aid in a particular sector, as set out by the Commission in a communication on its policy in that area ('discipline') and accepted by the Member States, have a binding effect. They constitute a measure of general application and may not be impliedly amended by an individual decision, which

---

was the first country to conclude a PCA with the European Union in June 1994, and this came into force in March 1998. A particularly strict (but never implemented) set of provisions can be found in the PCA with the Russian Federation at Article 53 (*Agreement on Partnership and Co-operation establishing a partnership between the European Communities and their Member States, of the one part, and the Russian Federation, of the other part*, OJ L 327 of 27 November 1997).

701. These principles include fundamental rights, proportionality, legal certainty, equality, subsidiarity and principles of procedural propriety.
702. Case C-22/70: *Commission v. Council* (ERTA), [1971] ECR 263.
703. C.D. Ehlermann: "*State aid Control – Success or Failure?*," *supra*, 18 January 1995.
704. For a detailed discussion of this evolution, *see* K.A. Lavdas & M.M. Mendrinou: "*Politics, Subsidies and Competition – The New Politics of State Intervention in the European Union*," Edward Elgar, Cheltenham UK, 1999, pp. 36–46.

> cannot be subsequently relied upon, on the basis of the principles of equal treatment and protection of legitimate expectations, in order to justify a further infringement of those rules.[705]

Accordingly, the various soft law measures require the Commission to follow its own rules and stated policies and they have mandatory effect once they are accepted by the Member States.

In progressing its soft law measures in the 1990s, apart from the procedural and *de minimis* developments reviewed earlier, the Commission established its rules on aid for research and development in 1996[706] which generally indicated a favourable position towards encouraging R&D across the EU in the context of new Treaty prerogatives inserted by the Maastricht Treaty to foster better exploitation of the industrial potential of policies of innovation, research and technological development and to do so "through the policies and activities it pursues under other provisions" of the Treaty.[707] In addition, further generally favourable guidelines were issued in respect of employment aid,[708] aid to small and medium-sized enterprises (SMEs),[709] industrial training supports,[710] aid for environmental protection measures[711] and regional investment and job creation measures.[712]

Taken together, these initiatives marked the beginning of a more explicit Commission policy in favour of horizontal State aid measures. They also reflected the general policy lines under which the Commission continued to approve most notified measures. By promoting greater clarity on the Commission's generally positive orientation, the Commission was also (i.e., in addition to its *de minimis* initiatives) seeking to at least simplify the ongoing process of notification and approval of horizontal measures. In doing so, the Commission also established distinct policy positions on what it preferred to see in horizontal measures (e.g., general training preferred to specific industrial training, support for environmental measures exceeding mandatory standards preferred to supports for mandatory standards, aid for innovative R&D preferred to pre-competitive research). Moreover, in the regional guidelines, the Commission established specific parameters designed to avoid the wide-ranging application of the regional exemptions of Article 107(3)(a) and (c) of the TFEU, to align

705. Case C-313/90: *CIRFS v. Commission*, [1993] ECR I-1125.
706. European Commission: *Community framework for State aid for Research and Development*, OJ C 45 of 17 February 1996.
707. TFEU, Article 173.
708. European Commission: *Guidelines on State aid for employment*, OJ C 334 of 12 December 1995 and Commission *Notice on an accelerated procedure for processing notifications of employment aid*, OJ C 218 of 27 July 1996.
709. European Commission: *Community Guidelines on State Aid to Small and Medium-sized enterprises*, OJ C 213 of 23 July 1996.
710. European Commission: *Community Framework on Training Aid*, OJ C 343 of 11 November 1998.
711. European Commission: *Community Guidelines on State Aid for Environmental Protection*, OJ C 72 of 10 March 1994.
712. European Commission: *Guidelines on National Regional Aid ("RAGS")*, OJ C 74 of 10 March 1998 as amended in 2000, OJ C 258 of 9 September 2000.

the State aid rules further with EU Regional and Cohesion Policy, to ensure payback if regional objectives were abandoned and to more distinctly define regional aid.

In contrast, Guidelines on State aid for the rescue and restructuring of firms in difficulty were issued in 1994[713] and substantially tightened up via revised guidelines in 1999.[714] In support of this new orientation, the Commission noted that:

> A major part of the increase in economic growth that should ultimately result from the Single Market will be due to the extensive structural change that it will induce in the Member States. While structural change is easier in an expanding economy, even in a recession it is undesirable that Member States should frustrate or unduly retard the process of structural adjustment through subsidies to firms which in the new market situation ought to disappear or restructure. Such aid would shift the burden of structural change on to other, more efficient firms and encourage a subsidy race. As well as preventing the full benefits of the Single Market for the Community as a whole, subsidies can place severe strain on national budgets and so impede economic convergence.[715]

The Commission also justified greater restrictions on aid for rescue and restructuring in the context of the EU's specific objective of economic and social cohesion and developments in State aid policies towards government capital injections, financial transfers to public enterprises and aid for SMEs.[716] While this might appear to constitute a scrambling around for justification and logic, it in fact shows the adaptability of the Commission in the new realities of the 1990s and its readiness to cite and apply new Treaty rules, new macro-policy objectives of the EU as a whole and the latest jurisprudence from the European Courts – especially concerning the notion of aid.

In a further and very political initiative, the Commission issued Guidelines on State aid for undertakings in deprived urban areas in 1997.[717] This was very much inspired by French proposals to reanimate deprived urban areas of Paris[718] and had been further endorsed by two preceding European Councils.[719] While a broadly

713. European Commission: *Community guidelines on State aid for rescuing and restructuring firms in difficulty*, OJ C 368 of 23 December 1994.
714. European Commission: *Community Guidelines on State aid for rescuing and restructuring firms in difficulty*, OJ C 288 of 9 October 1999.
715. *Ibid.*, Recital 1.
716. *Ibid.*, Recital 2. In regard to the objective of economic cohesion, the Commission specifically referenced Maastricht Treaty changes in what are now Articles 174 and 175 of the TFEU establishing this as an EU objective and requiring EU policies to contribute to this objective "*The formulation and implementation of the Union's policies and actions and the implementation of the internal market shall take into account the objectives set out in Article 174 and shall contribute to their achievement*" (Article 175 of the TFEU).
717. European Commission: *Guidelines on State aid for undertakings in deprived urban areas*, OJ C 146 of 14 May 1997.
718. European Commission: Decision *City Revival Pact* (State aid N 159/96, France), OJ C 215 of 25 July 1996.
719. European Council meeting on 9 and 10 December 1994 in Essen, Presidency Conclusions SI(94) 1000, p. 4 and European Council meeting on 26 and 27 July 1995 in Cannes, Presidency Conclusions SI(95) 500, pp. 4–5.

positive State aid policy towards such measures was indicated in the Guidelines which would apply for five years, there were important restrictions introduced to avoid the widespread use of quasi-regional or rural development aid measures in otherwise prosperous cities (e.g., designated deprived urban areas could not exceed 1% of total population). However, in repealing these Guidelines in 2002, the Commission noted that:

> Modernisation of State aid rules must include abolishing obsolete or inappropriate rules. Since no use has been made of this instrument after it was adopted by the Commission, it is suggested neither to prolong the guidelines on State aid for undertakings in deprived urban areas in its current form beyond May 2002 nor to propose a revision thereof.[720]

Moreover, specific clarifications were also issued in this period concerning the identification and/or calculation of State aid in respect of direct business taxation,[721] export credit insurance,[722] sales of public land and buildings,[723] aid to the aviation sector[724] and aid cases involving the postal sector.[725] Moreover, with a view to encouraging the greater use of national courts in assisting State aid enforcement, the Commission issued a dedicated Notice on this in 1995.[726]

In respect of sectors, major restrictions on shipbuilding aid emerged from the Council by 1998[727] and the special rules for the shipbuilding sector were eventually abolished in July 2014. This resulted from a substantially increased technological development and competitiveness of EU shipyards (coupled with many closures).[728] As early as 1996, however, the Commission view was that:

---

720. European Commission: *Notice on the expiry of the guidelines on State aid for undertakings in deprived urban areas*, OJ C 119 of 22 May 2002. Presumably to placate the French, the Notice adds "*Obviously, schemes or individual cases granting State aid to undertakings in deprived urban areas approved in the past under other legal bases will in no way be affected by the non-prolongation of the guidelines on State aid for undertakings in deprived urban areas.*"
721. European Commission: *Notice on the application of the State aid rules to measures relating to Direct Business Taxation*, OJ C 384 of 10 December 1998 – repealed in 2016.
722. European Commission: *Communication on Short-term Export-Credit Insurance*, OJ C 281 of 17 September 1997.
723. European Commission: *Commission Communication on State aid elements in sales of land and buildings by public authorities*, OJ C 209 of 10 July 1997.
724. European Commission: *Guidelines on the application of the State aid rules in the aviation sector*, OJ C 350 of 10 December 1994.
725. European Commission: *Notice from the Commission on the application of the competition rules to the postal sector and on the assessment of certain State measures relating to postal services*, OJ C 39 of 6 February 1998.
726. European Commission: *Notice on cooperation between national courts and the Commission in the State Aid field*, OJ C 312 of 23 November 1995.
727. Council Regulation No 1540/98/EC of 29 June 1998 establishing new rules on aid to shipbuilding, OJ L 202 of 18 July 1998.
728. The position now is that regional aid, and innovation aid can be given to the shipbuilding sector in accordance with the relevant horizontal Guidelines (Regional Aid 2014–2020 and the R&D&I Guidelines).

> The abolition of State aid on a global level appears to be justified as, in the light of the previous experience, State aid did not contribute to increase the competitiveness of European shipbuilders.[729]

Concerning the motor vehicle sector, in 1996, the Commission revised its framework for aid[730] making minor revisions to its earlier rules; increasing notification thresholds and in regard to the definition of the sector and the methods of carrying out related cost-benefit analysis. While continuing to recognise both the strategic and sensitive nature of the motor industry, the Commission pointed out that:

> The Commission does not intend, however, to impose an industrial strategy on the sector, it is preferable for a strategy to be defined within the sector and the market.[731]

Further refinements of the Code on synthetic fibres were also introduced in 1996[732] and a further initiative intended to allow the Commission to concentrate on large cases and eventually consolidate its sectoral State aid policies was issued in 1998 as the *Multisectoral Framework on Regional aid for large investment projects.*[733]

4.4.3 Commission Commences Banking Cases

In the 1990s, the European Commission, for the first time, applied the State aid rules in the banking sector in the highly controversial *Credit Lyonnais Decision* of 1995.[734] This was a conditional decision on restructuring aid to Credit Lyonnais.[735] This learning experience by the Commission was strongly reflected in the proceedings of a major State aid conference held in Florence in 1999 which critically examined several key issues regarding the application of the State aid rules in the sector, including "too-big-to-fail" arguments and the capability of the Commission to respond quickly to crisis cases in the banking sector to avoid contributing to a run on the banks.[736] This case and the subsequent Commission reflections would later prove crucial in preparing the State aid system for its response to the 2008 international financial crisis.

---

729. European Commission: Communication: "*Shaping Europe's Maritime future – a contribution to the competitiveness of maritime industries*," 25 March 1996.
730. European Commission: *Community Framework for State aid to the motor vehicle industry*, OJ C 279 of 15 September 1997.
731. *Ibid.*, Point 3.
732. European Commission: *Code on Aid to the Synthetic Fibres Industry*, OJ C 94 of 30 March 1996.
733. European Commission: *Multisectoral Framework on Regional aid for large investment projects*, OJ C 107 of 7 April 1998.
734. European Commission: Decision No 95/547/EC of 26 July 1995 giving conditional approval to the aid granted by France to the bank Crédit Lyonnais (Credit Lyonnais I), OJ L 308 of 21 December 1995 and Decision No 98/490/EC of 20 May 1998 concerning aid granted by France to the Crédit Lyonnais group (Credit Lyonnais II), OJ L 221 of 8 August 1998.
735. For a comprehensive review of banking sector cases in the period 1995–1999, *see* "*European Competition Law Annual 1999 – Selected Issues in the Field of State aids*," C.D. Ehlermann & M. Everson (eds): "*Robert Schumann Centre at the European University Institute*," Florence, Hart Publishing, 2001.
736. *Ibid.*

4.4.4 Cases Reinforcing Commission Policy on the Notion of Aid

Two significant Commission Decisions of 1994 firmly reinforced Commission policy on the elements of advantage and actual and potential effects on competition and intra-Community trade in the notion of aid in what is now Article 107(1) of the TFEU.

The *SST-Garngesellschaft mbH, Thuringen* decision illustrates the dogmatic position of the Commission on the relationship between State aid and competition.[737] According to the Commission, the object of the aid in the case was to cover the cost of the installation of new facilities for the production of polyester staple fibre. The entire output of the new plant was to serve as a supply for the company's spinning mill for the production of specialised polyester yarn, which was not produced elsewhere in the EU.[738] The Decision stated that:

> The aid in question undoubtedly constitutes aid within the meaning of [Article 107(1) of the TFEU], as it would allow SST-Garngesellschaft mbH to carry out the planned investment without having to bear all of the cost. Furthermore, as there is intra-Community trade in polyester staple... the proposed aid would be likely to distort competition and affect trade among the Member States.[739]

In a negative decision on *SITAS*, highlighting in its effect on trade assessment not only the potential advantage that an aid beneficiary would enjoy on exports markets, but also the advantage it could derive on its domestic market vis-à-vis foreign importers, the Commission stated:

> The measures to be regarded as constituting state aid constitute assistance to firms operating in Sicily. They benefit those firms inasmuch as the assistance is not provided outside the region.... The aid in question ... affects trade between Member States. Although it is not possible to assess the full impact of the aid as not all the recipients are known, import and export statistics ... reveal that a significant proportion of Sicilian products and services is exported to other Member States. In addition, trade between Member States is also affected in cases where the aid favours domestic output and services to the detriment of imports and the provision of services from other Member States.[740]

4.4.5 Jurisprudence in the 1990s

In the mid-1990s, the Commission started to pay more attention to the enforcement of the notification requirements and the recovery of illegal State aid. The Commission stated in 1995 that it intended to use all the powers it had under the Treaty to compel Member States to comply with the obligation to notify, in particular, by assisting

737. European Commission: Decision No 94/266/EC, *SST Garngesellschaft mbH, Thuringen* OJ L 114 of 5 May 1994.
738. *Ibid.*, para. 21.
739. *Ibid.*, para. 23.
740. European Commission: Decision No 94/374/EC, *Sicilian regional Law No 23/91 concerning assistance for industry and Article 5 of regional Law No 8/91 concerning financing for Sitas – Italy*, OJ L 170 of 5 July 1994.

national courts in their role of protecting the rights of firms affected by illegal aid that had been granted to competitors.[741] This policy was also aimed at encouraging economic operators to be more vigilant about the lawfulness of the aid granted to them. This strict position of the Commission was upheld and strengthened by the Court of Justice in its judgments in the *Tubemeuse, Boussac (1990)*[742] and *Deggendorf cases (1994)*.[743] At the same time, and particularly in the context of the difficult ratification of the Maastricht Treaty (signed in February 1992), several authors, including Judges of the Court, noted a more cautious approach in the Court's case law and its overall "lighter touch" with respect to State aid regulation (e.g., in the Sloman Neptun case considered *infra*).

The Commission's approach that unnotified aid was capable of being considered illegal per se was thrown into some confusion, by the Court in the *Boussac case (1990)*[744] which held, in effect, that unnotified aid was not per se unlawful as the lawfulness of aid depended on an assessment of its compatibility and a negative assessment under an Article 108(2) procedure was essential for aid to be held illegal vis-à-vis the Treaty.

In the same case, the Court strengthened the hand of the Commission by setting out the conditions under which interim relief could be obtained to oppose State aid. This has since become known as the "Boussac procedure." In effect, the Court held that the Commission may oppose an unnotified but notifiable aid by calling on the Member State to submit its comments and thereafter take an interim Decision requiring suspension of payment of the aid pending the outcome of the contentious procedure and the submission by that State of all information needed for a compatibility assessment. An interim Decision may also be taken where a Member State proceeds to implement an aid without either advising the Commission under the two month rule of the preliminary procedure or without awaiting the outcome of the contentious procedure. Where a Member State fails to provide the necessary information in response to an interim Decision, the Commission may take its final Decision on the basis of the information available to it. In the first use of the Boussac procedure, the Commission gave the French Government 15 days to advise of the steps taken to comply with its interim order and 30 days to provide the information required on the scheme at issue.[745] This procedure was also used in October 1995 against Germany for repeated failure to respond to questions raised by the Commission regarding aid to two new Volkswagen plants in the new German Lander.[746]

741. European Commission: *Twenty-Fifth Report on Competition Policy*, 1995, point 149.
742. Judgment of 21 March 1990, in Case C-142/87: *Belgium v. Commission (Tubemeuse)*, [1990] ECR I-959 and Case C-301/87: *France v. Commission (Boussac)*, [1990] ECR I-307.
743. Case C-188/92: *Textilwerke Deggendorf GmbH v. Commission*, [1994] ECR I-833.
744. Case C-310/87: *France v. Commission (Boussac)*, [1990] 1 ECR 307, 354–357.
745. European Commission: Decision No 92/35/EEC of 11 June 1991 requiring France to suspend the implementation of aid in favour of the Pari Mutuel Urbain (PMU), introduced in breach of what is now Article 108(3) of the TFEU, OJ L 14 of 21 January 1992.
746. European Commission: "Competition Policy Newsletter," Vol. 1 No 6 (Autumn/Winter 1995), p. 47.

In the *Tubemeuse case (1990)*,[747] the Court addressed *de minimis*. Belgium argued that Tubemeuse's production accounted for much less than 17% of EU production and pointed out that, since there was no rule defining in regard to State aid the threshold above which intra-Community trade was affected, reference should be made to the level of 5% of the market usually adopted by the Commission in its antitrust competition cases. The Court rejected this argument and stated that:

> The relatively small amount of aid or the relatively small size of the undertaking which receives it does not as such exclude the possibility that intra-Community trade might be affected.[748]

The *Sloman Neptun case (1993)*[749] again dealt with the matter of State resources in the context of what is now Article 107(1) of the TFEU. The ECJ in this case held that the partial non-application of German employment legislation to foreign crews of vessels flying the German flag did not constitute the grant of aid to the ship owners because:

> The system at issue does not seek, through its object and general structure, to create an advantage which would constitute an additional burden for the State or the above-mentioned bodies, but only to alter in favour of shipping undertakings the framework within which contractual relations are formed between those undertakings and their employees.[750]

While this exonerated the specific German measure, it established that any measure which confers an economic advantage on a specific undertaking, and which is the result of conduct attributable to the State, constitutes State aid regardless of whether there is a tangible transfer of resources. This case was and continues to be very significant for the State aid system. First, it removed all doubt that lost revenue to the State from tax aid measures was on a par with expenditure measures in regard to their being State aid. Second, it established the basic rule that a State aid measure must always involve a burden on the State.[751]

Some commentators note that this judgment of the Court was perceived as a reversal of the Court´s traditional case law.[752] As the Court had held on several occasions that State aids need not be financed through State resources, here the deviation from its earlier positions was difficult to clearly explain. There are different views on the reasons for this apparently new orientation by the Court. It has been suggested, for example, that the Court considered that if aids could be financed through

747. Case C-142/87: *Belgium v. Commission (Tubemeuse)*, [1990] ECR I-959.
748. *Ibid.*, paras 42–43.
749. Joined Cases C-72/91 and C-73/91: *Firma Sloman Neptun Schiffahrts AG v. Seebetriebsrat Bodo Ziesemer der Sloman Neptun Schiffahrts AG*, [1993] ECR I-887.
750. *Ibid.*, para. 21.
751. *See* A. Biondi, "*Some Reflections on the Notion of "State Resources" in European Community State Aid Law*" 30 Fordham International Law Journal, Issue 5/2006, Article 4, p. 24.
752. J.J. Piernas López: "Understanding the Notion of State Aid through Policy," *supra*, p. 22.

resources other than public ones, the Treaty rules would have provided for some reference to those resources and also that the Court had simply decided to pull back its expansive case law.[753]

A year later, in the *Deggendorf case (1994)*[754] the Court held that the approval of a new aid package should be subject to a suspension of the payment of the aid, where a prior illegal aid to the same company had not yet been recovered. This was based on the view that the cumulation of the incompatible aid and a new aid measure would render the totality of the aid incompatible. Accordingly, the Deggendorf principle establishes that no new aid can be granted before a previous illegal aid has been recovered.

In the second half of the 1990s the Commission and the Court payed more attention to the concept of selectivity in State aid determinations and, in particular, to the difficult distinction between State aid and some so-called *general measures*. The general position of the Commission was clear: Article 107(1) did not apply to general measures applicable to all undertakings in a Member State which meet objective, non-discriminatory and non-discretionary requirements.[755] The Court upheld a related understanding in the *FNE case (1996)*,[756] where it admitted for the first time that a generally applicable measure could be considered selective if the authorities enjoyed discretionary powers in its application. In other words, Member States should not discriminate between undertakings within its national territory in applying support measures as this would create selectivity and trigger the application of the State aid rules.

Concerning the requirement of advantage under Article 107(1), the Court decided, in the *SFEI case (1996)*[757] that the provision of logistical and commercial assistance by a public undertaking to its subsidiaries, which are governed by private law and carry on an activity open to free competition, is capable of constituting State aid within the meaning of Article 107 of the TFEU if the remuneration received in return is less than that which would have been demanded under normal market conditions. Here the Court extended its interpretation of the MEIP test beyond capital injections to any transaction involving public companies. This means that any transaction involving public undertakings, even a transaction within public undertakings, would have to be conducted under market conditions to avoid the transaction establishing an advantage and triggering the application of the State aid rules.

753. *See* opinion of AG Jacobs in Case C-379/98: *PreussenElektra AG v. Schleswag AG*, ECR 2001 p. I-2099 and J.J. Piernas López & M. Ross, "*State Aids: Maturing into a Constitutional Problem*" (1995), 15 YEL, p. 82.
754. Case C-188/92: *Textilwerke Deggendorf GmbH v. Commission*, [1994] ECR I-833.
755. European Commission: *Twenty-Fourth Report on Competition Policy*, 1994, point 347.
756. Case C-241/94: *France v. Commission*, [1996] ECR I-4551.
757. Case C-39/94: *Syndicat Français de l'Express international (SFEI) and others v. La Poste and others*, [1996] ECR I-3547.

In 1998, the *Renove I case*[758] allowed the Court to rule on aspects of the concepts of effect on competition and on trade, while also offering some endorsement of the Commission's *de minimis*[759] rule. In that case, the Court concluded that:

> the position of professional transport companies and companies which carry out transport only to meet their own needs are such that the latter cannot be considered to operate on the transport market or to form part of the transport sector. Therefore the exclusion, in the area of State aid, of the transport sector from the benefit of the de minimis rule laid down by the Commission's guidelines and notices, which are binding on it where they do not depart from the rules in the Treaty and are accepted by the Member States, does not apply to aid granted to undertakings which carry out transport only to meet their own needs to replace their commercial vehicles.[760]

The notion of selectivity was once again at the centre of the Court's deliberations in the *Belgium v. Commission (Maribel)* case in 1999.[761] This was an important case as, for the first time, it dealt with a Commission recovery order involving some 50,000 recipients of illegal aid in Belgium. On 17 June 1999, the Court of Justice confirmed the Commission's decision that the reduction of social security charges under the Belgian *Maribel bis/ter* scheme was a selective measure. This was based on the fact that undertakings belonging to sectors of manufacturing industry not specified in the royal decrees establishing the scheme and undertakings in the services and the building sectors were not eligible for the social security reductions under the scheme. Dismissing the Belgian appeal, the Court held that "neither the large number of eligible undertakings nor the diversity and importance of the industrial sectors to which those undertakings belonged warranted the conclusion that the Maribel bis/ter scheme constituted a general economic policy measure." Moreover, the intention of the Member State could not be taken into account to avoid the application of Article 107(1) of the Treaty, since such measures must be assessed solely in relation to their effects. Any opposite approach, in the view of the Court, would enable the Member State concerned to escape the application of the Community rules in this area simply by declaring its intention to generalise the contested measure in the future.

This was subsequently followed in the *Adria-Wien Pipeline case (2001)*[762] where the Court said that in applying Article 107 of the TFEU:

> it is irrelevant that the situation of the presumed beneficiary of the measure is better or worse in comparison with the situation under the law ... The only question to be determined is whether, under a particular statutory scheme, a State measure is such as to favour certain undertakings or the production of certain goods .... in comparison with other undertakings which are in a legal and factual situation that is comparable in the light of the objective pursued by the measure in question. However, a measure which, although conferring an advantage on its

---

758. Case C-351/98: *Spain v. Commission (Renove I)*, [2002] ECR I-8031.
759. *De minimis* was first established under the European Commission: *Community guidelines on State aid for SMEs*, 1992.
760. Case C-351/98: *Spain v. Commission (Renove I)*, [2002] ECR I-8031, para. 2.
761. Case C-75/97: *Belgium v. Commission*, [1999] ECR I-3671.
762. Case C-143/99: *Adria-Wien Pipeline GmbH and Wietersdorfer & Peggauer Zementwerke GmbH v. Finanzlandesdirektion für Kärnten*, [2001] ECR I-8365.

recipient, is justified by the nature or general scheme of the system of which it is part does not fulfil that condition of selectivity.[763]

4.5 PHASE 4 – 2000–2017 (THE MILLENNIUM ERA AND STATE AID REFORM)

The development of State aid law and policy in the period from 2000 to 2017 was strongly influenced by EU enlargements in 2004, 2007 and 2013 and the international financial crisis of 2007–2009. Changes of Commissioners for Competition brought about two phases of State aid reform and the Commission continued its quest to rationalise its caseload to concentrate on cases of major importance. At the same time, the Commission increasingly resorted to recovery orders, worked harder to ensure actual recovery and established one record after another in regard to the amounts to be recovered.

Policy also focussed on the increased transparency of the Commission, the adoption of clearer procedural and substantive rules, a concerted attack on State aid tax measures (in parallel with Commission policy on harmful business taxation) and reorganising the Commission's approach to compensation to public and private enterprises for the provision of services of general economic interest (SGEIs).[764] By mid-2016, the Commission was able to issue a new, comprehensive and detailed Notice on the notion of aid.[765]

4.5.1 Enlargement

The 2004 EU enlargement represented a challenge for the Commission as it required the application of State aid rules in very different economies from those of the older Member States. While the Europe Agreements and the pre-accession processes with each new Member State had certainly paved the way for an orderly transfer from national control to Commission control, the Commission certainly feared a massive influx of cases. New Member States, in turn, were looking to access EU structural funds

763. *Ibid.*, paras 5 and 42.
764. *See* Case C-280/00: *Altmark Trans GmbH and Regierungspräsidium Magdeburg v. Nahverkehrsgesellschaft Altmark GmbH, and Oberbundesanwalt beim Bundesverwaltungsgericht*, [2003] ECR I-7747; European Commission: *Communication from the Commission on the application of the European Union State aid rules to compensation granted for the provision of services of general economic interest*, OJ C 8 of 11 January 2012, pp. 4–14; Commission *Decision of 20 December on the application of Article 106(2) of the Treaty on the Functioning of the European Union to State aid in the form of public service compensation granted to certain undertakings entrusted with the operation of services of general economic interest*, OJ L 7 of 11 January 2012, pp. 3–10; Communication from the Commission, *European Union framework for State aid in the form of public service compensation*, [2011] OJ C 8 of 11 January 2012, pp. 15–22; *Commission Regulation on the application of Articles 107 and 108 of the Treaty on the Functioning of the European Union to de minimis aid granted to undertakings providing services of general economic interest*, OJ L 114 of 26 April 2012, p. 8.
765. European Commission: *Notice on the Notion of State aid as referred to in Article 107(1) TFEU*, 19 May 2016.

for national development and some have since taken the view that, while State aid was minimal prior to EU membership, the use of structural funds in fact required the creation of many hitherto unknown State aid schemes.[766] Moreover, as noted earlier, some specific concessions related to State aid matters featured in the accession treaties of some of the 2004 acceding countries.[767]

This was also the case in 2007 (the Bulgarian and Romanian accession) and in regard to the most recent enlargement in 2013 which added Croatia to the EU bloc.[768] In the case of Bulgaria and Romania, the accession treaties specifically flagged the fact that insufficient progress had been made on State aid and anti-corruption pre-accession requirements and delayed access to EU structural funds for these countries until those issues were rectified.[769]

In 2004, the Commission was already talking about State aid reform in the enlargement context and (*see infra*) had already embarked on its first round of block exemption initiatives:

> The reform process should result in light, predictable and transparent procedures and economically sound and legally robust criteria for the assessment of State aid measures. This should make State aid control after enlargement easier and enable the Commission to cope with the expected substantial increase in State aid measures in an enlarged Union.[770]

4.5.2 Banking Crisis

By August 2007, the worst financial crisis since 1930 struck the global economy and hit the stability of the banking sector across Europe. In response, EU Member States had to consider the rescue of banks but this could not be done within the Commission's Rescue and Restructuring Guidelines and, accordingly, the Commission rapidly issued three Communications on the role of State aid policy in the context of the crisis and the recovery process.[771]

This crisis once again underlined the highly political dimension of State aid. Indeed, the first political reaction of Britain, France, Germany and many other

766. A view held, in particular, by the authorities in the Baltic States (Estonia, Latvia and Lithuania).
767. *See* Chapter 3.
768. Currently, accession negotiations are under way with several countries. To join the European Union, a country needs to fulfil economic and political conditions known as the Copenhagen criteria (after the Copenhagen Summit of June 1993), which require a stable democratic government that respects the rule of law, and its corresponding freedoms and institutions. According to Article 49 of the TFEU, each current EU Member State and the European Parliament must agree to any enlargement.
769. European Commission: Communication from the Commission – Monitoring report on the state of preparedness for EU membership of Bulgaria and Romania, Brussels, COM (2006) 549 final, 26 September 2006.
770. European Commission: *Report on Competition Policy, 2004*, point 337.
771. European Commission: *Report on Competition Policy 2008*, p. 9.

European countries was to foster their national economic recovery through subsidy measures. State aid within the EU-27 rose sharply from less than 1% of EU GDP in 2007 to around 13% in 2011.[772]

The Commission first gave initial guidance on the application of State aid rules to measures taken in relation to financial institutions,[773] which, exceptionally, were based on what is now Article 107(3)(b) of the TFEU – allowing exemption for aid to remedy a serious disturbance in the economy of a Member State. Subsequently, the Commission supplemented and refined its guidance with a new Communication on how Member States could recapitalise banks during the financial crisis.[774] In addition, the Commission adopted a Temporary Framework[775] providing Member States with additional possibilities to tackle the effects of the credit squeeze on the real economy (i.e., the fact that banks had massively reduced lending or were no longer lending to the business sector). Among the provisions of the Temporary Framework, Member States could grant a lump sum of aid up to €500,000 per firm for two years in order to relieve their access to finance difficulties;[776] State guarantees for loans could be offered at a reduced premium; subsidised loans could be provided on certain conditions, risk capital financing for SMEs would be exempt up to the level of €2.5 million per SME per year (instead of the general €1.5 million limit) in cases where at least 30% (instead of the general requirement of 50%) of the investment cost came from private investors.

While the Commission's crisis measures can be perceived as complex manoeuvring which essentially threw away the State aid rules to allow Member States to address the needs of the banks and the knock on effects of diminished lending, this would be an over-simplification. First, as noted earlier, the Commission was largely ready for such a crisis since the late 1990s. Second, the temporary nature of the special rules introduced to address the crisis was stressed by the Commission from the outset. Thus, in 2009, the Commission highlighted that:

> It is clear that from the State aid control perspective, the most pressing issue is to manage the exit from the exceptional support measures adopted within the context of the crisis. We must prepare a strategy for gradually withdrawing aid whilst taking into account the market conditions and the still underlying risks to financial stability. And once the financial situation stabilises, the normal State aid instruments and, in particular horizontal aid instruments, will play a key role in helping the European economy emerge from the crisis by helping maintain a level playing field for business across the EU and preventing subsidy races between Member States.[777]

772. European Commission: Staff Working Document – *Facts and Figures on State Aid in EU Member States, 2012 Update*, SEC (2012) 443 final of 21 December 2012.
773. European Commission: Communication from the Commission – *The application of State aid rules to measures taken in relation to financial institutions in the context of the current global financial crisis*, OJ C 270 of 25 October 2008.
774. European Commission: *Communication on the Recapitalisation of financial institutions in the current financial crisis*, adopted on 5 December 2008, OJ C 10 of 15 January 2009.
775. European Commission: *Temporary Community Framework for State aid measures to support access to finance in the current financial and economic crisis*, OJ C 16 of 22 January 2009, as amended.
776. This was effectively an extension of the *de minimis* rule.
777. European Commission: *Report on Competition Policy, 2009*, COM (2010) 282 final.

The operations of State aid control in the context of the financial crisis are considered further in the context of cross-cutting issues with other EU policies.[778]

4.5.3 Recovery of Illegal State Aid

In 2000, the Commission again emphasised the need for the proper enforcement of Commission decisions, particularly concerning the recovery of State aid that has been unlawfully granted.[779] In line with the underlying jurisprudence and Commission policy, recovery of unlawful State aid is not a penalty, but a means to restore the situation prior to the granting of the illegal and unlawful aid in the interests of the competitive operations of the market. Since 2000, in particular, Commission policy sought to systematically apply the *Deggendorf principle*, whereby the Commission requires Member States to suspend the payment of new aid (even if compatible) to undertakings that have not repaid previous illegal and incompatible aid. This has effectively increased pressure on Member States to enforce recovery decisions in a more diligent manner, so as to be able to implement new State aid measures.[780]

In 2007, the Commission sought to reinvigorate its efforts to improve the enforcement and monitoring of State aid decisions and adopted a Notice on State aid Recovery with a view to achieving a more effective and immediate execution of recovery decisions.[781] The Notice stresses that, up to 2007, there was practically not a single case where recovery was completed within the deadline set out in the recovery decision.

By 2008, the Commission indicated, on the basis of information submitted by the Member States concerned, that good progress towards recovery was being made. The Commission noted, in particular, that, of the €10.3 billion of illegal and incompatible aid to be recovered under decisions adopted since 2000, some €9.3 billion (i.e., 90.7% of the total amount) had actually been recovered by the end of 2008. In addition, a further €2.5 billion in recovery interest had been recovered.

In 2009, the Commission pointed out that, by 31 December 2009, the amount of illegal and incompatible aid recovered had increased from €2.3 billion in December 2004 to €10.4 billion. The percentage of illegal and incompatible aid still to be recovered was 75% at the end of 2004, but only 12% at the end of 2009. The share of the total amount recovered had decreased, however, between 2008 and 2009 (from 90.9 to 88%), largely due, according to the Commission, to seven new recovery decisions adopted in 2009 and the high amounts of illegal aid identified in several 2008 decisions.[782]

---

778. *See* Chapter 6.
779. *See* European Commission: *Thirtieth Report on Competition Policy*, 2000 — SEC (2001) 694 FINAL.
780. M. Merola: "*The Forces Shaping State Aid Control in the EU*," *supra*.
781. European Commission: Notice from the Commission: "*Towards an effective implementation of Commission decisions ordering Member States to recover unlawful and incompatible State aid*," OJ C 272, 15.11.2007, p. 4.
782. European Commission: *Report on Competition Policy, 2009*, p. 22, COM (2010) 282 final.

By 2014, a somewhat different picture was emerging whereby only 52% of State aid recovery required by Commission Decisions was actually achieved in 10 years (€7.2 billion + interest); the Commission was still pursuing €5.1 billion plus interest (36%); and 12% of all State aid to be recovered was lost as a result of the bankruptcies of the undertakings concerned.[783]

The most recent 2016 statistics indicate that, in respect of 257 recovery decisions taken and finalised since 1999, almost €9.5 billion had been recovered and some €2.4 billion was categorised as non-recoverable ("aid lost").[784]

4.5.4 Pre-2005 Rule-Making

Prior to 2005, when the State aid Action Plan initiative was launched, State aid rule-making, which had advanced rapidly in the late 1990s, saw the Commission take advantage of the new Enabling Regulation and start the block exemption process in the State aid field for the first time.

Accordingly, certain forms of State aid to SMEs were first exempted from notification[785] together with certain types of training aid measures in 2001.[786] This approach was extended to employment aid in 2002.[787] R&D aids were added to the SME regulation in 2004,[788] when some further modifications to the training aid exemption regulation were also made.[789] Also in 2001, the Commission codified the *de minimis* rule for State aid at €100,000 per firm over a three-year period, thereby establishing legal certainty on this point for the first time.[790] Aid below the *de minimis* threshold was also exempt from notification, but this did not include export aid and aid contingent on local labour requirements (as these were banned under the WTO SCMA) and the agriculture, fisheries and aquaculture, and transport sectors were excluded.

These Regulations generally allowed EU Member States to grant aid immediately, without the need for prior notification to and authorisation by the Commission, provided that the conditions laid down in the block exemption regulation were met.

783. European Commission, DG Competition: *Statistics for 2004-2014, Recovery of illegal and incompatible State aid.*
784. European Commission: http://ec.europa.eu/competition/state_aid/studies_reports/recovery.html.
785. European Commission: Regulation No 70/2001/EC of 12 January 2001 on the application of Articles 87 and 88 of the EC Treaty to State aid to small and medium-sized enterprises, OJ L 10 of 13 January 2001.
786. European Commission: Regulation No 68/2001/EC of 12 January 2001 on the application of Articles 87 and 88 of the EC Treaty to training aid, OJ L 10 of 13 January 2001.
787. European Commission: Regulation No 2204/2002/EC of 12 December 2002 on the application of Articles 87 and 88 of the EC Treaty to State aid for employment, OJ L 337 of 13 December 2002.
788. European Commission: Regulation No 364/2004/EC of 25 February 2004 amending Regulation No 70/2001/EC as regards the extension of its scope to include aid for research and development, OJ L 63 of 28 February 2004.
789. European Commission: Regulation No 363/2004/EC of 25 February 2004 amending Regulation No 68/2001/EC on the application of Articles 87 and 88 of the EC Treaty to training aid, OJ L 63 of 28 February 2004.
790. European Commission: Regulation No 69/2001/EC of 12 January 2001 on the application of Articles 87 and 88 of the EC Treaty to de minimis aid, OJ L 10 of 13 January 2001.

However, the Commission was quick to argue that this procedural simplification did not entail a lesser degree of control or a relaxation of the rules on State aid.[791] This view was based on the fact that several provisions in the regulations required Member States to provide the Commission with summary information sheets and annual reports, thereby allowing it to monitor the application of the block exemptions. Moreover, as the regulations were directly applicable in the Member States, complainants could also go to national courts if their competitors had received aid which did not comply with the conditions laid down in the relevant block exemption regulation.

A Regional Aid regulation, which had been in preparation and consultation for some time, but was awaiting the parallel completion of new Regional aid Guidelines for 2007–2013 in December 2005, was adopted in 2006.[792] At the same time, the Commission extended the earlier block exemption regulations until 2008.[793]

In respect of the Regional Aid Regulation, Member States were exempt from notifying their regional investment aid schemes to the Commission if those schemes complied with the new Guidelines and the approved Regional aid map for 2007–2013.[794] According to the Commission, this was intended to considerably reduce the administrative burden of notifications for Member States and would simplify their work for the next programming period of the Structural Funds.[795] However, only "transparent forms" of regional investment aid were block exempted (i.e., schemes for which it is possible to calculate precisely the aid intensity as a percentage of the investment, and thus, e.g., excluding capital injections, risk capital measures and State guarantees). Non-transparent forms of regional aid remained subject to notification; although in the case of guarantees an approved methodology for the calculation of their aid intensity could also obviate the need to notify individual cases. State aid for large investment projects (i.e., planned support for an investment of over €50 million[796]) would continue to require individual notification in view of the potentially higher risk of serious distortions of competition.

These particular regulatory initiatives provided both the logic and experience for the Commission to more fully embark on a more generalised block exemption approach in 2008 which was further developed and expanded in the current GBER of 2014.[797]

---

791. European Commission: *XXXIst Report on Competition Policy*, 2001.
792. European Commission: Regulation No 1628/2006/EC of 24 October 2006 on the application of Articles 87 and 88 of the Treaty to national regional investment aid, OJ L 302 of 1 November 2006.
793. European Commission: Regulation No 1976/2006/EC of 20 December 2006 amending Regulations No 2204/2002/EC, No 70/2001/EC and No 68/2001/EC as regards the extension of the periods of application, OJ L 368 of 23 December 2006.
794. Under the Regional Aid Guidelines, each Member State was required to provide data and justification to the Commission for different maximum levels of regional investment or job creation aid to be applied in the individual regions of the country. This process of regional aid mapping culminated in a Commission decision approving the national and regional maps and aid levels for the period.
795. European Commission: Press Release: "*State aid: Commission simplifies procedures for approving regional aid with new block exemption Regulation,*" IP/06/1453 of 24 October 2006.
796. Commission Regulation No 1628/2006/EC, *supra*, Article 2.
797. The GBER of 2008 and the GBER of 2014 are considered further in Chapter 5.

4.5.5 Taxation Issues

Following the initiatives in regard to tax measures in the 1990s, then EU Competition Commissioner Mario Monti, in an address to the Universiteit Nyenrode in the Netherlands on 22 January 2002, pointed out that, since 11 July 2001, the European Commission had initiated 15 State aid procedures regarding the corporation tax regimes of 12 Member States, primarily concerning special tax regimes put in place for inward investment or financial services companies. Eight of these cases featured in the Commission Report on Competition Policy of 2006 – notably: Gibraltar (where the EU decided that the Gibraltar tax exempt companies scheme should be abolished by 2010), Greece (where an unnotified tax measure was subject, for the first time, to a suspension injunction) and Luxembourg (where the Commission ordered a 1929 Law providing tax exemptions for Luxembourg registered holding companies to be repealed). Shortly thereafter, the European Courts got more fully involved.

4.5.5.1 The AZORES Case

In its decision of 11 December 2002, the Commission ruled that reductions in the rates of income and corporation tax in the Autonomous Region of the (Portuguese) Azores, established by Decree No 2/99/A of the regional legislative assembly of the Azoress on 20 January 1999, was a selective measure of taxation constituting State aid and incompatible with the internal market.[798] On appeal in *Portugal v. Commission (2006)*, the European Court of Justice addressed the issue of the regional selectivity of these tax measures by focussing on whether the Azores tax measures were part of a regional system in its own right or whether they constituted, in fact, a derogation from the Portuguese tax system as a whole. As far as the Commission was concerned, the measure involved a reduction, applicable solely in the Azores territory, in the rate of tax that had been established by national legislation and applied to the rest of the Portuguese territory.

The ECJ rejected the Commission's interpretation of selectivity simply because measures apply in a given geographic area within a Member State, thereby allowing the possibility that the reference framework is not necessarily the territory of the Member State concerned. More precisely:

> it is appropriate . . . to examine whether that measure was adopted by that body in the exercise of powers sufficiently autonomous vis-à-vis the central power and, if appropriate, to examine whether that measure indeed applies to all the undertakings established in or all production of goods on the territory coming within the competence of that body.[799]

798. European Commission: Decision on Azores of 11 December 2002, OJ L 150 of 18 June 2003.
799. Case C-88/03: *Portugal v. Commission*, [2006] ECR I-7115, para. 62.

Thus, while the Court's judgment accepted that there was effective regional devolution within some Member States, three conditions had to be met if measures of this type were to be general measures rather than selective State aid tax measures:[800]

- *Institutional autonomy*: the infra-state authority must have, from the constitutional point of view, a political and administrative status separate from the central government.
- *Procedural autonomy:* the decision must have been taken without the possibility for the central government to intervene with regard to its content.
- *Financial responsibility*: the reduction of the national tax in the region must not be offset by aid or subsidies from other regions or central government.

The situation in the Azores did not meet these criteria as, in the Portuguese situation, there was a constitutional clause of solidarity allowing for financial compensation to the Azores Government if they actually got it wrong and they were short of money to deliver public services. In other words, while the Azores were autonomous from an institutional point of view, their decision on corporate taxation lacked both procedural and economic autonomy. Moreover, the reduction of the tax burden by the Azores authorities was inextricably linked to addressing the inequalities of the Azores region, and this was dependent on a budgetary transfer managed by the central government.[801]

Subsequently, on 10 September 2009, the Court of First Instance delivered a judgment in the *Banco Comercial dos Açores v. Commission (BCA) 2009* case.[802] This judgment concerned an annulment action brought by the Azorean-based credit institution against the Commission's 2002 Azores decision on the basis of partially similar grounds to those already dismissed by the ECJ in 2006. The BCA case again raised the question of the scope of Article 107(1) of the TFEU: *In what circumstances do variations in the national tax rate adopted solely for a designated geographical area of a Member State fall under the definition of State aid?* The CFI affirmed the ECJ position from 2006 and dismissed the case. BCA had benefited from the regional regime and paid corporate income tax at the reduced rate within the context of the challenged aid scheme. Following the 2006 judgment, the Portuguese tax authorities notified taxpayers, including BCA, that they were considered to have received illegal State aid and were required to pay additional corporate income tax in respect of previous years. Basically, the tax authorities made new tax assessments using the ordinary tax rate applicable to companies operating in Portugal, on the assumption that the rate used by the companies located in the Azores could not be applied, despite being set out as the applicable rate defined in the Portuguese official legal gazette. Portugal had specifically requested that BCA reimburse the difference between the ordinary tax rate and the rate applicable to companies operating in the Azores – a difference that varied between

800. Opinion of the Advocate General Geelhoed delivered on 29 October 2005 in case *Portugal v. Commission*, para. 54.
801. R. Greaves, "*Autonomous Regions, Taxation and EC State-Aid Rules*" (2009), 34 European Law Review, p. 785.
802. Case T-75/03: *Banco Comercial dos Açores v. Commission*, ECLI:EU:T:2009:322.

10.2% and 7.5% depending on the fiscal year[803] – together with compensatory interest.[804] In the BCA case, the Administrative Supreme Court of Portugal already ruled[805] that the case should be dismissed on the basis that the "tax assessment" was already a mere executor act of the European Commission decision and, as such, could not be challenged in court.[806]

The *Azores* judgment was subsequently applied in two other situations concerning the *Basque region* of Spain (September 2008)[807] and in respect of *Gibraltar* (December 2008).[808]

4.5.5.2 The Basque Case

In the Basque region, a trade union and two neighbouring autonomous communities brought an action in the Spanish courts for an annulment of the tax legislation. The Spanish court asked the ECJ in *Commidades Autonomas case (2008)* whether, in light of the Azores judgment, the setting of the corporation tax rate in the Basque Provinces satisfied the criteria of selectivity and consequently constituted a State aid. As was noted by one commentator, "... they [the ECJ] repeated the Azorean mantra and made it very clear that, in this particular case, where there was a procedural autonomy or an economic and financial autonomy or an institutional autonomy, it was a matter for the trial judge to decide on the facts. When it went back to Spain, it was the Supreme Court of the Basque country that then applied the ruling to the dispute, and they ruled that the Basque country had sufficient institutional, procedural and financial independence."[809]

The Court was concerned about a causal link between the tax measure and any compensation from the national government to the region. It also pointed out that there could be many reasons why a national government might wish to transfer money to a region, and raised questions as to where the burden of proof lay as regards demonstrating that the transfer of the money was direct because there had been a loss of revenue to the autonomous region. In the Basque case, the ECJ considered that it was for the national court to verify whether, taking into account the methodology and economic data available, the Spanish State would be providing compensation to the Basque province as a consequence of the tax measure.

803. In 1999, the Portuguese ordinary corporate income tax (CIT) rate was 34% and 23.8% under the Azores regime; since 2004 the ordinary CIT rate has been 25%, while in the Azores the rate has been 17.5%.
804. F. de Sousa da Câmara & M.R. da Fonseca, "*EU State Aid Rules and the Azores Cases*" (9 November 2009) Tax Notes International, p. 443.
805. Administrative Supreme Court of Portugal, file 1091/05, 24 May 2006.
806. F. de Sousa da Câmara and M.R. da Fonseca argue in "*EU State Aid Rules and the Azores Cases,*" *supra* that, while refusing to make an appraisal or an analysis about the substance of the case, the court had concluded that the sole procedural step to be taken by taxpayers could be an action for damages against Portugal in the national courts.
807. Joined Cases C-428/06 to C-436/06: *Commidades Autonomas*, judgment of 11 September 2008.
808. Cases T-211/04 and T-215/04: *Government of Gibraltar v. Commission*, [2008] ECR II-3745.
809. R. Greaves: "*Autonomous regions, taxation and EC state-aid rules,*" 34 European Law Review, 2009, p. 785.

4.5.5.3 *The Gibraltar Case*

In August 2002, the UK notified the Commission, pursuant to Article 108(3) of the TFEU, that Gibraltar proposed to make changes to its tax system that would involve the introduction of a Payroll Tax and a Business Property Occupation Tax (BPOT). The Commission's Decision of March 2004 found that the Payroll Tax and BPOT were materially selective because they would inherently favour offshore companies that had no physical presence in Gibraltar and which, as a consequence, would not incur corporation tax. The Commission also found that the proposed changes to Gibraltar's tax system were regionally selective on the grounds that they provided for a system under which companies in Gibraltar would be taxed, in general, at a lower rate than that applying in the UK.

The UK and the Government of Gibraltar both contested the Commission's Decision in respect of both material and regional selectivity. On 18 December 2008, the Court of First Instance (now the General Court) annulled the Commission's Decision. The Court accepted that the UK provided financial support to the Government of Gibraltar, but this support was to enable the UK to fulfil its international obligations, for example for the defence of Gibraltar. Gibraltar already had its own autonomous tax jurisdiction and the Court did not see a causal link between the financial support provided by the UK and the tax revenue foregone by Gibraltar. The General Court found, therefore, that Gibraltar's tax proposals did not breach EU rules on State aid on grounds of material selectivity. Moreover, the General Court ruled that the frame of reference for assessing whether Gibraltar's proposals were regionally selective corresponded exclusively to Gibraltar's territorial limits. The General Court, therefore, upheld as a matter of EU law, Gibraltar's freedom to set tax rates that are different from those in the UK.

The Commission and Spain both brought appeal actions asking the ECJ to set aside the General Court's judgment. The Commission's single ground of appeal was on the question of material selectivity. Spain appealed on both regional and material selectivity. The ECJ's judgment of 15 November 2011 held that Gibraltar's tax proposals were materially selective in that they granted selective advantages to offshore companies. It added that, in view of its finding on material selectivity, it was not relevant to examine whether Gibraltar's proposals were regionally selective.

After Gibraltar

Following the Gibraltar judgment, in January 2012, UK Foreign Secretary William Hague made a written statement to Parliament on the judgment.[810] He pointed out

810. Announcement "*Statement on European Court Judgement on taxation in Gibraltar,*" 12 January 2012, available at: https://www.gov.uk/government/news/statement-on-european-court-judgement-on-taxation-in-gibraltar.

that, as the ECJ's decision had not examined the issue of regional selectivity, this meant that there had been no change in the principles established by the Court in the Azores case; whereby autonomous regional bodies within an EU Member State could set lower levels of tax than in the rest of the Member State without giving rise to State aid, provided that certain criteria for determining the autonomous status of the regional body were met. The statement emphasised that, in accordance with its constitutional arrangements, Gibraltar is a fiscally autonomous entity with responsibility for the management of its economy, including taxation, vested in the Government of Gibraltar. Accordingly, the ECJ's judgment of 15 November 2011, in the UK Government's view, did not change Gibraltar's constitutional relationship with the UK or Gibraltar's freedom to set a tax regime that differed from that of the UK. Moreover, it was for the Government of Gibraltar, as the authority responsible for the tax system in Gibraltar, to consider the implications for Gibraltar of the ECJ's ruling on material selectivity.

4.5.5.4 Tax Ruling Investigations

One of the trickiest and most controversial issues in regard to tax measures concerns tax rulings. The function of a tax ruling is to establish in advance the application of the ordinary tax system to a particular case in view of its specific facts and circumstances. For reasons of legal certainty, many national tax authorities provide prior administrative rulings on how specific transactions will be treated fiscally. In practice, tax rulings may be issued by the tax authorities to establish in advance how the provisions of a bilateral tax treaty or national fiscal provisions will be applied to a particular case, especially in regard to a complex multinational tax payer; thereby providing additional legal certainty and predictability for both the State and the taxpayer on the application of general tax rules. From a State aid perspective, several Member States have for many years viewed countries which have deeper traditions of tax ruling practices with a degree of suspicion and considered the general practice of tax rulings to create *per se* selective tax reductions and thus to constitute both State aid and unfair tax competition. For its part, the Commission has consistently stated that tax rulings are perfectly legal, provided that they comply with the EU State aid rules and, ideally, when they are also published.[811] However, every decision of the administration that departs from the general tax rules to the benefit of individual undertakings in principle leads to a presumption of State aid and must be analysed in detail.[812]

Since 2013, the Commission has been carrying out an inquiry into tax ruling practices from the perspective of the State aid rules. By the end of 2014, all Member States had been asked to provide information about their tax ruling practice and the legal framework underlying that practice, as well as a list of tax rulings issued in the years 2010–2012 (and partly 2013). On the basis of this information, the Competition

811. *See*, for example, the discussion of discretionary administrative practices in taxation in European Commission: Notice on the application of the State aid rules to measures relating to direct business taxation, OJ C 384 of 10 December 1998 at paras 21 and 22.
812. *Ibid.*, para. 22.

requested details of specific tax rulings and, by 2016, had examined more than 1,000 tax rulings, including some 600 tax rulings which appeared in the public domain in November 2014 as a result of the "LuxLeaks" controversy.[813] In October 2015, the Commission concluded that Luxembourg and the Netherlands had granted selective tax advantages to *Fiat* and *Starbucks*,[814] respectively.[815] In January 2016, the Commission concluded that selective tax advantages granted by Belgium to least 35 multinationals, mainly from the EU, under its *"excess profit" tax scheme*[816] were illegal under EU State aid rules. Later in 2016, the Commission concluded that Ireland had granted undue tax benefits of up to €13 billion to *Apple Inc.* via two tax rulings concerning its Irish locations and ordered that this benefit should be paid back with interest.[817] This recent decision, which created a record as regards State aid recovery, is being appealed by both Apple and Ireland and is also the subject of Article 108(2) of the TFEU enforcement proceedings by the European Commission. In October 2017, the Commission concluded that a tax ruling issued by Luxembourg in 2003, and prolonged in 2011, lowered the tax paid by Amazon in Luxembourg without any valid justification and gave rise to a recovery order of some €250 million.[818] The Commission also has two further ongoing in-depth investigations into concerns that tax rulings may also have given rise to State aid issues in Luxembourg as regards *McDonald's*[819] and *GDF Suez.*[820]

Putting these cases in context, the Commission has argued that a fully functioning EU internal market requires that all market players – whether large or small, local or global – pay their fair share of tax. Therefore, the fight against tax evasion and tax fraud is declared to be one of the main priorities of the current Commission since 2015, and one of the most important initiatives for advancing the completion of the EU single

813. European Commission: *DG Competition Working Paper on State Aid and Tax rulings*, 3 June 2016.
814. European Commission: Press Release "*Commission decides selective tax advantages for Fiat in Luxembourg and Starbucks in the Netherlands are illegal under EU state aid rules,*" IP/15/5880 of 21 October 2015.
815. For each of these companies, a tax ruling issued by the respective national tax authority artificially lowered the tax paid by the company. Under EU State aid rules, tax rulings cannot use methods, no matter how complex, to establish transfer prices with no economic justification and which unduly shift profits to reduce the taxes paid by the company. Such practices would give the company concerned an unfair competitive advantage over other companies, typically SMEs that are taxed on their actual profits because they pay market prices for the goods and services they use.
816. European Commission: Press Release "*State aid: Commission concludes Belgian "Excess Profit" tax scheme illegal; around €700 million to be recovered from 35 multinational companies,*" IP/16/42 of 11 January 2016.
817. European Commission: Decision on State aid SA.38373 of 30 August 2016 on State aid implemented by Ireland to Apple, OJ L 187 of 19 July 2017 and Press Release "*State aid: Ireland gave illegal tax benefits to Apple worth up to €13 billion,*" IP/16/2923 of 30 August 2016.
818. Press release "*State aid: Commission investigates transfer pricing arrangements on corporate taxation of Amazon in Luxembourg,*" 7 October 2014 and most recently, Press release "*State aid: Commission finds Luxembourg gave illegal tax benefits to Amazon worth around €250 million,*" 4 October 2017.
819. European Commission: Decision of 3 December 2015 (SA.38945) *Alleged aid to Mc Donald's – Luxembourg*, OJ C 258 of 15 July 2016.
820. European Commission: Decision State aid SA.44888 (NN/2016) (ex EO/2016) – Luxembourg Possible State aid in favour of GDF Suez of 19 September 2016.

market.[821] In March 2015, the Commission unveiled a *Tax Transparency Package*,[822] aimed at ensuring that Member States have the information they need to protect their tax bases and effectively target companies that try to avoid paying their fair share of tax. In June 2015, the package was followed by a Commission *Action Plan for Fair and Effective Taxation*[823] which set out a series of initiatives to tackle tax avoidance, secure sustainable revenues and strengthen the single market for businesses. The Commission argues that, collectively, these measures aim to improve the corporate tax environment in the EU; making it fairer, more efficient and more growth-friendly. The Commission also emphasises that EU competition policy plays a key role in tackling this challenge.

The Commission has been criticised for various aspects of its pursuit of State aid tax measures. Some of these arguments focus on the use of the State aid rules as a mechanism of back-door tax harmonisation and the creation of legal uncertainty due to unclear reasoning – in particular via the reliance in these cases on the *"arm's length" principle*[824] and the (non-binding) *OECD Transfer Pricing Guidelines* to determine whether a given ruling created a selective advantage and thereby gave rise to State aid.[825]

4.5.6 Services of General Economic Interest (SGEI)

The undefined concept of "services of general economic interest" is mentioned in Articles 14 and 106(2) of the TFEU, in the Protocol on Public Broadcasting to the EU Treaty and in Article 36 of the EU Charter of Fundamental Rights of the Union. In short, these provisions create a right to public services and various Treaty rules (notably the transport, competition and State aid rules) are precluded from preventing the fulfilment of services of general economic interest by the undertakings responsible for their provision. In effect, Services of General Economic Interest (SGEI) are economic activities that public authorities identify as being of particular importance to citizens and that would not be supplied (or would be supplied under different conditions) if there were no public intervention. Examples of industries where SGEIs have been used and/or continue to be used in many countries are: telecommunications, broadcasting, water supply, electricity, gas, railways and postal services.

The complex issue of the treatment of SGEI supports by the State under the State aid rules arises from Article 106 of the TFEU which provides that, in respect of public undertakings and undertakings to which Member States grant special or exclusive rights, Member States shall neither enact nor maintain in force any measure contrary

821. European Commission: *Report on Competition Policy*, 2015, SWD (2016) 198 final.
822. *See* IP/15/4610 of 18 March 2015, available at http://europa.eu/rapid/press-release_IP-15-4610_en.htm.
823. *See* IP/15/5188 of 17 June 2015, available at http://europa.eu/rapid/press-release_IP-15-5188_en.htm.
824. That is, that profits must be allocated between companies in a corporate group, and between different parts of the same company, in a way that reflects economic reality and in line with arrangements that take place under commercial conditions between independent businesses.
825. The implications of the prioritised pursuit of State aid tax measures are considered further in Chapter 6.

to the rules contained in the Treaties, in particular to those rules provided for in Article 18 and Articles 101–109. Moreover, the Treaty provides that undertakings entrusted with the operation of services of general economic interest or having the character of a revenue-producing monopoly shall be subject to the rules contained in the Treaties, in particular to the rules on competition, in so far as the application of such rules does not obstruct the performance, in law or in fact, of the particular tasks assigned to them.

A European Court of Justice ruling in 1985[826] held that compensation for the extra obligation imposed on certain waste disposal firms to dispose of waste oil did not constitute State aid – it was compensation for SGEI. As a result, from 1985 until 1995, the European Commission took the view that compensation for the provision of services of general economic interest was not State aid. In 1995, this position became problematic following a Commission Decision which decided that tax concessions to certain postal service providers in France (to offset the cost of public service obligations) did not constitute State aid. On this occasion, the Court took the opposite view: the measure was a State aid which could, nonetheless, be deemed compatible under Article 106(2). Thereafter, the European Commission took the view that compensation for the provision of services of general economic interest was State aid that could, nonetheless, be exempted under either Article 106(2) or Article 107(3) of the TFEU. This view was subsequently challenged before the Court.

The *Ferring* case, decided in 2000, concerned a French Sales tax imposed on pharmaceutical companies selling directly to pharmacies. The tax was not imposed where distribution was made via wholesalers, resulting in the presumption of a selective advantage (and thus State aid) to the French wholesale pharmaceutical sector. However, the wholesalers were required to keep a permanent stock of certain products and to ensure speedy delivery in their geographic area. In this case, the Court held that the sales tax exemption for wholesalers might be compensation for the provision of services of general economic interest if the cost of the exemption was equivalent to the extra costs for wholesalers in meeting their additional legal obligations.[827]

In December 2000, the Nice European Council requested the Commission to report on the application of competition rules to services of general interest. In particular, the European Council requested the Commission to consider ways of ensuring greater predictability and increased legal certainty. In its report to the Laaken European Council in December 2001, the Commission pointed out that EU rules on State aid allow Member States to grant firms entrusted with operating services of general economic interest the financial assistance necessary to offset the additional costs generated by the specific tasks entrusted to them, and to enable the firms concerned to perform those tasks in conditions of economic equilibrium. On the other hand, EU law does not allow the amount of aid granted by the State to exceed what is necessary for the performance of the public service obligation or to be used by a firm

826. Case C-240/83: *Procureur de la Republique v. ADBHU*, [1985] ECR I-531.
827. Case C-53/00: *Ferring v. ACOS*, [2001] ECR 1-9067.

entrusted with operating a service of general interest for the purposes of cross-subsidising activities that are subject to competition.[828]

On 24 July 2003, the European Court of Justice issued a preliminary ruling confirming earlier case law in the *Ferring case*[829] to the effect that *financial support that merely represents compensation for public service obligations imposed by EU Member States does not constitute State aid.* The ECJ also further developed the substantive test for assessing when State funding of public services does go beyond compensation and so must be examined under the EU State aid rules. The new test appeared to be far stricter than that under earlier jurisprudence. Thus, the key issue as between Articles 106 and 107 became whether there was *over-compensation* to the SGEI provider.

In *Altmark (2003)*,[830] the Court developed the ideas of the *Ferring* judgment further *and* held that the State aid control regime does not apply to *compensation* given to any undertaking in consideration for public service obligations imposed on them (because there is no advantage conferred) where four conditions are met:

(1) the beneficiary has effectively been entrusted with clearly defined public service obligations;
(2) the parameters for calculating the compensation must be established in advance in an objective and transparent manner;
(3) the compensation does not exceed what is necessary to cover all or part of the costs incurred in discharging the public service obligations, taking into account the revenue such obligations may generate and the fact that the beneficiary is entitled to make a reasonable profit for discharging these obligations; and
(4) either the undertaking selected to discharge the public service obligation is chosen by means of a public procurement procedure or, failing this, the level of compensation is determined on the basis of an analysis of what it would cost a typical, well-run undertaking to discharge these obligations, again taking into account the revenue such obligations may generate and the right for the beneficiary to make a reasonable profit.

The judgment had several significant procedural and practical implications for EU State aid law enforcement and legal certainty. First, the judgment confirmed that necessary public service compensation falls outside the legal scope of State aid as defined under

828. European Commission: *XXXIst Report on Competition Policy*, 2001, p. 140.
829. Case C-53/00: *Ferring*, [2001] ECR I-9067.
830. Case C-280/00: *Altmark Trans GmbH and Regierungspräsidium Magdeburg v. Nahverkehrsgesellschaft Altmark GmbH, and Oberbundesanwalt beim Bundesverwaltungsgericht*, [2003] ECR I-7747. The Altmark case was referred to the ECJ for a preliminary ruling by the highest German administrative law court. In the first instance proceedings, a competitor sought annulment of licences granted to Altmark Trans GmbH to provide regional transport services. Altmark Trans had shown that the routes realised a loss of 0.58 DM per km and received compensation for this negative return. The competitor argued that Altmark Trans relied on illegal subsidies to provide the services, and that the licences were therefore illegal under German law. The national judges asked the court to decide whether compensation received by Altmark Trans for providing the transport services contained illegal State aid under what are now Article 93 or 107 of the TFEU.

Article 107 of the TFEU. This means that, where funding qualifies as compensation, there is no prior notification or standstill requirement. Second, the judgment provided a substantive test for judging when State funding of public services goes beyond necessary compensation and must be assessed under the State aid rules. Procedurally, this meant also that EU Member States need not notify Altmark compatible SGEI compensation to the Commission. However, the Commission remained free to take up cases on its own initiative or on the basis of a competitor's complaint.

The Altmark case led to a flurry of rule-making by the Commission designed to clarify policy on SGEIs, reinsert them into the State aid regulatory system and, at the same time, ensure that the Commission itself was not swamped with protective notifications.

Accordingly, in November 2005, the Commission adopted a Decision and a Framework on the application of Article 106(2) of the TFEU to State aid in the form of public service compensation (known as the "SGEI Package" or the "Monti-Kroes Package").[831] The conditions of compatibility set out in the Framework by and large corresponded to the conditions of the Decision. Both measures replicated the first three criteria of the Altmark judgment, which did not deal with Article 106(2) but with Article 107(1) of the TFEU. As a consequence, whenever the Altmark test was not satisfied, the test was to be repeated under Article 106(2) of the TFEU, with a slight relaxation as regards the fourth Altmark criterion. While Altmark required that the compensation be defined through a public tender procedure or a cost-benchmark based on the costs of a typical, well run and adequately equipped undertaking, it was sufficient under the SGEI Package that there was no over-compensation.

Analysis of the Commission's case law shows that the Commission has interpreted the Altmark test in a strict manner. As a consequence of the Commission's approach, the Altmark criteria are regularly considered not to be met. The Commission's point of view is based on the position that, while Altmark allows for a self-assessment by EU Member States of public service compensation, the assessment of whether compensation that qualifies as State aid meets the requirements for compatibility under Article 106(2) of the TFEU or other Treaty provisions is a matter falling under the exclusive competence of the Commission. In its practice, the Commission has had the tendency to find that State-financing of public service activities does not comply with the Altmark criteria; thereby bringing it within the ambit of Article 107(1) of the TFEU, and then, subsequently, declaring it compatible with the internal market on the basis of Article 106(2) or Article 107(3) of the TFEU. Hence, by its strict interpretation of the Altmark requirements, the Commission has seized control over Member States' spending in the context of what they consider to be a public service remit.

The main problem, however, has been the fourth Altmark criterion. In essence, the Commission's practice appears to be based on the premise that it can only be met if the provider is chosen on the basis of a competitive tender. However, even in those cases where the choice of undertaking to be entrusted with SGEI provision and the

831. European Commission: Press Release: *"State aid: Commission provides greater legal certainty for financing services of general economic interest."* IP/05/937 of 15 July 2005.

amount of compensation are affected by way of a procurement procedure perfectly in line with competition and public procurement rules, the compensation may fail the Commission's necessity test. The consequence of the Altmark test as interpreted by the Commission in these cases is that public service contracts that include incentives for the operator to increase its efforts, seek improvements in quality, attract more customers and retain additional revenues, require notification. Accordingly, the Commission has compelled the parties to agree on a more or less fixed margin that is not allowed to be increased depending on the economic success of the service in question.

In 2011, the European Commission adopted a revised package of EU State aid rules for the assessment of public compensation for services of general economic interest. The new package clarifies key State aid principles and introduces a new approach with simpler rules for SGEIs that are small, local in scope or pursue a social objective and provision for the detailed scrutiny of larger SGEI cases. The three replacement instruments (a new Communication, Decision and Framework) were augmented by an SGEI *de minimis* Regulation in 2012.

Accordingly, the present SGEI "package" in summary provides for the following.

Table 23 Main Features of the 2011–2012 SGEI Package

The ***2011 SGEI*** *Communication*[832] clarifies basic concepts of State aid, which are relevant for SGEI, such as the notion of aid, SGEI, economic activity, convergence between public procurement procedures, the absence of aid, etc. The ***2011 SGEI*** *Decision*[833] exempts Member States from the obligation to notify public service compensation for certain SGEI-categories to the Commission. The exemption is extended from hospitals and social housing to a much wider range of social services and a lower compensation threshold applies for triggering notifications for other SGEI activities. The notification threshold was lowered from €30 million to €15 million, taking account of stakeholders' concerns that the previous ceiling withdrew very sizeable contracts in important areas of the Internal Market from the Commission's scrutiny. Accordingly, all social services are now exempt from the obligation of notification to the Commission, regardless of the amount of the compensation received. The services concerned must meet "social needs as regards health and long term care, childcare, access to and

832. European Commission: *Communication from the Commission on the application of the European Union State aid rules to compensation granted for the provision of services of general economic interest*, OJ C 8 of 11 January 2012.

833. European Commission: *Decision of 20 December on the application of Article 106(2) of the Treaty on the Functioning of the European Union to State aid in the form of* public service compensation *granted to certain undertakings entrusted with the operation of services of general economic interest*, OJ L 7 of 11 January 2012.

reintegration in the labour market, social housing and the care and social inclusion of vulnerable groups." Previously only hospitals and social housing were exempted. Other SGEIs are exempted, provided that the compensation amount is less than €15 million a year.

The ***2011 SGEI*** *Framework*[834] sets out the approach to assessing large compensation amounts granted to operators outside the social services field. Those cases have to be notified to the Commission and may be declared compatible if they meet certain criteria. The new rules introduce, in particular, a more precise methodology to determine the amount of compensation, a requirement for Member States to introduce efficiency incentives in compensation mechanisms, a requirement to comply with EU public procurement rules and to ensure equal treatment of providers of the same service in the determination of compensation. Moreover, the Commission may require Member States to adopt measures to reduce the anti-competitive effects of certain compensations that present a particularly strong potential for distorting competition in the Internal Market. Accordingly, in future there will be a greater scrutiny of other SGEIs involving compensation amounts of more than €15 million a year and where the potential for distortions of competition within the internal market is higher. Whenever possible, the SGEI should be entrusted through an open and transparent public tender to ensure the best quality at the cheapest cost for taxpayers who pay for the services.

The ***2012 SGEI De Minimis Regulation***[835] exempts from EU State aid rules aid of up to €500,000 per company over a three-year period that is granted as compensation for the provision of SGEIs. Compensation of this magnitude is deemed unproblematic because it is too low to have any impact on trade and competition.

4.5.7 State Aid Action Plan, New Economic Approach and State Aid Modernisation (SAM) Initiative

In 2000, the EU adopted its Lisbon Strategy.[836] This was an action and development plan for the European Union intended to deal with the low productivity and stagnation of economic growth in the EU, through the formulation of various policy initiatives to be taken by all EU Member States. The broader objectives set out by the Lisbon Strategy were to be attained by 2010 and included the objective of transforming Europe into the world's largest knowledge-based economy by 2010. The dawn of the new millennium

834. European Commission: *Communication from the Commission – European Union framework for State aid in the form of public service compensation,* [2011] OJ C 8 of 11 January 2012.
835. European Commission: Regulation No 360/2012/EU on the application of Articles 107 and 108 of the Treaty on the Functioning of the European Union to *de minimis* aid granted to undertakings providing services of general economic interest, OJ L 114 of 26 April 2012.
836. "Presidency Conclusions," Lisbon European Council, 23 and 24 March 2000, Press Release Library, European Commission.

also saw a related and renewed interest in reducing State aid in the EU. Accordingly, in March 2001, the Stockholm European Council:

> asked EU Member States to demonstrate a downward trend in State aid in relation to GDP by 2003, taking into account the need to redirect aid towards horizontal objectives of common interest, including cohesion objectives.

This was important as it established a new objective indicator regarding aid reduction and set a political time-limit. At the same time, in order to improve transparency in the field of State aid and to more effectively monitor progress, the Commission was asked to ensure the provision of a publicly accessible State aid Register and Scoreboard by July 2001.[837] These objectives were confirmed by the Barcelona European Council in March 2002 where Member States again agreed to step up their efforts to reduce aid levels by eliminating aid particularly distortive of fair competition and reorienting resources towards horizontal objectives and targeting aid to identified market failures, i.e. environment, training, research and development and small and medium-sized enterprises.

By 2003, the Commission was able to report that:

> The level of State aid as a percentage of GDP decreased in twelve of the fifteen Member States between 1997 and 2001, in line with the undertaking at Stockholm to demonstrate a reduction in State aid by 2003. Greece, Italy, Portugal and Finland experienced the sharpest falls (by 0.3 percentage points or more) between 1997-1999 and 1999-2001. In contrast, aid in relation to GDP actually increased in Denmark, Luxembourg and the Netherlands. This was due largely to a rise in the level of aid granted for railway transport although in the case of Denmark, there was a substantial increase in aid for two horizontal objectives, employment and environment.[838]

With the 2003 position established by 2005, the Commission reported that the total amount of State aid granted by the then fifteen Member States was estimated at €53 billion in 2003 (0.57% of EU GDP).[839] Moreover, the underlying trend in the total amount of aid was "stable rather than downward," but there was a shift away from aid to individual companies and towards horizontal objectives and, in particular, R&D and the environment.

In 2005, the Commission's *State Aid Action Plan* was launched with the objective to provide more focused State aid rules and, thus, promote better targeted aid and better public spending. The emphasis of the work of the Commission placed on the new principle of "less and better targeted aid"[840] showed the Commission's desire not only

837. The State Aid Scoreboard was launched by the Commission in July 2001 to provide a transparent and publicly accessible source of information on the overall State aid situation in each of the EU Member States and on the Commission's current State aid control activities.
838. European Commission: *State Aid Scoreboard Spring 2003*, COM (2003) 225 final of 30 April 2003, p. 6.
839. European Commission: *State Aid Scoreboard Spring 2005*, COM (2005) 147 final of 20 April 2005.
840. European Commission: "*State aid action plan – Less and better targeted State aid: a roadmap for State aid reform 2005-2009*," (Consultation document – SEC (2005) 795), COM/2005/0107 final of 7 June 2005.

to reduce aid but to highlight good over bad aid i.e. aid should primarily reflect objectives of common interest (notably the Lisbon Strategy but primarily horizontal purposes in fact – such as regional development, supporting R&D and assisting environmental protection). The approach of the Action Plan was also designed to assist public finance management objectives and emphasised a linkage with market failures:

> Our Action Plan sets out a vision for a modernised state aid control regime to address these concerns. It is based on the twin principles of efficiency and equity. State aid should be efficient – it should promote overall growth in the size of the economic cake, by targeting the gaps that markets alone will not fill. But nothing in life is free, and that includes state aid. So the state aid rules should help Member States get the best value for money for their taxpayers, and make sure that scarce state resources are used where they can have most impact.[841]

Among the specific proposals in the Action Plan, the Commission indicated that it would, when relevant, strengthen its economic approach to State aid analysis as an economic approach to State aid control was one means of better focusing and targeting certain State aid towards the objectives of the EU Lisbon Strategy. This became generally known as the "new economic approach" in State aid regulation. Second, the Action Plan had a specific focus on improving research, development and innovation in the EU and announced that relevant State aid guidelines should be reformed. Third, in order to promote employment across the EU, the Action Plan indicated that the Commission intended to simplify and consolidate the block exemption regulations for training and employment aids, both of which were to expire at the end of 2006, in the context of a general block exemption regulation. Fourth, the Action Plan signalled unfinished business in regard to legal certainty and optimal control concerning SGEI compensations (*see* earlier). In addition, the Commission announced that it would adapt the Transparency Directive, to take account of the recent evolution of case law from the European Courts and simplify notification procedures.[842]

Following intensive work under the State Aid Action Plan, the Commission was ready again in 2012 to promote a further phase of reform and, in May 2012 announced its *State Aid Modernisation (SAM)* initiative. In the wake of the international financial crisis this emphasised the need for State aid control to contribute to a stronger financial discipline in Member States together with the need to streamline the enforcement of State aid rules, allowing the Commission to focus on the most distortive cases i.e. primarily the updating of the General Block Exemption Regulation (GBER). Moreover, reformed State aid control was seen as a means of supporting sustainable growth and contributing to improving the quality of public spending by discouraging aid that did not bring real added-value and distorted competition. The Commission also emphasised that "good" aid should support flagship initiatives of the *Europe 2020 Strategy* for smart, sustainable and inclusive growth in a pro-competitive way while also

841. "The State Aid Action Plan – Delivering Less and Better Targeted Aid," Neelie Kroes European Commissioner for Competition, SPEECH/05/440, London, 14 July 2005.
842. This resulted in European Commission: *Notice on a Simplified procedure for the treatment of certain types of State aid*, OJ C 136 of 16 June 2009.

maintaining a level playing field in the internal market. To this end, the Commission undertook to achieve wide-ranging reforms of substantive rules, procedures and decentralisation.[843]

4.5.7.1 *Progress of Rule-Making – Especially GBER*

Under the 2008 General Block Exemption Regulation, many categories or subcategories of aid were allowed to be granted immediately by EU Member States without prior notification to the Commission, up to the maximum aid amounts defined in the Regulation. In particular, the block exemption categories covered aid to small and medium-sized enterprises, aid in the form of risk capital, support to small enterprises newly created by female entrepreneurs, aid for research and development and innovation (R&D&I), aid for environmental protection, regional aid, training aid and aid for disadvantaged or disabled workers.[844]

Subject to some specific rules for each aid type and whether or not the place of the aid was in an assisted or deprived EU region, specific thresholds applied to the exemption from notification. If a measure was outside the scope of the GBER, it would have to be notified and would be examined under the prevailing guidelines e.g. the Regional aid Guidelines where the total amount of aid from all sources exceeded 75% of the maximum amount of aid which an investment with eligible costs of €100 million could receive, applying the standard aid threshold in force for large enterprises in the approved regional aid map on the date the aid was to be granted. Under the SAM reforms, all State aid guidelines and most regulations were updated between 2012 and 2016 – not least to coordinate them with the GBER.

As noted earlier, the 2008 GBER effectively covered 60% of all aid measures and almost 30% of all aid amounts in the EU and, in the most recent 2014 edition of the GBER,[845] several important changes were made which effectively further extended the scope of the GBER.[846] The Commission now hopes that at least 75% of all State aid measures, representing around 66% of total EU State aid by value, will no longer need to be notified.

In parallel with the elaboration of the GBERs, the Commission has been stepping up the *ex post* monitoring of the main types of aid covered by GBERs. This can be seen as a minimum trade-off against the decentralisation and the degree of exemption envisage by the GBER process. All Member States are apparently cooperating with the Commission on this, although many have submitted the requested monitoring

843. While several major areas of the SAM reforms are considered in this Chapter (e.g., the 2012 GBER and the Notice on the Notion of Aid of 2016) a fuller examination of the State aid reform processes can be found in Chapter 5.
844. European Commission: Regulation No 800/2008/EC of 6 August 2008 declaring certain categories of aid compatible with the common market in application of Articles 87 and 88 of the Treaty, OJ L 241 of 9 August 2008. This is also considered in further detail in Chapter 5.
845. European Commission: Regulation No 651/2014/EU of 17 June 2014 declaring certain categories of aid compatible with the internal market in application of Articles 107 and 108 of the Treaty, OJ L 187 of 26 June 2014.
846. *See* Chapter 5.

information with considerable delay. The CFI also handed down a judgment in 2009[847] which confirmed the legality of the monitoring exercises. Under the 2014 GBER, Member State monitoring was also introduced.

Another important outcome of the SAM reform was the elaboration of criteria for the application of the Article 107(3)(b) of the TFEU exemption in regard to *important projects of common European interest*. While certain earlier soft law instruments had previously dealt with the treatment of important projects of common European interest (IPCEI's), notably in regard to Research, Development and Innovation and concerning Environmental protection,[848] the Commission, as part of the State Aid Modernisation initiative, decided to clarify generally in 2014 how it would deal with State aid to promote the execution of such projects under the exemption of Article 107(3)(b) of the TFEU.[849] The policy background to this Communication has two distinct but inter-related elements. First, the State Aid Modernisation initiative (SAM)[850] calls for State aid to be directed towards objectives of common European interests in line with the priorities of the Europe 2020 agenda, so as to address market failures or other important systemic failures that hinder the promotion of growth and jobs and the development of an integrated, dynamic and competitive internal market. Second, the EU currently, and for the foreseeable future, has a range of strategies that are regarded as being of common European interest and per se important. These include the macro-policy initiatives set out in Table 24 *infra*.

Table 24 Important EU Strategies of Common Interest

The Europe 2020 Strategy[851] – This is a 10-year strategy proposed by the European Commission to advance the economy of the EU. It replaced the "Lisbon Strategy 2000-2010" and aims at "smart, sustainable, inclusive growth" with greater coordination of national and European policy. The strategy identifies five key targets the EU towards increasing growth and employment – raising the employment rate to at least 75%, investing 3% of GDP in R&D, reducing greenhouse gas emissions by between 20% and 30% coupled with a renewable

847. Case T-376/07: *Germany v. Commission*, [2009] ECR II-4293.
848. Under the earlier 2006 *Framework on State Aid for Research, Development and Innovation, supra* and the 2008 *Guidelines on State aid for Environmental Protection, supra* which pre-dated this Communication.
849. European Commission: *Communication from the Commission – Criteria for the analysis of the compatibility with the internal market of State aid to promote the execution of important projects of common European interest*, OJ C 188 of 20 June 2014.
850. European Commission: Communication from the Commission to the European Parliament, the Council, the European Economic and Social Committee and the Committee of the Regions – *EU State Aid Modernisation (SAM)* – COM (2012) 209 final of 8 May 2012.
851. European Commission: Communication from the Commission – *"Europe 2020 – A strategy for smart, sustainable and inclusive growth,"* COM (2010) 2020 final of 3 March 2010.

energy share of 20% in total energy consumption and a 20% increase in energy efficiency, increasing participation in secondary and third level education and bringing 20 million EU citizens above the poverty line. The Strategy is being implemented by a series of seven "flagship initiatives."

The European Research Area (ERA) – This is a system of scientific research programmes integrating the scientific resources of the European Union.[852] Since its inception in 2000, the structure has been concentrated on multinational cooperation in the fields of medical, environmental, industrial, and socio-economic research. The ERA can be likened to a research and innovation equivalent of the European "common market" for goods and services. Its purpose is to increase the competitiveness of European research institutions by bringing them together and encouraging a more inclusive way of working; similar to already existing systems among institutions in North America and Japan. Increased mobility of knowledge workers and deepened multilateral cooperation among research institutions across EU Member States are central goals of the ERA.[853]

The European Strategy for Key Enabling Technologies (KETs)[854] – In June 2012 the Commission launched its strategy to boost the industrial production of KETs-based products (e.g., innovative products and applications of the future). This strategy aims to keep pace with the EU's main international competitors, restore growth in Europe and create jobs in industry. Key Enabling Technologies (KETs) are investments and technologies that will allow European industries to retain competitiveness and capitalise on new markets. The Strategy has a particular focus on four KETs: nanotechnologies, advanced materials, advanced manufacturing and processing (production technologies) and biotechnology.

The Energy Strategy for Europe[855] – The Energy Union Strategy is a project of the European Commission to coordinate the transformation of European energy supply. It was launched in February 2015, with the aim of providing secure,

852. Article 179(1) of the TFEU provides that: "*the Union shall have the objective of strengthening its scientific and technological bases by achieving a European research area in which researchers, scientific knowledge and technology circulate freely, and encouraging it to become more competitive, including in its industry, while promoting all the research activities deemed necessary by virtue of other Chapters of the Treaties.*"

853. At http://ec.europa.eu/research/era/index_en.htm.

854. European Commission: Communication from the Commission to the European Parliament, the Council, the European Economic and Social Committee and the Committee of the Regions – "*A European strategy for Key Enabling Technologies – A bridge to growth and jobs*," COM (2012) 341 final of 26 June 2012.

855. European Commission: Communication from the Commission to the European Parliament, the Council, the European Economic and Social Committee and the Committee of the Regions – "*Energy 2020 — A strategy for competitive, sustainable and secure energy*" - COM (2010) 639 final.

sustainable, competitive, affordable energy. It was endorsed by the European Council in March 2015 and focuses on five priority areas: Energy security, solidarity and trust; a fully integrated European energy market; Energy efficiency contributing to moderation of demand; De-carbonising the economy and Research, innovation and competitiveness. The strategy includes a minimum 10% electricity interconnection target for all EU Member States by 2020, which the Commission hopes will put downward pressure energy prices, reduce the need to build new power plants, reduce the risk of black-outs, improve the reliability of renewable energy supplies, and encourage market integration.

The 2030 framework for climate and energy policies[856] – In 1997 the EU agreed to reduce its carbon dioxide emissions as part of the Kyoto Protocol, which runs until 2020. The 2030 Framework for Climate and Energy Policies, agreed in October 2014, sets out European targets beyond Kyoto and until 2030.

The European Energy Security Strategy[857] – This was launched by the European Commission in May 2014. The Strategy aims to ensure a stable and abundant supply of energy for European citizens and the economy. It seeks also to address key concerns e.g. that the EU imports more than half of all the energy it consumes (with a particularly high import dependency on crude oil (more than 90%) and natural gas (66%) and a total import bill of more than €1 billion per day) and that several Member States are heavily reliant on a single supplier, including some that rely entirely on Russia for their natural gas (with the risks of supply disruptions, whether caused by political or commercial disputes,[858] or infrastructure failure).

The Electronics Strategy for Europe[859] – This strategy was adopted in May 2013 and aims to maintain Europe at the leading edge in the design and manufacturing of micro and nano-electronics, and to provide benefits across the economy. The strategy facilitates industry investments of €100 billion and aims to create 250,000 jobs in Europe up to 2020.[860]

The Trans-European Transport and Energy networks[861] – The EU supports Trans-European Networks (TENs) within the Connecting Europe programme. The support is for transport networks, energy networks and telecommunication

856. European Commission: Communication from the Commission to the European Parliament, the Council, the European Economic and Social Committee and the Committee of the Regions, "*A policy framework for climate and energy in the period from 2020 to 2030*" - COM (2014) 15 final.
857. European Commission: Communication from the Commission to the European Parliament and the Council, "*European Energy Security Strategy*," COM (2014) 330 final.
858. For instance, the 2009 gas dispute between Russia and transit-country Ukraine which left many EU countries with severe shortages.
859. European Commission: "*The Electronics Strategy for Europe*," May 2013, accessed at: https://ec.europa.eu/digital-single-market/en/electronics-strategy-europe.
860. At https://ec.europa.eu/digital-single-market/en/electronics-strategy-europe.
861. *See* http://www.inforse.org/europe/eu_ten-e.htm.
On energy and http://ec.europa.eu/transport/infrastructure/tentec/tentec-portal/site/en/abouttent.htm on transport.

networks. The networks comprise infrastructure and priority corridor projects to link up integrated transport connections (roads, railways etc.), energy supply networks (pipelines etc.) and telecommunications connections.

The Innovation Union[862] – The "Innovation Union," created in 2010, sets out a strategic approach to innovation and is intended to focus EU efforts and co-operation with non-EU countries on challenges such as climate change, energy and food security, health and the ageing EU population. In particular, it recognises the need to use public sector intervention to stimulate the private sector and to remove bottlenecks (e.g., lack of finance, fragmented research systems and markets, under-use of public procurement for innovation and slow standard setting) which stop ideas reaching the market. The Innovation Union is one of the "flagship" initiatives under the Europe 2020 Strategy.

The Digital Agenda for Europe[863] – This is another "flagship" initiative under the Europe 2020 Strategy. The objective of this Agenda is to chart a course to maximise the social and economic potential of information technology (especially the internet) for business, work, recreation, communication and expression. Successful delivery of this Agenda is intended to spur innovation, economic growth and improvements in daily life for both citizens and businesses. In its specifics, it aims to use EU funds to increase internet coverage, to create a legal and safe internal market in online content and services and promote ICT innovation.

Resource Efficient Europe[864] – This (further) flagship initiative for a resource-efficient Europe provides a long-term framework for actions in many policy areas, supporting policy agendas for: climate change, energy, transport, industry, raw materials, agriculture, fisheries, biodiversity and regional development. This is designed to increase certainty for investment and innovation and to ensure that all relevant policies factor in resource efficiency in a balanced manner.

862. European Commission: Communication from the Commission to the European Parliament, the Council, the European Economic and Social Committee and the Committee of the Regions – "*Europe 2020 Flagship Initiative — Innovation Union*," COM (2010) 546 final of 6 October 2010.
863. European Commission: Communication from the Commission to the European Parliament, the Council, the European Economic and Social Committee and the Committee of the Regions – "*A Digital Agenda for Europe*," COM (2010) 245 final of 26 August 2010.
864. European Commission: Communication from the Commission to the European Parliament, the Council, the European Economic and Social Committee and the Committee of the Regions – "*A resource-efficient Europe — flagship initiative under the Europe 2020 strategy*," COM (2011) 21 of 26 January 2011.

The Integrated Industrial Policy for the Globalisation Era[865] – This highlights the need for industry to play a key role if Europe is to remain a leading economic power. The main policy document "An integrated industrial policy for the globalisation era" was accompanied by an EU Report on the competiveness performance of EU Member States and the European Competitiveness Report 2010. The Integrated Policy notes that a large part of the policy instruments which can improve industrial competitiveness are national, and the success of EU industry critically depends on national action. Thus, it is important, to keep an overview over national measures to foster industrial competitiveness because the design of EU level measures has to reflect the circumstances and existing national policies. While many of the necessary actions are in the Member States competency, the Commission will assist by monitoring progress and helping to organise the exchange of best practice.

4.5.7.2 *Notion of Aid*

On 19 May 2016, the Commission published, as a last part of its State Aid Modernisation initiative, a *Notice on the Notion of aid* which aims to give a guidance on when public spending falls within, and outside, the scope of EU State aid control and to help public authorities and companies to identify when public support measures can be granted without needing approval under EU State aid rules.[866] The Notice gives general guidance on all aspects of the definition of State aid via a categorised summary of the case law of the European Courts and the Commission's decision-making practice. This Notice is of particular importance for practitioners in the State aid field as previously many had argued, for example, that the interpretation of the substantive elements forming the notion of aid such "granted by the state or through state resources" and "selectivity" were far from clear.[867] While it is too early to assess whether this new Notice will put all questions of legal certainty on such points to rest, or if the Commission is trying to breath too much into its decisions and the case law of the Courts,[868] the 2016 Notice represents a valiant effort by the Commission to pull together 60 years of the conceptual development of the notion of aid into a single user document for practitioners and will undoubtedly constitute a key reference document in the years ahead.

865. European Commission: Communication from the Commission to the European Parliament, the Council, the European Economic and Social Committee and the Committee of the Regions, "*An Integrated Industrial Policy for the Globalisation Era – Putting Competitiveness and Sustainability as the Centre Stage*," COM (2010) 614 final of 28 October 2012.
866. *See*, European Commission: Press Release "*State aid: Commission clarifies scope of EU State aid rules to facilitate public investment*," IP/16/1782 of 19 May 2016.
867. *See*, for example, A. Biondi, "*State Aid is Falling Down, Falling Down: An Analysis of the Case Law on the Notion of Aid*" (2013), 50 Common Market Law Review, Issue 6, pp. 1719–1743.
868. A core argument in the Irish appeal on the 2016 Apple Inc. decision.

4.5.8 Data

As mentioned earlier, the Stockholm European Council in 2001 requested the Commission to ensure the provision of a publicly accessible State aid Register and Scoreboard by July 2001[869] in order to improve transparency in the field of State aid and to more effectively monitor progress. This was achieved on schedule with the online *State Aid Scoreboard*[870] presenting total data on the volume and objectives of State aid in the various countries. This achievement also encouraged policy makers to discuss State aid issues more freely.

The Scoreboard reveals that, until 2007, State aid decreased across EU Member States because the Commission acquired many more powers to promote State aid control and its role strengthened as part of European Monetary Union, the Lisbon Strategy and EU Enlargement. By the end of 2007, however, this positive trend ended as a result of the direct and indirect impacts of the international financial crisis.

The latest available data from State Aid Scoreboard relates to 2015[871] and shows that total State aid in the 28 EU Member States amounted to €98 billion, representing 0.67% of EU GDP. This represents a decrease of about 0.04% of GDP compared to 2014. In nominal terms, this represents a slight decrease of about 0.5% compared to 2014 expenditures (- €465 million). Across the 28 Member States, the overall change in reported State Aid expenditure in 2015 compared to 2014 was explained by the Commission with reference to the following factors:

(1) a strong reduction of State aid for regional development of €4.8 billion;
(2) a reduction of agricultural aid of €249 million;
(3) a reduction of State aid on research and development (including innovation) of €1 billion;
(4) an increase of State aid to environmental protection (including energy savings) of €3.3 billion;
(5) an increase of State aid for culture of €1.1 billion in 2015;
(6) an increase of State aid for employment of €400 million; and
(7) an increase of State aid for social support to individual consumers.

869. The State Aid Scoreboard was launched by the Commission in July 2001 to provide a transparent and publicly accessible source of information on the overall State aid situation in each of the EU Member States and on the Commission's current State aid control activities.
870. State Aid Scoreboard comprises aid expenditure made by Member States and which falls under the scope of Article 107(1) of the TFEU. The data is based on the annual reporting by Member States pursuant to Article 6(1) of Commission Regulation No 794/2004/EC. The archive is available at: http://ec.europa.eu/competition/state_aid/studies_reports/archive/scoreboard_arch.html.
871. Available at: http://ec.europa.eu/competition/state_aid/scoreboard/index_en.html.

4.5.9 Other Jurisprudence

In addition to those mentioned already in regard to the millennium period, a number of further landmark cases have emerged since 2000.

4.5.9.1 The **Adria-Wien Pipeline Case** *(2001)*[872]

In this case, the Austrian Constitutional Court asked the Court of Justice for a preliminary ruling concerning the interpretation of what is now Article 107 of the TFEU – whether legislative measures adopted by a Member State which provide for a rebate of energy taxes on natural gas and electricity, but grant that rebate only to undertakings whose activity is shown to consist primarily in the manufacture of goods, are to be regarded as State aid. The Court of Justice concluded that, although objective, the criterion applied by the national legislation was not justified by the nature or general scheme of that legislation and could not therefore save the measure from being State aid.

In particular, the Court stated that:

> a State measure which benefits all undertakings in national territory, without distinction, cannot therefore constitute State aid ... For the application of [Article 107 of the TFEU] ... the only question to be determined is whether, under a particular statutory scheme, a State measure is such as to favour certain undertakings or the production of certain goods within the meaning of [Article 107 of the TFEU] in comparison with other undertakings which are in a legal and factual situation that is comparable in the light of the objective pursued by the measure in question. However, a measure which, although conferring an advantage on its recipient, is justified by the nature or general scheme of the system of which it is part does not fulfil that condition of selectivity.[873]

This further clarified the selectivity criterion and the Court again departed from the effects principle in ruling that the *objective* pursued by a Member State was to be regarded as decisive for the determination of whether a State measure could be seen as *prima facie* materially selective. Among the views on this case, it has been suggested that the Court avoided a two-step assessment of selectivity (asking first if one group of undertakings is in receipt of an advantage denied to another group and second whether such differentiation is justified by the nature or general scheme of the measure of which it forms part), but merely merged them and accepted a clearly objective-based approach in the area of material selectivity.[874] Others have taken the view that the

872. Case C-143/99: *Adria-Wien Pipeline GmbH and Wietersdorfer & Peggauer Zementwerke GmbH v. Finanzlandesdirektion für Kärnten*, [2001] ECR I-8365.
873. Case C-143/99: *Adria-Wien Pipeline GmbH and Wietersdorfer & Peggauer Zementwerke GmbH v. Finanzlandesdirektion für Kärnten*, [2001] ECR I-8365, paras 34–36, 41–42, 48–52, 55.
874. A. Bartosh: "*The concept of selectivity?*," in edited by Erika Szyszczak, "*Research Handbook on European State Aid Law*," 2011, p. 180.

methodology used in *Adria-Wien Pipeline* did not alter the basic structure of the selectivity test; it just incorporated the comparability exercise into the selectivity examination.[875]

4.5.9.2 **Preussen Elektra** *(2001)*[876]

This case involved a dispute over the compatibility with EU law of a German scheme for subsidising renewable electricity generation. The scheme obliged generators to pay premium prices for electricity from renewables, and to share the cost of doing so between themselves. The Court found that the State aid rules could not apply as the companies involved were under private ownership and that the subsidies provided by the scheme were not at any time State resources. The Court stated that only advantages granted directly or indirectly through State resources are to be considered aid within the meaning of Article 107 of the TFEU. The distinction made in that provision between "aid granted by a Member State" and aid granted "through State resources" did not signify that all advantages granted by a State, whether financed through State resources or not, constitute aid but was intended merely to bring within that definition both advantages which are granted directly by the State and those granted by a public or private body designated or established by that State.

4.5.9.3 ***The* Chronopost Case** *(2003)*[877]

The *Chronopost case* focused on whether the access granted to Chronopost (an express parcels delivery company which is a subsidiary of the French State post office organisation La Poste) to La Poste's national network was an advantage given via State resources and constituting State aid. The Commission had found that there was no State aid. However, Ufex and other competitors of Chronopost appealed the decision and the CFI supported them, annulling the Commission decision on 14 December 2000. In the subsequent appeal lodged by Chronopost, La Poste and France, the European Court of Justice on 13 July 2003 annulled the CFI decision, finding that the CFI had erred in law in setting out the relevant test for the existence of State aid, and referred the matter back to the CFI.[878] On 7 June 2006, the CFI annulled the Commission decision again, this time for inadequate reasoning and because the Commission had

875. K. Driurdz & C. Marchgraber, "*Non-discrimination in European and Tax Treaty Law. Open Issues and Recent Challenges*" (2015) International Tax Law, p. 317.
876. Case C-379/98: *PreussenElektra AG v. Schhleswag AG*, judgment of 13 March 2001, ECLI-:EU:C:2001:160.
877. Joined Cases C-83/01 P, C-93/01 P and C-94/01 P: *Chronopost SA, La Poste and French Republic v. Ufex and others*, [2003] ECR I-6993.
878. In effect, the ECJ found that the CFI had erred in law in using a test based on comparisons with normal market conditions, because La Poste's network, built to meet non-commercial public service requirements and on the basis of a reserved sector, was too dissimilar to a commercial network to enable the comparisons in the CFI's test. Paragraph 38 of the ECJ judgment notes the "absence of any possibility" of using the CFI's test. Instead, the ECJ held (paras 39–40) that the relevant test was whether Chronopost had been charged on an objectively rational basis for the full costs of its use of the network.

been wrong to disregard the value of goodwill in the transfer of Postadex (including a customer database) from La Poste to Chronopost. On 1 July 2007, the ECJ annulled the CFI's new decision and definitively restored the Commission's finding of no aid.

4.5.9.4 The **British Aggregates Association Cases** *(2006–2012)*

The British Aggregates Association ("BAA") submitted a complaint to the European Commission that the UK levy on aggregates breached Article 107(1) of the TFEU. The aggregates levy was a tax on aggregates (a material often used in construction), which aimed to encourage the use of recycled aggregates and reduce environmental damage. It was levied on rock, sand or gravel on their first extraction as well as on processed products. Derogations applied to certain extraction processes and to materials with certain geological features. BAA complained that it breached Article 107. However, the Commission decided[879] on 24 April 2002 not to object to the levy, finding it did not comprise any elements of State aid within the meaning of Article 107 as its scope was justified by the logic and nature of the tax system.

BAA appealed to the General Court of the European Union. In the *BAA 1 case*[880] the General Court dismissed the appeal. BAA further appealed to the CJEU, which in the *BAA 2 case*,[881] upheld three of BAA's six complaints and referred the case back to the General Court. Following reconsideration, the General Court held that the Decision not to open an investigation must be annulled: *BAA 3 case.*[882]

A continuing and difficult issue in regard to tax measures is the tension between European rules against Member States conferring advantages on certain undertakings or products and the discretion that Member States retain to determine their own tax systems. This was central to these cases and the question of how, in practice, selectivity is to be assessed with reference, in particular, to undertakings or products "in a comparable legal and factual situation" – and whether or not "justified by the nature or general scheme of the tax system of which it is a part" – is now illustrated by the BAA 3 case where the General Court identified five steps:

(i) Identify what is the *"normal" taxation* under the specific tax regime, against which the impugned measure is to be compared.
(ii) Identify the *objective* pursued by the specific tax regime.
(iii) Consider whether the situations of the undertakings/products in question are *comparable.*
(iv) If so, consider whether they are *taxed differently.*
(v) If so, consider whether that difference in tax treatment is *justified* by the objective pursued by the regime.

879. European Commission: Decision C(2002) 1478 of 24 April 2002 United Kingdom Aggregates Levy, OJ C 133 of 5 June 2002.
880. Case T-210/02: *British Aggregates Association v. Commission*, [2006] ECR II-2789.
881. Case C-487/06: *British Aggregates Association v. Commission*, [2008] ECR I-10515.
882. Case T-210/02: *British Aggregates Association v. Commission*, [2006] ECR II-2789.

While the Commission has persisted in limiting the rights of third parties in State aid proceedings (based on a fundamental view that State aid regulation is a matter between the Commission and Member States) the European Courts have assisted the rights of third parties, especially the position of claimants. Thus, cases such as *Athinaiki (2008), NDSHT (2011)* and *Ryanair (2010)* have had a strong impact on enforcement practice.[883] Similarly, case law has strengthened parties' defence rights by: (a) imposing limits on the Commission's control of the correct execution of its recovery decisions (*Mediaset*);[884] and (b) maintaining access to justice for all undertakings receiving a recovery order. In particular, it is directly as a result of ECJ action that beneficiaries of individual aid granted under an aid scheme can challenge the Commission's decision before the EU courts, declaring an aid scheme incompatible with the common market and seeking recovery of the aid paid out.[885]

4.5.9.5 The **Lufthansa Case** *(2013) on the Role of National Courts*

National courts are in a position to play a significant role in applying EU State aid law, ranging from actions brought by a Member State against the beneficiary of aid, to actions brought by private parties against Member States, or aid recipients, alleging that the aid granted in a specific case was unlawful. Actions before national courts can offer a means of redress for competitors and other third parties affected by unlawful State aid. Remedies available before these courts include preventing the payment of unlawful aid; recovering unlawful aid; and demanding damages for competitors and other third parties.[886] The number of cases in which private parties have brought direct actions alleging that competitors have received aid has grown, especially since the new millennium.[887]

In relation to one such case, the landmark judgment in the *Lufthansa* case saw the European Court of Justice create an important precedent in 2013 in regard to the role of national courts.[888] According to that judgment, when the Commission opens an in-depth investigation, national courts in the EU must assume the existence of aid. Furthermore, where the measure is challenged before the national court, the national court must take all necessary steps to stop the implementation of the aid, which may include ordering its suspension and repayment, before the Commission reaches its final

883. Case C-521/06: *Athinaiki Techniki v. Commission*, [2008] ECR I-5829; Case C-322/09 P: *NDSHT Nya Destination Stockholm Hotell & Teaterpaket AB v. Commission*, [2010] ECR I-11911 and Case T-423/07: *Ryanair v. Commission*, [2011] ECR II-2397.
884. Case C-403/10 P: *Mediaset SpA v. Commission*, [2011] ECR I-117.
885. Joined Cases C-71/09 P, C-73/09 P and C-76/09 P: *Comitato "Venezia vuole vivere" and Hotel Cipriani Srl and Società Italiana per il gas SpA (Italgas) v. Commission*, [2011] ECR I-4727.
886. European Commission: *Commission notice on the enforcement of State aid law by national courts*, OJ C 85 of 9 April 2009.
887. European Commission: "*Enforcement of EU State aid law by national courts: the Enforcement Notice and other relevant materials*," Competition Handbook, 2010, available at: http://ec.europa.eu/competition/publications/state_aid/national_courts_booklet_en.pdf.
888. Case C-284/12: *Deutsche Lufthansa v. Flughafen Frankfurt-Hahn GmbH*, judgment of 21 November 2013, ECLI:EU:C:2013:755.

decision. This is despite the fact that, at the point of starting the in-depth investigation, the Commission will not have reached any definite conclusion about whether the measure in question does indeed constitute aid and it is possible that the measure could be found not to constitute aid when the Commission reaches its final decision. Indeed, in the case in question the Commission did conclude that the arrangements at issue did not constitute State aid.[889]

This judgment could lead to an increasing role for courts in State aid proceedings, and a further rise in private actions in State aid, as it allows competitors of alleged aid recipients to adversely affect the operations of these recipients while the Commission is still continuing its investigation. The assessment of the quantum of aid to be repaid, therefore, represents a key issue to be addressed by courts in such State aid proceedings. While the judgment is silent on what is to happen if the national court acts and the final Commission decision finds that there is no aid involved, it does recognise that the national court may itself consider that there is no aid involved or that the Commission's basis for the opening of the investigation procedure might be unsound. In those circumstances, the judgment held that the national court may seek clarification from the Commission and, in accordance with Article 267(2) and (3) of the TFEU, it may or must refer a question to the Court for a preliminary ruling.

4.5.9.6 The **Irish Travel Tax Case** *(2016) Concerning Recovery*

Another landmark judgment from the General Court was the *Irish Air Travel Tax* (ATT) case, which challenged existing practice in determining the amount of aid to be recovered. For several years from March 2009, an Irish ATT was payable by commercial airlines for every passenger (excluding transfer and transit passengers) departing from an Irish airport. In July 2012 the Commission concluded that, as the tax rates were based on the distance travelled from Dublin Airport, the rates constituted incompatible State aid and conferred a selective economic advantage on domestic flights over most cross-border flights.[890] The Commission ordered the recovery of unlawful aid from three Irish airlines, Ryanair, Aer Lingus and Aer Arann. The Commission concluded that the amount of recoverable State aid was the difference between the lower rate of €2 and the standard rate of €10 levied on each passenger. In February 2015, following an appeal by Ryanair and Aer Lingus, the General Court annulled the Commission's Decision, stating that:

> It must be held that, in a situation such as that in the present case, where the ATT was intended to be passed on to the passengers and where the economic advantage arising from the application of the reduced tax could also have been

889. In relation to the Lufthansa case, the European Commission concluded in late 2014 that Ryanair's arrangements with Frankfurt-Hahn GmbH did not constitute State aid. For further details, *see* European Commission: Decision State Aid: Commission decisions on public financing of airports and airlines in Germany, Belgium, Italy and Sweden – further details', memo, 1 October, http://europa.eu/rapid/press-release_MEMO-14-544_en.htm.

890. European Commission: Decision of 25 July 2012 on State aid case SA.29064 (2011/C, ex 2011/NN), "*Differentiated air travel tax rates implemented by Ireland,*" OJ L 119 of 30 April 2013.

> passed on to the passengers, the Commission cannot presume that the advantage actually obtained and retained by the airlines amounted, in all cases, to €8 per passenger.[891]

This judgment had potentially significant implications for State aid cases, as it indicated that passing-on effects needed to be taken into account (subtracted) when calculating the amount of State aid to be recovered. In contrast, the standard approach in Commission State aid decisions was that the alleged competitive advantage equalled the "negative" amount of incremental cash flows and that the recovery of this negative amount was required in full, in order to re-establish the status quo. Accordingly, there was typically no consideration of whether any aid was passed on e.g. in the form of lower prices to customers.

However, on 21 December 2016, the CJEU overturned the General Court's ruling on this; holding that recovery entails the restitution of the advantage procured for the beneficiary, not the restitution of any economic benefit it may have enjoyed as a result of exploiting the advantage. Thus, the advantage which had to be recovered was the difference between the normal rate and the lower rate actually applied to the beneficiaries of the aid, i.e. the sum of €8 per passenger for each of the flights concerned. In so ruling, the Court rejected the notion of "economic passing on" used by the General Court. Accordingly, there was no need to assess whether and to what extent the airlines actually utilised the economic advantage e.g. whether it enabled them to offer more competitive ticket prices.[892]

After 60 years, both State aid law and State aid policy have moved on dramatically. The core "notion of aid" is a far more complex and sophisticated concept than could ever have been imagined by the Treaty founders. While the application of the prohibition on State aid has arguably tightened and enforcement has benefitted from innovative methods and clearer law, the fact remains that the system is still largely permissive rather than prohibitive. Accordingly, what has probably changed most in 60 years is the balance of power in regard to State aid policy. This is reflected, in particular, in the heavy enforcement of State aid rules in the taxation sphere – which clearly is a cause for concern among many Member States – and in the Commission's emphasis on major cases (which it defines) and the new policy of regulated decentralisation via block exemptions.

At the same time, and with the support of the Courts generally, State aid policy has managed to repeatedly reinvent itself in response to various crises and the developmental stages of the EU itself and to align its logic closely with the latest macro-policy initiatives of the EU. In place of its original peripheral conception as a possibly necessary adjunct to competition policy, State aid regulation has become a core policy of the EU itself and a field that now deals more with the alignment of national economic policies than with spillover effects that could damage the common/internal market or impact negatively on cohesion.

891. Case T-473/12: *Aer Lingus and Ireland v. European Commission*, judgment of 5 February 2015, not yet reported.
892. Case C-164/15 P: *Commission v. Aer Lingus Ltd and Ryanair*, ECLI:EU:C:2016:990.

Law and policy over the years has also reflected the emergence of laissez-faire economics as a single economic philosophy and this is strongly seen in the new primary focus of State aid regulation on the economics of measures rather than their per se legal compliance. State aid law, in turn, has conveniently shifted and evolved to facilitate this trend. A related development from recent years is the Commission's orientation towards delineating good aid versus bad aid – a matter that would have been inconceivable prior to 1990. And armed with this philosophy and a huge confidence in its validity, the Commission has gone global with the State aid regime via the WTO (but only to a point) and more so via trade agreements with the close neighbours of the EU. It has also succeeded in reducing inefficient and expensive sectoral aid with a focus on horizontal measures while also using the bureaucracy and power of the State aid system to leverage new economic approaches in national policies which are closely aligned with its core philosophies.

These are among the elements to be considered further in the following Chapters.

CHAPTER 5

The Process and Progress of State Aid Reforms

5.1 INTRODUCTION

EU law and policy in respect of the application of the State aid rules has changed in many ways over a 60-year period. On this there are two types of changes – incremental and fundamental:

- Incremental change of law and policy in the EU primarily results from new European Court decisions on actual cases and new policy directions resulting from new decisions by the European Commission.
- Fundamental change of law and policy in the EU results from active efforts to reform law and policy in regard to the regulation of State aid.

The importance of incremental change has already been seen in earlier coverage of the development of the State aid system of the EU via Commission decisions and European Court judgments. Moreover, up to the 1999 State Aid Procedural Regulation, all procedural aspects of the application of Article 108 emerged from contested decisions before the European Courts and procedural constraints and best practices imposed by these cases.

In regard to fundamental change, prior to the late 1990s, there was an underlying political problem in that the European Commission and the Council of Ministers seemed unlikely to agree on any measures under what is now Article 109 of the TFEU. The Commission suspected that its powers would be diluted by the Member States in the Council and the Council feared an expansion of the Commission's remit in the field of State aid control. Accordingly, the provision of Article 109 of the TFEU was only used once up to that point.[893]

In 1966, the Commission presented a draft Regulation to the Council on the conditions and methods of application of certain provisions of what is now Article 108 of the TFEU.[894] This text proposed an eight-week preliminary procedure period after the expiry of which approval of notified aid could be assumed. It also proposed a definitive list of exemptions related to Article 107(2) including social aid, cultural aid, and aid supporting certain public services (such as water, gas, electricity and telecommunications). The reduction or abolition of identified existing aids in the agricultural sector was also proposed. Within months, this proposal was amended to change the agricultural aid list. Faced with little likelihood of progress, the Commission formally withdrew the proposal by a decision of 28 February 1975. A similar fate met a further Article 109 based proposal put forward in the interim in 1970 and designed to introduce a quarterly system of reporting on the application in significant cases of regional aid.[895] This proposal was withdrawn by Commission Decision on 14 December 1976.

The Council of Industry Ministers examined a proposal in 1990 to invite the Commission to propose a draft Regulation under what is now Article 109 of the TFEU which would comprehensively define the scope and criteria of application of Articles 107 and 108. This was known as the "Battaglia initiative." However, Council agreement on the initiative foundered on the point of whether the Council was competent to ask the Commission to make an Article 109 based proposal. This, of course, suggests in turn that there was little Commission enthusiasm and the matter concluded with, the then Competition Commissioner, Sir Leon Brittan agreeing that the Commission would henceforth present to the Industry Council the draft annual Report on Competition Policy, that a multilateral consultative group on State aid would be established and meet twice yearly and that the Commission would publish a compendium of the rules in force regarding State aid control.[896]

5.2 THE FIRST PHASE OF REFORM 1996–2005 (THE "IRISH INITIATIVE")

Against this difficult political background, the first phase of fundamental change commenced in 1996, following proposals from the Irish Council Presidency to open up for discussion the efficiency and effectiveness of EU State aid controls, including issues related to predictability, administrative simplification and legal certainty. At the time,

893. Council Regulation No 1107/70/EEC on the granting of aids for transport by rail, road and inland waterway, OJ L 130 of 1970.

894. Draft Council Regulation on the conditions and methods of application of certain provisions of Article 93 of the Treaty; COM (66) 95 Final of 30 March 1966.

895. European Commission: *Proposal for a Council Regulation laying down in accordance with Article 94 EEC the methods of supervision by the Commission of the application in the central regions of the Community of the principles for the coordination of general regional aid schemes*, COM (72) 1523 Final of 4 December 1972.

896. On the Battaglia initiative, *see* generally European Commission: *Twentieth Report on Competition Policy* (1990), point 170.

this was highly politically sensitive and was initially blocked by Germany and Spain at the Council of Ministers. However, this initiative steadily made an impact in subsequent years resulting in an important Procedural Regulation, the first use of Block Exemption Regulations in the EU State aid control system and political agreement to reduce overall State aid levels. The subsequent manifestation of the reform process was the European Commission State Aid Action Plan of 2005.

The adoption by the Council of the so-called Enabling Regulation[897] was an important product of this phase of reform. In 1998, Council Regulation No 994/98/EC was adopted using Article 109 of the TFEU as its legal basis and this gave the Commission, for the first time, the power to issue block exemption (Commission) Regulations declaring categories of horizontal State aid (regional aid, aid for SMEs, aid for research and development, aid for employment, aid for environmental protection and training aid) compatible with the internal market and exempt from notification. A range of such Commission Regulations followed between 2001 and 2006.[898] It also facilitated the first *De Minimis* Regulation,[899] at a time when the Commission's policy on *de minimis* was still in doubt before the European Courts, and a further *De Minimis* Regulation was later adopted for Agriculture.[900]

In the relations between the Commission and the Member States, the Enabling Regulation was a political and legal breakthrough that established that reforms were needed but that their substance should remain under the control of the Commission. By facilitating a solution on *de minimis* and the first development of block exemptions, Council Regulation No 994/98/EC also allowed the Commission to commence a strategy to prepare for the accession of 10 new Member States in 2004 on the basis of the first transfer of State aid regulatory responsibilities to Member States.

Separately, in the context of this first phase of reform, the Procedural Regulation of 1999[901] was an important achievement as it codified the process of assessing the legality of State aid, specified criteria and exemptions in more detail, strengthened the

897. Council Regulation No 994/98/EC of 7 May 1998 on the application of Articles 92 and 93 of the Treaty establishing the European Community (now Articles 107 and 108 of the TFEU) to certain categories of horizontal State aid, OJ L 142 of 14 May 1998, as amended in 2013 by Council Regulation No 733/2013/EU of 22 July 2013, OJ L 204 of 31 July 2013.
898. European Commission: Regulation No 68/2001/EC of 12 January 2001 on the application of Articles 87 and 88 of the Treaty to training aid, OJ L 10 of 13 January 2001 as amended in 2004; Commission Regulation No 70/2001/EC of 12 January 2001 on the application of Articles 87 and 88 of the Treaty to State aid to small and medium-sized enterprises, OJ L 10 of 13 January 2001 as amended in 2004; Commission Regulation No 2204/2002/EC of 12 December 2002 on the application of Articles 87 and 88 of the Treaty to State aid for employment, OJ L 337 of 13 December 2002 and Commission Regulation No 1628/2006/EC of 24 October 2006 on the application of Articles 87 and 88 of the Treaty to national regional investment aid (Block Exemption Regulation for regional aid), OJ L 302 of 1 November 2006.
899. European Commission: Regulation No 69/2001/EC of 12 January 2001, OJ L 10 of 13 January 2001 and European Commission: Regulation No 1998/2006/EC on the application of Articles 87 and 88 of the Treaty to *de minimis* aid, OJ L 379 of 28 December 2006.
900. European Commission: Regulation No 1535/2007/EC of 20 December 2007 on the application of Articles 87 and 88 of the Treaty to de minimis aid in the sector of agricultural production, OJ L 337 of 21 December 2007.
901. Council Regulation No 659/1999/EC of 22 March 1999 laying down detailed rules for the application of Article 93 of the EC Treaty (now Article 108 of the Treaty on the Functioning of the European Union), OJ L 83 of 27 March 1999.

Commission's monitoring and recovery instruments and established deadlines and a range of consequences for procedural breaches and in respect of powers of recovery. The Regulation also formalised the earlier multilateral consultative group on State aid as an Advisory Committee made up of representatives of Member States and headed by the Commission.[902] The Advisory Committee was given a role in regard to such matters as the form and content of notifications and annual reports, time limits, extensions, and interest calculations while, at the same time excluding any Member State veto. On this, the Regulation provided that: "the Commission shall take the utmost account of the opinion delivered by the Committee. It shall inform the Committee of the manner in which its opinion has been taken into account."

In respect of the rights of interested parties, the Regulation defined these as Member States, firms, persons, or associations "whose interests might be affected by the granting of aid"[903] and established the right for those parties to complain to the Commission about unlawful aid, to provide more information when the Commission decided to open a formal investigation of a case and to challenge State aid decisions in national courts.[904]

The Regulation strengthened monitoring powers by allowing the Commission to demand data on all existing aid schemes on an annual basis. This addressed a particular problem whereby some governments, such as Greece in the 1980s, refused to cooperate with monitoring requirements. It also paved the way for more substantial monitoring and transparency initiatives (such as the State Aid Scoreboard). On State aid recovery, the Regulation introduced injunctive powers of interim recovery and conceded a 10-year recovery limitation period to Member States, thereby promoting greater legal certainty for them in regard to previous measures and ongoing contested cases.

In overall terms, the Procedural Regulation strengthened Commission powers and discretions concerning State aid control while also delivering limited, but nonetheless important, concessions to Member States. In particular, the Regulation represented a move to hard law to promote legal certainty and uniformity and thereby increased the role of legal rules and decreased the scope for political deal-making in State aid cases.

A further effect of the first phase of reform was reflected in renewed political consideration of how to reduce overall State aid levels in the EU. It became clear that, even assuming full legal compliance by Member States and allowing for enhanced Commission enforcement powers, this alone might not achieve substantial reductions in the overall volumes of State aid in the EU. Accordingly, in March 2001, and in a new atmosphere of trust between the Commission and the Member States, the Stockholm European Council:

> asked EU Member States to demonstrate a downward trend in State aid in relation to GDP by 2003, taking into account the need to redirect aid towards horizontal objectives of common interest, including cohesion objectives.

902. 1999 Procedural Regulation, Article 28.
903. 1999 Procedural Regulation, Article 1(h).
904. 1999 Procedural Regulation, Article 20.

This was important as it established a new objective indicator regarding aid reduction and set a political time limit. At the same time, in order to improve transparency in the field of State aid and to more effectively monitor progress, the Commission was asked to ensure the provision of a publicly accessible State aid Register and Scoreboard by July 2001.[905] These objectives were confirmed by the Barcelona European Council in March 2002 where Member States again agreed to step up their efforts to reduce aid levels by eliminating aid particularly distortive of fair competition, reorienting resources towards horizontal objectives and targeting aid to identified market failures, i.e., for environment, training, research and development and small and medium-sized enterprises.

By 2003, the Commission was able to report that:

> The level of State aid as a percentage of GDP decreased in twelve of the fifteen Member States between 1997 and 2001, in line with the undertaking at Stockholm to demonstrate a reduction in State aid by 2003. Greece, Italy, Portugal and Finland experienced the sharpest falls (by 0.3 percentage points or more) between 1997-1999 and 1999-2001. In contrast, aid in relation to GDP actually increased in Denmark, Luxembourg and the Netherlands. This was due largely to a rise in the level of aid granted for railway transport although in the case of Denmark, there was a substantial increase in aid for two horizontal objectives, employment and environment.[906]

With the 2003 position established by 2005, the Commission reported that the total amount of State aid granted by the then fifteen Member States was estimated at €53 billion in 2003 (0.57% of EU GDP).[907] Moreover, the underlying trend in the total amount of aid was "stable rather than downward," but there was a shift away from aid to individual companies and towards horizontal objectives and in particular R&D and the environment.

5.3 THE STATE AID ACTION PLAN[908]

The second stage of reform centred on the Commission's 2005 "State Aid Action Plan – *Less and better targeted State aid: A Roadmap for State Aid Reform 2005 – 2009.*" This was based on the following objectives:

- *Less distortive and better targeted State aid,* in line with the European Council's repeated declarations, so that public money is used effectively to the benefit of EU citizens in terms of improving economic efficiency, generating more

905. The State Aid Scoreboard was launched by the Commission in July 2001 to provide a transparent and publicly accessible source of information on the overall State aid situation in each of the EU Member States and on the Commission's current State aid control activities.
906. European Commission: *State Aid Scoreboard Spring 2003,* COM (2003) 225 final of 30 April 2003, p. 6.
907. European Commission: *State Aid Scoreboard Spring 2005,* COM (2005) 147 final of 20 April 2005.
908. European Commission: *State Aid action plan: Less and better targeted State aid: a roadmap for State aid reform 2005 - 2009* – Consultation document adopted on 7 June 2005.

growth and sustainable jobs, social and regional cohesion, improving services of general economic interest, sustainable development and cultural diversity.
- *A more refined economic approach*, so that less distortive aid, particularly where money is less easily available from financial markets, can be approved more easily and quickly and so that the Commission concentrates its resources on the cases liable to create more serious distortions of competition and trade.
- *More streamlined and efficient procedures, better enforcement, higher predictability and enhanced transparency*, including the exemption of more measures from the notification obligation and the simplification of procedures.
- *A shared responsibility between the Commission and Member States* based on the view that the Commission cannot improve State aid rules and practices without the effective support of Member States and their full commitment to comply with their obligations to notify any envisaged aid and to enforce the rules properly.

Among the specific proposals in the Action Plan, the Commission indicated that it would, when relevant, strengthen its economic approach to State aid analysis as an economic approach to State aid control was one means of better focusing and targeting certain State aid towards the objectives of the EU Lisbon Strategy. Second, the Action Plan had a specific focus on improving research, development and innovation in the EU and announced that relevant State aid guidelines should be reformed. Third, in order to promote employment across the EU, the Action Plan indicated that the Commission intended to simplify and consolidate the block exemption regulations for training and employment aids, both of which were to expire at the end of 2006, in the context of a general block exemption regulation. Fourth, in regard to public services and continuing controversies concerning services of general economic interest, the Commission stated that it would adopt a new Decision on this matter, in the interests of legal certainty, together with guidelines to specify under which conditions public service compensations which constitute State aid would be considered compatible with the Treaty. The Action Plan also signaled a wish to grant an exemption from notification of small-scale compensations and provide special conditions in regard to hospitals and social housing companies. In addition, the Commission announced that it would adapt the Transparency Directive, to take account of the recent evolution of case law from the European Courts and simplify notification procedures.[909]

On the generality of the Action Plan, the Commission announced on 9 February 2006 that there was broad stakeholder support for the principles and direction of the intended reforms, especially as regards:

- the revision of rules applicable to State aid for R&D and innovation;
- the proposal to create a general block exemption regulation which would authorise State aid without a need to notify the measure to the Commission;

909. This resulted in European Commission: *Notice on a Simplified procedure for the treatment of certain types of State aid*, OJ C 136 of 16 June 2009.

- the review of the regulation specifying the amount below which a subsidy is not considered State aid (the *de minimis* regulation); and
- the new rules on services of general economic interest and regional aid.

5.3.1 The New Economic Approach

In regard to the so-called *refined economic approach*, earlier attempts by the Commission to adopt a per se approach to State aid cases (i.e., to assume that they always involved negative impacts on competition and trade) gave way to European Court requirements for the Commission to specify the impacts on competition and trade that brought a government measure within the scope of Article 107(1). However, except in the case of large investment projects, rescue and restructuring cases – and to a limited degree the analysis of incentive effects under the R&D Guidelines – the Commission had never really embarked on the extensive economic analysis needed to demonstrate or balance these effects, especially in decisions concerning the exemption of State aid from prohibition. Indeed, the European Court of First Instance held in 2000 that:

> the Commission is not required to carry out an economic analysis of the actual situation on the relevant market, of the market share of the undertakings in receipt of the aid, of the position of competing undertakings and of trade flows of the services in question between Member States, provided that it has explained how the aid in question distorted competition and affected trade between Member States.[910]

At the same time, the European Courts had adopted an approach which was more sophisticated and geared towards the economic circumstances of a particular case. This was especially so in regard to public service obligations. In addition, the Commission had developed certain economic tests for certain State aid situations – notably the "market economy investor principle" and the "private creditor principle"[911] – to address questions in the application of Article 107(1) as to whether a particular measure conferred a commercial advantage.

One critique in 2006 of the dearth of economic analysis in State aid control pointed out that:

> The resulting approach – while arguably being relatively simple to administer – does not seek to identify the effectiveness of aid and the actual impact on markets. In combination with a rather broad approach taken when considering whether a measure constitutes State aid or not, the State aid approval system thus bears the risk of being overly broad (to look at too many measures) and at the same time to be too imprecise, in the sense of not discriminating enough between "good" aid

910. Case T-55/99: *Confederación Espanola de Transporte de Mercancías v. Commission*, [2000] ECR II-3207, para. 7.

911. This was affirmed by the European Court of Justice in the Fogosa Case (Case C-480/98: *Spain v. Commission*, [2000] ECR I-8717) where it was held that, to eliminate any State aid in the State's dealings with a debtor, the State must follow *the private creditor principle* by insisting on rescheduling debt, payments by installment or forced bankruptcy in order to avoid an escalation of unpaid debt.

> measures and "bad" aid measures. One of the main aspects in which a more economic approach bears promise in the context of State aid control is that it has the potential to improve the level of precision in State aid control.[912]

Moreover, it was relevant that, well into the twenty-first century, DG Competition of the European Commission was somewhat strong on lawyers and short of modern economists.[913]

The State Aid Action Plan pointed out that:

> State aid should only be used when it is an appropriate instrument for meeting a well defined objective, when it creates the right incentives, is proportionate and when it distorts competition to the least possible extent. For that reason, appreciating the compatibility of State aid is fundamentally about balancing the negative effects of aid on competition with its positive effects in terms of the common interest.

Thus, there was a need for a thorough modification of rules and procedures including a refined economic approach in order to allow for an effective assessment of the allocation or distribution effects of State aid, taking account of the actual contribution of State aid measures to commonly agreed, politically desirable objectives. Accordingly:

> it is likely, as well as intended, that an effects-based approach will shift the argumentation from legal and accounting battles towards a battle over the impact of the aid on markets and ultimately on consumers. Such a change would not only greatly contribute towards precision and effectiveness of European State aid control, but in fact enhance predictability...and holds the potential to reduce – at least to some extent – the scope for politics in the field of State aid control and the potential to increase cooperation across Member States.[914]

In terms of the specifics of an economic framework for the analysis of State aid cases, the following new three Step Test was outlined [915] for assessing the compatibility of a State aid measure under Article 107(3) of the TFEU based on the assessment of consumer welfare.

---

912. H.W. Friederiszick, L.A. Röller & V. Verouden: "*European State Aid Control - An Economic Framework*" in P. Buccirossi (ed.): "*Handbook of Antitrust Economics*," MIT Press, February 2006, *supra*, pp. 10–11.
913. In L.A. Röller: "*Economic Analysis and Competition Policy Enforcement in Europe*" in Edward Elgar (ed.): "*Modelling European Mergers: Theory, Competition Policy and Case Studies*," 2005 where the Chief Competition Economist pointed out that, of 700 officials at DG Competition, 200 had an economics background but only 20 of these (including the 10 economists on his own staff) had an advanced modern education in economics.
914. H.W. Friederiszick, L.A. Röller & V.Verouden: "*European State Aid Control - An Economic Framework*," February 2006, *supra*.
915. *Ibid.*, p. 37.

Table 25 The Three-Step Balancing Test

STEP A – Is there a market failure or another objective of common interest? (e.g., social or regional cohesion);
STEP B – Is the aid measure targeted, i.e. does the proposed aid address the market failure or other objective? In particular:
i. is the aid measure an appropriate instrument, i.e. are there other, better placed instruments?
ii. is there an incentive effect, i.e. does the aid change the behaviour of firms?
iii. is the aid measure necessary, i.e. could the same change in behaviour be obtained with less aid?
STEP C – Are the distortions of competition and effect on trade limited, so that the overall balance is positive?

The idea was that this would allow a balancing of costs and benefits, including appropriate consideration of efficiency and equity aspects and a focus on the effects and effectiveness of State aid in comparison with the largely rule based assessments which had generally applied in the past. However, this would run in parallel with the rule based assessments which, for legal reasons, would retain their fundamental importance. Moreover, the view of the Commission in advocating this new approach was that it could also be regarded as a refinement of the traditional policy principles in State aid control centred on whether a State aid was *necessary, proportional and of limited duration*. In terms of the practical application of this approach, the Commission prioritised the use of the new balancing tests to State aid for Innovation and in regard to Risk Capital for Small and Medium Enterprises and later developed versions of this approach for the assessment of several other categories of State aid.

In its new emphasis on economic impacts, the Commission improved its basis for identifying "good" aid by focussing on the identification and assessment of market failures (including externalities, imperfect information, or coordination problems). The proper identification of market failures, in turn, was intended to facilitate a better evaluation of whether State aid could be justified and considered acceptable, whether it represented the most appropriate solution, and how it should be implemented to achieve the desired objective without distorting competition and trade to an extent contrary to the common interest.[916] The alternative reasoning related to *objectives of common interest*, such as social or regional cohesion, also recognised that State aid control was relevant to other EU policies (whether as a directing factor or to allow flexibility in the State aid regime to facilitate the attainment of those other policy objectives).[917]

In the application of this new approach, the Commission gradually promoted a move away from a purely form-based approach towards an effects-based and

916. A. Biondi: "*Some Reflections on the Notion of 'State Resource'*," *supra*, p. 25.
917. Several key aspects of these policy interactions are explored in Chapter 6.

efficiency-based approach which emphasised the economic implications of State aid.[918] This was also more consistent with the antitrust approach in EU competition policy and eventually moved the burden of proof concerning need, legality and positive/negative impacts from the European Commission to the notifying Member States.

5.3.2 *De Minimis* Adjustments

Under the State Aid Action Plan, the Commission recognised that "in an EU of 25 or more, it will be impossible for the Commission to assess every single distortion of competition resulting from aid awarded at national level" and the Commission proposed, in effect, to concentrate on State aids likely to pose the most serious threats to competition and trade (specifically: fiscal advantages, unlimited or implicit State guarantees: especially in the financial services, energy and recently liberalised sectors). Moreover, the State Aid Action Plan noted that the 2004 Enlargement posed a particular challenge creating a need for adaptations to State aid policy based on better governance and effective control. In the context of these reforms, and despite calls from some Member States to raise the *de minimis* threshold to €4,000,000, a new *de minimis* ceiling of €200,000 was introduced with effect from 1 January 2007.[919] The 2006 Regulation also applied to the transport sector and to the processing and marketing of agricultural products (but not agricultural production). Nevertheless, since many companies in the road transport sector are relatively small, a specific ceiling of €100,000 was applied to this sector. For the same reason, and in view of the overcapacity of the sector, *de minimis* aid could not be used to buy road freight vehicles.

In 2004, the Commission had established specific *de minimis* rules for the agriculture sector.[920] Under that Regulation, which covered both primary production and the processing and marketing of agricultural products, the total amount of de minimis aid granted to one undertaking was regarded as not meeting all the criteria of Article 107(1) of the TFEU where it did not exceed €3,000 per beneficiary over any period of three years or a cumulative amount laid down for each Member State representing 0.3% of annual output in the agriculture sector. On account of the similarities between activities in the processing and marketing of agricultural products and industrial activities, activities in the processing and marketing of agricultural products were included in the scope of Regulation No 1998/2006/EC, creating an exclusion from the scope of Regulation No 1860/2004/EC.

918. M. Merola: "*The Forces Shaping State Aid Control in the EU*," *supra*.
919. European Commission: Regulation No 1998/2006/EC of 15 December 2006 on the application of Articles 87 and 88 of the Treaty to *de minimis* aid, OJ L 379 of 28 December 2006. This applied until 2013.
920. European Commission: Regulation No 1860/2004/EC of 6 October 2004 on the application of Articles 87 and 88 of the EC Treaty to de minimis aid in the agriculture sector, OJ L 325 of 28 October 2004.

In 2007, Regulation No 1860/2004/EC was repealed and replaced by a specific *de minimis* Regulation regarding agricultural production.[921] This also increased the earlier thresholds to €7,500 and 0.75% of annual output in the agriculture sector.

5.3.3 Increased Monitoring

As noted earlier, the Commission initially introduced individual block exemption regulations for training aid, employment aid, environmental aid, research and development and innovation aid and regional aid with respect to both SMEs and large enterprises between 2001 and 2006 via Commission Regulations applying the 1998 Enabling Regulation. From 2006, the Commission increased its ex post monitoring of the main types of aid covered by these Block Exemption Regulations. The analysis of the results of the first three years monitoring exercises showed that, overall, the system had functioned in a satisfactory manner. All Member States were cooperating with the Commission, even though many continued to submit requested information with considerable delay. The CFI also handed down out a judgment in 2009[922] which confirmed the legality of the monitoring exercises.

5.3.4 The SGEI Package

Following the *Altmark* judgment in 2003, there was a perceived need to further clarify the application of the State aid rules to the financing of SGEIs. Accordingly, the Commission adopted a Decision and a Framework on the application of Article 106(2) of the TFEU to State aid in the form of public service compensation (known as the "SGEI Package" or the "Monti-Kroes Package") in November 2005.[923] The conditions of compatibility set out in the Framework by and large corresponded to the conditions of the Decision. Both measures replicated the first three criteria of the Altmark judgment, which did not deal with Article 106(2) but with Article 107(1) of the TFEU. As a consequence, whenever the Altmark test was not satisfied, the test was to be repeated under Article 106(2) of the TFEU, with a slight relaxation as regards the fourth Altmark criterion. While Altmark required that the compensation should be defined through a public tender procedure or a cost-benchmark based on the costs of a typical, well run and adequately equipped undertaking, it was sufficient under the SGEI Package that there was no over-compensation.

921. European Commission: Regulation No 1535/2007/EC of 20 December 2007 on the application of Articles 87 and 88 of the EC Treaty to *de minimis* aid in the sector of agricultural production, OJ L 337 of 21 December 2007.
922. Case T-376/07: *Germany v. Commission*, [2009] ECR II-4293.
923. European Commission; Press Release: "*State aid: Commission provides greater legal certainty for financing services of general economic interest*," IP/05/937 of 15 July 2005.

5.3.5 Further Development of Block Exemptions

In 2006, the Commission adopted a Regulation allowing the block exemption of regional aid granted in line with the prevailing 2007 RAGs and an approved regional aid map for the period 2007–2013, provided that the aid was transparent (meaning aid schemes where it was possible to calculate precisely the gross grant equivalent as a percentage of eligible expenditure ex ante without a need to undertake a risk assessment – notably grants, interest rate subsidies, capped fiscal measures and public loans that were backed by normal security and did not involve abnormal risk giving rise to State guarantee elements). While the Regulation applied to aid schemes and individual aids, it did not apply to regional aid measures supporting the coal, steel, shipbuilding, synthetic fibres and agriculture and fisheries sectors or to export aid or aid contingent upon the use of domestic goods.

In addition, the regional aid block exemption for regional investment aid schemes only applied if, before the start of work on the project, the beneficiary had submitted an application for aid, the project had been approved for support and an express reference to both conditions was included in the aid scheme.

The Commission's initial sorties into block exempting certain categories of horizontal State aid accelerated significantly with the adoption of the first General Block Exemption Regulation in 2008, which both consolidated and extended the measures introduced between 2001 and 2006.

Under the 2008 *General Block Exemption Regulation*,[924] 26 categories or subcategories of aid were allowed to be granted immediately by EU Member States without prior notification to the Commission, up to the maximum aid amounts as defined in the Regulation:

- ***Small and medium-sized enterprises aid*** – Beyond the categories of aid available for all enterprises, different types of aid were specifically designed to help SMEs to overcome the specific "market failures" they faced. Thus, SMEs could be subsidised in their different development stages viz. SME investment and employment aid, consultancy aid in favour of SMEs and aid for SME participation in fairs.
- The General Block Exemption Regulation also covered ***aid in the form of risk capital*** as risk capital was seen as constituting an important instrument for the financing of SMEs. The Regulation, accordingly, exempted from notification aid for risk capital in the formation of private equity investment funds in which the State is a partner, investor or participant; even if on less advantageous terms than other investors. The investment fund could invest up to €1.5 million per target undertaking over a twelve month period.

924. European Commission: Regulation No 800/2008/EC of 6 August 2008 declaring certain categories of aid compatible with the common market in application of Articles 87 and 88 of the Treaty, OJ L 241 of 9 August 2008.

- The Regulation allowed EU Member States to support ***small enterprises newly created by female entrepreneurs*** to allow these entrepreneurs to overcome the specific market failures which they were perceived as facing, especially access to finance. In particular, the Regulation allowed support for different kinds of operating costs including child and parent care costs.
- ***Aid for Research & Development & Innovation (R&D&I)*** – Beyond the more traditional categories of R&D aid, the GBER also included a series of innovation measures to foster the competitiveness of European industry via more money spent on R&D&I including:
  - o Aid for research and development projects.
  - o Aid for technical feasibility studies.
  - o Aid for industrial property right costs for SMEs.
  - o Aid for young innovative enterprises.
  - o Aid for innovation advisory services and for innovation support services.
  - o Aid for the loan of highly qualified personnel.
  - o Aid for research and development in the agricultural and fisheries sectors.
- ***Environmental aid*** – The Regulation facilitated national authorities granting an important number of aid measures favouring environmental protection and tackling climate change, notably:
  - o Investment aid to go beyond EU standards for environmental protection.
  - o Aid for the acquisition of transport vehicles which go beyond EU environmental standards.
  - o Aid for early adaptation to future EU environmental standards for SMEs.
  - o Investment aid in energy savings measures.
  - o Investment aid in high efficiency co-generation.
  - o Investment aid for the promotion of energy from renewable energy sources.
  - o Aid for environmental studies.
  - o Aid in the form of reductions in environmental taxes.
- ***Regional aid*** – As national regional aid was seen as promoting the economic, social and territorial cohesion of the EU by addressing the handicaps of disadvantaged regions, the block exemption covered:
  - Regional investment and employment aid.
  - Aid for newly created small enterprises in assisted regions.
- ***Training aid*** – The Regulation authorised aid for general training as well as for specific training.
- ***Aid for disadvantaged and disabled workers*** – The Regulation covered aid that incentivised companies to hire disabled or otherwise disadvantaged workers viz:
  - Aid for the recruitment of disadvantaged workers in the form of wage subsidies.
  - Aid for the employment of disabled workers in the form of wage subsidies.
  - Aid for compensating the additional costs of employing disabled workers.

Subject to some specific rules for each aid type and whether or not the place of the aid was in an assisted or deprived EU region, the following thresholds applied to the exemption from notification.

Table 26 2008 GBER Limits to Block Exemptions for Horizontal State Aids

Commission Regulation No 800/2008/EC *did not apply* to any individual aid, whether granted ad hoc or on the basis of a scheme, the gross grant equivalent of which exceeded the following thresholds:

(a) SME investment and employment aid: €7.5 million per undertaking per investment project;
(b) investment aid for environmental protection:€7.5 million per undertaking per investment project;
(c) aid for consultancy in favour of SMEs: €2 million per undertaking per project;
(d) aid for SME participation in fairs: €2 million per undertaking per project;
(e) research and development project aid and feasibility studies:
  (i) if the project is predominantly fundamental research €20 million per undertaking, per project/feasibility study;
  (ii) if the project is predominantly industrial research, €10 million per undertaking, per project/feasibility study;
  (iii) for all other projects, €7.5 million per undertaking, per project/feasibility study;[925]
  (iv) if the project is a EUREKA project twice the amounts laid down in points (i), (ii) and (iii) respectively.
(f) aid for industrial property rights costs for SMEs: €5 million per undertaking per project;
(g) training aid: €2 million per training project;
(h) aid for the recruitment of disadvantaged workers: €5 million per undertaking per year;
(i) aid for the employment of disabled workers in the form of wage costs: €10 million per undertaking per year;
(j) aid compensating for additional costs of employing disabled workers: €10 million per undertaking per year.

Regional investment aid awarded in favour of large investment projects was required to be notified to the Commission if the total amount of aid from all sources exceeded 75% of the maximum amount of aid which an investment with eligible costs of €100 million could receive, applying the standard aid threshold in force for large enterprises in the approved regional aid map on the date the aid was to be granted.

925. For the purposes of determining the appropriate threshold applicable to research and development project aid and feasibility studies pursuant to point (e), a project was required to be considered to consist "predominantly" of fundamental research or "predominantly" of industrial research, if more than 50% of the eligible project costs were incurred through activities which fall within the category of fundamental research or industrial research respectively. In cases where the predominant character of the project cannot be established, the lower threshold would apply.

5.3.6 Simplification

In line with the Action Plan, the European Commission's State aid "Simplification Package" entered into force on 1 September 2009. The Package is composed of a *Best Practice Code*[926] and a *Notice on a Simplified Procedure*,[927] both aimed at improving the effectiveness, transparency and predictability of the Commission's State aid procedures.

Overall, the State Aid Action Plan primarily succeeded in reducing the Commission's case load in response to the 2004 and 2007 Enlargements which added 12 new Member States to the European Union. This emerged principally from increasing the *de minimis* threshold and the adoption of the GBER which also established the areas which the Commission would regard as more important cases requiring notification and, where appropriate, a much more detailed economic assessment and a higher burden of proof from notifying Member States.

The reform initiative under the Action Plan was somewhat interrupted with the emergence of the international financial crisis which required a further package of initiatives by 2007–2008. The important changes of policy and law in response to the crisis were not reforms, as such, but emergency measures,[928] and the Commission returned to State aid reform in 2012.

5.4 THE STATE AID MODERNISATION PROGRAMME (2012–2016)[929]

On 8 May 2012, the European Commission launched a third reform initiative called the *State Aid Modernisation programme* (SAM). The SAM was based on the Commission view that modernisation of State aid control was needed to strengthen the quality of the Commission's scrutiny and to shape State aid control into a tool which promoted a sound use of public resources for growth-oriented policies and limited competition distortions that would undermine a level playing field in the internal market. The Commission also pointed out that the complexity of the prevailing substantive rules and the procedural framework, applying equally to smaller and bigger cases, were challenges to State aid control. Accordingly, the stated objectives of the SAM were:

1. to foster sustainable, smart and inclusive growth in a competitive internal market;

926. European Commission: *Code of Best Practice for the conduct of State aid control procedures*, OJ C 136 of 16 June 2009.
927. European Commission: *Notice from the Commission on a simplified procedure for treatment of certain types of State aid*, OJ C 136 of 6 June 2009, pp. 3–12.
928. These are considered in Chapter 6.
929. European Commission: Communication from the Commission to the European Parliament, the Council, the Economic and Social Committee and the Committee of the Regions – *EU State Aid Modernisation (SAM)*, COM/2012/0209 final of 8 May 2012.

2. to focus Commission *ex ante* scrutiny on cases with the biggest impact on the internal market while also strengthening the Member States cooperation in State aid enforcement;
3. to streamline the rules and provide for faster decisions.

The Commission's proposals and the implementation of the SAM to date are summarised in the following Table.

Table 27 Progress of the State Aid Modernisation Programme

(A) *The revision, streamlining and consolidation of State aid guidelines to make them consistent with common principles for assessing the compatibility of aid with the internal market:*

- Revised Regional State aid Guidelines (2013).
- Revised Guidelines on Broadband (2013).
- Revised Guidelines on Rescue and Restructuring State aid (2014).
- Revised Framework for Research, Development and Innovation aid (2014).
- Revised Guidelines on Environmental and Energy aid (2014).
- Revised Guidelines on Risk Finance for SMEs (2014).
- New Guidelines on Criteria for the analysis of the compatibility with the internal market of State aid to promote the execution of important projects of common European interest (2014).
- State aid Guidelines on Aviation (2014).
- In parallel, State aid rules relating to agriculture, forestry and rural areas (including *de minimis* aspects) were revised.

(B) *Specific revisions of relevant Council and Commission Regulations:*

- Revised Council Enabling Regulation (2013).
- Revised Commission General Block Exemption Regulation (2014).
- Revised Commission *De Minimis* Regulation (2014).

(C) *Clarification and better explanation of the* concept of State aid:

- Commission Notice on the Notion of Aid (2016).

(D) *Modernisation of the* **Procedural Regulation** *(with regard to complaint-handling and to introduce market information tools and sector inquiries in State aid assessments) and of the* **Implementing Regulation** *in regard to the calculation of certain time limits, the handling of complaints and the identification and protection of confidential information:*

- Council Regulation No 734/2013/EU of 22 July 2013 amending Regulation No 659/1999/EC laying down detailed rules for the application of Article 108 of the TFEU, OJ L 204 of 31 July 2013.
- Commission Regulation No 372/2014/EU of 9 April 2014 amending Regulation No 794/2004/EC as regards the calculation of certain time limits, the handling of complaints and the identification and protection of confidential information, OJ L 109 of 12 April 2014.

(E) *Increasing the* transparency *of State aid awards:*

- Communication from the Commission amending the Communications from the Commission on EU Guidelines for the application of State aid rules in relation to the rapid deployment of broadband networks, on Guidelines on regional State aid for 2014–2020, on State aid for films and other audiovisual works, on Guidelines on State aid to promote risk finance investments and on Guidelines on State aid to airports and airlines (2014).

(F) *Requiring Member States to* evaluate *their main aid schemes:*

- Commission Staff Working Document: "Common methodology for State aid evaluation" (2014).

From a procedural perspective, in view of the Commission's increased powers, stakeholders more acutely felt the need for greater transparency in State aid procedures. However, the Commission and Member States failed to address this need when amending the Procedural Regulation.[930] The ECJ's case law once again significantly contributed to this trend, especially regarding the position of claimants. In this respect, cases such as *Athinaiki, NDSHT* and *Ryanair* have had a strong impact on enforcement practice.[931] Similarly, case law has strengthened parties' defence rights by: (a) imposing limits on the Commission's control of the correct execution of its recovery decisions (*Mediaset*);[932] and (b) maintaining access to justice for all undertakings receiving a recovery order.

It is indeed thanks to the CJEU[933] that the actual beneficiaries of individual aid granted under an aid scheme can challenge the Commission's decision before the EU courts where an aid scheme is held to be incompatible with the common market and a recovery of the aid paid out is sought. After a ten-year battle, and despite the Commission's efforts to persuade the EU courts that these claims should be dealt with at a national level, the CJEU has refused to accept the Commission's view that this solution was in the best interest of the EU's legal system. Without such a strong stance by the EU courts, the shape of EU State aid control would have been very different from the current one. Nonetheless, many commentators continue to view the CJEU as being unduly cautious in defending the bilateral nature of State aid proceedings (i.e., as between the Commission and Member States) with the effect that transparency and procedural rights for third parties remain two of the principal unresolved issues in State aid control.

In its 2015 Annual Report on Competition Policy, the Commission noted that the State aid rules had been overhauled in the context of the State aid modernisation (SAM)

930. Council Regulation No 734/2013/EU of 22 July 2013 amending Regulation No 659/1999/EC, setting out detailed rules for the application of Article 108 of the TFEU, OJ L 204 of 31 July 2013.
931. Case C-521/06: *Athinaiki Techniki v. Commission*, [2008] ECR I-5829; Case C-322/09 P: *Nya Destination Stockholm Hotell & Teaterpaket AB v. Commission*, [2010] ECR I-11911 and Case T-423/07: *Ryanair v. Commission*, [2011] ECR II-2397.
932. Case C-403/10 P: *Mediaset SpA v. Commission*, [2011] ECR I-117.
933. Joined Cases C-71/09 P, C-73/09 P and C-76/09 P: *Comitato "Venezia vuole vivere" and Hotel Cipriani Srl and Società Italiana per il gas SpA (Italgas) v. Commission*, [2011] ECR I-4727.

initiative and again stressed that the initiative had been aimed at helping Member States to better target aid measures towards economic growth, job creation and social cohesion. The Report also noted that work was continuing on one final item – providing detailed and up to date guidance on the notion of aid.[934]

The Commission also notes that the SAM reforms ensure more efficient decision-making and procedures for granting growth supporting aid that is not distortive to market functioning in the EU and that this has been achieved by tangible cuts in red tape, the promotion of a better use of limited public resources by Member States and of a higher contribution of aid measures to investment. The revised rules on State aid for R&D&I are held out as a particular example of the latter.

5.4.1 GBER 2014 in Context

In respect of the new GBER,[935] this is seen by the Commission as one of the cornerstones of the State Aid Modernisation reform as it simplifies aid granting procedures for Member States by authorising, without prior notification, a wide range of measures fulfilling horizontal common interest objectives. Thus, only cases with the biggest potential to distort competition in the internal market continue to require notification, leaving a significantly larger number of "smaller and unproblematic measures" exempt from prior notification, "in exchange for strengthened controls at Member State level, greater transparency and better evaluation of the impact of aid."

The Commission comments that:

> Following the State Aid modernisation and the entry into force of the new GBER, Member States made extensive use of the possibilities offered by the comprehensive modernisation of State aid rules. Notably, a surge in aid excluded from prior Commission scrutiny indicates an important reduction of red tape. Indeed, ... about 90 % of new measures in 2014 were registered as exempted from prior notification according to GBER. As regards the share of GBER expenditure in total aid measures, this amounted to approximately 40% in 2014, and is expected to increase even further in 2015.[936]

Several indications are given which suggest also that, despite the "partnership" with Member States, the Commission is carefully working on these new arrangements to ensure that they are not misused or mis-interpreted by Member States. First, the Commission is providing pro-active support to Member States through advocacy work and trainings. The Commission services have also set up a High Level Group on State Aid Modernisation with EU Member States, together with other dedicated working groups and a network of State aid country coordinators, to oversee implementation and facilitate compliance with the new requirements for transparency and evaluations. In

934. Commission Staff Working Paper 2015, *supra*, p. 4.
935. European Commission: Regulation No 651/2014/EU of 17 June 2014 declaring certain categories of aid compatible with the internal market in application of Articles 107 and 108 of the Treaty on the Functioning of the European Union (TFEU), OJ L 187 of 26 June 2014. A summary of the 2014 GBER is set out in Table 8 in Chapter 2.
936. European Commission: Staff Working Paper 2015, *supra*, p. 5.

particular, the role of the State aid country coordinators is to help to address systemic issues in State aid enforcement at Member State level, help Member States prioritise their portfolio of cases and assist with providing training and guidance. In 2016, the Commission also launched Bilateral Partnerships with certain Member States in order to address existing compliance problems and challenges in these Member States. The Bilateral Partnerships aim to build a structured bilateral dialogue between the Commission and the Member State concerned to allow the identification and tackling of obstacles that may still hinder compliance with the State aid rules. In 2016, the Commission agreed on Bilateral Partnership work programmes on State aid with Italy, Bulgaria and Romania and similar arrangements with other Member States were being examined.

Moreover, all Member States have committed to participating in the development of the *Transparency Award Module* – an IT platform designed to facilitate data collection, storage and access by all stakeholders.[937] In addition, work is continuing with Member States to elaborate further on the institutional set up of granting authorities, national information systems for State aid and the development of a methodology for encoding information required by the transparency provisions of Article 9 and Annex III of the 2014 GBER.

The Commission also sees the new evaluation requirements as complementing the major expansion of the GBER and as a necessary *ex post* safeguard, alongside transparency and monitoring. Thus, since July 2014, evaluation is required for GBER aid schemes with an average annual State aid budget above €150 million in the fields of regional aid, aid for SMEs and access to finance, aid for research and development and innovation, energy and environmental aid and aid for broadband infrastructures. By the end of 2016, the Commission had approved evaluation plans covering 28 State aid schemes submitted by the Czech Republic, Germany, Spain, France, Hungary, Italy, Lithuania, Austria, Poland, Portugal, Finland, and the United Kingdom, mostly in regard to regional or R&D&I aid schemes and broadband support measures, accounting for some €36 billion of annual State aid.[938]

5.4.2 Extending the GBER

Recital 1 of the 2014 GBER indicated that the Commission planned to propose criteria for exempting port and airport infrastructure provided that sufficient case experience was developed. In 2016, the Commission adopted a series of State aid decisions (in particular relating to investment aid to ports)[939] and these were considered to have provided sufficient experience to support the extension of the scope of the GBER to

937. *See*: https://webgate.ec.europa.eu/competition/transparency/public?lang=en.
938. European Commission: Commission Staff Working Paper accompanying the *Report on Competition Policy 2016*, p. 22.
939. Including European Commission: Decision of 20 April 2016 in Case SA.44846 – *Investment aid for Berth 9 in Cuxhaven port*, OJ C 220 of 17 June 2017, European Commission: Decision of 4 May 2016 in Case SA.44479 – *Extension of the Rostock Overseas Port*, OJ C 220 of 17 June 2016; European Commission: Decision of 14 July 2016 in Case SA.40680 – *Offshore-Terminal*

facilitate the grant of aid to port and airport infrastructure in unproblematic cases. On this basis, the GBER was extended in June 2017.[940]

Under this amendment to GBER 2014, Member States can now make public investments in regional airports handling up to three million passengers per year without prior control by the Commission, thereby facilitating public investment in more than 420 airports across the EU (which account for about 13 % of air traffic). The GBER has also been extended to allow public authorities to cover operating costs of small airports (almost half of all airports in the EU which only account for less than 1 % of air traffic) handling up to 200,000 passengers per year to improve the connectivity of regions. The new exemption conditions for airports complement the Commission's Guidelines on State aid to airports and airlines[941] which will apply to cases above the thresholds which will continue to require notification and advance approval.

In regard to ports, investment aid of up to €150 million for sea ports and up to €50 million for inland ports is block exempt and designed, in particular, to promote the dredging of ports and inland waterways. This is also seen as consistent with the newly adopted Regulation No 2017/352/EU of the European Parliament and of the Council of 15 February 2017 establishing a framework for the provision of port services and common rules on the financial transparency of ports.

The amendment of GBER 2014 also goes further by extending the exemption of State aid for cultural projects and for sports facilities and in the EU's outermost regions. The increased thresholds for measures supporting culture and sports/multifunctional recreational infrastructure are based on the view that higher amounts of aid do not pose a threat to competition if the conditions set out in the General Block Exemption Regulation for those measures are complied with.

5.4.3 The 2016 Notice on the Notion of Aid

On 19 May 2016, the Commission published, as a last part of its State Aid Modernisation initiative, a *Notice on the Notion of aid* with the intention of providing guidance on when public spending falls within, and outside, the scope of EU State aid control and to assist public authorities and companies to identify when public support measures can be granted without needing approval under EU State aid rules.[942]

The Notice provides a categorised summary of the case law of the European Courts and the Commission's decision-making practice on all key aspects of the

---

Bremerhaven, OJ C 406 of 4 November 2016 and European Commission: Decision of 19 August 2016 in Case SA.45848 – *Extension of cruise ship terminal Putbus-Lauterbach*, OJ C 369 of 7 October 2016.

940. European Commission: Regulation No 2017/1084/EU of 14 June 2017 amending Regulation No 651/2014/EU as regards aid for port and airport infrastructure, notification thresholds for aid for culture and heritage conservation and for aid for sport and multifunctional recreational infrastructures, and regional operating aid schemes for outermost regions and amending Regulation No 702/2014/EU as regards the calculation of eligible costs, OJ L 156 of 20 June 2017.
941. European Commission: *Guidelines on state aid to airports and airlines*, OJ C 99 of 4 April 2014.
942. *See*, European Commission: Press Release "*State aid: Commission clarifies scope of EU State aid rules to facilitate public investment*," IP/16/1782 of 19 May 2016.

identification of State aid measures under Article 107(1) of the TFEU. It also stresses that, on issues that have not yet been considered by the Courts, it reflects the Commission view as to how the notion of State aid should be construed and that these views are without prejudice to any subsequent interpretation of the notion of State aid by the EU Courts.

In particular, the Notice deals extensively with the concept of undertaking and cases where economic activities do and do not arise. Thus, for example, the Notice makes clear that the exercise of public power by the State in regard to the army and police, air navigation safety and control, maritime traffic control and safety, anti-pollution surveillance, the organisation, financing and enforcement of prison sentences, the development and revitalisation of public land by public authorities and the collection of data to be used for public purposes on the basis of a statutory obligation do not give rise to State aid concerns, unless carried out via an economic activity that is separable from the exercise of public power.[943] The Notice also examines the extent to which social security, healthcare, education, research and cultural services do not give rise to State aid concerns and the rarer cases when they do.

Similarly, the Notice explores in detail when a measure is imputable to the State (meaning that it is provided by or through State resources for the purposes of Article 107(1)) and especially the more indirect cases. The Notice points out that the imputability to the State of a measure taken by a public undertaking may be inferred from a set of indicators arising from the circumstances of the case and the context in which the measure was taken. These indicators can include those showing that the public authority cannot act independently in regard to the measure, the nature of the market operations of the public authority, the degree of supervision that the public authorities exercise over the management of the undertaking, etc.[944]

The conditions for a measure to give rise to an advantage and when the State is or is not acting in a manner similar to a market economic operator are reviewed in detail. The Notice also brings together the latest thinking a case law on selectivity and the issue of differentiating between State aid and general measures, noting, in particular, that "a Member State which introduces a differentiation between undertakings needs to be able to show that this differentiation is actually justified by the nature and general scheme of the system in question."[945] In regard to regional selectivity, the case law on Gibralter and Azores is central to the analysis. The Notice also looks at specific issues concerning tax measures,[946] and this new material extensively updates and replaces the earlier 1998 Notice on the application of State aid rules to measures relating to direct business taxation.[947]

In its examination of competition and trade effects, the Notice confirms that, while these are two distinct and necessary elements of the notion of aid, in practice, however, these criteria are often treated jointly in the assessment of State aid as they

943. European Commission: *Notice on the Notion of Aid*, May 2016, *supra*, paras 17–18.
944. *Ibid.*, paras 40–43.
945. *Ibid.*, paras 117–155.
946. *Ibid.*, paras 156–184.
947. OJ C 384 of 10 December 1998. The considerations relating to tax measures are examined further in Chapter 6.

are, as a rule, considered inextricably linked.[948] In regard to effects on trade specifically, the Notice points out that an effect on trade between Member States cannot be merely hypothetical or presumed, and it must be established why the measure distorts or threatens to distort competition and is liable to have an effect on trade between Member States, based on the foreseeable effects of the measure. On the other hand, it is not necessary to define the market or to investigate in detail the impact of the measure on the competitive position of the beneficiary and its competitors.[949] At the same time, the Notice avoids clarifying a particular grey area in the decisional practice and jurisprudence by pointing out that:

> In principle, an effect on trade can also occur even if the recipient exports all or most of its production outside the Union, but in such situations the effect is less immediate and cannot be assumed from the mere fact that the market is open to competition.[950]

The Notice also refers to the fact that the Commission has in a number of decisions considered, in view of the specific circumstances of the cases, that the measure had a purely local impact and consequently had no effect on trade between Member States. It notes that, while it is not possible to define general categories of measures that typically meet these criteria, past decisions providing examples of these situations include:

- sports and leisure facilities serving predominantly a local audience;
- cultural events and entities performing limited economic activities;
- hospitals and other health care facilities providing the usual range of medical services aimed at a local population;
- news media and/or cultural products which, for linguistic and geographical reasons, have a locally restricted audience;
- small airports or ports that predominately serve local users;
- the financing of certain cable ways (and in particular ski lifts) in areas with few facilities and limited tourism capability.[951]

In a section of the Notice dedicated to clarifying when State aid arises in the context of infrastructure projects,[952] the Commission indicates that infrastructure projects often involve several categories of actors and any State aid involved may potentially benefit the construction (including extensions or improvements), the operation or the use of the infrastructure. While the funding of infrastructure that is not meant to be commercially exploited is in principle excluded from the application of the State aid rules, several factors, such as liberalisation, privatisation, market integration and technological progress have, however, increased the scope for commercial exploitation

948. European Commission: Notice on the Notion of Aid, May 2016, *supra*, para. 186.
949. *Ibid.*, paras 190 et seq.
950. *Ibid.*, para. 193.
951. *Ibid.*, paras 196–198.
952. *Ibid.*, paras 199 et seq.

of infrastructures, as confirmed especially by recent General Court rulings on airport projects.[953] These clarifications end, however, with a rather unclear message:

> Due to the uncertainty that existed prior to the Aéroports de Paris judgment, public authorities could legitimately consider that the public funding of infrastructure granted prior to that judgment did not constitute State aid and that, accordingly, such measures did not need to be notified to the Commission. It follows that the Commission cannot put such funding measures definitively adopted before the Aéroports de Paris judgment into question on the basis of State aid rules. This does not imply any presumption as regards the presence or absence of State aid or legitimate expectations as regards funding measures not definitively adopted before the Aéroports de Paris judgment, which will have to be verified on a case by case basis.[954]

The Notice definitively repeals several previous Notices (notably on Business Direct Taxation and on the Sale of Public Land and Buildings) but ends with another obscure point as follows:

> The present Communication replaces any opposing statements relating to the notion of State aid included in any existing Commission Communications and Frameworks, save for statements pertaining to specific sectors and justified by their particular features.[955]

Nonetheless, this Notice is of particular importance for practitioners in the State aid field as previously many had argued, for example, that the interpretation of the substantive elements forming the notion of aid – such "granted by the State or through State resources" and "selectivity" – was far from clear.[956] While it is too early to assess whether this new Notice will put all questions of legal certainty on such points to rest, or if the Commission is trying to breath too much into its decisions and the case law of the Courts,[957] the 2016 Notice represents a valiant effort by the Commission to pull together 60 years of the conceptual development of the notion of aid into a single user document for practitioners and will undoubtedly constitute a key reference document in the years ahead.

As one commentator has noted:

> Attempts to clarify the notion of State aid and the European Commission's position is welcomed. It should however be noted that the Commission's interpretation of

953. Notably, Case T-128/98: *Aéroports de Paris v. Commission*, [2000] ECR II-3929, para. 125, confirmed on appeal in Case C-82/01 P: *Aéroports de Paris v. Commission*, [2002] ECR I-9297 and Joined Cases T-443/08 and T-455/08: *Freistaat Sachsen and Land Sachsen-Anhalt and Others v. Commission*, [2011] ECR II-1311 upheld on appeal in Case C-288/11 P: *Mitteldeutsche Flughafen AG and Flughafen Leipzig-Halle GmbH v. Commission*, ECLI:EU:C:2012:821.
954. European Commission: *Notice on the Notion of Aid*, May 2016, *supra*, para. 209.
955. *Ibid.*, para. 230.
956. *See*, for example, A. Biondi, *"State Aid is Falling Down, Falling Down: An Analysis of the Case Law on the Notion of Aid"* (2013), 50 Common Market Law Review, Issue 6, pp. 1719–1743.
957. A core argument in the Irish appeal on the 2016 Apple Inc decision.

> EU State aid is not necessarily shared by EU Member States nor the European Courts, and should be considered critically.[958]

It would seem that the State Aid Modernisation process is now complete – at least for now. Even before the recent changes to the 2014 GBER, Commissioner Margrethe Vestager noted that:

> Last month, we adopted our Notice on the Notion of Aid. It's the final step in a journey that started almost exactly four years ago, when the Commission launched State aid Modernisation.... Less than one in ten State aid measures now come to us for a decision. The rest fall under the general block exemption regulation.[959]

However, and continuing to reflect some reticence about the "Partnership" discussed above, she also stressed that:

> even with the best intentions, we can't always be sure whether State aid is doing good. I am often asked, does taxpayers' money actually deliver faster development in our poorest regions, or do companies just pocket the money, and go on doing exactly what they were doing before? ...If we're serious about getting the best out of State aid, we need to know what it really achieves. It is therefore very positive that you're already evaluating the effect of one-fifth of the State aid that you give, under the evaluation rules that are part of State aid Modernisation. Evaluation will, over time, help companies invest without hurting competition.

Commissioner Vestager's speech concluded with a strong attack on the impact of tax avoidance on internal market competition and signalled the importance of addressing State aid arising from tax rulings. This is one of the several cross-cutting policy areas that are addressed in the next Chapter.

958. KPMG: "*Commission issues Notice on the Notion of State Aid,*" Tax Flash, Issue 284 of 23 May 2016 accessible at: https://assets.kpmg.com/content/dam/kpmg/pdf/2016/05/etf-284-state-aid-clarification-from-commission.pdf.
959. "The EU State aid rules: working together for fair competition," Speech by Competition Commissioner Margrethe Vestager to the High Level Forum on State Aid Modernisation, Brussels, 3 June 2016.

CHAPTER 6

State Aid Regulation and Other EU Policies

6.1 INTRODUCTION

The development of EU State aid law and policy has been influenced by the evolution and development of a wide range of other EU policies over the last 60 years. While the key regulatory articles of the Treaty have remained largely unchanged since the 1950s, Treaty changes in other policy areas created new possibilities and new imperatives which have been pursued, *inter alia*, via the application of the State aid rules. Moreover, in some areas, perceived shortcomings in Treaty mandates have also been addressed via reinvigorated efforts to extend the application of State aid law and policy to try to fill gaps.

Here we examine a selection of policy areas where State aid regulation has evolved in particular to assist the implementation of other Treaty objectives; demonstrating indeed that the very basis of the Treaty rules on State aid regulation has undergone some important fundamental shifts in its 60-year history.

The selection here looks at the impact of evolving EU policies concerning: (a) environment, energy and steel, (b) regional development and cohesion, (c) the banking sector, and (d) taxation on the application of the State aid rules. While these are not the only EU policy areas which have underpinned the development of State aid law and policy, the selected fields are important because some of them (notably environment, cohesion and banking) emerged as new EU policy imperatives, the pursuit of which was taken up as a core element of State aid policy, given the Commission's strong regulatory powers under its State aid mandate. They also include areas which could not have been imagined when the founding Treaty rules were conceived and which indeed show the imaginative dimension which the Commission has brought to bear in applying the State aid rules. In respect of coal and steel, these have largely been absorbed into mainstream State aid regulation since 2002 but, given the importance of these industries in the EU, they remain areas of sectoral policy priority and economic and political sensitivity. Moreover, while the application of State aid rules in the tax arena is eminently logical (given that many State aid measures are tax benefits rather than expenditure measures), the European Commission has developed a specific interest in the taxation area which is arguably driven by the failure of political consensus on the harmonisation of direct taxation and the resultant political fears of unfair tax competition.

Other EU policy areas of significant importance to the evolution of the State aid rules in the last 60 years have already been reviewed and include developments under the common agricultural and transport policies, audiovisual policy, the EU information society, etc.

6.2 STATE AID LAW AND POLICY AND EU POLICIES ON ENERGY, STEEL AND ENVIRONMENT

While the ECSC and Euratom Treaties put energy issues to the forefront of European integration since the 1950s, EU energy policy developed rather sporadically in the last 60 years. First, the importance of coal (and therefore the ECSC) diminished as oil became the most important energy source. Second, differences in energy mixes, transport routes or structures of energy markets resulted in the differing interests of the Member States hindering energy policy cooperation. While this improved over time, the speed of this development varied strongly and many of the more ambitious plans of the European Commission for a coherent policy often failed in the face of opposition from Member States.[960]

The challenges for EU energy policy relate in large measure to the structure of the energy market in Europe. In 2014 the EU gross energy consumption was 1,606 million tonnes, 3.6% lower than in 2013. The structure of consumption was primarily petroleum products (34.4%), followed by gas (21.4%) and solid fossil fuels (16.7%). The share of nuclear heating was 14.1% and renewables accounted for only 12.5%. At the same time, renewable energy sources have increased their share from 4.3% in 1990 to 12.5% in 2014, while gas has risen from 17.9% in 1990 to 21.4% in 2014. The mixture of fuels and their shares in energy consumption in different countries depends on the natural resources available, the structure of their economies and also national choices in energy systems. In 2014, 73.3% of all energy in the EU was produced from fossil sources (coal, crude oil, natural gas, non-renewable wastes). In 2014, 69.1% of EU imports of natural gas and 43.5% of EU crude oil imports came from Russia or Norway, representing a growing dependence on these two exporters, while 70.7% of EU imports of solid fuels originated in Russia, Colombia and the United States.[961]

This structure has raised important policy issues about energy security and about the potential for renewable energy sources to support solutions (both at EU and

960. For a fuller discussion, *see* S. Langsdorf: "*EU Energy Policy: From the ECSC to the Energy Roadmap 2050*," European Green Foundation, December 2011.
961. European Commission: Eurostat statistical books: Energy, transport and environment indicators. Publications Office of the European Union: Luxembourg, 2016.

national levels) in regard to both energy and environmental protection policies. In turn, EU State aid policy has been influenced by evolving policy responses in regard to energy and environmental protection.

6.2.1 Aid to the Coal Sector

It emerges as curious that, after 60 years, the coal-mining sector in the EU continues to receive substantial State aid. Such aid has traditionally been used to maintain local employment, especially in periods of economic turmoil or transition. The political imperative to protect jobs has been a major factor in the aid provided to the German,[962] Polish and Spanish coal industries. Reforms to subsidies are resisted for a range of reasons and those in receipt of economic support often engage in rent-seeking behaviour; using their economic and political influence to maintain particular industrial supports. National governments also find it difficult to roll back existing measures for fear of ceding markets to other nations not pursuing a similar agenda. Moreover, it is frequently argued that the removal of subsidies, especially in the coal sector, will not result in positive effects in the short term (e.g., the abolition of domestic coal subsidies may lead to a switch to cheaper imported coal, rather than cleaner technologies) and that subsidised industries return more to the State in taxation than they receive in subsidies.

The European Coal and Steel Community (ECSC) Treaty regulated the common European market in coal and steel until its expiry in July 2002. Subsidies under Article 4 of the ECSC Treaty were prohibited and Article 95 of the ECSC allowed the Commission to approve certain subsidies and, in practice, this tended to arise during crises periods in both industries.

Since the 1960s, the Commission adopted several frameworks allowing temporary State aid for the coal sector, primarily for the purposes of restructuring, modernisation and rationalisation. In 1994, the Commission adopted Decision No 3632/93/ECSC which regulated State aid to the coal sector until the ECSC expired in 2002.[963] Under that Decision, the Commission recognised that the rationalisation and restructuring of the sector required further action and that the coal mines and the EU itself did not have sufficient resources for this. Moreover, the coal sector was seen as an element of energy security for the EU and a trade issue, with a considerable volume of coal being imported into the EU. The policy context of this Decision also recognised that:

> despite the inevitable restructuring and closures, care must be taken to minimise the social and regional impact of these changes, when continuing the

962. The German Federal Environment Agency (2003) compared the subsidies received by the German coal industry with the number of employees in this sector. It concluded that safeguarding employment in the coal sector for 2001 was costing €82,000 a year in subsidies for each coal miner's job saved. Cited in: "*Energy subsidies in the European Union: A brief overview,*" European Environment Agency, Copenhagen 2004, p. 9.
963. European Commission: Decision No 3632/93/ECSC of 28 December 1993 establishing Community rules for State aid to the coal industry, OJ L 329 of 30 December 1993.

> Community's policy in this sector, which must take account of the precarious social situation of mining regions, in particular in the context of the principle of economic and social cohesion.

Accordingly, continuing State aid for the sector was needed and new rules should apply.[964] Under the terms of the Decision, aid granted to the coal industry could be considered compatible with the proper functioning of the internal market provided that it helped to achieve at least one of the following objectives:

- to make, in the light of coal prices on international markets, further progress towards economic viability with the aim of achieving a general reduction of State aid;
- to solve the social and regional problems created by total or partial reductions in the activity of production units;
- to help the coal industry adjust to environmental protection standards.[965]

Operating aid could be granted under specific conditions and Member States which intended to grant operating aid between 1994 and 2002 were required to submit to the Commission in advance a modernisation, rationalisation and restructuring plan designed to improve the economic viability of the undertakings concerned by reducing production costs. So-called closure aid could also be permitted to address specific regional and social impacts of coal mine closures. In addition, research and development aid and aid for environmental protection could be provided in the coal sector, as long as it complied with the applicable frameworks at the time for aids of these types.[966] In 2001, under the ECSC Treaty, the amount of aid granted was approximately €6.3 billion.

The expiry of the ECSC in 2002 was followed by Council Regulation No 1407/2002/EC which noted, in particular that:

> Strengthening the Union's energy security, which underpins the general precautionary principle, therefore justifies the maintenance of coal-producing capability supported by State aid. However implementing this objective does not put into question the need to continue the restructuring process of the coal industry given that, in the future, the bulk of Community coal production is likely to remain uncompetitive vis-à-vis imported coal.[967]

Following the expiry of the ECSC Treaty, State aid in the coal sector in the EU, apart from Article 107 of the TFEU, was regulated initially by Council Regulation No 1407/2002/EC,[968] the so-called *Coal Regulation*, which allowed Member States to grant certain State aid to the coal sector. This was based on Article 107(3)(e) and 109 of the TFEU and allowed Member States to grant aid to the coal industry up to 31 December

964. *Ibid.*, Preamble.
965. *Ibid.*, Article 2.
966. *Ibid.*, Articles 3–9.
967. Council Regulation No 1407/2002/EC of 23 July 2002 on *State aid to the coal industry*, OJ L 205 of 2 August 2002.
968. *Ibid.*

2010.[969] With a focus on reducing coal-mining activity and restructuring the coal industry, only aid to cover production losses (closure aid), for accessing coal reserves (investment aid and operating aid) and to cover exceptional costs that were not related to current production (aid for inherited liabilities) were permitted and the overall amount of closure aid and operating aid had to follow a downward trend and be limited by the amount authorised by the Commission in 2001. In 2007, the Commission produced a Report on the application of the Coal Regulation concluding that, between 2003 and 2006, energy security had not been achieved and pointing out that the coal mines in EU Member States providing operating aid would not survive without subsidies (these were in Bulgaria, Germany, Hungary, Romania, Slovenia and Spain).[970]

In 2010, the European Commission presented a proposal for a revised Council Regulation on State aid to facilitate the closure of uncompetitive coal mines, reaffirming that State aid has for many years been considered necessary to maintain a certain amount of indigenous primary energy sources, ensuring the Union's energy security and keeping the European hard coal industry alive. This initiative failed, however, and in 2010 Council Decision No 2010/787/EU[971] (the "*Coal Decision*") was adopted, giving Member States greater flexibility, including the possibility to continue granting State aid to the coal sector, provided that it related to closures of production units no later than 31 December 2018 or to defined exceptional costs until 31 December 2027. The main concerns of the EU Member States, supported by industry stakeholders, were both the risk of the immediate closure of many European mines (and the resultant pressure of specific regional labour markets with a flood of redundant mine workers) and the prospect of endangering Europe's energy security and energy supply.[972]

In 2010, the coal sector involved some 100,000 workers in Europe: 42,000 in the coal sector itself and over 55,000 in related industries. The mines that rely on operating subsidies are located mostly, but not only, in the Ruhr region, in Germany, in north-west Spain and in the Jiu Valley in Romania.[973] More than 40% of electricity in Germany and Romania was produced from hard coal burning and in Spain the share was around 25%.[974] Moreover, EU coal production accounts for approximately 288 million tonnes of coal which is used for electricity generation, heat generation, steel production and other industrial processes.[975]

969. *Ibid.*, Article 14(3).
970. European Commission: "*Commission Report on the Application of Council Regulation 1407/2002/EC on State aid to the Coal Industry,*" COM (2007) 253 final of 21 May 2007.
971. Council Decision No 2010/787/EU on State aid to facilitate the closure of uncompetitive coal mines, OJ L 336 of 21 December 2010.
972. M. Lang, "*State Aid for the Coal Sector - Inevitable or Dispensable?*" EstAL, 1|2012, p. 114.
973. European Commission: Proposal for a Council Regulation on State aid to facilitate the closure of uncompetitive coal mines, COM (2010) 372 final, 20 July 2010, p. 2.
974. European Commission: Press Release: "*State aid: Commission proposes Council Regulation on State aid to close uncompetitive coal mines,*" IP/10/984 of 20 July 2010.
975. European Economic and Social Committee: Opinion on the Proposal for a Council Regulation on State aid to facilitate the closure of uncompetitive coal mines, OJ C 54 of 19 February 2011.

Table 28 Recent Coal Industry Decisions

By February 2017, the European Commission made 15 Decisions under the 2010 Coal Decision.[976] Closure aid and aid to cover exceptional costs were approved for coal mines in Poland, Slovakia, Romania, the United Kingdom, the Czech Republic, Hungary, Italy and Germany.
On 29 June 2011 the Commission approved the first State aid under the Coal Decision by Slovenia to support the closure of the Trbovlje Hrastnik coal mine located in the central region of Zasavska.[977] The Slovenian plan involved financing towards a social programme to re-qualify workers and help them find a new job or create their own as well as to co-finance the pensions of those who had reached retirement age. According to the plan, the mine had to be closed by the end of 2012 but the aid could, nevertheless, be granted until the end of 2015. The support was also destined to cover costs linked with the rehabilitation of the site, including removing waste water from the mine and ensuring safety underground.
The Commission's latest decision, on 18 November 2016, found that Poland's plans to provide PLN with €7.95 billion of support to alleviate the social and environmental impact of closing uncompetitive coal mines by 2018 to be in line with the EU State aid rules.[978] In particular, the State support will fund severance payments, compensatory pensions and social security benefits for the workers who have lost, or will lose, their jobs due to the closures. Furthermore, it will be used to secure mine shafts and the decommissioning of mine infrastructure, repair damage to the environment caused by mining and re-cultivate land after the mine closures. The remainder of the aid will cover the production losses of the mines until closure.

6.2.2 Aid to the Steel Sector

As with the coal sector, the Steel sector is also subject to a special regime in the field of State aid. In part, this goes back to the earliest days of the EU when subsidies to both sectors were specifically regulated under Article 4 of the ECSC Treaty. Following the expiry of the ECSC Treaty in 2002, State aid to the steel sector is now regulated by the TFEU rules.

Under current State aid rules, regional aid to the steel sector is excluded from the scope of the GBER and the Regional Aid Guidelines. Aid to the steel sector is also excluded from the Rescue and Restructuring Guidelines. However, the Environmental Aid guidelines, Research, Development and Innovation Framework and Risk Capital

976. Accessible at: http://ec.europa.eu/competition/elojade/isef/index.cfm?fuseaction=dsp_result.
977. European Commission: Press Release: "*State aid: Commission approves Slovenian aid towards the closure of the Trbovlje Hrastnik coal mine*," IP/11/804 of 29 June 2011.
978. European Commission: Decision No SA.41161 of 18 November 2016 – *State aid to Polish coal mining in the period 2015-2018* of 18 November 2016, OJ C 51 of 17 February 2017.

Guidelines do apply to the steel sector. Accordingly, aid to the steel sector remains notifiable and is generally viewed negatively by the Commission on the basis of declining global demand coupled with the risks of uncompetitive subsidised supply.

Specifically, the EU State aid rules prohibit both investment aid and rescue and restructuring aid to the steel sector. Indeed, while this was previously allowed, the Commission and the Council agreed in the 1990s that no further decisions of this nature would be taken to rescue EU steel firms or to facilitate their expansion.

While Article 107(3)(c) of the TFEU provides the discretionary basis to allow aid to facilitate the development of certain economic activities, the Commission considers that, because of the existing overcapacities at European and world level and the consequent inefficiencies as well as the prohibition of rescue and restructuring aid to the steel industry, only aid to facilitate structural adjustment can contribute to the development of a healthier steel industry. Therefore, the following aid for firms in the steel industry *may* be regarded as compatible with the internal market:

(1) Aid to cover payments payable by steel firms to workers made redundant or accepting early retirement (provided that the payments actually arise from the partial or total closure of steel plants which have not already been taken into account for the approval of aid and the payments do not exceed those customarily granted under the rules in force in the Member States, and the aid does not exceed 50% of those payments).
(2) Aid to steel firms which permanently cease production of steel products, provided that certain conditions are met.
(3) Aid to steel firms which satisfy the conditions set out above but which are directly or indirectly controlled by, or which themselves directly or indirectly control, a firm that is itself a steel firm. Such aid may also be deemed compatible with the internal market provided certain conditions are met.

The latest Decisions of the Commission concerning the State aid to the steel sector were negative. Having previously ordered the recovery of illegal State aid to the steel sectors in Belgium, Germany, Italy and Poland, in 2016, the Commission adopted a final negative decision requiring Belgium to recover €211 million of aid granted to companies within the "Duferco group"[979] and opened a formal investigation into possible aid measures granted by Italy to "Ilva,"[980] which amount to approximately €2 billion of financial support in total. Commenting on these cases, the current Competition Commissioner, Margaret Vestager, noted that the world currently faces overcapacity in the steel sector and that the EU has to compete by investing in new technologies and innovations:

979. European Commission: Press Release "State aid: Commission orders Belgium to recover €211 million from several steel companies within the Duferco group," IP/16/113 of 20 January 2016.
980. European Commission: Decision No SA.38613 – Italian support for steel producer Ilva in Taranto, 20 January 2016, OJ C 241 of 1 July 2016.

> The European steel industry needs to be competitive globally and it needs to take the steps to ensure that it is. It cannot rely on public funds to survive... It is in this context that EU state aid rules don't allow public support for the rescue and restructuring of failing steelmakers, but they do enable EU countries to boost the global competitiveness of steel companies. In particular, EU state aid rules allow support to steelmakers to make them more competitive in the long-term for objectives such as research, development and innovation.[981]

In addition, the Commission view is that this type of aid distorts competition, risks leading to harmful subsidy races between Member States, keeps uncompetitive capacity on the market and transfers problems to other Member States.

6.2.3 Aid for Environmental Protection and Energy

While EU energy policy started with the ECSC regulation of the coal industry under the ECSC Treaty, EU energy policy has changed considerably over the years, although, as seen earlier, the coal sector has a continuing importance for both employment and energy in several EU Member States. Prior to the Lisbon Treaty in 2007 (TFEU), which recognised the importance of solidarity in matters of energy supply and changes to energy policies within the EU, energy policy was largely viewed in terms of common market rules (including those deriving from the ECSC and Euratom treaty rules) and from the standpoint of environmental policy. Environmental policy, in turn, only emerged as an official EU policy area in 1987 under the Single European Act, although there had been earlier actions by the EU to advance a common environmental policy on the basis that national environmental policies could result in trade barriers in the EU and as a result of initial green party policies, notably from Germany in the 1980s.[982]

As early as 1973, the concept that the polluter pays was first introduced and, in 1975, the Council issued specific recommendations to Member States on environmental matters noting that "environmental protection should not in principle depend on policies which rely on grants of aid and place the burden of combating pollution on the Community,"[983] while also pointing out that a range of environmental measures should not be regarded as breaching the polluter pays principle, i.e.:

981. European Commission: Statement by Commissioner Vestager on EU State aid rules in the steel sector and Commission State aid decisions concerning Duferco in Belgium and Ilva in Italy, Brussels, 20 January 2016, Statement/16/118.
982. A declaration on environmental and consumer policy was adopted at the Paris Summit of October 1972 which requested the European Commission to draw up an action programme for environmental protection. This (first) Environmental Action Programme was adopted in July 1973 setting out general principles and focussed on the prevention, reduction and containment of environmental damage, the conservation of an ecological equilibrium, the rational use of natural resources and the need for a comprehensive assessment of the impacts of other policies on the environment. It concentrated largely on water and air pollution. The Second Programme in 1977 continued the same approach while adding nature protection. These programmes achieved some limited progress in EU environmental legislation but political support was generally weak due to the economic recession in this period.
983. Council Recommendation 45/436 of 3 March 1975 regarding cost allocation and action by public authorities on environmental matters, 1975, OJ L 149 of 25 July 1975, para. 2.

(a) financial contributions which might be granted to local authorities for the construction and operation of public installations for the protection of the environment, the cost of which could not be wholly covered in the short term from the charges paid by polluters using them. In so far as other effluent as well as household waste is treated in these installations, the service thus rendered to undertakings should be charged to them on the basis of the actual cost of the treatment concerned;

(b) financing designed to compensate for the particularly heavy costs which some polluters would be obliged to meet in order to achieve an exceptional degree of environmental cleanliness;

(c) contributions granted to foster activities concerning research and development with a view to implementing techniques, manufacturing processes and products causing less pollution.[984]

By the late 1980s, a specific impetus to EU environmental policy emerged from the 1987 Treaty changes which declared environmental policy to be a joint responsibility of the EU and its Member States,[985] provided for the specifics of EU environmental policy aimed at a high standard of environmental protection[986] and further provided that:

> Environmental protection requirements must be integrated into the definition and implementation of the Union's policies and activities, in particular with a view to promoting sustainable development.[987]

In 1994, the Commission adopted the Community Guidelines on State aid for environmental protection,[988] representing one of the first EU responses to the mandate to integrate environmental policies into other EU policy areas.[989] These Guidelines set out Commission policy in this area while stressing that further progress needed to be made towards the full application of the "polluter pays" principle. This principle means that those who cause environmental damage should be forced to bear the costs which they would otherwise impose on the rest of society. However, both incentives such as State aids and disincentives such as taxes and levies were recognised as being necessary in the environmental protection field.

Under the 1994 Guidelines, operating aid was allowed under certain circumstances, and aid for investment was allowed not only for investment in new equipment to reduce or eliminate pollution, but also in energy-saving technology and for the use of renewable energy sources.

---

984. *Ibid.*
985. TFEU, Article 4.
986. TFEU, Articles 191 et seq.
987. TFEU, Article 11.
988. European Commission: *Community Guidelines on State Aid for Environmental Protection*, OJ C 72 of 10 March 1994.
989. Later, the Commission also set out its commitment to integrating environmental policy into other policy areas in its working paper of 26 May 1999 entitled *"Integrating environmental aspects into all relevant policy areas"* and in its report to the Helsinki European Council on integrating environmental concerns and sustainable development into Community policies (SEC (1999) 1941 final).

In regard to aid for investments to enable firms to adapt to new mandatory environmental standards, aid intensities of up to 15% of eligible investment costs were acceptable if the investment was necessary to comply with new mandatory standards or legal obligations. This was conditional, however, on the fact that the plants or installations concerned must have been operating for at least two years before the introduction of the relevant new environmental standards. In regard to aid for investment that allowed firms to achieve significantly higher levels of environmental protection than required, or aid in fields where there was no legal obligation at all, these could be accepted up to a maximum intensity of 30%. In all cases of environmental aid, an extra 10% for SMEs was allowed and investments in environmental protection by SMEs in assisted regions could receive an extra 15% (for A Regions) and 10% (in C Regions).

The Guidelines also stipulated that, in line with the "polluter pays" principle, no aid should be given towards the operating costs of complying with mandatory requirements. However, the Commission recognised two possible exceptions. The first concerned the introduction of environmental taxes to better reflect the true costs of production. Such a tax might harm certain sectors, particularly if introduced in only one Member State. Therefore, a temporary relief of these taxes, although an operating aid, was seen as being potentially justifiable. The second exception to the general rule concerned grants to cover parts or all of the operating costs of waste disposal or recycling facilities, often accompanied by green levies.

In accordance with point 4.3 of the Guidelines, the Commission conducted a review in 1996 and concluded that there was no need to make any amendments in the meantime. On 22 December 1999 it decided to extend the validity of the Guidelines until 30 June 2000[990] and, on 28 June 2000, this was further extended to 31 December 2000.[991]

However, following the adoption of the 1994 Guidelines, action in the field of the environment policy evolved considerably at the initiative of national governments, at the EU level and globally, in particular following the adoption of the 1997 Kyoto Protocol. In 1998 the EU Member States and the Community signed the Kyoto Protocol to the United Nations Framework Convention on Climate Change[992] and EU environmental policy then shifted towards achieving the goals of reducing greenhouse gas emissions by 2012. In parallel, Member States granted State aid more frequently in the energy sector, for example, and the aid they provided was frequently in forms which had not previously been used, such as tax reliefs and exemptions. New forms of operating aid were also on the increase.

990. European Commission: Extension of the validity of the Community guidelines on State aid for environmental protection, OJ C 14 of 19 January 2000, p. 8.
991. European Commission: Extension of the validity of the Community guidelines on State aid for environmental protection, OJ C 184 of 1 July 2000, p. 25.
992. The Kyoto Protocol treaty was negotiated in December 1997 at the city of Kyoto, Japan and came into force 16 February 2005. All related documents can be found at: http://unfccc.int/kyoto_protocol/items/2830.php.

In 2001 new Environmental Aid Guidelines were introduced and the Commission pointed out that:

> Ensuring that prices reflect costs at all stages of the economic process is the best way of making all parties aware of the cost of protecting the environment. Apart from its potentially adverse effects on trade and competition, State aid generally undermines that aim because it enables certain firms to reduce costs artificially and not to reveal the costs of environmental protection to consumers. In the long term, therefore, some forms of State aid run counter to the objectives of sustainable development.[993]

Accordingly, the Commission's new position was that aid should no longer be used to make up for the absence of cost internalisation and aid could no longer be justified for investments designed merely to bring companies into line with new or existing EU technical standards. However, in order to address the special difficulties encountered by SMEs, this approach was relaxed to allow State aid to these firms for a period of three years from the adoption of such standards. Moreover, State aid was also permissible where it served as an incentive to achieve levels of protection which were higher than those required by EU standards e.g. in a situation where a Member State decided to adopt standards which were more stringent than the EU standards in order to achieve a higher level of environmental protection. Aid also continued to be permissible where firms invested in environmental protection over and above the strictest existing EU standards or where no EU standards existed.

Thus the following general rules applied to environmental State aids from 1999 to 2008:

- For a period of three years from the adoption of new compulsory EU standards, investment aid to help SMEs meet new standards could be authorised up to a maximum of 15% of eligible costs.
- Investment aid enabling firms to improve on applicable EU standards could be authorised up to not more than 30% of eligible investment costs.
- A 30% limit also applied to aid where firms undertook investment in the absence of mandatory EU standards or where they had to undertake investment in order to comply with national standards that were more stringent than the applicable EU standards.
- Investments in energy saving were deemed equivalent to investments to promote environmental protection and such investments, together with investments in the combined production of electric power and heat, were eligible for investment aid at the basic rate of 40% of eligible costs.
- The rate of aid for investment to promote renewable sources of energy could also be allowed up to 40% of eligible investment costs.

993. European Commission: *Community guidelines on State aid for environmental protection*, OJ C 37 of 3 February 2001, para. 16.

- Investments made in regard to renewable energy installations serving all the needs of an entire community (such as an island or residential area) could qualify for a bonus of 10% points on top of the basic rate of 40% of eligible costs.
- In cases where it could be shown to be necessary, Member States would be permitted to grant investment aid to support renewable energy, up to 100% of eligible costs. (However, the installations concerned would not be entitled to receive any further support).
- An SME bonus of 10% points could be added to all of the above limits to encourage additional investment by SMEs in environmental protection or energy saving development.
- A separate bonus system was provided for this type of aid in assisted regions although SMEs in assisted regions could not benefit from both the SME and the assisted region top up.
- In regard to the Kyoto Protocol commitments to reduce greenhouse gases, the Guidelines stipulated that it was for each Member State to formulate the policies, measures and instruments it wished to adopt in order to comply with the targets set under the Kyoto Protocol. While some of the means adopted by Member States in that regard could constitute State aid, the Commission indicated that it was still too early to lay down the conditions for authorising any such aid in the Guidelines.

Further updated Guidelines were adopted on 1 April 2008, following a reform process of roughly two years[994] and certain environmental State aids were included in the 2008 GBER.[995] The 2008 Guidelines also reflected the approach set forth in the State Aid Action Plan[996] with respect to a more refined economic approach to State aid analysis and the introduction of a balancing test. As a result, the Guidelines established rules under which the Commission would perform either a standard assessment (where State aid may be found compatible if it fulfilled the simpler criteria set out in the Guidelines) or a detailed assessment, which required a more thorough analysis of the measures and the performance of a balancing test on a case by case basis in major cases. As a matter of principle, the Guidelines provided for the Commission to look at the incentive effect, necessity and proportionality of State aid measures in the environmental area. For all forms of environmental aid, the idea was that the aid must be limited strictly to the extra investment costs borne by firms to achieve the environmental policy result, e.g. in the case of the introduction of higher standards, the costs of cleaning up pollution where the actual polluter cannot be identified, the extra costs of using renewable energy.

994. European Commission: *Community Guidelines on State aid for environmental protection*, OJ C 82 of 1 April 2008.
995. European Commission: Regulation No 800/2008/EC of 6 August 2008 declaring certain categories of aid compatible with the common market in application of Articles 87 and 88 of the Treaty (General Block Exemption Regulation or GBER), OJ L 214 of 9 August 2008, Articles 17–25.
996. Considered earlier in Chapter 5.

Under the 2008 GBER, environmental aids were compatible and exempt from notification where the aid did not exceed €7.5 million per firm and:

- In respect of aid for investment which went beyond EU standards for environmental protection or to increase the level of environmental protection in the absence of EU standards, the aid intensities did not exceed – 35% for large enterprises, 45% for Medium enterprises and 55% for Small enterprises.
- In respect of aid for the acquisition of transport vehicles which went beyond EU environmental protection standards the aid intensities did not exceed – 35% for large enterprises, 45% for Medium enterprises and 55% for Small enterprises.
- In respect of aid for the early adaptation to future environmental standards by SMEs, the aid intensities did not exceed – 15% for small enterprises or 10% for medium enterprises (if implemented at least three years before required to do so) and 10% for small enterprises implementing the standards nearer the required date.
- In respect of aid for investment in energy saving measures, net extra investment costs did not exceed – 60% for Large enterprises (20% gross), 70% for Medium enterprises (30% gross) and 80% for Small Enterprises (40% gross).
- In respect of aid for investment in high efficiency co-generation, the aid intensities did not exceed – 45% for large enterprises, 55% for Medium enterprises and 65% for Small enterprises.
- In respect of aid for investment in the promotion of energy from renewable energy, the aid intensities did not exceed – 45% for large enterprises, 55% for Medium enterprises and 65% for Small enterprises.
- In respect of aid for environmental studies, the aid intensities did not exceed – 50% for large enterprises, 60% for Medium enterprises and 70% for Small enterprises.
- In respect of aid for the environment, in the form of tax reductions, this was only allowed if at least the EU minimum is paid and the aid is only allowed for a maximum period of 10 years.

The 2008 Guidelines were much more generous than their predecessor in that they increased the possibilities to provide State aid; both by allowing higher aid levels and by broadening the scope of the Guidelines. Thus, under the 2008 Guidelines, there was a considerable increase in acceptable aid limits e.g. the threshold for investment aid became 60–80%. This, of course, meant that the State could cover as much as 100% of the extra costs, if the project at stake had been subject to a competitive bidding process. In addition, the new Guidelines expanded their scope and also included, among other new features, specific rules for aid to district heating. 60–80% of the eligible investment costs entailed in a district heating installation could be financed by the State if the installation ran on a renewable energy source. If the installation ran on fossil energy, the State could only cover 50–70% of the costs. Also here, 100% of extra costs could be funded if this was part of a competitive bidding process.

The more generous limits emerged both from consultations with stakeholders and as a reflection of a deepening EU environment/climate policy. The inclusion of the specific State aid rules on the issue of district heating was done primarily in response to the problems of the new Eastern European Member States and their large but highly inefficient district heating installations. Thus, the 2008 Guidelines signaled that State aid could, and perhaps should, be used to upgrade this sector.[997] Indeed, the primary driver of the 2008 Guidelines was the European Commission; not least to ensure that there was coherence with parallel policy-processes, such as the proposal for a new renewable energy Directive.[998]

In 2014, a new set of *Guidelines on State aid for Environmental Protection and Energy* were adopted[999] in parallel with changes in the 2014 GBER[1000] in regard to environmental State aid. While the linkage to energy issues, especially renewable energy, was clear in earlier guidelines, the title of the new Guidelines fully establishes that link. The 2014 Guidelines set out the Commission's policy on the compatibility of public support for environmental and energy sector related measures under EU State aid provisions. These Guidelines focus more on investments in sustainable energy in order to achieve the EU 2020 targets: the shift towards a low-carbon economy in all sectors as well as a strong emphasis on renewable energy and energy efficiency, resulting in almost a doubling of investment amounts in sustainable energy in the period 2014–2020. Since the scope of the Guidelines has been extended to the energy field, they now include measures related to energy infrastructure projects, generation adequacy measures and energy intensive users.

The key policy features of the new Guidelines on environmental protection and energy are the following:

- *The need for a gradual introduction of market based mechanisms* – Some renewable energy technologies have reached a stage of maturity and, therefore, in the view of the Commission, market principles (not State aid) in this area must be applied. Thus, as regards renewable energy, the new Guidelines foresee the gradual introduction of competitive bidding processes in this area. Such procedures must be introduced by Member States for allocating public support for renewable energy, while offering Member States some flexibility to take account of national circumstances. The Guidelines also foresee the gradual replacement of feed-in tariffs by feed-in premiums, which are intended to expose renewable energy sources more to market forces. Small

997. European Commission: Review of the Guidelines for State Aid for Environmental Protection, 2005. Questionnaire Issued in October 2005, accessible at: http://ec.europa.eu/comm/competition/state_aid/reform/00910_questionnaire_env_en.pdf.

998. K. Flåm, *"EU Environmental State Aid Policy. Wide Implications, Narrow Participation?"* CANES Working Paper, FNI Report 13/2008, p. 12.

999. European Commission: *Guidelines on State aid for environmental protection and energy 2014-2020*, OJ C 200 of 28 June 2014.

1000. European Commission: Regulation No 651/2014/EU of 17 June 2014 declaring certain categories of aid compatible with the internal market in application of Articles 107 and 108 of the Treaty, OJ L 187 of 26 June 2014.

installations may benefit from a special regime and can still be supported with feed-in tariffs or equivalent forms of support.

- *Promoting the competitiveness of European industry* – Charges levied for the funding of renewable energy support make up an increasing proportion of the energy bill for industry. This constitutes a very high burden for some energy intensive companies; in particular those exposed to strong international competition. Accordingly, the Guidelines allow for a reduction of this burden for a limited number of energy intensive sectors across the EU. Member States may also reduce the burden on highly energy intensive companies in other sectors.
- *Supporting cross-border energy infrastructure to further the Single European Energy Market* – The new Guidelines include criteria for supporting energy infrastructure, focusing on projects that improve cross-border energy flows and promote infrastructure in Europe's less-developed regions.
- *Permission to grant aid to secure adequate electricity generation where there is a real risk of insufficient electricity generation capacity* – This is designed to allow Member States to encourage producers to build new generation capacity or to prevent them from shutting down existing plants or to reward consumers to reduce electricity consumption in peak hours.

At the same time, the Commission also has simplified procedures to implement certain aid measures in the field of environmental protection and energy, e.g. in respect of certain forms of aid to promote the use of renewable energies or district heating, to clean up contaminated sites or to improve energy efficiency in buildings. The 2014 Guidelines establish the current conditions under which the Commission will consider notifiable State aid for environmental protection and energy (i.e., in those cases not covered by the GBER) compatible with the internal market. They apply to State aid granted for environmental protection and energy in all sectors including those which are subject to specific EU rules on State aid, unless such rules provide otherwise (such as agriculture and fishery, aquaculture, forestry, coal and transport). It is also clarified that environmental and energy aid may not be awarded to firms in difficulty. In addition, the Guidelines do not apply to:

- the design and manufacture of environmentally friendly products, machines or means of transport with a view to operating with fewer natural resources and action taken within plants or other production units with a view to improving safety or hygiene;
- the financing of environmental protection measures relating to air, road, railway, inland waterway and maritime transport infrastructure;
- stranded costs;[1001]

1001. "*Stranded Costs*" refer to the existing investments in infrastructure for the incumbent utility which may become redundant in a competitive environment. For instance, a large, incumbent monopoly electric power utility will have made substantial investments over the years and will carry debt. The market cost of electricity includes payments on this debt.

- State aid for research, development and innovation;
- State aid to biodiversity measures.[1002]

Individual aid granted on the basis of an aid scheme remains subject to the notification obligation if the aid exceeds certain notification thresholds and if it is not granted on the basis of a competitive bidding process. The main thresholds under the 2014 Guidelines are:[1003]

- investment aid: where the aid amount exceeds €15 million for one undertaking;
- aid for energy infrastructure: where the aid amount exceeds €50 million for one undertaking, per investment project;
- aid for Carbon Capture and Storage: where the aid amount exceeds €50 million per investment project;
- aid in the form of a generation adequacy measure: where the aid amount exceeds €15 million per project per undertaking;
- operating aid for the production of renewable electricity and/or combined production of renewable heat or operating aid for the production of biofuel where the resulting renewable electricity generation capacity per site exceeds 250 megawatts and where the resulting production exceeds 150,000 tonnes per year, respectively.

Reflecting the continued application of the balancing test, the common assessment principles in respect of State aid for environmental protection and energy are the following:[1004]

- *Existence of the objective of common interest.* Aid should contribute to the achievement of the Europe 2020 Strategy for delivering sustainable growth to support the shift towards a resource-efficient, competitive low-carbon economy.
- *Need for State intervention.* Member States should explain how the aid measure can effectively mitigate the market failure associated with reaching the objective of common interest without that aid.
- *Appropriateness of State aid.* The Guidelines note that State aid is not the only policy instrument available to Member States to promote increased levels of environmental protection or to achieve a well-functioning secure, affordable and sustainable European energy market. Regulation and market-based instruments are also important tools to achieve environmental and energy objectives. Soft instruments, such as voluntary eco-labels, and the diffusion of environmentally friendly technologies may also play an important role in achieving a higher level of environmental protection.

1002. *Guidelines on State aid for environmental protection and energy* 2014–2020, op.cit. paras 14–16.
1003. *Ibid.*, para. 20.
1004. *Ibid.*, paras 26–240.

- *Incentive effect*. An incentive effect occurs where the aid changes the behaviour of an undertaking in such a way that it engages in additional activities, which it would not carry out or it would carry out in a restricted or different manner without the aid. For example, the Commission considers that aid does not present an incentive effect for the beneficiary in all cases where work on the project had already started prior to the aid application by the beneficiary to the national authorities.
- *Proportionality of the aid*. Environmental and energy aid is considered to be proportionate if the aid amount per beneficiary is limited to the minimum needed to achieve the environmental protection or energy objective aimed for. The level of aid is the minimum needed when the aid corresponds to the net extra cost necessary to meet the objective, compared to the counter-factual scenario in the absence of aid.
- *Avoidance of undue negative effects on competition and trade*. For aid to be compatible with the internal market, the negative effects of the aid measure in terms of distortions of competition and impact on trade between Member States must be limited and outweighed by the positive effects in terms of the contribution of the measure to the objective of common interest.
- *Transparency*. To ensure that Member States, the Commission, economic operators, and the public, have easy access to all relevant acts and to pertinent information about the aid awarded, Member States must ensure the publication of the following information on a "comprehensive State aid website," at national or regional level in respect of aid awards greater than €500,000, including: the full text of the approved aid scheme or the individual aid granting decision and its implementing provisions, or a link to it, the identity of the granting authority/ies, the identity of the individual beneficiaries, the form and amount of aid granted to each beneficiary, the date of granting, the type of undertaking (SME/large company), the region in which the beneficiary is located (at NUTS level II) and the principal economic sector in which the beneficiary has its activities (at NACE group level).

Under the 2014 Guidelines, the eligible costs for environmental aid are the extra investment costs in tangible and/or in intangible assets which are directly linked to the achievement of the common objective. The eligible costs are determined as follows:

- where the costs of achieving the common interest objective can be identified in the total investment costs as a separate investment, for instance, because the green element is a readily identifiable "add-on component" to a pre-existing facility, the costs of the separate investment constitute the eligible costs;
- in all other cases, the eligible costs are the extra investment costs established by comparing the aided investment with the counter-factual situation in the absence of State aid. In principle, reference can be made to the cost of a technically comparable investment that would credibly be realised without aid

and which does not achieve the common interest objective or that only attains that objective to a lesser degree. Eligible costs are set out depending on the scenario chosen.

Under the Guidelines, the limits of State aid for environmental protection and energy are the following.[1005]

Table 29 2014 Guidelines – Limits of State Aid for Environmental Protection and Energy

	Small Enterprise (Intensities May Be Increased by a Bonus of 5% or 15% Points up to Maximum 100%)	*Medium-Sized Enterprise (Intensities May Be Increased by a Bonus of 5% or 15% Points up to Maximum 100%)*	*Large Enterprise (Intensities May Be Increased by a Bonus of 5% or 15% Points up to Maximum 100%)*
Aid for undertakings going beyond Union standards or increasing the level of environmental protection in the absence of Union standards (aid for the acquisition of new transport vehicles)	60% 70% if eco-innovation, 100% if there is a bidding process	50% 60% if eco-innovation, 100% if there is a bidding process	40% 50% if eco-innovation 100% if there is a bidding process
Aid for environmental studies	70%	60%	50%
Aid for early adaptation to future Union standards			
more than three years	20%	15%	10%
between one and three years before the entry into force of the standards	15%	10%	5%

1005. *Ibid.*, para. 241 and Annex.

	Small Enterprise (Intensities May Be Increased by a Bonus of 5% or 15% Points up to Maximum 100%)	*Medium-Sized Enterprise (Intensities May Be Increased by a Bonus of 5% or 15% Points up to Maximum 100%)*	*Large Enterprise (Intensities May Be Increased by a Bonus of 5% or 15% Points up to Maximum 100%)*
Aid for waste management	55%	45%	35%
Aid for renewable energies Aid for co-generation installations	65%, 100% if there is a bidding process	55%, 100% if there is a bidding process	45%, 100% if there is a bidding process
Aid for energy efficiency	50%, 100% if there is a bidding process	40%, 100% if there is a bidding process	30%, 100% if there is a bidding process
Aid for district heating and cooling using conventional energy	65%, 100% if there is a bidding process	55%, 100% if there is a bidding process	45% 100% if there is a bidding process
Aid the remediation of contaminated sites	100%	100%	100%
Aid for relocation of undertakings	70%	60%	50%
Aid in the form of tradable permits	100%	100%	100%
Aid for energy infrastructure District heating infrastructure	100%	100%	100%
Aid for Carbon Capture & Storage (CCS)	100%	100%	100%

The 2014 GBER applies to environmental State aid granted for the following purposes (provided all other conditions laid down in GBER are met):

- to increase the level of environmental protection in the absence of EU standards;
- investment aid for early adaptation to future EU standards;
- investment aid for energy efficiency measures;

- investment aid for energy efficiency projects in buildings;
- investment aid for high efficiency co-generation;
- investment aid for the promotion of energy from renewable sources;
- operating aid for the promotion of electricity from renewable sources;
- operating aid for the promotion of energy from renewable sources in small-scale installations;
- aid in the form of reductions in environmental taxes;
- investment aid for renewal of contaminated sites;
- investment aid for energy-efficient district heating and cooling;
- investment aid for waste recycling and reutilisation;
- investment aid for energy infrastructure;
- aid for environmental studies.

Many of the GBER conditions reflect those of the 2014 Environmental Guidelines e.g. the measures exempted must still fulfil the incentive effect, transparency, proportionality and cumulation rules, as reflected in the assessment criteria of the Guidelines. However, in the case of block exempted measures, a more simplified method of calculation of extra investment costs is used (operating costs and benefits are not taken into account). In the case of block exempted measures, lower maximum aid intensities apply compared to those of the Guidelines.

Under the GBER rules, environmental aid measures may benefit from the presumed compatibility with the internal market, and the consequent exemption from prior notification, where they are within the threshold limits for notification exemption and the aid intensity limits are respected. The threshold levels are up to the following (depending on the type of measure):

- €15 million per undertaking per investment project for investment aid for environmental protection, excluding investment aid for the renewal of contaminated sites and aid for the distribution network part of an energy-efficient district heating and cooling installation;
- €10 million for investment aid for energy efficiency projects;
- €20 million per undertaking per investment project for investment aid for the renewal of contaminated sites;
- €15 million per undertaking per project for operating aid for the production of electricity from renewable sources and operating aid for the promotion of energy from renewable sources in small-scale installations (or €150 million when the aid is granted on the basis of a competitive bidding process);
- €20 million per undertaking per investment project for investment aid for a district heating or cooling distribution network;
- €50 million per undertaking, per investment project for investment aid for energy infrastructure.

In turn, the State aid intensity limits under GBER 2014 are the following:

Table 30 State Aid for Environmental Protection and Energy – State Aid Intensity Limits under GBER 2014

Aid Intensities for Investment Aid	*Competitive Bidding*	*Small Enterprises*	*Medium-Sized Enterprises*	*Large Enterprises*
Going beyond EU standards / Absence of EU Standards		60%	50%	40%
Investment aid for waste recycling and reutilisation		55%	45%	35%
Early adaptation to future EU standards > three years before entry into force of standard		20%	15%	10%
Early adaptation to future EU standards > one but < three years before entry into force of standard		15%	10%	5%
Environmental studies		70%	60%	50%
Investment aid for energy efficiency measures		50%	40%	30%
Investment aid for the promotion of energy from renewable sources	100%	65% 50%	55% 40%	45% 30% (of the total investment costs)

Aid Intensities for Investment Aid	*Competitive Bidding*	*Small Enterprises*	*Medium-Sized Enterprises*	*Large Enterprises*
Investment aid for high-efficiency co-generation		65%	55%	45%
Investment aid for energy efficiency projects in buildings	The nominal value of the loan or the amount guaranteed shall not exceed €10 million per project at the level of the final beneficiaries. Additional investment from private investors reaching at minimum 30%.			
Investment aid for energy infrastructure	The aid amount shall not exceed the difference between the eligible costs and the operating profit of the investment.			
Operating aid for the promotion of electricity from renewable sources	Aid shall be granted in a competitive bidding process (with some exceptions). Aid shall be granted as a premium in addition to the market price.			
Operating aid for the promotion of energy from renewable sources in small-scale installations	The aid per unit of energy shall not exceed the difference between the total costs of producing energy from the renewable source in question and the market price of energy.			
Aid in the form of reductions in environmental taxes	The beneficiaries shall pay at least the respective minimum level of taxation.			
Renewal of contaminated sites		100%	100%	100%
Investment aid for energy-efficient district heating and cooling		65%	55%	45%
In most cases the aid intensity may be increased by 15% points for investments located in assisted areas fulfilling the conditions of Article 107(3)(a) of the Treaty and by 5% points for investments located in assisted areas fulfilling the conditions of Article 107(3)(c) of the Treaty.				

It is clear from the above review that a serious and concerted effort was made to incorporate environmental protection and energy policy in the State aid rules as a matter of EU policy. This is further reflected in the Commission's 2014 Communication setting *criteria for the analysis of the compatibility with the internal market of State aid to promote the execution of important projects of common European interest.*[1006] In that regard, the EU currently, and for the foreseeable future, has a range of strategies that are regarded as being of common European interest and *per se* important. These include the following in relation to environment and energy.

Table 31 Important EU Strategies of Common Interest in Regard to Environment and Energy

The Energy Strategy for Europe[1007] – The Energy Union Strategy is a project of the European Commission to coordinate the transformation of European energy supply. It was launched in February 2015, with the aim of providing secure, sustainable, competitive, affordable energy. It was endorsed by the European Council in March 2015 and focuses on five priority areas: Energy security, solidarity and trust; a fully integrated European energy market; Energy efficiency contributing to moderation of demand; De-carbonising the economy and Research, innovation and competitiveness. The strategy includes a minimum 10% electricity interconnection target for all EU Member States by 2020, which the Commission hopes will put downward pressure energy prices, reduce the need to build new power plants, reduce the risk of black-outs, improve the reliability of renewable energy supplies, and encourage market integration.
The 2030 framework for climate and energy policies[1008] – In 1997 the EU agreed to reduce its carbon dioxide emissions as part of the Kyoto Protocol, which runs until 2020. The 2030 Framework for Climate and Energy Policies, agreed in October 2014, sets out European targets beyond Kyoto and until 2030.

1006. European Commission: Communication from the Commission – *Criteria for the analysis of the compatibility with the internal market of State aid to promote the execution of important projects of common European interest*, OJ C 188 of 20 June 2014. *See* earlier review of this in Chapter 2.

1007. European Commission: Communication from the Commission to the European Parliament, the Council, the European Economic and Social Committee and the Committee of the Regions – *"Energy 2020 – A strategy for competitive, sustainable and secure energy"* – COM (2010) 639 final.

1008. European Commission: Communication from the Commission to the European Parliament, the Council, the European Economic and Social Committee and the Committee of the Regions, *"A policy framework for climate and energy in the period from 2020 to 2030"* – COM (2014) 15 final.

The European Energy Security Strategy[1009] – This was launched by the European Commission in May 2014. The Strategy aims to ensure a stable and abundant supply of energy for European citizens and the economy. It seeks also to address key concerns e.g. that the EU imports more than half of all the energy it consumes (with a particularly high import dependency on crude oil (more than 90%) and natural gas (66%) and a total import bill of more than €1 billion per day) and that several Member States are heavily reliant on a single supplier, including some that rely entirely on Russia for their natural gas (with the risks of supply disruptions, whether caused by political or commercial disputes,[1010] or infrastructure failure).

The Trans-European Transport and Energy networks[1011] – The EU supports Trans-European Networks (TENs) within the Connecting Europe programme. The support is for transport networks, energy networks and telecommunication networks. The networks comprise infrastructure and priority corridor projects to link up integrated transport connections (roads, railways, etc.), energy supply networks (pipelines, etc.) and telecommunications connections.

Resource Efficient Europe[1012] – This (further) flagship initiative for a resource-efficient Europe provides a long-term framework for actions in many policy areas, supporting policy agendas for: climate change, energy, transport, industry, raw materials, agriculture, fisheries, biodiversity and regional development. This is designed to increase certainty for investment and innovation and to ensure that all relevant policies factor in resource efficiency in a balanced manner.

Moreover, the EU Seventh Environment Action Programme to 2020: "Living well, within the limits of our planet" guides European environment policy until 2020.[1013] The Programme states that ensuring the Union's long-term prosperity requires further action to address such challenges as population dynamics, urbanisation, disease and pandemics, accelerating technological change and unsustainable economic growth. Its priority objectives are: to protect, conserve and enhance the Union's natural capital; to turn the Union into a resource-efficient, green and competitive low-carbon economy; to safeguard the Union's citizens from environment-related pressures and risks to health and well-being; to maximise the benefits of Union environment legislation by

1009. European Commission: Communication from the Commission to the European Parliament and the Council, "*European Energy Security Strategy*," COM (2014) 330 final.
1010. For instance, the 2009 gas dispute between Russia and transit-country Ukraine, which left many EU countries with severe shortages.
1011. *See* http://www.inforse.org/europe/eu_ten-e.htm on energy and http://ec.europa.eu/transport/infrastructure/tentec/tentec-portal/site/en/abouttent.htm on transport.
1012. European Commission: Communication from the Commission to the European Parliament, the Council, the European Economic and Social Committee and the Committee of the Regions – "*A resource-efficient Europe – flagship initiative under the Europe 2020 strategy*," COM (2011) 21 of 26 January 2011.
1013. Decision No 1386/2013/EU of the European Parliament and of the Council of 20 November 2013 on a General Union Environment Action Programme to 2020 "Living well, within the limits of our planet," OJ L 354 of 28 December 2013, pp. 171–200.

improving implementation; to improve the knowledge and evidence base for Union environment policy; to secure investment for environment and climate policy and address environmental externalities; to improve environmental integration and policy coherence; to enhance the sustainability of the Union's cities and to increase the Union's effectiveness in addressing international environmental and climate-related challenges.[1014] Moreover, the Programme stresses that:

> It is essential that Union priority objectives for 2020 are established, in line with a clear long-term vision for 2050. This would also provide a stable environment for sustainable investment and growth. The 7th EAP should build on policy initiatives in the Europe 2020 strategy,[1015] including the Union climate and energy package,[1016] the Commission Communication on a Roadmap for moving to a low-carbon economy in 2050,[1017] the EU Biodiversity Strategy to 2020,[1018] the Roadmap to a Resource Efficient Europe,[1019] the Innovation Union Flagship Initiative[1020] and the European Union Strategy for Sustainable Development.[1021]

Even before the 2014 Guidelines and GBER were adopted, in 2013 many politicians were emphasising the important role of State aid regulation in the EU and, in particular, its potential to transform markets to become more "green" oriented and ecologically friendly. Thus, there was considerable lobbying for the State aid regime to allow and facilitate the evolution of new, appropriate public policy tools which would balance the desirability of proportionality against the need to control climate risk and ensure economic flexibility in the face of short-term impacts against "ideal" market structures.[1022] Moreover, there was a strong lobby evident in the consultative process in favour of simplifying State aid rules and allowing exemptions in areas with pervasive market failures; allowing the use of State aid to address missing markets and excessive market concentration in most national markets and to ensure that government support did not flow to fossil fuel investments and incentivise countries to transition their energy-intensive industries into the low-carbon alternatives.[1023]

In 2014, State aid for *environmental protection, including energy saving* measures, across the EU amounted to €43.6 billion. Of this, €7.7 billion (17.6%) was covered by the pre-existing GBER arrangements. The latest statistics indicate that some 46% of total spending on State aid across the EU in 2015 was attributable to State aid

1014. *Ibid.*, Article 2.
1015. According to the Stern Review on the Economics of Climate Change, without action, the overall costs of climate change will be equivalent to losing at least 5% of global gross domestic product (GDP) each year. Including a wider range of risks and impacts, this figure could increase this to 20% of GDP.
1016. OECD: *Environmental Outlook to 2050: The Consequences of Inaction* (Report, 2012).
1017. COM (2011) 244.
1018. COM (2011) 571.
1019. COM (2011) 112.
1020. COM (2011) 885.
1021. Decision No 1386/2013/EU of the European Parliament and of the Council of 20 November 2013 on a General Union Environment Action Programme to 2020 "Living well, within the limits of our planet," OJ L 354 of 28 December 2013, pp. 171–200, para. 8.
1022. Green European Foundation: "*The role of State aid in creating a green economy*," November 2013.
1023. *Ibid.*, p. 20.

supporting environmental protection and energy savings (i.e., €47 billion in total), mainly following the introduction of renewable energy systems in line with the 2014 Guidelines and the improved accuracy of accounting for aid in respect of renewables. Thus, State aid for environmental protection including energy savings increased by €3.3 billion in 2015 compared with 2014 and €10.2 billion of total State aid supporting environmental protection and energy savings in 2015 (21.6%) was covered by the current GBER.[1024]

From 1996 to 2000, State aid to *gas infrastructure* was approved by the EU for projects in Denmark, Greece, Ireland, and Spain coupled with on-budget subsidies given to the gas industry by the EU. From 1996 to 2000, these included structural funds of €2 billion and €3 billion in preferential loans from the European Investment Bank. In addition, *tax incentives for the exploration and production of oil and gas* were also used and producer countries, such as Denmark, Ireland, the Netherlands and the UK, have continued to support the exploration and production of oil and gas via tax incentive measures e.g. in Denmark the payment of royalties on gas and oil production was abolished; Ireland introduced a pre-exploration preferential tax scheme for oil; in the Netherlands, tax exemptions were provided to less profitable Dutch gas fields and UK taxation on new gas fields has been repeatedly lowered to create an incentive for investment, especially for smaller gas fields or fields where exploration is difficult.[1025]

While several strategy papers underpin current EU energy policy, the most important ones are: "*Energy 2020 – A strategy for competitive, sustainable and secure energy*"[1026] and the "*Energy Roadmap 2050.*"[1027] The former emphasises the urgent need to act in order to both restructure the energy market in the EU and to reach the climate targets, while also remaining competitive into the future. In order to meet these challenges, the Commission estimates the need for further investment of some €1 trillion, especially for creating or rebuilding infrastructure. Five priority areas are identified, especially to reach the 2020 goals:

- achieving an energy-efficient Europe;
- completing the internal energy market;
- empowering consumers and achieving the highest level of safety and security;
- extending Europe's leadership in energy technology; and
- innovation and strengthening the external dimension of the EU energy market.

However, due to its continuing focus on fossil fuels and nuclear energy, the Energy Roadmap 2050 has been criticised by many environmental activists as a retrograde step and a lost opportunity. In particular, there is concern that the new strategy of the European Commission on the future of Europe's energy supply of February 2016 is to

1024. European Commission: State Aid Scoreboard 2016, accessible at: http://ec.europa.eu/competition/state_aid/scoreboard/index_en.html.
1025. European Environment Agency: "*Energy subsidies in the European Union: A brief overview,*" Copenhagen 2004 and State aid Scoreboard.
1026. European Commission: "*Energy 2020 – A strategy for competitive, secure, and sustainable energy,*" COM (2010) 639 of 10 November 2010.
1027. European Commission: "*Energy Roadmap 2050,*" COM/2011/885 of 15 December 2011.

rely heavily on natural gas for the coming two decades and beyond.[1028] Critics also contrasted the continued role of fossil fuels with commitments to cut carbon dioxide made by the EU at the Paris Climate Summit in December 2015. Moreover, the continued high level of gas imports from Russia, Norway, Qatar and other Gulf States and the requisite multi-billion euro investment in infrastructure (including new cross-border pipelines and the development of terminals for the import of liquefied natural gas) raised particular concerns.[1029] In addition, others argued that the Commission was hugely over-estimating the demand for gas[1030] and that, instead of pumping millions into projects that are doomed to fail, EU policy should wait until new, more credible estimates for gas demand can be formulated. Others more bluntly criticised this strategy as "rolling out the red carpet for Gazprom," Russia's national energy giant. Faced with this level of concern, as noted by one commentator, it seems likely that, in the coming years, green energy policy makers will lobby more intensively for legislation that leads the way to a truly sustainable energy system with 100% renewables and a phasing-out of fossil fuels and nuclear energy.[1031]

For its part, the European Commission argues that its strategy consists of a package of measures which include moderating energy demand, increasing energy production in Europe (including from renewables), further developing a well-functioning and fully integrated internal energy market, as well as diversification of energy sources, suppliers and routes. The proposals are also intended to bring more transparency to the European energy market and to create more solidarity between EU Member States. In that regard, Commissioner for Climate Action and Energy, Miguel Arias Cañete said that:

> After the gas crises of 2006 and 2009 that left many millions out in the cold, we said: 'Never again'. But the stress tests of 2014 showed we are still far too vulnerable to major disruption of gas supplies. And the political tensions on our borders are a sharp reminder that this problem will not just go away. Today's proposals are about a reliable, competitive and flexible system in which energy flows across borders and consumers reap the benefits. They are about standing together to protect the most vulnerable. And they are about securing our clean energy future: I can assure that our commitment to a clean energy transition is irreversible and non-negotiable.[1032]

In any event, current EU policy, as set out in recent EU Commission strategy papers, sees the EU relying on elements such as a high share of renewable energies, high energy efficiency, energy savings, carbon capture and storage and nuclear energy to transform Europe's energy market in the long run. Some of these elements are highly contested. Public and political opinion has also been increasingly critical about nuclear energy, an

1028. European Commission: Press Release "*Towards Energy Union: The Commission presents sustainable energy security package*," IP/16/307 of 16 February 2016.
1029. F. Harvey, "*Europe Places Bets on Natural Gas to Secure Energy Future*" (16 February 2016), the Guardian.
1030. European Court of Auditors: Special Report "*Improving the security of energy supply by developing the internal energy market: more efforts needed*," European Union, 2015.
1031. S. Langsdorf: "*EU Energy Policy: From the ECSC to the Energy Roadmap 2050*," European Green Foundation, December 2011, p. 9.
1032. *Ibid.*

option which green energy activists have dismissed since their political beginnings as too high-risk and high-cost to provide a viable basis for a sustainable energy system. Thus, while the long-term goal of the EU is clear – to restructure its economy to a low-carbon economy – the means of achieving this remain contentious.

One recent view of the interaction between EU State aid policy and energy and environmental policy is that where regulation has failed, the magic relentless force of European integration is still able to push public spending towards common interests, such as sustainable growth and social responsibility, under the supervision and assistance of an independent controller.[1033] Thus, after 60 years, State aid control is still about ensuring "that resources are channeled to industries which contribute to growth and competitiveness, that State intervention does not permit any company or sector to gain an unfair advantage over its competitors in another Member State and that State aid policy is consistent with other Community policies."[1034] This view also highlights that this is even truer at a time when more efficient and targeted European action is considered essential to control "the negative externalities that unsound public finances in a Member State can generate for its neighbours."[1035]

It is certainly clear that the 2014 Guidelines on State aid for environmental protection and energy, applicable until 2020, mark a new era for the application of the EU State aid rules in the energy sector. The Commission expects that established renewable energy sources will become grid-competitive; implying that subsidies and exemptions from balancing responsibilities should be phased out in a degressive way between 2020 and 2030. The Commission's aim is to abolish all subsidies for established renewables in the longer term. The 2014 Guidelines introduce two fundamental shifts in energy policy. The transition from feed-in tariffs to market premiums and from statutory tariffs to competitive bidding processes will have a substantial impact on the future of renewables support schemes in the EU. With some exceptions (in particular in respect of aid already granted under existing schemes), Member States were required to align existing aid schemes with the new Guidelines no later than 1 January 2016. Accordingly, at least to some extent, Member States support to renewable energy systems must now reflect the energy market and take due account of competition between technologies.

The 2014 Guidelines also aim to achieve climate change objectives and simultaneously lower retail prices for the benefit of consumers. To achieve this, energy cost increases must be contained, price signals for investments in electricity must be ensured and the internal energy market must function without impediments. However, given the controversial nature of these issues and the extensive negotiations before the adoption of the 2014 Guidelines, much of the guidance is fairly vague and open ended. Outside the scope of the 2014 Guidelines, the European Commission will decide how Member States can support new nuclear generation projects.

1033. E. Righini: "*State Aid Control: An Evolutionary Theory of Resilience and Adaptation,*" European University Institute, 2016, p. 138.
1034. P. Sutherland: "*Foreword,*" in *Competition Rules in the EEC and the ECSC Applicable to State Aids* Brussels-Luxembourg, Commission of the European Communities 1987, p. 6.
1035. M. Draghi: "*Memorial Lecture in Honour of Tommaso Padoa-Schioppa,*" speech delivered in London on 9 July 2014.

6.3 REGIONAL DEVELOPMENT AND COHESION

EU regional policy accounts for the single largest share of the EU budget for 2014–2020 (€351.8 billion out of a total of €1,082 billion)[1036] and is the main investment instrument of the EU. These resources are used to finance strategic transport and communication infrastructures, to favour a transition to a more environmentally friendly economy, to support small and medium-sized enterprises (SMEs) in becoming more innovative and more competitive, to create new and lasting job opportunities, to reinforce and modernise education systems and to build a more inclusive society. In so doing, regional policy serves as a catalyst for further public and private funding by obliging EU countries to co-finance projects from their national budgets and by boosting investor confidence. Taking into account this national contribution, and the leverage effect of financial instruments, the overall impact of EU investment for 2014–2020 is estimated at over €500 billion.

From a broader policy perspective, EU regional policy is seen as an expression of solidarity between EU Member States as the bulk of funding is targeted towards the less developed regions of the EU. Thus, EU regional policy aims, in particular, to assist these regions to fulfil their economic potential, in the light of regional disparities both across the EU and within EU Member States. According to the latest available statistical data,[1037] EU regional policy funding has financed tens of thousands of projects over the years, benefiting all EU countries individually and the EU as a whole in terms of economic growth and jobs. Between 1989 and 2013, over €800 billion was allocated from the EU budget to co-fund projects targeting regional growth.

There are 274 EU regions covered by EU regional policy in the period 2014–2020.

Table 32 EU Regional Funding 2014–2020

Type of Region	*Basis*	*Targeted Funding*
Less Developed Regions	Per capita GDP < 75% of EU-27 average	€182.2 billion
Transition Regions	Per capita GDP > 75% and < 90% of EU-27 average	€35.4 billion
More Developed Regions	Per capita GDP > 90% of EU-27 average	€54.3 billion

1036. Funding for regional and cohesion policy in the 2014–2020 period amounts to €351.8 billion. Detailed data and charts are available in the Cohesion Policy Data portal.

1037. *See* all the financed projects on the Inforegio page of the European Commission, accessible at: http://ec.europa.eu/regional_policy/en/projects.

Other sources of funding envisaged for the same period include the Cohesion Fund (€65.3 billion), European territorial cooperation (€10.2 billion), the "Youth employment initiative" (€3.2 billion) and specific allocations for the outermost and sparsely populated regions (€1.6 billion).[1038]

The evolution of EU regional policy dates back to 1957 when it was first mentioned in the Treaty of Rome. In 1958 the European Social Fund (ESF)[1039] was created and the European Regional Development Fund (ERDF) was established in 1975.[1040] The specific legal basis for regional policy was established in the Single European Act in 1986. Two years later, and to adapt to the accession of Greece (1981), Spain and Portugal (1986), the Structural Funds were integrated into an over-arching cohesion policy with a budget of some €64 billion. The EU cohesion policy of 1988 commenced with a specific focus on the poorest and most underdeveloped regions, the introduction of multi-annual programming, the strategic orientation of investments and the involvement of regional and local partners. This process was further enhanced in 1993 when the Maastricht Treaty established the Cohesion Fund, the Committee of the Regions and the principle of subsidiarity (whereby decision-making must always be made at the least centralised/most local level able to address the matter appropriately). In the 1994–1999 period, the resources for regional funds were doubled.

In 2000, the EU Lisbon Strategy shifted the priorities towards growth, jobs and innovation and the priorities of cohesion policy were shifted to reflect this. Up to 2004, pre-accession instruments made EU funding and know-how available to countries engaged in the process of joining the EU. The 10 new countries that joined the EU in 2004 increased EU population by 20%, but EU GDP only rose by 5%. In the 2004–2006 period, the budget of the cohesion fund was €213 billion for the 15 existing Member States and €22 billion for the new Member States. From 2007 to 2013, the EU budget for regional development was €347 billion, of which 25% was dedicated to research and innovation and 30% for environmental infrastructure and measures to combat climate change. Available information in respect of this period points to an estimated 400,000 projects implemented by SMEs receiving direct investment aid; effective support for 121,400 start-ups, 94,955 research projects, 33,556 cooperation projects and the creation of an estimated 1 million new jobs from 2007 to 2014.[1041] In the current programming period of 2014–2020, the EU budget for its regional development and cohesion programmes is €351.8 billion, with a particular focus on four key investment

1038. For more data, *see* European Commission: Regional Policy website at: http://ec.europa.eu/regional_policy/en/funding/available-budget/.

1039. The ESF funds local, regional and national employment-related projects throughout Europe: from small projects run by neighbourhood charities to help local disabled people find suitable work, to nationwide projects that promote vocational training among the whole population. For more information, *see* the ESF website at: http://ec.europa.eu/esf/main.jsp?catId = 35&langId = en.

1040. The ERDF aims to strengthen economic and social cohesion in the European Union by correcting imbalances between its regions. Further information is accessible from the ERDF website at: http://ec.europa.eu/regional_policy/en/funding/erdf/.

1041. *See* European Commission: Regional Policy web page: http://ec.europa.eu/regional_policy/en/policy/what/key-achievements/.

priorities: research and innovation, the digital agenda, support for SMEs and the low-carbon economy. Some €100 billion is to be dedicated to these sectors, of which €26.7 billion will support the shift to a low-carbon economy (energy efficiency and renewable energies).[1042]

The European Regional Development Fund (ERDF) and the European Social Fund (ESF) are now jointly known as the "EU Structural Funds" as they are designed to invest in economic and social restructuring across the EU and thereby reduce gaps in development between European regions, for example in terms of infrastructure and employment. Together with the Cohesion Fund, the European Agricultural Fund for Rural Development (EAFRD) and the European Maritime and Fisheries Fund (EMFF), they make up the European structural and investment funds (ESIFs) and each of these funds is intended to contribute in its own way to delivering the growth goals of the Europe 2020 strategy – the EU's over-arching strategy for growth and jobs in the period to 2020.

6.3.1 The State Aid Dimension of Regional Development and Cohesion Policy

As these policies and funds developed over the years, a core question arose – did such funds, entirely or in part, constitute State aid? If they did, they were, of course, eligible for exemption under Article 107 of the TFEU and with particular reference to two exemption grounds:

> (a) aid to promote the economic development of areas where the standard of living is abnormally low or where there is serious underemployment, and of the regions referred to in Article 349, in view of their structural, economic and social situation; (the so-called **"A" Regions** of the EU with per capita GDP at less than 75% of the EU average);
> (c) aid to facilitate the development of certain economic activities or of certain economic areas, where such aid does not adversely affect trading conditions to an extent contrary to the common interest; (the so-called **"C" Regions** of the EU);[1043]

Under EU regional policy in coordination with the State aids rules, the EU refers to "assisted regions" as those where investment and job creation aids are seen as justified based on different degrees of national or regional handicaps and general market failures. In 2015, some €10 billion of regional development State aid was granted across the 28 EU Member States amounting to 10% of all State aid[1044]

Initially, the European Commission insisted that Member States give advance notice of all significant cases of general regional aid. Later, the Commission agreed to draw up general criteria for the review of regional aid schemes. This was first done in 1971, following a Council Resolution that represented the first ever document on the

1042. More on the history of the regional and cohesion policy can be found on the European Commission: Regional Policy website at http://ec.europa.eu/regional_policy/en/policy/what/history/.
1043. *See* earlier discussion of these exemptions in Chapter 2.
1044. European Commission: State Aid Scoreboard 2016, accessible at: http://ec.europa.eu/competition/state_aid/scoreboard/index_en.html.

implementation of the regional aid rules of the EEC Treaty,[1045] and later in 1975,[1046] and 1978[1047] (after the accession of Denmark, Ireland and the UK, at which time it adopted the first communication on the method of coordination of regional aid). In the eighties, after the accession of Greece, Portugal, and Spain, and following the reinforcement of the objective of economic and social cohesion via the Single European Act, the Commission laid down new rules in the 1988 guidelines on regional aid, which introduced, quantitative, statistical criteria for the definition of the eligible regions for the first time, and made a first attempt to ensure coordination with the objectives of the structural funds.[1048]

6.3.2 The Relevant State Aid Rules

In a more comprehensive attempt to coordinate structural policies with Regional State aid rules, the European Commission adopted Regional Aid Guidelines in 1998 ("RAGs 1998").[1049] These Guidelines formalised several well-established regional aid issues, notably:

- the basic distinction between Article 107(3)(a) and 107(3)(c) regions, as confirmed by the Courts;[1050]
- the uniform maximum ceilings of aid intensity;
- the concept of regional specificity;
- the attention to sectoral repercussions;
- the principle of transparency;
- the *ex ante* assessment of aid schemes and exemption for individual aid; and
- the concept of a comprehensive regional aid policy (i.e., that regional aid should be granted under a multisectoral aid scheme which forms part of a regional development strategy with clearly defined objectives).

At the same time, the 1998 RAGS introduced new elements stemming from Commission practice.[1051] First, a basic innovation was the setting of a global coverage ceiling in

1045. First Resolution of 20 October 1971 of the Representatives of the Governments of the Member States, meeting within the Council, on general systems of regional aid, OJ C 111 of 4 November 1971, p. 1.
1046. European Commission: Communication to the Council on *General Regional Aid Schemes*, COM (75) 77 of 26 February 1975.
1047. European Commission: Communication of the Commission on Regional Aid Schemes, OJ C 31 of 3 February 1979.
1048. European Commission: Communication on the method for the application of Article 92(3)(a) and (c) to regional aid, OJ C 212 of 12 August 1988.
1049. European Commission: *Guidelines on Regional aid*, OJ C 74 of 10 March 1998.
1050. Case C-248/84, *Germany v. Commission*, [1987] ECR 2671.
1051. *See* M. Merola, "*Regional Aid: Recent Trends and Some Historical Background – with special Focus on large Investment Projects*" EstAL, 3/2010, p. 591.

terms of population eligible for regional aid throughout the EU. The underlying idea was to reinforce the principle that Article 107(a) and (c) exemptions were to be used sparingly to support the most disadvantaged regions. This innovation, coupled with the requirement imposed on Member States to notify the Commission of national regional aid maps, was the model on which the Commission's modern regional aid policy was to be based from 1998 to the present day.

Regional State Aid Mapping[1052]

The basic approach to regional aid was based on early German proposals suggesting that, based on German experience and practice, it was desirable to divide up territorial maps and examine the economic needs and relative economic handicaps of each territorial unit on the basis of detailed statistics and economic indicators for each unit. This approach was pursued, somewhat independently at first, at EU level by the EU Regional Policy, the EU Statistics Office (EUROSTAT) and DG Competition of the European Commission in regard to the application of the Article 107(3) State aid control exemptions. In the 1990s, the different approaches to the economic mapping were the subject of serious efforts of coordination and convergence and there is now a reasonable consistency of approach in regard to EU regions for different purposes. The importance of this exercise can be seen in the manner in which EU regions, big and small, are now identified and classified for the purposes of different EU policies, including State aid control. In the State aid field, the regions, subregions, etc. of all Member States are now classified as *assisted regions* or *non-assisted regions*.

Assisted regions include both Article 107(3) (a) and Article 107(3) (c) regions for the purposes of State aid control. While some State aid can still be granted in non-assisted regions, including small levels of SME aid for example, State aid exemptions on the basis of Article 107(3) (a) and Article 107(3) (c) may only be approved in regions of Member States formally recognised as A or C Regions in the European Commission's periodic State aid mapping exercise.

Regional mapping for State aid and structural fund purposes in the EU is based on the *Nomenclature of Territorial Units for Statistics (NUTS)* which was established by Eurostat to provide a single uniform breakdown of territorial units for the production of regional statistics for the European Union. Although the NUTS classification lacked legal force until relatively recently, it was used since 1988 in EU

1052. The present approved Regional State Aid Maps for all EU Member States for the period 2014–2020 can be accessed at: http://ec.europa.eu/competition/state_aid/regional_aid/regional_aid.html.

legislation.[1053] In 2003, Regulation No 1059/2003/EC[1054] normalised the status of NUTS regions in EU Law. Normally NUTS 1 regions mean large Member States of the EU (population in excess of 3 million) and internal regions are sub-divided into smaller NUTS II regions (population from 800,000 to 3 million), even smaller NUTS III regions (150,000–800,000 population), etc. Because of size, some Member States start the statistical regional units at NUTS II level.

The second important innovation in the 1998 RAGs was a new method for identifying regions covered by Article 107(3)(c) based on a two-step analysis.[1055] The first involved setting a population ceiling covered by both Article 107(3)(a) and 107(3)(c) across the EU. The second step allowed Member States to use qualitative criteria indicated in the Guidelines to specify Article 107(3)(c) regions, but with a wide margin of discretion to determine the methodology and parameters to be applied for the selection of the eligible regions.

Based on its experience with regional aid up to then, the Commission was aware that the richer Member States continued to grant large amounts of aid for large projects in depressed or underdeveloped regions and was increasingly uneasy with the implicit approval given to these projects when authorising regional aid schemes. Having initially tried to control these via approval conditions, in the late 1990s the Commission sought to devise more sophisticated mechanisms to capture and assess cases of regional aid to large projects or large cases of aid.[1056]

The experiment to address this issue emerged as the Multisectoral Framework on Regional aid for Large Investment Projects (LIPs).[1057] Under the LIPs Framework, individual notifications of regional investment aid to assist large investments i.e. investments of over €50 million were to be subjected to a complex analysis that represented, to some degree, a precursor of the "new economic approach" developed in subsequent years. However, this initiative failed overall, gave rise to insurmountable problems when applied in practice, resulted in few notifications and was not effective in reducing the level of aid to large projects. Among its practical difficulties were

1053. For example in Council Regulation No 2052/88/EEC of 24 June 1988 on the tasks of the Structural Funds and their effectiveness and on coordination of their activities between themselves and with the operations of the European Investment Bank and the other existing financial instruments, OJ L 185 of 15 July 1988.
1054. Regulation No 1059/2003/EC of the European Parliament and of the Council of 26 May 2003 on the establishment of a common classification of territorial units for statistics (NUTS), OJ L 154 of 21 June 2003.
1055. Annex III of the 1998 Guidelines.
1056. *See* F.G. Wishlade, "*The Control of Regional Aid to Large Investment Projects: Workable Compromise or Arbitrary Constraint?*" EstAL, 3/2008, p. 495 and M. Merola, "*Regional Aid: Recent Trends and Some Historical Background – with special Focus on large Investment Projects*" EstAL, 3/2010, p. 592.
1057. European Commission: *Multisectoral Framework on regional aid for Large Investment Projects*, OJ C 107 of 7 April 1998.

problems in obtaining appropriate information on apparent consumption and total production capacity and problems in accurately assessing the number of safeguarded and indirect jobs in a reliable way.

A revised LIPs Framework was adopted in 2002 aimed at simplifying the system and decreasing the global volume of regional aid to large investments projects, an objective that the previous framework had failed to achieve. Under the new system, the reduction of the permissible aid level for large investment projects was obtained through the automatic adjustment of regional aid ceilings. Thus, where the investment was between €50 and €100 million euros, the relevant RAGS ceiling was reduced by 50% and, for any investment value over €100 million, the ceiling was reduced to 34% of the relevant RAGS ceiling. Thus, a €160 million investment in a region with a 25% Rags ceiling could receive no more than €24 million of aid or 15% of the investment value. Investment aid in the steel and synthetic fibres sectors was specifically prohibited and, for the motor vehicle sector, the limit was 30% of the RAGS ceiling for all projects over €50 million or all aid awards over €5 million. Member States were obliged to notify all LIPS aid where the proposed aid exceeded 50% of the RAGs ceiling and no aid could be given if the market share of the beneficiary exceeded 25% or the new capacity of the project was more than 5% of total market capacity.

Although the 2002 LIPs Framework was planned to operate until 2009, a few years later they were again revised in the context of the second reform of regional aid, and ultimately incorporated into the Guidelines on National Regional Aid for 2007–2013 (RAGs 2006).[1058]

While the 1998 RAGS[1059] were adopted for an unlimited period of time, in April 2003, the Commission decided to apply these guidelines until 2006, and to proceed to their review for the period after 2006. Following a consultation process with Member States, which began in April 2003, the Commission adopted the Regional Aid Guidelines for the period 2007–2013 on 21 December 2005[1060] which applied to all economic sectors except basic agricultural production, fisheries, the coal and steel sectors and the synthetic fibres industry.

This approach is again taken in the newest Regional Aid Guidelines of 2014 which came into force on 1 July 2014 and apply to all economic sectors except agricultural production, fisheries, aquaculture, the steel, energy and transport sectors, airports and the synthetic fibres industry.[1061] Where regional aid seeks to assist a firm in financial difficulty, the rules in the Rescue and Restructuring Guidelines apply and take precedence.[1062] Moreover, operating aid to address regional handicaps and specific

1058. European Commission: *Guidelines on National Regional Aid for 2007-2013*, OJ C 54 of 4 March 2006.
1059. European Commission: *Guidelines on National Regional Aid*, OJ C 74 of 10 March 1998 as amended in 2000, OJ C 258 of 9 September 2000.
1060. Guidelines on National Regional Aid for 2007–2013, op.cit.
1061. European Commission: *Guidelines on Regional State Aid for 2014 to 2020*, OJ C 209 of 23 July 2013, paras 9–11.
1062. *Ibid.*, para. 18.

market failures may be granted to SMEs and in the Outermost Regions of the EU. However, operating aid to support financial and insurance services, business consultancy services and the locations of corporate headquarters is not permitted as the EU views support for such sectors as not assisting regional development.[1063]

In addition, regional investment aid to broadband networks or to research infrastructures may be considered compatible with the internal market if, in addition to the general conditions laid down in the Regional Aid Guidelines, it complies also with certain specific conditions (e.g., on giving transparent and non-discriminatory access to this infrastructure).

In accordance with a prevailing principle of EU Law, Treaty exceptions are meant to be applied restrictively. Thus, for example, all of the EU regions should not, in practice, qualify for State aid regional exemptions under Article 107(3)(a) and (c). Under the 1998 Regional Aid Guidelines, the mapping approach that had already been developed was elaborated further via population scope limits on eligibility for Article 107(3)(a) and (c) exemptions. Thus, the 1998 Guidelines specified that, based on detailed national statistical data, 52.2% of the EU (25 Member States) population lived in regions eligible for regional State aid, with 34.2% of the EU population living in A Regions eligible for the highest rates of aid (40%–50%), and 18% living in relatively less disadvantaged C Regions which were eligible for lower aid rates of 10%–20%. Under the 2006 Guidelines, the overall population coverage for regional State aid was fixed at 43.1% of the EU population across all Member States. This included a safety net to ensure that no Member State lost more than 50% of its previous entitlement. Regions with less than 75% of the EU average per capita GDP (i.e., disadvantaged) qualified for the highest rates of aid under Article 107(3)(a), as well as for possible operating aid (regional aid aimed at reducing a firm's current expenses). In 2006, these regions covered some 30% of the EU population and, because of the huge disparity in wealth between these regions, ranging from 32.2% to 74.9% of the EU average, they were divided into three categories with maximum ceilings fixed between 30% and 50%.

This approach is continued in the 2014 Regional Aid Guidelines, but with minor adjustments to the maximum aid levels (essentially 25%–50%), and three forms of Regional aid are permitted: investment aid, aid for job creation and operating aid (in exceptional cases). The Guidelines provide that regional aid may be granted to A, C and other regions – provided that the limits of the amounts of regional aid are in compliance with the accepted regional maps. Accordingly, the current permissible regional State aid limits are the following.[1064]

1063. Regional Aid Guidelines, 2014, paras 16 and 17.
1064. Regional Aid Guidelines, 2014, paras 171–177.

Table 33 State Aid Limits under the 2014 Regional Aid Guidelines

Assisted Area (% GDP per Capita)	*Large Firms (% of Eligible Costs)*	*Medium Firms (% of Eligible Costs)*	*Small Firms (% of Eligible Costs)*
A Regions < 45%	50	60	70
A Regions (45–60%)	35	45	55
A Regions (60–75%)	25	35	45
Former A Regions until the end of 2017, sparsely populated and external border areas	15	25	35
Other C Regions	10	20	30

According to the Commission, the overall scope of application of the Guidelines now applies to some 47% of the EU population.[1065] Under the GBER, regional State aid is exempt from notification up to the following limits connected to the applicable maximum aid intensity:

Table 34 Regional Aid Notification Thresholds under the GBER

Applicable Maximum Aid Intensity	*Threshold for Notification € million*
10%	7.5
15%	11.25
25%	18.75
35%	26.25
50%	37.5

Accordingly, while regional aid up to the amount that an investment of €100 million may receive is generally exempt from notification under the GBER, individual aid granted under a scheme remains subject to the notification obligation pursuant to Article 108(3) of the Treaty, if the aid from all sources exceeds these notification thresholds or if it is granted to a beneficiary that has closed down the same or similar activity in the previous two years or intends to close down such an activity. In addition,

1065. Regional Aid Guidelines, 2014, para. 147.

investment aid granted to a large undertaking to diversify an existing establishment in a "C" region into new products, remains subject to the notification.

Where notification is required, its compatibility will be determined having regard to the following criteria, the content of which is described in detail in the Guidelines:

(a) There is a contribution to a *well-defined objective of common interest*: a State aid measure must aim at an objective of common interest in accordance with Article 107(3) of the Treaty.
(b) There is an *established need* for State intervention to remedy a market failure or address an equity or cohesion concern.
(c) The proposed aid measure is an *appropriate policy instrument* to address the objective of common interest.
(d) There is an *incentive effect*: the aid must change the behaviour of the undertaking(s) concerned in such a way that it engages in additional activity which it would not carry out without the aid or it would carry out in a restricted or different manner or location. (Aid will only be authorised if it actually changes the behaviour of an undertaking in a way that it engages in additional activity contributing to the development of an area so that it is clear that the aid influenced the beneficiary's investment or location decision.)
(e) The aid amount must be limited to the minimum needed to induce the additional investment or activity in the area concerned (*proportionality*).
(f) There are *no undue negative effects on competition and trade* between Member States.
(g) Member States, the Commission, economic operators and the public must have easy access to all relevant acts and to pertinent information about the aid awarded thereunder (*transparency*).

The Guidelines specify that notified regional aid will be permitted when all of these criteria are met.[1066]

For example, the Commission will presume that regional aid cannot be considered compatible and will normally not approve aid under the Regional Aid Guidelines if it gives rise to one of the following negative effects on competition and trade (the so-called "*black list*"):

- *relocation:* where the beneficiary relocates an activity to the target area and closes down that same or a similar activity elsewhere, if there is a causal link between the aid and the relocation;
- *"relocation" from certain other regions:* where, in the absence of the aid, the investment would take place in a region with the same or higher aid intensity;
- *markets in structural decline:* where the aid creates capacity in a market that is structurally in absolute decline.

1066. Regional Aid Guidelines, 2014, para. 26.

In calculating the aid intensities for regional aid, this can be done either with reference to the investment costs of an initial investment project or by reference to the expected wage costs for two years arising from job creation linked to an initial investment. Where the aid is calculated on the basis of investment costs the Commission also requires:

- that the aid beneficiary provides a financial contribution of at least 25% either through its own resources or by external financing free of any public support;
- that the investment which is to be subsidised should be maintained in the region for a minimum period of five years (for large enterprises) or three years (for SMEs);
- formal application for aid is also required before works on the project can be started (incentive effect).

Where the aid is calculated on the basis of wage costs, the posts must be filled within three years of the completion of the investment and each job created through the investment must be maintained within the area concerned for a period of five years from the date the post was first filled. For investments carried out by SMEs, Member States may reduce this five-year period for the maintenance of jobs to a minimum of three years.

For the purposes of "regional aid mapping," each Member State is required to notify a single regional aid map covering its entire national territory to the Commission, in accordance with Article 108(3) of the TFEU. On this basis, the Commission examines and approves the mapping to apply in the 2014–2020 period and these become an integral part of the new Regional Aid Guidelines. As noted earlier, the mapping exercise was completed in 2014/early 2015 and the detailed regional aid maps for all EU Member States were published by the European Commission as a series of decisions not to raise objections to the maps proposed.

The 2006 and 2014 RAGs reflected specific priorities of EU State aid reform under the State Aid Action Plan and the subsequent State Aid Modernisation initiative. The former, in particular, sought to achieve a codification of the principle of "less, and better targeted State aid," increased attention to market failures and a more refined economic assessment of notified measures. However, the 2006 RAGs were mainly intended to cope with the challenges relating to the enlargement of the EU to include countries characterised by a long-lasting history of planned economies, and therefore limited market experience. It was expected that the Commission's workload in the State aid field would increase substantially in the first years after the 2004 enlargement. To address this situation, the Member States and the Commission agreed to exempt not only individual aids, but also transparent aid schemes meeting the conditions of the Guidelines and this resulted in the first and more recent GBERs.

The process of rule-making in respect of regional State aid eventually coordinated the purposes, amounts and the spatial application of regional aid exemptions with the various EU fund regulations. Arguably, the evolution of the regional State aid rules had a wider impact on the procedures and methods of the funds, than vice versa. An exception to this, however, was the spatial dimension where funding priority regions had to be fully integrated into State aid mapping. While these matters are much better coordinated now than previously, the remaining challenges are evident from the fact that the application of State aid rules has been identified as a continuing risk area in the management of the European Structural and Investment Funds (ESIF).[1067]

6.3.3 State Aid and Structural Funds

Returning to a basic question in this area, it was not always clear when or if EU Structural funds constituted State aid. Confusion on this point arose from three considerations:

- The concept of "by and through State resources" in Article 107(1) of the TFEU.
- Updates and revisions of various Guidelines and Notices since the late 1990s that stipulated the need to add EU funds with national resources in determining the amount of aid.
- The practice of the Commission that required national authorities to obtain from the Commission two authorisations for projects combining structural funds with State resources that were classified as State aid. One approval had to be granted by DG Regional Policy and covered structural funds and another was granted by DG Competition and covered the State aid used to co-finance projects.

In 2003, the European Commission, in its Annual Competition Report, made the following observation:

> with respect to competition rules, it should be noted that Community support does not represent State aid within the meaning of Article 87(1) EC [Article 107(1) TFEU], but it must follow the same rules and must be taken into account – where it concurs with Member State funding – for the purpose of determining the compatible amount of aid.[1068]

This is a rather confusing comment that states that EU support funding is not State aid but, when combined with national funding it becomes part of the total State aid calculation. Nonetheless, this position has been consistently pursued by the Commission. This is despite the fact that it is a stretch of logic to view EU structural fund co-financing as "by or through State resources." The Commission position is partly supported by a general principle set out in the *Ladbroke Racing case (2000)*, which did not involve structural funds, but where the Court held that:

> [Article 107(1)] of the Treaty covers all the financial means by which the public sector may actually support undertakings, irrespective of whether or not those means are permanent assets of the public sector. Consequently, even though the sums...are not permanently held by the Treasury, the fact that they constantly

1067. The European Court of Auditors concluded in its Annual Report of 2012 that non-compliance with State aid rules is one of the four main areas of error in the implementation of the European Regional Development Fund and the Cohesion Fund.
1068. European Commission: XXXIII Annual Competition Policy Report, 2003, para. 393.

remain under public control, and therefore available to the competent national authorities, is sufficient for them to be categorised as State aid and for the measure to fall within [Article 107(1)] of the Treaty.[1069]

At the same time, a contrary view is that structural funds are not under the constant control of the Member States, given the fact that the allocation of structural funds per Member State and the eventual release of those funds are determined by the Council and the Commission, respectively. Moreover, even if there still is a residual degree of control by the State when it disburses structural funds, that is not a sufficient criterion because structural funds do not come out of public budgets, creating in the process an additional burden for the State.[1070]

However, it is unhelpful to this viewpoint that some State aid Guidelines specifically stipulated or continue to imply that structural funds must be added in calculating State aid amounts.[1071] In respect of earlier versions of Guidelines, more developed EU Member States actively lobbied to have structural funds included in State aid calculations on the basis that the exclusion of structural funds was inequitable towards those Member States and gave a competitive advantage to assisted countries.

The structural fund regulations now recognise additionally that, when EU structural funds are combined with State aid, the Member State concerned has to comply also with the relevant State aid rules if a State aid situation arises. This was explicitly stipulated in Regulation No 1260/99/EC, then Regulation No 1083/2006/EC and Regulation No 1303/2013/EU (the basic Regulations for structural funds). Thus, the view is that there is a State aid situation when structural funds are combined with national funding in situations where the national funding meets the requirements of Article 107(1) of the TFEU. At the same time, the standard structural fund requirement for national co-financing does not create a State aid situation in three cases. First, where a project is funded solely by the EU and/or private funds without any public funds from a national source, there is no State aid. Second, if national co-financing is below the *de minimis* level it is not classified as State aid and, as a consequence, no State aid situation arises. Third, if national co-financing above the *de minimis* level

1069. Case C-83/98P: *France v. Ladbroke and Commission*, [2000] ECR I-03271, para. 50.

1070. *See* P. Nicolaides, *"Puzzles of State Aid: Structural Funds, Cumulation and De Minimis"* EstAL, 3/2005, pp. 436–437.

1071. *See* for example: European Commission: *Community guidelines on State aid for small and medium-sized enterprises*, which provided that: "The aid ceiling will apply regardless of whether the aid is provided entirely from domestic sources or is part-financed by the Community from the Structural Funds, and more especially the European Regional Development Fund (ERDF)," OJ C 213 of 23 July 1996; European Commission: Regulation No 1407/2013/EU of 18 December 2013 on the application of Articles 107 and 108 of the Treaty on the Functioning of the European Union to *de minimis* aid which stipulates that: "Union funding centrally managed by the Commission which is not directly or indirectly under the control of the Member State does not constitute State aid and should not be taken into account in determining whether the relevant ceiling is complied with," OJ L 352 of 24 December 2013 and European Commission: Regulation No 651/2014/EU of 17 June 2014 (GBER 2014) which provides that "Union funding centrally managed by the institutions, agencies, joint undertakings or other bodies of the Union, that is not directly or indirectly under the control of Member States, does not constitute State aid. Where such Union funding is combined with State aid, only the latter should be considered for determining whether notification thresholds and maximum aid intensities are respected," OJ L 187 of 26 June 2014.

does not satisfy all the criteria of Article 107(1) of the TFEU, again there is no State aid. An example of this situation is where the recipient of the combined EU and State funds is not an undertaking (as is the case with certain infrastructure projects) or where the aid goes directly to individuals such as unemployed persons. Therefore, if the measure financed is not State aid (i.e., granted to individuals, not granted through state resources, etc.) the EU grants may exceed those State aid levels of intensity. However, if the EU funds are combined with State aid then the aid intensities have to be respected as those funds are deemed to come under the control of the State.

According to the Commission's 2016 Notice on the Notion of Aid:

> The origin of the resources is not relevant provided that, before being directly or indirectly transferred to the beneficiaries, they come under public control and are therefore available to the national authorities, even if the resources do not become the property of the public authority.[1072]

Moreover, the Commission clarifies its view that:

> Resources coming from the Union (for example from structural funds), from the European Investment Bank or the European Investment Fund, or from international financial institutions, such as the International Monetary Fund or the European Bank for Reconstruction and Development, are considered as State resources if national authorities have discretion as to the use of these resources (in particular the selection of beneficiaries). By contrast, if such resources are awarded directly by the Union, by the European Investment Bank or by the European Investment Fund, with no discretion on the part of the national authorities, they do not constitute State resources (for example funding awarded in direct management under the Horizon 2020 framework programme, the EU programme for the Competitiveness of Enterprises and Small and Medium-sized Enterprises (COSME) or the Trans-European Transport Network (TEN-T) funds)...[and] A transfer of State resources is also present if the resources are at the joint disposal of several Member States who decide jointly on the use of those resources. This would be the case, for example, for funds from the European Stability Mechanism (ESM).[1073]

While the case law of the European Union clarifies many aspects concerning the attribution of resources to the State,[1074] there are no cases directly addressing the inclusion of structural funds in State aid calculations or the circumstances in which Member States exercise a sufficient degree of control to create a State aid situation and/or justify the counting of EU funds together with State resources. Accordingly, much of this may still be contestable in the future.

In the meantime, the Commission has taken several recent decisions in pursuit of its particular viewpoint. In its *Decision on the National broadband project in Greece*

1072. European Commission: *Notice on the notion of State aid pursuant to Article 107(1) TFEU*, OJ C 262 of 19 July 2016.
1073. *Ibid.*, paras 59 and 60.
1074. *See*, for example, Case C-345/02: *Pearle BV, Hans Prijs Optiek Franchise BV and Rinck Opticiëns BV v. Hoofdbedrijfschap Ambachten*, [2004] ECR I-07139, para. 35; Case C-303/88: *ENI-Lanerossi*, [1991] ECR I-1433; Case C-126/01: *Ministère de l'Économie, des Finances et de l'Industrie v. GEMO SA*. [2003] ECR I-13769; and Case C-482/99: *France v. Commission (Stardust Marine)*, [2002] ECR I-4397.

(2006), the Commission approved State aid of €210 million in Greece, which was intended to be partly financed by the Cohesion fund, to increase broadband penetration and coverage in regions of the country where citizens and businesses currently had difficulties in gaining access to the benefits of broadband technology. That Decision noted that: "The measure is partly financed with European structural funds, which qualify as State resources once they come under the control of Member States."[1075] In its *Decision on the Investment aid scheme for the reduction of VOC emissions in the Czech Republic (2008)* the Commission pointed out that:

> In the case at issue the resources from the Cohesion Fund will be made available to the competent national authorities and made available to the competent national authorities and constantly remain under their control. [...]. No direct transfer between the Community budget and the beneficiaries may take place. Therefore, in the case at issue, the resources from the Cohesion Fund qualify as State resources. For obvious reasons, this is also the case for the resources of national origin.
>
> The award of grants under the notified scheme will be imputable to the State. The activities of the Cohesion Fund [...] take the form of Operational Programmes, one of them being the Environmental Operational Programme. Operational programmes [...] set out general objectives and priorities, and consequently leave significant margin of discretion to the Member States for the use of the resources from the Structural Funds. In the case at issue, the Ministry of the Environment [...] will be responsible for the selection of the projects and the attribution of financial means to the beneficiaries. Therefore, the measures [...] will be imputable to the State.[1076]

In the light of the analysis here, it is clear that the European Commission has worked hard over the years to coordinate its development funding programmes under the EU Regional and Cohesion policies with the State aid rules and, in particular, with the Treaty bases for exemption of State aid for regional development. Following the most recent RAGs, the scope for regional State aid has been firmly coordinated spatially with structural fund programming via the spatial rules of the RAGs and the Regional aid mapping requirements. The structural fund regulations, in turn, have reinforced the imperative to separately ensure State aid compliance and approvals, where necessary. In addition, the Commission has taken a creative position on the cumulation of structural funds with national State aid funding although, as seen in the analysis, this has not been directly challenged.

6.4 BANKING REGULATION AND THE RESPONSE TO THE INTERNATIONAL FINANCIAL CRISIS

The EU system of State aid control came under considerable pressure on account of the widespread impact of the international financial crisis since late 2008. This required an

1075. European Commission: Decision No 201/2006: *National broadband project in Greece*, OJ C 296 of 6 December 2006.
1076. European Commission: Decision No SA.24320 – N 672/2007 of 5 June 2008 – *Investment aid scheme for the reduction of VOC emissions (Czech Republic)*, OJ C 218 of 27 August 2008.

unprecedented relaxation of many of the State aid rules to allow for bank rescues and recapitalisations and to ensure that State aid measures could, at least in some cases, substitute for business finance in the real economy where bank lending was not happening in the normal way. These arrangements are regarded as temporary (and some have already been removed) and as a particular exception to the normal application of State aid control by the European Commission on the basis of special exemptions to allow State aid "to remedy a serious disturbance in the economy of a Member State."[1077]

However, the interaction between the State aid rules and the banking sector dates back to an important first experience by the European Commission in dealing with a State aid case involving the rescue and restructuring of a major bank. Between 1995 and 1998, the Commission adopted its decisions approving State aid to rescue and restructure the ailing French bank Credit Lyonnais.[1078] This case was the first of its kind in the EU State aid system and arose from a combination of supervisory failure and market failure. Among the considerations in the Credit Lyonnais case were the urgency of the case, its high political profile in France and the need for flexibility beyond what was then allowable under the applicable Rescue and Restructuring State aid Guidelines.

In Credit Lyonnais, France argued that any rejection of its aid proposals would trigger a potential systemic crisis in the banking sector. However, this was rejected by the Commission and an overall compromise deal was made with the French. As the Commission noted one year later:

> there was no better example of the "too big to fail" problem than in the Credit Lyonnais case, where the argument that there was a severe risk of systemic crisis simply did not hold true. In 1992, we were on the brink of taking a negative decision. If the French had not signalled their acceptance of our minimum conditions at the very last hour, the decision would have been negative.[1079]

While Credit Lyonnais resulted in a later revision of the Rescue and Restructuring Guidelines to allow additional measures in the banking sector, it also prompted some serious reflection by the Commission and experts as to how rescue and restructuring cases in the sector might be better handled under the State aid rules – especially if there was indeed a potential for a systemic banking crisis.[1080] The regulatory dilemma and the general tone and vision of these reflections was aptly summarised by one of the contributors to that debate:

1077. TFEU, Article 107(3)(b). For a fuller discussion of this exemption, *see* Chapter 2.
1078. European Commission: Decision No 95/547/EC of 26 July 1995 giving conditional approval to the aid granted by France to the bank Crédit Lyonnais (Credit Lyonnais I), OJ L 308 of 21 December 1995 and Decision No 98/490/EC of 20 May 1998 concerning aid granted by France to the Crédit Lyonnais group (Credit Lyonnais II), OJ L 221 of 8 August 1998.
1079. A. Petersen: "*State aid problems in the Banking Sector*" in C.D. Ehlermann & M. Everson (eds): "*European Competition Law Annual 1999 – Selected issues in the field of State Aid,*" Oxford, 2001, p. 177.
1080. On this see the extensive discussion covered in C.D. Ehlermann & M. Everson (ed.): "*European Competition Law Annual 1999 – Selected Issues in the Field of State Aid,*" Oxford, 2001.

> it is worth recalling that the history of banking is marked by many episodes of crisis and panic. We might think that technological and financial advance has changed the banking industry: I nonetheless conclude that banks are still very fragile financial intermediaries... Crucially, regulatory and competition authorities must ascertain whether increased competition will intensify the fragility of individual banks or of the banking system as a whole. In the latter case, macroeconomic stability is at stake. In general, there is no clear-cut answer. However, a presumption can be established: stronger competition will encourage banks to undertake riskier activities and this may increase the probability of their failure.[1081]

These reflections prepared the Commission for speed and flexibility in the context of what was to emerge as a serious systemic crisis in 2008/2009: otherwise known as the international financial crisis.

The first signs of the financial crisis arriving in the EU were seen in early Autumn 2008. Some banks, e.g. Northern Rock, Sachsen LB, IKB, required State intervention to stabilise their business and State aid was approved under the applicable rescue and restructuring rules.[1082] However, as the Commission had known for many years, this approach was unlikely to be sustainable in the face of a real systemic crisis in the banking sector. Indeed, between September and October 2008, the UK, Germany, Belgium, France Luxembourg, the Netherlands and Ireland were all in crisis in regard to the survival of some or all of their main banks.

As the existing framework was considered too difficult to meet the challenges ahead, the Commission issued a number of Communications which provided detailed guidance on the criteria for the compatibility of Member States' support to banks and non-financial firms with the requirements of Article 107(3)(b) of the TFEU – allowing State aid in the context of the need to remedy a serious disturbance in the economy of a Member State. While this was seen initially as an almost complete abandonment of State aid control in the sector, its evolution displays an interesting logic and can be summarised as follows:

Development of State Aid Financial Crisis Measures

Phase 0 – in the period prior to October 2008 when all cases were dealt with under Article 107(3)(c) of the TFEU and the 2004 Rescue and Restructuring Guidelines;

Phase 1 – from October 2008 to February 2009 when the Commission applied Article 107(3)(b) of the TFEU to approve a large number of aid measures at unprecedented speed and subject to very limited conditions and introduced the first Temporary Framework to allow State aid to promote access to finance;

1081. M. Sarcinelli: "*State Aid Problems in the Banking Sector*" in C.D. Ehlermann & M. Everson (eds): "*European Competition Law Annual 1999 – Selected issues in the field of State Aid,*" Oxford, 2001, p. 178.

1082. European Commission: DG Competition Autumn 2008 *State aid Scoreboard*, Chapter 5, p. 51 (http://ec.europa.eu/competition/state_aid/studies_reports/archive/scoreboard_arch.html).

Phase 2 – from February to July 2009 when the Commission started to assess restructuring plans for ailing banks and applied requirements similar to those under the Rescue and Restructuring Guidelines, extending them into the field of Article 107(3)(b) of the TFEU;

Phase 3 – from July 2009 to July 2013 when the Commission applied its Financial Crisis restructuring Guidelines,[1083] thereby progressively increasing the restructuring obligations on aid assisted banks, including divestiture requirements;

Phase 4 – from August 2013 to date when policy has moved back towards the general application of Article 107(3)(c) of the TFEU and the Rescue and Restructuring Guidelines once again.[1084]

In its *Banking Communication of October 2008,*[1085] the Commission laid down the basic rules and conditions under which financial institutions in difficulty could receive State aid in the form of (i) guarantees to cover their liabilities and (ii) recapitalisation measures. The Framework also provided for measures in the event of a controlled winding-up of operations. The Commission put the focus on fundamentally sound and systemic banks, while at the same time trying to prevent free riders from receiving crisis aid. In respect of systemic banks there was a concern that the Member States would try to call even small banks systemic and try to rescue them with crisis aid as the notion of "systemic" was important to apply Article 107(3)(b) of the TFEU.[1086]

In response to further deterioration in credit lending conditions in late 2008 which threatened to affect the real economy, many EU Member States considered supporting financial institutions with capital injections to ensure that financial institutions continued lending to the real economy. In its *Recapitalisation Communication of December 2008,*[1087] the Commission provided detailed guidance on recapitalisation measures, building on the criteria already set out in the Banking Communication. The Communication aimed to ensure that such measures would be designed in a way to take the individual situation of the financial institution concerned fully into account.

At the same time, the Commission introduced the *Temporary Framework for State aid Measures to support access to finance in the current financial and economic crisis*

1083. European Commission: *Communication from the Commission – the return to viability and the assessment of restructuring measures,* OJ C 195 of 2009.
1084. This was intended to commence in early 2011 but was only achieved under the July 2013 Banking Communication.
1085. European Commission: *Communication on the application of State aid rules to measures taken in relation to financial institutions in the context of the current global financial crisis,* adopted on 13 October 2008, OJ C 270 of 25 October 2008.
1086. For more on the crisis aid *see* R.M. D'Sa, "*Instant State Aid Law in a Financial Crisis – A U-Turn?*" EstAL, 2/2009, pp. 145–159.
1087. European Commission: *Communication on the Recapitalisation of financial institutions in the current financial crisis,* adopted on 5 December 2008, OJ C 10 of 15 January 2009.

[1088] because of the need to counteract the increasing difficulty of the real economy to obtain credit and other types of financial support. Under the Temporary Framework, EU Member States were allowed to grant aid under existing instruments for all sectors of the economy through higher limits on grants, credit guarantees, loans and risk capital.

In recognition that major structural reforms of some individual banks would be an inevitable result of the crisis, the Commission concluded that cleaning up impaired assets was an additional measure that many banks would need to undertake, often in combination with restructuring measures, to ensure long-term viability. Accordingly, the Commission's *Impaired Assets Communication* of February 2009[1089] set out to provide guidance for State interventions in the context of efforts of financial institutions to clean their balance sheets of "toxic assets."

In 2009, the Commission adopted the *Restructuring Communication.*[1090] This Communication complemented the three previously issued communications on State aid to banks, outlining the criteria that the Commission would apply to restructuring aid for banks in the crisis period in order to ensure long-term viability of financial institutions in the EU. Where a financial institution had received State aid, the Member State should submit a viability plan, or a more fundamental restructuring plan, in order to confirm or re-establish the individual bank's long-term viability without reliance on State support. Criteria had already been established to delineate the conditions under which a bank might need to be subject to more substantial restructuring and when measures would therefore be needed to cater for distortions of competition resulting from the aid. The Communication required Member States to provide a restructuring plan where it had recapitalised a distressed bank or when a bank, in connection with the crisis, had received aid (except for participation in a guarantee scheme) exceeding 2% of the bank's total risk-weighted assets. For banks that were not distressed, i.e. fundamentally sound and had received a limited amount of aid, no restructuring plan would be required. However, Member States would have to submit a viability review enabling the Commission to assess viability of these banks and the Communication explained what type of information the Commission would expect to receive in these cases.

Among the detailed requirements of the *Restructuring Communication*, it was clarified that the costs associated with the restructuring must be borne not only by the State but also by capital holders. Nonetheless, thresholds concerning burden-sharing are not fixed in advance. Where significant burden-sharing was not immediately possible due to market circumstances at the time of the rescue, this should be addressed at a later stage. Measures to limit distortion of competition by a rescued bank

1088. European Commission: *Temporary framework for State aid measures to support access to finance in the current financial and economic crisis,* adopted on 17 December 2008; OJ C 16 of 22 January 2009 (Consolidated version OJ C 83 of 7 April 2009).
1089. European Commission: *Communication from the Commission on the treatment of impaired assets in the Community banking sector,* OJ C 72 of 26 March 2009.
1090. European Commission: Communication from the Commission "*The return to viability and the assessment of restructuring measures in the financial sector in the current crisis under the State aid rules,*" OJ C 195 of 19 August 2009.

in the same Member State or in other Member States should be designed in a way that limits any competitive disadvantage to other banks while taking into account the systemic nature of the current crisis. Moreover, a key principle of the EU rescue and restructuring rules on State aid – the "one time last time" rule – would not necessarily apply to banks assisted out of the crisis if such non-application could be justified. The Restructuring Communication applied until the end of 2010.[1091]

While the other instruments had no expiry date, it was necessary in early 2011 to review the position of the Restructuring Communication. This resulted in a new Communication which generally extended the Restructuring Communication.[1092] The 2011 Communication notes that the re-emergence of tensions in sovereign debt markets forcefully illustrated the continued volatility in financial markets. Second, the high level of inter-connectedness and interdependence within the financial sector in the EU justified market concerns about contagion. Third, the high volatility of financial markets and the uncertainty about the economic outlook justified maintaining, as a safety net, the possibility for Member States to argue the need to have recourse to crisis-related support measures on the basis of Article 107(3)(b) of the TFEU.[1093]

For these reasons, the Commission argued that the Banking, Recapitalisation and Impaired Assets Communications (setting out guidance on the compatibility criteria for crisis-related aid to banks on the basis of Article 107(3)(b) of the Treaty – most notably in the form of government guarantees, recapitalisations and asset relief measures) needed to stay in place beyond 31 December 2010. Moreover, the Restructuring Communication, which addressed the follow-up to such support measures, also needed to remain applicable until end-2011.[1094] The Communication also anticipated a return to normal non-crisis approaches from 2012.[1095]

But this was not to be. In 2012, the Commission adopted a further Communication[1096] which kept in place the four Communications that set the conditions for the compatibility with the Treaty rules on State aid of support in the form of funding guarantees, recapitalisation and asset relief, as well as the requirements for a restructuring or viability plan (the Restructuring Communication).[1097]

1091. For a critical review of these financial sector State aid measures, *see* C. Ahlborn & D. Piccinin, "*The Application of the Principles of Restructuring Aid to Banks during the Financial Crisis*" (2010), 1 European State Aid Law Quarterly, p. 47 and C. Ahlborn & D. Piccinin: "*The Great Recession and Other Mishaps: The Commission's Policy of Restructuring Aid in a Time of Crisis*" in E. Szyszczak (ed.): "*Research Handbook on European State Aid Law Edward Elgar Publishing,*" 2011, pp. 124 et seq.
1092. European Commission: *Communication from the Commission on the application, from 1 January 2011, of State aid rules to support measures in favour of banks in the context of the financial crisis*, OJ C 329 of 7 December 2010.
1093. *Ibid.*, para. 6.
1094. *Ibid.*, para. 7.
1095. *Ibid.*, para. 8.
1096. European Commission: *Communication from the Commission on the application, from 1 January 2012, of State aid rules to support measures in favour of banks in the context of the financial crisis*, OJ C 356 of 6 December 2011.
1097. For a critical review of these financial sector State aid measures, *see* C. Ahlborn & D. Piccinin, "*The Application of the Principles of Restructuring Aid to Banks during the Financial Crisis*" (2010), 1 European State Aid Law Quarterly, p. 47 and C. Ahlborn & D. Piccinin: "*The Great*

In July 2013, the Commission replaced the 2008 Banking Communication and supplemented the remaining crisis rules.[1098] The main changes are aimed at improving the restructuring process and restoring competition between banks. In particular, banks are now required to work out a sound plan for their restructuring or orderly winding-up before they can receive recapitalisations or asset protection measures. Moreover, in the case of capital shortfalls, bank owners and other creditors will be required to contribute as a first resort, before banks can receive public funding.

In particular, the current Communication insists that a bank needs to work out a restructuring plan, including a capital raising plan, convincingly demonstrating how it will become profitable in the long term before it can receive recapitalisation measures. If the viability of the bank cannot be restored, an orderly winding-up plan needs to be submitted instead. Second, the new rules also envisage the possibility for Member States and the Commission, in cooperation with the competent banking supervisory authority, to explore ways of filling capital shortfalls with contributions from the bank itself, from private investors or the bank's owners. At the same time, if a public recapitalisation is urgently necessary to avert risks to financial stability, this can still be approved temporarily before the full restructuring plan is ready; provided that the competent banking supervisory authority confirms that an immediate intervention is necessary. Third, the new rules provide that failed banks should apply strict executive remuneration policies and set a cap on total remuneration as long as the entity is under restructuring or relying on State support. The idea here is to give management the proper incentives to implement the restructuring plan and repay the aid.

State Aid to Banks under the Crisis Rules in Context

The importance of these crisis measures in the EU State aid regulatory system can be understood with reference to the scale of crisis supports in the period. Between 1 October 2008 and 1 October 2014, the Commission took more than 450 decisions authorising State aid measures to the financial sector. The bulk of this aid represented guarantees on liabilities. In fact, a total aid of €3,893 billion (29.8% of EU GDP in 2013) was approved for guarantees on liabilities in order to help re-establish confidence on the financial markets. Of this, financial institutions have actually used less than a quarter of the amount approved. The outstanding amount peaked in 2009 at €836 billion (6.4% of EU 2013 GDP), and has decreased since. In 2013, outstanding guarantees amounted to €352 billion (2.7% of EU 2013 GDP). Thus, it is clear that EU Member States have not actually used (implemented) all the aid approved. Moreover, since 2008, only €3.13 billion of the total guarantees provided have been called.

Recession and Other Mishaps: The Commission's Policy of Restructuring Aid in a Time of Crisis" in E. Szyszczak (ed.): "*Research Handbook on European State Aid Law Edward Elgar Publishing,*" 2011, pp. 124 et seq.

1098. European Commission: *Communication from the Commission on the application, from 1 August 2013, of State aid rules to support measures in favour of banks in the context of the financial crisis* ("*Banking Communication*"), OJ C 216 of 30 July 2013.

Recapitalisation was the second most used crisis instrument to support the financial sector and the Commission has authorised an overall aid amount of €821 billion (6.3% of EU 2013 GDP) in the last six years. From 2008 to 2013, EU Member States have actually granted an overall amount of €448 billion (3.4% of EU 2013 GDP) in recapitalisation measures. In that regard, the four countries which supported their banks the most in the 2008–2013 period were the UK (€100 billion), Germany (€64 billion), Ireland (€63 billion), and Spain (€62 billion). The top receiving banks were the Royal Bank of Scotland (€50 billion), Anglo Irish Bank (€32 billion), and Bankia (€22 billion). It is also relevant to point out that some financial institutions that were recapitalised at the outset of the crisis have already started repaying the assistance received.

Some Member States have also provided direct short-term liquidity support to banks and other troubled financial institutions. Since 2008, the Commission approved aid amounting to €380 billion (2.9% of EU 2013 GDP) for liquidity measures. However, EU Member States have actually used only a very small amount in comparison to the total approved. Thus, the outstanding liquidity measures peaked in 2009 at €70 billion (0.5% of EU 2013 GDP) with Spain and the Netherlands providing more than 50% of the aid, and, by 2012, the outstanding amount had decreased to €34.5 billion (0.26% of EU 2013 GDP).

In respect of asset relief measures, in the period 2008–2013, EU Member States provided asset relief measures reaching €188 billion (1.4% of EU 2013 GDP) in aid of this type while approved measures amounted to €669 billion in total (5.1% of EU 2013 GDP).

Latest data for 2016 show that 40 further State aid banking decisions were taken in by the Commission in 2016. These involved Austria, Croatia, Cyprus, Estonia, France, Germany, Greece, Hungary, Ireland, Italy, Malta, Poland, Portugal and the United Kingdom. Many of these cases focused on prolongations of earlier approvals, especially concerning guarantee schemes.

Since the adoption of the *Temporary Framework* in December 2008, EU Member States have also made considerable use of the new facilities offered to support access to finance in the current financial and economic crisis. By the end of 2009, the Commission had authorised 61 schemes under the Temporary Framework (involving all EU Member States except Bulgaria and Cyprus):

- 21 schemes for aid up to €500,000 per company proposed by Czech Republic, Germany, Estonia, Ireland, Greece, Spain, France, Italy, Latvia, Lithuania, Luxembourg, Hungary, Malta, Netherland, Austria, Poland, Portugal, Slovenia, Slovak, Finland and the United Kingdom;
- 16 guarantee measures in Belgium, Czech Republic, Germany, Greece, France, Italy, Latvia, Luxembourg, Hungary, Romania, Slovenia, Finland, Sweden and the United Kingdom;
- 7 schemes for subsidised loans in Germany, Greece, France, Italy, Hungary and France;

- 5 schemes offering reduced interest loans to businesses investing in the production of green products in Germany, Spain, France, Italy and the United Kingdom;
- 5 risk-capital schemes in Germany, France, Italy and Austria;
- 7 export-credit schemes in Belgium, Denmark, Germany, France, Luxembourg, Netherlands and Finland.[1099]

Germany emerged as the Member State with the highest number of approved measures under the Temporary Framework. By the end of September 2009, Germany had adopted 7 schemes involving all the instruments (two different schemes were put in place for reduced-interest rate loans as well as two amendments to the scheme for aid of up to €500,000 per company). The Commission has also authorised several measures for France, Italy and the United Kingdom. At the same time, Belgium, Denmark, Estonia, Ireland, Lithuania, Malta, Netherland, Poland, Portugal, Romania, Slovakia and Sweden only put in place one of the different possibilities offered in the Temporary Framework and, of these, most related to schemes for aid of up to €500,000 per company – the de facto temporary expansion of *de minimis* State aid under the crisis rules.

By end-2013, of a further €83 billion approved aid under the Temporary Framework between 2009 and 2011, approximately €36 billion had been used by 10 Member States, with Germany accounting for €17 billion and France the second largest user spending almost €5 billion.[1100]

The Temporary Framework expired in December 2011.

At the wider level of EU policy, in June 2012, Heads of State and Government agreed to create a Banking Union, completing the economic and monetary union, and allowing for the centralised application of EU-wide rules for banks in the euro area (and any non-euro Member States that would want to join). The new regulatory framework with common rules for banks in all 28 Member States, set out in a single rulebook, is the foundation of the banking union. Common rules are intended to help to prevent bank crises in the future (especially via the Capital Requirements Directive[1101] and Regulation)[1102] and, if banks do end up in difficulty, set out a common framework to manage the process, including a means to wind them down in an orderly way (via the Directive on Bank Recovery and Resolution (BRRD)).[1103] Common rules are also designed to safeguard deposits up to €100,000 (per depositor/per bank) at all times and

1099. European Commission: Autumn 2009 State aid Scoreboard, *supra*, p. 48.
1100. European Commission: State Aid Scoreboard 2014.
1101. Directive No 2013/36/EU of the European Parliament and of the Council of 26 June 2013 on access to the activity of credit institutions and the prudential supervision of credit institutions and investment firms, amending Directive 2002/87/EC and repealing Directives 2006/48/EC and 2006/49/EC, OJ L 176 of 27 June 2013.
1102. Regulation No 575/2013/EU of the European Parliament and of the Council of 26 June 2013 on prudential requirements for credit institutions and investment firms and amending Regulation (EU) No 648/2012, OJ L 176 of 27 June 2013.
1103. Directive No 2014/59/EU of the European Parliament and of the Council of 15 May 2014 establishing a framework for the recovery and resolution of credit institutions and investment firms and amending Council Directive 82/891/EEC, and Directives 2001/24/EC, 2002/47/EC,

everywhere in the EU (via the Directive on Deposit Guarantee Schemes).[1104] In addition, the Commission has issued a proposal for a European Deposit Insurance Scheme (EDIS) to provide a stronger and more uniform degree of insurance cover for all retail depositors in the banking union.

In its recent Annual Report on Competition Policy, the Commission points out that:

> Businesses and households need sound financial intermediaries – typically banks – to underpin investment and consumption decisions. The crisis showed that when banks in Europe have problems, the effects can reach far beyond the immediate threat to depositors and shareholders. It can severely affect a country's financial stability, and almost inevitably has spillover effects on other Member States and even beyond the EU. In this context, State aid control remained an essential tool to ensure a safer and sounder banking sector in the EU.
> State aid rules are an integral part of the Banking Union, guaranteeing equal treatment between the Member States that are in the Banking Union and those that are not. The role of State aid control is to ensure that the choices made by the national government do not unduly burden the public purse or distort the level playing field in the EU.[1105]

The speed and adaptability of the EU State aid system in the face of the international financial crisis is generally seen as a success story.[1106] As seen in the analysis here, the role of State aid regulation in a possible systemic banking crisis was considered a decade earlier and undoubtedly facilitated the Commission's speed of action. Nonetheless, the banking crisis brought systemic weaknesses in the State aid rescue and restructuring rules to the fore and required an entirely new rulebook for a sector which was too big to fail. The reliance on the application of Article 107(3)(b) of the TFEU and the abandonment of the core principle in rescue and restructuring aid of "one-time; last-time" were creative policy moves that facilitated a huge State aid response across most EU Member States. Thus, the exceptional circumstances resulting from the global financial crisis have led the Commission to consider the failure of almost any bank to be sufficient to disturb the entire economy of a Member State and thus to justify the application of Article 107(3)(b) of the TFEU.[1107]

2004/25/EC, 2005/56/EC, 2007/36/EC, 2011/35/EU, 2012/30/EU and 2013/36/EU, and Regulations No 1093/2010/EU and No 648/2012/EU, of the European Parliament and of the Council, OJ L 173 of 12 June 2014.

1104. Directive No 2014/49/EU of the European Parliament and of the Council of 16 April 2014 on deposit guarantee schemes, OJ L 173 of 12 June 2014.

1105. European Commission: *Report on Competition Policy 2016*, COM (2017) 285 final of 31 May 2017.

1106. *See* F.C. Laprévote & M. Paron, "*The Commission's Decisional Practice on State Aid to Banks: An Update*" EstAL, 1/2015, pp. 88–116.

1107. *See*, for example, European Commission: Decision No C 37/2010 of 22 February 2012: *FHB Jelzálogbank Nyrt*, OJ L 152 of 22 May 2014.2012, para. 71, in which the Commission merely considered that "given the specific circumstances on the financial markets [...] the measures can be examined under Article 107(3)(b)" and European Commission: Decision No SA.35709 of 18 December 2013: *NKBM*, OJ C 162 of 7 June 2013.

At the same time, the role of the State aid system in the response to the financial and banking crisis provided a pivotal impetus for Banking Union, especially in regard to the Eurozone where contagion risks were at their highest.

6.5 EU TAXATION POLICY AND THE PURSUIT OF STATE AID TAX MEASURES

EU Member States are free to decide on the economic policy which they consider most appropriate and, in particular, to design tax systems and spread the tax burden as they see fit across the various factors of production. Nonetheless, EU Member States must exercise this competence in line with EU law.[1108]

Under EU Law, with the exception of value added taxation, certain aspects of excise taxes and some minor direct taxation directives, taxation generally falls within the competence of EU Member States who are left to devise systems of taxation that best suit the needs of their economies.

Thus, EU Member States can determine the scope and application of corporation, income, consumption, property, wealth, inheritance and other taxes on the basis of their own political and economic realities, including wealth distribution policy, ability to pay factors, environmental protection considerations. The need for unanimity on tax issues, especially direct taxation, is preserved by TFEU Article 223(2):

> All rules or conditions relating to the taxation of Members or former Members shall require unanimity within the Council.

As a result, approximation progress in regard to EU direct tax legislation has been limited. Following the removal of a German veto linked to the effective establishment of the principle of the free movement of capital in the EU, three measures on direct taxation (which required the unanimous agreement of all EU Member States) were adopted in 1990 – two Directives[1109] and a Convention.[1110] Two further Directives were adopted in 2003.[1111] To avoid the introduction of new EU tax legislation (which, as noted, requires political unanimity), the Commission also proposed a tax policy based on voluntary harmonisation of Member States' tax systems to recommended standards. Its 2003 strategy on liberating the internal market from company tax

1108. European Commission: *Communication from the Commission – Commission Notice on the Notion of State aid pursuant to Article 107(1) of the TFEU*, May 2016, p. 40.

1109. Council Directive No 90/434/EEC of 23 July 1990 on the common system of taxation applicable to mergers, divisions, transfers of assets and exchanges of shares concerning companies of different Member States, O J L 225 of 20 August 1990 and Council Directive No 90/435/EEC of 23 July 1990 on the common system of taxation applicable to parent companies and their subsidiaries in different Member States, O J L 225 of 20 August 1990. These Directives were based on European Commission proposals from 1969.

1110. Convention No 90/436/EEC on the elimination of double taxation in connection with the adjustment of transfers of profits between associated undertakings ("*Arbitration Convention*"), O J L 225 of 20 August 1990..

1111. Council Directive No 2003/48/EC of 3 June 2003 on the taxation of savings income in the form of interest payments and Council Directive No 2003/49/EC of 3 June 2003 on a common system of taxation applicable to interest and royalty payments made between associated companies of different Member States, O J L 157 of 26 June 2003.

obstacles[1112] set out a series of recommendations to Member States to amend their respective tax systems. The schemes recommended for transposition into national law ranged from Home State Taxation rules for newly created small and medium enterprises to the development of a Common EU Tax Base for EU multinationals based on International Accounting Standards principles; they include an EU tax regime for the "Societas Europae."[1113]

While the EU has for a long time aspired to a common tax system in respect of business taxes, certain Member States strongly resist this as an encroachment into their national sovereignty. One effect of differences in tax systems is that major industries sometimes decide to relocate to lower tax countries creating jobs in the second country and losing jobs in the first country. The EU debate on direct tax harmonisation commenced in the early 1960s and the 1962 *Neumark Report* first proposed a single corporation tax rate to apply across the EU.[1114] Subsequently, the *Tempel Report* of 1970,[1115] based on the examples of some Member States, took a different direction, recommending the introduction of a classical dividend taxation system. Both reports in effect reopened the question of the founding treaties as to whether the harmonisation of direct taxation was necessary for the creation of the single EU market. The consensus in both reports was, *inter alia*, that the unharmonised tax treatment of cross-border dividend payments was a major problem within an internal market.

In 1975, the European Commission proposed a directive on the harmonisation of corporate and capital income taxes with a tax rate between 45% and 55% on retained earnings. This was rejected by the European Parliament in 1980 and withdrawn by the Commission in 1990. In 1969, the proposals for the Merger Directive and the Parent subsidiary Directive were launched by the Commission. These were adopted with modifications in 1990. In the late 1980s, further proposals for a directive on cross-border losses and a uniform tax base for enterprises were presented and subsequently withdrawn for lack of political consensus.

On 18 March 1992, the *Ruding Report*[1116] was published by the European Commission. The Ruding Report found that the average cost of capital in every Member

1112. Communication from the Commission to the Council and the European Parliament "*Some Key Issues in Europe's Competitiveness – Towards an Integrated Approach*," Brussels, 21 November 2003, COM (2003) 704 final.

1113. *See* P. Rossi-Maccanico, "'*State Aid Review of Member States' Measures Relating to Direct Business Taxation*" EstAL, 2/2004, pp. 229–251.

1114. Neumark Report: "*Rapport du Comite Fiscal et Financier*," 1962. Available at: http://bookshop.europa.eu/eubookshop/FileCache/PUBPDF/CB6208070FRC/CB6208070FRC_002.pdf. The rate proposed was based on a split rate system involving 50% on retained earnings and 15%–25% on distributed profits without giving credits to shareholders against their personal income tax liability.

1115. Tempel Report: "*Impôt sur les sociétés et impôt sur le revenu dans les Communautés Européennes*," Tempel, A.J. van den, Luxembourg, CE 1970.

1116. European Commission: "*Report of the Committee of Independent Experts on Company Taxation*" (1992). This Report was prepared for the European Commission by the "Ruding Committee," a committee of independent experts on company taxation, chaired by the former Dutch Minister for Finance, Dr Otto Ruding. The Committee were asked to evaluate the importance of taxation for business decisions with respect to the location of investment and the international allocation of profits between enterprises, in order to determine whether

State was lowest for purely domestic investments, that tax differences can affect the location of investment and cause distortion of competition and that the main distortions could not be reduced solely through market forces or through the independent actions of Member States. The Report made a large number of recommendations (focussed on the elimination of double taxation and on corporation tax systems) which included proposals for:

- a general regulation on deductions based on losses of subsidiaries in other countries;
- the harmonisation of Double Tax Agreements;
- the harmonisation of Member State corporation tax systems;
- minimum rates for corporation tax; and
- common standards for loss deductions in corporation tax assessment.

Following the Report, the Commission tabled a proposal for a Directive to eliminate withholding taxes on cross-border payments of interest and royalties between companies, a proposal for a Directive on cross-border loss compensation and proposals to extend the scope of the parent subsidiary and merger Directives, but all these proposals were blocked in the Council – at least until the 2003 (*see* Directives 2003/48/EC and 2003/49/EC above).

Perhaps the most controversial proposal from Ruding was the suggestion that common rates of corporation taxation should be set at around 30%. This was the high end of average Member State rates at the time and it deeply angered several Member States which had low rates or were seeking to progressively reduce rates in the interests of foreign investment and to improve the general risk/reward ratio in the national business environment. On the other hand, some of the larger Member States and others with strongly developed (and hence continuously fixed and expensive) social welfare regimes supported upward harmonisation as proposed by Ruding – if only because downward movements in rates were seen as virtually impossible.

Between 1990 and 1997, the further development of EU direct taxation initiatives was stalled for political reasons linked to vetoes, sovereignty issues and the principle of subsidiarity. With the veto positions very clear after Ruding, the following years saw a shift in the rhetoric and the approach in the debate between these countries centred on the argument that, in the absence of harmonisation, there was a problem of tax competition in the EU that was damaging the EU market and that should be addressed at EU level. This was a controversial change of direction by the European Commission which had been previously agnostic as to tax competition *per se*.[1117] However, to regain momentum on direct taxation harmonisation, and to pursue a Commission viewpoint on the apparent damage to national employment policies, national tax regimes and the

existing differences in corporate taxation and the burden of business taxes among Member States led to major distortions affecting the functioning of the Internal Market.

1117. *See*, in particular, C.M. Radaelli: "*Policy Narratives in the European Union – the Case of Harmful Tax Competition*," European University Institute, Working Paper RSC No 98/34 accessible at https://www.eui.eu/DepartmentsAndCentres/RobertSchumanCentre/Publications/WorkingPapers/9834t.

smooth functioning of the EU single market of a range of allegedly harmful direct tax measures, it was necessary to reach agreement that many tax measures were unfair on, or harmful to, other countries to the degree that they could:

- Be penalised in terms of significant erosion of the tax base.
- See capital income taxes spiral down to zero and corporations move profits to special tax regimes, leaving governments with the sole option of asking for more revenue from low skilled labour.
- Over time damage redistributive policies and bring the whole mechanism of the welfare state to a halt.

Moreover, without raising political efforts in regard to tax coordination to a maximum, the argument was that the ambitions for EU coordinated action in the fight against unemployment would be impossible. This new approach, launched by the Commission in a reflection paper for the Verona EU Summit in April 1996,[1118] replaced the failed approach (which had limited political backing) that direct tax harmonisation was needed to facilitate international companies operating in the EU Single Market and the European Commission positioned itself at the centre of the then required coordinated response.

In October 1997, the Commission launched its "direct tax package"[1119] which included the proposal for the Savings Directive and the Interest and Royalties Directive, the Code of Conduct for Business Taxation and a Commission Notice on the interpretation and application of the EC Treaty State Aid Rules to Business Taxation.[1120]

An amended version of the Code of Conduct was adopted by the Council in the form of a resolution on 1 December 1997.[1121] As a resolution it was not legally binding, but a political declaration. Under the Code of Conduct, harmful tax measures are "*measures (including administrative practices) which affect or may affect in a significant way the location of business activity in the Community*" and which provide for a significantly lower effective level of taxation than the general level of taxation in the Member State concerned. The criteria for identifying potentially harmful measures include:

- an effective level of taxation which is significantly lower than the general level of taxation in the country concerned;
- tax benefits reserved for non-residents;
- tax incentives for activities which are isolated from the domestic economy and therefore have no impact on the national tax base;
- granting of tax advantages even in the absence of any real economic activity;

1118. European Commission: "*Taxation in the European Union*," SEC(96) 487 final of 20 March 1996.
1119. European Commission: "*Towards tax co-ordination in the European Union*," COM (1997) 495.
1120. European Commission: "*Notice on the application of the State Aid rules to measures relating to direct business taxation*," OJ C 384 of 10 December 1998.
1121. Conclusions of the ECOFIN Council Meeting on 1 December 1997 concerning taxation policy ("*Code of Conduct on Business Taxation*"), OJ C 98 of 6 January 1998.

- a basis of profit determination for companies in a multinational group which departs from internationally accepted rules, in particular those approved by the OECD;
- lack of transparency;

Under the Code of Conduct, the Member States undertook to:

- refrain from introducing any new harmful tax measures;
- re-examine their existing laws and established practices and amend them as necessary with a view to eliminating any harmful measures as soon as possible, taking into account the Council's discussions following the review process;
- inform each other of tax measures which may fall within the scope of the code and oversee the provision of information on those measures;
- promote the adoption of principles aimed at abolishing harmful tax measures in third countries and in territories to which the Treaty does not apply. In particular, Member States with dependent and associated territories or which had special responsibilities or taxation prerogatives in respect of other territories undertook, within the framework of their constitutional arrangements, to ensure that these principles were applied in those territories.

The Code of Conduct left it to a high-level political group (the Primarolo Group), supported by the Commission, to examine nearly 300 potentially harmful tax measures and eventually 66 of these were listed as harmful.[1122] However, this Group's Report and its 66 apparently harmful tax measures were not agreed by all EU Member States.[1123] At this point, the importance of the cross-linkage to the State aid rules in the Code of Conduct became clear and, with the transfer of Commissioner Monti to become the new Competition Commissioner, the State aid rules were used to subsequently and progressively attack the majority of the 66 allegedly harmful tax measures. This fulfilled the hard law dimension of the otherwise non-binding Code:

> Without prejudice to Community Law and the objectives of the Treaty, the Council notes that the Commission... commits itself to the strict application of the aid concerned, taking into account, inter alia, the negative effects of aid that are brought to light in the application of this code. The Council also notes that the Commission intends to examine or re-examine existing tax arrangements and

1122. Council of the European Union: *"Report from the Code of Conduct Group to the ECOFIN Council of 29 November 1999 on the Code of Conduct for Business Taxation" (Primarolo Report)*, SN 4901/99 of 23 November 1999.

1123. The Conclusions of the ECOFIN Council Meeting on 9 March 1998 point out that the Report can reflect either the unanimous opinion of the members of the group or the various opinions, not necessarily unanimous, expressed in the course of the group's discussions. *See also* C.M. Radaelli: "*The Code of Conduct Against Harmful Tax Competition – Open Method of Coordination in Disguise*," European University Institute, EUI Working Papers, 2002, RSC No 2002/43.

> proposed new legislation by Member States case by case, thus ensuring that the rules and objectives of the Treaty are applied consistently and equally to all.[1124]

The first major action against the Irish Corporation Tax regime was finalised in 1996 but only published after the Code of Conduct[1125] and was, in many ways, a test case for potential future action using the State aid rules. By early 2003, however, the Commission had taken negative decisions on German, Spanish (Biscaye Province), Luxembourgois and Belgian coordination centres, Societes de financement schemes, Finnish captive insurance schemes for the Aland Islands, the French Centrales de tresorerie scheme, the Greek Foreign companies offices scheme, the Italian Trieste financial and insurance services scheme, the Swedish Foreign Insurance companies scheme, the international financing activities scheme in the Netherlands and the Irish Foreign Income tax scheme.[1126] These cases were followed by a range of further high profile tax cases – notably concerning the Azores and Gibraltar tax systems and the Luxembourgois preferential tax regime for financial holdings which had existed since 1929. Moreover, the preferential tax arrangements for France Telecom in the French tax code and Italian tax benefits for newly listed companies were declared illegal State aids in 2004 and 2005 respectively, recovery orders were issued and legal proceedings were taken to the European Court of Justice in 2006 for failure to recover illegal aid in regard to both of these cases.

The European Court of Justice largely supported this line of Commission action against allegedly harmful tax measures via the State aid rules by focussing on the free movement principles and by accepting very flexible interpretations of the selectivity of such measures. Accordingly, certain commentators not only see the application of the State aid rules by the Commission as the new force in achieving progress regarding harmonisation in direct taxation (without political unanimity) but point to the Court of Justice itself as the author of gradual tax harmonisation without political consent.[1127]

It was not always clear that a tax benefit was a State aid in terms of the TFEU. This was resolved by the European Court of Justice Case of *Sloman Neptun*[1128] which held that a benefit from public expenditure or from a tax saving were both equally State aid

1124. Code of Conduct for Business Taxation, *supra,* Article J.
1125. European Commission: Decision No 98/C 395/08 of 22 July 1998: *International Financial Services Centre (IFSC) and Shannon Customs Free Airport Zone (SCAZ) – Irish Corporation Tax (ICT)*, OJ C 395 of 18 December 1998.
1126. European Commission Press Release "*Final negative State aid decisions on special tax schemes in Belgium, the Netherlands and Ireland*" IP/703/242 of 18 February 2003.
1127. *See* for example: J. Keuchel & A. Schrinner: "*Gradual Harmonisation of Tax Law by the European Court of Justice,*" Linklaters, Oppenhoff and Radler in "Legal500.com," June 2001.
1128. Joined Cases C-72/91 and C-73/91, *Sloman Neptun Schiffahrts AG and Seebetriebsrat Bodo Ziesemer der Sloman Neptun Schiffahrts AG,* [1993] I ECR 887. As early as 1974, the European Court of Justice had established that tax measures which are open to all economic agents operating within a Member State are, in principle, general measures and not State aid. In turn, the Court ruled that any decision that departed from the general tax rules to the benefit of individual undertakings lead, in principle, to a presumption of State aid (Case C-173/73: *Italy v. Commission,* [1974] ECR 709).

in certain circumstances. Moreover, in the WTO Subsidies Agreement, the definition of "subsidy,"[1129] for which the EU claims primary credit,[1130] puts the matter beyond doubt also in the WTO context.

The application of the State aid rules to taxation presents particular difficulties since schemes of taxation tend to be expressed generally while producing effects unequally on taxpayers according to their circumstances.[1131] Across EU Member States, 44% of all State aid was given by means of tax measures in 2011.[1132] More recently, in 2015, tax measures still accounted for 30% of total State aid.[1133] As a result, there is detailed EU experience in regard to such measures, including quite imaginative Member State practice in the creation and implementation of tax aids. Indeed, the very first State aid case to reach the European Courts was a tax aid case under the original European Coal and Steel Community[1134] and the most recent Commission Decisions have a targeted focus on tax measures.

One of the main issues with tax measures, however, is whether and to what extent they may be regarded as general measures (thus not involving State aid) or as creating sufficient selective advantages to amount to State aid. Thus, it is important to differentiate "selective" tax incentives from general rules which are either not "aids" at all or which apply not only to "certain" undertakings or goods but to the whole economy. These "general measures" cannot be challenged in the context of Article 107(1) of the TFEU.[1135] If they lead to major distortions of the competitive situation within the European Union, the Commission and the Council are in a position to act under Articles 116 and 117 of the TFEU.[1136]

This issue became particularly unclear as a result of a European Court ruling in 1974 which established that a tax measure did create a selective advantage and would constitute State aid if there was a departure from the somewhat nebulous concept of the "nature or general scheme of the system."[1137]

In a major effort to clarify the distinction between general measures and State aids in these areas and in parallel with the Code of Conduct on Unfair Tax Measures, the Commission issued a *Notice on the application of the State Aid rules to measures relating to direct business taxation* in 1998.[1138] This Notice, now superseded by the May

1129. Article 1 of the WTO Subsidies and Countervailing Measures Agreement of 1994 defines a subsidy, *inter alia,* to include circumstances where "government revenue that is otherwise due is foregone or not collected (e.g., fiscal incentives such as tax credits)."
1130. C.D. Ehlermann, *"State Aid Control – Success or Failure?"* (18 January 1995), Fordham International Law Journal, 1995.
1131. R. Plender: "Definition of Aid" in *The Law of State Aid in the European Union,* Published online March 2012 | e-ISBN: 9780191699030 | DOI: http://dx.doi.org/10.1093/acprof:oso/9780199265329.003.0001.
1132. European Commission: DG Competition State Aid "Scoreboard," 2012.
1133. European Commission: DG Competition State Aid "Scoreboard," 2016 accessed at: http://ec.europa.eu/competition/state_aid/scoreboard/index_en.html.
1134. Case C-30/59: *Gezamenlijke Steenkolenmijnen,* [1961] ECR 5.
1135. C. Quigley: "General Taxation" in *The Law of State Aid in the European Union,* Oxford, 2003, pp. 207–217.
1136. Case C-88/03: *Portugal v. Commission,* [2006] ECR I-7115, paras 46, 58.
1137. Case C-173/73: *Italy v. Commission,* [1974] ECR 709.
1138. European Commission: *Notice on the application of the State aid rules to measures relating to direct business taxation,* OJ C 384 of 10 December 1998.

2016 *Notice on the Notion of Aid,*[1139] was based on the policy position (and interpretation of Article 107 of the TFEU) that any measure that relieved a firm of charges that were normally met from its budget created an advantage e.g. special tax reductions, accelerated depreciation allowances, deferrals of tax payments. Moreover, the loss of State revenue arising from such measures was regarded as equivalent to State expenditure and, as such, created advantages.

The Notice made clear that, to constitute State aid, those advantages must be selective (i.e., specific) and that this would generally arise where the measure created an exception to general tax or social security legislation, regulations or administrative provisions or where there was a discretionary decision by a government authority on what was to be paid. Accordingly, the Notice declared that this was not the case where there is an economic rationale involved which made the exception necessary for the functioning and effectiveness of the tax system.[1140] On this basis, the Notice indicated that the following *did not* constitute State aid:

- *tax measures of a purely technical nature (e.g., setting the rate of taxation, depreciation rules and rules on loss carry-overs; provisions to prevent double taxation or tax avoidance);*
- *measures pursuing general economic policy objectives through a reduction of the tax burden related to certain production costs (research and development (R&D), the environment, training, employment);*[1141]
- *the progressive nature of an income tax scale or profit tax scale which can be justified by the redistributive purpose of the tax;*
- *measures for the calculation of asset depreciation and stock valuation and arrangements for the collection of fiscal debts (which vary from one Member State to another) and which can be regarded as inherent in the tax systems to which they belong;*
- *measures creating some advantages which can be justified by objective differences between taxpayers e.g. special rates of tax for small businesses and different approaches to the taxation of farmers and fishermen;*
- *exemption of non- profit undertakings from tax laws.*

1139. European Commission*: Notice on the notion of State aid pursuant to Article 107(1) TFEU,* OJ C 262 of 19 July 2016.

1140. According to the Notice, the common system applicable should first be determined. It must then be examined whether the exception to the system (or differentiations within that system) is justified "by the nature or general scheme" of the tax system: "that is to say, whether they derive directly from the basic or guiding principles of the tax system in the Member State concerned. If this is not the case, then State aid is involved."

1141. The Notice pointed out that the fact that some firms or some sectors benefit more than others from some of these tax measures does not necessarily mean that they are caught by the State aid rules. Thus, measures designed to reduce the taxation of labour for all firms have a relatively greater effect on labour-intensive industries than on capital-intensive industries, without necessarily constituting State aid. Similarly, tax incentives for environmental, R&D or training investment favour only the firms which undertake such investment, but again do not necessarily constitute State aid.

On the other hand, the Notice indicated that the following *would normally* constitute State aid:

- *measures which are regional or local in scope and, therefore, may favour certain undertakings as a departure from the general system;*[1142]
- *tax measures where the main effect is to promote one or more sectors of activity, including measures that favour only national products which are exported, which target all of the sectors that are subject to international competition or which create a derogation from the base rate of corporation tax for an entire section of the economy (e.g., manufacturing versus the services sector);*[1143]
- *preferential tax rules for public versus private enterprises;*
- *measures which create undue discretion in the hands of the administering authority to decide the levels of actual payments;*
- *measures allowing non-resident companies to be treated more favourably than resident ones or if tax benefits are granted to head offices or to firms providing certain services (e.g., financial services) within a group.*[1144]

Moreover, according to the 1998 Notice, any decision of the administration that departed from the general tax rules to the benefit of individual undertakings would lead, in principle, to a presumption of State aid and must be analysed in detail by the Commission.

More generally, where a fiscal aid is granted in order to provide an incentive for firms to embark on certain specific projects (investment in particular) and where its intensity is limited with respect to the costs of carrying out the project, it was viewed as no different from any other subsidy and to be accorded the same treatment. Nevertheless, such arrangements needed to lay down sufficiently transparent rules to enable the benefit conferred to be quantified. In most cases, however, tax relief provisions were to be seen as general in nature but this would normally not prevent their classification as State aid because:

> they are not linked to the carrying-out of specific projects and reduce a firm's current expenditure without it being possible to assess the precise volume involved when the Commission carries out its ex-ante examination. Such measures constitute 'operating aid'. Operating aid is in principle prohibited.[1145]

The Notice also pointed out that tax rules that are, for example, aimed at a certain region or a certain sector or a certain function within an enterprise (such as financial

---

1142. The key issues in the *Gibraltar* and *Azores* cases (Joined Cases C-106/09 P and C-107/09 P: *Commission and Spain v. Government of Gibraltar and United Kingdom,* [2011] ECR I-11113 and Case C-88/03: *Portugal v. Commission,* [2006] ECR I-7715, respectively).
1143. *See* European Commission: Decision No 98/C 395/08 of 22 July 1998: *International Financial Services Centre (IFSC) and Shannon Customs Free Airport Zone (SCAZ) – Irish Corporation Tax (ICT)*, OJ C 395 of 18 December 1998.
1144. These two points were central in the Apple case – European Commission: Decision of 30 August 2016 on State aid implemented by Ireland to Apple, OJ L 187 of 19 July 2017.
1145. European Commission: *Notice on the application of the State Aid rules to measures relating to direct business taxation, supra,* at point 32.

services) would be regarded as specific. However, the specific nature of these tax rules did not automatically turn them into State aid. If there was an economic rationale that made them necessary to the functioning and effectiveness of the tax system, then these specific tax rules would not be regarded as State aid. This could be the case, for example, for some specific tax provisions that take account of different accounting requirements in certain sectors.

Finally, the Notice specified that, even if a tax measure constituted State aid under Article 107(1) of the TFEU, it could nevertheless qualify for one of the derogations from the principle of incompatibility with the internal market provided for in Article 107(2) and (3). Furthermore, where the recipient, whether a private or public undertaking, had been entrusted by the State with the operation of services of general economic interest, the aid might also benefit from assessment under Article 106 of the Treaty.

The European Commission *Notice on the notion of State aid pursuant to Article 107(1) TFEU*[1146] finalised in May 2016 repealed the 1998 *Notice on the application of the State Aid rules to measures relating to direct business taxation* and looks at various issues concerning tax measures, including an expansion of some of the points in the previous 1998 Notice. In particular, the interpretative guidance in the new Notice incorporates the judgments of the Azores and Gibraltar judgments[1147] and notes that:

> A measure which derogates from the reference system (prima facie selectivity) may still be found to be non-selective if it is justified by the nature or general scheme of that system. This is the case where a measure derives directly from the intrinsic basic or guiding principles of the reference system or where it is the result of inherent mechanisms necessary for the functioning and effectiveness of the system. On the contrary, external policy objectives which are not inherent to the system cannot be relied upon for that purpose....The basis for a possible justification could, for instance, be the need to fight fraud or tax evasion, the need to take into account specific accounting requirements, administrative manageability, the principle of tax neutrality, the progressive nature of income tax and its redistributive purpose, the need to avoid double taxation, and the objective of optimising the recovery of fiscal debts.[1148]

Looking at other additional aspects of taxation, the May 2016 Notice points out that:

- *Cooperatives* – cooperatives can be regarded as not being in a comparable factual and legal situation to that of commercial companies, so that preferential tax treatment for cooperatives may fall outside the scope of the State aid rules on certain conditions.[1149]
- *Collective investment taxation* – Tax measures aimed at ensuring tax neutrality for investments in collective investment funds/companies should not be viewed as selective where those measures do not have the effect of favouring

1146. European Commission: Communication – *Commission Notice on the notion of State aid pursuant to Article 107(1) TFEU*, 19 May 2016.
1147. *Ibid.*, points 120–156.
1148. *Ibid.*, points 138–139.
1149. *Ibid.*, point 159.

certain collective investment undertakings or certain types of investments, but rather of reducing or eliminating double economic taxation in accordance with the overall principles inherent to the tax system in question.[1150]

- *Tax amnesties* – In general, a tax amnesty measure that applies to undertakings can be considered a general measure if several conditions are met. First, the measure should be of an exceptional nature, providing a strong incentive for undertakings to voluntarily comply with the tax obligations, and enhancing tax debt collection. Second, it should effectively be open to any undertaking of any sector or size that has outstanding tax liabilities due at the date set by the measure, without favouring any predefined group of undertakings. Third, it should not entail any de facto selectivity in favour of certain undertakings or sectors. Fourth, the tax administration's action should be limited to administering the implementation of the tax amnesty without any discretionary power to intervene in the granting or intensity of the measure. Fifth, the measure should not entail a waiver from verification. Finally, tax amnesty measures may also be considered as general measures if they follow the policy objective of ensuring compliance with a general principle of law, such as the principle that a judgment must be given within a reasonable period of time.[1151]
- *Tax rulings* – If in daily practice tax rules need to be interpreted, they should not leave room for the discretionary treatment of undertakings. Every decision by the administration that departs from the general tax rules and benefits individual undertakings leads in principle to a presumption of State aid and must be analysed in detail.[1152]
- *Tax settlements* – Tax settlements generally occur in the context of disputes between the taxpayer and the tax authorities concerning the amount of tax owed and are a common practice in many EU Member States. Tax settlements allow tax authorities to avoid long-standing legal disputes before national jurisdictions and ensure quick recovery of the tax due. While the competence of Member States in this field is not disputed, the Commission takes the view that State aid may be involved where it appears that the amount of taxes due has been significantly reduced without a clear justification (such as optimising the recovery of debt) or in a disproportionate manner to the benefit of the taxpayer e.g. by making disproportionate concessions to a taxpayer or where the settlement is contrary to the applicable tax provisions and has resulted in a lower amount of tax.[1153]
- *Administrative Tax Rulings* – For reasons of legal certainty, many national tax authorities provide prior administrative rulings on how specific transactions will be treated for tax purposes. Administrative rulings that merely contain an interpretation of the relevant tax provisions without deviating from the case

1150. *Ibid.*, point 163.
1151. *Ibid.*, points 165–169.
1152. *Ibid.*, point 171.
1153. *Ibid.*, points 172–173.

law and administrative practice do not give rise to a presumption of aid. However, an absence of transparency on this coupled with a high degree of administrative discretion on tax rulings can reverse this position.[1154]

- *Depreciation rules* – Continuing the approach under the 1998 Notice, the Commission view is that tax measures of a purely technical nature, such as depreciation/amortisation rules, generally do not constitute State aid and are general measures. However, some depreciation arrangements can depart from the general tax policy on depreciation. Thus, depreciation incentives (such as a shorter term of depreciation, a more favourable depreciation method, early depreciation, etc.) for certain types of assets or undertakings, which are not based on the guiding principles of the depreciation rules in question, may give rise to the existence of State aid. By contrast, accelerated and early depreciation rules for leased assets may be seen as general measures if the lease contracts in question are really accessible to companies of all sectors and sizes. But again, if the tax authority has discretionary freedom to set different depreciation periods or different valuation methods, firm by firm or sector by sector, there is a presumption of selectivity. Likewise, prior authorisation from a tax administration as a condition for applying a depreciation scheme involves selectivity if the authorisation is not limited to the prior verification of the legal requirements.[1155]
- *Flat-rate taxation for specific activities* – Specific provisions that do not contain discretionary elements, allowing, for example, income tax to be determined on a fixed basis, may be justified by the nature and general scheme of the system e.g. where they take account of specific accounting requirements or of the importance of land in assets which are specific to certain sectors; reflecting a concern to avoid a disproportionate administrative burden on certain types of undertakings because of their small size and/or sector of activity (e.g., in the agriculture or fisheries sectors). However, such arrangements do become selective if their effect is to create a lower tax burden for them as compared to other undertakings excluded from its scope of application.[1156]
- *Anti-abuse rules* – The provision of anti-abuse rules may be justified by the logic of preventing tax avoidance by taxpayers. However, such rules might be selective if they provide for a derogation (non-application of the anti-abuse rules) to specific undertakings or transactions, which would not be consistent with the logic underlying the anti-abuse rules in question.[1157]
- *Excise duty relief* – Although excise duties are largely harmonised at EU level, this does not automatically imply that any duty relief in these areas would fall outside the scope of the State aid rules. In fact, a reduced excise duty can grant

1154. *Ibid.*, points 175–177.
1155. *Ibid.*, points 178–181.
1156. *Ibid.*, points 182–183.
1157. *Ibid.*, point 184.

a selective advantage for the undertakings which use the product in question as an input or sell it on the market.[1158]

While these interpretations are now part of a general Commission Notice, they reflect decisional practice[1159] and a range of supporting judgments from the European Courts over the last decade that have had a strong focus on tackling what are perceived as harmful tax measures and some of the impacts of a lack of harmonisation of direct taxation in the EU. As one commentator concludes:

> From a complementary tool to the Code of Conduct in the fight against harmful tax competition, year after year State aid control became a key area of the fight against harmful tax competition at the EU level. Such evolution required a remarkable hermeneutical effort by the Commission and the Court... Still, the structure of an aid, as defined under Article 107 TFEU, cannot be indefinitely stretched.... State aid, alone, can do little to avoid tax erosion resulting from this lack of coordination. State aid is a useful tool in the fight against harmful tax competition. Nevertheless,

1158. *Ibid.*, point 185.
1159. These include the State aid Decision of the EFTA Surveillance Authority of 18 March 2009 with regard to the taxation of investment undertakings in Lichtenstein (*on tax neutrality*), Commission Decision of 12 May 2010, N 131/2009, Finland, Residential Real Estate Investment Trust (REIT) scheme, OJ C 178 of 3 July 2010 (on collective versus individual investments), Commission Decision of 11 July 2012 on the *tax amnesty* measure notified by Latvia (SA.331830), OJ C 1 of 4 January 2013, Commission Decision in Case No SA.38374 of 21 October 2015: State aid implemented by the Netherlands to Starbucks, OJ C 460 of 19 December 2014, Commission Decision of 21 October 2015 in Case No SA.38375 – Fiat and Commission Decision of 11 January 2016 in Case No SA.37667 – excess profit exemption state aid scheme (the latter three Decisions concerning *tax rulings accepting transfer pricing arrangements not at "arm's length"* are under appeal), Commission Decision No 2003/757/EC of 17 February 2003 on the aid scheme implemented by Belgium for coordination centres established in Belgium, OJ L 282 of 30 October 2003 (*also concerning tax rulings* and upheld on appeal in Joined Cases C-182/03 and C-217/03: *Belgium and Forum 187 ASBL v. Commission*, [2006] ECR I-5479 decided on 22 June 2006), Commission Decision No 2003/601/EC of 17 February 2003 on the Foreign Income aid scheme implemented by Ireland, OJ L 204 of 13 August 2003 (*establishing that the misapplication of national law via tax rulings resulting in a lower amount of tax confers a selective advantage*), Commission Decision No 2003/438/EC of 16 October 2002 on State aid C 50/2001, Luxembourg Finance Companies, OJ L 153 of 20 June 2003, Commission Decision No 2003/501/EC of 16 October 2002 on State aid C 49/2001, Luxembourg Coordination centres, OJ L 170 of 9 July 2003, Commission Decision No 2004/76/EC of 13 May 2003, French Headquarters and Logistic Centres, OJ L 23 of 28 January 2004, and the above Fiat, Starbucks and Belgian Coordination Centres Decisions (*concerning the endorsement of questionable profit calculation methods via tax rulings*), Commission Decision No 2011/276/EU of 26 May 2010 on State aid C-76/03, Umicore SA, OJ L 122 of 11 May 2011 (*concerning tax settlements*), Commission Decision of 20 November 2012 on SA.34736 on the early depreciation of certain assets acquired through a financial leasing, OJ C 384 of 13 December 2012, Commission Decision No 2007/255/EC of 20 December 2006 on the aid scheme implemented by France under Article 39 CA of the General Tax Code, OJ L 112 of 30 April 2007 (both *concerning accelerated depreciation arrangements*) and Commission Decision No 1999/779/EC of 3 February 1999 on an Austrian aid granted in the form of an exemption from beverage tax of wine and other fermented beverages sold directly on the place of production to the consumer, OJ L 305 of 30 November 1999 (*concerning State aid via excise duty exemptions*). Moreover, the following additional Decisions on tax rulings are listed on a new "tax ruling" page of the DG Competition website: (1) Alleged aid to Amazon (Case No SA.38944), (2) Alleged aid to McDonalds (Case No SA.38945 of 3 December 2015: Alleged aid to Mc Donald's – Luxembourg, OJ C 258/2016 of 15 July 2016) and (3) Possible State aid in favour of GDF Suez (ENGIE) (Case No SA.44888).

> it cannot be intended as a full substitute for the positive approximation of the corporate tax system of the Member States.[1160]

Since June 2013, the Commission has been investigating the tax ruling practices of Member States and it extended this information inquiry to all Member States in December 2014. In these investigations, the Commission was able to use, for the first time, new information request powers under the updated Procedural Regulation of 2013 which allows the Commission, if information provided by a Member State subject to a State aid investigation is deemed insufficient, to ask any other Member State as well as companies (including the company benefitting from the aid measure or its competitors) to provide directly to the Commission all market information necessary to enable it to complete its State aid assessment.[1161] These new powers arose from the State Aid Modernisation initiative launched by the Commission in 2012[1162] to allow it to concentrate its enforcement efforts on State aid that is considered most liable to distort competition.

On the basis of this new-style investigation, the Commission concluded, in October 2015, that Luxembourg and the Netherlands had granted selective tax advantages to Fiat and Starbucks, respectively.[1163] Then, in January 2016, the Commission concluded that selective tax advantages granted by Belgium to least 35 multinationals, mainly from the EU, under its "excess profit" tax scheme were illegal under EU State aid rules.[1164] In August 2016, the Apple Decision was announced as further progress in this series of State aid investigations.

The Apple Case

On 30 August 2016, the European Commission announced that it had concluded that Ireland granted undue tax benefits of up to €13 billion to Apple and that this was illegal under EU State aid rules because it allowed Apple to pay substantially less tax than other businesses. Ireland was ordered to recover the illegal aid. Competition Commissioner Margrethe Vestager pointed out that:

1160. E. Traversa & A. Flamini, "*Fighting Harmful Tax Competition through EU State Aid Law: Will the Hardening of Soft Law Suffice?*" (2015), 14 European State Aid Law Quarterly, Issue 3, p. 331.
1161. Council Regulation No 734/2013/EU of 22 July 2013 amending Regulation No 659/1999/EC laying down detailed rules for the application of Article 93 of the EC Treaty, OJ L 204 of 31 July 2013.
1162. European Commission: Communication from the Commission to the European Parliament, the Council, the European Economic and Social Committee and the Committee of the Regions – EU State Aid Modernisation (SAM), COM/2012/0209 final of 8 May 2012.
1163. Commission Decision No 2016/2326/EU of 21 October 2015 on State aid SA.38375 (2014/C ex 2014/NN) which Luxembourg granted to Fiat (notified under document C (2015) 7152), OJ L 351 of 22 December 2016 and Commission Decision No SA.38374 of 21 October 2015: State aid implemented by the Netherlands to Starbucks, OJ C 460 of 19 December 2014.
1164. Commission Decision No 2016/1699//EU of 11 January 2016 on the excess profit exemption State aid scheme SA.37667 (2015/C) (ex 2015/NN) implemented by Belgium (notified under document C (2015) 9837), OJ L 260 of 27 September 2016.

> *Member States cannot give tax benefits to selected companies – this is illegal under EU state aid rules. The Commission's investigation concluded that Ireland granted illegal tax benefits to Apple, which enabled it to pay substantially less tax than other businesses over many years. In fact, this selective treatment allowed Apple to pay an effective corporate tax rate of 1 per cent on its European profits in 2003 down to 0.005 per cent in 2014.*[1165]

Apple Sales International and Apple Operations Europe are two Irish incorporated companies that are fully-owned by the Apple group and ultimately controlled by the US parent, Apple Inc. The taxable profits of Apple Sales International and Apple Operations Europe in Ireland were found to have been determined by a tax ruling granted by Ireland in 1991, which in 2007 was replaced by a similar second tax ruling. This later tax ruling was terminated when Apple Sales International and Apple Operations Europe changed their structures in 2015.[1166] In effect, the Irish Revenue Commissioners had issued two rulings (advance opinions) on the method for determining the net profit of the Irish branches of both Apple Sales International and Apple Operations Europe. According to the Decision, these rulings endorsed a way to establish the taxable profits for two Irish incorporated companies of the Apple group (Apple Sales International and Apple Operations Europe), which the Commission decided did not correspond to economic reality: as almost all sales profits recorded by the two companies were internally attributed to a "head office." The Commission's assessment highlighted that these "head offices" existed only on paper and could not have generated such profits. These profits allocated to the "head offices" were not subject to tax in any country under specific provisions of the Irish tax law, which are no longer in force. The Commission noted also that the tax treatment in Ireland enabled Apple to avoid taxation on almost all profits generated by sales of Apple products in the entire EU Single Market. This was due to Apple's decision to record all sales in Ireland, rather than in the countries where the products were sold. As a result of the allocation method endorsed in the tax rulings, Apple only paid an effective corporate tax rate that declined from 1% in 2003 to 0.005% in 2014 on the profits of Apple Sales International:

> *In short, about 90% of Apple's foreign profits are earned by Irish subsidiaries, which are highly profitable because they hold rights to Apple's intellectual property. However, these Irish entities paid very little tax because they were not tax resident anywhere - a structure that exploited differences between the US and Irish definitions of tax residence.*[1167]

1165. European Commission: Press Release *"State aid: Ireland gave illegal tax benefits to Apple worth up to €13 billion,"* 30 August 2016.
1166. Point 136 of the Decision notes that Apple put in place a new corporate structure in Ireland with effect from 1 January 2015 as a consequence of the modification of Irish tax law, whereby an Irish incorporated company could no longer declare its tax residence to be outside of Ireland, while not having any place of tax residency anywhere else, as was the case for ASI and AOE.
1167. Financial Times, 30 August 2016.

On the basis of its findings that the tax rulings issued by Ireland were illegal under EU State aid rules as they endorsed an artificial allocation of Apple Sales International and Apple Operations Europe's sales profits to their "head offices," where they were not taxed (thereby enabling Apple to pay substantially less tax than other companies), the Commission applied its powers to order the recovery of unpaid taxation under these arrangements over the ten-year period 2003 to 2014. The recovery amount, which is not specifically included in the Decision, has been assessed and publicised by the Commission as being of the order of €13 billion, plus interest.[1168]

Following the Apple Decision, the Irish Government and Apple indicated their intention to appeal the Decision and, on 19 December 2016, the Irish Government published the main lines of the argumentation to be presented in the case.[1169] In general terms, the appeal will argue that the Commission's Decision of 30 August 2016 has misunderstood the relevant facts and Irish law in that it wrongly asserts that two "Opinions" (the disputed tax rulings) given in 1991 and 2007 by the Irish Revenue Commissioners "renounced" tax revenue that Ireland would have otherwise been entitled to collect from the Irish branches of Apple Sales International and Apple Operations Europe. In the Irish view, the opinions involved no departure from Irish law because the ordinary tax rules applicable to branches in Ireland of non-resident companies are in the Taxes Consolidation Act 1997 and the opinions simply applied those rules, which in accordance with the territoriality principle, taxes only the profits attributable to the branch, not the non-Irish profits of the company.

In addition, the Irish authorities argue that the Commission has no competence, under the State aid rules, unilaterally to substitute its own view of the geographic scope and extent of the Member State's tax jurisdiction for those of the Member State itself – "As the purpose of the State aid rules is to tackle State interventions which confer a selective advantage, the State aid rules by their nature cannot remedy mismatches between tax systems on a global level."

Meanwhile, the Commission announced the commencement of Article 108(2) of the TFEU enforcement proceedings against Ireland in October 2017 for failure to recover the illegal aid from Apple.[1170] Moreover, in October 2017, the Commission concluded that a tax ruling issued by Luxembourg in 2003, and prolonged in 2011, lowered the tax paid by Amazon in Luxembourg without any valid justification and gave rise to a

1168. The Decision requires the recovery from Apple of unpaid tax for the period since 2003, which amounts to up to €13 billion, plus interest. Around €50 million in unpaid taxes relate to the undue allocation of profits to the "head office" of Apple Operations Europe. The remainder results from the undue allocation of profits to the "head office" of Apple Sales International. The recovery period stops in 2014, as Apple changed its structure in Ireland as of 2015 and the tax ruling of 2007 no longer applies.

1169. Irish Department of Finance: Apple State Aid Case – *Explanation of the main lines of argument in Ireland's annulment application lodged with the General Court of the European Union on 9 November 2016*, 19 December 2016.

1170. European Commission: Press Release "*State aid: Commission refers Ireland to Court for failure to recover illegal tax benefits from Apple worth up to €13 billion,*" 4 October 2017.

recovery order of some €250 million.[1171] The Commission also continues two similar in-depth investigations into concerns that tax rulings may give rise to State aid issues in Luxembourg, as regards McDonald's and GDF Suez.[1172]

Moreover, in all of these cases, the Commission highlights that the fight against tax evasion and tax fraud is one of the top priorities of this Commission and that this provides at least part of the policy context for these investigations. In particular, in June 2015, the Commission unveiled a series of initiatives to tackle tax avoidance, secure sustainable tax revenues and strengthen the Single Market for businesses. The proposed measures are part of the *Commission's Action Plan for fair and effective taxation*,[1173] and aim to significantly improve the corporate tax environment in the EU, making it fairer, more efficient and more growth-friendly. Key proposed actions include a framework to *ensure effective taxation where profits are generated* and a strategy to relaunch the Common Consolidated Corporate Tax Base (CCCTB) on which a fresh proposal is envisaged.

Another element of this new policy drive is the so-called *Tax Transparency Package* which was launched by the Commission in March 2015. The central component of this initiative was a legislative proposal to improve cooperation between Member States in terms on their cross-border tax rulings by requiring Member States to automatically exchange information on their tax rulings (something which was previously voluntary and discretionary). The idea here was that a strict timeline should be set whereby, every three months, national tax authorities will have to send a short report to all other Member States on all cross-border tax rulings that they have issued. Member States will then be able to ask for more detailed information on a particular ruling. This initiative was adopted in the form of an amending Directive and entered into force on 1 January 2017.[1174] According to the European Commission:

> This legislation will contribute to bringing about a much greater degree of transparency and will act as a deterrent from using tax rulings as an instrument for tax abuse - good news for businesses and for consumers who will continue to benefit from this very useful tax practice but under very strict scrutiny in order to ensure a framework for fair tax competition.[1175]

1171. European Commission: Press release "*State aid: Commission investigates transfer pricing arrangements on corporate taxation of Amazon in Luxembourg*," 7 October 2014 and most recently, Press release "*State aid: Commission finds Luxembourg gave illegal tax benefits to Amazon worth around €250 million*," 4 October 2017.
1172. State aid SA.38945 of 3 December 2015: Alleged aid to Mc Donald's – Luxembourg, OJ C 258 of 15 July 2016: Invitation to submit comments pursuant to Article 108(2) of the Treaty on the Functioning of the European Union, OJ C 258 of 15 July 2015 and State aid SA.44888 (NN/2016) (ex EO/2016) – Luxembourg Possible State aid in favour of GDF Suez of 19 September 2016.
1173. European Commission: Communication from the Commission to the European Parliament and the Council: *A Fair and Efficient Corporate Tax System in the European Union: 5 Key Areas for Action*, COM (2015) 302 final of 17 June 2015.
1174. Council Directive No 2015/2376/EU of 8 December 2015 amending Directive No 2011/16/EU as regards mandatory automatic exchange of information in the field of taxation, OJ L 332 of 18 December 2015.
1175. European Commission: Press Release on the entry into force of Council Directive 2015/2376/EU.

The Tax Transparency Package also includes a proposed review and tightening of the Code of Conduct on Unfair Tax Competition and indicates that the Commission will work with EU Member States to review the Code of Conduct, to make it more effective in ensuring fair and transparent tax competition within the EU.

The European Courts have continued to be supportive of the pursuit of fiscal aid by the Commission and of the more recent concepts created to establish the tests for State aid in tax measures and the grounds for illegality. Among the important cases in recent years, the following selected summary is of interest as it covers the main substantive argumentation used in the Apple Case.

Table 35 Some Leading Recent Cases on Fiscal State Aid

Case	*Main Points*
C-311/97 Royal Bank of Scotland[1176]	The fact that non-resident and resident companies are in a comparable situation as regards the method of determining their taxable base is further supported by the case law of the Court of Justice on the taxation of branches in the context of Article 49 of the Treaty.
C-446/03 *Marks & Spencer v. Halsey*[1177]	Where the Court of Justice recognised that resident and non-resident companies are not in the same legal or factual position.
Case C-253/03 CLT-UFA[1178]	"It is necessary to apply a tax rate to the profits made by a branch which is equivalent to the overall tax rate which would have been applicable in the same circumstances to the distribution of the profits of a subsidiary to its parent company."
Case C-169/08 Presidente del Consiglio dei Ministri[1179]	By renouncing tax revenue that a Member State would otherwise have been entitled to collect under its tax rules, a tax ruling gives rise to a loss of State resources.
C-182/08: Glaxo Wellcome[1180]	Member States are free to decide on the economic policy which they consider most appropriate and, in particular, to spread the tax burden as they see fit across the various factors of production. Nonetheless, Member States must exercise this competence in accordance with Union law.

1176. Case C-311/97: *Royal Bank of Scotland plc v. Elliniko Dimosio (Greek State)*, [1999] ECR I-2651, para. 29.
1177. Case C-446/03: *Marks & Spencer plc v. David Halsey (Her Majesty's Inspector of Taxes)*, [2005] ECR I-10837.
1178. Case C-253/03: *CLT-UFA SA v. Finanzamt Köln-West*, [2006] ECR I-1831, para. 29.
1179. Case 169/08: *Presidente del Consiglio dei Ministri v. Regione Sardegna*, [2009] ECR I-1821, para. 58.
1180. Case C-182/08: *Glaxo Wellcome GmbH & Co. KG v. Finanzamt München II*, [2009] ECR I-8591, para. 34 and the case law cited.

Case	*Main Points*
C-66/02 *Italy v. Commission*;[1181] C-222/04 Cassa di Risparmio di Firenze and Others;[1182] C-522/13 Ministerio de Defensa and Navantia.[1183]	As regards fiscal measures, an advantage may be granted through different types of reduction in an undertaking's tax burden and, in particular, through a reduction in the taxable base or in the amount of tax due.
C-270/15 *P Belgium v. Commission*[1184] and C-15/14 *P Commission v. MOL*[1185]	As regards the selective nature of an advantage in the case of an individual aid measure, as opposed to a scheme, "the identification of the economic advantage is, in principle, sufficient to support the presumption that it is selective."
Joined Cases C-182/03 and C-217/03, Belgium and Forum 187 *ASBL v. Commission*,[1186] Joined Cases C-106/09 P and C-107/09 *P Commission v. Government of Gibraltar and United Kingdom*,[1187] C-417/10 3M Italia,[1188] C-529/10 Safilo[1189] and T-538/11 *Belgium v. Commission*.[1190]	Any fiscal measure a Member State adopts, including a tax ruling endorsing a profit allocation method for determining a branch's taxable base, must comply with the State aid rules, which bind the Member States and enjoy primacy over their national legislation. Moreover, under Cases C-182/03 and C-217/03: "in order to decide whether a method of assessment of taxable income such as that laid down under the regime for coordination centres confers an advantage on them, it is necessary, [...], to compare that regime with the ordinary tax system, based on the difference between profits and outgoings of an undertaking carrying on its activities in conditions of free competition."[1191]

State aid in the form of tax measures has received considerable attention in the last few years as a result of Commission decisions since 2014 concerning *Apple* in Ireland, *Starbucks* in the Netherlands, and *Fiat Finance and Trade* and *Amazon* in Luxembourg,

1181. Case C-66/02: *Italy v. Commission*, [2005] ECR I-10901, para. 78.
1182. Case C-222/04: *Ministero dell'Economia e delle Finanze v. Cassa di Risparmio di Firenze SpA, Fondazione Cassa di Risparmio di San Miniato and Cassa di Risparmio di San Miniato SpA*, [2006] ECR I-289, para. 132.
1183. Case C-522/13: *Ministerio de Defensa and Navantia SA v. Concello de Ferrol*, ECLI-:EU:C:2014:2262, paras 21–31.
1184. Case C-270/15 P: *Belgium v. Commission*, ECLI:EU:C:2016:489, para. 49.
1185. Case C-15/14 P: *Commission v. MOL Magyar Olaj- és Gázipari Nyrt*, ECLI:EU:C:2015:362, para. 60.
1186. Cases C-182/03 and C-217/03: *Belgium and Forum 187 ASBL v. Commission*, [2006] ECR I-5479, para. 81.
1187. Joined Cases C-106/09 P and C-107/09 P: *Commission and Spain v. Government of Gibraltar and United Kingdom*, [2011] ECR I-11113.
1188. Case C-417/10: *Ministero dell'Economia e delle Finanze and Agenzia delle Entrate v. 3M Italia SpA*, ECLI:EU:C:2012:184, para. 25.
1189. Case C-529/10: *Ministero dell'Economia e delle Finanze and Agenzia delle Entrate v. Safilo Spa* ECLI:EU:C:2012:188, para. 18.
1190. Case T-538/11: *Belgium v. Commission*, ECLI:EU:T:2015:188, para. 66.
1191. The basis for the application of the "arm's length principle."

where the Commission is challenging national tax rulings concerning multinational companies' taxation and transfer pricing arrangements. The four Decisions have given rise to considerable debate on the Commission's powers in the field of taxation and have indeed taken many politicians, lawyers and commentators by surprise.[1192] Many commentators argue that these Decisions go beyond the boundaries of existing case law and constitute an attempt by the Commission to test – and arguably also push – the limits of Article 107 of the TFEU.[1193]

In the face of the adage that nothing is certain except death and taxes, it is argued by some that the present drive by the Commission creates significant legal uncertainty in regard to important aspects of national tax policies and that the State aid rules cannot achieve what the Commission is surreptitiously trying to do.[1194] Critics of the present approach include former European Competition Commissioner Neelie Kroes who (after the Apple case was decided by the Commission) publicly stated that State aid rules were not the right tool to fight tax avoidance. In particular:

> State aid is not a cure for all ills. It is a tool to address instances where a Member State has made an exception to its own rules and given a specific company an advantage... EU Member States have a sovereign right to determine their own tax laws. State aid cannot be used to rewrite those rules. However, the current State aid investigations into tax rulings appear to do exactly that, by suggesting a radical new approach to so-called transfer-pricing rules that determine where profits shall be allocated. You cannot change the rules of the game through ad hoc State aid enforcement, and then seek retroactive recovery for unpaid taxes. Doing so would be fundamentally unfair and would harm competition, growth and tax income in Europe. And it raises serious questions about legal certainty and the rule of law.[1195]

Moreover, the Commission has been criticised for relying on the *OECD Transfer Pricing Guidelines*[1196] to determine whether a given ruling contained a selective advantage and

1192. Commission Decision No 2016/2326/EU of 21 October 2015 on State aid SA.38375 (2014/C ex 2014/NN) which Luxembourg granted to Fiat (notified under document C (2015) 7152), OJ L 351 of 22 December 2016; Commission Decision No SA.38374 of 21 October 2015: State aid implemented by the Netherlands to Starbucks, OJ C 460 of 19 December 2014; Commission Decision No 2016/1699/EU of 11 January 2016 on the excess profit exemption State aid scheme SA.37667 (2015/C) (ex 2015/NN) implemented by Belgium (notified under document C (2015) 9837), OJ L 260 of 27 September 2016; Commission Decision No SA.38944 (2014/C) (2014/NN) – Alleged aid to Amazon: Invitation to submit comments pursuant to Article 108(2) of the Treaty on the Functioning of the European Union, OJ C 44 of 6 February 2015, Commission Decision No SA.38945 of 3 December 2015: Alleged aid to Mc Donald's – Luxembourg: Invitation to submit comments pursuant to Article 108(2) of the Treaty on the Functioning of the European Union, OJ C 258 of 15 July 2015 and Commission Decision No SA.44888 (NN/2016) (ex EO/2016) – Luxembourg Possible State aid in favour of GDF Suez of 19 September 2016.

1193. *See*: State Aid and Taxation – All Clear?," Editorial, European State Aid Law Quarterly, Vol. 3/2015.

1194. *See* R. Luja, "*Does the Modernization of State Aid Control Put Legal Certainty in Risk?*" EstAL, 4/2012, p. 765 and G. Matsos, "*Systematic Misconceptions of State Aid Law in the Area of Taxation*" EstAL, 3/2014, p. 495.

1195. Neelie Kroes, "*Why EU State Aid is Not the Right Tool to Fight Tax Avoidance*" (1 September 2016), The Guardian magazine.

1196. OECD Transfer Pricing Guidelines for Multinational Enterprises and Tax Administrations 2010, 16 August 2010.

therefore gave rise to State aid in the abovementioned cases on transfer pricing (*Fiat, Starbucks and the Belgian excess profit ruling system*). While the Commission officially labels the OECD Transfer Pricing Guidelines as a tool among others to assess whether a given tax ruling requires further assessment under State aid rules, in practice the Commission applies them aggressively and any deviation from those is likely to raise problems from a State aid perspective.

It will take some further time to clarify if the Commission's aggressive approach to certain State aid tax measures will be sustained by the European Courts. If it is, further political debate may well raise additional issues concerning back-door harmonisation of direct taxation. This would justifiably rekindle earlier fears that the Lisbon Treaty (2007) would enable tax harmonisation across the EU without political consensus. Ironically, such misgivings about EU-wide taxation were a significant factor in Ireland's rejection of the Lisbon Treaty at a referendum in 2008 and negotiations to encourage Irish voters to accept the Treaty at a second referendum in 2009 included a promise not to move towards tax harmonisation.[1197]

At the same time, it is clear that, given the balance of competence between Member States and the Commission and the precise TFEU unanimity requirements on tax harmonization, economic distortions in the internal market do arise from the operations of 28 national tax systems – in particular in respect of corporation profits taxes, transfer pricing arrangements and other aspects of business taxation. The proper choice, however, is either to achieve legislative harmonisation pursuant to primary EU law or to do nothing and accept the reality of a problem in the EU that, in fact, has no viable solution. There is little doubt that the Commission is working in the shadows between these options and that its State aid regulatory function is being mobilised to the fullest to address tax distortions, whether Member States support this politically or not.

1197. For more on taxation *see CIVITAS – Institute for the Study of Civil Society* fact sheets on EU law.

CHAPTER 7

Assessment, Conclusions and Future Directions

7.1 INTRODUCTION

Sixty years of State aid law and policy have demonstrated remarkable development built on the initial idea that economic spillover effects of sovereign economic policies of Member States should be regulated in the interests of competition. This initial idea resulted in the emergence of a globally unique EU State aid system which has unmistakenly grown stronger. However, the system as it has evolved is not necessarily supported by the Member States and, despite some influence on the multilateral trading system, it has not fully convinced other countries as to its merits. As a supranational system, the EU State aid law and policy has given rise to a range of issues which can be abstracted as political, economic, legal and administrative. Indeed, the main issues concern the sovereignty of national economic policies under the regulatory regimes, taxation dilemmas, political factors in decision-making, political imperatives in the evolution of the regulatory systems themselves, boundary issues between economic and social considerations and impacts and the capacity of the European Commission to regulate in accordance with substantive law.

Accordingly, these political, economic, legal and administrative considerations constitute a general framework here to draw some broader conclusions regarding what has happened under the umbrella of EU State aid regulation in the last six decades.

7.2 POLITICAL ASSESSMENT

7.2.1 Politics and Regulation

It is axiomatic that law is the written expression of political will and consensus. However, as *Middlemas* notes, the notion that international law and treaties "lay down what has been agreed by the sovereign players and what therefore will be" is a higher fiction on account of the gaps:

- between what the law says and what actually happens;
- between the public version of how a public authority operates and the reality; and
- between the grandiose aims constantly referred to in a rhetoric and incremental, and often informal, progress.[1198]

This is explained by a deep, multifaceted and complex political process, especially in the context of the European Union. It is similar in regard to the WTO but the informal politics of the WTO are more obvious and more generally acceptable as such on account of the diplomatic basis for multilateral trade accords, the largely per se approach of regulation, (once adopted and once acted upon by WTO Members) and the extensive and political bargaining to ultimately agree or disagree on the multilateral rules.

The traditional approach of tripartite bargaining in international relations (involving State to State bargains, State to business bargains and business to business bargains)[1199] has been developed by *Lawton* into the notion of "Pentagonal Diplomacy" for the purpose of analysing the evolution and content of various EU economic policies:

> In analysing, within an EC context, how firms and governments relate to and negotiate with one another over defined mutual goals, one must include another player or level of "governance" within the paradigm, i.e. the European Commission.[1200]

Thus, two other lines can be added to the traditional triangle to reflect the fact that governments must negotiate, not only with other governments and with firms but also with the European Commission; and firms, in turn must bargain with other firms, governments and with the European Commission. This five-sided political analytical framework is complex, because the interplay varies according to the specificities of a particular bargain, it entails five inter-linked sets of negotiating bargains (State-State, firm-firm, State-firm, firm-European Commission, and European Commission-State),

---

1198. K. Middlemas, *supra*, p. 668.

1199. S. Strange, "*States, Firms and Diplomacy*" (1992), 68 International Affairs, Issue 1 and J.B. Tucker, "*Partners and Rivals: A Model of International Collaboration*" (1991), 45 International Organisation, Issue 1, Winter.

1200. T.C. Lawton, "*The Creation and Control of EC Industrial Policy – Lessons from the Electronics Sector*" (1995–1996), DCUBS Research Papers, Issue 7, Department of Government, University of Essex accessible at http://www.dcu.ie/dcubs/research_papers/no.7html.

all five bargaining sets come into play for each issue area although the policy impact of the individual sets vary according to the issue area. In this way, in regard to policy development in certain spheres, the firm-Commission interplay may be negligible, while, for others, it may be the State-State bargain which has little input into policy development. Similarly, Government-Commission bargaining (usually an intra-institutional procedure, between the Commission and the Council) may be pivotal, or it may merely constitute the Council "rubber stamping" a particular policy. In turn, business and Commission negotiating can be central to the development of a particular policy, or it may be peripheral, if not irrelevant, to the particular policy process. On this basis, *Lawton* argues, in his analysis of EU policy on the electronics sector, that the *Pentagonal Diplomacy conceptual framework* can be used to comprehensively analyse and assess EU industrial policy bargains over time. Moreover, due to the emerging pivotal role of the European Commission (at least in the electronics sector):

> the actual policy agenda-setting, trade tool utilisation, rules governing competition, and concentration of resources, remain largely the domain of the European Commission, in partnership with certain large corporate enterprises.[1201]

While the value of the pentagonal diplomacy model is accepted here, it is also to be noted that a further line could be added ("Hexagonal Diplomacy") to reflect internal Commission bargaining as between different Directorates General (European Commission Departments) which has had a profound effect on various EU "flagship" economic policies over the years and has been very influential in the "common interest" positions taken in regard to State aid issues.

In regard to the EU State aid system generally, it is clear that limited EU competence in regard to industrial policy has been progressively expanded via a comprehensive range of informal bargains using the State aid rules (and other policy instruments) to create a de facto and growing common industrial policy that was never envisaged in the Treaties, which was actively opposed at the inception of the EU[1202] and which, in formal political and legal terms, is still broadly resisted as an intrusion on the sovereignty of EU Member States and anathema to the principle of subsidiarity. Second, while higher politics helps to explain much of the evolution of law and policy in EU State aid control, this evolution has also been paradoxically enhanced by the Commission's successful efforts to largely depoliticise the decision-making process in regard to State aid cases. And finally, the process has been assisted further by a long-term Commission process of "rewriting the narrative" in regard to the objectives and the rationale for the use of the State aid rules and various aspects of their substantive content.

1201. *Ibid.*
1202. Meaning the rejection of a common industrial policy apart from the ECSC and Euratom exceptions regarding the steel, coal and atomic energy sectors which were fully ceded to EU policy control.

7.2.2 The Erosion of the Sovereignty of National Industrial Policies and the EU State Aid Control Regime

The sovereignty of national industrial policies of EU Member States has been steadily eroded since the 1950s by the interactions within the Lawton Pentagon, compromises and initiatives within the European Commission and by various processes inherent in the EU common market and the evolution and redefinition of the "common interest." By and large, the European Courts, by taking a broad, evolutionary and teleological approach to the interpretation of EU Law have supported this progression, although, on occasion, they have felt bound to curb Commission expansionist policies.

Typically, the increased role of the EU as a supranational body (generally meaning the Commission but also closer coordination between Member States at the initiative of larger and net financial contributor Member States, in particular) coincided over the years with periods of crisis[1203] or periods anticipating major change in the structure and composition of the EU.[1204] In some cases, there was an eventual consensus that a strong EU role – or at least one coordinated under EU auspices – was desirable on account of the scale of the problems to be dealt with (e.g., EU unemployment, low performing R&D and technology sectors, crises in major industrial (or "sensitive") sectors and competitiveness in the face of economic globalisation). Nonetheless, the overall role of the EU in regard to industrial policies remains officially what is set out in Article 173 of the TFEU.

TITLE XVII – INDUSTRY

Article 173

"1. The Union and the Member States shall ensure that the conditions necessary for the competitiveness of the Union's industry exist.

For that purpose, in accordance with a system of open and competitive markets, their action shall be aimed at:

- speeding up the adjustment of industry to structural changes,
- encouraging an environment favourable to initiative and to the development of undertakings throughout the Union, particularly small and medium-sized undertakings,
- encouraging an environment favourable to cooperation between undertakings,
- fostering better exploitation of the industrial potential of policies of innovation, research and technological development.

1203. Middlemas, *supra*.
1204. Most notably in the setting of each proposed Enlargement.

> 2. The Member States shall consult each other in liaison with the Commission and, where necessary, shall coordinate their action. The Commission may take any useful initiative to promote such coordination, ***in particular initiatives aiming at the establishment of guidelines and indicators, the organisation of exchange of best practice, and the preparation of the necessary elements for periodic monitoring and evaluation***. The European Parliament shall be kept fully informed.
>
> 3. The Union shall contribute to the achievement of the objectives set out in paragraph 1 through the policies and activities it pursues under other provisions of the Treaties. The European Parliament and the Council, acting in accordance with the ordinary legislative procedure and after consulting the Economic and Social Committee, may decide on specific measures in support of action taken in the Member States to achieve the objectives set out in paragraph 1, ***excluding any harmonisation of the laws and regulations of the Member States.***
>
> This Title shall not provide a basis for the introduction by the Union of any measure which could lead to a distortion of competition or ***contains tax provisions or provisions relating to the rights and interests of employed persons.***"[1205]

This Article was introduced in the Maastricht Treaty, and the highlighted text in the second part of paragraph 3 was added by the Nice Treaty. Other highlighted parts of the Article reflect refinements made in concluding the Lisbon Treaty (TFEU). Viewed strictly, the scope of involvement of the EU is on promoting competitiveness, with a focus on open markets, structural change in industry, promoting a positive business environment for SMEs and R&D and innovation, and it is a joint role with the Member State governments. The Nice amendments reflect national concerns that the Article could be used as a back-door alternative to avoid the political unanimity required by the Treaty in respect of tax and social issues in the context of the qualified majority rule also introduced in the Nice amendments. However, the important element in Article 173, from a State aid point of view, is the phrase: "The Community shall contribute to the achievement of the objectives set out in paragraph 1 through the policies and activities it pursues under other provisions of this Treaty." This has effectively allowed the Commission, in particular, to use State aid policy to support any initiatives in regard to EU Industry Policy, and it has also allowed Member States to lobby for such action in the context of competitiveness. This is indeed further reinforced by Article 6 of the TFEU which provides that the EU shall have competence to carry out actions to support, coordinate or supplement the actions of the Member States in regard, *inter alia*, to industry.

These Treaty provisions, and their subsequent application, in effect consolidated much of what had in fact evolved in the form of EU policy action regarding industrial policy under various programmes.

While the ECSC Treaty and the EURATOM Treaty may be regarded as having established a policy basis for supranational control over three key industrial sectors,

1205. TFEU, Article 173.

the TFEU preserved national sovereignty and control in regard to all other sectors. Nonetheless, the Treaty does contain many provisions, including the State aid rules, from which a common industrial policy has evolved via the overall application to industry or to certain sectors of industry of all the general Treaty provisions with a view to accelerating the process of resource allocation among and within the various sectors. More specifically, this has involved the interplay of:

- general measures for the further development of the internal market and for the establishment of a European economic and monetary union;
- external commercial policy (anti-dumping policy, bilateral and multilateral trade agreements with implications for individual industrial sectors);
- social and regional policy (when the industrial reconversion process has unacceptable social and regional consequences);
- competition policy (legal instruments for intervention in market mechanisms that are not functioning well and for controlling State aid);
- research and development policy;
- the strengthening of cooperation among European enterprises;
- Specific EU policy measures for certain industrial sectors and the resources provided for this purpose.

An underlying view has also developed in regard to the economic development narrative of the EU that, faced with current competitive challenges in both high technology and traditional industries, these challenges can no longer be met by national industrial policies and that resultant industrial restructuring is thus closely linked to the phenomenon of economic interdependence. All of the above policy consolidations into a "common industrial policy" have been supported by, or even lead by, the development of the EU State aid rules. This was initially noticeable in State aid policies regarding the so-called *sensitive industrial sectors* (motor vehicles, shipbuilding, textiles, coal, steel, air transport, agriculture and fisheries) where crises, overcapacity, subsidised international competition and structural adjustment problems were addressed by various frameworks in regard to the adjusted application of State aid rules to those sectors. It also became evident in regard to horizontal State aid rules, especially regarding SME development and the subsidisation of research and development. Moreover, the State aid rules have also worked in tandem with many, if not most, of the EU policy activity areas set out in Articles 3–6 of the TFEU.

Whether or not the elaboration of specific policy positions as to the use of State aids in these areas was pivotal or ancillary has depended on internal bargaining within the European Commission. However, the use of special State aid regimes has been important in several areas as the most powerful instrument available to the European Commission to achieve a desired policy effect on account of the Commission's exclusive competence under Articles 107 and 108 in regard to any State aid issues which (invariably) arose in considering responses to the various sectoral crises or economic policy areas perceived to be in need of coordinated development at EU level. Accordingly, *Holmes and Smith* note that EU competition policy has always involved an implicit common industrial policy and that, due to difficulties in reaching a commonly accepted and well-specified industrial policy, "competition policy is being called upon to perform tasks far removed from supporting the principles of anti-trust and free trade."[1206]

Over the years, the European Commission reduced its sectoral focus in the State aid system. In part, this was because most crisis sectors in all Member States had been rescued and restructured at least once. It was also due to globalisation influences and an increasing policy perspective that a horizontal framework industrial policy was a more coherent response. Thus, it was unsurprising that the 2000 Lisbon Competitiveness Strategy, for example, became a central pillar of all major EU policy areas and the specific policy context of the State Aid Action Plan and the changes to State aid regulation arising from it.

More recently, the State Aid Modernisation programme followed suit; in particular in regard to its orientation of many reforms towards a renewed emphasis on other EU policy imperatives. With the express priority objective of modernising State aid control to foster sustainable, smart and inclusive growth in a competitive internal market,[1207] the State Aid Modernisation initiative noted that State aid control already underpinned the Europe 2020 flagship policies in areas such as broadband guidelines supporting the achievement of the objectives of "Digital agenda for Europe," policy on infrastructure aid assisting the achievement of smart, upgraded and fully interconnected transport and energy networks as foreseen by "Resource efficient Europe" and the framework for State aid to research, development and innovation facilitating the achievement of "Innovation Union" as well as "An industrial policy for the globalisation era" objectives. It also pointed out that the Europe 2020 growth Strategy recognised the role of State aid for growth and its capacity "to actively and positively contribute to the Europe 2020 objectives by prompting and supporting initiatives for more innovative, efficient and greener technologies, while facilitating access to public support for investment, risk capital and funding for research and development"[1208] and noted that:

> Policies to achieve the Europe 2020 objectives can make an important contribution to ending the crisis and re-igniting sustainable growth. Member States and the Union will prioritise budgetary outlays to that effect, some of which will contain State aid... [and that] Modernised State aid control should facilitate the treatment of aid which is well-designed, targeted at identified market failures and objectives of common interest, and least distortive ("good aid"). This shall ensure that public support stimulates innovation, green technologies, human capital development, avoids environmental harm and ultimately promotes growth, employment and EU competitiveness.[1209]

1206. P. Holmes & A. Smith: "*Automobile Industry*" in P. Buigues, A. Jacquemin & A. Sapir (eds): "European Policies on Competition, Trade and Industry – Conflict and Complementaries," Aldershot, Edward Elgar.
1207. European Commission: *EU State Aid Modernisation (SAM)*, COM/2012/0209 final of 8 May 2012 at para. 8.
1208. *Ibid.*, para. 10 referring to European Commission: Communication "*Europe 2020 – a strategy for smart, sustainable and inclusive growth,*" COM (2010) 2020 final of 3 March 2010, p. 20.
1209. *Ibid.*, paras 11 and 12.

It is also worth noting that the authority of the Commission in regard to State aid regulation was incrementally strengthened on the run-up to each EU Enlargement by the Commission's elaboration of policies to reorient or strengthen State aid control in response to the fears of existing Member States that their industrial policies could be undermined by new countries unimpeded by disciplines on their government supports to undertakings. Thus, the compliance requirements of new Member States in regard to the State aid rules became stricter with every phase of EU Enlargement. Furthermore, the constant redefinition of the core political logic of the State aid regime (the process of "redefining the narrative" discussed further in the next section) has allowed the Commission the greatest flexibility to apply the rules and to orient them into a changing policy context or direction. From this process something closely resembling a common industrial policy emerged even before the GBER initiatives began in 2008. However, this remained a "framework" industrial policy of action coordinated at EU level, which still left certain aspects fully under the sovereign control of the EU Member States. Since then fewer and fewer areas of industrial policy would remain fully or largely under national competence[1210] as this trend to coordinate progressed and where, using the State aid rules, the test was no longer one of formal legality but of formal legality coupled with the requirement to prove economic need and the absence of other non-State aid options to address industrial policy problems.[1211] Thus, while the framework viewpoint is more consistent with Article 173 of the TFEU, the ever-strengthened frame was progressively also taking over the picture; and with it the sovereignty and freedom of action of national industrial policies.

Viewed from this perspective, the GBER initiatives simply furthered a process that had already advanced significantly. Moreover, as recently as September 2017, the Commission launched its new Industrial policy strategy: "Investing in a smart, innovative and sustainable Industry"[1212] which notes that:

> Improving framework conditions for investment, including regulatory predictability, fair competition and the rule of law, must also remain a key theme of the Commission's work with Member States on reforms ...as part of the third pillar of the Investment Plan for Europe. Greater efforts should be undertaken by national and regional authorities with fiscal space to support quality investment and close the investment gap accumulated since the crisis... EU and Member States' funds should be deployed as incentives to create added value in the economy without jeopardising the development of a vibrant private market for project financing. The Union ensures that State aid properly incentivises firms to invest in Research & Development... and other competitiveness-enhancing measures, and that selected companies are not given economic advantages which negatively affect competition and trade between Member States.

1210. The most obvious policy subarea of remaining primary sovereignty was SME development.
1211. This was a core effect of the new economic approach which emerged from the State Aid Action Plan (*see* Chapter 5 *supra*).
1212. European Commission: Communication from the Commission – *"Investing in a smart, innovative and sustainable Industry – A renewed EU Industrial Policy Strategy,"* COM (2017) 479 final of 13 September 2017.

7.2.3 The Erosion of the Sovereignty of National Direct Taxation and the EU State Aid Control Regime

The consolidation of Commission power and the rewriting of the policy narrative in a State aid control setting have been most obvious in regard to tax measures involving State aid considerations. While various aspects of fiscal aid measures and important cases have been examined earlier, the manner in which the State aid rules have emerged as a back-door instrument of direct tax harmonisation deserves close examination.

The importance of the policy narrative and the emergence of a dominant or asymmetrical narrative is described by *Roe* in the following terms:

> It is only by watching who ends up 'telling the better story' or 'making the better case'- that is, who ends up on the side of the scenario that actually underwrites and stabilises the decision making in the face of controversy - that we come to any kind of understanding as to who has more or less power in getting people to 'change their stories', when changing them matters for decision making. In such circumstances, asymmetrical narratives do not reflect or mediate power relations: rather, they instantiate them. It isn't that what is 'behind' narratives are the power relations that form them as much as what is 'in front of' us is power in the form of winning and losing narratives. When all else remains uncertain in a controversy, our knowledge of asymmetrical narratives is our knowledge of power.[1213]

Radaelli (1998)[1214] examines policy change and the creation of an advocacy coalition in regard to EU policy on direct taxation in the period leading up to the adoption of the EU Code of Conduct on Harmful Tax Competition in 1997.[1215] Against the background of political deadlock on advancing harmonisation in regard to direct taxation because of Treaty requirements on unanimity, this analysis shows how the European Commission effectively reshaped the preferences of EU Member States by providing conceptual innovation, exploiting the short-term horizon of national policy makers in conditions of uncertainty, complexity and polarisation and by engaging in reasoned persuasion. In short, it is a study on how an EU viewpoint on the apparent damage to national employment policies, national tax regimes and the smooth functioning of the EU single market of a range of allegedly harmful direct tax measures replaced the failed approach (which had limited political backing) that direct tax harmonisation was needed to facilitate international companies operating in the EU Single Market. In so doing, moreover, the European Commission positioned itself at the centre of the then required coordinated response. Thus, EU Commissioner Mario Monti, in an attempt to regain momentum in regard to direct taxation, presented a reflection document to the informal ECOFIN meeting in Verona on 13 April 1996 during the Italian Presidency of

1213. E. Roe: "*Narrative Policy Analysis*," Duke University Press, Durham, 1994.
1214. C.M. Radaelli, "*Policy Narratives in the European Union – The Case of Harmful Tax Competition*" European University Institute, Working Paper RSC No 98/34 accessible at https://www.eui.eu/DepartmentsAndCentres/RobertSchumanCentre/Publications/WorkingPapers/9834t.
1215. Council of the European Union: Conclusions of the ECOFIN Council Meeting on 1 December 1997 concerning taxation policy ("*Code of Conduct on Business Taxation*"), OJ C 98/2 of 6 January 1998.

the EU. This paper[1216] argued that "in the past too often discussions were confined to taxation proposals seen in isolation, thus limiting proper consideration of wider tax issues and of the framing of taxation policy within the wider context of EU policies." As a result, Radaelli argues that:

> An important political consequence has been ...a more cooperative attitude of member states toward tax coordination, culminated with the adoption of a code of conduct and precise commitments on tax-related state aid rules and capital income taxation... By re-presenting itself not as a component of an advocacy coalition, but as a forum for inter-governmental deliberation, the Commission has curbed adversarial politics and created the pre-conditions for problem-solving politics.[1217]

This analysis recognises that the European Commission was previously agnostic as to tax competition per se but, to regain direct taxation momentum, it was necessary to reach agreement that many tax measures were unfair on, or harmful to, other countries to the degree that they could:

- Be penalised in terms of significant erosion of the tax base.
- See capital income taxes spiral down to zero and corporations move profits to special tax regimes, leaving governments with the sole option of asking for more revenue from low skilled labour.
- Over time damage redistributive policies and bring the whole mechanism of the welfare state to a halt.

Moreover, without raising political efforts in regard to tax coordination to a maximum, the argument was that the ambitions for EU coordinated action in the fight against unemployment would be impossible:

> In the old strategy of tax neutrality, European direct taxation was a policy in search of a 'drive'. At that time, the single market was chosen as the drive that - according to the Commission - could have assisted the launch of EU tax coordination. With the narrative of harmful tax competition, instead, EU tax policy becomes itself an important drive to the rescue of the welfare state and employment.[1218]

This progression is consistent with a degree of unease on the part of many analysts as regards the role of the European Commission in the entirety of the EU Legal Order. As *Middlemas* notes:

> The Commission's aim, in the simplest terms, is to confound Engel's view of history that the product of many separate wills is something that no one willed... It must search for the elements of a general will and define it where it does not already exist, and lead mutually antagonistic players to accept commonality in

1216. European Commission: "*Taxation in the European Union,*" SEC(96) 487 final of 20 March 1996.
1217. *Supra*, p. 6.
1218. *Ibid.*, p. 7.

> Community aims and ideals, on the assumption that its members continue to accept the Treaties as the best available means of achieving what they want.[1219]

The Code of Conduct left it to a high level political Group (the Primarolo Group), supported by the Commission, to examine nearly 300 potentially harmful tax measures and eventually 66 of these were listed as harmful.[1220] However, this Group's Report and its 66 apparently harmful tax measures were not agreed by all EU Member States.[1221] At this point, the importance of the cross-linkage to the State aid rules in the Code of Conduct became clear and the State aid rules were quickly used to subsequently and progressively attack the majority of the 66 allegedly harmful tax measures. This fulfilled the hard law dimension of the otherwise non-binding Code.

Moreover, the European Court of Justice has largely supported this line of Commission action against allegedly harmful tax measures via the State aid rules by focussing on the free movement principles in the TFEU and by accepting very flexible interpretations of the selectivity of such measures. Accordingly, certain commentators not only see the application of the State aid rules by the Commission as the new force in achieving progress regarding harmonisation in direct taxation without political unanimity but also point to the Court of Justice itself as the author of gradual tax harmonisation without political consent.[1222] This is also consistent with the view of *Lavdas and Mendrinou*[1223] that an unresolved political dispute can readily be transformed in the EU system into a legal question and that:

> The Commission has taken very seriously the possibility that its enforcement strategies may benefit from reinvigoration or clarification through the Court's case-law, especially with cases suited to the Commission's evolving policy agenda.[1224]

Several commentators have noted that State aid law has become an all-purpose tool to camouflage policy-making. Its application is not limited to certain sectors nor to

---

1219. *Supra*, p. 213. Church and Phinnemore describe the Commission as a somewhat shadowy body despite its clear importance – "What it is there for is not wholly clear ...but, incontrovertibly, it matters both because of its specific roles and because it has become the workhorse of the EU. This reminds us that the Commission cannot be just an executive, let alone a civil service. It is a politico-administrative body which crosses the normal boundaries of the separation of powers, straying into the legislative and the judicial as well as the executive (and) its nature and its on-going governance and management reforms ensure that it will remain controversial." C.H. Church and D. Phinnemore: "Guide to the European Treaties – from Rome to Maastricht, Amsterdam, Nice and Beyond," 2002, Penguin, London, p. 398.
1220. Primarolo Report, *supra*.
1221. The Conclusions of the ECOFIN Council Meeting on 9 March 1998 point out that the Report can reflect either the unanimous opinion of the members of the group or the various opinions, not necessarily unanimous, expressed in the course of the group's discussions. *See also* C.M. Radaelli: "*The Code of Conduct Against Harmful Tax Competition – Open Method of Coordination in Disguise*," European University Institute, EUI Working Papers, 2002, RSC No 2002/43.
1222. *See* for example: J. Keuchel & A. Schrinner: "*Gradual Harmonisation of Tax Law by the European Court of Justice*," Linklaters, Oppenhoff and Radler in "Legal500.com," June 2001.
1223. *Supra*, pp. 142–144.
1224. *Supra*, p. 143.

harmonised or non-harmonised areas. This view emphasises that State aid law has evolved to a regulatory and policy-making tool rather than a mere monitoring and law enforcement tool preventing isolated distortive State aid measures granted by Member States. While the Commission is generally keen to deny any wider policy-making and regulatory intent or objective, wider policy-making and regulation by virtue of State aid law is an undeniable fact experienced, at least, by EU Member State's governments. At present, and in particular, non-harmonised taxation is seen to have evolved into a laboratory of State aid policy-making and regulation.[1225]

Taken together, it is clear that EU competences in regard to industrial policy and direct taxation have been progressively expanded via a comprehensive range of informal bargains to rewrite the narrative in important areas of Member State relations. This process has benefited from the absence of a State aid definition together with the practice, since the 1970s, of reorienting the political objectives of State aid control and has used the State aid rules (and other policy instruments) to effectively expand the provisions of the Treaty or to bypass its constraints. In the absence of express political consent, these developments in the last two decades represent a considerable intrusion on the sovereignty of EU Member States in regard to industrial and taxation policy and, accordingly, can be construed as anathema to the principle of subsidiarity in EU Law, the intentions of the drafters of the TFEU and its predecessors and the express terms of the Treaty itself. While EU Member States (or on occasion some of them) have been to some degree complicit in these developments, it would appear that this back-door incrementalism has been used instead of the proper political recourse to amending the Treaty to achieve this degree of new policy and political momentum.

7.2.4 Political Factors in Decision-Making

For many years, the operation of the EU State aid regime was perceived in very political terms. Indeed, this was probably true in the period up to the 1980s when the application of the EU regime was more exceptional than commonplace. The founding Member States in that early period seem to have operated on the premise that if one State complained about another then the supports of the former would be likely to be counter-attacked later. Moreover, this "prisoners dilemma" situation was clearly added to as individual countries followed the lead of others in regard to the type of supports they offered to undertakings allowing them, under national sovereignty, to correct the effects of subsidy competition between states. Matters changed, however, when new Member States joined and when the recessions of the 1970s, the 1980s and the more recent international financial crisis put increased pressure on the ability of national policies to respond to crises and when the fear of migration of industry to low wage underdeveloped Member States emerged for the first time as a political consideration.

When the application of the EU State aid regime started to take serious effect (approximately from the late 1970s), the absence of detailed substantive and

1225. C. Koenig, "*Where is State Aid Law Heading to?*" European State Aid Law Quarterly, 4/2014, p. 611.

procedural rules facilitated "back-room" negotiations related to State aid notifications. Moreover, as the system lacked much real transparency until the mid-1990s, the scope for political fixing in State aid cases was considerable, whether or not perceptions to that effect were predominantly correct.

This changed considerably when, from the mid-1980s, the application of the State aid rules became a Commission priority in the run-up to the completion of the EU Single Market by 1992[1226] and under Competition Commissioners Peter Sutherland (1985–1989) and Sir Leon Brittan (1989–1993) an actual State aid policy gradually took shape. However, as already seen, the legal development to support State aid policy was hampered by political fears that the Council of Ministers would actually dilute rather than reinforce the Treaty orientations in regard to government supports. The challenge here was met by two developments which succeeded in largely bypassing the need for political consensus to elaborate legislation in support of a toughening policy regarding State aid. The first factor was the supportive development of case law by the European Courts which largely allowed the concept of aid to be expanded and the Court of Justice, rather than the Council of Ministers, to progressively write the rules of procedure. As *Cini* notes, the "Commission-Court relationship ... replaced the more conventional inter-institutional policy-making triangle involving the Commission, the Parliament and the Council in this policy area."[1227] The second factor was the alternative development by the Commission of soft law measures which eventually emerged as having binding effect. On the importance of this, *Rawlinson* pointed out that:

> Experience has shown that aid levels tend to rise if there are no hard and fast rules but only a vaguely formulated policy... The Commission needs rules to discipline itself. Rules are the best safeguard against political decisions which, if they were to proliferate, would destroy all state aid control.[1228]

The political sensitivity of these developments cannot be underestimated as State aid policy is perhaps the most politicised of EU regulatory policies because Commission decisions can intrude, sometimes very dramatically, to prevent Member States from applying aspects of their national industrial policies:

> This is after all an area which pits the Commission directly against the Member States, with governmental authorities rather than firms the targets of Commission regulation. While EU governments in principle agree that a state aid regime is necessary....this does not stop them contesting both Commission policy and Commission decisions in individual cases of aid, particularly when national or governmental interests are perceived to be at stake. This point is crucial as it

1226. A. Petersen: "*State Aid and European Union – State Aid in the Light of Trade, Competition, Industrial and Cohesion Policies*" in I. Harden (ed.): "*State Aid – Community Law and policy,*" Cologne, Bundesanzeiger, 1993.
1227. M. Cini, "*From Soft Law to Hard Law? – Discretion and Rule-making in the Commission's State Aid Regime*" (2000), European University Institute, EUI Working Papers, RSC No 2000/35, p. 8.
1228. F. Rawlinson: "*The Role for Policy Frameworks, Codes and Guidelines in the Control of State Aid*" in I. Harden (ed.): "*State Aid – Community Law and Policy,*" Cologne, Bundesanzeiger, 1993, p. 58.

demonstrates the fine line that the state aid officials tread when vigorously enforcing a policy which is both central to the single market objective and highly politically sensitive.[1229]

The Commission has very wide discretion in the handling of State aid cases, especially when they are notified under Article 108(3) of the TFEU. In the first instance, the Commission officials must ascertain whether there is State aid involved and, if there is, whether the Commission should indicate doubts as to the eventual compatibility of the aid with the exemption criteria of Article 107(3). While the experience and professionalism of Commission officials is brought to this exercise, there is very little transparency in this process vis-à-vis any third party interests as the Commission dialogues largely with the notifying Member State. Moreover, at this initial stage, political lobbying and dialogue remains very important, as most Member States realise that a positive decision without conditions is rarely the result of the commencement of the formal procedure. In practice, this can lead to the amendment of the substance of a support measure (to make it not State aid or to eliminate possible compatibility concerns) or to the withdrawal of the notification.

When a formal procedure commences, the final decision may involve wider third party inputs (if they are contributed), and the scope for political lobbying in formal procedure cases is confined to more controversial and singular cases. In regard to the latter, Member States will lobby the Commission through their national Commissioner,[1230] and there is still scope for some politicking on this basis. At the same time, the increased elaboration of soft law rules since the 1990s and more recent Regulations have reduced what *Petersen* described in regard to controversial cases as a process akin to Council decision-making with "bargaining, log-rolling and consensus building part-and-parcel of the Commission's decision-taking process."[1231]

The process of depoliticisation by rule-making was given a particular boost under Competition Commissioner Van Miert (1993–1996) via the adoption of the Council's Procedural Regulation to largely codify the State aid procedural law of the European Courts (in exchange for a 10-year limit on recovery orders) and the Council's Enabling Regulation which created the missing legal basis for much of the Commission's soft law measures (and for Member States created the basis for eventual State aid block exemptions from the requirement to pre-notify aid measures).

Clearly, it has increasingly emerged as in the interests of the Commission to reduce the extent of political lobbying and interference in its State aid decision-making. While important successes in that regard have been achieved, it would be wrong to suggest that the EU State aid control regime has been fully depoliticised. State aid decisions by the European Commission remain politically sensitive vis-à-vis the EU Member States (whether as aid notifiers or as competitors for industrial locations,

1229. M. Cini, *supra*, p. 9.
1230. At the present time every EU Member State nominates one member of the European Commission.
1231. J. Petersen, "*Decision Making in the European Union – Towards a Framework for Analysis*" (1995), 2 Journal of European Public Policy, pp. 69–93.

foreign investments, etc.) and the reduction of scope for political lobbying has not reduced mutual suspicions nor has it fully foreclosed all scope for political action in the process.

7.3 THE EVOLUTION OF LEGAL RULES

The EU State aid system has at least tried to address a range of legal issues that have arisen over the years. These mainly concern legal certainty and definitional clarity, uniform application, effectiveness of control, enforcement practice and deterrent effect.

7.3.1 Legal Certainty and Definitional Clarity

According to *Raitio*, the definition and scope of application of legal certainty is controversial and it is easily mixed up with the concept of "rule of law":

> The avoidance of arbitrariness has traditionally been regarded as a basic norm for the judge. The formal aspect of legal certainty refers to the requirement of eliminating randomness from the legal decision-making activity, which intertwines with the concept of predictability. .. The reliance on formal legal certainty, principle of legality and rule of law are often related to an attempt to safeguard overriding public interests. The substantive aspect of legal certainty requires in turn that the solutions of the judicial decision-making must also be substantially right, which can be called the demand of acceptability. .. However, the principle of legal certainty has often been used in a formal sense implying the idea of the predictability of legal decisions. .. As an underlying principle of law legal certainty cannot be formulated in a specific way, because the circumstances to which it is supposed to be applied are difficult to determine...Principles are often intertwined and suitable for 'weighing up and balancing', which in turn implies that principles do not necessarily have any specific scope of application. However, one can determine the typical situations in which legal certainty has been applied in practice.[1232]

In particular, Raitio points out that the principle of legal certainty focuses on the non-retroactivity of law and the protection of legitimate expectations.[1233] Non-retroactivity covers the non-application of a legislative measure to the effects in the future of a situation which has arisen either without law or under a former law or to a situation which is fully completed. The issue of retroactivity also arises where, for example, the date of entry into force of legislation precedes the date of publication. In regard to the protection of legitimate expectations, this involves a minimum requirement that an individual must be able to point either to a transaction which has been entered into between the individual and the authorities, or to a course of conduct or a "specific assurance" on the part of the relevant authorities. Moreover, it is clear that the

1232. J. Raitio: "*Legal Certainty*," IVR – *Encyclopaedia of Jurisprudence, Legal Theory and Philosophy of Law*, http://www.ivr-enc.info/en/article. J. Raitio is also the author of "*The Principle of Legal Certainty in EC Law*," Kluwer Academic Publishers, 2003.
1233. *Ibid.*

principle of legal certainty applies to legislation, its execution and to judicial decision-making concerning its implementation. Nonetheless, Raitio takes the view that the principle of legal certainty cannot be expressed by definitions alone, because it is an underlying general principle of law. As well as relating to the principle of non-retroactivity and the protection of legitimate expectations, it can and should also be related to the conceptual scale for weighing up and balancing between predictability and acceptability, between formal justice and material fairness:

> The idea of legal certainty as a scale from predictability to acceptability is not merely a question of legal theory, but it is also a question of legal politics.

Peczenik[1234] has listed a range of requirements for legal certainty in decision-making. These include the principle of legality (the legal decisions must be based on law); the view that legal texts must be clear and precise, the principle of objectivity (similar cases must be treated and decided in a similar way); the prohibition of arbitrariness in judicial decision-making; the idea that decisions must be given in reasonable time and the principle of openness in decision-making.

If legal certainty was a pure concept and standard, there would be limited scope for judicial disputes. Thus, taken together, these theoretical perspectives point out correctly that pure legal certainty is impossible and that the principle is a relative one creating a flexible standard that can be applied using indicators or a range of qualitative assessments.

In the State aid context, the fundamental legal certainty of State aid law, using the above indicators from *Peczenik,* cannot be questioned, and it has substantially improved in recent years. However, it is clear that the predictability of State aid decisions remains a difficult issue and that this is linked to the absence of a definition, the density of the case law of the European Commission and the European Courts and the extent and growing complexity of secondary regulations and soft law measures in the State aids field. Specific issues arise as regards the absence of a State aid definition, the European Commission's review of existing aids and the security of undertakings vis-à-vis the recovery of illegal State aid.

7.3.2 Legal Certainty and the Absence of a State Aid Definition

It is clear from the earlier examination of Article 107(1) of the TFEU that the scope of the basic prohibition on State aid, on which the system of EU control is based, is paradoxically both narrow and flexible. The development of the provision in jurisprudence and Commission practice shows that it is a "living instrument" of European law. Accordingly, there is a clear need to maximise legal certainty in regard to the central concept of "aid" in the Treaty or "State aid" as it is more conventionally called. This need is shared by the Commission as regulator, the Member States as parties to uncertain Treaty rules and the final beneficiaries of a vast amount of money being

1234. A. Peczenik, Alexander: "*What is Right? On Democracy, Legal Safety, Ethics and Legal Argumentation,*" (Vad är rätt? Om demokrati, rättssäkerhet, etik och juridisk argumentation) Stockholm, Fritze, 1995, p. 89.

passed to them under literally thousands of schemes and operations in 28 EU Member States and further afield that they could, in a worst case, be obliged to repay.

This issue has been recognised by the Commission's 2016 Notice on the Notion of Aid[1235] which does provide some much needed guidance – but this is not absolute, it is not unarguable, and it remains subject to any further conceptual changes that can happen at any time from new Commission decisions, Court judgments or specific interpretations of those judgments by the Commission.

The tests developed to determine whether "State aid" falls within the prohibition generally fail to provide a sufficient degree of predictability for Member States, aid recipients or competitors thereby exacerbating the legal uncertainty created by the absence of a definition of "aid." First, the market investor principle was developed from economic science as a generalised methodology to establish advantage above and beyond payments at market rates or beyond a direct State response to the market failures of classical economics. While some guidance can be derived from such a principle, it is to be observed that economic science generally provides a basis for the multifaceted analysis of situations rather than a prescriptive solution. Concentration on the market investor principle may thus increase debate on the presence or absence of advantage causing the essence of the condition to become impenetrable and Commission discretion to be absolute. The unpredictability and uncertainty surrounding the advantage test is exacerbated further by the fact that the market investor principle is not used consistently in all cases of State aid assessment by the Commission and that no precise legal tests on the acceptability of market failure arguments to justify State aids have been developed.

Second, the specificity test is also problematic in so far as the distinction between a general measure and specific aid remains unresolved. While greater policy clarity on this distinction has emerged in recent years, the use of the "nature or general scheme of the system" as a dynamic criterion continues to fail to provide adequate certainty or clarity to Member States in regard to tax issues in particular.

Third, while the effect on trade test is a clear-cut one, the test of distortion of competition remains somewhat unclear because of an unresolved debate as to whether or not a per se approach is to be applied. Moreover, after 60 years, it is not obvious whether the distortion of competition being addressed is either between competing firms or the competing policies of EU Member States. At the same time, increased reasoning requirements on the European Commission have undoubtedly improved the focus of the distortion test where it is applied and this assists the coherence of State aid policy with other aspects of competition policy under the Treaty.

Fourth, the continuing indirect assessment of distortion of competition without consistent reference to the "relevant market" on which such distortion may arise is serious source of concern to economists and practitioners and to those wishing to see State aid control develop fully and consistently as a branch of competition policy at EU level. While there have been strong efforts since 2005 to focus more on economic tests

1235. European Commission: *Notice on the notion of State aid pursuant to Article 107(1) TFEU*, 19, May 2016, *supra*.

under the refined economic approach, it is equally arguable, especially from a non-economist perspective, that this type of reform in fact impedes legal certainty further by adding complexity.

Finally, the relatively recent introduction of requirements on notifying Member States to prove the need for and anticipated future effects of proposed State aids is an innovation akin to the removal of the right to silence or the presumption of innocence in State aid cases. This was introduced to address the fact that the Commission always considered that Member States had more information on proposed State aids than they were willing to disclose[1236] or alternatively to reduce the risk (based on public choice economic theory) of third party market distortions resulting from the rent-seeking behaviour of powerful economic actors.[1237]

7.3.3 The European Commission's Review of Existing Aids and Legal Certainty

The European Commission has the power and the duty under Article 108 of the TFEU and under the Procedural Regulation to keep existing aid under constant review and, where it considers it necessary, to propose appropriate measures to Member States required by the progressive development and functioning of the internal market. One important effect of this is that there can be cases where something formally decided *not* to fall within the scope of Article 107(1) may do so by a reoriented Commission policy applied via a review of existing aid. This practice was first used in the Irish Corporation Tax Decision finalised in 1996.[1238] In that case, a 1979 assurance by the Commission that a single 10% corporation tax applicable to all manufacturing undertakings in Ireland did not constitute State aid was reversed on the basis that, due to the increasing convergence between the manufacturing and services sectors, a State aid advantage arose by the mid-1990s for Irish manufacturers vis-à-vis Irish services undertakings which were taxed at a rate of 38% on profits. Notwithstanding any flexible interpretation of Article 108, it seems bizarre that a *non-State aid* could be reviewed as an *existing State aid*. In this Decision, the Commission was careful to respect legitimate expectations, but it was quick, in turn, to include this strange interpretation in the Procedural Regulation in 1999 to confirm its right to embark on a similar course in the future.[1239] On the other hand, the Treaty rules and case law have made clear that

1236. On this, *see*, for example, A. Houtman: "*EC State Aid Control: In search of the Right Balance*" in Ehlermann and Everson (eds): "*European Competition Law Annual 1999 – Selected Issues in the Field of State Aids*," Oxford, 2001, p. 92.

1237. R. Behboodi, *supra*, p. 33 et seq. and WTO World Trade Report, 2006, *supra*, pp. 63–64.

1238. European Commission: Decision No 98/C 395/08 of 22 July 1998 – *International Financial Services Centre (IFSC) and Shannon Customs Free Airport Zone (SCAZ) – Irish Corporation Tax (ICT)*, OJ C 395 of 18 December 1998.

1239. Council Regulation No 659/1999/EC of 22 March 1999 laying down detailed rules for the application of Article 93 of the EC Treaty (now Article 108 of the Treaty on the Functioning of the European Union), OJ L 83 of 27 March 1999, at Article 1(b)(v) and continued in Article 1(b)(v) of the current Council Regulation No 1589/2015/EU of 13 July 2015 laying down detailed rules for the application of Article 108 of the Treaty on the Functioning of the European Union, OJ L 248 of 24 September 2015.

the qualification of an aid as "existing aid" provides legal certainty both to the Member State granting the aid and to the beneficiary of the aid, in so far as, even if reviewed by the Commission and found to be incompatible with the internal market, any Commission decision thereafter will have only future effect and therefore existing aid cannot be subject to a recovery order.

Nonetheless, the view here is that any power of the Commission to intervene via the State aid rules of the TFEU in a non-State aid is a serious infringement of legal certainty and legality, regardless of whether or not this is endorsed by the Council, the Court or by the apparent imperatives of the progressive development and functioning of the internal market. At its simplest, the very large number of government measures that have never given rise to State aid issues, or which were deemed to not constitute State aid, remain open to a politically based challenge which has a high degree of arbitrariness. Legal certainty in this situation is low as regards the sovereignty of Member States and is only relieved by the limitation on recovery in these situations to preserve the legitimate expectations of beneficiary undertakings.

The overuse of discretion to the detriment of legal certainty also arises in regard to a number of other areas notably the issue of *de minimis* measures (if they are too small to materially affect competition or trade, then they should be fully and de jure excluded from the State aid regime and not merely deemed not to meet the criteria of Article 107 – subject to conditions and different levels in different sectors) and some conceptual issues regarding the locus of State aids in Member State resources, particularly as regards EU Structural Funds and similar funds applied by Member States.

7.3.4 Legal Certainty and the Security of Undertakings vis-à-vis the Recovery of Illegal State Aid

While beneficiary undertakings are protected against recovery vis-à-vis any existing aid review by the European Commission, the legal security of undertakings in regard to aid recovery in cases of illegal aid or misused aid is very limited. This begins with the duty of care on business undertakings requiring them to know that they have received State aid and that it is, in fact, compatible with the TFEU requirements.[1240] Second, business firms have limited protection against recovery decisions as the only, and limited defences, available to Member States are the impossibility of executing recovery (e.g., the beneficiary is bankrupt and assets cannot be recovered) or the protection of legitimate expectations (which cannot exclude the duty of care on the part of the recipient of State aid noted above).

Nonetheless, reforms since 1999 have limited the exposure of firms to recovery decisions to a period of 10 years[1241] and recent Commission Regulations and soft law

1240. Case C-5/89: *Germany v. Commission (BUG-Alutechnik)*, [1990] I ECR 3453 at 3457.
1241. First introduced in Article 15 of Council Regulation No 659/1999/EC of 22 March 1999 laying down detailed rules for the application of Article 93 of the EC Treaty (now Article 108 of the Treaty on the Functioning of the European Union), OJ L 83 of 27 March 1999 and retained in

measures,[1242] together with the very new *State Aid Transparency Public Search* facility of the European Commission,[1243] have increased the transparency requirements on Member States in regard to the disclosure of State aid facts to beneficiary undertakings. Taken together, these improvements increase the legal security of beneficiary undertakings. Nonetheless, it still does not seem to be common practice for most firms to check their tax incentives or public grants vis-à-vis EU State aid controls and the introduction of increased transparency in this way may increase the exposure of recipient undertakings to litigation from competitors before national courts.[1244]

7.3.5 The Promotion of Legal Certainty via State Aid Reforms

The Commission's 2005 State Aid Action Plan recognised, at least to some degree, that legal certainty needed to be improved. In regard to the new challenges facing EU State aid policy, the Action Plan notes that:

> the increasing complexity and number of documents progressively adopted by the Commission over time have created a need to streamline state aid policy, focus attention on the most distortive types of aid and make state aid control more

the current Council Regulation No 1589/2015/EU of 13 July 2015 laying down detailed rules for the application of Article 108 of the Treaty on the Functioning of the European Union, OJ L 248 of 24 September 2015 at Article 17.

1242. For example: European Commission: Regulation No 651/2014/EU of 17 June 2014 declaring certain categories of aid compatible with the internal market in application of Articles 107 and 108 of the Treaty, OJ L 187 of 26 June 2014, Article 5; Commission Regulation No 1407/2013/EC of 18 December 2013 on the application of Articles 107 and 108 of the Treaty on the Functioning of the European Union to *de minimis* aid, OJ L 352 of 24 December 2013 at Article 6 and European Commission: Guidelines on Regional State aid for 2014–2020, OJ C 209 of 23 July 2013 at para. 141.

1243. European Commission: *State Aid Transparency Public Search* at: https://webgate.ec.europa.eu/competition/transparency/public?lang=en.

1244. The involvement of national courts in State aid control has been a policy objective since 1995 (*Commission Notice on cooperation between national courts and the Commission in the State Aid field*, OJ C 312 of 23 November 1995). Under these arrangements, and the background European Court jurisprudence, the role of national courts is twofold – the national court must ensure that aid measures are not introduced without an approval by the Commission and that approved State aid is properly applied in line with positive or conditional decisions. In the "Study on the Enforcement of State Aid Law at National Level," March 2006, Jones Day, Lovells, Allen & Overy, it is noted that there has been a sharp increase in the number of State aid related cases brought before national courts – "National judges take seriously their responsibilities in the State aid arena, and are increasingly willing to take a firm stand against illegal aid and to protect individual businesses against violations of the EU rules. Regrettably, however, the powers of national courts are still not being used to the full. Companies are often hesitant to launch proceedings at national level to put an end to the illegal granting of aid to their competitors, or to assert their rights to claim compensation. In some cases, national courts themselves seem uncertain about the powers that they have in the State aid arena, and the locus standi of competitors." (p. 3) In its most recent Notice (European Commission notice on the enforcement of State aid law by national courts, OJ C 85 of 9 April 2009), largely prepared to update the Notice on case references and newer legislation, the Commission notes that: "genuine private enforcement before national courts has played a relatively limited role in State aid to date" (Recital 5).

> predictable and user-friendly, thereby minimising legal uncertainty and the administrative burden both for the Commission and for Member States.[1245]

It also recognised the need to specifically adopt new guidelines regarding the conditions when public service compensations which constitute State aid are compatible with the Treaty in order to increase legal certainty.[1246]

One year later, the Commission was more defensive, rejecting any suggestion that there was a legal certainty problem generally in the system:

> I don't think it is true that there is a poor legal certainty in the field of State aid. First of all, the Commission makes guidelines, frameworks, notices etc. to explain how it interprets the notion and the compatibility of "State aid" under the EC Treaty. Second, Member States are well aware that they cannot grant any State aid unless the aid has been authorised by the Commission. It may be authorised under a scheme or as an individual notification. The aid can also fall under a block exemption regulation allowing Member State to grant the aid without notifying it to the Commission. In my view there is legal certainty if Member States respect the principles to only grant aid in accordance with an authorised scheme, individual notification or a scheme which is clearly covered by an exemption regulation.[1247]

Notwithstanding this degree of optimism, the extent of concern on legal certainty was very evident from a range of the comments received on the Draft State Aid Action Plan. The UK government comments, for example, raised three significant issues of legal certainty.[1248] First, in regard to R&D State aid, the UK pointed out the need for a relaxed approach to most university R&D activity in order to provide "more clarity and legal certainty on where the universities stand." The suggestion here was that the Commission should clearly state that most such activities be block exempted to the extent that they might involve State aid at the level of the University, bearing in mind, in particular, that risks of distortion of competition at the level of the university are very low and the benefits for European economic competitiveness are substantial.[1249] Second, the UK argued that a way must be found for more potential State aid cases to be taken outside the notification obligation, where the risk of serious distortion of competition is low – "This would allow increased legal certainty for those cases currently not notified at all and, if done properly, a greater likelihood that genuinely distortive aid would come to the Commission's attention." On this, the core suggestion was to extend the scope of Block Exemptions.[1250] Third, in a very distinct reaction

1245. State Aid Action Plan, *supra*, at para. 17.
1246. As noted earlier, this was done via a range of measures from 2005 related to the Altmark ruling.
1247. In Revue des Droits de la Concurrence: "*Delivering the State aid Reform – Interview with Lowri Evans, Deputy Director General for State Aid, European Commission,*" Institut de droit de la concurrence, No 3-2006 pp. 7–9 accessible at https://www.concurrences.com/en/review/issues/No-4-2006/interview/lowri-evans-new-state-aid-deputy-director-general-delivering-the-state-aid-12589.
1248. UK Response to Commission Roadmap for State Aid Reform at: http://ec.europa.eu/competition/state_aid/reform/comments_environmental_protection_revision/wrap2.pdf.
1249. *Ibid.*, paras 18–22.
1250. *Ibid.*, para. 82.

against the suggestion in the Action Plan that the Commission might introduce a provisional recovery order in all detected cases of unnotified State aid, the UK stated that:

> The introduction of provisional recovery orders could lead to malicious complaints combined with legal uncertainties leading to administrative paralysis and a flood of new notifications to the Commission...Until the Commission can make the State aid rules far less intrusive and provide effective legal certainty, it should not lightly impose automatic provisional recovery for non-notified aid.[1251]

While most of these concerns were subsequently dealt with, the State Aid Modernisation initiative of 2012 again noted that:

> Over time, State aid rules have developed into a complex legal framework. There is scope to clarify and simplify the rules, enhance consistency and streamline the assessment process. There is a need to better explain State aid concepts and to consolidate our horizontal and substantive rules.[1252]

It is clear that the SAM initiative actively sought to address these matters, culminating in the extensive Commission Notice on the Notion of Aid produced in 2016. Nonetheless, the SAM initiative resulted in over 2,000 pages of State aid regulatory documents, a complex GBER Regulation that is not easy to navigate and updated instruments for the notification of non-GBER measures containing increasingly complex (and often legally uncertain) economic analytical and assessment concepts.[1253]

7.3.6 Whither Legal Certainty in the EU State Aid Regime?

As pure legal certainty is impossible and can only be approached using indicators or a range of qualitative assessments, views may objectively or subjectively differ as to the level of legal certainty to be achieved and the methods to be applied to improve legal certainty. The view here is that, as with the evolution of EU procedural rules, the time must come when further definitional clarity is provided by a codifying Regulation as regards what is and what is not State aid. After 60 years of control, hundreds of cases focused on the "notion of aid" and an EU inspired definition of subsidy in the WTO

1251. *Ibid.*, at para. 125.
1252. *Supra,* at para. 22.
1253. *See*, for example, European Commission: Communication from the Commission – Framework for State aid for research and development and innovation, OJ C 198 of 27 June 2014 which points out that "R&D&I aid may distort the dynamic incentives to invest of competitors of the aid beneficiary. When an undertaking receives aid, the likelihood of successful R&D&I activities on its part generally increases, leading to an increased presence on the relevant product market(s) in the future. That increased presence may lead competitors to reduce the scope of their original investment plans (crowding out effect). Furthermore, the presence of aid may make potential beneficiaries complacent or more risk seeking. The long term effect on the overall performance of the sector is in this case likely to be negative. R&D&I aid may therefore, if not correctly targeted, support inefficient undertakings and lead to market structures where many market players operate significantly below efficient scale." (paras 99 and 100).

SCMA, the Commission's persistent desire to retain flexibility with no definition of "aid" becomes less defensible and more of a problem than a solution.

Moreover, when a measure has been declared to not constitute aid within the meaning of Article 107(1) of the TFEU, there should be a total barrier on any reopening of this question. This would curb the expansionism of the Commission in the application of the State aid rules and, at the same time, allow Member States the right to develop such measures without future risk. Finally, a serious effort towards simplification remains elusive. To address the sheer complexity of case law, secondary regulation and soft law, it would be desirable for Member States to work with the Commission to elaborate a basis for a consolidated Regulation every 7 or 10 years on substantive and procedural law on the control of State aids and to aim for real simplification.

7.3.7 Uniform Application, Enforcement Practice and Deterrent Effect

An important test of the effectiveness of the State aid regime relates to the uniform application of the relevant legal norms. Indeed, in the legal order of the EU, the issue of uniform application of EU law dates back to the early days of the Treaties in the European Court of Justice's development of the doctrine of direct effect and the related principle of the supremacy of EU law which remains contentious. These principles were created by the Court precisely to ensure the uniform application of EU law.[1254] However, as *Kowalik-Bacczyk* points out,[1255] the principle of supremacy, or primacy of European Community law, is not expressly contained in any of the founding Treaties.[1256] However, according to the constant jurisprudence of European Court of Justice, the primacy of EU law applies to all national norms, including constitutional norms.[1257] Therefore, any conflict between a Community norm and a national norm that has the same scope of application should be resolved by the non-application of conflicting national law, otherwise the notion of unified application of European law would be endangered and the European Court of Justice consequently insists on this idea.

In this setting, the recovery of State aid poses a difficulty in regard to the uniform application of the EU State aid rules. In some Member States, for example, a recipient undertaking faced with a decision to repay illegal State aid has a range of appeal options under both administrative and civil law[1258] which may or may not result in

1254. Case C-26/62; *Van Gend En Loos,* [1963] ECR 3 and Case C-6/64: *Costa v. ENEL,* 1964.
1255. K. Kowalik-Bacczyk, *"Should We Polish up?, Polish Constitutional Tribunal and the Idea of the Supremacy of EU Law"* (1 October 2005), 6 German Law Journal, Issue 10.
1256. It would have been solved by the Treaty Establishing a Constitution for Europe, where it was defined in Article I-6.
1257. Case C-11/70: *Internazionale Handelsgesellschaft,* [1970] ECR 1125.
1258. J. Kühling & J.D. Braun: *"State Aid: The Effective Application of EC State Aid Procedures: From a Plan to Grant Aid to the Recovery of Illegal Aid – The Role of National Law and Practice in Germany,"* in P.F. Nemitz (ed.): *"The Effective Application of EU State Aid Procedures – The Role of National Law and Practice,"* Kluwer Law International, 2007.

effective recovery and which may delay effective recovery for many years. This was brought out clearly in the *Kvaerner case* in 2005.[1259]

State Aid Recovery in the Kvaerner case (2005)

In the Kvaerner case, the Commission found that State aid granted by Germany for the benefit of the Kvaerner Warnow Werft GmbH by a private law agreement was incompatible with the common market and ordered recovery. The beneficiary company (Kvaerner) refused to repay the aid. The competent German authority did not bring an action against Kvaerner for repayment of the aid before the civil courts but issued an administrative act ordering immediate repayment of the amount in question. This act was declared immediately enforceable (in line with the State aid Procedural Regulation of 1999, Article 14.3). Kvaerner brought an action against this immediate enforceability before the Verwaltungsgericht Berlin (Administrative Court of Berlin) and this court annulled the decision declaring the administrative act immediately enforceable; arguing that under German law any claim for reimbursement of aid must have a statutory basis which did not exist in this case.[1260] Furthermore, the court held that the use of an administrative procedure by the German authorities was unlawful, given that the aid was granted by a private law agreement. However, the Oberverwaltungsgericht Berlin-Brandenburg (Higher Administrative Court of Berlin-Brandenburg) set aside the decision of the Administrative Court of Berlin.[1261] The Higher Administrative Court of Berlin-Brandenburg argued that the competent authority was not bound to recover the aid in the same manner in which it was granted in the first place. It held that the effet utile of the Commission decision required that the competent authority be allowed to recover the aid by way of an administrative act. Thus, the German Court implied that Article 14(3) of the Procedural Regulation is not satisfied if a Member State – instead of issuing an administrative decision which is to be executed immediately – decides to seek a court decision in a civil law proceeding to obtain an enforceable order of a national court which then can be used to execute the Commission Decision.

In any event, the Commission's decision in the case was overturned by the General Court in 2009 on its substance, but without addressing the arguments advanced in regard to recovery.[1262]

The chronic problem with recovery as a matter of State aid enforcement was highlighted in the Commission's Recovery Notice of 2007,[1263] which indicated that there

1259. European Commission: Decision No 2005/374/EC of 20 October 2004 on a State aid measure implemented by Germany for Kvaerner Warnow Werft, OJ L 120/21 of 12 May 2005.
1260. *Verwaltungsgericht Berlin*, 15 August 2005, Case VG 20 A 135.5, EuZW 2005, pp. 659 et seq.
1261. *Oberverwaltungsgericht Berlin-Brandenburg*, 7 November 2005, Case 8 S 93/05, EuZW 2006, pp. 91 et seq.
1262. Case T-68/05: *Aker Warnow Werft GmbH and Kvaerner ASA v. Commission*, [2009] ECR II-00355.
1263. European Commission: *Notice from the Commission – Towards an effective implementation of Commission decisions ordering Member States to recover unlawful and incompatible State aid*, OJ C 272 of 15 November 2007, pp. 4–17, para. 3.

was practically not a single case where recovery was completed within the deadline set out in the recovery decision. While the Notice set out to improve and speed-up the execution of its recovery decisions, it essentially reiterated the principles underlying its recovery policy, set out the measures taken by the Commission to facilitate the execution of recovery decisions and outlined the actions that Member States should take to ensure that they reach full compliance with the rules and principles as established by EU law in that regard. It also highlighted the importance of the so-called *Deggendorf* procedure[1264] for the enforcement of recovery. This was an additional means to put pressure both on Member States and beneficiaries to comply with recovery decisions and is apparently being more actively applied since 2007.[1265]

By 2014, the Commission was still pursuing 36% of illegal aid which was to be recovered in the period 2004–2014. The most recent 2016 statistics indicate that in respect of 257 recovery decisions taken and finalised since 1999, full recovery had been achieved in only 165 cases, involving the recovery of almost €9.5 billion, with some €2.4 billion categorised as non-recoverable ("aid lost"). Reflecting a generally consistent pattern over the years, founding EU Member States and Spain accounted for 76% of all recovery orders issued in this period.[1266]

In practice, the process of recovery of incompatible State aid is a lengthy process and one of the real problems is estimating the value of the illegal aid, especially in tax cases and in regard to aid measures involving guarantees. Nonetheless, and recognising a problem here as regards the uniform application of the State aid rules, the State Aid Action Plan pointed out that the effectiveness and credibility of State aid control presupposes a proper enforcement of the Commission's decisions. For that reason, the Commission signalled its intention to achieve a more effective and immediate execution of recovery decisions, ensuring equality of treatment of all beneficiaries, and to monitor more closely the execution of the recovery decisions by Member States. Where Member States did not take all measures available to implement such decisions, the Commission intended to more actively pursue non-compliance under what are now Articles 108(2), 258 and 260(2) of the TFEU.[1267]

Hancher et al. (2007) point out, however, that the methodology for recovery remains a matter for the national laws of the Member States, that persistent obstacles exist in national procedural rules and that the ECJ has confirmed the sovereignty of the

1264. Arising from Joined Cases: T-244/93 and T-486/93: *Textilwerke Deggendorf GmbH (or TWD) v. Commission*, [1995] ECR II-2265 and the ECJ judgment of 15 May 1997 in Case C-355/95 P: *TWD v. Commission*, [1997] ECR I-2549. This case law confirmed that, when assessing a new aid measure, the Commission has the power to take into account the fact that the beneficiary of this new aid has not fully repaid earlier unlawful and incompatible aid that was the subject of a recovery decision. In such cases, the Commission may eventually decide that, otherwise compatible, aid cannot be paid out as long as previous illegal aid has not been fully reimbursed by a beneficiary or a related undertaking.

1265. European Commission: *State Aid Scoreboard, Spring 2007*, p. 6.

1266. European Commission: http://ec.europa.eu/competition/state_aid/studies_reports/recovery.html.

1267. *Supra*, para. 53.

national courts in this respect.[1268] This situation indicates that there is a particular problem regarding the uniform application of sanctions under the EU State aids regime that is constitutionally linked to national court attitudes towards supremacy and the cautious position of the ECJ that national procedural remedies must apply in regard to State aid recovery. Thus, no matter how well intentioned or how firmly grounded in the Procedural Regulation, the effectiveness and credibility of State aid control is questionable, especially as regards the uniform application of law, where 100% compliance with recovery sanctions cannot be achieved within a reasonably short time.

It is also peculiar that, following the initial clarification by the European Court of Justice in 1973 that illegal State aid could be the subject of a recovery decision, the Commission waited nearly 10 years to apply this remedy generally in such cases. Throughout the 1980s and 1990s there were numerous examples in negative decisions of recovery being demanded with interest back-dated to the date on which the aid was first granted.[1269] By 1991, the Commission attributed a quantum surge in its

1268. L. Hancher, T. Ottervanger and P.J. Slot: "*EC State Aids*," 3rd edition, Thomson/Sweet & Maxwell, 2006, p. 12, referring, in particular, to Case C-526/04: *Labaratoires Boiron SA*, judgment of 7 September 2006, [2006] ECR I-07529.

1269. For example: European Commission: Decision No 91/144/EEC of 2 May 1990 on aid granted by the Greek government to a cement manufacturer (Halkis Cement Company), OJ L 73 of 20 March 1991; Commission Decision No 91/389/EEC of 18 July 1990 on aid granted by the city of Hamburg, OJ L 215 of 2 August 1991; Commission Decision No 91/75/EEC of 25 July 1990: concerning aid provided for in Italian law No 120/87 to assist certain areas of the Mezzogiorno affected by natural disaster, OJ L 86 of 6 April 1991; Commission Decision No 92/329/EEC (*IOR*), OJ L 183 of 3 July 1992; Commission Decision No 91/390/EEC of 26 March 1991 on aid granted by the French Government to the undertaking Saint-Gobain (Eurofloat) at Salaise-sur-Sanne (glass sector), OJ L 215 of 20 June 1991; Commission Decision No 91/391/EEC of 26 March 1991 on aid granted by the German Government to Deggendorf GmbH, a producer of polyamide and polyester yarns located in Deggendorf, OJ L 215 of 20 June 1991; Commission Decision No 92/11/EEC of 31 July 1991 concerning aid provided by the Derbyshire County Council to Toyota Motor Corporation, an undertaking producing motor vehicles, OJ L 6 of 11 January 1992; Commission Decision No 92/296/EEC *Nuova Cartiera di Arbatax*, OJ L 159 of 12 June 1992; Commission Decision No 91/304/EEC of 17 December 1990 on aid granted by the German Government and the Government of the Land of Bavaria to the producer of polyamide and polypropylene yarns, Reinhold KG, situated in Selbitz, OJ L 156 of 20 June 1991; Commission Decision No 92/330/EEC of 18 December 1991 on aid by Germany to the Deggendorf textile works, (*Deggendorf II*), OJ L 183 of 3 July 1992; Commission Decision No 92/318/EEC of 25 March 1992 on aid granted by Spain to Industrias Mediterraneas de la Piel SA (Imepiel), OJ L 172 of 27 June 1992; Commission Decision No 92/465/EEC of 14 April 1992 concerning aid granted by the Land of Berlin to Daimler- Benz AG Germany, OJ L 263 of 9 September 1992; Commission Decision No 92/483/EEC of 24 June 1992 concerning aid provided by the Brussels Regional Authorities (Belgium) in favour of the activities of Siemens SA in the data-processing and telecommunications sectors, OJ L 288 of 3 October 1992; Commission Decision No 93/349/EEC of 9 March 1993 concerning aid provided by the United Kingdom Government to British Aerospace for its purchase of Rover Group Holdings over and above those authorized in Commission Decision No 89/58/EEC authorising a maximum aid to this operation subject to certain conditions (*British Aerospace*), OJ L 143 of 15 June 1993; Commission Decision No 93/412/EEC of 6 April 1993 concerning aid awarded by the German Government to Hibeg and by Hibeg via Krupp GmbH to Bremer Vulkan AG, facilitating the sale of Krupp Atlas Elektronik GmbH from Krupp GmbH to Bremer Vulkan AG (*Bremer Vulkan*), OJ L 185 of 27 July 1993; Commission Decision No 94/374/EEC (*Sicilian Regional Aid*), OJ L 170 of 5 July 1994 and Commission Decision No 94/814/EEC of 14 September 1994 on aid in respect of exports of mushrooms, granted in connection with the Market Development Fund in Ireland (Irish Mushrooms), OJ L 335 of 23 December 1991.

notification and complaints workload to the impact of the threat of recovery orders.[1270] Moreover, from 1987 (when the Commission stated its general satisfaction with recovery as an enforcement method)[1271] to 2000, the Commission, probably for political reasons, ceased to report on its achievements in this regard. This changed, however, in recent years as part of the process of State aid reforms.

With regard to the deterrent effect of the State aid regulatory system, one early commentator on the impetus on Member States to notify aid observed that:

> Member States are not always eager to notify plans of state aids especially when they have reason to think that such plans may be turned down by the Commission or that they may be authorised only with considerable delay. Since Member States do not keep national registers of state aids, the Commission must rely on complaints by other Member States and third interested parties or on information from other sources in order to learn of unnotified aids.[1272]

Since the 1990s, however, registers of State aid have emerged,[1273] and these have been actively encouraged under recent soft law instruments and block exemption regulations, in particular. With the growth in enforcement powers (and also due to EU Enlargement) the difficulty for the Commission's system by the mid-1990s became not so much one of ignorance but of overload. Nonetheless, the political and economic advantages of silence remained important factors (evidenced by some 100 detected cases of unnotified aid per year at one point) necessitating the continuing use by the Commission of complaints, parliamentary debates and the media as sources of information regarding possible unnotified aid. However, any breaches of Article 108(3) of the TFEU – whether accidental or otherwise – had to be increasingly and carefully weighed against the risks of subsequent complaints, litigation (before national courts), negative Decisions and possible back-dated recovery orders with interest.

Accordingly, it may be tentatively concluded that the deterrent effect of the EU regime vis-à-vis unnotified aid has been strengthened by increasingly vigilant enforcement. Moreover, in these conditions, "good faith" failure to notify became less important over time as the insistence of the European Commission on notification become ever clearer to EU Member States. On the other hand, increasingly effective enforcement has not acted as a particular deterrent on EU Member States continuing to act as subsidising States. This is clear from the extent of positive decisions in the system, without conditions (which reached a level of some 95% before the introduction of the first GBER in 2008) and the persisting volumes of State aid throughout the EU.

1270. European Commission: *Twenty-First Report on Competition Policy (1991)*, point 159.
1271. European Commission: *Seventeenth Report on Competition Policy (1987)*, point 173.
1272. D. Schina *supra*, p. 139.
1273. This system was first introduced in the 1990s by the Commission in order to improve monitoring and to facilitate Commission Surveys on State Aid. Arrangements were standardised by a Commission letter to Member States of 22 February 1994 and subsequently changed into a joint annual reporting format on existing aid to cover EC Treaty reporting requirements and those arising from Article 25 of the WTO SCMA, 1994.

7.4 ECONOMIC ISSUES AND IMPACTS

The EU State aid system gives rise to a range of economic issues. The main issues concern the contribution of State aid control to competition nationally and internationally, economic development, and international trade and investment. A further important issue relates to the application of EU State aid control rules in transition economies. While these issue areas are essentially issues of political economy, an over-arching issue concerns the application of economic theory and principles by the EU State aid regulatory system.

Classical economic theory has a general importance in regard to EU State aid policy. Thus, many economists will argue simply that State aid is bad as it quite simply distorts competition and markets. However, more recent developments in economic theories create a wider basis for discussion and are now beginning to be influential in State aid control and in regard to the key question: when is State aid good or bad?

From the early 1900s, economists developed the analytical tool of a *social welfare function* which resulted in fundamental theorems of welfare economics. These point to the conditions under which the market mechanism results in a "Pareto efficient allocation" of economic resources. On the basis of these approaches, economic theory now suggests ways of increasing social welfare or total welfare through State intervention. The first is by increasing the efficiency of an economy ("making the cake bigger") and the second concerns the redistribution of available resources in order to maximise the preferences of society for equity and redistribution ("dividing the cake better").

Taken together with public economy theory, public choice theory, competition economics and continuously developing international trade theory, economics now has a lot to say about the actual and potential effects of State aids and subsidies.

7.4.1 The Economic Rationale for Government Supports to Undertakings

From a welfare economics perspective, public intervention (including subsidisation) should be implemented when total welfare increases by more than the cost of the intervention. Thus, State intervention may improve the functioning of markets (and thereby be acceptable to the rationale of welfare economics) when competition or the market are unlikely to produce economically efficient outcomes. These circumstances are known as "market failures" and economics suggests that the proper role for public policy should be directed at improving the efficient functioning of markets by correcting market failures, as long as the benefits of intervention outweigh the costs.

As *Fingleton*[1274] points out, State aid is one of a number of general instruments which a government may use to achieve certain objectives. For some interventions, a State aid may be the most efficient instrument from an economic perspective. At the same time, it is generally assumed that the objective of a State aid is either to rectify a market failure caused by an economic externality (the efficiency argument) or to

1274. J. Fingleton, F. Ruane & V. Ryan: *"Market Definition and State Aid Control"* (1999), European Economy, Issue 3 – "State Aid and the Single Market," (European Commission), pp. 77–79.

redistribute resources (the redistribution argument). In the case of market failures, it is also assumed in this type of economic analysis that the government can calculate the net benefit associated with any intervention and that its objective is to grant aid where that net benefit is positive – in other words, the government will only give State aid where the benefits exceed the cost.

In regard to market efficiency, the main market failures considered relevant to State aid issues[1275] are:

> *Externalities* – meaning positive or negative side effects of the actions of one or more market actors on other market actors (foreign or domestic).[1276]
> *Public goods* – a public good is one whose full benefits cannot be priced in the market as it is difficult or impossible to exclude anyone from using the goods. Examples of this include national defence, public broadcasting services and certain services of general economic interest. For many public goods, such as street lighting, education, etc. the traditional model has consisted of State ownership and funding from taxation. Increasingly, however, the provision of such goods is left to the (often regulated) private sector with subsidies paid to producers if required. Such subsidies may take the form of direct support to an existing firm (e.g., a firm-specific subsidy) or the option to provide the service may be put out to tender.
> *Information asymmetries / missing markets – meaning situations where there is a discrepancy between the information available to one side of the market (e.g., the supply-side) and the information available to the other side of the market (the demand-side). This is often advocated as a market failure rationale for supports for foreign direct investment and State aids for SMEs related to their market relationship with bank lenders.*

1275. Friederiszick, Röller & Verouden: "*European State Aid Control- An Economic Framework,*" February 2006, *supra*, pp. 13–15. These same points are also covered in European Commission: "*Communication on a Pro-Active Competition Policy for a Competitive Europe,*" COM (2004) 293 Final of 20 April 2004.

1276. The Fingleton analysis, *supra*, indicates that government support to promote R&D can be efficient especially where it is activity-specific and available to all firms engaged in a particular production activity in the context of *Production externalities* (where firms do not adequately provide for future investment, as can be the case with R & D). He also refers to the efficient use of subsidisation (via sectoral, horizontal or regional supports) in the context of *Cluster externalities* (where, in certain industries, the profitability of a firm is greater if it is physically close to its horizontal competitors or to its suppliers, clusters of producers are economically efficient) to aid initial firms to commence production and effectively create the conditions for the cluster. In a third aspect of externalities, he points to *Time related externalities* (potentially significant in relation to SME development and to certain types of government supports to maintain investments or to move production from a national to an international/export focus) where subsidisation may be one of a number of policies that can be used to enhance incentives to achieve optimal investment in circumstances where firms operate in industries where long-term investments are required, but existing managers may be short sighted and this results in under-investment. A final example is that of *Environmental externalities.* In that case, activity or sector specific intervention subsidies can be efficiently used to remedy environmental damage where production imposes pollution costs on society.

Coordination problems – meaning a situation where markets may not function efficiently when there is a coordination problem between market actors e.g. in regard to setting market standards.
Market Power or Dominance – meaning the case of a failure of competition where, for example, the dominance of one or a few firms results in market inefficiency in the form of reduced output and prices that are too high from society's point of view.

In regard to externalities, these can be negative or positive. An example of a negative externality is the situation where environmental side effects are not taken into account by producers. As an example of a positive externality, when a company undertakes R&D, this activity may have positive spillover effects for other companies (in the form of diffusion of knowledge; technological breakthroughs, etc.). Public goods are also a type of extreme externality as suppliers of such goods cannot appropriate the benefits to other people. As a result, public goods are not normally provided by the market. According to welfare economics, the public financing of such goods or services may then be an efficient response to correct the problem of underprovision of public goods and to achieve a more efficient outcome.

This now seems to be a more refined and somewhat consolidated list vis-à-vis an earlier list of 10 market failures considered relevant to the analysis of State aid by European Commission officials in 1999.[1277]

A second set of considerations involves distributional reasons for intervention. Economic theory is emphatic that functioning markets establish an efficient allocation of goods and provide the opportunity for individuals to engage in an open and fair competitive process. However, when the outcome of the free market as a result of this process is perceived as inequitable, Governments often wish to intervene in order to create a more equitable outcome of the market process. This provides an economic rationale for State intervention on grounds of equity, e.g. in the form of social or regional aid and a range of social welfare type measures including pensions, education, unemployment assistance payments, public health and housing. Thus, in addition to the efficiency rationale for government supports, modern economics recognises that

1277. *See* F. Ilzkovitz, R. Meiklejohn & J.H. Schmidt: "*The Control of State Aid – A proposal for a Co-ordinated approach*" in Ehlermann & Everson (eds): "*European Competition Law Annual 1999 – Selected Issues in the Field of State aids,*" Oxford, 2001, p. 157 where the listed market failures are: (1) public goods, including lighthouses, (2) merit goods, including cultural and educational services, (3) increasing returns to scale – leading to monopolistic or oligopolistic markets, (4) positive and negative externalities in regard to pollution and environmental damage, vocational training and R&D, (5) imperfect or asymmetric information, notably on capital markets, (6) institutional rigidities, notably in labour markets, (7) imperfect factor mobility, relevant to problems of unemployment and regional disparities, (8) frictional problems of market adjustment – a special case of imperfect factor mobility, (9) subsidisation of foreign competitors e.g. in regard to the shipbuilding and aviation sectors, and (10) income redistribution.

there may be distributional reasons for government supports. Again, the view is that there are many instruments available to the State to achieve redistribution and, in some instances, State aid-type interventions may be the economist's preference.

In the case of so-called universal services, including some essential services such as postal services, electricity supply or telecommunications, it is implicit that it is considered desirable that everybody in society should have access at the same price, regardless of whether the cost of supply varies.[1278] Provision of such a service may require that the price be lower than the cost for some consumers and direct aid to suppliers may be economically legitimate to cover the extra cost. In other cases, the suppliers may be allowed to charge a margin above cost to some customers in order to cross-subsidise those for whom supply is more costly. Moreover, this approach, which is ideologically neutral as between public and private enterprise as supplier, provides the basis for sector liberalisation and the logic for the *Altmark* situations considered earlier.

A second form of redistribution concerns regional equality: where State aid can be used (explicitly or implicitly) to transfer resources from richer regions of the economy to poorer regions. In this scenario, the economic view is that, rather than make per capita payments in the poorer regions, the State may legitimately choose to grant subsidies to producers, in order to increase or maintain employment levels. A particular case arises in respect of industrial restructuring where, for example, a region has a predominant industry that goes into decline and, if the labour is immobile geographically and in terms of skills, the decline of the industry will have long-term repercussions on the wealth of the region that market forces will not quickly rectify. Economically rational redistribution in this case may take the form of support to the declining industry as a short-term measure or for the retraining of the workforce or as subsidies to new firms to encourage new employment in the region.

At the same time, economic theory is not able to identify a determinative basis for the "optimal" redistribution of wealth and resources, as this depends on the citizens' preferences, or in other words it is a political issue. Accordingly, economists tend to shy away from the equity area (e.g., in competition analysis) and to focus primarily, or even exclusively, on the relatively neutral concepts associated with allocative efficiency in markets, thereby avoiding political distributional concerns – even if relevant to the issues, as they can be in cases involving the analysis of State aid proposals:

> In principle, integrating equity considerations into the analysis undermines the normative strength of economic concepts such as of "perfect competition", or the idea of Adam Smith's invisible hand.[1279]

Of course, while this overall typology of the rationality of government action adds clarity to the approach of economics, in reality, it is often the case that both efficiency and equity considerations are simultaneously present in a decision to provide State aid.

1278. For example, provision of such services is more expensive in rural areas but connection charges are often the same for both rural and urban subscribers.

1279. Friederiszick, Röller & Verouden: "*European State Aid Control – An Economic Framework,*" February 2006, *supra*, p. 15.

Fingleton indicates, for example, that granting an airline aid to provide a daily service to a regional airport may have an equity rationale, such as mitigating the higher transport costs, and may also bring prices closer to marginal cost if there are economies of scale. Moreover, the granting of State aid to firms that invest in production facilities in regions where the previous industry declined might improve equity, but might also have the type of pump-priming rationale of creating a sustainable and effective economic cluster.[1280]

7.4.2 The Underdevelopment of Economic Analysis in the Application of State Aid Law and Policy and the Argument for Change

In addition, there are several arguments pointing to particular reasons for the underdevelopment of economic analysis in the State aid field (at least until 2005), including:

- The fact that the application of economic theories to State aid control is, of its very nature, more challenging than in other fields (e.g., antitrust); not least because of the inter-relationships between and the potential conflicts of economic efficiency as well as equity objectives.
- The fact that, in practice, several relevant theories of competitive harm can be applied.
- The complications associated with including tax payer costs and preferences in the economic analysis of State aids.
- The very political environment of State aid measures and State aid controls – part of this argument is that State aid procedures are largely based on a desire to limit political influence on markets rather than to ensure the economic logic or the ultimate effectiveness of State aid measures.
- The perception that the legal framework for State aid control in the EU treaties never provided much scope for a more sophisticated analysis of economic effects in the sense that State aid is illegal, unless certain criteria are met. As a result of this strict legal tradition, it was suggested in the past that an approach based more on economic analysis would be inappropriate and that predictability and legal certainty in the State aid field are better served by an essentially legalistic approach.

Arising from a process that began in 1998, the emerging thinking in regard to the economic analysis of State aid cases since 2005 began to suggest that limiting attention to the efficiency of markets was inadequate in the context of State aid control. Thus, as redistribution concerns are often among the main objectives of some State aid measures, redistributional concerns should be taken into account in the approval of State aid and should not be disregarded in its assessment by the European Commission. Moreover, social and regional cohesion policy, explicitly mentioned in the TFEU as among the grounds for exempting State aid measures from prohibition, and equity

1280. *Supra*, at p. 79.

oriented State aid measures – in particular horizontal regional development and connected vertical sectoral adjustment measures – account for up to half of all State aid granted across the European Union.

To achieve the right mix or balance in future economic assessment, the so-called new economic approach was designed to allow EU State aid control, at least in larger cases, to explicitly address the trade-off between equity and efficiency considerations via a new type of economic analysis focused on balancing costs and benefits, transparency on equity considerations and balancing these on the basis of impacts on consumer welfare. Increasingly, this now involves a detailed assessment of alternatives to equity based State aids (e.g., general measures or regulation), the analysis of incentive effects and market impacts of State aid measures, oversight of the possibility that addressing some market failures may actually create others and at least some consideration of distribution impacts such as "subsidy shopping" across the EU.

7.4.3 The Traditional Economic Approach of the European Commission

As already explained, a key element in the evaluation of a government measure to determine the application of Article 107 of the TFEU is the consideration of the actual or potential effects of the proposed measure on competition and trade. European Commission practice in regard to economic analysis in these assessments has been much less sophisticated than in regard to the analyses in antitrust type competition cases under Articles 101 and 102 of the Treaty.

In the antitrust field, a key device that has been used is the economic assessment of the actual or potential effects of particular business behaviours on the so-called relevant market. This has meant that, in considering anticompetitive agreements, mergers and alleged abuses of dominant market power, the Commission has examined the markets in the goods or services at the centre of the case together with markets in substitute and complementary goods or services and the potential responses of both the supply and demand sides of the market to the issues in the case.[1281]

In regard to State aid cases, earlier attempts by the Commission to adopt a per se approach to State aid cases (i.e., to assume that they always involved negative impacts on competition and trade) gave way to European Court requirements for the Commission to specify the impacts on competition and trade that brought a government measure within the scope of Article 107(1). However, prior to 2005 and except in the case of large investment projects, rescue and restructuring cases – and to a limited degree the analysis of incentive effects under the R&D Guidelines – the Commission had never really embarked on the extensive economic analysis needed to demonstrate or balance these effects, especially in decisions concerning the exemption of State aid from prohibition. Indeed, the European Court of First Instance held in 2000 that:

> the Commission is not required to carry out an economic analysis of the actual situation on the relevant market, of the market share of the undertakings in receipt

1281. European Commission: *Notice on the definition of the relevant market for the purposes of Community Competition Law*, OJ C 372 of 9 December 1997.

> of the aid, of the position of competing undertakings and of trade flows of the services in question between Member States, provided that it has explained how the aid in question distorted competition and affected trade between Member States.[1282]

At the same time, the European Courts gradually adopted an approach which is more sophisticated and geared towards the economic circumstances of a particular case. This was especially so in regard to public service obligations where the Court held that subsidies given to a company providing the public service do not constitute State aid in the sense of Article 107(1) when specific conditions are met relating to, among other things, the amount of the subsidy and the way in which it has been granted.[1283] In addition, as noted earlier, the Commission has developed certain economic tests for certain State aid situations – notably the "market economy investor principle" and the "private creditor principle"[1284] to address questions in the application of Article 107(1) as to whether a particular measure confers a commercial advantage. This has been important, for example, in looking at the effects of financial transfers to, or the cancellation of debts of, ailing public companies e.g. airlines.

However, the generally limited economic analysis in State aid cases is very clear from the following Commission statement in 1997 footnoted to a Commission Notice on the definition of the relevant market:

> The focus of assessment in state aid cases is the aid recipient and the industry/ sector concerned rather than identification of competitive restraints faced by the aid recipient ...When consideration of market power and, therefore, of the relevant market are raised in any particular case, the elements of the approach outlined here (i.e. in anti-trust cases) might serve as a basis for the assessment of state aid cases (emphasis added).[1285]

Some commentators have pointed out that the crude and expedient approach of sector or industry analysis has, in effect, been used as a proxy for the market in most State aid cases in combination with a presumption of impact on competition and trade.[1286]

In a critique of the dearth of economic analysis in State aid control at the commencement of the Commission's refined economic approach in 2006, it was pointed out that:

1282. Case T-55/99: *Confederación Espanola de Transporte de Mercancías v. Commission*, [2000] ECR II-3207, para. 7.
1283. Case C-280/00: *Altmark Trans GmbH and Regierungspräsidium Magdeburg v. Nahverkehrsgesellschaft Altmark GmbH*, [2003] ECR I-7747, para. 95.
1284. This was affirmed by the European Court of Justice in the Fogosa Case (Case C-480/98: *Spain v. Commission*, [2000] ECR I-8717) where it was held that, to eliminate any state aid in the State's dealings with a debtor, the State must follow *the private creditor principle* by insisting on rescheduling debt, payments by installment or forced bankruptcy in order to avoid an escalation of unpaid debt.
1285. European Commission: *Notice on the definition of the relevant market for the purposes of Community Competition*, *supra*, at footnote 1281.
1286. *See*, for example, J. Fingleton: "*How to Apply Anti-Trust Market Definition Rules to State Aid*" in Ehlermann & Everson (eds): "*European Competition Law Annual 1999 – Selected Issues in the Field of State Aids*," Oxford, 2001, p. 72.

> The resulting approach – while arguably being relatively simple to administer – does not seek to identify the effectiveness of aid and the actual impact on markets. In combination with a rather broad approach taken when considering whether a measure constitutes state aid or not, the state aid approval system thus bears the risk of being overly broad (to look at too many measures) and at the same time to be too imprecise, in the sense of not discriminating enough between "good" aid measures and "bad" aid measures. One of the main respects in which a more economic approach bears promise in the context of state aid control is that it has the potential to improve the level of precision in state aid control.[1287]

On the other hand, there was also a recognition among some commentators and practitioners that advanced economic analysis in State aids cases had limitations, could be very time-consuming and expensive and could fail to fully recognise the broader political context in which much State aid is created. Moreover, it is relevant that, at least prior to 2005, DG Competition of the European Commission was somewhat strong on lawyers and short of modern economists.[1288] On the limitations of economics in this field, one senior WTO official highlighted the fact that:

> The simple argument that all subsidies are undesirable because they distort economic activity and reduce welfare is based on excessively simplistic assumptions about perfectly functioning markets. A theoretical case can be made for welfare-enhancing subsidisation, built around the existence of market imperfections of various kinds. In particular, the notion at the heart of the problem facing competition policy is market power, or imperfect competition. The basic economic problem associated with market power is under-production. Hence, subsidisation could, in principle, be seen as a substitute for competition policy interventions.[1289]

The same commentator also pointed out that more analysis was required to clarify the divergences between subsidy rules and economic logic and that this should address the following:

(1) The shortcomings of economics in providing clear *ex ante* prescriptions from theory that would allow optimal rules to be drawn up and applied automatically and avoiding the fact that so much economic welfare analysis depends on the circumstances of each particular case or situation.
(2) The difficulty of welfare economics in providing any meaningful prescriptions where governments are pursuing public policy (or equity) objectives, apart from advising on the relative efficiencies of different intervention options.
(3) The lessons from public choice economic theory that demonstrate that even the best intentions can be frustrated through political capture, leading to

1287. Friederiszick, Röller & Verouden: "*European State Aid Control- An Economic Framework*," February 2006, *supra*, pp. 10–11.
1288. In L.A. Röller: "*Economic Analysis and Competition Policy Enforcement in Europe*" in Edward Elgar (ed.): "*Modelling European Mergers: Theory, Competition Policy and Case Studies*," 2005 the then Chief Competition Economist pointed out that, of 700 officials at DG Competition, 200 had an economics background but only 20 of these (including the 10 economists on his own staff) had an advanced modern education in economics.
1289. P. Lowe: "*The Treatment of Subsidies in the WTO Framework*," in "*European Competition Law Annual 1999 – Selected Issues in the Field of State aids*," *supra*, p. 119.

> outcomes from interventions that do not correspond to the apparent intentions of governments, nor to recognisable welfare prescriptions.[1290]

From a legal perspective, the EU State aid control system has faced the additional problem that the control system itself has its own public policy dimension – established by the Treaty – that precludes an exclusively economic efficiency based assessment of State aid cases. Thus, for example, the application of the State aid rules must have regard to various other EU policy objectives (especially economic and social cohesion, various common policies – such as transport agriculture and fisheries, the development of competitiveness and small and medium enterprises and environment policy) which require it to balance its State aid assessments at EU level as between efficiency and equity (political, legal and administrative) considerations. This is confirmed by the analysis of a senior State aid control official:

> The Commission, which has broad discretion in doing so, must balance the objective of undistorted competition in the internal market with other Community objectives that the aid may promote. When searching for the right balance, the Commission performs a double test of the necessity and proportionality of the aid. Contrary to the way it is often phrased, the first test is not a test of whether aid is necessary to correct market failures, but a statement that market failures are a necessary pre-condition for the granting of aid.[1291]

7.4.4 The Beginnings of the "New Economic Approach"

From the late 1990s, the European Commission came under pressure from the European Courts to improve its economic analysis in *antitrust cases* when several of its assessments in individual cases were held to be errors of reasoning by the Courts.[1292] This resulted in a serious internal appraisal of the European Commission's own capacity to carry out increasingly complex economic assessments and ultimately to the establishment of the Office of the Chief Competition Economist at the European Commission's DG Competition.

At the same time, some analysts even question whether there is anything new in the so-called new economic approach that has emerged in antitrust and was then developed following the 2005 State Aid Action Plan reform:

> The role and scope of modern economic analysis in competition policy in Europe has been changing. Characterising this change as one towards a "more economic approach" could be misleading. Indeed, antitrust and merger analysis has been based on economics for a long time. The question for effective enforcement is not one of "more" or "less" economics, but rather what kind of economics and especially how the economic analysis is used – or indeed sometimes may be abused – in the context of guidelines or cases. The change in the practice of

1290. *Ibid.*, p. 121.
1291. A. Houtman: "*EC State aid Control – In search of the right balance*" in "*European Competition Law Annual 1999 – Selected Issues in the Field of State Aids,*" *supra*, p. 95.
1292. For example, Case T-342/99: *Airtours plc v. Commission*, [2002] ECR II-2585.

> European competition policy is all about the way in which economic principles and economic evidence are brought to bear in the context of decision making.[1293]

The State Aid Action Plan: *"Less and Better Targeted State Aid – A Roadmap for State Aid Reform 2005 to 2009"* pointed out that:

> state aid should only be used when it is an appropriate instrument for meeting a well defined objective, when it creates the right incentives, is proportionate and when it distorts competition to the least possible extent. For that reason, appreciating the compatibility of state aid is fundamentally about balancing the negative effects of aid on competition with its positive effects in terms of the common interest.

In order to face the new challenges of State aid control, including its contribution to the Lisbon Competitiveness Strategy, the impact of enlargement, economic and social cohesion and legal complexity, the Action Plan proposed a thorough modification of rules and procedures including *a refined economic approach* in order to allow for an effective assessment of the allocation and distribution effects of State aid, taking account of the actual contribution of State aid measures to commonly agreed, politically desirable objectives.

Among the initial ideas set out in the Action Plan concerning the refined economic analysis of State aid were a deeper analysis of market failures (with an obligation on Member States to provide the necessary data), an analysis of the appropriateness of State aid as a solution to alleged market failures and an analysis of how particular State aid measures should be applied in order to limit distortions of competition and trade.

According to the earlier (2004) *Communication on a Pro-Active Competition Policy for a Competitive Europe,* the indication was that the type of detailed economic analysis being indicated would only apply to individual or sectoral State aid measures.[1294] By 2006, this idea had broadened, envisaging its application to all notifiable cases lying above the half-way point between block exemption levels and maximum State aid levels and perhaps also on the basis of lower allowable State aid maxima.[1295]

7.4.5 The Development of a More Economic Based Assessment of State Aids

The new economic approach envisaged for State aid cases thus sought to create an economic framework of assessment for European State aid control as a means of achieving more precision in State aid control, i.e. a means to better distinguish "good aid" from "bad aid." While this was partly the result of an increasing number of economists in DG Competition, it also sought to address the perceived problem that the focus of the Treaty rules on State aid were predominantly seen as reflecting the desire

1293. L.A. Röller: *"Economic Analysis and Competition Policy Enforcement in Europe," supra.*
1294. European Commission: *"Communication on a Pro-Active Competition Policy for a Competitive Europe,"* COM (2004) 293 Final of 20 April 2004 para. 4.2.
1295. This is discussed in Friederiszick, Röller & Verouden: *"European State Aid Control - An Economic Framework,"* February 2006, *supra,* p. 50 and following.

to limit political influence, rather than to promote economic effectiveness. Consequently, the main assessments in State aid cases were seen as centred traditionally on formal legal compatibility with the legislation and evolving practice under the case law and that the actual legal approach of the Treaty could even preclude examination of the eventual effects of State aid. In the view of DG Competition, an appropriate economic framework for the assessment of State aid would contribute to its policy goal of "less and better targeted aid," would not lead to an overall softening of State aid control and could, in fact, enhance predictability and legal certainty:

> Moreover, it is likely, as well as intended, that an effects-based approach will shift the argumentation from legal and accounting battles towards a battle over the impact of the aid on markets and ultimately on consumers. Such a change would not only greatly contribute towards precision and effectiveness of European state aid control, but in fact enhance predictability...and holds the potential to reduce – at least to some extent – the scope for politics in the field of state aid control and the potential to increase cooperation across Member States.[1296]

Initial pilots of the new economic approach emerged in the creation of balancing tests to be applied in the Guidelines on State aid for Research, Development and Innovation and in regard to Risk Capital for Small and Medium Enterprises and were further elaborated in some of the updated guidelines under the State Aid Action Plan reforms. As the Commission's State aid caseload was running at over 1,000 cases per year in 2005, it was clear that this level of analysis could not be applied to all cases. It was equally clear at the time that few notified cases gave rise to substantial regulatory or economic concerns (with 95% + of cases being approved without conditions). Moreover, the Commission had long sought to concentrate its efforts on the cases most likely to distort competition and trade. These considerations came together in 2008 with the first GBER (essentially a pilot exercise) and the later refinement of the current (2014) GBER.

The GBER approach also allowed for the application of the balancing tests of the new economic approach in respect of non-GBER State aids which still had to be notified together with the placing of a substantially increased burden on Member States, via updated regulations and soft law measures, to prove, when required to notify, the actual or likely impacts of new State aid measures, their response to market failures and the necessity and proportionality of the proposed State aid. This process was completed under the State Aid Modernisation initiative from 2012 to 2016.[1297]

7.4.6 Regulation as a Contribution to Competition Nationally and Internationally

One of the fundamental ideas of EU State aid regulation is to avoid *undue* distortions of competition and trade. Accordingly, it is not the objective to fully eliminate all

1296. H.W. Friederiszick, L.A. Röller & V.Verouden: "*European State Aid Control - An Economic Framework*," February 2006, *supra*.

1297. For a fuller and recent analysis, *see*: P. Werner and V. Verouden (eds): "*EU State Aid Control – Law and Economics*," Kluwer Law International, 2016.

distortions of competition and/or trade arising from State aid. In contrast, and with the exception of so-called cases of minor importance or with no cross-border effects, the EU antitrust regime does seek to eliminate all anticompetitive behaviours of business undertakings, whether in express or implicit agreements, via mergers, in regard to monopoly power and, in particular abuses of dominant market positions. Moreover, by the parallel application of similar rules in most of the EU Member States, the minor cases are also generally regulated and the broad thrust of the antitrust rules transposed into national laws.

It is clear that the EU State aid rules were originally a second-best Treaty solution to a lack of consensus on a common industrial policy at the inception of the EU and with a focus on avoiding any spillovers from government supports which might replicate or replace market distortions otherwise removed via the anti-trust rules. This is also the reason why the State aid rules appear in the Competition Chapter of the TFEU and its predecessors, why they appear in similarly titled chapters of third country trade agreements and why they are primarily overseen by DG Competition of the European Commission.

While the Commission has in the past sought, at least to some degree, to apply a per se approach in State aid cases – and this has had some considerable support in the European Courts – any distinctly competition or efficiency driven policy lines have had to give way in practice to a range of additional considerations including:

- The political dynamic of the EU.
- The equity considerations reflected in Article 107(2) and (3).
- The very limited capacity of the Commission to examine all State aids.
- The need to balance the approach to State aids with other EU objectives and policies (a matter arising from specific Treaty provisions and very much reflected in soft law measures, more recent Commission regulations and GBER rules on State aid).

In addition, with the exception of Denmark, Portugal and the 13 new EU Member States, there has never been any parallel national regulation of State aids similar to that which developed since the 1980s in the anti-trust field.[1298] Second, the Commission has endeavoured, via different approaches over the years, to reduce its State aid case load (while retaining as much of its powers as possible) in order to focus on (the still undefined) cases likely to create *major* distortions of competition. Third, from the pattern of the vast majority of notified State aid cases being approved without conditions, it is clear how far away from per se regulation of the competitive distortions of competition the EU State aid regime actually is, and the dominance of political, legal and equity considerations in regard to applying the concept that competition is not unduly distorted. At the same time, existing EU regulation in some areas is very strict. A particular example is in regard to aid for rescue and restructuring. However, the

1298. Among the 13 new Member States, pre-accession control systems have now become monitoring, reporting and national coordination systems.

present strictness was in fact introduced (largely from the late 1990s), after almost all major EU industries had been rescued/restructured at least once with unimpeded government support.

In these circumstances, it is arguable that the regulation of State aids in the EU is misconceived as a major instrument of competition policy, and despite the persistent use of "competition" as a European Commission mantra in State aid cases. Even with a new/refined economic approach increasing the burden of proof on Member States in regard to the linkages between proposed State aids and identified market failures, the factors cited above are unlikely to change this reality – although they have achieved a degree of convergence between the assessment methodologies in the State aid control and the anti-trust fields. Moreover, with the revised wording of the TFEU, intended to remove "free and undistorted competition" as an EU Treaty objective, it seems likely that the pursuit of competition based economically rational efficiency in the State aids field will face further political pressures in the future.[1299]

At the international level, the efforts of the EU to promote subsidy regulation in a manner akin to the State aid regime have been paralleled by EU advocacy of international anti-trust regulation at the multilateral level. To date, however, the latter has been resisted, primarily by developing countries via the UNCTAD. Accordingly, it is clear that there is no real competition policy base either in the WTO regime of regulation of government supports to undertakings, or at least not in the sense of exclusive economic efficiency arguments advocated by many economists.

On the other hand, and with a very clear trade policy focus, the EU has been broadly successful in extending the reach of its unique State aid system to non-EU countries – in the wider context of removing indirect barriers to trade and via a range of mostly bilateral agreements. The operational success of these initiatives has varied, depending largely on whether or not eventual EU membership is included in the agreement. However, major trade negotiations with Canada and the USA have tended to avoid the issue.

1299. As press comments on the Brussels Summit of 21–22 June 2007 note, President Nicolai Sarkozy celebrated the removal of references to "free and undistorted competition" from the EU's stated objectives as a victory for French voters who rejected the Constitution in a referendum two years previously: "Competition as an ideology, as a dogma, what has it done for Europe?" Sarkozy asked, saying it only brought "fewer and fewer people who vote in European elections and fewer and fewer people who believe in Europe." (http://www.euroactiv.com). The TFEU simply refers to the exclusive competence of the EU in regard to establishing the competition rules necessary for the functioning of the internal market (Article 3.1), whereas the Treaty had previously provided for a system ensuring that competition in the internal market is not distorted as an EU activity (Article 2 of the Maastricht Treaty on European Union), reinforced by the statement of principle in Article 4 that, for the purposes set out in Article 2, the activities of the Member States and the Community shall include "...the adoption of an economic policy which is based on the close coordination of Member States' economic policies ... and conducted in accordance with the *principle of an open market economy with free competition.*"

7.4.7 Regulation as a Contribution to International Trade and Investment

In his analysis of the relationship between subsidies and trade measures, *Messerlin* outlines three conflicting economic points of view on the effects of subsidies. The "mercantilist" approach focuses on the effects of foreign subsidies on the interests of domestic producers and disregards the interests of domestic consumers. This approach favours countervailing subsidies or other retaliatory measures to discipline foreign subsidies. The "pure trade theory" approach, on the other hand, tends to emphasise the benefits that foreign subsidies confer on domestic consumers and stresses that subsidies are less distortive than alternative forms of protection (import duties or non-tariff barriers). Finally, the "political economy" approach leads to the conclusion that subsidies should be constrained in the interest of economic efficiency in the country granting the aids, because they are easily captured by vested interests.[1300]

In relation to the trade approach to State aids and subsidies, the Messerlin analysis provides evidence that trade policies (including the WTO Agreements relevant to government supports) tend to treat trade restriction and trade expansion asymmetrically. Thus, under GATT rules import tariffs are, within limits, regarded as an acceptable instrument of protection while export subsidies are forbidden per se. Using political economy theory, the Messerlin analysis also highlights the unintended effects of government supports with reference to an economic analysis of two cases. First, the farm subsidies under the EU CAP, which via price supports was intended to help farmers, in fact, increased farm output and resulted in higher land prices. Thus, the CAP benefited landowners more than farmers per se, farm subsidies benefited traders more than farmers, and the CAP actually eliminated farmers more rapidly than might have been the case in its absence. Second, as government supports via subsidies tend to be "input" subsidies, he suggests that a simple case can be easily built to demonstrate that subsidies given to Airbus Industries could have benefited Boeing: this possibility merely would require that the price of aircraft engines declines because of scale economies associated with Airbus's activities. Thus, production and export subsidies to Airbus could have turned into input subsidies to Boeing.

More generally, it is argued, especially by Australian economists, that without trade barriers, the budgetary cost of providing significant protection through subsidies is too high and, thus, subsidies tend to be greatest in the presence of moderate trade barriers. When trade barriers are very high, subsidies are unnecessary. When trade barriers have been abolished, subsidies are too costly. Hence, the most effective way of eliminating subsidies is to ensure free trade. On the basis of this approach, EU State aids in manufacturing tend now to be marginal for the industries where single market liberalisation has been achieved and concentrated in manufacturing sectors where EU protection remains substantial, and where it still offers room for Member State protection. Moreover, State aids tend to increase in services sectors which are just

1300. P. Messerlin: *"External Aspects of State Aids"* (1999) European Commission: European Economy, Issue 3 – "State Aid and the Single Market," pp. 77–79.

beginning the liberalisation process. Accordingly, subsidies tend to be substitutable for other trade measures only when the global level of protection of the sector in question is still high.

On the basis of this analysis, trade liberalisation per se tends to reduce the rationality of subsidisation. In this situation, State aid control can best be regarded as an interim instrument which is useful on the way to free trade and one which tends to become increasingly irrelevant with market liberalisation. However, the important point here is the rationality of subsidisation. From one economic view, only market failures that call for functional interventions (i.e., market-friendly interventions aimed at addressing market failures without directly modifying resource allocation between specific activities e.g. improvements in physical infrastructure, human capital or the functioning of capital markets, or the provision of information and technical support to potential investors or exporters) should be addressed by governments and failures (whether perceived or real) which require selectivity are either unimportant or cannot be remedied by government action.[1301] A second narrower viewpoint is that getting the prices right is sufficient for an economy to reach optimality, suggesting that neither functional nor selective measures are justified. A third and probably prevalent approach assumes that market failures are important and pervasive, and that effective remedies can be devised involving a crucial role for governments, including through selective interventions.

Of course, much of this debate is driven by the implications of public choice theory that governments cannot properly assess economic problems in devising interventions and that, when they do act, government interventions are captured by special interests and become permanent. However, while most economists would agree that the results from these "public choice" models are useful to understand the effect of industrial policies, they would not all agree with the broad policy conclusions that have been derived from those models. Significantly, the prescriptiveness of public choice theory has been challenged by the view that government capabilities can be improved, that the degree of selectivity can be adapted to the level of capabilities, and that governments can be helped to intervene efficiently.[1302] *Rodrik* points to the danger that academic economists' views on State capabilities can be superficial and that there is much to be learned by undertaking systematic analytical studies of State capabilities.[1303] Subsequently, his analysis went one step further by proposing an institutional framework for "redeploying industrial policy in a more effective manner" involving a more flexible form of strategic collaboration between the public and private sectors, designed to elicit information about objectives, distribute responsibilities for solutions,

1301. M. Noland & H. Pack: "*Industrial Policy in an Era of Globalisation – Lessons from Asia,*" Institute for International Economics, Washington DC, 2003.

1302. S. Lall: "*Selective Policies for Export Promotion – Lessons from the Asian Tigers*" in G.K. Helleiner (ed.): "*Non-traditional Export Promotion in Africa – Experiences and Issues,*" Palgrave Macmillan, New York, 2002.

1303. D. Rodrik: "*Trade and Industrial Policy Reform in Developing Countries – A Review of Recent Theory and Evidence*" in J. Behrman & T.N. Srinivasen (eds): "*Handbook of Development Economics,*" Vol III, Amsterdam, Netherlands, 1993.

and evaluate outcomes as they appear.[1304] Thus, it can be argued that present State aid control policy, however interim on the path to free trade, is making an important contribution to improving the logic, rationality and potential for success of specific Government State aid measures.

As to the contribution of State aid regulation to investment, especially foreign direct investment for development, empirical evidence is scarce.[1305] However, various (and mostly unpublished) surveys indicate that direct government supports tend not to be in the top considerations of a foreign investor seeking a location for a mobile international investment project. Key factors are: macroeconomic and political stability, a positive business environment (including a predictable tax regime – which under EU State aid rules may increasingly involve tax aid measures and well developed infrastructure) education levels, workforce factors (including skills, languages and wage rates) and access to (especially new) markets. Accordingly, while any State aid being offered will generally be accepted by foreign investors, they do not tend to be the most persuasive factor and competition between investment attraction agencies only tends to arise when all the other factors are otherwise favourably balanced and the choice of investment locations is short-listed on that basis.[1306] In addition, the growing impact of State aid recovery mechanisms now requires the prudent foreign investor to carry out due-diligence procedures on the legality of proffered aid. At the same time, the progressive shift in the emphasis of EU Member States State aid programmes towards "horizontal aids" (and regional development aid in particular) indicates a continuing belief on the part of governments in the value of government supports for general industrial development and the promotion of investment. This is mirrored in the generally permissive attitude of the EU State Aid regime towards regional aid and other horizontal forms of support.

An important point is that international regulation, whether at the EU or multilateral levels, does restrict the use of some selective interventions and, in the case where government supports for investment have a negative impact on third parties, the risk of retaliation now has to be taken into account in practice. In recent years, the EU has increased its surveillance and discipline of horizontal regional investment aid to large projects in order to avoid emerging inter-state conflicts concerning a pattern of industrial relocation that became evident in the 1990s. This has strengthened the application of EU rules in regard to foreign direct investment. Second, government action in many EU countries has improved along the lines suggested by Rodrik. Finally, government action in the EU in regard to the business environment has increased dramatically in the last 10 years. For these reasons, it is likely, but not conclusive, that government supports to undertakings have decreased in overall significance as a factor in foreign direct investment location decisions and that this trend has been promoted, at least in part, by the increasing impact and sophistication of the regulatory regime.

1304. D. Rodri, "*Industrial Policy for the Twenty-First Century*" (2004), CEPR Discussion Paper No 47, London, Centre for Economic Policy Research.
1305. WTO: *World Trade Report 2006, supra*, pp. 80–82.
1306. This, in particular, has been the consistent analysis of the Irish Industrial Development Authority since the 1980s.

7.4.8 The (Mostly Economic) Challenges of Regulation in Transition Economies

Against the background of the above analysis, it is worth considering the implications of the regulation of government supports at national level, based on the general lines of the EU system.[1307] In general, the primary reason for the transposition of EU State aid rules into national laws in various transition countries is that this is set out, for many countries, as a clear pre-condition for advancing in the EU accession process. Where the incentive of future EU membership is absent,[1308] the extent of the parallel introduction of State aid rules in national law has been very limited. A second reason, of course, and again mostly in regard to aspiring EU members, is that the introduction of a national State aid regime advances readiness for WTO membership also.

There can be little doubt that this type of law approximation is complex and difficult for transition countries, and the difficulties are exacerbated by the absence of a model law on national State aid regulation for use in such countries.[1309] At the same time, the transposition of EU State aid rules in transition economies is facilitated by: (a) the general classification of those countries in full, at least for a period, as Article 107(3)(a) regions,[1310] (b) the relative flexibility of applying the EU *de minimis* threshold in the circumstances of transition countries[1311] and the exclusion of the agriculture sector. In the former case, this can generally allow greater flexibility in regard to the granting of State aid than is likely to be possible in the overall economic circumstances of transition countries. In the second case, €200,000 per firm is big money in a transition economy if fully transposed at that level while it is a relatively minor level of aid in developed countries. The exclusion of agriculture, moreover, reflects, in particular, the non-application of the EU CAP system in third countries.

On the other hand, the transposition of EU State aid rules in transition countries gives rise to three particular problems. The first is the application of the very strict EU rescue and restructuring State aid rules (designed for advanced economies in the context of the completion of most major industrial reconstruction in those economies) in the circumstances of the transition economy. The second is the interface between State aid regulation and fledgling industrial development policies in those countries. The third concerns the potential use of GBER rules in the national State aid systems of transition countries.

1307. As seen in Chapter 3, this is a distinct requirement of the EU in its relations with various third countries, including those aspiring to future membership. In the unusual cases of Denmark and Portugal, the rationale for national legislation was the control of State aid below the EU *de minimis* threshold (Denmark) and improved national coordination on State aid issues (Portugal).

1308. For example, under the Partnership and Cooperation Agreements with the countries of the former Soviet Union – *see* Chapter 3.

1309. *See* the implicit systemic model for transition countries set out in Chapter 3.

1310. This allows the highest levels of State aid for regional economic development and other inter-linked categories of horizontal State aid.

1311. For the most express provisions on *de minimis*, *see* the EU Association Agreements with Ukraine, Georgia and Moldova.

In general, it is virtually impossible for a transition economy to properly and fully apply the current rescue and restructuring rules in the circumstances of transition. While anecdotal evidence suggests that the Commission does not push this point too far in practice, it would be appropriate if these particular rules were fully excluded from, or at least modified in, EU agreements with third countries. As regards fledgling industrial policies, the problem is that, in the case of many countries,[1312] the externally imposed requirement to regulate can precede the actual development of industrial development policy and may, thus, have the tendency to strangle it at birth. The GBER problem is that if national systems in transition countries (e.g., Ukraine. Georgia and Moldova) were to apply the GBER thresholds in addition to the EU *de minimis* threshold, they would have almost nothing to control. Contrariwise, if EU agreements with transition countries specifically excluded the use of GBER methods by third countries, this would paradoxically put them at a trading disadvantage vis-à-vis the EU. Again, anecdotal evidence suggests that the Commission is not encouraging block exemption arrangements in transition countries. However, a distinct position on this point has yet to be elaborated.

Aside from integration imperatives and the above areas of difficulty, the main argument for a national State aid policy and a regulatory system is to ensure that government money and non-monetary benefits are not wasted. This is firstly about value for money – limiting the amount of State aid to what is necessary and proportional to the problem being assisted. Moreover, there are additional public expenditure advantages arising from achieving compatibility with EU standards in this field. A functioning national State aid regulatory system can assist the rationalisation of spending on development programmes in the country and the better targeting of public expenditures. It can also assist the avoidance of over-spending in regard to, for example, the attraction of foreign direct investment to the country as its economic transition evolves.[1313]

More generally – and this applies to any national regime – a functioning control and regulatory system helps to avoid persistent subsidisation. It can also help to reduce ad-hoc political decisions to subsidise, in response to an economic or industrial policy issue, in the absence of a careful analysis of the problem and a real expectation that State aid can actually help to solve the problem. Indeed a system of control, in line with EU standards, can create the checks necessary to ensure that the economically important questions are asked and answered before State aids are created and before public money is actually committed or spent.

Overall, then, some delicate issues arise from the transposition of EU State aid rules into the circumstances of transition economies and there is a need for greater

1312. A particularly good example was the case of Bosnia and Herzegovina which, while required to develop a State aid regulatory system for SAA purposes, had no actual industrial development policy – a point that was separately demanded under the EU/BiH European Partnership of 2005.

1313. The present degree of inter-State competition for internationally mobile investment projects is evidenced by the existence of approximately 1,000 agencies in Europe in 1995 – Ernst & Young Survey *"Regions of the New Europe,"* as reported in the Financial Times of 24 October 1995 – a situation that is unlikely to have decreased since then.

precision and sensitivity in what the EU demands in that regard. Second, the advantages of national regulation are such that they constitute an argument for national regulation of government supports, independently of any international regime or its specific demands on national governments. This point adds credibility to the ideas first advanced in the 2005 State Aid Action Plan regarding national authorities[1314] although the approach suggested by the European Commission was and continues to be directed more at decentralisation of EU controls rather than towards the independent evolution of national regimes. Indeed, it remains to be seen if, especially in the GBER context, EU Member States begin to evolve their own separate national control regimes by e.g. building on the example of Denmark and/or using the scope of below threshold flexibility to apply national legal rules to promote greater rationality and improved public finance management in decentralised decisions to grant block exempted or *de minimis* State aid.

7.5 ADMINISTRATION OF THE SYSTEM

Substantive law needs to be clear and fully applied. Otherwise there is an inherent flaw in any body of law. While best practice law making advocates that detailed consideration is given to implementation in the making of law,[1315] the EU State aid system did not begin as a well thought out legal regime that was planned to be workable in terms of implementation and enforcement. It was undoubtedly an experiment based on Havana Charter thinking and resulted in an evolution of the system, frequent ad-hoc shifts of policy and the creation of significant complexity in rule-making as the system operated over the last 60 years.

While this is a fundamental explanation for significant administrative weaknesses in the application of the State aid regulatory system, other reasons connected with the capacities of the European Commission also hampered its ability to fully, fairly and uniformly apply the State aid rules.

7.5.1 Capacity of the European Commission in the EU System to Regulate in Accordance with Substantive Law

As noted earlier, an important factor which caused the Commission to revisit its traditional per se approach and to recognise a *de minimis* concept in the State aid control regime has been administrative. The increasing impact of reasoning requirements by the Court and the success of Commission enforcement against infringements of Articles 107 and 108 created an administrative problem for the Commission obliging an increasing recognition that it did not have the resources to give the same attention to important and minor notifications of aid. This position was exacerbated in the run-up to the recent EU Enlargements with the prospect of detailed supervision of State

1314. European Commission: "*State aid action plan – Less and better targeted State aid: a roadmap for State aid reform 2005-2009,*" *supra*, at para. 51.

1315. E. Stuart & S. Bruen-Nilsen: "*International and European Best Practices for the Preparation of Legislation,*" Astana, January 2005.

aid in an EU with almost twice as many Member States as prior to 2004. In addition, the Commission's own experience through the years eventually testified to the apparent conformity of most notifications with the Treaty rules.

The EU State aid Action Plan referred to the need to streamline State aid policy and focus attention on the most distortive types of aid.[1316] Moreover, in regard to its intention to bring forward a General State Aid Block Exemption Regulation, the Commission pointed out:

> To ensure better governance and facilitate the granting of aid, which is clearly compatible with the Treaty, the Commission will issue a general block exemption regulation to exempt certain categories of aid from the obligation to notify to the Commission. The regulation will be based on the principle that state aid policy should <u>focus on the most distortive types of aid</u> (emphasis added) and that it should set clear 'positive' and 'negative' priorities.[1317]

This was again one of the main themes of the 2012 State Aid Modernisation initiative which focussed on three objectives: (i) to foster sustainable, smart and inclusive growth in a competitive internal market; (ii) to focus Commission *ex ante* scrutiny on cases with the biggest impact on the internal market while strengthening Member States' cooperation in State aid enforcement; and (iii) to streamline the rules and provide for faster decisions.

The persistent problem for the Commission, however, was that it is legally responsible for the clearance of all measures of government support to undertakings which meet the tests necessary for the application of Article 107 of the TFEU. Down through the years, and especially in response to more serious enforcement by the Commission, the Commission's limited State aid control administration (although considerably increased in the last 15 years) has, therefore, been obliged to receive and consider all cases, major and minor, notified to it which do or might constitute State aid. It has also developed wider and deeper responsibilities in its supranational control of State aid as the EU system has evolved; notably as regards the administration of the new economic approach, the application and lengthy follow up of recovery decisions and as a result of the enlargement of the EU itself. These fundamental pressures on the Commission have caused it to seek various reliefs for its own system (paradoxically often in tandem with attempts to expand its scope of action) usually using euphemistic language concerning administrative simplification and the need to focus attention on the cases of State aid likely to create the greatest distortions of competition. In almost every case of such administrative simplification, it is *the Commission's* administrative burden that the Commission is seeking to relieve, and there is a concomitant tendency to increase the administrative burden on Member States by the invention of safeguards or pseudo-safeguards presented on the basis of not weakening the effectiveness of control. Equally, the orientation towards cases of State aid likely to create the greatest distortions of competition means, in practice, that the Commission wishes to reduce its caseload.

1316. *Supra*, p. 5.
1317. *Ibid.*, p. 10.

The emergence of the *de minimis* concept in State aid regulation was an important first step by the Commission to reduce its administrative burdens. However, to benefit from *de minimis* in the system, Member State have to apply safeguards and create complex systems of record-keeping. In the early stages of this development, the UK refused to apply this concept and insisted on continuing protective and necessary notifications to the Commission to avoid the transfer of the administrative burden to its national administration.

In the 1990s, the European Commission more publicly admitted that, despite its efforts, levels of State aid in Member States remained high and renewed efforts were made to ensure progressive reductions in overall levels. At the same time, the ineffectiveness of notifications per se in the supervision of damaging State aids was not directly addressed. This undoubtedly related to continuing tensions and mutual suspicions between the Commission and the Member States in this area but a second likely factor is the opposition of certain Member States (traditionally Denmark, in particular) to any weakening of supranational control.

Thus, while the Commission had succeeded in getting more and more State aid measures properly notified, it had become a victim of its own success. In trying to relieve its administrative pressures and burdens, the Commission built on earlier decentralisation achieved in the anti-trust area and evidently saw no option other than to move politically and cautiously to shift the burden back to the Member States – or else run the risk that supranational control would be seen to be unduly diluted.

As the vast majority of State aid notifications up to 2005 were approved unconditionally,[1318] there is no doubt that the supranational control of State aid by the Commission involved primary attention to cases where, overall, there is no infringement of the Treaty rules. Moreover, the extent of practical non-opposition to notified aid measures raised the questions of whether the State aid rules are a de facto exception to the legal maxim that Treaty exemptions are to be applied restrictively, or whether the case records indicated a significant degree of ineffective, or perhaps politically skewed, enforcement. The view here is that each of these factors contributed to the reality as regards notifications but that administrative ineffectiveness and political influence were at most marginal. Thus, the pivotal factor was that the EU regime had fundamentally become not a prohibition system but a generally permissive one. In this situation, both the Member States and the Commission shared an excessive administrative burden that could best be addressed as a joint problem. Under the State Aid Modernisation initiative, the Commission's continuing devolution strategy was applied more explicitly and with an indication that the GBER system was not working particularly well:

> Should the Commission decide to increase the size and scope of aid measures exempt from notification obligation, responsibilities of Member States for ensuring the correct enforcement of State aid rules would increase. With more measures exempt from the notification requirement, Member States will have to ensure the

1318. Eighty-nine per cent of all notified cases in 2005 were approved without an investigation procedure (preliminary assessment only). A further 8% were approved after the formal investigation and only 3% were the subject of a negative decision.

> ex ante compliance with State aid rules of de minimis measures and block-exempted schemes and cases, in strict coordination with the Commission which will continue to exercise ex post control of such measures. The Commission will expect better cooperation from Member States in terms of quality and timeliness of submission of information and notifications' preparation, as well as effective national systems (including private enforcement) to ensure that State aid measures exempt from ex ante notification obligation comply with Union law. A lower administrative burden through less notification obligations can only be envisaged if it is accompanied by increased commitment and delivery on the part of the national authorities in terms of compliance. Consequently, ex post control by the Commission will have to be increased, also because the current results of the monitoring of the implementation of block exempted measures by Member States reveal frequent lack of compliance with State aid rules. In such a way, effectiveness of enforcement can be ensured.[1319]

Thus, even as the reform progressed and shifted much of the administrative burden from the Commission to the EU Member States via a continuation of the cautious approach to block exemptions, there were doubts as to future effectiveness in parallel with a degree of silence as to the equity of the burden shift.

A further complication in salvaging the Commission's administrative and regulatory capacity concerned the identification of most distortive cases and the setting of "clear 'positive' and 'negative' priorities" (as referred to in the State Aid Action Plan). Apart from a general policy that horizontal aids are less distortive of competition than sectoral or ad-hoc interventions and its approach to regional aid to large investment projects, it was only after the State Aid Modernisation initiative that the Commission actually identified the priority cases where there could be no question of relinquishing control and upon which it would wish to target its efforts and limited resources.

Thus, after 60 years, the Commission has identified *de minimis* and block exempt measures as essentially "good aid," with an expectation that most State aid in the future will increasingly be in these categories. "Bad aid" or potentially bad aid is apparently all State aid lying above these various thresholds and in the areas not covered by either *de minimis* or the 2014 GBER,[1320] notably:

- Export aid.
- Aid contingent upon the use of domestic over imported goods.
- Aid for the closure of coal mines.
- Certain categories of regional aid excluded by the GBER[1321] (especially regional aid measures supporting the steel, coal, shipbuilding, synthetic fibres and transport sectors, related infrastructure, energy generation, distribution and infrastructure, regional schemes targeting a limited number of specific sectors of economic activity, certain types of regional aid to compensate the

1319. European Commission: Communication from the Commission – *EU State Aid Modernisation (SAM)*, COM/2012/0209 final of 8 May 2012, para. 21.
1320. European Commission: Regulation No 1407/2013/EC of 18 December 2013 on the application of Articles 107 and 108 of the Treaty on the Functioning of the European Union to *de minimis* aid, OJ L 352 of 24 December 2013, Article 1 and GBER 2014, *supra*, Article 1.
1321. GBER 2014, *supra*, Article 13.

transport costs of goods produced in the outermost regions or in sparsely populated areas, operating aid to financial or insurance undertakings, individual aid to firms that recently liquidated).
- Aid to firms which are the subject of an uncompleted State aid recovery order.
- Aid to firms in difficulty, except in the case of natural disaster aid.

7.6 OVERALL CONCLUSIONS

In addition to the assessment of the EU State aid system in regard to its political, legal, economic and administrative dimensions, the following more generalised conclusions can be drawn from the review of the development of EU State aid law and policy in the last 60 years:

(1) The overall development of EU State aid law, policy and practice is a story of how a relatively simple and novel idea from the 1950s has evolved into a highly complex mechanism of supranational control and a very specialised field of law.
(2) Every aspect of the system has changed and arguably deepened in the last 60 years. Even though the original EEC Treaty rules have changed little in their current TFEU formulations, almost every phrase (notably the notion of "aid," the bases for exemptions from prohibition and the generally couched procedures) have evolved hugely. These developments were primarily driven, in different ways, by the Commission and the European Courts; while external developments and the role of EU Member States also played a part. After 60 years, therefore, the original design of the system is virtually unrecognisable in the present system.
(3) Important strains in the EU State aid regulatory system emerged over the years in at least three respects. First, the emergence of the GBER was a dramatic step back from earlier efforts by the European Commission to increasingly expand State aid control since the 1980s. Second, it has become ever clearer that negative Commission decisions will be contested (often over many years) before the European Courts; indicating that after 60 years there is little real national support for the system in operation (although, of course, Member States are formally committed to it under the Treaty). Third, if the recovery system in regard to illegal State aid fails (and there is limited evidence that it is succeeding fully), the system as a whole risks turning into a Potemkin village of EU law.
(4) At the international level, international law concerns about the trade effects of State aids and subsidies have been the major driver of the various international, regional and national systems of regulation, dating right back to the fifteenth century. While the European Union has developed a unique, complex and far-reaching system of State aid control over the last 60 years, the regulation of subsidies under international trade law has developed in

parallel. However, the content of international regulation is different, it has developed more slowly and cautiously and today it operates quite differently to the EU State aid system. Both systems, however, have the same conceptual roots in the Havana Charter and liberal economic philosophy has played an important part, especially in justifying the control of the relatively recent "subsidising State." From 1960, but more particularly since 1990, the EU has been expanding the scope of its system into non-EU countries, including those aspiring to EU association or eventual membership. Nonetheless, the current iteration of international regulation (the WTO system) displays continuing weaknesses in addressing the non-tariff trade barriers represented by some State aid and subsidy interventions. The separately developed EU system of State aid regulation, in contrast, is more robust and effective.

(5) Effectively addressing the impacts of State aids and subsidies via international treaties is not an easy process. For one thing, the resistance of national governments to subsidy regulation under international law is clear – unless there is a wider imperative such as the prospect of EU membership. Even then, however, the implementation of national systems applying the EU system is fraught with difficulty as this type of regulation regularly results in conflict with national economic policies and business interests. At the same time, the expansion of the EU system into third countries has widened and deepened in many respects, obliging the latter to comply with, not only the general principles of State aid law, but also the detailed rules including their future development via Commission regulatory instruments and the case law of the European Courts.

(6) The 60 years of EU State aid policy can be divided into four phases, each of which was quite different in terms of the intensity of developments, their specific direction and the relative influence of different stakeholders, actors and factors. Thus, the early years began with little controls until the 1970s oil crises and State aid rules were again tightened in the recession period of the 1980s. This was followed in the 1990s with the greater development of legal rules in the EU State aid system and new policy orientations regarding enforcement and interaction with other EU policies. The period from 2000 to 2017 saw real efforts to reform the system, for a range of reasons and in parallel with the expansion of the scope of the system's regulatory reach.

(7) The core "notion of aid" is a far more complex and sophisticated concept than could ever have been imagined by the Treaty founders. While the application of the prohibition on State aid has arguably tightened and enforcement has benefitted from innovative methods and clearer law, the fact remains that the system is still largely permissive rather than prohibitive. Accordingly, what has probably changed most in 60 years is the balance of power in regard to State aid policy. This is reflected in particular in the heavy enforcement of State aid rules in the taxation sphere – which clearly is a cause for concern among many Member States – and in the Commission's emphasis on major cases (which it defines) and the new policy of regulated decentralisation via block exemptions.

(8) At the same time and with the support of the Courts generally, State aid policy has managed to repeatedly reinvent itself in response to various crises and the developmental stages of the EU itself and to align its logic closely with the latest macro-policy initiatives of the EU. In place of its original peripheral conception as a possibly necessary adjunct to competition policy, State aid regulation has become a core policy of the EU itself and a field that now deals more with the alignment of national economic policies than with spillover effects that could damage the common/internal market or impact negatively on cohesion.

(9) Law and policy over the years has also reflected the emergence of *laissez-faire* economics as a single economic philosophy, and this is strongly seen in the new primary focus of State aid regulation on the economics of measures rather than their per se legal compliance. State aid law in turn has conveniently shifted and evolved to facilitate this trend. A related development from recent years is the Commission's orientation towards delineating good aid versus bad aid – a matter that would have been inconceivable prior to 1990. And armed with this philosophy and a huge confidence in its validity, the Commission has gone global with the State aid regime via the WTO (but only to a point) and more so via trade agreements with the close neighbours of the EU. It has also succeeded in reducing inefficient and expensive sectoral aid with a focus on horizontal measures while also using the bureaucracy and power of the State aid system to leverage new economic approaches in national policies which are closely aligned with its core philosophies.

(10) The imperatives for State aid reform in the last 20 years were quite varied – ranging from demands for greater legal certainty to a perceived need to assess important cases more fully from an economic standpoint. It is also clear that the Commission was determined to jettison its standard workload (where most notified cases were approved in any event without conditions) and especially in the context of significant EU Enlargement in 2004 and 2007. However, it is also clear that the Commission would not relinquish its powers in the system without sufficient safeguards against Member State mischief and that the reforms evolved towards a type of decentralisation – building on the experience with pre-accession requirements for national State aid controls and recently completed decentralisation in the antitrust field – while granting some (mostly nominal) control concessions to Member States.

(11) As a result, the European Commission has a generally reduced caseload of more significant cases, it continues to monitor closely how Member States are applying GBER cases and *de minimis* and it has more scope to pursue new areas of interest – especially concerning unfair tax competition in the context of the State aid rules.

(12) From the Member State perspective, the reforms have increased legal certainty (especially on State aid recovery), increased the burden of what is required in notifiable cases and, at the same time, reduced the necessity to

obtain advance approval for a wide range of measures covered by the GBER. The extent of take-up of GBER measures indicates that Member States are increasingly following the parameters of this decentralisation in designing and implementing measures that are centrally defined by the GBER, in order to avoid notification and control.

(13) While the key regulatory articles of the Treaty have remained largely unchanged since the 1950s, Treaty changes in other policy areas created new possibilities and new imperatives which have been pursued, *inter alia*, via the application of the State aid rules. Moreover, in some areas, perceived shortcomings in Treaty mandates have also been addressed via reinvigorated efforts to extend the application of State aid law and policy to try to fill gaps. These areas include developments under the common agricultural and transport policies, audiovisual policy, the EU information society, evolving EU policies concerning environment, energy and steel, regional development and cohesion, the banking sector and taxation. Some of these areas are of particular importance because, as they emerged as new EU policy imperatives (e.g., policies on environment, cohesion and banking), they were quickly taken up as core elements of State aid policy on account of the Commission's strong regulatory powers under its State aid mandate. This is most notable in respect of the interactions between the State aid system and taxation policy. While the application of State aid rules in the tax arena is eminently logical (given that many State aid measures are tax benefits rather than expenditure measures), the European Commission has developed a specific interest in the taxation area which is arguably driven by the failure of political consensus on the harmonisation of direct taxation and the resultant political fears of unfair tax competition.

7.7 FUTURE DIRECTIONS

By 2017, EU State aid law and policy has taken a distinct shift towards sharing the burden of regulation with the current 28 EU Member States – largely by means of extensive block exemption from notifications of the vast majority of State aid measures across the EU. De facto, this has created the essence of a common industrial policy with a distinct focus on other EU policies and economic theory and rationality. This is expected to grow in importance as Member States increasingly adapt economic policy measures to eschew EU State aid control. This important impact of the recent evolution of the system is probably partly accidental (as the reasons are partly administrative) and partly by design (as the European Commission, having failed in its earlier sectoral development efforts, focuses increasingly on economic initiatives related to new definitions of priorities in the common EU interest).

That this is set to continue is clear from the Commission's most recent initiative in the context of the Europe 2020 Agenda – the September 2017 new Industrial policy strategy: "Investing in a smart, innovative and sustainable Industry."[1322] While this makes only limited reference to State aid control, it quietly reflects the position that the EU State aid system is seen as an instrument to ensure that State aid properly incentivises firms to invest in research and development and other competitiveness-enhancing measures. With a range of new initiatives set out in regard to various industries (including steel, defence, the motor industry and digital industries), overall investment in infrastructure and environmental protection, this is likely to become part of a new macro-context for future State aid law and policy in the coming decade.

As seen earlier, a cautious partnership with EU Member States is developing in the context of the devolution of State aid responsibilities coupled with the Commission's new dialogue, transparency and ex-post evaluation initiatives. Undoubtedly, however, the Commission has achieved its long-standing aim of freeing itself up to address major cases.

These new arrangements have also allowed the Commission to map out the essence of what it regards as potentially "good" and "bad" State aid. This is heavily driven by economic theory which, valid or not, is to be firmly applied in respect of potentially bad State aid and is also reflected in the general rules (especially the GBER) in respect of potentially good State aid. Moreover, the Commission has now definitively prioritised its continuing work on tax measures, especially tax rulings considered to give rise to State aid concerns.

It seems reasonable to assume that EU Member States will avail of the flexibilities of State aid devolution as far as possible, although Brexit and post-Brexit considerations, together with other tensions emerging in international trade and the increasing importance of mobilising State aid law and policy to buttress continuously developing EU policies in the common interest, are likely to pose new challenges for both the regulator and the regulated in the coming years.

1322. European Commission: Communication from the Commission – "*Investing in a smart, innovative and sustainable Industry – A renewed EU Industrial Policy Strategy,*" COM (2017) 479 final of 13 September 2017.

Annexes

ANNEX 1

Main Provisions of EU Law: Articles 106 to 109 of the Treaty on the Functioning of the European Union (TFEU)

(Article 106 and Articles 107 – 109 of the TFEU)

Article 106

1. In the case of public undertakings and undertakings to which Member States grant special or exclusive rights, Member States shall neither enact nor maintain in force any measure contrary to the rules contained in the Treaties, in particular to those rules provided for in Article 18 and Articles 101 to 109.
2. Undertakings entrusted with the operation of services of general economic interest or having the character of a revenue-producing monopoly shall be subject to the rules contained in the Treaties, in particular to the rules on competition, in so far as the application of such rules does not obstruct the performance, in law or in fact, of the particular tasks assigned to them. The development of trade must not be affected to such an extent as would be contrary to the interests of the Union.
3. The Commission shall ensure the application of the provisions of this Article and shall, where necessary, address appropriate directives or decisions to Member States.

Article 107

1. Save as otherwise provided in the Treaties, any aid granted by a Member State or through State resources in any form whatsoever which distorts or threatens to distort competition by favouring certain undertakings or the production of certain goods shall, in so far as it affects trade between Member States, be incompatible with the internal market.
2. The following shall be compatible with the internal market:

(a) aid having a social character, granted to individual consumers, provided that such aid is granted without discrimination related to the origin of the products concerned;
(b) aid to make good the damage caused by natural disasters or exceptional occurrences;
(c) aid granted to the economy of certain areas of the Federal Republic of Germany affected by the division of Germany, in so far as such aid is required in order to compensate for the economic disadvantages caused by that division. Five years after the entry into force of the Treaty of Lisbon, the Council, acting on a proposal from the Commission, may adopt a decision repealing this point.
3. The following may be considered to be compatible with the internal market:
(a) aid to promote the economic development of areas where the standard of living is abnormally low or where there is serious underemployment, and of the regions referred to in Article 349, in view of their structural, economic and social situation;
(b) aid to promote the execution of an important project of common European interest or to remedy a serious disturbance in the economy of a Member State;
(c) aid to facilitate the development of certain economic activities or of certain economic areas, where such aid does not adversely affect trading conditions to an extent contrary to the common interest;
(d) aid to promote culture and heritage conservation where such aid does not affect trading conditions and competition in the Union to an extent that is contrary to the common interest;
(e) such other categories of aid as may be specified by decision of the Council on a proposal from the Commission.

Article 108

1. The Commission shall, in cooperation with Member States, keep under constant review all systems of aid existing in those States. It shall propose to the latter any appropriate measures required by the progressive development or by the functioning of the internal market.
2. If, after giving notice to the parties concerned to submit their comments, the Commission finds that aid granted by a State or through State resources is not compatible with the internal market having regard to Article 107, or that such aid is being misused, it shall decide that the State concerned shall abolish or alter such aid within a period of time to be determined by the Commission.
If the State concerned does not comply with this decision within the prescribed time, the Commission or any other interested State may, in derogation from the provisions of Articles 258 and 259, refer the matter to the Court of Justice of the European Union direct.
On application by a Member State, the Council may, acting unanimously, decide that aid which that State is granting or intends to grant shall be considered to be compatible with the internal market, in derogation from the provisions of Article 107 or from the regulations provided for in Article 109, if such a decision is justified by exceptional circumstances. If, as regards the aid in question, the Commission has already initiated

the procedure provided for in the first subparagraph of this paragraph, the fact that the State concerned has made its application to the Council shall have the effect of suspending that procedure until the Council has made its attitude known.
If, however, the Council has not made its attitude known within three months of the said application being made, the Commission shall give its decision on the case.
3. The Commission shall be informed, in sufficient time to enable it to submit its comments, of any plans to grant or alter aid. If it considers that any such plan is not compatible with the internal market having regard to Article 107, it shall without delay initiate the procedure provided for in paragraph 2. The Member State concerned shall not put its proposed measures into effect until this procedure has resulted in a final decision.
4. The Commission may adopt regulations relating to the categories of State aid that the Council has, pursuant to Article 109, determined may be exempted from the procedure provided for by paragraph 3 of this Article.

Article 109

The Council, on a proposal from the Commission and after consulting the European Parliament, may make any appropriate regulations for the application of Articles 107 and 108 and may in particular determine the conditions in which Article 108(3) shall apply and the categories of aid exempted from this procedure.

ANNEX 2

Extracts from the WTO Subsidies and Countervailing Measures Agreement, 1994

Article 1

Definition of a Subsidy

1.1 For the purpose of this Agreement, a subsidy shall be deemed to exist if:

(a) (1) there is a financial contribution by a government or any public body within the territory of a Member (referred to in this Agreement as "government"), i.e. where:

(i) a government practice involves a direct transfer of funds (e.g. grants, loans, and equity infusion), potential direct transfers of funds or liabilities (e.g. loan guarantees);

(ii) government revenue that is otherwise due is foregone or not collected (e.g. fiscal incentives such as tax credits)[1];

(iii) a government provides goods or services other than general infrastructure, or purchases goods;

(iv) a government makes payments to a funding mechanism, or entrusts or directs a private body to carry out one or more of the type of functions illustrated in (i) to (iii) above which would normally be vested in the government and the practice, in no real sense, differs from practices normally followed by governments;

or

1. In accordance with the provisions of Article XVI of GATT 1994 (Note to Article XVI) and the provisions of Annexes I through III of this Agreement, the exemption of an exported product from duties or taxes borne by the like product when destined for domestic consumption, or the remission of such duties or taxes in amounts not in excess of those which have accrued, shall not be deemed to be a subsidy.

(a) there is any form of income or price support in the sense of Article XVI of GATT 1994;
and
(b) a benefit is thereby conferred.

1.2 A subsidy as defined in paragraph 1 shall be subject to the provisions of Part II or shall be subject to the provisions of Part III or V only if such a subsidy is specific in accordance with the provisions of Article 2.

Article 2

Specificity

2.1 In order to determine whether a subsidy, as defined in paragraph 1 of Article 1, is specific to an enterprise or industry or group of enterprises or industries (referred to in this Agreement as "certain enterprises") within the jurisdiction of the granting authority, the following principles shall apply:

(a) Where the granting authority, or the legislation pursuant to which the granting authority operates, explicitly limits access to a subsidy to certain enterprises, such subsidy shall be specific.

(b) Where the granting authority, or the legislation pursuant to which the granting authority operates, establishes objective criteria or conditions[2] governing the eligibility for, and the amount of, a subsidy, specificity shall not exist, provided that the eligibility is automatic and that such criteria and conditions are strictly adhered to. The criteria or conditions must be clearly spelled out in law, regulation, or other official document, so as to be capable of verification.

(c) If, notwithstanding any appearance of non-specificity resulting from the application of the principles laid down in subparagraphs (a) and (b), there are reasons to believe that the subsidy may in fact be specific, other factors may be considered. Such factors are: use of a subsidy programme by a limited number of certain enterprises, predominant use by certain enterprises, the granting of disproportionately large amounts of subsidy to certain enterprises, and the manner in which discretion has been exercised by the granting authority in the decision to grant a subsidy.[3] In applying this subparagraph, account shall be taken of the extent of diversification of economic activities within the jurisdiction of the granting authority, as well as of the length of time during which the subsidy programme has been in operation.

2.2 A subsidy which is limited to certain enterprises located within a designated geographical region within the jurisdiction of the granting authority shall be specific. It is understood that the setting or change of generally applicable tax

2. Objective criteria or conditions, as used herein, mean criteria or conditions which are neutral, which do not favour certain enterprises over others, and which are economic in nature and horizontal in application, such as number of employees or size of enterprise.
3. In this regard, in particular, information on the frequency with which applications for a subsidy are refused or approved and the reasons for such decisions shall be considered.

rates by all levels of government entitled to do so shall not be deemed to be a specific subsidy for the purposes of this Agreement.

2.3 Any subsidy falling under the provisions of Article 3 shall be deemed to be specific.

2.4 Any determination of specificity under the provisions of this Article shall be clearly substantiated on the basis of positive evidence.

Article 5

Adverse Effects

No Member should cause, through the use of any subsidy referred to in paragraphs 1 and 2 of Article 1, adverse effects to the interests of other Members, i.e.:

(a) injury to the domestic industry of another Member[4];

(b) nullification or impairment of benefits accruing directly or indirectly to other Members under GATT 1994 in particular the benefits of concessions bound under Article II of GATT 1994[5];

(c) serious prejudice to the interests of another Member.[6]

This Article does not apply to subsidies maintained on agricultural products as provided in Article 13 of the Agreement on Agriculture.

Article 6

Serious Prejudice

6.1 Serious prejudice in the sense of paragraph (c) of Article 5 shall be deemed to exist in the case of:

(a) the total ad valorem subsidization[7] of a product exceeding 5 per cent[8];

(b) subsidies to cover operating losses sustained by an industry;

(c) subsidies to cover operating losses sustained by an enterprise, other than one-time measures which are non-recurrent and cannot be repeated for that enterprise and which are given merely to provide time for the development of long-term solutions and to avoid acute social problems;

4. The term "injury to the domestic industry" is used here in the same sense as it is used in Part V.
5. The term "nullification or impairment" is used in this Agreement in the same sense as it is used in the relevant provisions of GATT 1994, and the existence of such nullification or impairment shall be established in accordance with the practice of application of these provisions.
6. The term "serious prejudice to the interests of another Member" is used in this Agreement in the same sense as it is used in paragraph 1 of Article XVI of GATT 1994, and includes threat of serious prejudice.
7. The total ad valorem subsidization shall be calculated in accordance with the provisions of Annex IV.
8. Since it is anticipated that civil aircraft will be subject to specific multilateral rules, the threshold in this subparagraph does not apply to civil aircraft.

(d) direct forgiveness of debt, i.e. forgiveness of government-held debt, and grants to cover debt repayment.[9]

6.2 Notwithstanding the provisions of paragraph 1, serious prejudice shall not be found if the subsidizing Member demonstrates that the subsidy in question has not resulted in any of the effects enumerated in paragraph 3.

6.3 Serious prejudice in the sense of paragraph (c) of Article 5 may arise in any case where one or several of the following apply:

(a) the effect of the subsidy is to displace or impede the imports of a like product of another Member into the market of the subsidizing Member;

(b) the effect of the subsidy is to displace or impede the exports of a like product of another Member from a third country market;

(c) the effect of the subsidy is a significant price undercutting by the subsidized product as compared with the price of a like product of another Member in the same market or significant price suppression, price depression or lost sales in the same market;

(d) the effect of the subsidy is an increase in the world market share of the subsidizing Member in a particular subsidized primary product or commodity[10] as compared to the average share it had during the previous period of three years and this increase follows a consistent trend over a period when subsidies have been granted.

6.4 For the purpose of paragraph 3(b), the displacement or impeding of exports shall include any case in which, subject to the provisions of paragraph 7, it has been demonstrated that there has been a change in relative shares of the market to the disadvantage of the non-subsidized like product (over an appropriately representative period sufficient to demonstrate clear trends in the development of the market for the product concerned, which, in normal circumstances, shall be at least one year). "Change in relative shares of the market" shall include any of the following situations: *(a)* there is an increase in the market share of the subsidized product; *(b)* the market share of the subsidized product remains constant in circumstances in which, in the absence of the subsidy, it would have declined; *(c)* the market share of the subsidized product declines, but at a slower rate than would have been the case in the absence of the subsidy.

6.5 For the purpose of paragraph 3(c), price undercutting shall include any case in which such price undercutting has been demonstrated through a comparison of prices of the subsidized product with prices of a non-subsidized like product supplied to the same market. The comparison shall be made at the same level of trade and at comparable times, due account being taken of any

9. Members recognize that where royalty-based financing for a civil aircraft programme is not being fully repaid due to the level of actual sales falling below the level of forecast sales, this does not in itself constitute serious prejudice for the purposes of this subparagraph.

10. Unless other multilaterally agreed specific rules apply to the trade in the product or commodity in question.

other factor affecting price comparability. However, if such a direct comparison is not possible, the existence of price undercutting may be demonstrated on the basis of export unit values.

6.6 Each Member in the market of which serious prejudice is alleged to have arisen shall, subject to the provisions of paragraph 3 of Annex V, make available to the parties to a dispute arising under Article 7, and to the panel established pursuant to paragraph 4 of Article 7, all relevant information that can be obtained as to the changes in market shares of the parties to the dispute as well as concerning prices of the products involved.

6.7 Displacement or impediment resulting in serious prejudice shall not arise under paragraph 3 where any of the following circumstances exist[11] during the relevant period:

(a) prohibition or restriction on exports of the like product from the complaining Member or on imports from the complaining Member into the third country market concerned;

(b) decision by an importing government operating a monopoly of trade or state trading in the product concerned to shift, for non-commercial reasons, imports from the complaining Member to another country or countries;

(c) natural disasters, strikes, transport disruptions or other *force majeure* substantially affecting production, qualities, quantities or prices of the product available for export from the complaining Member;

(d) existence of arrangements limiting exports from the complaining Member;

(e) voluntary decrease in the availability for export of the product concerned from the complaining Member (including, *inter alia*, a situation where firms in the complaining Member have been autonomously reallocating exports of this product to new markets);

(f) failure to conform to standards and other regulatory requirements in the importing country.

6.8 In the absence of circumstances referred to in paragraph 7, the existence of serious prejudice should be determined on the basis of the information submitted to or obtained by the panel, including information submitted in accordance with the provisions of Annex V.

6.9 This Article does not apply to subsidies maintained on agricultural products as provided in Article 13 of the Agreement on Agriculture.

11. The fact that certain circumstances are referred to in this paragraph does not, in itself, confer upon them any legal status in terms of either GATT 1994 or this Agreement. These circumstances must not be isolated, sporadic or otherwise insignificant.

Article 8

Identification of Non-Actionable Subsidies

8.1 The following subsidies shall be considered as non-actionable[12]:

(a) subsidies which are not specific within the meaning of Article 2;

(b) subsidies which are specific within the meaning of Article 2 but which meet all of the conditions provided for in paragraphs 2(a), 2(b) or 2(c) below.

8.2 Notwithstanding the provisions of Parts III and V, the following subsidies shall be non-actionable:

(a) assistance for research activities conducted by firms or by higher education or research establishments on a contract basis with firms if:[13, 14, 15]

- the assistance covers[16] not more than 75 per cent of the costs of industrial research[17] or 50 per cent of the costs of pre-competitive development activity[18, 19];
- and provided that such assistance is limited exclusively to:

---

12. It is recognized that government assistance for various purposes is widely provided by Members and that the mere fact that such assistance may not qualify for non-actionable treatment under the provisions of this Article does not in itself restrict the ability of Members to provide such assistance.
13. Since it is anticipated that civil aircraft will be subject to specific multilateral rules, the provisions of this subparagraph do not apply to that product.
14. Not later than 18 months after the date of entry into force of the WTO Agreement, the Committee on Subsidies and Countervailing Measures provided for in Article 24 (referred to in this Agreement as "the Committee") shall review the operation of the provisions of subparagraph 2(a) with a view to making all necessary modifications to improve the operation of these provisions. In its consideration of possible modifications, the Committee shall carefully review the definitions of the categories set forth in this subparagraph in the light of the experience of Members in the operation of research programmes and the work in other relevant international institutions.
15. The provisions of this Agreement do not apply to fundamental research activities independently conducted by higher education or research establishments. The term "fundamental research" means an enlargement of general scientific and technical knowledge not linked to industrial or commercial objectives.
16. The allowable levels of non-actionable assistance referred to in this subparagraph shall be established by reference to the total eligible costs incurred over the duration of an individual project.
17. The term "industrial research" means planned search or critical investigation aimed at discovery of new knowledge, with the objective that such knowledge may be useful in developing new products, processes or services, or in bringing about a significant improvement to existing products, processes or services.
18. The term "pre-competitive development activity" means the translation of industrial research findings into a plan, blueprint or design for new, modified or improved products, processes or services whether intended for sale or use, including the creation of a first prototype which would not be capable of commercial use. It may further include the conceptual formulation and design of products, processes or services alternatives and initial demonstration or pilot projects, provided that these same projects cannot be converted or used for industrial application or commercial exploitation. It does not include routine or periodic alterations to existing products, production lines, manufacturing processes, services, and other on-going operations even though those alterations may represent improvements.
19. In the case of programmes which span industrial research and pre-competitive development activity, the allowable level of non-actionable assistance shall not exceed the simple average of

(i) costs of personnel (researchers, technicians and other supporting staff employed exclusively in the research activity);
(ii) costs of instruments, equipment, land and buildings used exclusively and permanently (except when disposed of on a commercial basis) for the research activity;
(iii) costs of consultancy and equivalent services used exclusively for the research activity, including bought-in research, technical knowledge, patents, etc.;
(iv) additional overhead costs incurred directly as a result of the research activity;
(v) other running costs (such as those of materials, supplies and the like), incurred directly as a result of the research activity.

(b) assistance to disadvantaged regions within the territory of a Member given pursuant to a general framework of regional development[20] and non-specific (within the meaning of Article 2) within eligible regions provided that:
(i) each disadvantaged region must be a clearly designated contiguous geographical area with a definable economic and administrative identity;
(ii) the region is considered as disadvantaged on the basis of neutral and objective criteria[21], indicating that the region's difficulties arise out of more than temporary circumstances; such criteria must be clearly spelled out in law, regulation, or other official document, so as to be capable of verification;
(iii) the criteria shall include a measurement of economic development which shall be based on at least one of the following factors:
- one of either income per capita or household income per capita, or GDP per capita, which must not be above 85 per cent of the average for the territory concerned;

the allowable levels of non-actionable assistance applicable to the above two categories, calculated on the basis of all eligible costs as set forth in items (i) to (v) of this subparagraph.

20. A "general framework of regional development" means that regional subsidy programmes are part of an internally consistent and generally applicable regional development policy and that regional development subsidies are not granted in isolated geographical points having no, or virtually no, influence on the development of a region.

21. "Neutral and objective criteria" means criteria which do not favour certain regions beyond what is appropriate for the elimination or reduction of regional disparities within the framework of the regional development policy. In this regard, regional subsidy programmes shall include ceilings on the amount of assistance which can be granted to each subsidized project. Such ceilings must be differentiated according to the different levels of development of assisted regions and must be expressed in terms of investment costs or cost of job creation. Within such ceilings, the distribution of assistance shall be sufficiently broad and even to avoid the predominant use of a subsidy by, or the granting of disproportionately large amounts of subsidy to, certain enterprises as provided for in Article 2.

- unemployment rate, which must be at least 110 per cent of the average for the territory concerned;

as measured over a three-year period; such measurement, however, may be a composite one and may include other factors.

(c) assistance to promote adaptation of existing facilities[22] to new environmental requirements imposed by law and/or regulations which result in greater constraints and financial burden on firms, provided that the assistance:

(i) is a one-time non-recurring measure; and

(ii) is limited to 20 per cent of the cost of adaptation; and

(iii) does not cover the cost of replacing and operating the assisted investment, which must be fully borne by firms; and

(iv) is directly linked to and proportionate to a firm's planned reduction of nuisances and pollution, and does not cover any manufacturing cost savings which may be achieved; and

(v) is available to all firms which can adopt the new equipment and/or production processes.

8.3 A subsidy programme for which the provisions of paragraph 2 are invoked shall be notified in advance of its implementation to the Committee in accordance with the provisions of Part VII. Any such notification shall be sufficiently precise to enable other Members to evaluate the consistency of the programme with the conditions and criteria provided for in the relevant provisions of paragraph 2. Members shall also provide the Committee with yearly updates of such notifications, in particular by supplying information on global expenditure for each programme, and on any modification of the programme. Other Members shall have the right to request information about individual cases of subsidization under a notified programme.[23]

8.4 Upon request of a Member, the Secretariat shall review a notification made pursuant to paragraph 3 and, where necessary, may require additional information from the subsidizing Member concerning the notified programme under review. The Secretariat shall report its findings to the Committee. The Committee shall, upon request, promptly review the findings of the Secretariat (or, if a review by the Secretariat has not been requested, the notification itself), with a view to determining whether the conditions and criteria laid down in paragraph 2 have not been met. The procedure provided for in this paragraph shall be completed at the latest at the first regular meeting of the Committee following the notification of a subsidy programme,

22. The term "existing facilities" means facilities which have been in operation for at least two years at the time when new environmental requirements are imposed.

23. It is recognized that nothing in this notification provision requires the provision of confidential information, including confidential business information.

provided that at least two months have elapsed between such notification and the regular meeting of the Committee. The review procedure described in this paragraph shall also apply, upon request, to substantial modifications of a programme notified in the yearly updates referred to in paragraph 3.

8.5 Upon the request of a Member, the determination by the Committee referred to in paragraph 4, or a failure by the Committee to make such a determination, as well as the violation, in individual cases, of the conditions set out in a notified programme, shall be submitted to binding arbitration. The arbitration body shall present its conclusions to the Members within 120 days from the date when the matter was referred to the arbitration body. Except as otherwise provided in this paragraph, the DSU shall apply to arbitrations conducted under this paragraph.

Article 14

Calculation of the Amount of a Subsidy in Terms of the Benefit to the Recipient

For the purpose of Part V, any method used by the investigating authority to calculate the benefit to the recipient conferred pursuant to paragraph 1 of Article 1 shall be provided for in the national legislation or implementing regulations of the Member concerned and its application to each particular case shall be transparent and adequately explained. Furthermore, any such method shall be consistent with the following guidelines:

(a) government provision of equity capital shall not be considered as conferring a benefit, unless the investment decision can be regarded as inconsistent with the usual investment practice (including for the provision of risk capital) of private investors in the territory of that Member;

(b) a loan by a government shall not be considered as conferring a benefit, unless there is a difference between the amount that the firm receiving the loan pays on the government loan and the amount the firm would pay on a comparable commercial loan which the firm could actually obtain on the market. In this case the benefit shall be the difference between these two amounts;

(c) a loan guarantee by a government shall not be considered as conferring a benefit, unless there is a difference between the amount that the firm receiving the guarantee pays on a loan guaranteed by the government and the amount that the firm would pay on a comparable commercial loan absent the government guarantee. In this case the benefit shall be the difference between these two amounts adjusted for any differences in fees;

(d) the provision of goods or services or purchase of goods by a government shall not be considered as conferring a benefit unless the provision is made for less than adequate remuneration, or the purchase is made for more than adequate remuneration. The adequacy of remuneration shall be determined in relation to prevailing market conditions for the good or service in question in the country of provision or purchase (including price, quality, availability, marketability, transportation and other conditions of purchase or sale).

PART VII: NOTIFICATION AND SURVEILLANCE

Article 25
Notifications

25.1 Members agree that, without prejudice to the provisions of paragraph 1 of Article XVI of GATT 1994, their notifications of subsidies shall be submitted not later than 30 June of each year and shall conform to the provisions of paragraphs 2 through 6.

25.2 Members shall notify any subsidy as defined in paragraph 1 of Article 1, which is specific within the meaning of Article 2, granted or maintained within their territories.

25.3 The content of notifications should be sufficiently specific to enable other Members to evaluate the trade effects and to understand the operation of notified subsidy programmes. In this connection, and without prejudice to the contents and form of the questionnaire on subsidies[24], Members shall ensure that their notifications contain the following information:

(i) form of a subsidy (i.e. grant, loan, tax concession, etc.);
(ii) subsidy per unit or, in cases where this is not possible, the total amount or the annual amount budgeted for that subsidy (indicating, if possible, the average subsidy per unit in the previous year);
(iii) policy objective and/or purpose of a subsidy;
(iv) duration of a subsidy and/or any other time-limits attached to it;
(v) statistical data permitting an assessment of the trade effects of a subsidy.

25.4 Where specific points in paragraph 3 have not been addressed in a notification, an explanation shall be provided in the notification itself.

25.5 If subsidies are granted to specific products or sectors, the notifications should be organized by product or sector.

25.6 Members which consider that there are no measures in their territories requiring notification under paragraph 1 of Article XVI of GATT 1994 and this Agreement shall so inform the Secretariat in writing.

25.7 Members recognize that notification of a measure does not prejudge either its legal status under GATT 1994 and this Agreement, the effects under this Agreement, or the nature of the measure itself.

24. The Committee shall establish a Working Party to review the contents and form of the questionnaire as contained in BISD 9S/193-194.

25.8 Any Member may, at any time, make a written request for information on the nature and extent of any subsidy granted or maintained by another Member (including any subsidy referred to in Part IV), or for an explanation of the reasons for which a specific measure has been considered as not subject to the requirement of notification.

25.9 Members so requested shall provide such information as quickly as possible and in a comprehensive manner, and shall be ready, upon request, to provide additional information to the requesting Member. In particular, they shall provide sufficient details to enable the other Member to assess their compliance with the terms of this Agreement. Any Member which considers that such information has not been provided may bring the matter to the attention of the Committee.

25.10 Any Member which considers that any measure of another Member having the effects of a subsidy has not been notified in accordance with the provisions of paragraph 1 of Article XVI of GATT 1994 and this Article may bring the matter to the attention of such other Member. If the alleged subsidy is not thereafter notified promptly, such Member may itself bring the alleged subsidy in question to the notice of the Committee.

25.11 Members shall report without delay to the Committee all preliminary or final actions taken with respect to countervailing duties. Such reports shall be available in the Secretariat for inspection by other Members. Members shall also submit, on a semi-annual basis, reports on any countervailing duty actions taken within the preceding six months. The semi-annual reports shall be submitted on an agreed standard form.

25.12 Each Member shall notify the Committee *(a)* which of its authorities are competent to initiate and conduct investigations referred to in Article 11 and *(b)* its domestic procedures governing the initiation and conduct of such investigations.

Article 26

Surveillance

26.1 The Committee shall examine new and full notifications submitted under paragraph 1 of Article XVI of GATT 1994 and paragraph 1 of Article 25 of this Agreement at special sessions held every third year. Notifications submitted in the intervening years (updating notifications) shall be examined at each regular meeting of the Committee.

26.2 The Committee shall examine reports submitted under paragraph 11 of Article 25 at each regular meeting of the Committee.

ANNEX I (to the SCMA)

ILLUSTRATIVE LIST OF EXPORT SUBSIDIES

(a) The provision by governments of direct subsidies to a firm or an industry contingent upon export performance.

(b) Currency retention schemes or any similar practices which involve a bonus on exports.

(c) Internal transport and freight charges on export shipments, provided or mandated by governments, on terms more favourable than for domestic shipments.

(d) The provision by governments or their agencies either directly or indirectly through government-mandated schemes, of imported or domestic products or services for use in the production of exported goods, on terms or conditions more favourable than for provision of like or directly competitive products or services for use in the production of goods for domestic consumption, if (in the case of products) such terms or conditions are more favourable than those commercially available[25] on world markets to their exporters.

(e) The full or partial exemption remission, or deferral specifically related to exports, of direct taxes[26] or social welfare charges paid or payable by industrial or commercial enterprises.[27]

---

25. The term "commercially available" means that the choice between domestic and imported products is unrestricted and depends only on commercial considerations.

26. For the purpose of this Agreement: The term "direct taxes" shall mean taxes on wages, profits, interests, rents, royalties, and all other forms of income, and taxes on the ownership of real property;The term "import charges" shall mean tariffs, duties, and other fiscal charges not elsewhere enumerated in this note that are levied on imports;The term "indirect taxes" shall mean sales, excise, turnover, value added, franchise, stamp, transfer, inventory and equipment taxes, border taxes and all taxes other than direct taxes and import charges; "Priorstage" indirect taxes are those levied on goods or services used directly or indirectly in making the product; "Cumulative" indirect taxes are multi-staged taxes levied where there is no mechanism for subsequent crediting of the tax if the goods or services subject to tax at one stage of production are used in a succeeding stage of production;

    "Remission" of taxes includes the refund or rebate of taxes; "Remission or drawback" includes the full or partial exemption or deferral of import charges.

27. The Members recognize that deferral need not amount to an export subsidy where, for example, appropriate interest charges are collected. The Members reaffirm the principle that prices for goods in transactions between exporting enterprises and foreign buyers under their or under the same control should for tax purposes be the prices which would be charged between independent enterprises acting at arm's length. Any Member may draw the attention of another Member to administrative or other practices which may contravene this principle and which result in a significant saving of direct taxes in export transactions. In such circumstances the Members shall normally attempt to resolve their differences using the facilities of existing bilateral tax treaties or other specific international mechanisms, without prejudice to the rights and obligations of Members under GATT 1994, including the right of consultation created in the preceding sentence.

    Paragraph (e) is not intended to limit a Member from taking measures to avoid the double taxation of foreign-source income earned by its enterprises or the enterprises of another Member.

(f) The allowance of special deductions directly related to exports or export performance, over and above those granted in respect to production for domestic consumption, in the calculation of the base on which direct taxes are charged.

(g) The exemption or remission, in respect of the production and distribution of exported products, of indirect taxes in excess of those levied in respect of the production and distribution of like products when sold for domestic consumption.

(h) The exemption, remission or deferral of prior-stage cumulative indirect taxes on goods or services used in the production of exported products in excess of the exemption, remission or deferral of like prior-stage cumulative indirect taxes on goods or services used in the production of like products when sold for domestic consumption; provided, however, that prior-stage cumulative indirect taxes may be exempted, remitted or deferred on exported products even when not exempted, remitted or deferred on like products when sold for domestic consumption, if the prior-stage cumulative indirect taxes are levied on inputs that are consumed in the production of the exported product (making normal allowance for waste).[28] This item shall be interpreted in accordance with the guidelines on consumption of inputs in the production process contained in Annex II.

(i) The remission or drawback of import charges in excess of those levied on imported inputs that are consumed in the production of the exported product (making normal allowance for waste); provided, however, that in particular cases a firm may use a quantity of home market inputs equal to, and having the same quality and characteristics as, the imported inputs as a substitute for them in order to benefit from this provision if the import and the corresponding export operations both occur within a reasonable time period, not to exceed two years. This item shall be interpreted in accordance with the guidelines on consumption of inputs in the production process contained in Annex II and the guidelines in the determination of substitution drawback systems as export subsidies contained in Annex III.

(j) The provision by governments (or special institutions controlled by governments) of export credit guarantee or insurance programmes, of insurance or guarantee programmes against increases in the cost of exported products or of exchange risk programmes, at premium rates which are inadequate to cover the long-term operating costs and losses of the programmes.

(k) The grant by governments (or special institutions controlled by and/or acting under the authority of governments) of export credits at rates below those which they actually have to pay for the funds so employed (or would have to pay if they borrowed on international capital markets in order to obtain funds of the same maturity and other credit terms and denominated

28. Paragraph (h) does not apply to value-added tax systems and border-tax adjustment in lieu thereof; the problem of the excessive remission of value-added taxes is exclusively covered by paragraph (g).

in the same currency as the export credit), or the payment by them of all or part of the costs incurred by exporters or financial institutions in obtaining credits, in so far as they are used to secure a material advantage in the field of export credit terms.

Provided, however, that if a Member is a party to an international undertaking on official export credits to which at least twelve original Members to this Agreement are parties as of 1 January 1979 (or a successor undertaking which has been adopted by those original Members), or if in practice a Member applies the interest rates provisions of the relevant undertaking, an export credit practice which is in conformity with those provisions shall not be considered an export subsidy prohibited by this Agreement.

(l) Any other charge on the public account constituting an export subsidy in the sense of Article XVI of GATT 1994.

ANNEX 3

References and Citations

INTERNATIONAL TREATIES

Treaty of Tordesillas, 7 June 1494 accessed at: http://avalon.law.yale.edu/15th_century/mod001.asp

Havana Charter, **United Nations Conference on Trade and Employment, 1947 accessed at:** https://www.wto.org/english/docs_e/legal_e/prewto_legal_e.htm

General Agreement on Tariffs and Trade, 1947 ("GATT 1947"), **accessed at: http://www.worldtradelaw.net/uragreement/gatt.pdf**

The Treaty establishing the European Coal and Steel Community **(Treaty of Paris or ECSC Treaty), 1951, accessed at: https://www.consilium.europa.eu/uedocs/cmsUpload/Treaty%20constituting%20the%20European%20Coal%20and%20Steel%20Community.pdf**

The Treaty establishing the European Economic Community **(Treaty of Rome or EEC Treaty), 1957, accessed at http://www.equalrightstrust.org/ertdocumentbank//rometreaty.pdf.**

Treaty establishing the European Atomic Energy Community **(EURATOM Treaty), 25 March 1957 – 2010 consolidated text accessed at: http://europa.eu/eu-law/decision-making/treaties/pdf/consolidated_version_of_the_treaty_establishing_the_european_atomic_energy_community/consolidated_version_of_the_treaty_establishing_the_european_atomic_energy_community_en.pdf**

EFTA Agreement on Government Aid, **EFTA Bulletin, October 1968.**

Agreement on the interpretation and application of Articles VI, XVI and XXIII of the General Agreement on Tariffs and Trade (Subsidies Code), 1979– **accessed at: http://www.worldtradelaw.net/tokyoround/subsidiescode.pdf**

Treaty on European Union (Maastricht Treaty), **OJ C 191 of 29 July 1992.**

Council of Europe: European Convention on Cinematographic Co-production, **Strasbourg, 2 October 1992, accessed at: http://www.coe.int/en/web/conventions/full-list/-/conventions/rms/090000168007bd2d.**

WTO: Subsidies and Countervailing Measures Agreement, 1994 **(accessed at: wto.org).**

WTO: Agreement on Agriculture, 1994 **(accessed at: wto.org).**

WTO: General Agreement on Trade in Services, 1994 **(accessed at: wto.org).**

WTO: Trade-Related Investment Measures Agreement, 1994 **(accessed at: wto.org).**

Agreement between the EFTA States **on the establishment of a Surveillance Authority and a Court of Justice on 2 May 1992, OJ L 344 of 31 January 1994 and EFTA States' official gazettes, accessed at: http://secretariat.efta.int/Web/legaldocuments/EsaAndEFTACourtAgreement/Documents**

Interim Association Agreement **between the European Communities and their Member States, of the one part, and Palestinian Authority of the West Bank and the Gaza Strip, OJ L 187 of 16 July 1997.**

Agreement on Partnership and Co-operation **establishing a partnership between the European Communities and their Member States, of the one part, and the Russian Federation, of the other part, OJ L 327 of 27 November 1997.**

Euro-Mediterranean Agreement **establishing an association between the European Communities and their Member States, of the one part, and the Republic of Tunisia, of the other part, OJ L 97 of 30 March 1998.**

Charter of Fundamental Rights of the European Union, **OJ C 364 of 18 December 2000.**

Euro-Mediterranean Agreement **establishing an association between the European Communities and their Member States, of the one part, and the Kingdom of Morocco, of the other part, OJ L 70 of 18 March 2000.**

Euro-Mediterranean Agreement **establishing an Association between the European Communities and their Member States, of the one part, and the Hashemite Kingdom of Jordan, of the other part, OJ L 129of 15 May 2002.**

Stabilisation and Association Agreement **between the European Communities and their Member States, of the one part, and the former Yugoslav Republic of Macedonia, of the other part of 26 March 2001, OJ L 84 of 20 March 2004.**

Euro-Mediterranean Agreement **establishing an association between the European Communities and their Member States, of the one part, and the Arab Republic of Egypt, OJ L 345 of 31 December 2003**

Stabilisation and Association Agreement **between the European Communities and their Member States, of the one part, and the Republic of Croatia, of the other part (October 2001), OJ L 26 of 28 January 2005.**

Energy Community Treaty 2005, **as amended, accessed at: https://www.energy-community.org/portal/page/portal/ENC_HOME/ENERGY_COMMUNITY/Legal/Treaty**

The Kyoto Protocol Treaty, 2005 **accessed at: http://unfccc.int/kyoto_protocol/items/2830.php**

Central European Free Trade Agreement (CEFTA) 2006 **(accessed at http://cefta.int/)**.

Treaty on the Functioning of the European Union, **OJ C 115 of 9 May 2008.**

Stabilisation and Association Agreement **between the European Communities and their Member States, of the one part, and the Republic of Albania SAA (2006), OJ L 107 of 28 April 2009.**

Stabilisation and Association Agreement **between the European Communities and their Member States, of the one part, and the Republic of Montenegro (March 2007), OJ L 108 of 29 April 2010.**

Treaty on the Eurasian Economic Union, 2014 **accessed at: http://www.un.org/en/ga/sixth/70/docs/treaty_on_eeu.pdf**

Association Agreement **between the European Union and its Member States, of the one part, and Ukraine, of the other part, 2014, OJ L 161 of 29 May 2014.**

Association Agreement **between the European Union and the European Atomic Energy Community and their Member States, of the one part, and Georgia, of the other part, OJ L 261 of 30 August 2014.**

Association Agreement **between the European Union and the European Atomic Energy Community and their Member States, of the one part, and the Republic of Moldova, of the other part, OJ L 260 of 30 August 2014.**

Bibliography

C. Ahlborn and D. Piccinin: "*The application of the Principles of Restructuring Aid to Banks during the Financial Crisis*" in European State Aid Law Quarterly, Vol. 1 2010.

C. Ahlborn and D. Piccinin: "*The Great Recession and other mishaps: the Commission's policy of restructuring aid in a time of crisis*" in E. Szyszczak (Ed.) Research Handbook on European State Aid Law, Edward Elgar Publishing, 2011.

F. Andriessen: "*The Role of Anti-Trust in the Face of Economic Recession: State Aids in the EEC*"', European Competition Law Review, 1983.

P. Anestis & S. Drakakakis Howrey: "*State aid policy and services of general economic interest: shedding some light on a controversial area*", European Antitrust Review, 2006.

William C. Atkinson: "*A History of Spain and Portugal*", Penguin, London, 1960.

A. Bartosh: '*The concept of selectivity?*', in E. Szyszczak (Ed.) Research Handbook on European State Aid Law, Edward Elgar Publishing, 2011 p. 180.

R. Behboodi: "*Industrial Subsidies and Friction in World Trade*", Routledge Publishing, London & New York, 1994.

A. Biondi: "*Some Reflections on the Notion of "State Resources" in European Community State Aid Law*", Fordham International Law Journal, Vol. 30, Issue 5/2006.

A. Biondi, '*State aid is falling down, falling down: An analysis of the case law on the notion of aid*', Common Market Law Review, Issue 6/2013.

Sir Leon Brittan*: "European Competition Policy - Keeping the Playing-Field Level*", Brassey's (UK) for the Centre for European Policy Studies, 1992.

J. Broche, O. Chatterjee, I Orissich and N. Tosics in "*State Aid for Films – a policy in motion?*", Competition Policy Newsletter, DG Competition, Spring 2007.

K. Brown and T. Tiemann: "EU State aid policy and the EC – Airbus case", Maastricht University, 2012.

A. Campbell: "*Common Market Law*", Longman (London), 1975.

M. Cini: "*From Soft Law to Hard Law? – Discretion and Rule-making in the Commission's State Aid Regime*", European University Institute, EUI Working Papers, RSC No 2000/35, 2000.

C. H. Church and D. Phinnemore: "Guide to the European Treaties - from Rome to Maastricht, Amsterdam, Nice and Beyond", 2002, Penguin, London.

Copenhagen Think Tank/European Audiovisual Observatory: http://www.dfi.dk/NR/rdonlyres/1BE19F2D-F61F-403F-934C-B0AB2447D9D8/0/CTT_Information_Notes_300606.pdf.

F. de Sousa da Câmara and M.R. da Fonseca: *"EU State Aid Rules and the Azores Cases"*, in Tax Notes International, November 9, 2009.

R. M. D'Sa: *"Instant State Aid Law in a Financial Crisis – A U-Turn?"*, European State Aid Law Quarterly, Vol. 2/2009.

S. Dillon: "International Trade and Economic Law and the European Union", Hart Publishing, Oxford and Portland Oregon, 2002.

M. Draghi: *Memorial Lecture in Honour of Tommaso Padoa-Schioppa*, speech delivered in London on 9 July 2014.

K. Driurdz and C. Marchgraber: *"Non-discrimination in European and Tax Treaty Law. Open Issues and Recent Challenges"*, International Tax Law, Vienna, 2015, p. 317.

J. Edelman Spero: *"The Politics of International Economic Relations"*, London, 1982.

R. E. Edwards and S. Lester: *"Towards a More Comprehensive World Trade Organisation Agreement on Trade Related Investment Measures"*, Stanford Journal of International Law, 1997, Vol. 33, p. 169.

C.D.Ehlermann: *"State aid Control – Success or Failure?"*, 18 January 1995, Fordham International Law Journal, 1995.

C. D. Ehlermann and M. Everson (Ed): *"European Competition Law Annual 1999 – Selected issues in the field of State Aid"*, Oxford, 2001.

M. Emerson: *"After the UK's Brexit. White Paper – What's the next move towards a CFTA?"*, CEPS Policy Insights, No 2017/07, February 2017.

Ernst & Young Survey: *"Regions of the New Europe"*, as reported in the Financial Times of 24 October 1995.

"State Aid and Taxation – All Clear?", Editorial, European State Aid Law Quarterly, Vol. 3/2015.

A. Evans and S. Martin: *"Socially acceptable distortion of competition: Community Policy on State Aids"*, European Law Review, April 1991.

J. Faull: *"Prospects for Decentralisation of EU State Aid Control"* in European Competition Annual 1999: Selected Issues in the Field of State Aids, Ehlermann & Everson (eds.), Hart Publishing, 2001.

J. Fingleton, F. Ruane and V. Ryan: *"Market Definition and State Aid Control"* in European Commission: "European Economy", No 3. 1999 - "State Aid and the Single Market".

J. Fingleton: *"How to apply anti-trust market definition rules to state aid"* in European Competition Law Annual 1999 – Selected Issues in the Field of State aids, Ehlermann and Everson (eds.), Oxford, 2001.

K. Flåm: *"EU Environmental State Aid Policy. Wide Implications, Narrow Participation?"*, CANES Working Paper, FNI Report 13/2008.

H.W. Friederiszick, L. A. Röller and V. Verouden: *"European State Aid Control- An Economic Framework"*, in Handbook of Antitrust Economics, P. Buccirossi (ed), MIT Press, February 2006.

R. Greaves: *"Autonomous regions, taxation and EC state-aid rules"*, European Law Review, 2009.

Green European Foundation: *"The role of State aid in creating a green economy"*, November 2013.

S. Hamilton: *"The WTO Ruling against Boeing is Meaningless"*, Forbes Magazine, 28 November 2016, accessed at: https://www.forbes.com/sites/scotthamilton5/2016/11/28/wto-boeing-ruling-gives-airbus-good-pr-but-its-meaningless/#25700c937d7c.

L. Hancher, T. Ottervanger and P.J. Slot: *"EC State Aids"* (First Edition), Chancery Law Publications, 1993.

L. Hancher, T. Ottervanger and P.J. Slot: *"EC State aids"*, (Third edition), Thomson/ Sweet & Maxwell, 2006.

L. Hancher, T. Ottervanger and P.J. Slot: *"EC State Aids"* (Fourth Edition), Thomson/ Sweet & Maxwell, 2012.

F. Harvey: *"Europe places bets on natural gas to secure energy future"*, The Guardian, 16 February 2016.

G. E. Luengo Hernandez de Madrid, "Regulation of subsidies and State aids in WTO and EC law", Kluwer Law International, 2006.

P. Holmes and A. Smith: *"Automobile Industry"* in P. Buigues, A. Jacquemin and A. Sapir (Eds): *"European Policies on Competition, Trade and Industry - Conflict and Complementaries"*, Aldershot, Edward Elgar, 1994.

A. Houtman: *"EC State Aid Control: In search of the right balance"* in European Competition Law Annual 1999 – Selected Issues in the Field of State aids, Ehlermann and Everson (eds), Oxford, 2001.

R. Hudec: *"GATT Dispute Settlement after the Tokyo Round: An Unfinished Business"*, Cornell International Law Journal, 1980, Vol. 13, Issue 2.

R. Hudec: *"Regulation of Domestic Subsidies under the MTN Subsidies Code"* in *"Interface Three – Legal Treatment of Domestic Subsidies"*, Wallace et al. (eds.), Washington, International Law Institute, 1984.

R. Hudec: *"Legal issues in US-EC Trade Policy: GATT litigation 1960-1985"* in *"Issues in US-EC Trade Relations"*, Baldwin, Hamilton and Sapir (eds), Chicago, Chicago University Press, 1988.

F. Ilzkovitz, R. Meiklejohn and J. H. Schmidt: *"The Control of State Aid – A proposal for a Co-ordinated approach"* in European Competition Law Annual 1999 – Selected Issues in the Field of State aids, Ehlermann and Everson (eds), Oxford, 2001.

Irish Department of Finance: *Programme for Peace and Reconciliation in Ireland and Northern Ireland*, (Stationery Office, Dublin) 1995.

Irish Department of Finance: *"Apple State Aid Case - Explanation of the main lines of argument in Ireland's annulment application lodged with the General Court of the European Union on 9 November 2016"*, 19 December 2016.

Jones Day, Lovells, Allen & Overy: *"Study on the Enforcement of State Aid Law at National Level"*, March 2006.

W. Jinglian, *"A Key Step to Establish the Fundamental Status of Competition Policies"*, Chinese Government Network, 22 June 2016, accessible at: http://finance.sina.com.cn/roll/2016-06-22/doc-ifxtfsae6008165.shtml.

Karim, Md. Rezaul: *"The EU Market Economy Investor Principle: A Good Paradigm?"*, University of Birmingham – School of Law, 28 April 2014.

J. Keuchel and A. Schrinner: "*Gradual harmonisation of tax law by the European Court of Justice*", Linklaters, Oppenhoff and Radler in "*Legal500.com*", June 2001.

C. Koenig: "*Where is State aid law heading to?*", European State Aid Law Quarterly, Vol. 4/2014, p. 611.

M. Köhler: "*New Trends Concerning the Application of the Private Investor Test*", European State Aid Law Quarterly, Vol. 1/2011, p. 21.

K. Kowalik-Bacczyk: "*Should we Polish up?, Polish Constitutional Tribunal and the idea of the Supremacy of EU Law*", German Law Journal, Vol. 10, 1 October 2005.

KPMG: "*Commission issues Notice on the Notion of State Aid*", Tax Flash, Issue 284 of 23 May 2016 accessible at: https://assets.kpmg.com/content/dam/kpmg/pdf/2016/05/etf-284-state-aid-clarification-from-commission.pdf.

N. Kroes: "*The State Aid Action Plan – Delivering Less and Better Targeted Aid*", SPEECH/05/440, London, 14th July 2005.

N. Kroes: '*Why EU state aid is not the right tool to fight tax avoidance*', The Guardian magazine, 1 September 2016.

J. Kühling and J.D. Braun: "*State Aid: The effective application of EC State aid procedures: From a plan to grant aid to the recovery of illegal aid – the role of national law and practice in Germany*", in "The Effective Application of EU State Aid Procedures – The Role of National Law and Practice", P.F. Nemitz (ed.), Kluwer Law International, 2007.

S. Lall: "*Selective policies for export promotion – lessons from the Asian Tigers*", in "Non-traditional export promotion in Africa – experiences and issues", G. K. Helleiner (ed), New York, Palgrave Macmillan, 2002.

M. Lang: "*State Aid for the Coal Sector - Inevitable or Dispensable?*", European State Aid Law Quarterly, Vol. 1/2012.

S. Langsdorf: "*EU Energy Policy: From the ECSC to the Energy Roadmap 2050*", European Green Foundation, December 2011.

F. C. Laprévote and M. Paron: "*The Commission's Decisional Practice on State Aid to Banks: An Update*", European State Aid Law Quarterly, 1/2015, pp. 88–116.

K. A. Lavdas and M. M. Mendrinou: "*Politics, subsidies and competition: the new politics of state intervention in the European Union*", Cheltenham, UK, Edward Elgar, 1999.

T. C. Lawton: "*The creation and control of EC Industrial Policy – Lessons from the Electronics Sector*", DCUBS Research Papers, No 7/1995-1996, Department of Government, University of Essex accessible at: http://www.dcu.ie/dcubs/research_papers/no.7html.

Loman, Mortelmans, Post and Watson: "*Culture and Community Law*", Walters Kluwer, 1992.

F. Louis and A. Vallery: "*State aid and financing of public services – a comment on the Altmark judgment of the Court of Justice*" Competition Law Insight, September 2003.

P. Lowe: "*The treatment of Subsidies in the WTO Framework*", in European Competition Law Annual 1999 – Selected Issues in the Field of State aids, Ehlermann and Everson (eds), Oxford, 2001.

R. Luja: "'*Does the Modernization of State Aid Control Put Legal Certainty in Risk?*", European State Aid Law Quarterly, 4/2012.

G. Matsos: "*Systematic Misconceptions of State Aid Law in the Area of Taxation*", European State Aid Law Quarterly, 3/2014.

T. May: Speech of Prime Minister Teresa May of 17 January 2017, accessible at: http://www.independent.co.uk/news/uk/home-news/full-text-theresa-may-brexit-speech-global-britain-eu-european-union-latest-a7531361.html.

M. Merola: "*Regional Aid: Recent Trends and Some Historical Background – with special Focus on large Investment Projects*", European State Aid Law Quarterly, 3/2010.

M. Merola: "*The Forces Shaping State Aid Control in the EU*" in '*What Shapes the Law – Reflections on the History, Law, Politics and Economics of International and European Subsidy disciplines*', L. Rubini and J. Hawkins (ed.), University of Birmingham, European University Institute, 2016.

P. Messerlin: "*External aspects of State Aids*", European Commission: European Economy, No 3/1999.

K. Middlemas: "*Orchestrating Europe – the Informal Politics of European Union 1973-1995*", Fontana, London, 1995.

R. Middleton: "*Negotiating on Non-Tariff Distortions of Trade – the EFTA Precedent*", London, Macmillan, 1975.

K. A. Miller: "*Why did Columbus sail?*" in Christian History, Issue 35, Volume XI, No 3.

P. Morici: "*Resolving the North American Subsidies War*", Journal of Canadian-American Public Policy, No 27 of September 1996.

P. Nicolaides: "*Puzzles of State Aid: Structural Funds, Cumulation and De Minimis*"', European State Aid Law Quarterly, 3/2005.

P. Nicolaides: "*State aid on the day after the exit of the UK from the EU*", 4 February 2017 accessible at: http://www.stateaidhub.eu/blogs/stateaiduncovered/post/8330.

M. Noland and H. Pack: "*Industrial Policy in an era of globalisation – Lessons from Asia*", Washington DC, Institute for International Economics, 2003.

OECD: *Transfer Pricing Guidelines for Multinational Enterprises and Tax Administrations*, 16 August 2010.

OECD Report: Environmental Outlook to 2050: The Consequences of Inaction, 2012.

A. Peczenik, Alexander: "*What is Right? On Democracy, Legal Safety, Ethics and Legal Argumentation*" (Vad är rätt? Om demokrati, rättssäkerhet, etik och juridisk argumentation), Fritze, Stockholm, 1995.

P. Pescatore: "*The Doctrine of 'Direct Effect': An Infant Disease of Community Law*", European Law Review Vol. 155/1983.

A. Petersen: "State aid problems in the Banking Sector" in *European Competition Law Annual 1999 – Selected issues in the field of State Aid*, C.D. Ehlermann and M. Everson, M. (ed), Oxford, 2001, p. 177.

A. Petersen: "*State aid and European Union – state aid in the light of trade, competition, industrial and cohesion policies*" in "State aid - Community Law and policy", I. Harden (ed.), Bundesanzeiger, Cologne, 1993.

J. Petersen: "*Decision making in the European Union – towards a framework for analysis*", Journal of European Public Policy, Vol. 2/1995.

J. J. Piernas López and M. Ross: "*State Aids: Maturing into a Constitutional Problem*", YEL, 1995, p. 82.

J. J. Piernas López: "*Understanding the Notion of State Aid through Policy*", European University Institute, Dubrovnik, April 2012.

J. J. Piernas López: "*The Concept of State Aid under EU Law: From internal market to competition and beyond*", Oxford University Press, 2015.

J. J. Piernas López: "*The Evolving Nature of the Notion of Aid under EU Law*", European State Aid Law Quarterly 3/2016.

R. Plender: "*Definition of Aid*" in *The Law of State Aid in the European Union*, Published online, March 2012, available at: http://dx.doi.org/10.1093/acprof:oso/9780199265329.003.0001.

V. Price-Curzon: "*Free trade areas: The European Experience*", Howe Institute, Toronto, 1987.

C. Quigley: "*General Taxation*" in *The Law of State Aid in the European Union*, Oxford, 2003, pp. 207–217.

C. Quigley and A. M. Collins: "*EC State Aid Law and Policy*", Hart Publishing, Portland, Oregon, USA, 2003.

C. Quigley: "*European State Aid Law and Policy*" (Third Edition), Hart Publishing, Oxford and Portland, Oregon, 2015.

C. M. Radaelli: "*Policy Narratives in the European Union – the Case of Harmful Tax Competition*", European University Institute, Working Paper RSC No 98/34 accessible at: https://www.eui.eu/DepartmentsAndCentres/RobertSchuman Centre/Publications/WorkingPapers/9834t.

C. M. Radaelli: "*The Code of Conduct Against Harmful Tax Competition - Open Method of Coordination in Disguise*", European University Institute, EUI Working Papers, RSC No 2002/43.

J. Raitio: "*Legal Certainty*", IVR – Encyclopaedia of Jurisprudence, Legal Theory and Philosophy of Law, available at: www.ivr-enc.info/en/article.

J. Raitio: "*The Principle of Legal Certainty in EC Law*", Kluwer Academic Publishers, 2003.

F. Rawlinson: "*The role for policy frameworks, codes and guidelines in the control of state aid*", in "State Aid – Community Law and Policy", I. Harden (ed.), Bundesanzeiger, Cologne, 1993.

Revue des Droits de la Concurrence: "*Delivering the State aid Reform – Interview with Lowri Evans, Deputy Director General for State Aid, European Commission*", Institut de droit de la concurrence, No 3/2006, pp. 7–9 accessible at: https://www.concurrences.com/en/review/issues/No-4-2006/interview/lowri-evans-new-state-aid-deputy-director-general-delivering-the-state-aid-12589.

E. Righini: "*State Aid Control: An Evolutionary Theory of Resilience and Adaptation*", European University Institute, 2016.

D. Rodrik: "*Trade and Industrial policy reform in developing countries – a review of recent theory and evidence*" in "Handbook of Development Economics", J. Behrman and T.N. Srinivasen (eds.), Amsterdam, Netherlands, Vol III/1993.

D. Rodrik: "*Industrial Policy for the twenty-first century*", CEPR Discussion Paper No 47, London, Centre for Economic Policy Research, 2004.

E. Roe: *Narrative Policy Analysis*, Duke University Press, Durham, 1994.

L. A. Röller: *"Economic Analysis and Competition Policy Enforcement in Europe"* in *Modelling European Mergers: Theory,* Competition Policy and Case Studies, Edward Elgar (ed.), 2005.

P. Rossi-Maccanico: *"State Aid Review of Member States' Measures Relating to Direct Business Taxation"*, European State Aid Law Quarterly, 2/2004.

L. Rubini: *"The Definition of Subsidy and State Aid: WTO and EC Law in Comparative Perspective"*, Oxford University Press, 2009.

M. Sarcinelli: *"State aid problems in the Banking Sector"* in *"European Competition Law Annual 1999 – Selected issues in the field of State Aid"*, C.D. Ehlermann and M. Everson, M. (ed), Oxford, 2001, p. 178.

Despina Schina: *"State Aids under the EEC'*, Oxford, 1987.

Adam Smith: *"Inquiry into the Nature and Causes of the Wealth of Nations"*, Glasgow, 1776.

S. Strange: *"States, Firms and Diplomacy"*, International Affairs, Vol. 68/1992, No 1.

E. Stuart and S. Bruen-Nilsen: *"International and European Best Practices for the Preparation of Legislation"*, Astana, January 2005.

E. Stuart and D. Vuletić: *"Introduction to the Regulation of State aid under the Law of the European Communities – A Handbook for Bosnia and Herzegovina"*, Sarajevo, 2006.

E. Stuart: *"Analysis and Assessment of key issues in the regulation of government supports to undertakings under international law"*, Belgrade, 2008 (unpublished).

E. Stuart, S. Cemnolonskis and I. Roginska: *Report on State Aid Mapping for Ukraine*, November 2014, accessible at: www.eupublicprocurement.org.ua.

E. Stuart and I. Roginska: *"State aid regulation and Ukrainian Industrial Policy"* European State Aid Law Quarterly, Vol. 15, No 1, March 2016.

J. Stuart Mill: *"Essays on Some Unsettled Questions of Political Economy"*, 1844.

J. Stuart Mill: *"Principles of Political Economy"*, 1848.

P. Sutherland, *"Foreword"*, in Competition Rules in the EEC and the ECSC Applicable to State Aids, Brussels-Luxembourg, Commission of the European Communities, 1987.

J. Thiesing in Wohlfarth, Everling, Glaesner and Sprung: *"Die Europaische Wirtschaftsgemeinschaft, Kommentar zum Vertrag"*, Verlag Franz, 1960, Artikel 92, p. 276.

J. B. Tucker: *"Partners and Rivals: A model of international Collaboration"*, International Organisation, Vol. 45, No 1, Winter 1991.

UK House of Lords Select Committee on the European Communities: *State Aids to Agriculture*, 1981-82, Seventh Report, HMSO London.

UK Government: *'Response to Commission Roadmap for State Aid Reform'*, accessible at: http://ec.europa.eu/competition/state_aid/reform/comments_environmental_protection_revision/wrap2.pdf.

UK Government: *'Statement on European Court Judgement on taxation in Gibraltar'*, 12 January 2012, available at: https://www.gov.uk/government/news/statement-on-european-court-judgement-on-taxation-in-gibraltar.

UK Government White Paper: "*The United Kingdom's exit from and new partnership with the European Union*", Cm. 9417, 2 February 2017.

D. Vaughan (Ed.): *The Law of the European Communities*, Vol. I, Butterworths, London, 1986.

M. Vestager: "*The EU State aid rules: working together for fair competition*", Speech by Competition Commissioner to the High Level Forum on State Aid Modernisation, Brussels, 3 June 2016.

P. Werner and V. Verouden (Eds.): "*EU State Aid Control – Law and Economics*" Kluwer Law International, 2016.

M. Wall and d Vis-Dunbar: "*The Standstill in Subsidies – Update*", International Institute for Sustainable Development, November 2005, accessible at http://www.iisd.org.

R. Whish: "*Competition Law*", Butterworths, London, 1994.

F. G. Wishlade: "*Subsidies and State Aids – the definition of acceptable measures under the EU and WTO rules*", European Policies research Centre, University of Strathclyde, September 1996.

F. G. Wishlade: "*The Control of Regional Aid to Large Investment Projects: Workable Compromise or Arbitrary Constraint?*", in European State Aid Law Quarterly, 3/2008.

WTO: "*World Trade Report 2006 – exploring the links between subsidies, trade and the WTO*", Geneva, 2006.

S. Zhang: "*China's Fair Competition Review System: China Takes Another Significant Step Eight Years After Enacting the Anti-Monopoly Law*", Anti-Trust Watch, 1 July 2016, accessible at: http://blogs.orrick.com/antitrust/2016/07/01/chinas-fair-competition-review-system-china-takes-another-significant-step-eight-years-after-enacting-the-anti-monopoly-law.

Table of European Court Cases

European Court of Justice/Court of Justice of the European Union

Case C-311/97: *Royal Bank of Scotland plc v. Elliniko Dimosio (Greek State)*, [1999] ECR I-2651., 322
Case C-327/97: *Italy v. Commission*, [2004] ECR I-3679., 44
Cases C-15/98 and 105/99: *Italy and Sardegna Lines*, [2000] ECR I-8855., 44
Case C-83/98P: *France v. Ladbroke and Commission*, [2000] ECR I-03271., 293
Case C-156/98: *Germany v. Commission*, [2000] ECR I-6857., 60
Joined Cases C-180/98 to C-184/98: *Pavlov and Others v. Stichting Pensioenfonds Medische Specialisten*, [2000] ECR I-6451., 40
Case C-351/98: *Spain v. Commission (Renove I)*, [2002] ECR I-8031., 193
Case C-378/98: *Commission v. Belgium*, [2001] ECR I-5107., 87
Case C-379/98: *PreussenElektra AG v. Schleswag AG*, [2001] ECR I-2099., 192, 222
Case C-480/98: *Spain v. Commission*, [2000] ECR I-8717., 86, 235, 360
Case C-143/99: *Adria-Wien Pipeline GmbH and Wietersdorfer & Peggauer Zementwerke GmbH v. Finanzlandesdirektion für Kärnten*, [2001] ECR I-8365., 40, 193, 221
Case C-310/99: *Italy v. Commission*, [2002] ECR I-2289., 45, 180
Case C-334/99: *Germany v. Commission*, [2003] ECR I-1139., 60
Case C-482/99: *France v. Commission (Stardust)*, [2002] ECR I-4397., 34, 294
Case C-53/00: *Ferring v. ACOS*, [2001] ECR 1-9067., 20, 207, 208
Cases C-57/00P and C-61/00 P: *Freistaat Sachsen v. Commission*, [2003] ECR I-9975., 60
Case C-277/00: *Germany v. Commission*, [2004] ECR I-3925., 60, 86
Case C-278/00: *Greece v. Commission*, [2004] ECR I-3997., 57
Case C-280/00: *Altmark Trans GmbH and Regierungspräsidium Magdeburg v. Nahverkehrsgesellschaft Altmark GmbH, and Oberbundesanwalt beim Bundesverwaltungsgericht*, [2003] ECR I-7747., 18, 30, 50, 194, 208, 360
Case C-298/00: *Italy v. Commission*, [2004] ECR I-4087., 44
Case C-82/01P: *Aéroports de Paris v. Commission*, [2002] ECR I-9297., 251
Joined Cases C-83/01 P, C-93/01 P and C-94/01 P: *Chronopost SA, La Poste and French Republic v. Ufex and others*, [2003] ECR I-6993., 222
Case C-126/01: *Ministère de l'Économie, des Finances et de l'Industrie v. GEMO SA.*, [2003] ECR I-13769., 294
Case C-66/02: *Italy v. Commission*, [2005] ECR I-10901., 323
Joined Cases C-183/02 and C-187/02: *P Demesa v. Commission*, [2004] ECR I-10609., 87
Case C-345/02: *Pearle BV, Hans Prijs Optiek Franchise BV and Rinck Opticiëns BV v. Hoofdbedrijfschap Ambachten*, [2004] ECR I-7139., 294
Case C-88/03: *Portugal v. Commission*, [2006] ECR I-7115., 112, 200, 311, 313
Case C-172/03: *Heiser*, [2005] ECR I-1627., 45, 180
Cases C-182/03 and C-217/03: *Belgium and Forum 187 ASBL v. Commission*, [2006] ECR I-5479., 317, 323
Case C-253/03: *CLT-UFA SA v. Finanzamt Köln-West*, [2006] ECR I-1831., 322,
Joined Cases C-346 and 529/03: *Atzeni v. Regione autonoma della Sardegna*, [2006] ECR I-1875., 44, 87
Case C-399/03: *Commission v. Council*, [2006] ECR I-5629., 16

Court of First Instance/General Court

European Commission State Aid Decisions

Other Case Law Citations

Germany

Italy

Portugal

Administrative Supreme Court of Portugal, file 1091/05, 24 May 2006., 202

World Trade Organisation

The Domestic International Sales Corporation, Panel Report, (1976), BISD, 23rd Supplement, 98., 105

Administration of the Foreign Investment Review Act (FIRA), 1984, BISD, 30th Supplement, 140 et seq., 115

Ecuador, US and others v. EC: Regime for the Importation, Sale and Distribution of Bananas, Panel Report, 22 May 1997, WT/DS27/R., 116

European Communities – Regime for the importation, sale and distribution of bananas, Report of the Appellate Body of 25 September 1997, WT/D27/AB/R., 116

US, EC and Japan v. Indonesia: Certain Measures Affecting the Automobile Industry, Panel Report of 2 July 1998, WT/DS54, 55, 59 and 64/R., 116

EC and Japan v. Canada: Measures Affecting the Automotive Industry, Panel Report of 11 February 2000, WT/D139, 142/R., 116

Foreign Sales Corporation Case - EC v. US: Tax Treatment for Foreign Sales Corporations, Report of the Panel, 8 October 1999, WT/DS108/R and Appellate Body Report, 24 February 2000, WT/DS108/AB/R., 105

European Communities - Measures Affecting Trade in Large Civil Aircraft, Panel Report, 22 September 2016, DS316., 124

United States — Conditional Tax Incentives for Large Civil Aircraft, Panel Report, 28 November 2016, DS487., 122

Other EU Documents

European Council and Council of the European Union

Intergovernmental Committee on European Integration: The Brussels Report on the General Common Market (the Spaak Report), 1956. An English summary is available at http://aei.pitt.edu/995/1/Spaak_report.pdf., 4, 97

European Council: Conclusions of the European Council meeting on 9 and 10 December 1994 in Essen, Presidency Conclusions SI(94) 1000., 186

European Council: Conclusions of the European Council meeting on 26 and 27 July 1995 in Cannes, Presidency Conclusions SI(95) 500., 186

European Council: Presidency Lisbon Council Conclusions of 23 and 24 March 2000, Press Release Library, European Commission., 99

European Council: Conclusions of the Stockholm European Council, 23–24 March 2001, SN 100/01., 220

European Council: Conclusions of the European Council of 4 February 2011, accessible at: https://www.consilium.europa.eu/uedocs/cms_data/docs/pressdata/en/trans/119253.pdf., 102

European Commission Policy Documents

Thirty-First Report on Competition Policy, 2001., 56
Thirty-Third Report on Competition Policy, 2003., 287
Report on Competition Policy, 2004., 195
Report on Competition Policy, 2008., 195
Report on Competition Policy, 2009, COM (2010) 282 final., 196, 197
Report on Competition Policy, 2015, SWD (2016) 198 final., 206
Report on Competition Policy, 2016, COM (2017) 285 final of 31 May 2017., 304
Neumark Report: "*Rapport du Comite Fiscal et Financier,*" 1962., 306
Tempel Report: "*Impôt sur les sociétés et impôt sur le revenu dans les Communautés Européennes,*" Tempel, A.J. van den, Luxembourg, CE 1970., 306
Commission *Proposal for a Council Regulation laying down in accordance with Article 94 EEC the methods of supervision by the Commission of the application in the central regions of the Community of the principles for the coordination of general regional aid schemes,* COM (72) 1523 Final of 4 December 1972., 162, 230
"*Reorganisation of the Community Shipbuilding Industry,*" Communication from the Commission to the Council of 9 December 1977., 160
"*Completing the Internal Market,*" COM (85) 310, http://europa.eu/documents/comm/white_papers/pdf/com1985_0310_f_en.pdf., 171
First Survey on State aids in the European Community, 1989., 171
Communication of the Commission to the Council and to the European Parliament – "Industrial policy in an open and competitive environment - Guidelines for a Community approach," COM (90) 556 final, 16 November 1990., 98
"*Report of the Committee of Independent Experts on Company Taxation*" (1992)., 306
"*Growth, competitiveness, and employment - The challenges and ways forward into the 21st century,*" 5 December 1993 COM (93) 700 final., 99
"Competition Policy Newsletter," Vol. 1 No 6 (Autumn/Winter 1995), p. 47., 190
Communication: "*Shaping Europe's Maritime future - a contribution to the competitiveness of maritime industries,*" 25 March 1996., 188
"*Taxation in the European Union,*" SEC(96) 487 final of 20 March 1996., 308, 336
"*Towards tax co-ordination in the European Union,*" COM (1997) 495., 308
Sixth Survey on State Aid in the European Union in the Manufacturing and Certain Other sectors, COM (98) 417, 1998., 181
Seventh Survey on State Aid in the European Union in the Manufacturing and Certain Other sectors, Brussels, 30 March 1999., 181
Working Paper "*Integrating environmental aspects into all relevant policy areas*" of 26 May 1999., 261
Report to the Helsinki European Council on integrating environmental concerns and sustainable development into Community policies (SEC (1999) 1941 final)., 261
"*European Economy,*" 1999., 77
Communication on the future of the Cinema and the Audiovisual Industry in Europe, 27 September 2001., 78
Communication from the Commission to the Council, the European Parliament, the Economic and Social Committee and the Committee of the Regions on certain legal aspects relating to cinematographic and other audiovisual works, OJ C 43 of 16 February 2002., 78

Communication from the Commission to the Council and the European Parliament *"Some Key Issues in Europe's Competitiveness – Towards an Integrated Approach,"* Brussels, 21 November 2003, COM (2003) 704 final., 306

State Aid Scoreboard Spring 2003, COM (2003) 225 final of 30 April 2003., 212, 233

"Communication on a Pro-Active Competition Policy for a Competitive Europe," COM (2004) 293 Final of 20 April 2004., 355, 363

State Aid Scoreboard Spring 2005, COM (2005) 147 final of 20 April 2005., 212, 233

"State aid action plan - Less and better targeted State aid: a roadmap for State aid reform 2005-2009," (Consultation document –SEC (2005) 795), COM/2005/0107 final of 7 June 2005., 212, 233, 372

Review of the Guidelines for State Aid for Environmental Protection, 2005. Questionnaire Issued in October 2005, accessible at: http://ec.europa.eu/comm/competi tion/state_aid/reform/00910_questionnaire_env_en.pdf., 266

Analytical Report for the Opinion on the application from the Former Yugoslav Republic of Macedonia for EU membership, [COM (2005) 562 final] of 9 November 2005., 135

Croatia 2005 Progress Report, [COM (2005) 561 final] of 9 November 2005., 135

Communication from the Commission - Monitoring report on the state of preparedness for EU membership of Bulgaria and Romania, Brussels, COM (2006) 549 final, 26 September 2006., 195

Report on the Application of Council Regulation 1407/2002/EC on State aid to the Coal Industry," COM (2007) 253 final of 21 May 2007., 257

State Aid Scoreboard, Spring 2007., 351

Notice from the Commission - Towards an effective implementation of Commission decisions ordering Member States to recover unlawful and incompatible State aid, OJ C 272 of 15 November 2007., 86, 87, 89, 197, 350

DG Competition Autumn 2008 *State aid Scoreboard*, accessible at: http://ec.europa.eu/competition/state_aid/studies_reports/archive/scoreboard_arch.html., 297

Communication from the Commission – *"Europe 2020 - A strategy for smart, sustainable and inclusive growth,"* COM (2010) 2020 final of 3 March 2010., 215, 333

Proposal for a Council Regulation on State aid to facilitate the closure of uncompetitive coal mines, COM (2010) 372 final, 20 July 2010., 257

Communication from the Commission to the European Parliament, the Council, the European Economic and Social Committee and the Committee of the Regions - *'A Digital Agenda for Europe'*, COM (2010) 245 final of 26 August 2010., 218

Communication from the Commission to the European Parliament, the Council, the European Economic and Social Committee and the Committee of the Regions - *'Europe 2020 Flagship Initiative — Innovation Union'*, COM (2010) 546 final of 6 October 2010., 218

Communication from the Commission to the European Parliament, the Council, the European Economic and Social Committee and the Committee of the Regions - *'Energy 2020 — A strategy for competitive, sustainable and secure energy'* – COM (2010) 639 final of 10 November 2010., 216, 275

Commission Staff Working Document: Facts and Figures on State aid in the EU Member States - 2010 Update of 1 December 2010., 13

Commission: Communication from the Commission to the European Parliament and the Council: *A Fair and Efficient Corporate Tax System in the European Union: 5 Key Areas for Action*, COM (2015) 302 final of 17 June 2015., 321

*DG Competition Working Paper on State Aid and Tax rul*ings, 3 June 2016., 205

Commission Staff Working Paper accompanying the *Report on Competition Policy 2016.*, 247

Proposal for a Council Decision on the provisional application of the Comprehensive Economic and Trade Agreement between Canada of the one part, and the European Union and its Member States, of the other part, COM/2016/0470 final of 5 July 2016., 145

"Guide to the Draft text on Investment Protection and Investment Court System in the Transatlantic Trade and Investment Partnership (TTIP)," accessible at: http://trade.ec.europa.eu/doclib/press/index.cfm?id = 1365., 146

Commission: State Aid Scoreboard, 2016 available at: http://ec.europa.eu/competition/state_aid/scoreboard/index_en.html., 146

Memorandum of Understanding on a dialogue in the area of the State aid control regime and the Fair Competition Review System between on one side the Directorate-General for Competition of the European Commission and on the other side the National Development and Reform Commission of The People's Republic of China, 2 June 2017, accessible at: http://ec.europa.eu/competition/international/bilateral/mou_china_2017.pdf., 152

Communication from the Commission – "Investing in a smart, innovative and sustainable Industry - A renewed EU Industrial Policy Strategy," COM (2017) 479 final of 13 September 2017., 334, 380

ECOSOC

Opinion on the Proposal for a Council Regulation on State aid to facilitate the closure of uncompetitive coal mines, OJ C 54/16/2011 of 19 February 2011., 257

European Court of Auditors

Special Report *'Improving the security of energy supply by developing the internal energy market: more efforts needed'*, European Union, 2015., 279

European Environment Agency

"Energy subsidies in the European Union: A brief overview," Copenhagen 2004., 255, 278

Eurostat

Statistical books: Energy, transport and environment indicators. Publications Office of the European Union: Luxembourg, 2016., 254

European Commission Press Statements

Press Release: *"Commission announces Decision on Dutch Electricity Market,"* IP/90/267 of 28 March 1990., 101

Press Release: *"Final negative State aid decisions on special tax schemes in Belgium, the Netherlands and Ireland,"* IP/703/242 of 18 February 2003., 310

Press Release: *"State aids: Commission opens formal investigation into UK Nuclear Decommissioning Authority,"* IP/04/1430 of 1 December 2004., 102

Press Release: *"State aid: Commission provides greater legal certainty for financing services of general economic interest,"* IP/05/937 of 15 July 2005., 209, 239

Press Release: *"State aid: Commission authorises transfer of nuclear assets from British Nuclear Fuels to Nuclear Decommissioning Authority subject to conditions,"* IP/06/428 of 4 April 2006., 102

Press Release: *"State aid: Commission simplifies procedures for approving regional aid with new block exemption Regulation,"* IP/06/1453 of 24 October 2006., 199

Press Release: *"State aid: Commission proposes Council Regulation on State aid to close uncompetitive coal mines,"* IP/10/984 of 20 July 2010., 257

Press Release: *"State aid: Commission approves Slovenian aid towards the closure of the Trbovlje Hrastnik coal mine,"* IP/11/804 of 29 June 2011., 258

Press Release: *"State aid: Commission consults on new film support rules,"* 30 April 2013., 79

Press Release: *"State aid: Commission exempts more aid measures from prior notification,"* 21 May 2014., 12, 84

Press Release: *"State aid: Commission investigates transfer pricing arrangements on corporate taxation of Amazon in Luxembourg,"* 7 October 2014.

Press Release: *"A single rulebook for the resolution of failing banks will apply in the EU as of 1 January 2015"* of 31 December 2014., 68

Press Release: *"Combatting Corporate Tax Avoidance - Commission presents Tax Transparency Package,"* IP/15/4610 of 18 March 2015., 206

Press Release: "Commission presents Action Plan for Fair and Efficient Corporate Taxation in the EU," IP/15/5188 of 17 June 2015., 206

Press Release: *"Commission decides selective tax advantages for Fiat in Luxembourg and Starbucks in the Netherlands are illegal under EU state aid rules,"* IP/15/5880 of 21 October 2015., 205

Statement by Commissioner Vestager on EU state aid rules in the steel sector and Commission State aid decisions concerning Duferco in Belgium and Ilva in Italy, Brussels, 20 January 2016, Statement/16/118., 260

Press Release: *"State aid: Commission concludes Belgian "Excess Profit" tax scheme illegal; around €700 million to be recovered from 35 multinational companies,"* IP/16/42 of 11 January 2016., 205

Press Release: *"State aid: Commission orders Belgium to recover €211 million from several steel companies within the Duferco group,"* IP/16/113 of 20 January 2016., 259

Press Release: *"Towards Energy Union: The Commission presents sustainable energy security package,"* IP/16/307 of 16 February 2016., 279

Press Release: "*State aid: Commission clarifies scope of EU State aid rules to facilitate public investment,*" IP/16/1782 of 19 May 2016., 219, 248

Press Release: "*State aid: Commission decides Spanish professional football clubs have to pay back incompatible aid,*" 4 July 2016., 88

Press Release: "*State aid: Ireland gave illegal tax benefits to Apple worth up to €13 billion,*" IP/16/2923 of 30 August 2016., 205, 319

Press Release: "*Major Win for the EU in the WTO Dispute on Boeing,*" IP/16/3947 of 28 November 2016., 123

Press Release: "*State aid: Commission and China start dialogue on State aid control,*" 2 June 2017., 153

Press Release: "*State aid: Commission finds Luxembourg gave illegal tax benefits to Amazon worth around €250 million,*" 4 October 2017., 205, 321

Press Release: "*State aid: Commission refers Ireland to Court for failure to recover illegal tax benefits from Apple worth up to €13 billion,*" 4 October 2017., 320

Specific Web Pages

On early negative decisions: http://ec.europa.eu/competition/state_aid/register/state_aid_negative_decisions_1969-1994_en.pdf., 158, 169

On State aid recovery: http://ec.europa.eu/competition/state_aid/studies_reports/recovery.html., 89, 198, 351

Other WTO and EFTA Documents

World Trade Organisation

"*World Trade Report 2006 – Exploring the links between subsidies, trade and the WTO,*" 24 July 2006, Geneva., 113

WTO Press Statements

WTO Press Release of 11 February 1988: "*GATT Provisions on Subsidies need clarifications,*" Geneva accessible at http://www.sunsonline.org/trade/process/during/uruguay/other/01110088.htm., 106

WTO Press Release of 4 July 1988: "*U.S. call for new GATT rules on subsidies,*" Geneva accessible at: http://www.sunsonline.org/trade/process/during/uruguay/country/07040088.htm., 106

European Free Trade Area

EFTA, Economic Committee, *Working Party on Government Aids, Final Report*, Geneva, 1986., 129

"*The EFTA Surveillance Authority's State aid Guidelines*" of 19 January 1994 accessible at: http://www.eftasurv.int/fieldsofwork/fieldstateaid/legaltexts., 130

Table of Legislation

Council and European Parliament

Regulations

Directives

Directive 2014/49/EU of the European Parliament and of the Council of 16 April 2014 on deposit guarantee schemes Text with EEA relevance., 304

Decisions

Council Decision of 19 December 1960 on the system of aid in existence in France for certain types of paper pulp, OJ No 84 of 31 December 1960., 15

Council Decision No 68/160/EEC of 27 March 1968 extending until 30 June 1968 the authorisation granted in Article 1 of the Decision of 19 December 1960 on the system of aid in existence in France for certain types of paper pulp, OJ L 76 of 28 March 1968., 15

Council Decision No 271/65/EEC, on the clarification of the application of Articles 107 to 109 in regard to taxation, social security and State intervention in relation to competition in rail, road, and inland waterway transport (1965-1966), OJ 1500 Spec. Ed. 67., 28

Council Decision No 70/355/EEC of 13 July 1970 concerning the implementation by the Federal Republic of Germany of compensation measures for cereal producers, OJ L 157 of 18 July 1970., 15

Council Decision of 24 July 1973 on *a system of aids existing in the United Kingdom for refining raw sugar* (1973), OJ L 207/47 of 16 August 1973., 16

Council Decision of 27 February 1975 on *the system of aid for the slaughter of beef cattle in the United Kingdom* (1975), OJ L 52/35 of 28 February 1975., 16

Council Decision of 21 April 1975 *on the system of aids to be applied in France for the private storage of table wines*, OJ L 103/24 of 23 April 1975., 15

Council Decision of 15 March 1976 *on the system of aid to be applied in France for certain wine-growers*, OJ L 72/15 of 18 March 1976., 15

Council Decision of 22 June 1976 *on the system of aid applicable to the slaughter of hens in Denmark*, OJ L 168/12 of 28 June 1976., 15

Council Decision No 257/2000/EC of 20 March 2000 on *aid granted in Italy by RIBS SpA on the restructuring of the Italian sugar beet sector*, OJ L 328/51 of 23 December 2000., 16

Council Decision No 808/2000/EC of 19 December 2000 on *the distillation of certain German wine products*, OJ L 328/49 of 23 December 2000., 16

Council Decision No 809/2000/EC of 19 December 2000 on *the distillation of certain Italian wine products*, OJ. L 328/51 of 23 December 2000., 16

Council Decision No 530/2003/EC: *Italian aid to milk producers*, OJ L 184 of 23 July 2003., 16

Council Decision No 39/2006/EC: *Cypriot farmers*, OJ L 23 of 27 January 2006., 16

Council Decision No 2010/787/EU of 10 December 2010 on State aid to facilitate the closure of uncompetitive coal mines, OJ L 336 of 21 December 2010., 80, 257

Other

European Commission

Regulations

Directives

Decisions

Other

Guidelines on Regional aid, OJ C 74 of 10 March 1998, as amended in 2000, OJ C 258 of 9 September 2000., 284

Multi-sectoral Framework on Regional aid for large investment projects OJ C 107 of 7 April 1998., 188, 286

Community Framework on Training Aid, OJ C 343 of 11 November 1998., 185

Notice on the application of the State aid rules to measures relating to Direct Business Taxation, OJ C 384 of 10 December 1998., 182, 187, 204, 308, 311

Community Guidelines on State aid for rescuing and restructuring firms in difficulty, OJ C 288 of 9 October 1999., 186

Guidelines on National Regional Aid ("RAGS"), OJ C 74 of 10 March 1998 as amended in 2000, OJ C 258 of 9 September 2000., 185, 287

Communication on the repercussions of the terrorist attacks in the United States on the air transport industry, COM (2001) 574 Final., 58

Extension of the validity of the Community guidelines on State aid for environmental protection, OJ C 14 of 19 January 2000., 262

Extension of the validity of the Community guidelines on State aid for environmental protection, OJ C 184 of 1 July 2000., 262

Commission Communication relating to the methodology for analysing State aid linked to stranded costs, adopted by the Commission on 26 July 2001 and issued as Commission letter SG (2001) D/290869 of 6 August 2001 –accessible at: http://ec.europa.eu/competition/state_aid/legislation/specific_rules.html., 74

Community guidelines on State aid for environmental protection, OJ C 37 of 3 February 2001., 263

Communication from the Commission: Rescue and restructuring aid and closure aid for the steel sector, OJ C 70 of 19 March 2002., 74

Notice on the expiry of the guidelines on State aid for undertakings in deprived urban areas, OJ C 119 of 22 May 2002., 187

Communication from the Commission concerning certain aspects of the treatment of competition cases resulting from the expiry of the ECSC Treaty, OJ C 152 of 26 June 2002., 8

Community guidelines on State aid to maritime transport, OJ C 13 of 17 January 2004., 28, 74

Community guidelines on financing of airports and start-up aid to airlines departing from regional airports, OJ C 312 of 9 December 2005., 29

Guidelines on National Regional Aid for 2007-2013, OJ C 54 of 4 March 2006., 287

Notice from the Commission - Towards an effective implementation of Commission decisions ordering Member States to recover unlawful and incompatible State aid, OJ C 272 of 15 November 2007., 89, 350

Notice from the Commission (2007/C 272/05) - *Towards an effective implementation of Commission decisions ordering Member States to recover unlawful and incompatible State aid*, OJ C 272 of 15 November 2007., 86, 87

Community Guidelines on State aid for environmental protection, OJ C 82 of 1 April 2008., 102, 264

Communication from the Commission on the application of State aid rules to public service broadcasting, OJ C 257 of 27 October 2009., 75
Communication from the Commission on the application, from 1 January 2011, of State aid rules to support measures in favour of banks in the context of the financial crisis, OJ C 329 of 7 December 2010., 300
Communication of the Commission - Temporary Union framework for State aid measures to support access to finance in the current financial and economic crisis, OJ C 6 of 11 January 2011., 46, 67, 181
Communication from the Commission on the application, from 1 January 2012, of State aid rules to support measures in favour of banks in the context of the financial crisis, OJ C 356 of 6 December 2011., 300
Framework on State aid for shipbuilding, OJ C 364 of 14 December 2011., 80
Communication on the application of the European Union State aid rules to compensation granted for the provision of services of general economic interest, OJ C 8 of 11 January 2012., 73
Communication from the Commission: *European Union framework for State aid in the form of public service compensation* (2011), OJ C 8 of 11 January 2012., 73
Communication from the Commission - *Guidelines on State aid for environmental protection and energy* 2014-2020, OJ C 200 of 28 June 2014 and *Guidelines on certain State aid measures in the context of the greenhouse gas emission allowance trading scheme post 2012*, OJ C 154 of 5 June 2012., 73
Guidelines on Regional State aid for 2014-2020, (2013/C 209/01), OJ C 209 of 23 July 2013., 63
Communication from the Commission to the Member States on the application of Articles 107 and 108 of the Treaty on the Functioning of the European Union to short-term export-credit insurance, OJ C 392 of 19 December 2012, as amended., 73, 173
EU Guidelines for the application of state aid rules in relation to the rapid deployment of broadband networks of 15 January 2013, OJ C 25 of 26 January 2013., 75
Communication from the Commission on the application, from 1 August 2013, of State aid rules to support measures in favour of banks in the context of the financial crisis ("Banking Communication"*)*, OJ C 216 of 30 July 2013., 75, 301
Guidelines on Regional State aid for 2014-2020, OJ C 209 of 23 July 2013., 68, 73, 80, 346
Communication from the Commission on State aid for films and other audio-visual works, OJ C 332 of 15 November 2013., 75
Guidelines on risk finance aid for 2014-2020, OJ C 19 of 22 January 2014., 73
Guidelines on State aid to airports and airlines, OJ C 99 of 4 April 2014., 29, 74, 248
Communication from the Commission - *Criteria for the analysis of the compatibility with the internal market of State aid to promote the execution of important projects of common European interest*, OJ C 188 of 20 June 2014., 65, 215, 275
Framework for State aid for research and development and innovation, OJ C 198 of 27 June 2014., 73, 80, 348
Guidelines on State aid for environmental protection and energy 2014-2020 OJ C 200 of 28 June 2014., 73, 102, 266

National Legislation

Index

C

D

E

INTERNATIONAL COMPETITION LAW SERIES

1. Ignacio De Leon, *Latin American Competition Law and Policy: A Policy in Search of Identity*, 2001 (ISBN 90-411-1542-0).
2. Wim Dejonghe & Wouter Van de Voorde (eds), *M & A in Belgium*, 2001 (ISBN 90-411-1594-3).
3. Yang-Ching Chao, Gee San, Changfa Lo & Jiming Ho (eds), *International and Comparative Competition Law and Policies*, 2001 (ISBN 90-411-1643-5).
4. Martin Mendelsohn & Stephen Rose, *Guide to the EC Block Exemption for Vertical Agreements*, 2002 (ISBN 90-411-9813-X).
5. Clifford A. Jones & Mitsuo Matsushita (eds), *Competition Policy in the Global Trading System: Perspectives from the EU, Japan and the USA*, 2002 (ISBN 90-411-1758-X).
6. Christian Koenig, Andreas Bartosch, Jens-Daniel Braun & Marion Romes (eds), *EC Competition and Telecommunications Law*. Second Edition, 2009 (ISBN 978-90-411-2564-4).
7. Jürgen Basedow (ed.), *Limits and Control of Competition with a View to International Harmonization*, 2002 (ISBN 90-411-1967-1).
8. Maureen Brunt, Economic Essays on Australian and New Zealand Competition Law, 2003 (ISBN 90-411-1991-4).
9. Ky P. Ewing, Jr., *Competition Rules for the 21st Century: Principles from America's Experience*, Second Edition, 2006 (ISBN 90-411-2477-2).
10. Joseph Wilson, *Globalization and the Limits of National Merger Control Laws*, 2003 (ISBN 90-411-1996-5).
11. Peter Verloop & Valérie Landes (eds), *Merger Control in Europe: EU, Member States and Accession States*, Fourth Edition, 2003 (ISBN 90-411-2056-4).
12. Themistoklis K. Giannakopoulos, *Safeguarding Companies' Rights in Competition and Anti-dumping/Anti-subsidies Proceedings*, Second Edition, 2011 (ISBN 978-90-411-3404-2).
13. Marjorie Holmes & Lesley Davey (eds), *A Practical Guide to National Competition Rules across Europe*, Second Edition, 2007 (ISBN 978-90- 411-2607-8).
14. Sigrid Stroux, *US and EU Oligopoly Control*, 2004 (ISBN 90-411-2296-6).
15. Tzong-Leh Hwang and Chiyuan Chen (eds), *The Future Development of Competition Framework*, 2004 (ISBN 90-411-2305-9).

16. Phedon Nicolaides, Mihalis Kekelekis and Maria Kleis, *State Aid Policy in the European Community: Principles and Practice,* Second Edition, 2008 (ISBN 978-90-411-2754-9).
17. Doris Hildebrand, *Economic Analyses of Vertical Agreements: A Self- Assessment,* 2005 (ISBN 90-411-2328-8).
18. Frauke Henning-Bodewig, *Unfair Competition Law: European Union and Member States,* 2005 (ISBN 90-411-2329-6).
19. Duarte Brito & Margarida Catalão-Lopes, *Mergers and Acquisitions: The Industrial Organization Perspective,* 2006 (ISBN 90-411-2451-9).
20. Nikos Th. Nikolinakos, *EU Competition Law and Regulation in the Converging Telecommunications, Media and IT Sectors,* 2006 (ISBN 90-411- 2469-1).
21. Mihalis Kekelekis, *The EC Merger Control Regulation: Rights of Defence. A Critical Analysis of DG COMP Practice and Community Courts' Jurisprudence,* 2006 (ISBN 90-411-2553-1).
22. Mark R. Joelson, *An International Antitrust Primer: A Guide to the Operation of United States, European Union and Other Key Competition Laws in the Global Economy,* Third Edition, 2006 (ISBN 90-411-2468-3).
23. Themistoklis K. Giannakopoulos, *A Concise Guide to the EU Anti-dumping/ Anti-subsidies Procedures,* 2006 (ISBN 90-411-2464-0).
24. George Cumming, Brad Spitz & Ruth Janal, *Civil Procedure Used for Enforcement of EC Competition Law by the English, French and German Civil Courts,* 2007 (ISBN 978-90-411-2471-5).
25. Jürgen Basedow (ed.), *Private Enforcement of EC Competition Law,* 2007 (ISBN 978-90-411-2613-9).
26. Jung Wook Cho, *Innovation and Competition in the Digital Network Economy: A Legal and Economic Assessment on Multi-tying Practices and Network Effects,* 2007 (ISBN 978-90-411-2574-3).
27. Akira Inoue, *Japanese Antitrust Law Manual: Law, Cases and Interpretation of the Japanese Antimonopoly Act,* 2007 (ISBN 978-90-411-2627-6).
28. René Barents, *Directory of EC Case Law on Competition,* 2007 (ISBN 978-90-411-2656-6).
29. Paul F. Nemitz (ed.), *The Effective Application of EU State Aid Procedures: The Role of National Law and Practice,* 2007 (ISBN 978-90-411-2657-3).
30. Jurian Langer, *Tying and Bundling as a Leveraging Concern under EC Competition Law,* 2007 (ISBN 978-90-411-2575-0).
31. Abel M. Mateus & Teresa Moreira (eds), *Competition Law and Economics – Advances in Competition Policy and Antitrust Enforcement,* 2007 (ISBN 978-90-411-2632-0).
32. Alberto Santa Maria, *Competition and State Aid: An Analysis of the EC Practice,* 2007 (ISBN 978-90-411-2617-7).
33. Barry J. Rodger (ed.), *Article 234 and Competition Law: An Analysis,* 2007 (ISBN 978-90-411-2605-4).
34. Alla Pozdnakova, *Liner Shipping and EU Competition Law,* 2008 (ISBN 978-90-411-2717-4).

35. Milena Stoyanova, *Competition Problems in Liberalized Telecommunications: Regulatory Solutions to Promote Effective Competition*, 2008 (ISBN 978-90-411-2736-5).
36. *EC State Aid Law/Le Droit des Aides d'Etat dans la CE. Liber Amicorum Francisco Santaolalla Gadea*, 2008 (ISBN 978-90-411-2774-7).
37. René Barents, *Directory of EC Case Law on State Aids*, 2008 (ISBN 978- 90-411-2732-7).
38. Ignacio De Leon, *An Institutional Assessment of Antitrust Policy: The Latin American Experience*, 2009 (ISBN 978-90-411-2478-4).
39. Doris Hildebrand, *The Role of Economic Analysis in EU Competition Law: TheEuropean School*, Fourth Edition, 2016 (ISBN 978-90-411-6245-8).
40. Eugène Buttigieg, *Competition Law: Safeguarding the Consumer Interest. A Comparative Analysis of US Antitrust Law and EC Competition Law*, 2009 (ISBN 978-90-411-3119-5).
41. Ioannis Lianos & Ioannis Kokkoris (eds), *The Reform of EC Competition Law: New Challenges*, 2010 (ISBN 978-90-411-2692-4).
42. George Cumming & Mirjam Freudenthal, *Civil Procedure in EU Competition Cases before the English and Dutch Courts*, 2010 (ISBN 978-90-411-3192-8).
43. A.E. Rodriguez & Ashok Menon, *The Limits of Competition Policy: The Shortcomings of Antitrust in Developing and Reforming Economies*, 2010 (ISBN 978-90-411-3177-5).
44. Mika Oinonen, *Does EU Merger Control Discriminate against Small Market Companies? Diagnosing the Argument with Conclusions*, 2010 (ISBN 978-90-411-3261-1).
45. Eirik Østerud, *Identifying Exclusionary Abuses by Dominant Undertakings under EU Competition Law: The Spectrum of Tests*, 2010 (ISBN 978-90-411-3271-0).
46. Marco Botta, *Merger Control Regimes in Emerging Economies: A Case Study on Brazil and Argentina*, 2011 (ISBN 978-90-411-3402-8).
47. Jürgen Basedow & Wolfgang Wurmnest (eds), *Structure and Effects in EU Competition Law: Studies on Exclusionary Conduct and State Aid*, 2011 (ISBN 978-90-411-3174-4).
48. George Cumming (ed.), *Merger Decisions and the Rules of Procedure of the European Community Courts*, 2012 (ISBN 978-90-411-3671-8).
49. Eduardo Molan Gaban & Juliana Oliveira Domingues (eds), *Antitrust Law in Brazil: Fighting Cartels*, 2012 (ISBN 978-90-411-3670-1).
50. Giandonato Caggiano, Gabriella Muscolo & Marina Tavassi (eds), *Competition Law and Intellectual Property: A European Perspective*, 2012 (ISBN 978-90-411-3447-9).
51. Ben Van Rompuy, *Economic Efficiency: The Sole Concern of Modern Antitrust Policy? Non-efficiency Considerations under Article 101 TFEU*, 2012 (ISBN 978-90-411-3870-5).
52. Liyang Hou, *Competition Law and Regulation of the EU Electronic Communications Sector: A Comparative Legal Approach*, 2012 (ISBN 978-90-411-4047-0).

53. Barry Rodger, *Landmark Cases in Competition Law: Around the World in Fourteen Stories*, 2012 (ISBN 978-90-411-3843-9).
54. Andreas Scordamaglia-Tousis, *EU Cartel Enforcement: Reconciling Effective Public Enforcement with Fundamental Rights*, 2013 (ISBN 978-90-411-4758-5).
55. Bernardo Cortese (ed.), *EU Competition Law: Between Public and Private Enforcement*, 2014 (ISBN 978-90-411-4677-9).
56. Barry Rodger (ed.), *Competition Law: Comparative Private Enforcement and Collective Redress across the EU*, 2014 (ISBN 978-90-411-4559-8).
57. Nada Ina Pauer, *The Single Economic Entity Doctrine and Corporate Group Responsibility in European Antitrust Law*, 2014 (ISBN 978-90-411-5262-6).
58. Urška Petrovčič, *Competition Law and Standard Essential Patents: A Transatlantic Perspective*, 2014 (ISBN 978-90-411-4960-2).
59. David Telyas, *The Interface between Competition Law, Patents and Technical Standards*, 2014 (ISBN 978-90-411-5418-7).
60. Katerina Maniadaki, *EU Competition Law, Regulation and the Internet: The Case of Net Neutrality*, 2014 (ISBN 978-90-411-4140-8).
61. Horacio Vedia Jerez, *Competition Law Enforcement and Compliance across the World: A Comparative Review*, 2015 (ISBN 978-90-411-5815-4).
62. Kadir Ba, *The Substantive Appraisal of Joint Ventures under the EU Merger Control Regime*, 2015 (ISBN 978-90-411-5816-1).
63. Alberto Santa Maria, *Competition and State Aid: An Analysis of the EU Practice*, Second Edition, 2015 (ISBN 978-90-411-5818-5).
64. Lúcio Tomé Feteira, *The Interplay between European and National Competition Law after Regulation 1/2003: "United (Should) We Stand?"*, 2016 (ISBN 978-90-411-5663-1).
65. Giovanni Pitruzzella & Gabriella Muscolo(eds), *Competition and Patent Law in the Pharmaceutical Sector: An International Perspective*, 2016 (ISBN 978-90-411-5927-4).
66. Małgorzata Cyndecka, *The Market Economy Investor Test in EU State Aid Law: Applicability and Application*, 2016 (ISBN 978-90-411-6102-4).
67. Damiano Canapa, *Trademarks and Brands in Merger Control: An Analysis of the European and Swiss Legal Orders*, 2016 (ISBN 978-90-411-6717-0).
68. Inge Graef, *EU Competition Law, Data Protection and Online Platforms: Data as Essential Facility*, 2016 (ISBN 978-90-411-8324-8).
69. Anders Jessen, *Exclusionary Abuse after the* Post Danmark I *Case: The Role of the Effects-Based Approach under Article 102 TFEU*, 2017 (ISBN 978-90-411-8996-7).
70. Baskaran Balasingham, *The EU Leniency Policy: Reconciling Effectiveness and Fairness*, 2017 (ISBN 978-90-411-8479-5).
71. Eugene Stuart & Iana Roginska-Green, *Sixty Years of EU State Aid Law and Policy: Analysis and Assessment*, 2018 (ISBN 978-90-411-8869-4).